Taiyo Matsumoto is best known to English-reading audiences as the creator of *Tekkonkinkreet*, which in 2006 was made into an animated feature film of the same name, directed by Michael Arias. In 2007, Matsumoto was awarded a Japan Media Arts Festival Excellence Award, and in 2008 he won an Eisner Award for the English publication of *Tekkonkinkreet*.

ALSO AVAILABLE IN ENGLISH BY TAIYO MATSUMOTO:

Tekkonkinkreet
GoGo Monster
Sunny

CATS OF THE LOUVRE
VIZ Signature Edition
Story & Art by Taiyo Matsumoto

Translation & English Adaptation . . . Michael Arias
Touch-Up Art & Lettering . . . . Deron Bennett
Cover & Graphic Design . . . . Adam Grano
Editor . . . . Mike Montesa

LOUVRE NO NEKO Vol. 1–2 by Taiyou MATSUMOTO
© 2017 Taiyou MATSUMOTO
Futuropolis / Musée du Louvre éditions, Paris
All rights reserved. Original Japanese edition published by SHOGAKUKAN.
English translation rights in the United States of America, Canada, the United
Kingdom, Ireland, Australia and New Zealand arranged with SHOGAKUKAN.

Printed in China | Published by VIZ Media, LLC,
P.O. Box 77010, San Francisco, CA 94107 | viz.com

1 2 3 4 5 6 7 8 9 10
First printing, September 2019

PARENTAL ADVISORY
CATS OF THE LOUVRE is rated T for Teen
and is recommended for ages 13 and up.

VIZ MEDIA
VIZ SIGNATURE

research assistance:

the staff of
musée du louvre

special thanks:

fabrice douar
sebastien gnaedig
ilan nguyen
ayako takahashi
yasuki hori
kumaichiro naka

book design
(japanese edition):

junzi takahashi

CATS
OF THE
LOUVRE

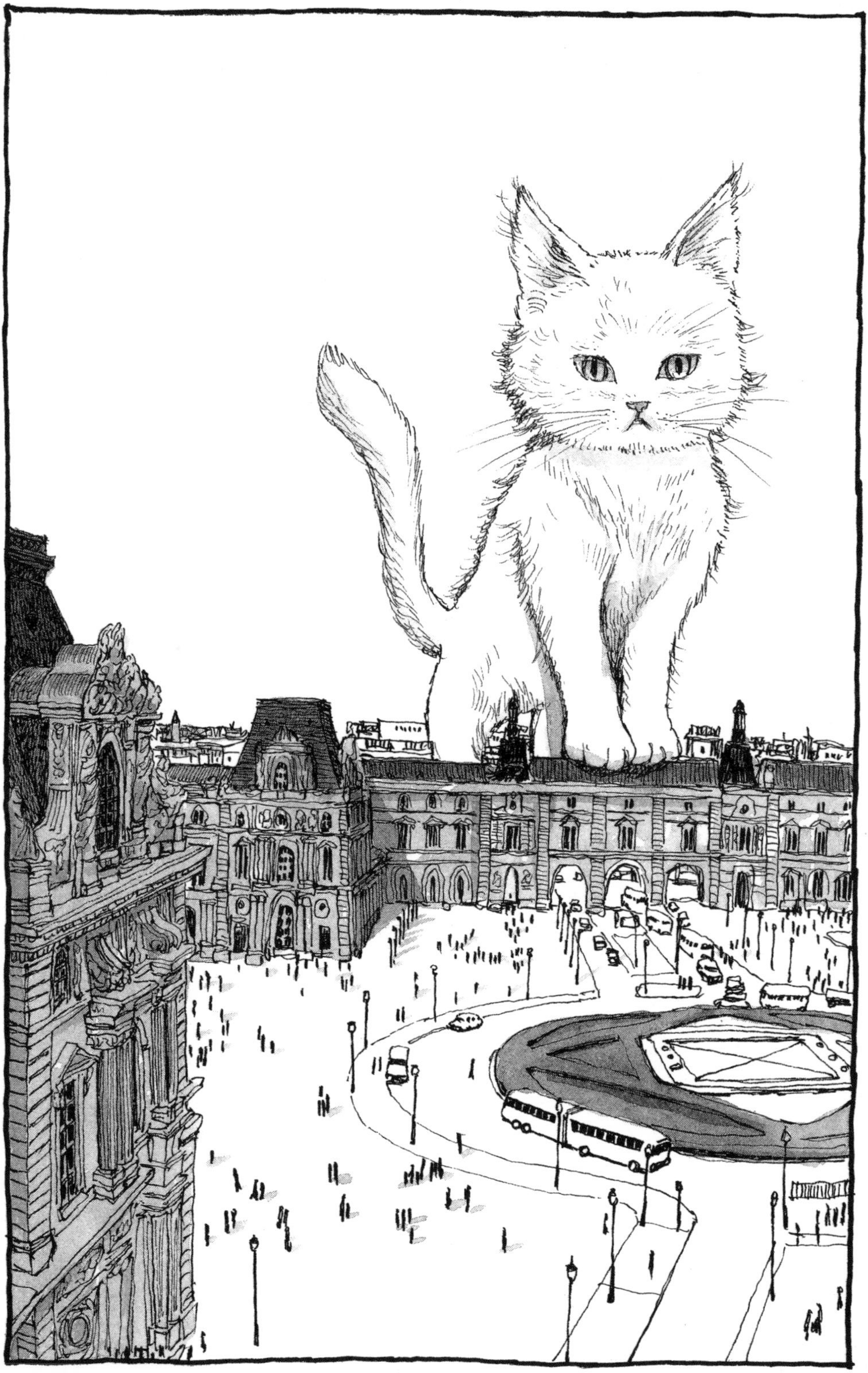

Cats of the Louvre

by TAIYO MATSUMOTO

VIZ MEDIA

Contents

PART ONE

PART TWO

PART ONE

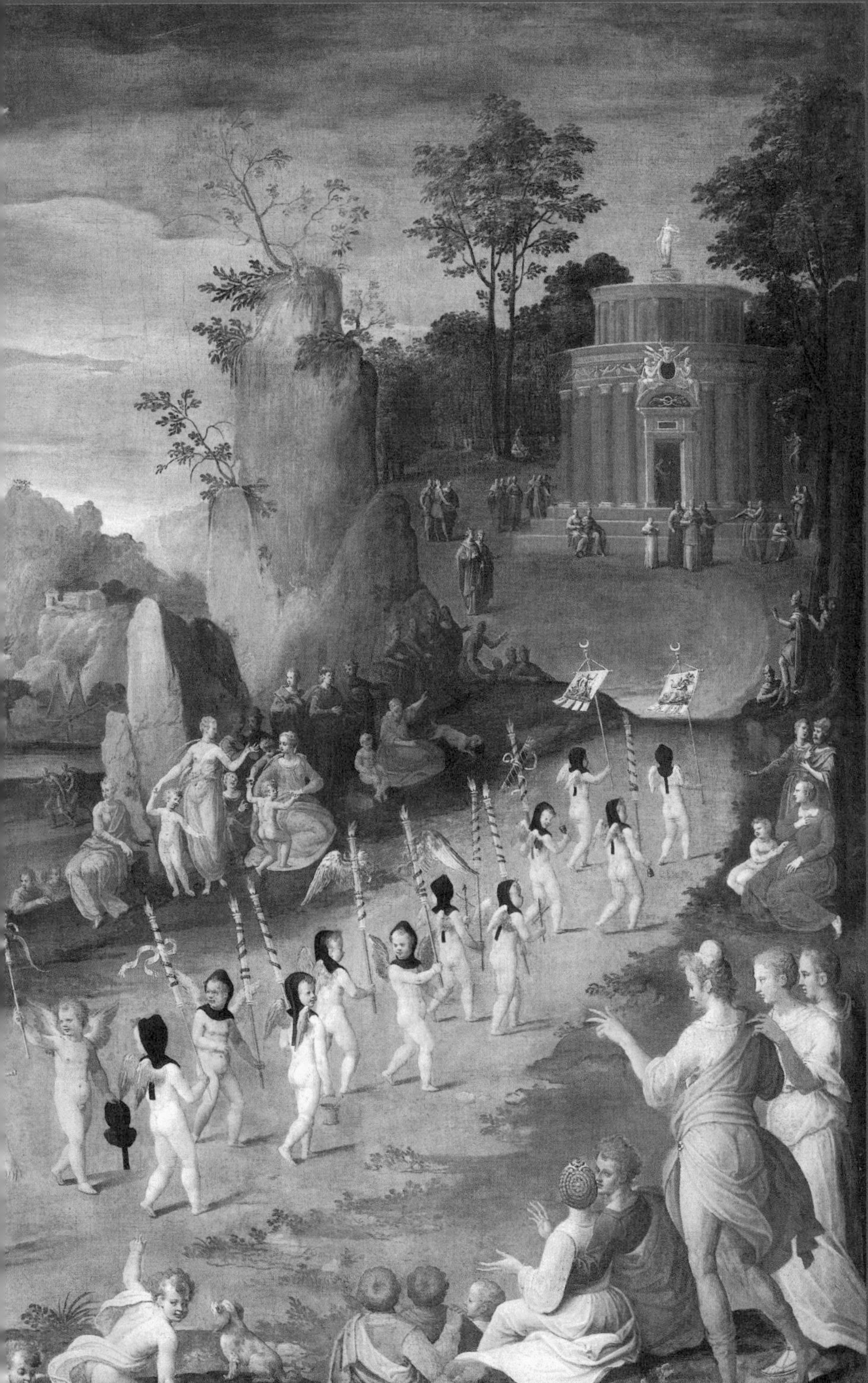

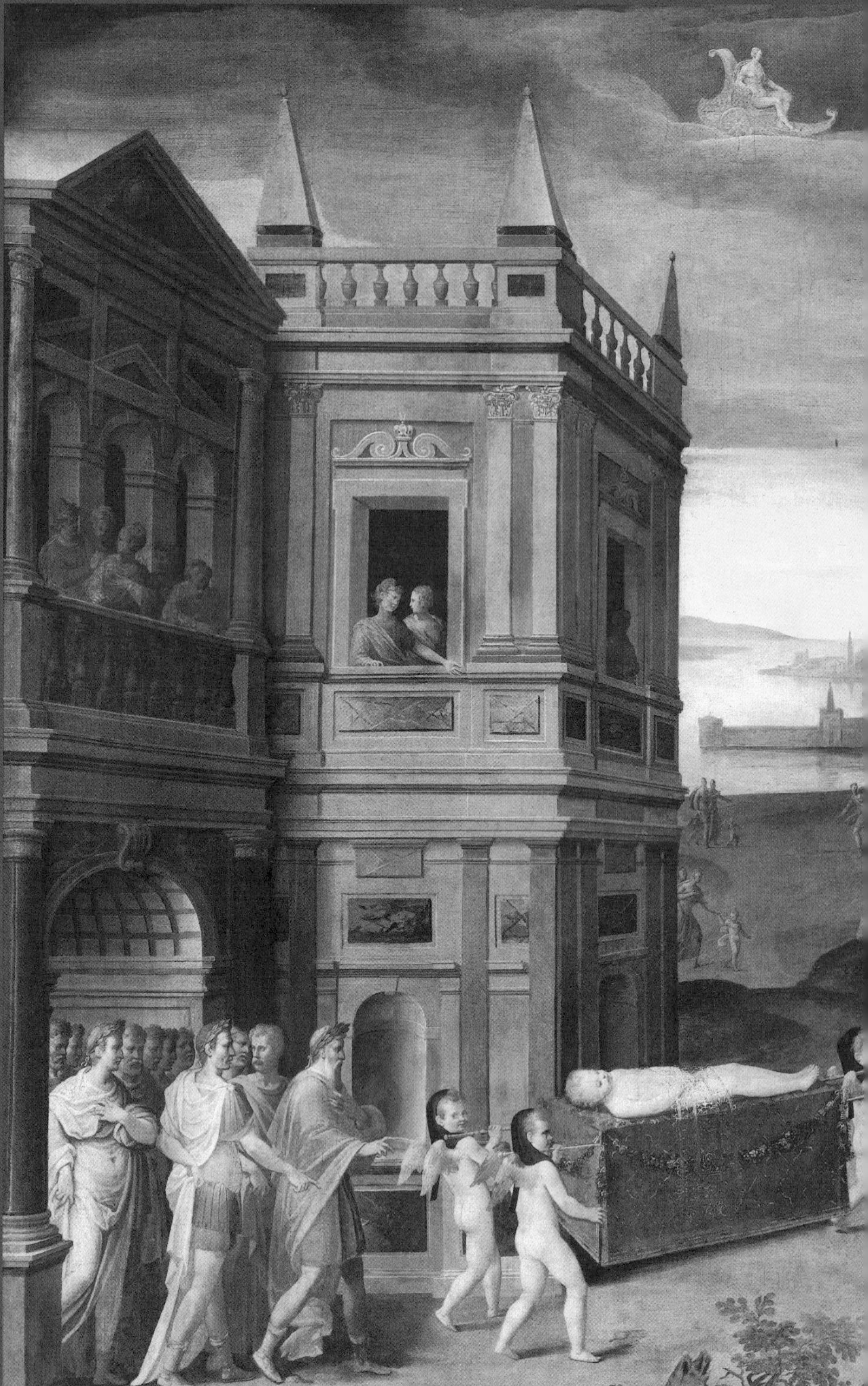

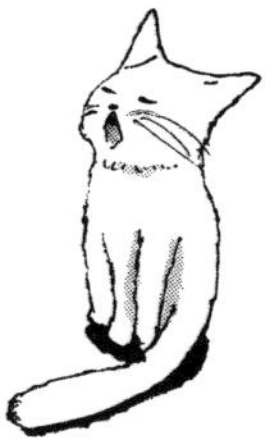

ILLUSTRATION ON PREVIOUS SPREAD:

The Funeral Procession of Love, Louvre permanent collection

Les Funérailles de l'Amour, circa 1580. Attributed to Henri Lerambert (known to Fontainebleau 1568–1570—Paris 1608), collaborator of Antoine Caron. Paris, Musée du Louvre, Department of Paintings

SPRING

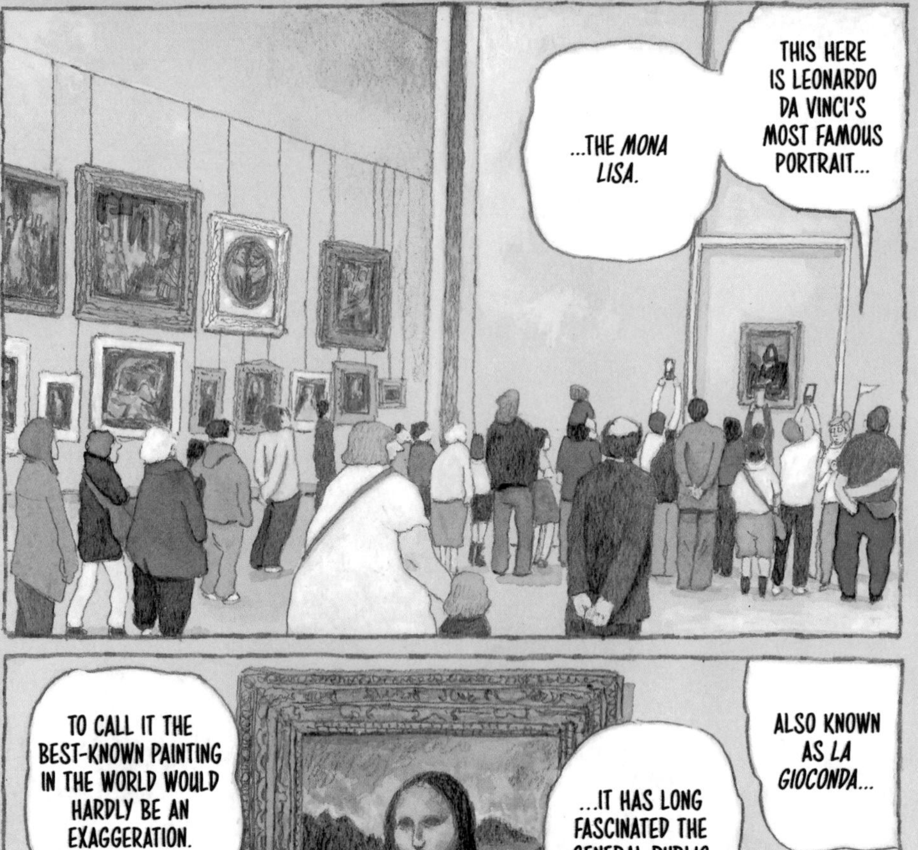
THIS HERE IS LEONARDO DA VINCI'S MOST FAMOUS PORTRAIT...
...THE *MONA LISA.*

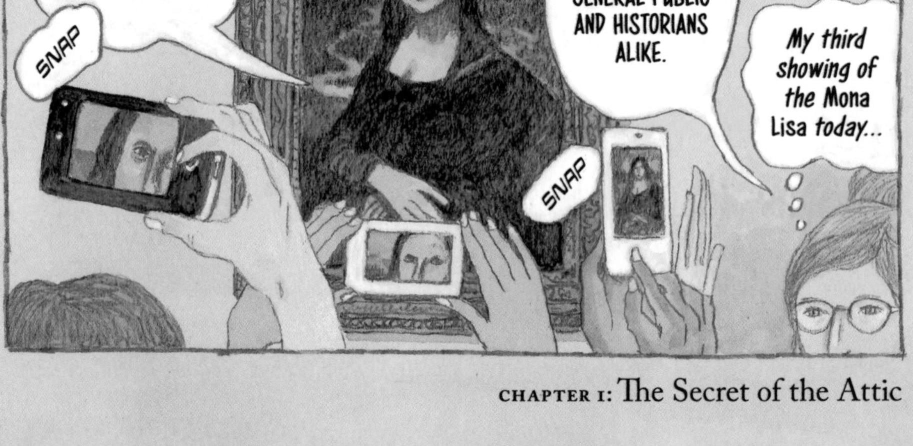
ALSO KNOWN AS *LA GIOCONDA*...
...IT HAS LONG FASCINATED THE GENERAL PUBLIC AND HISTORIANS ALIKE.
TO CALL IT THE BEST-KNOWN PAINTING IN THE WORLD WOULD HARDLY BE AN EXAGGERATION.
My third showing of the Mona Lisa *today...*
SNAP
SNAP

CHAPTER 1: The Secret of the Attic

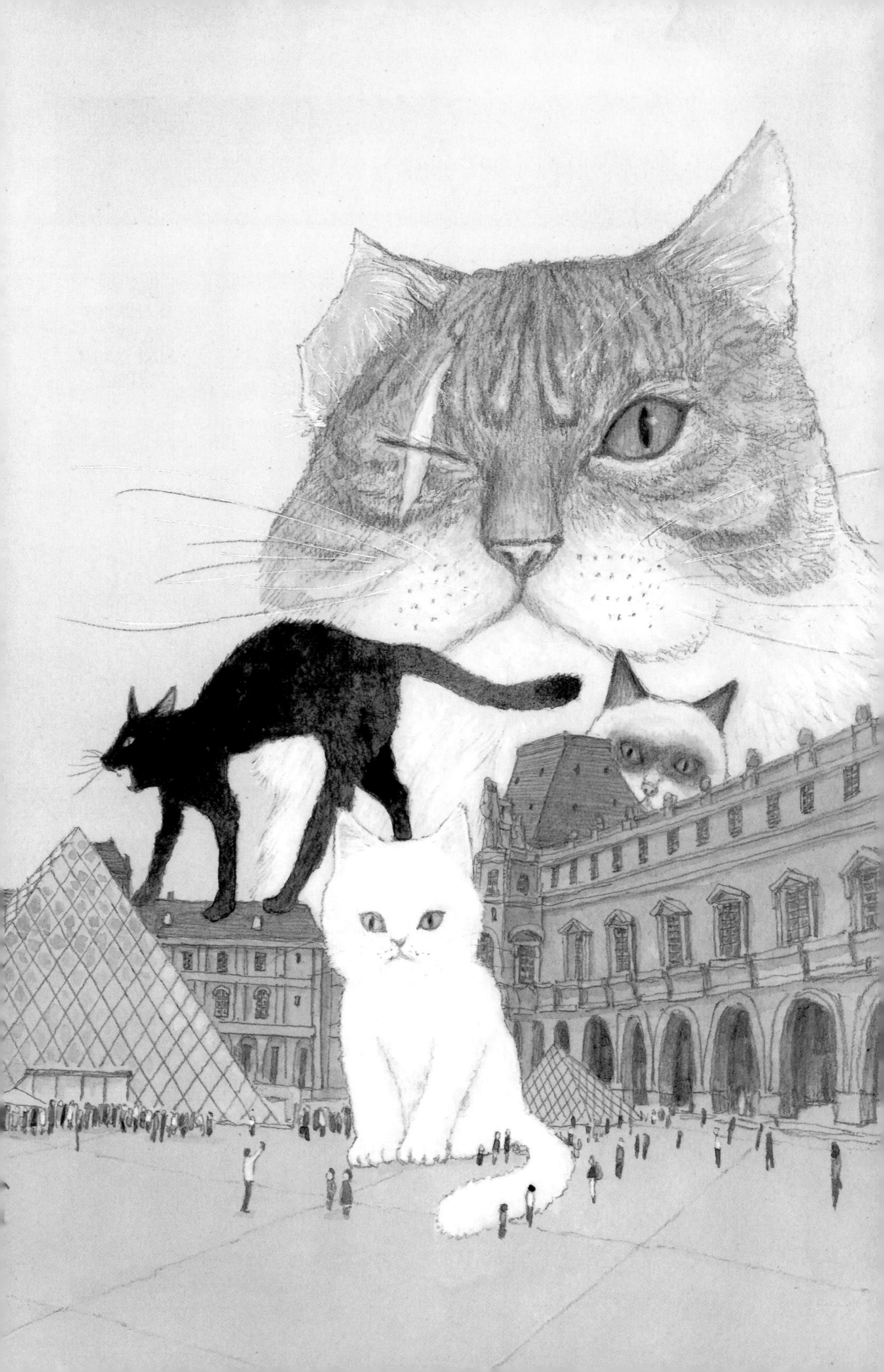

CHAPTER 1
The Secret of the Attic

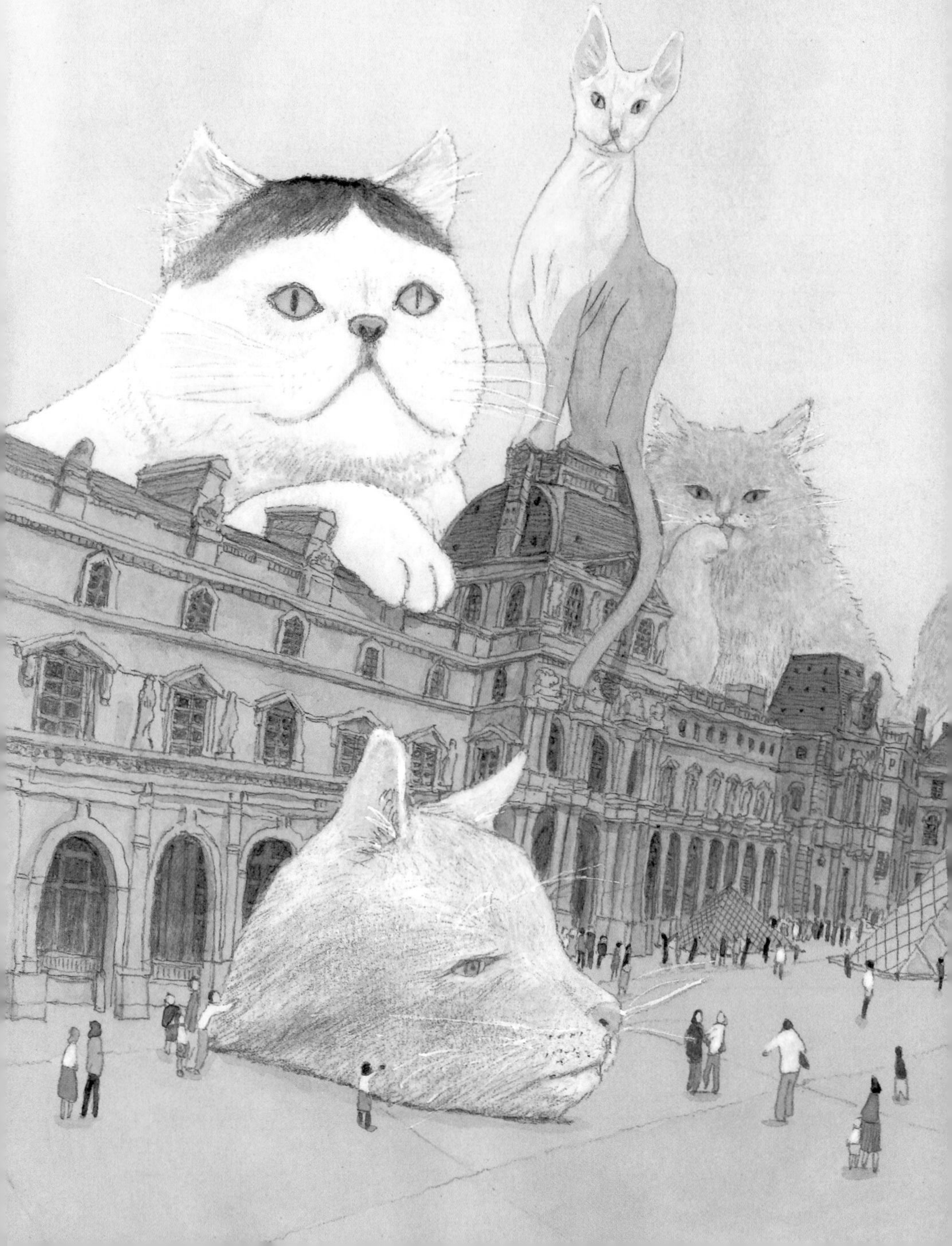

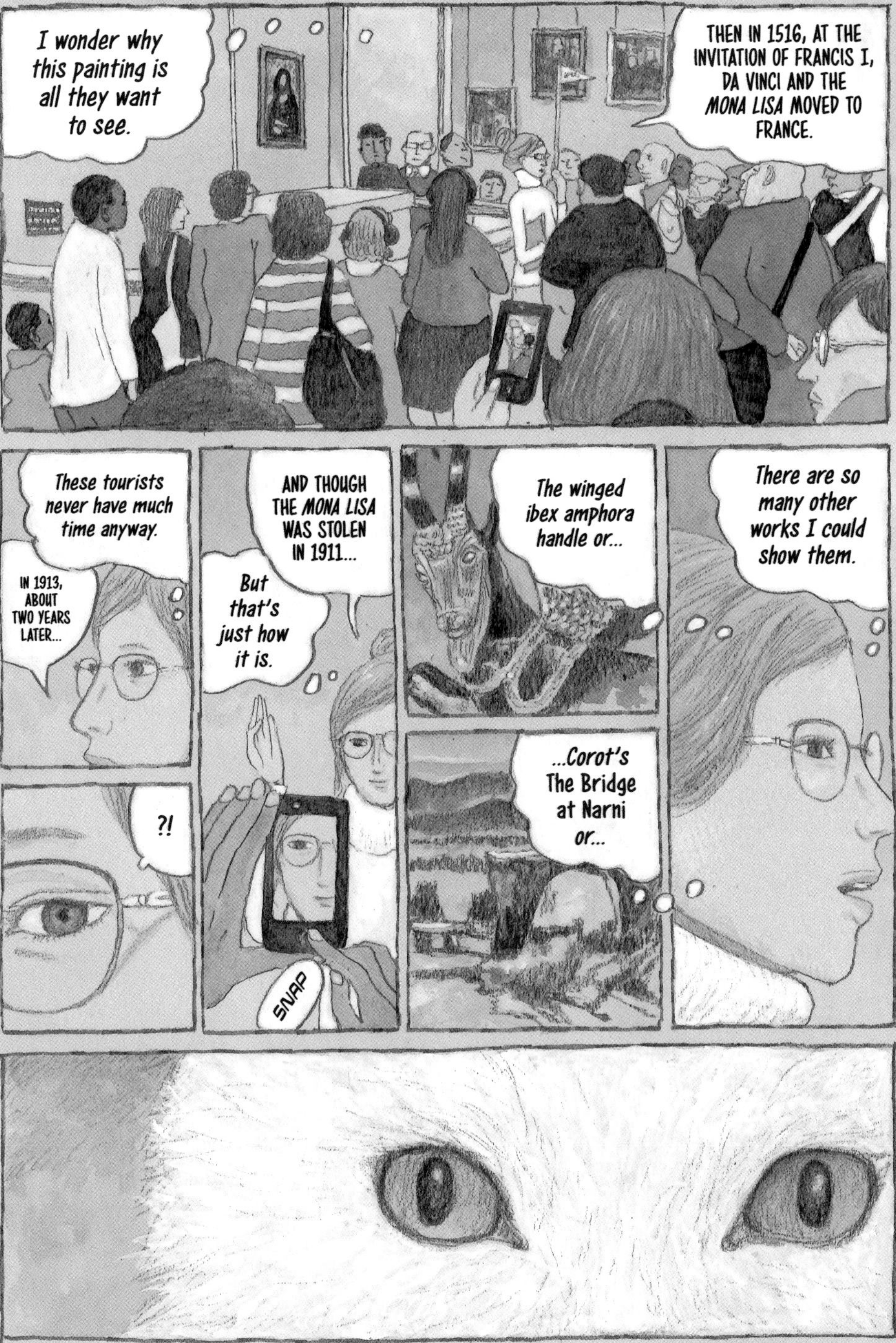
THEN IN 1516, AT THE INVITATION OF FRANCIS I, DA VINCI AND THE *MONA LISA* MOVED TO FRANCE.
I wonder why this painting is all they want to see.
There are so many other works I could show them.
The winged ibex amphora handle or...
...Corot's The Bridge at Narni or...
AND THOUGH THE *MONA LISA* WAS STOLEN IN 1911...
But that's just how it is.
SNAP
These tourists never have much time anyway.
IN 1913, ABOUT TWO YEARS LATER...
?!

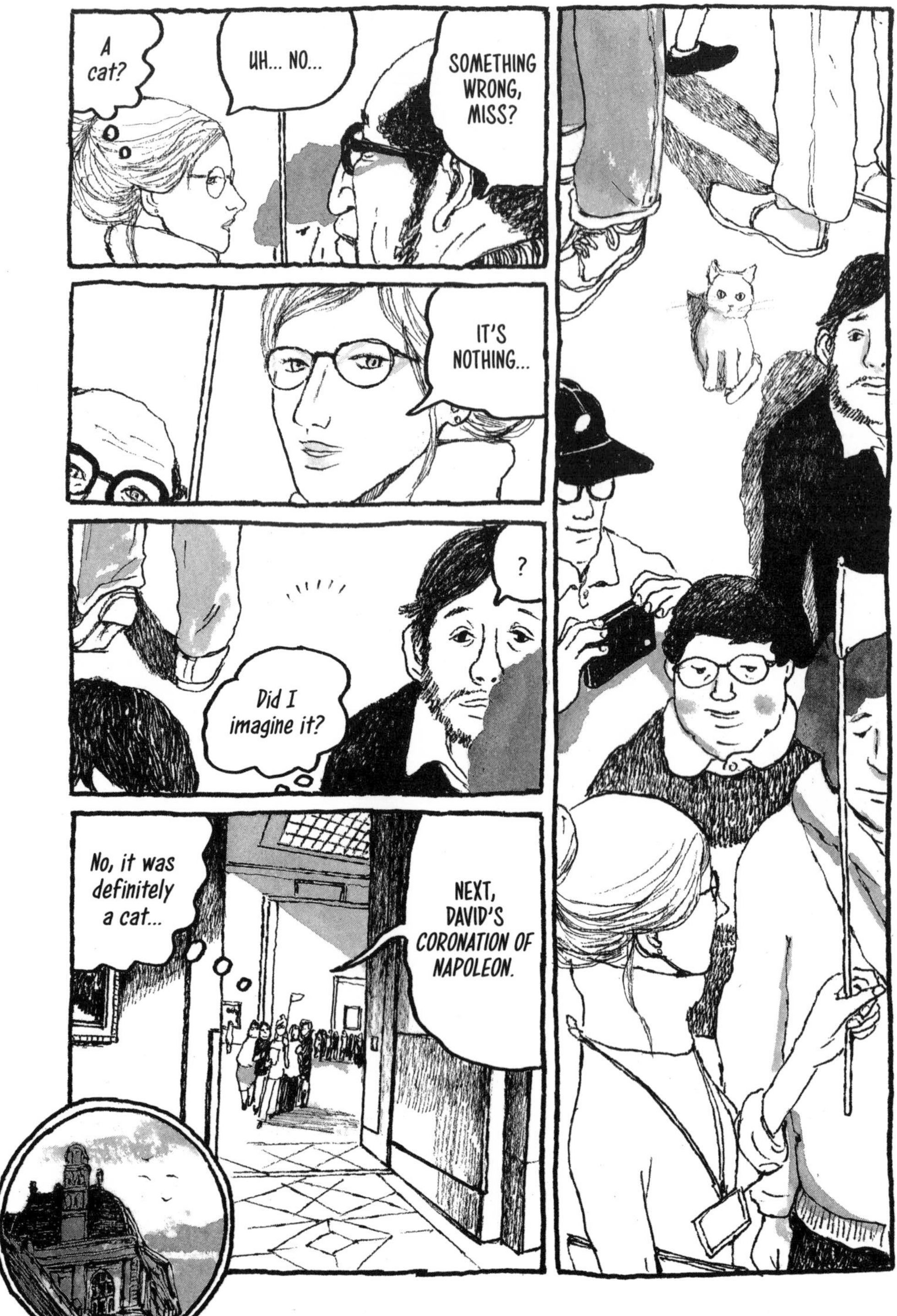
SOMETHING WRONG, MISS?
UH... NO...
A cat?
IT'S NOTHING...
?
Did I imagine it?
NEXT, DAVID'S CORONATION OF NAPOLEON.
No, it was definitely a cat...

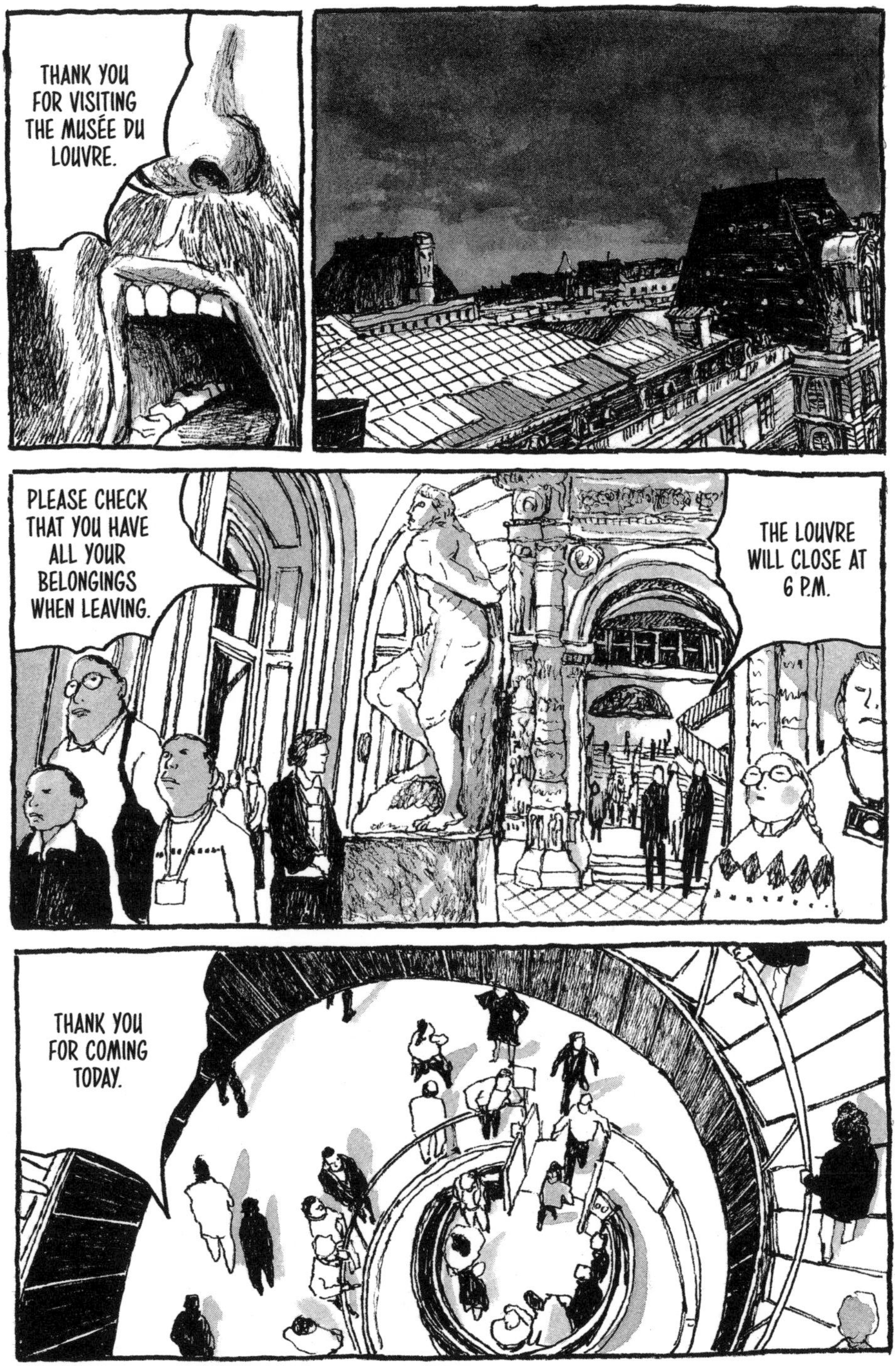
THANK YOU FOR VISITING THE MUSÉE DU LOUVRE.
THE LOUVRE WILL CLOSE AT 6 P.M.
PLEASE CHECK THAT YOU HAVE ALL YOUR BELONGINGS WHEN LEAVING.
THANK YOU FOR COMING TODAY.

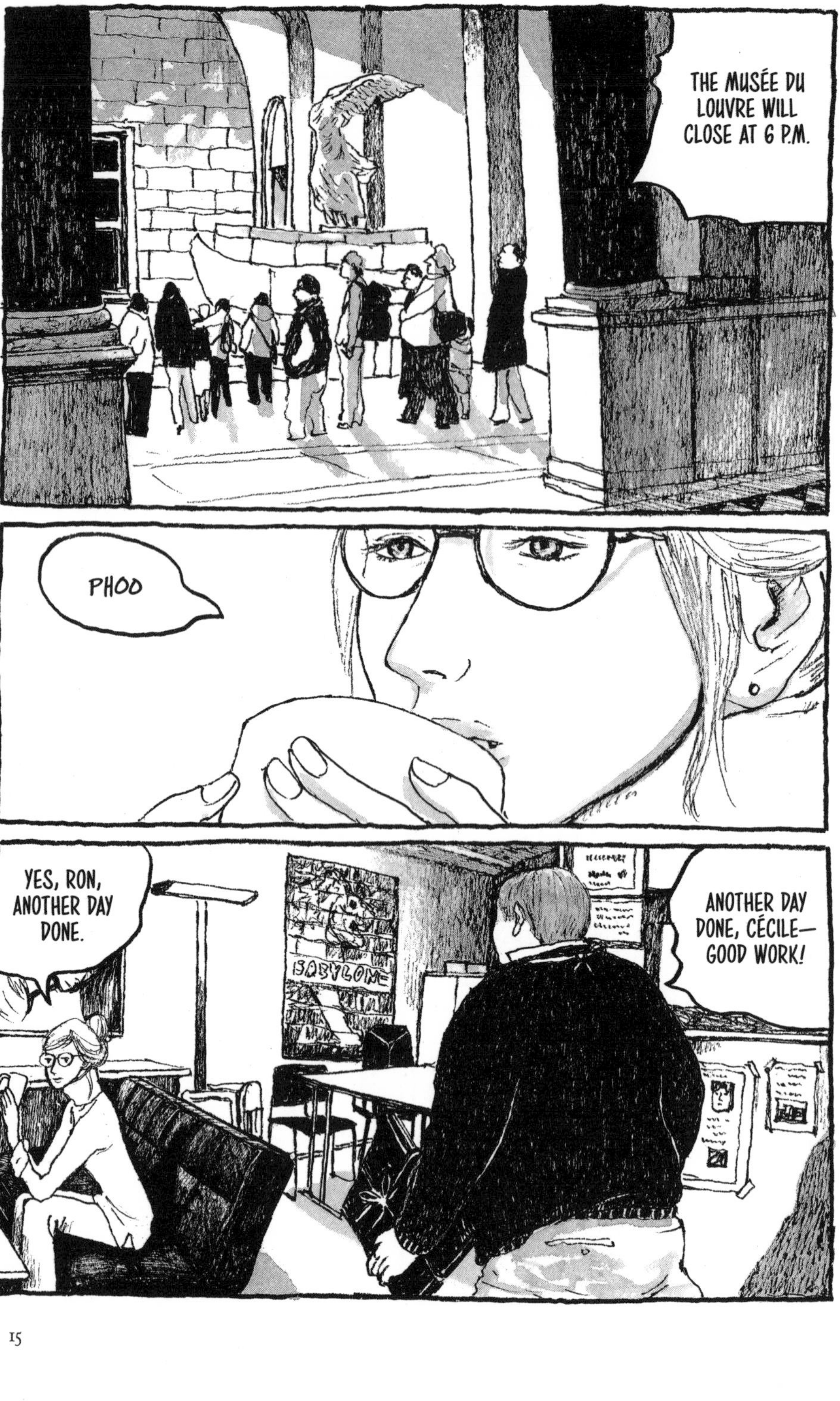
THE MUSÉE DU LOUVRE WILL CLOSE AT 6 P.M.
PHOO
ANOTHER DAY DONE, CÉCILE— GOOD WORK!
YES, RON, ANOTHER DAY DONE.

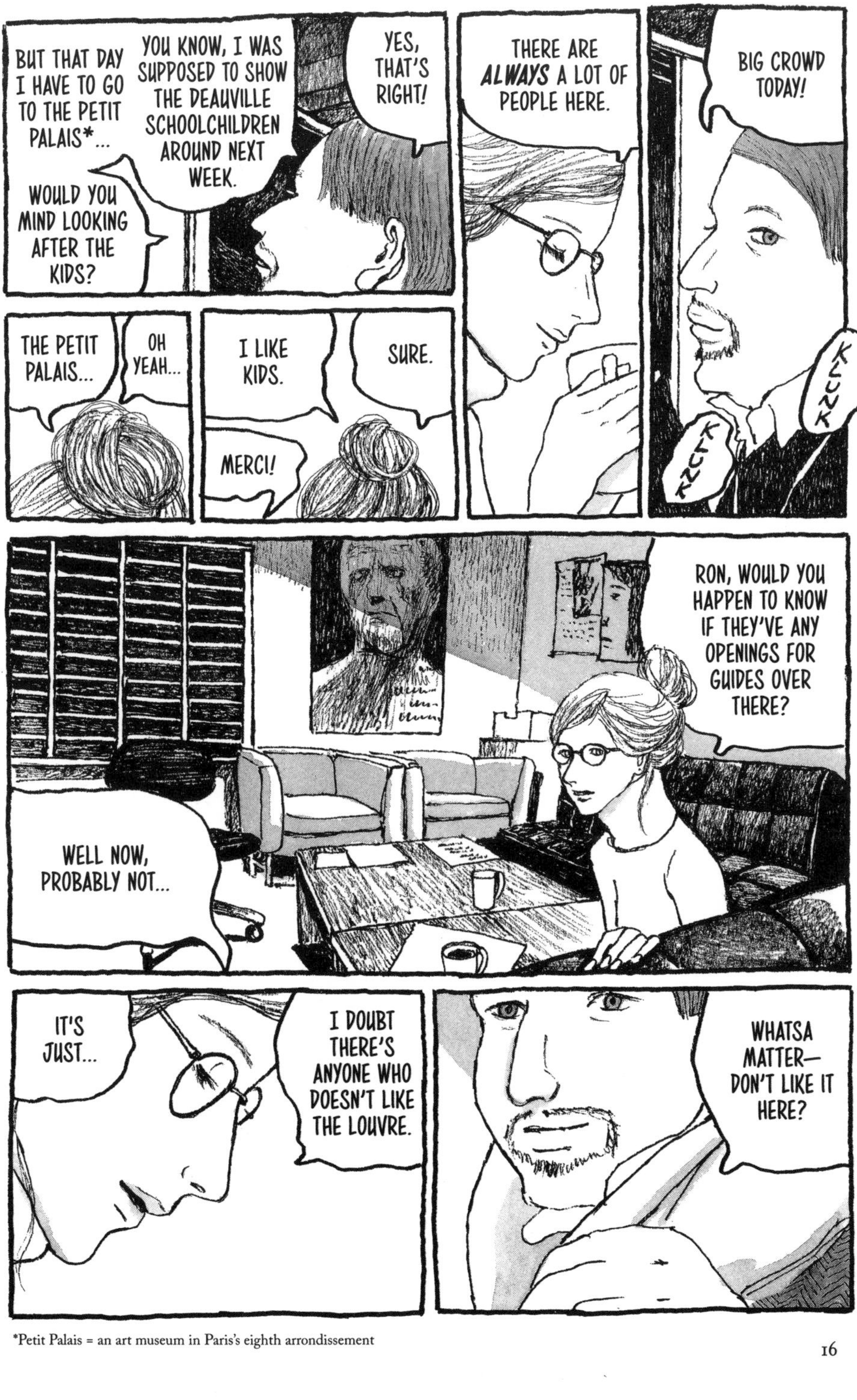
BIG CROWD TODAY!
KLUNK
KLUNK
THERE ARE *ALWAYS* A LOT OF PEOPLE HERE.
YES, THAT'S RIGHT!
YOU KNOW, I WAS SUPPOSED TO SHOW THE DEAUVILLE SCHOOLCHILDREN AROUND NEXT WEEK.
BUT THAT DAY I HAVE TO GO TO THE PETIT PALAIS*...
WOULD YOU MIND LOOKING AFTER THE KIDS?
SURE.
I LIKE KIDS.
MERCI!
OH YEAH...
THE PETIT PALAIS...
RON, WOULD YOU HAPPEN TO KNOW IF THEY'VE ANY OPENINGS FOR GUIDES OVER THERE?
WELL NOW, PROBABLY NOT...
WHATSA MATTER— DON'T LIKE IT HERE?
I DOUBT THERE'S ANYONE WHO DOESN'T LIKE THE LOUVRE.
IT'S JUST...

*Petit Palais = an art museum in Paris's eighth arrondissement

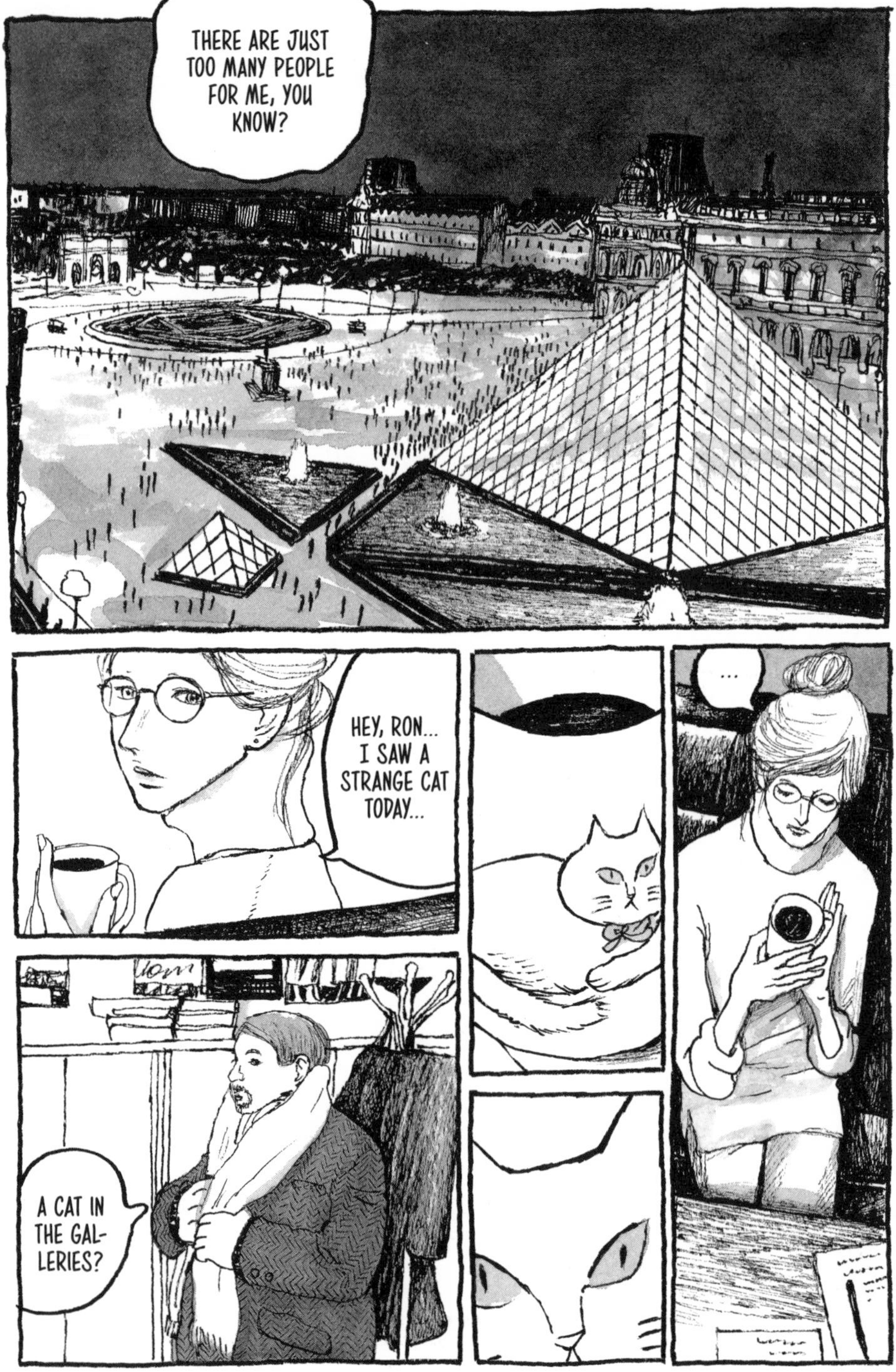
THERE ARE JUST TOO MANY PEOPLE FOR ME, YOU KNOW?
...
HEY, RON... I SAW A STRANGE CAT TODAY...
A CAT IN THE GAL-LERIES?

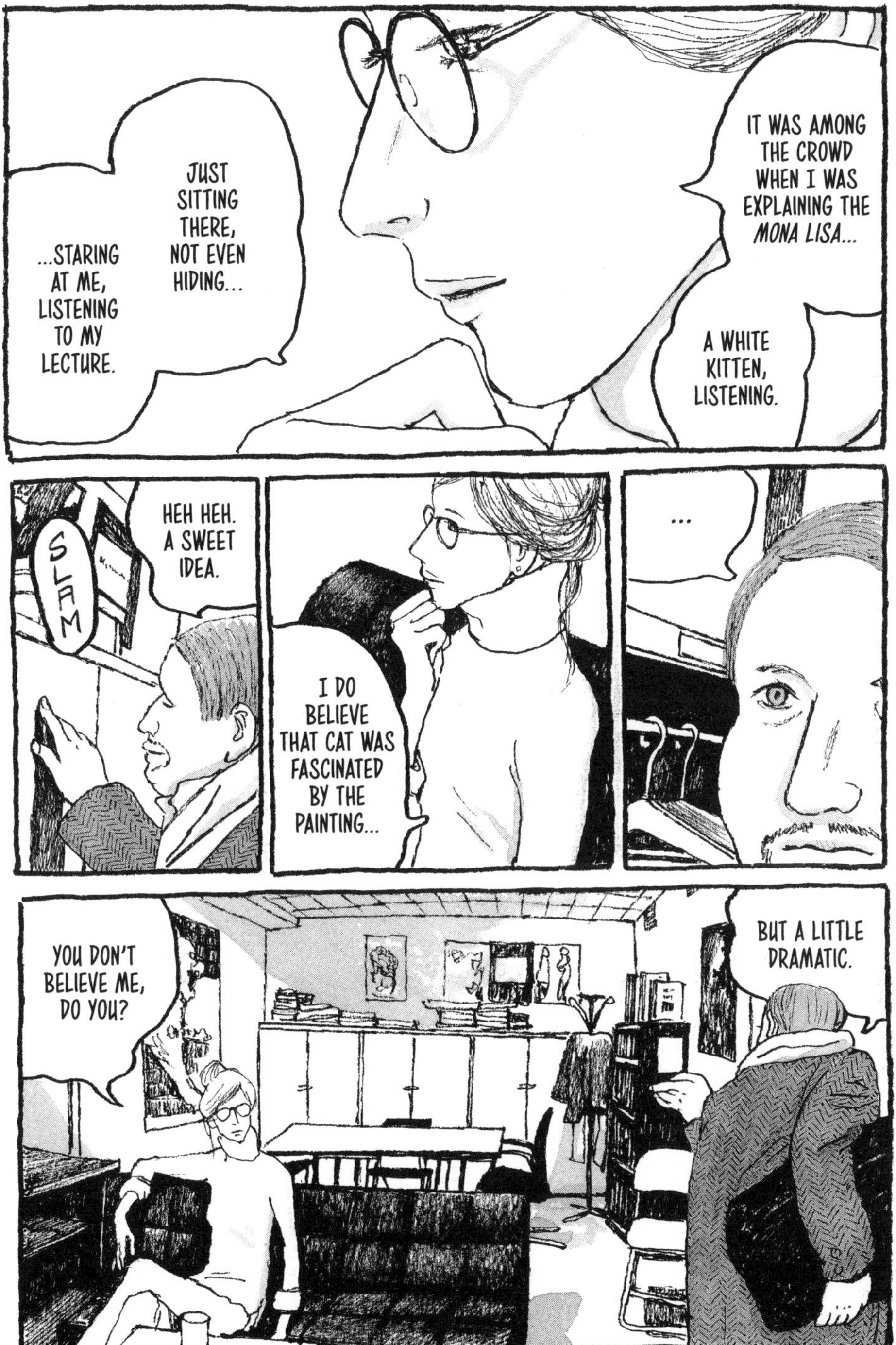
IT WAS AMONG THE CROWD WHEN I WAS EXPLAINING THE *MONA LISA*...
A WHITE KITTEN, LISTENING.
JUST SITTING THERE, NOT EVEN HIDING...
...STARING AT ME, LISTENING TO MY LECTURE.
...
I DO BELIEVE THAT CAT WAS FASCINATED BY THE PAINTING...
HEH HEH. A SWEET IDEA.
SLAM
BUT A LITTLE DRAMATIC.
YOU DON'T BELIEVE ME, DO YOU?

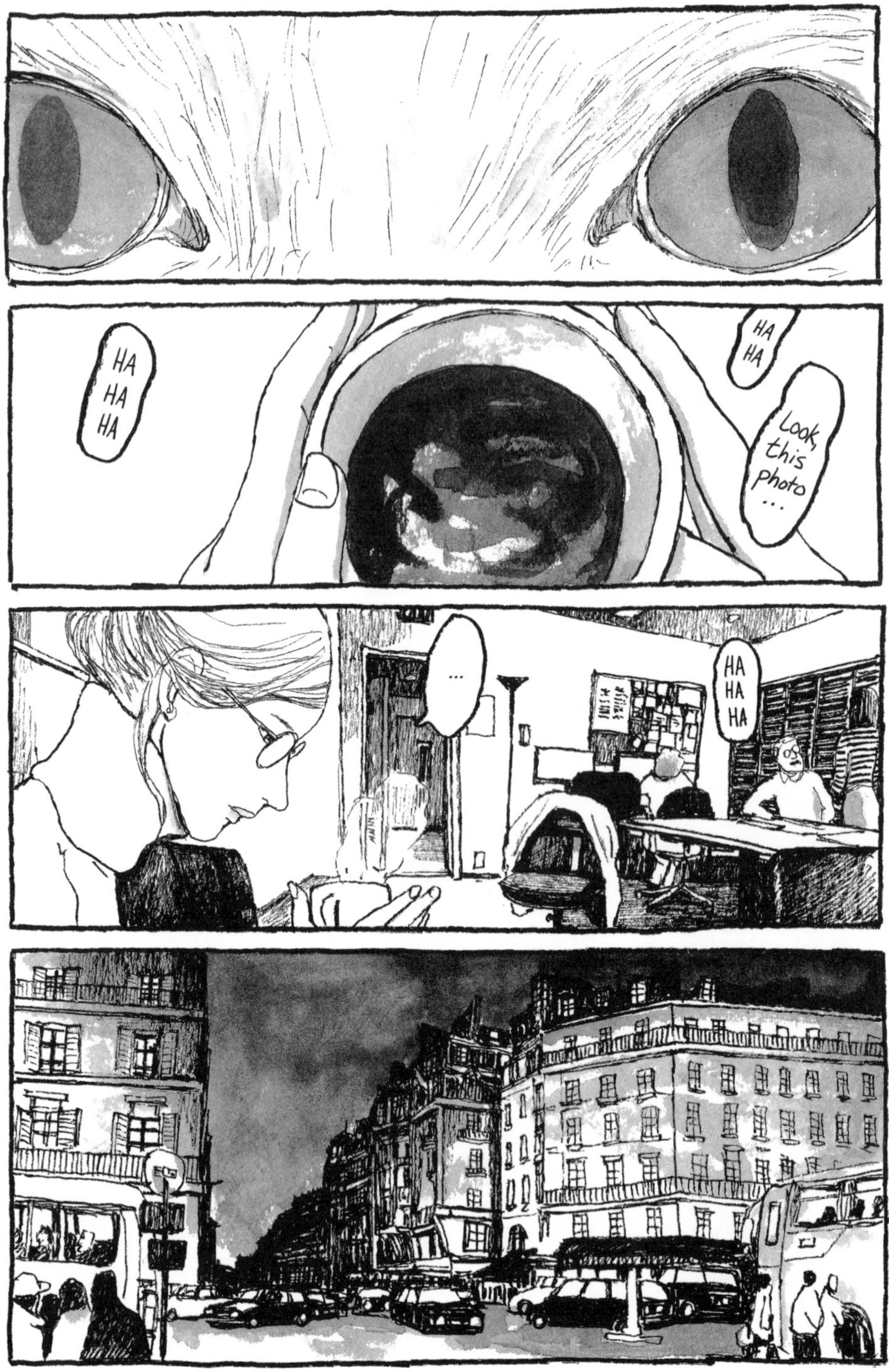
HA HA
Look, this photo ...
HA HA HA
HA HA HA
...

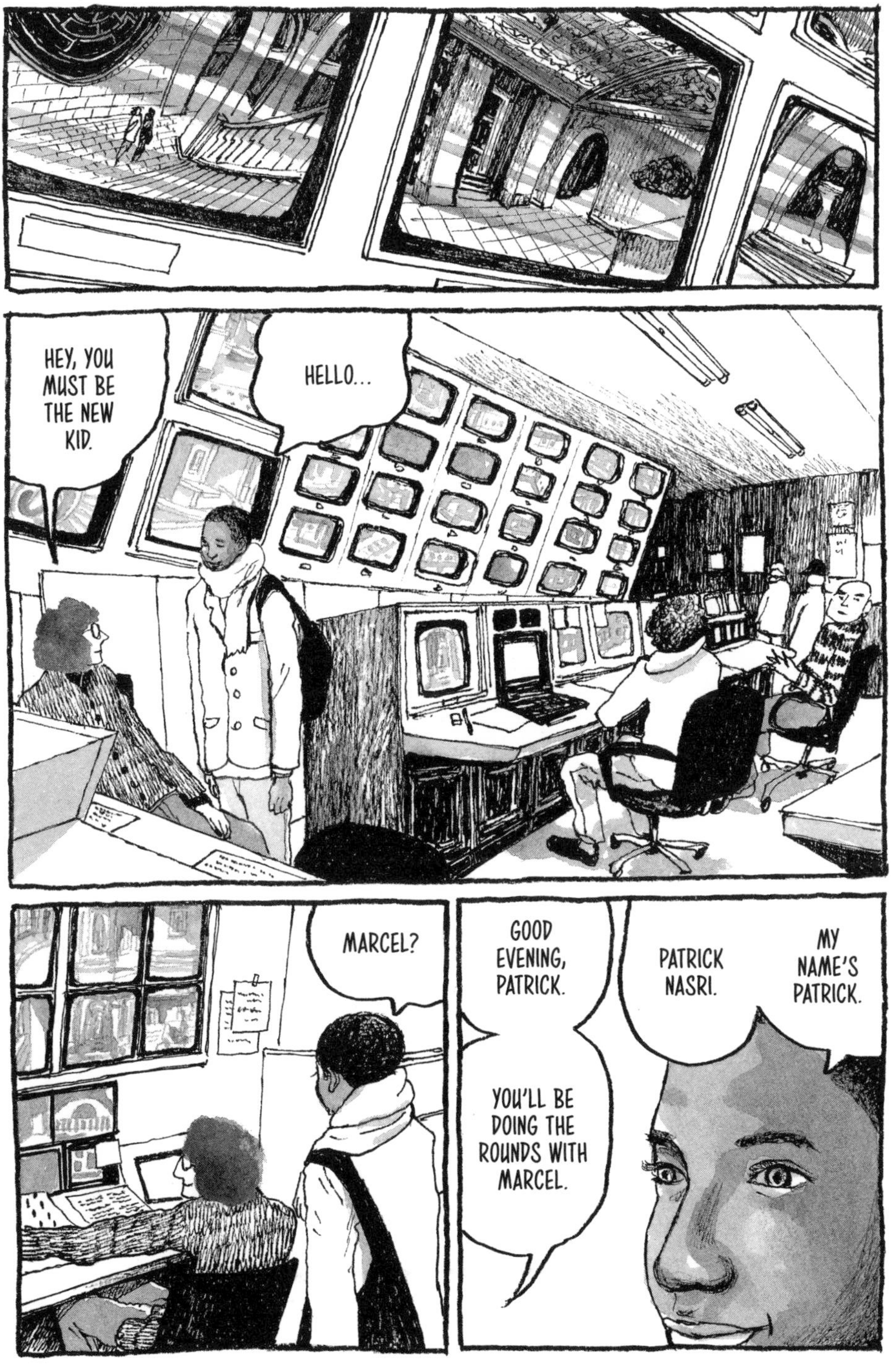
HELLO...
HEY, YOU MUST BE THE NEW KID.
MY NAME'S PATRICK.
PATRICK NASRI.
GOOD EVENING, PATRICK.
YOU'LL BE DOING THE ROUNDS WITH MARCEL.
MARCEL?

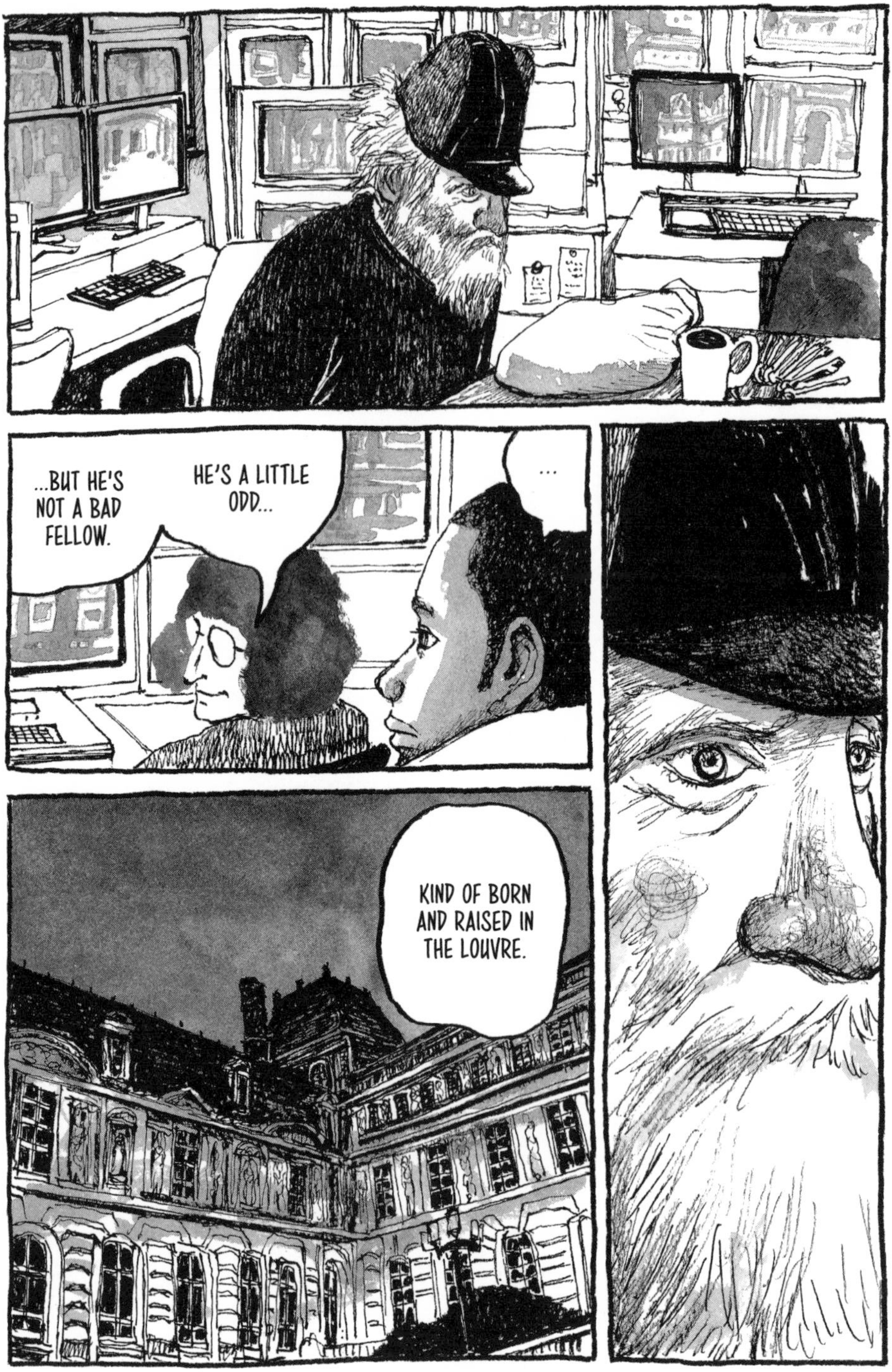
...
HE'S A LITTLE ODD...
...BUT HE'S NOT A BAD FELLOW.
KIND OF BORN AND RAISED IN THE LOUVRE.

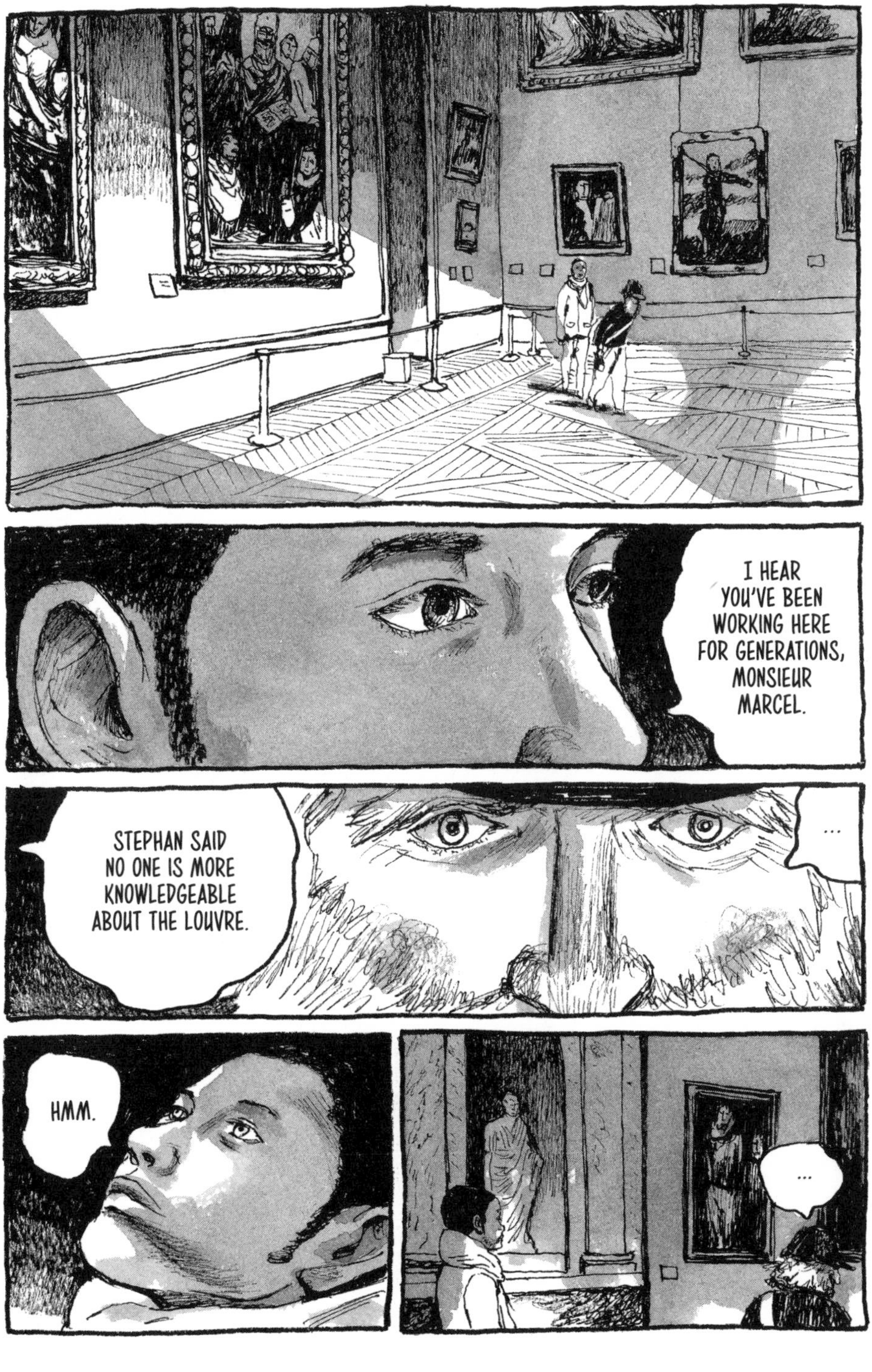
I HEAR YOU'VE BEEN WORKING HERE FOR GENERATIONS, MONSIEUR MARCEL.
...
STEPHAN SAID NO ONE IS MORE KNOWLEDGEABLE ABOUT THE LOUVRE.
...
HMM.

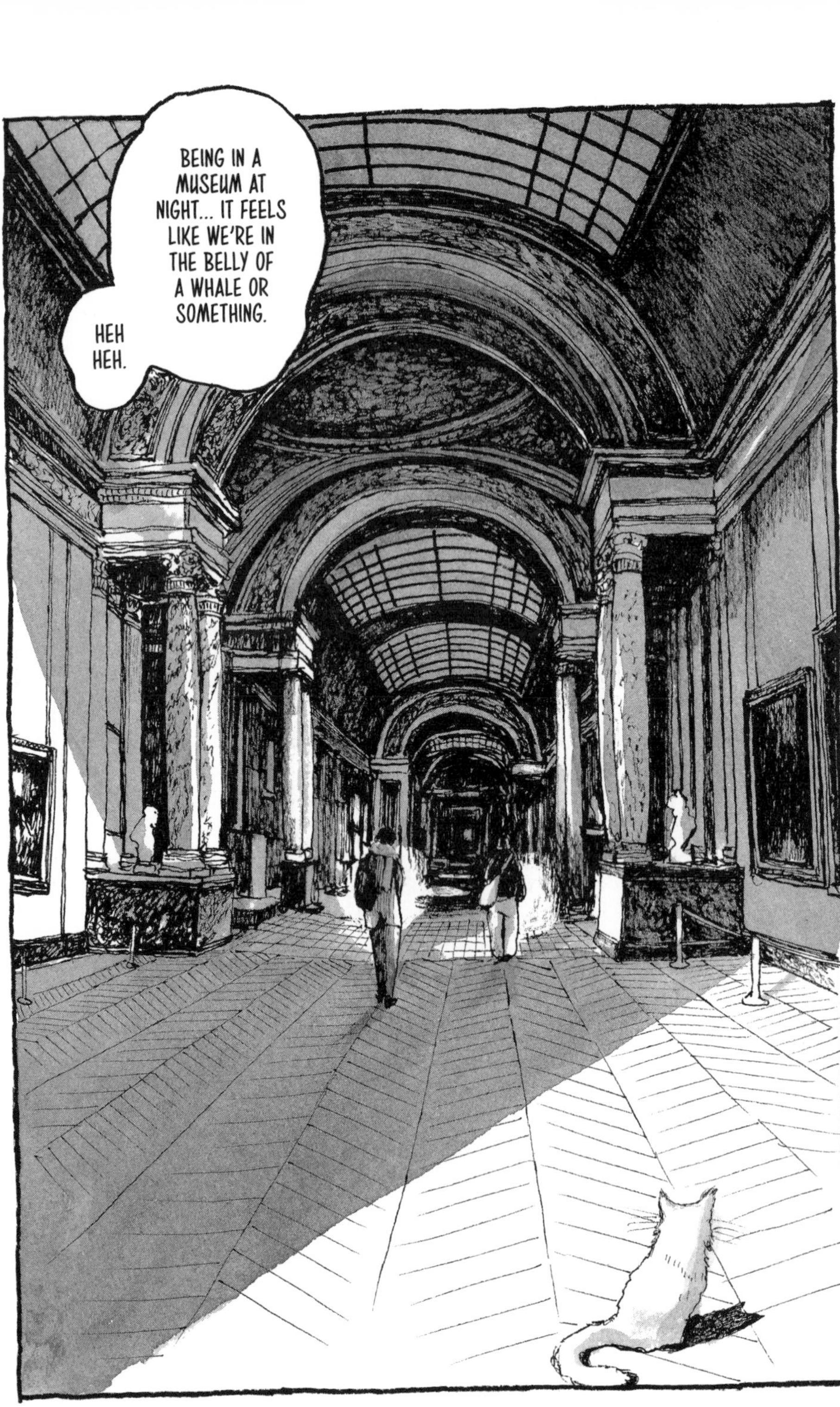
BEING IN A MUSEUM AT NIGHT... IT FEELS LIKE WE'RE IN THE BELLY OF A WHALE OR SOMETHING.
HEH HEH.

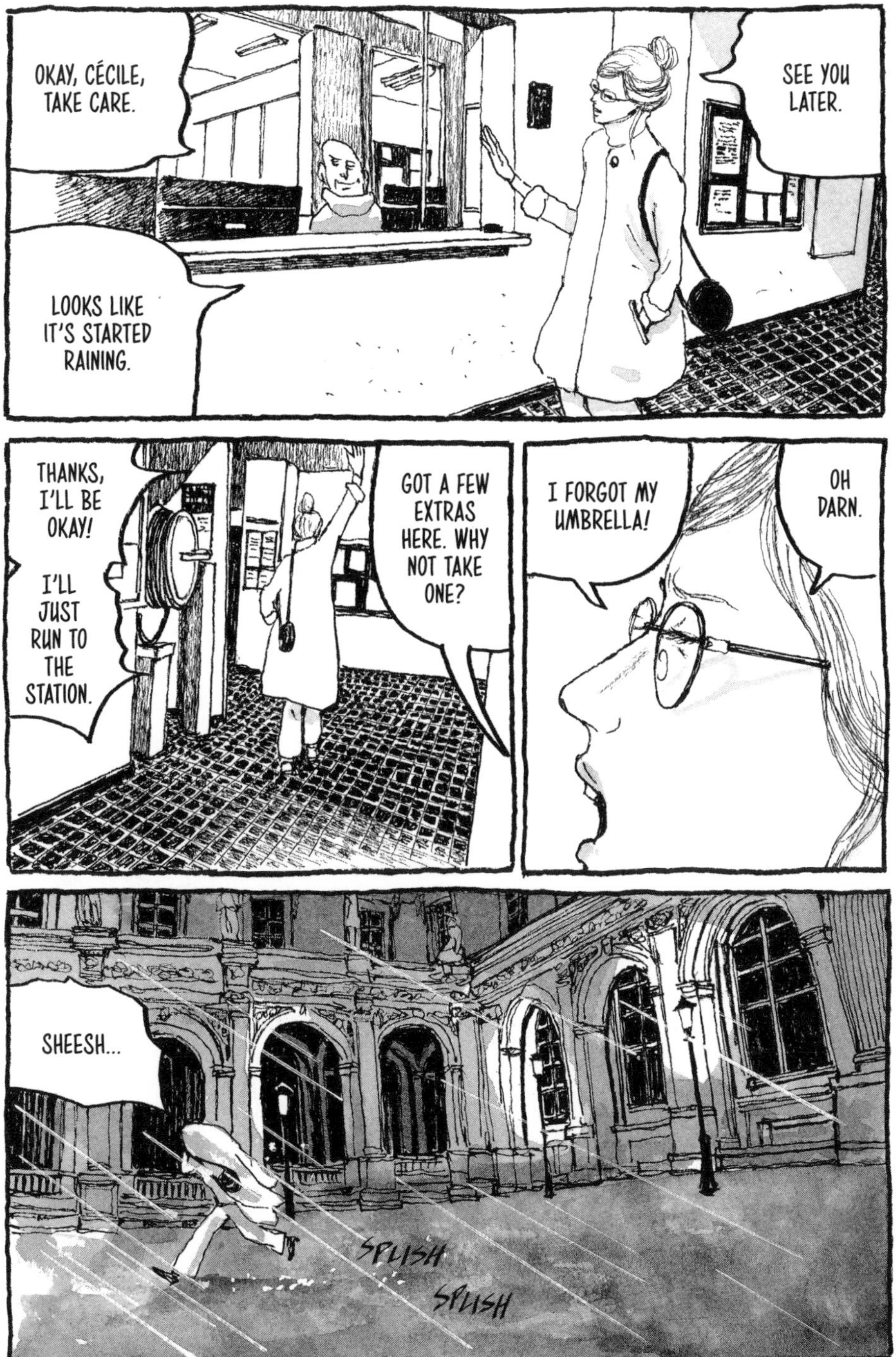
SEE YOU LATER.
OKAY, CÉCILE, TAKE CARE.
LOOKS LIKE IT'S STARTED RAINING.
OH DARN.
I FORGOT MY UMBRELLA!
GOT A FEW EXTRAS HERE. WHY NOT TAKE ONE?
THANKS, I'LL BE OKAY!
I'LL JUST RUN TO THE STATION.
SHEESH...
SPLISH
SPLISH

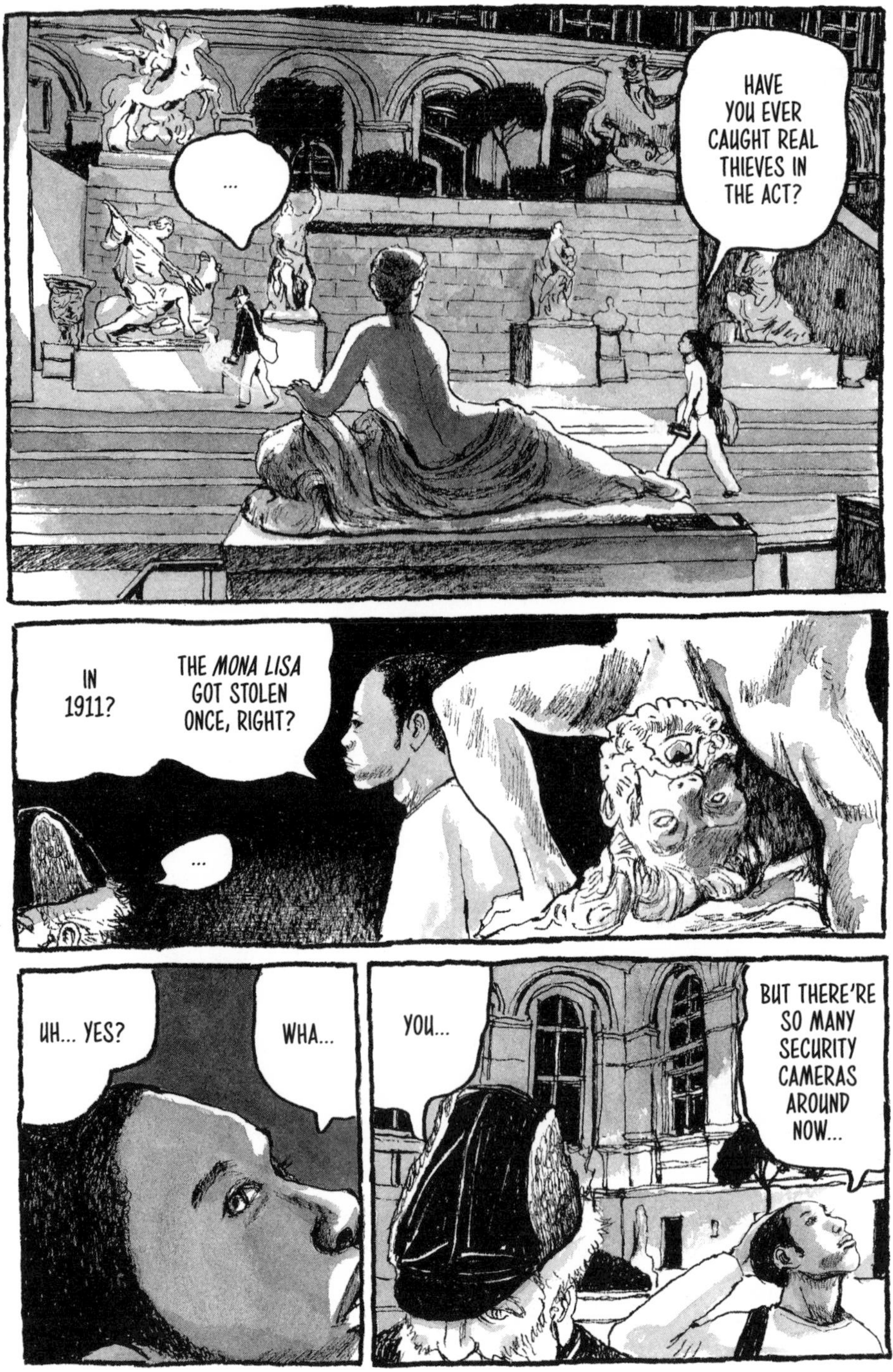
HAVE YOU EVER CAUGHT REAL THIEVES IN THE ACT?
...
THE *MONA LISA* GOT STOLEN ONCE, RIGHT?
IN 1911?
...
BUT THERE'RE SO MANY SECURITY CAMERAS AROUND NOW...
YOU...
WHA...
UH... YES?

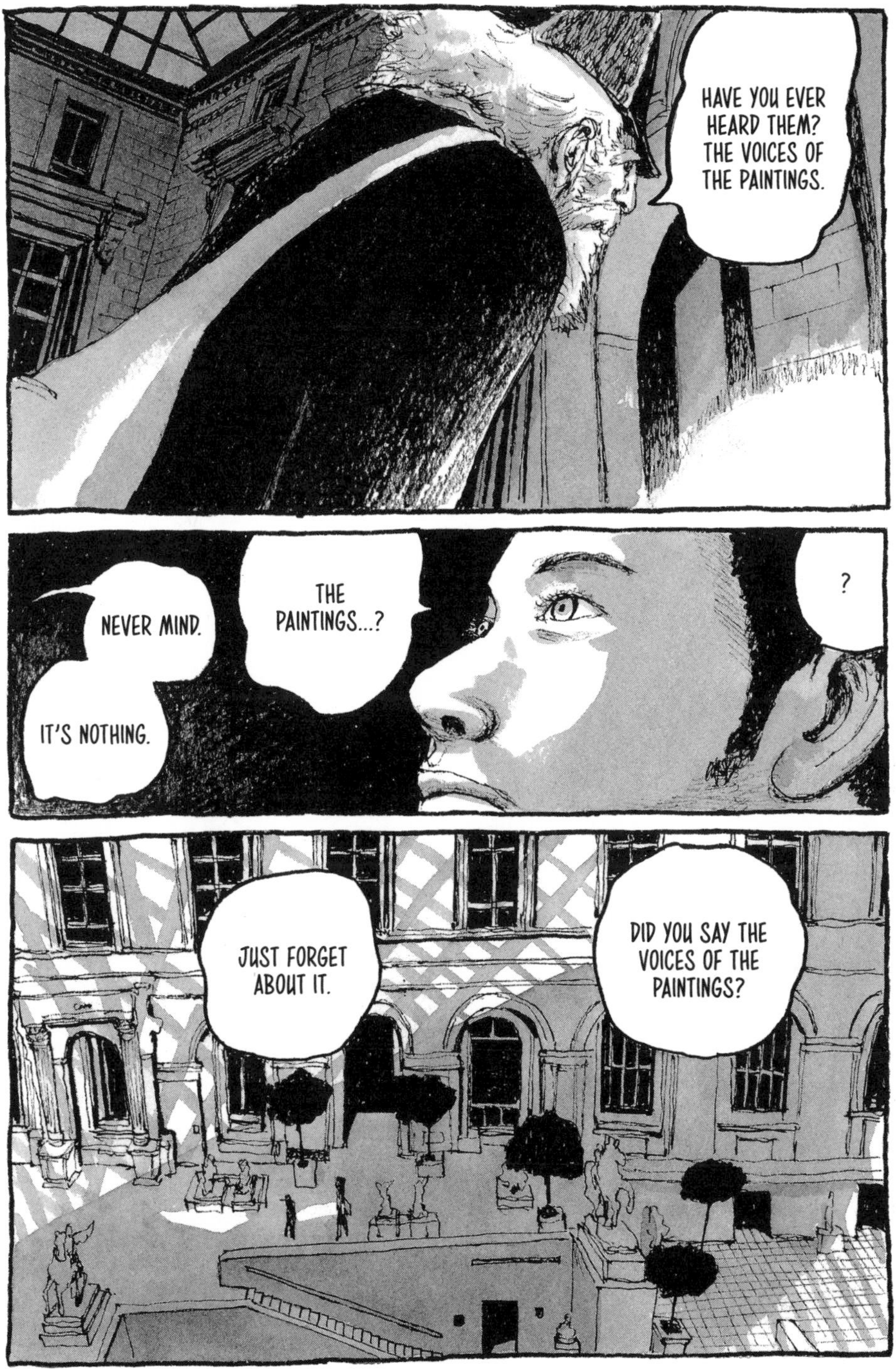
HAVE YOU EVER HEARD THEM? THE VOICES OF THE PAINTINGS.
?
THE PAINTINGS...?
NEVER MIND.
IT'S NOTHING.
DID YOU SAY THE VOICES OF THE PAINTINGS?
JUST FORGET ABOUT IT.

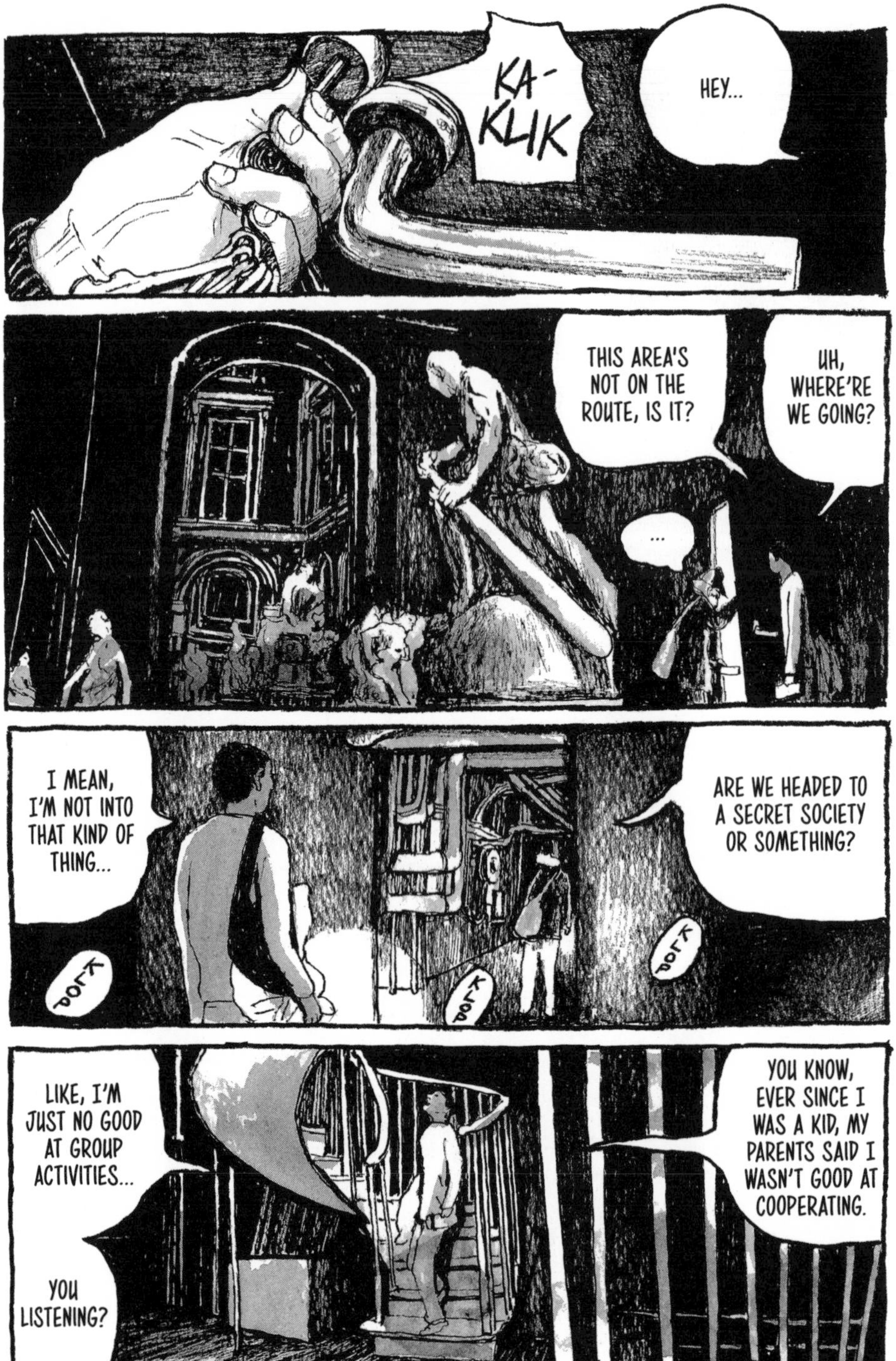
HEY...
KA-KLIK
UH, WHERE'RE WE GOING?
THIS AREA'S NOT ON THE ROUTE, IS IT?
...
ARE WE HEADED TO A SECRET SOCIETY OR SOMETHING?
I MEAN, I'M NOT INTO THAT KIND OF THING...
KLOP
KLOP
KLOP
YOU KNOW, EVER SINCE I WAS A KID, MY PARENTS SAID I WASN'T GOOD AT COOPERATING.
LIKE, I'M JUST NO GOOD AT GROUP ACTIVITIES...
YOU LISTENING?

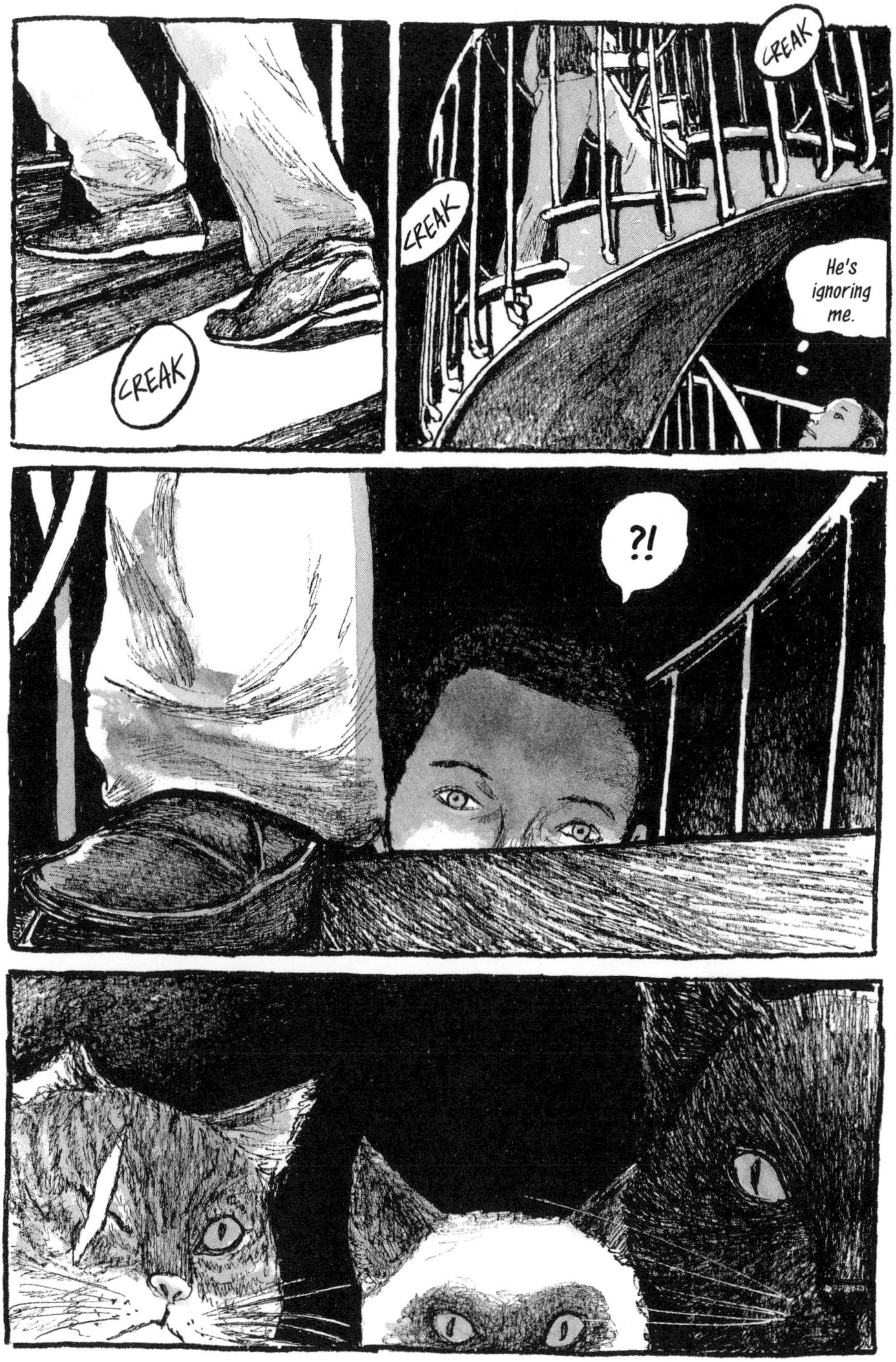
CREAK
CREAK
He's ignoring me.
CREAK
?!

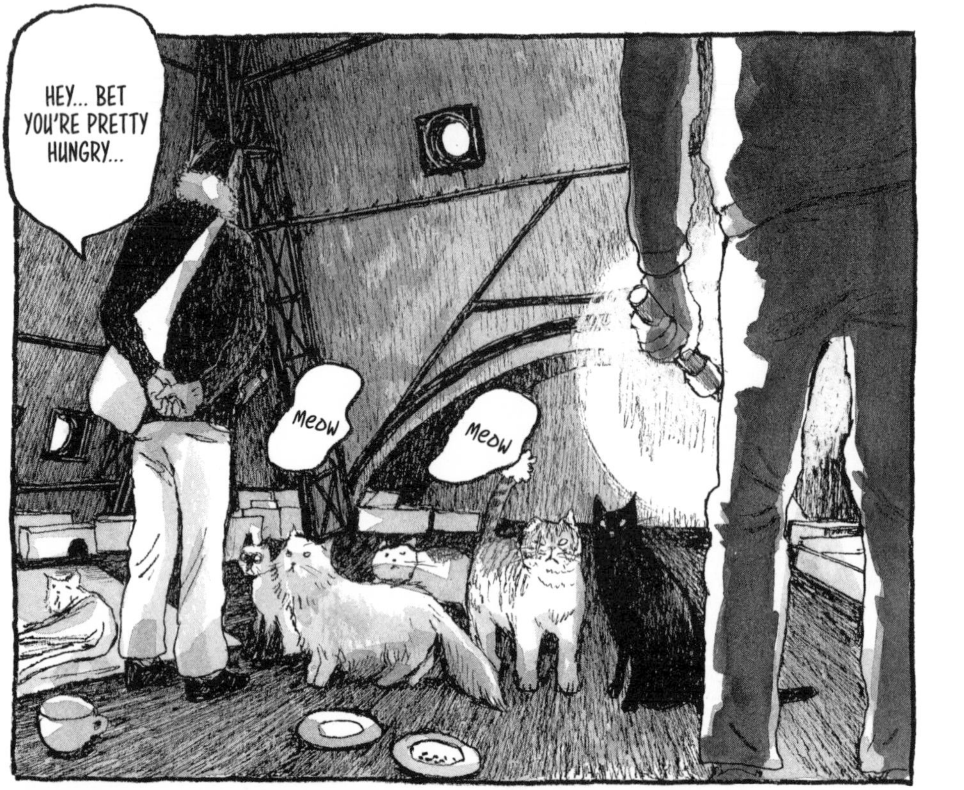
HEY... BET YOU'RE PRETTY HUNGRY...
meow
meow

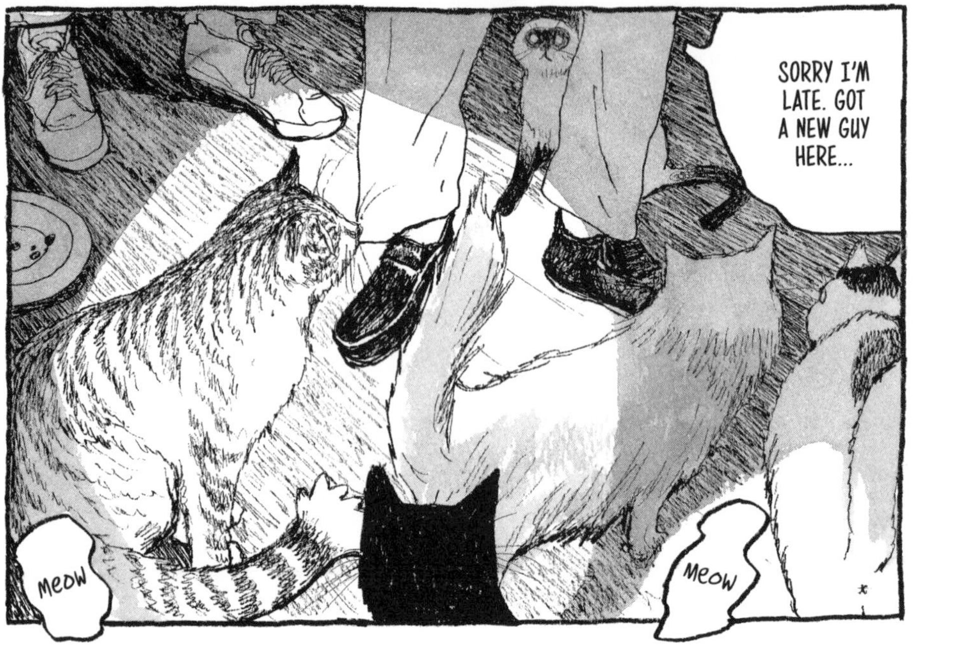
SORRY I'M LATE. GOT A NEW GUY HERE...
meow
meow

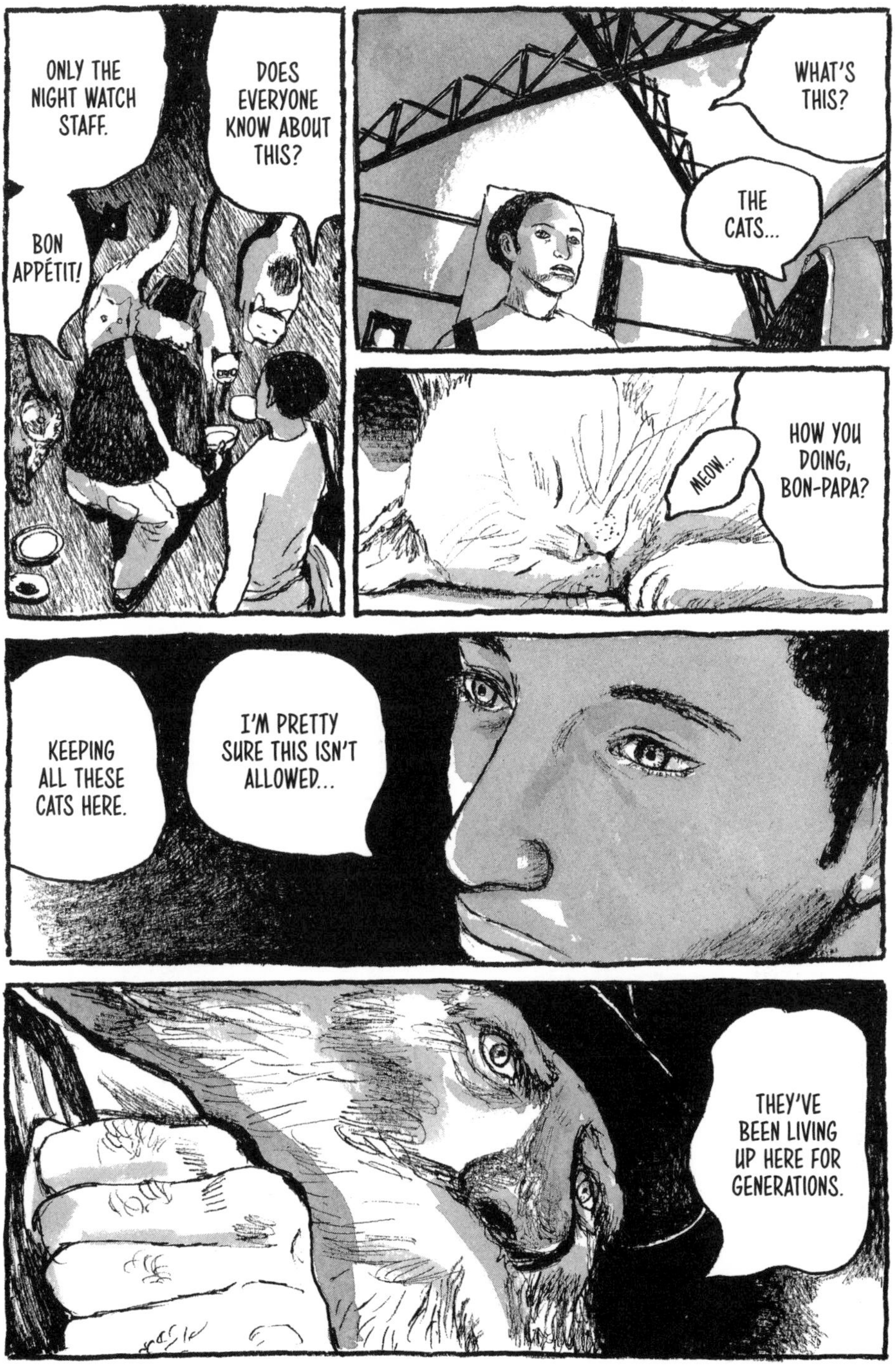
WHAT'S THIS?
THE CATS...
HOW YOU DOING, BON-PAPA?
MEOW...
DOES EVERYONE KNOW ABOUT THIS?
ONLY THE NIGHT WATCH STAFF.
BON APPÉTIT!
I'M PRETTY SURE THIS ISN'T ALLOWED...
KEEPING ALL THESE CATS HERE.
THEY'VE BEEN LIVING UP HERE FOR GENERATIONS.

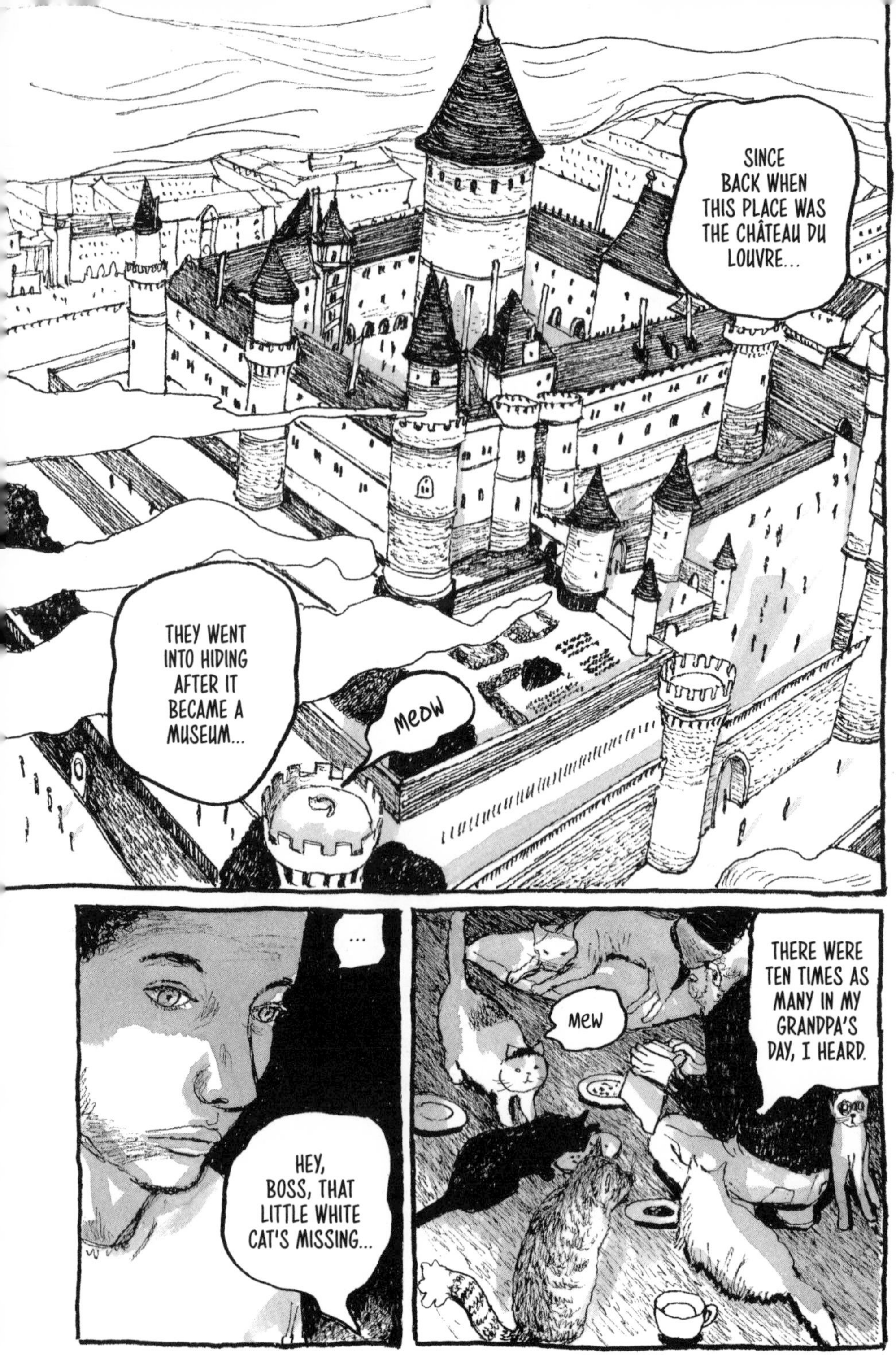
SINCE BACK WHEN THIS PLACE WAS THE CHÂTEAU DU LOUVRE...
THEY WENT INTO HIDING AFTER IT BECAME A MUSEUM...
MEOW
THERE WERE TEN TIMES AS MANY IN MY GRANDPA'S DAY, I HEARD.
MEW
...
HEY, BOSS, THAT LITTLE WHITE CAT'S MISSING...

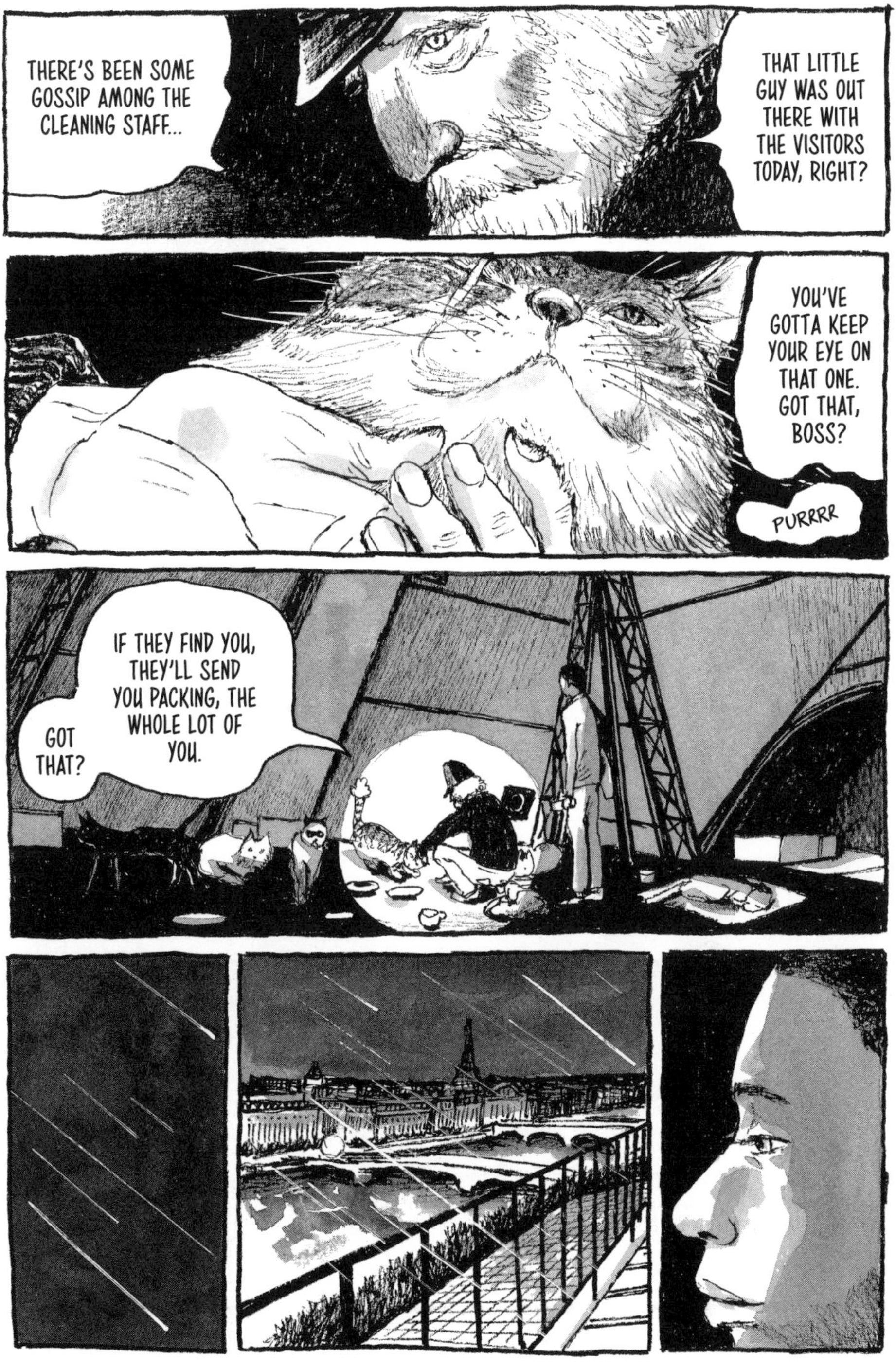
THAT LITTLE GUY WAS OUT THERE WITH THE VISITORS TODAY, RIGHT?
THERE'S BEEN SOME GOSSIP AMONG THE CLEANING STAFF...
YOU'VE GOTTA KEEP YOUR EYE ON THAT ONE. GOT THAT, BOSS?
PURRRR
IF THEY FIND YOU, THEY'LL SEND YOU PACKING, THE WHOLE LOT OF YOU.
GOT THAT?

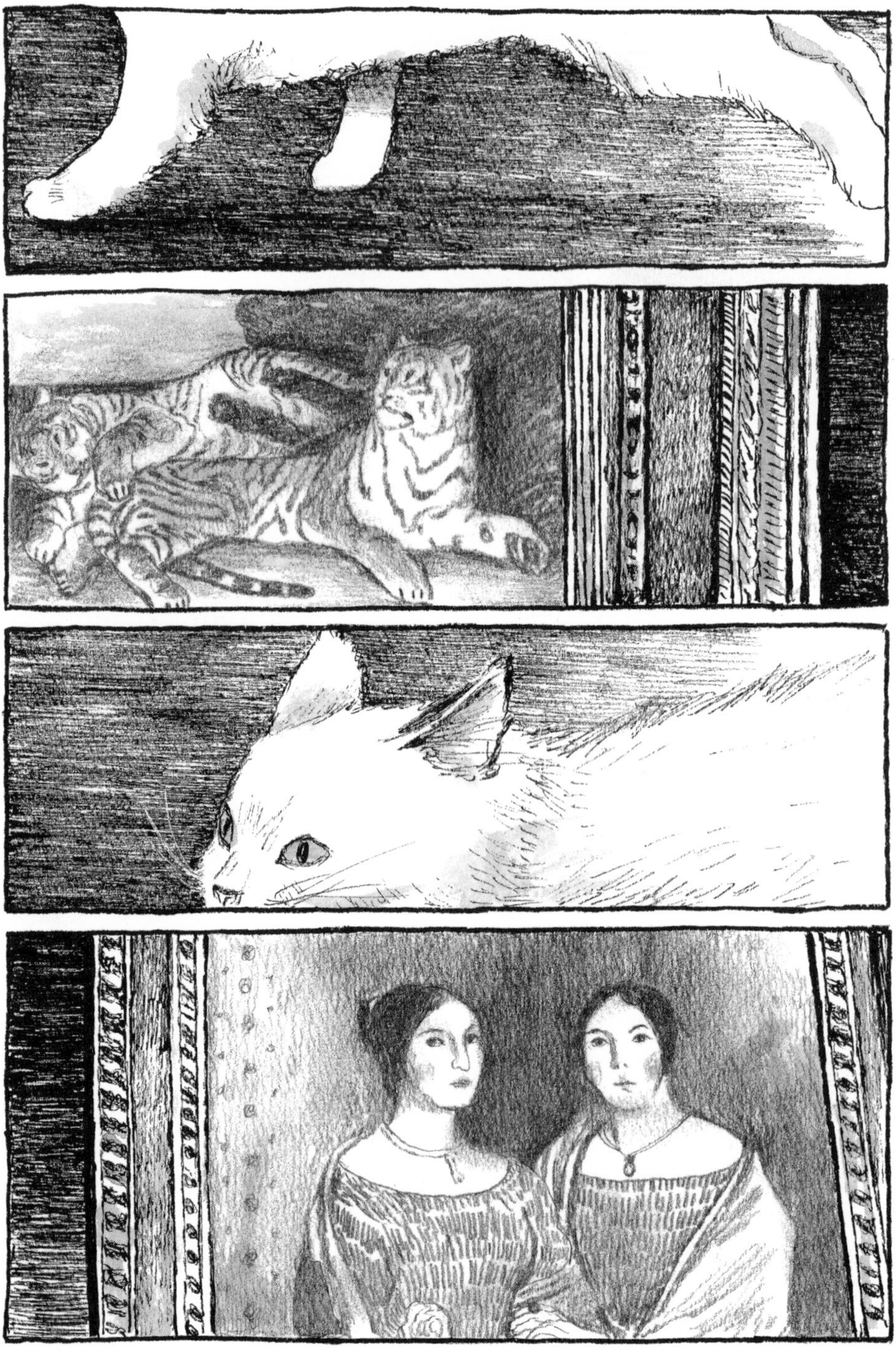

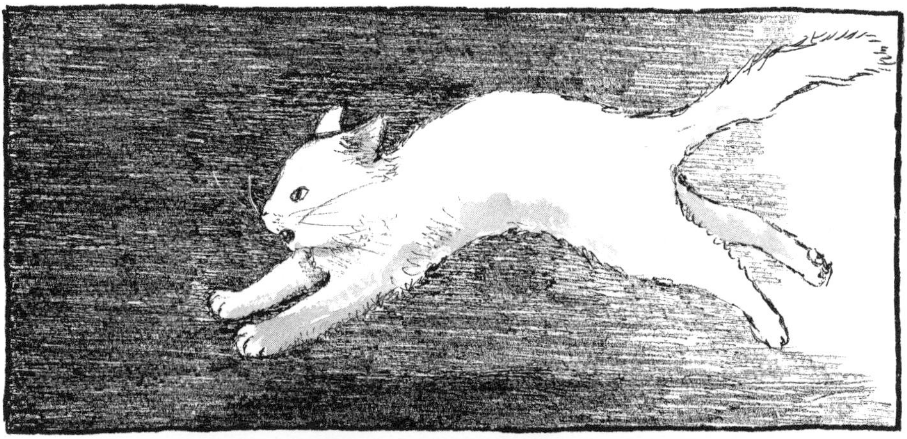
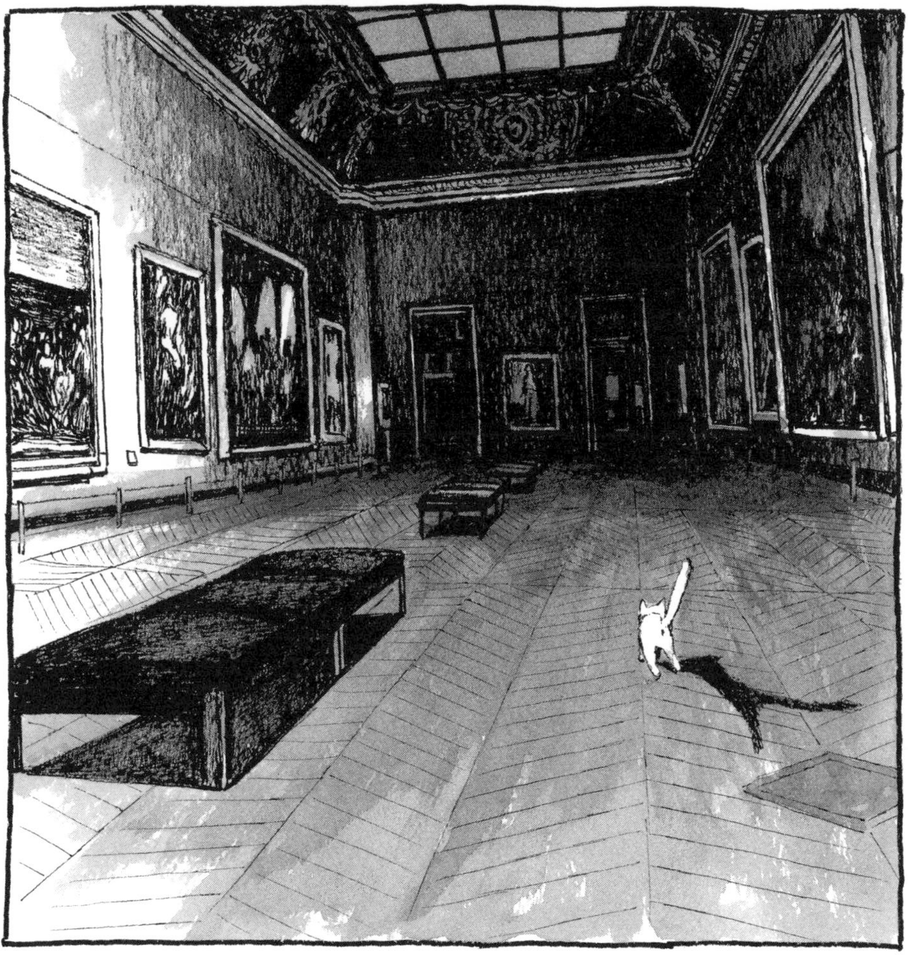

CHAPTER 2

The Secret of the Full Moon

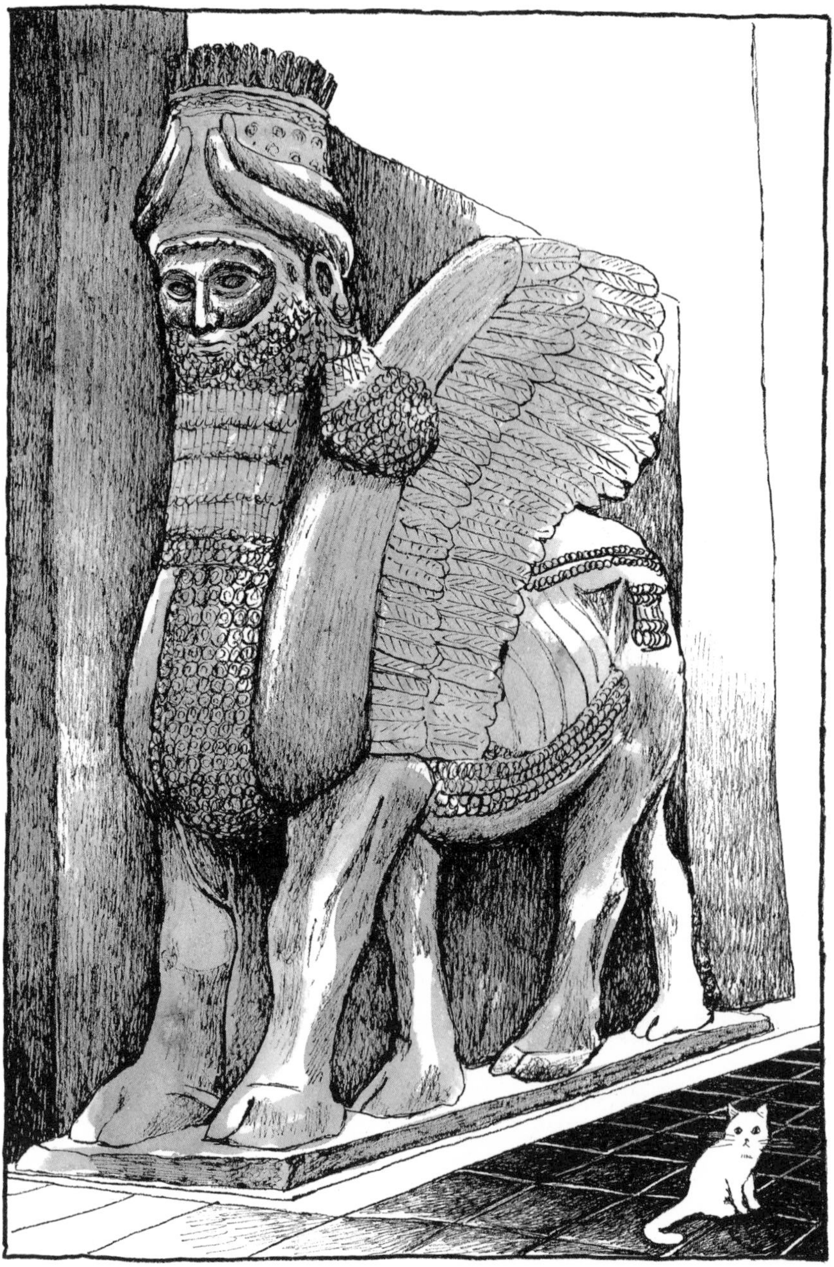

▲ Lamassus, Assyrian deity with human head, bull body and wings (Near Eastern Antiquities)

BONSOIR
BONSOIR,
SNOWBÉBÉ.

I WATCHED YOU
YESTERDAY.

I KNOW
YOU.

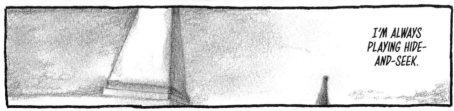

I'M ALWAYS
PLAYING HIDE-
AND-SEEK.

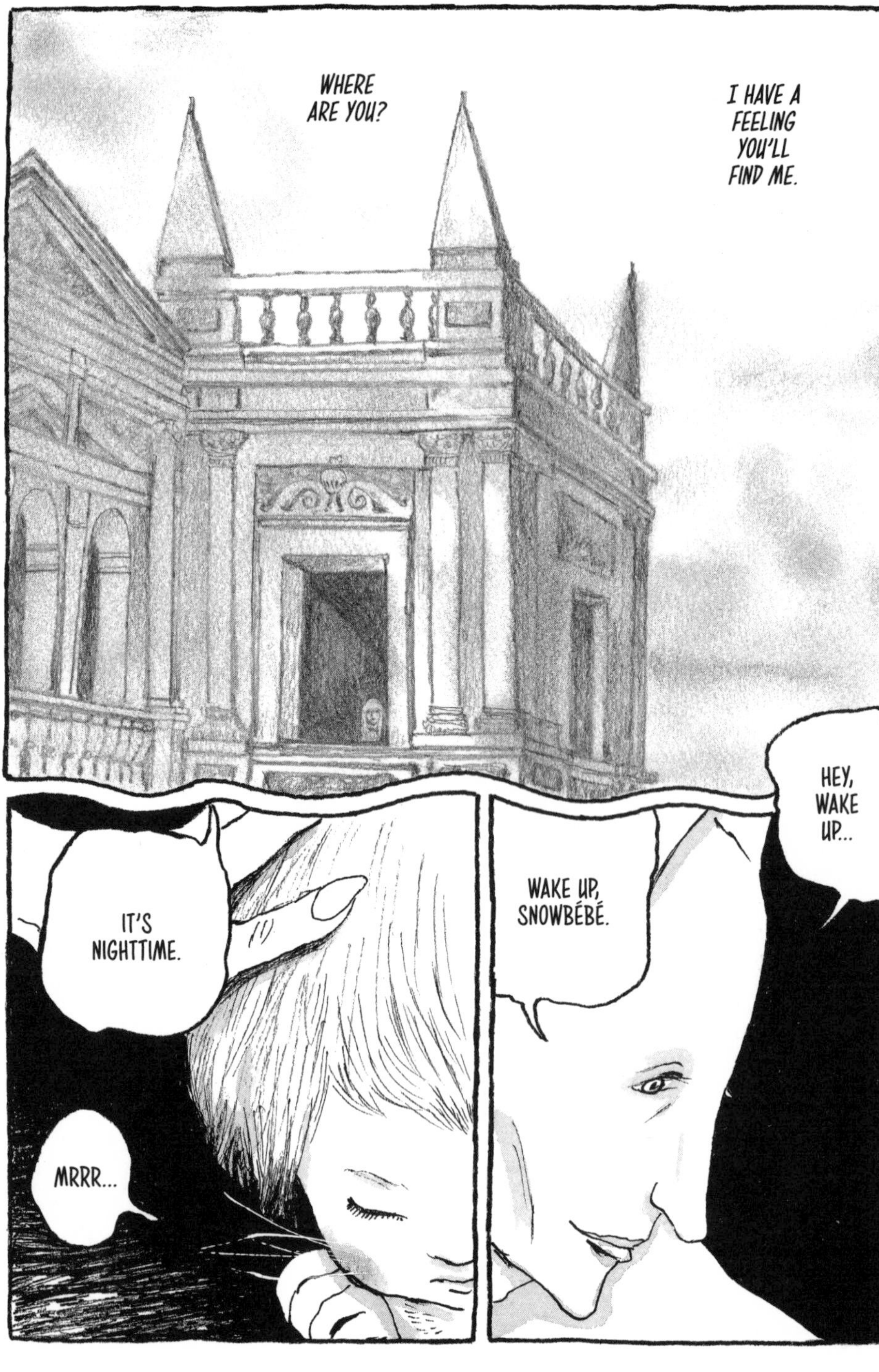
I HAVE A FEELING YOU'LL FIND ME.
WHERE ARE YOU?
HEY, WAKE UP...
WAKE UP, SNOWBÉBÉ.
IT'S NIGHTTIME.
MRRR...

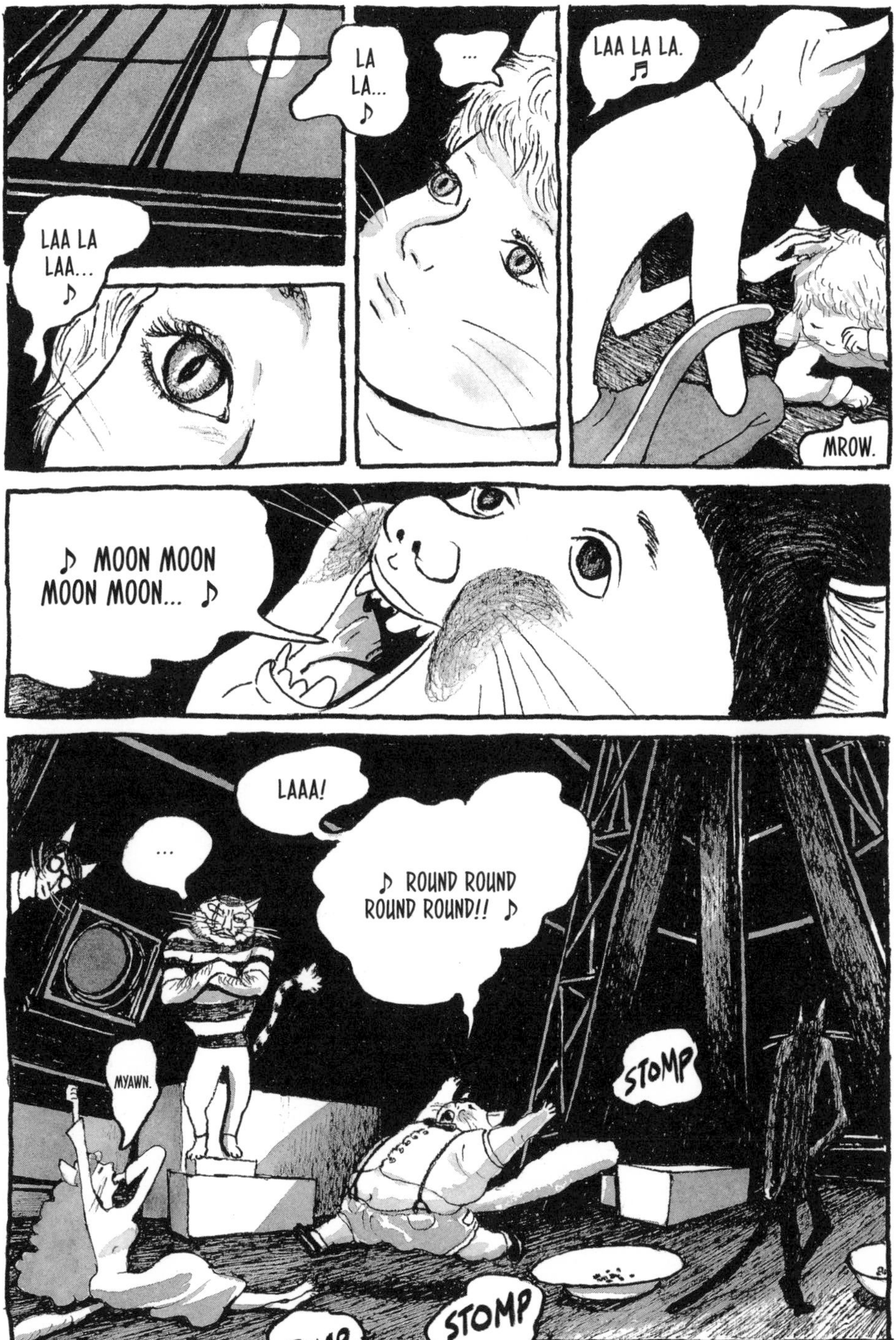
LAA LA LA. ♬
MROW.
LA LA... ♪
...
LAA LA LAA... ♪
♪ MOON MOON MOON MOON... ♪
LAAA!
♪ ROUND ROUND ROUND ROUND!! ♪
STOMP
...
MYAWN.
STOMP
STOMP

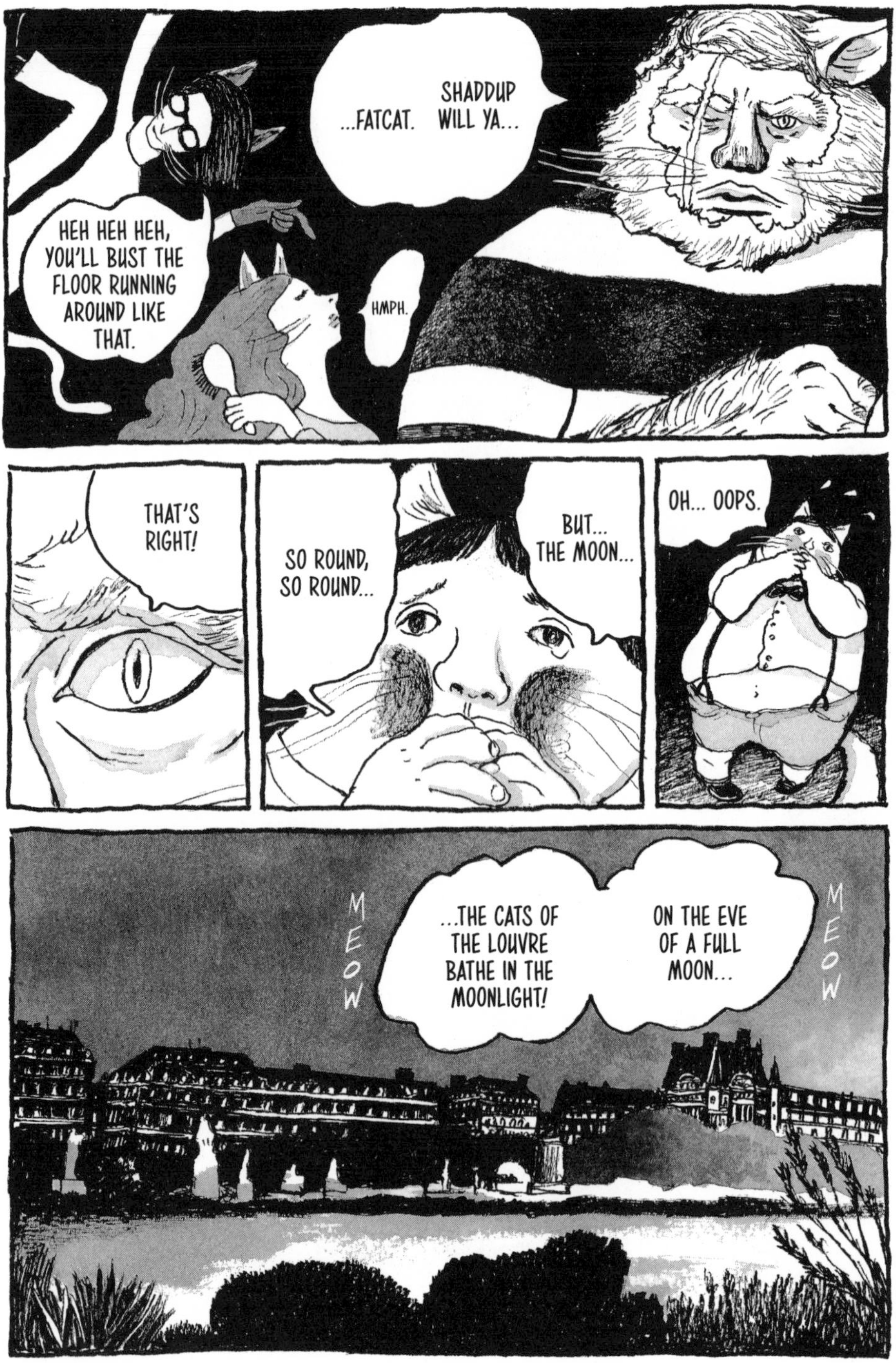
SHADDUP WILL YA... ...FATCAT.
HMPH.
HEH HEH HEH, YOU'LL BUST THE FLOOR RUNNING AROUND LIKE THAT.
OH... OOPS.
BUT... THE MOON...
SO ROUND, SO ROUND...
THAT'S RIGHT!
MEOW
ON THE EVE OF A FULL MOON...
...THE CATS OF THE LOUVRE BATHE IN THE MOONLIGHT!
MEOW

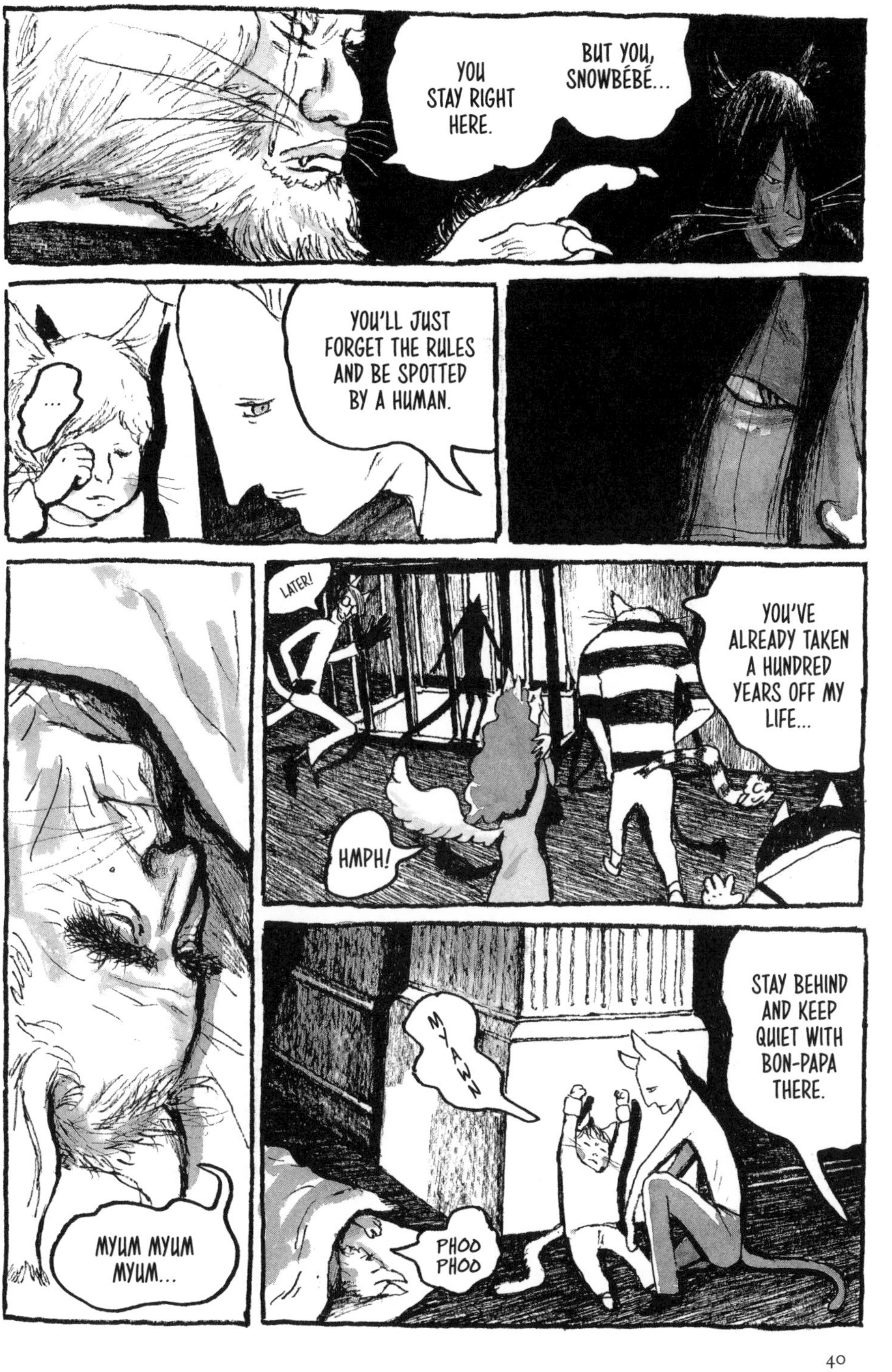
BUT YOU, SNOWBÉBÉ...
YOU STAY RIGHT HERE.
YOU'LL JUST FORGET THE RULES AND BE SPOTTED BY A HUMAN.
...
YOU'VE ALREADY TAKEN A HUNDRED YEARS OFF MY LIFE...
LATER!
HMPH!
STAY BEHIND AND KEEP QUIET WITH BON-PAPA THERE.
MYAWN
PHOO PHOO
MYUM MYUM MYUM...

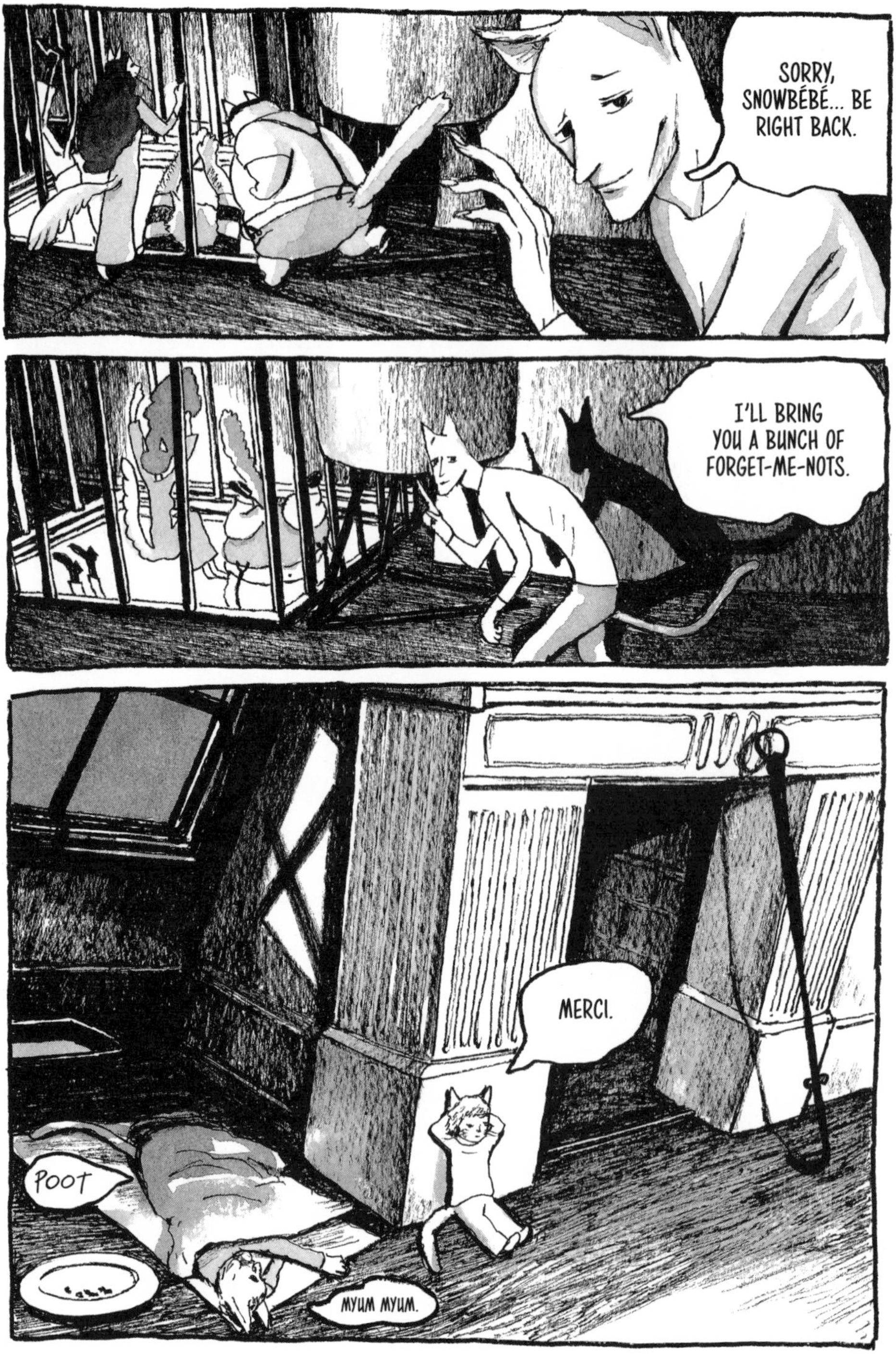
SORRY, SNOWBÉBÉ... BE RIGHT BACK.
I'LL BRING YOU A BUNCH OF FORGET-ME-NOTS.
MERCI.
POOT
MYUM MYUM.

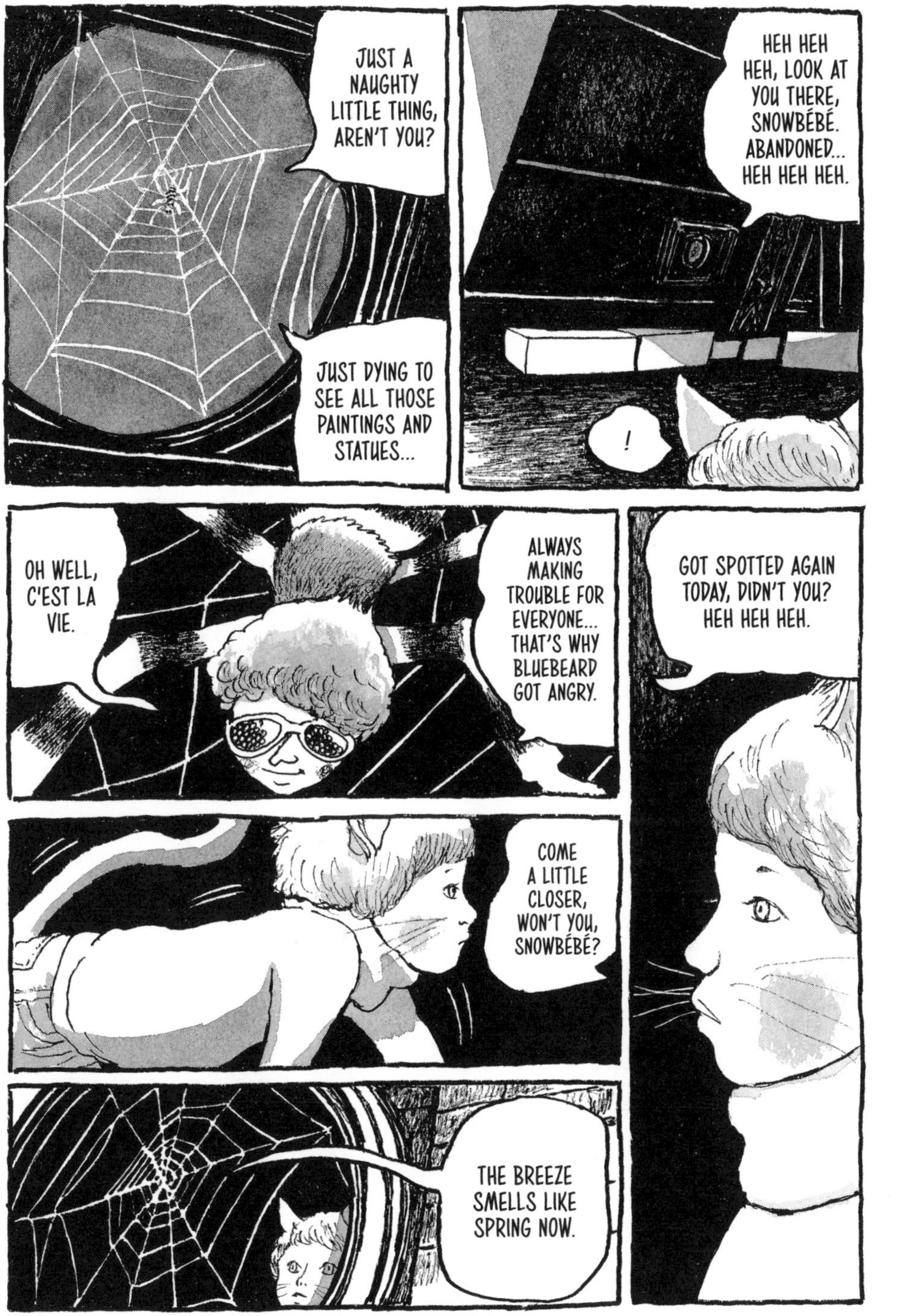
HEH HEH HEH, LOOK AT YOU THERE, SNOWBÉBÉ. ABANDONED... HEH HEH HEH.
!
JUST A NAUGHTY LITTLE THING, AREN'T YOU?
JUST DYING TO SEE ALL THOSE PAINTINGS AND STATUES...
GOT SPOTTED AGAIN TODAY, DIDN'T YOU? HEH HEH HEH.
ALWAYS MAKING TROUBLE FOR EVERYONE... THAT'S WHY BLUEBEARD GOT ANGRY.
OH WELL, C'EST LA VIE.
COME A LITTLE CLOSER, WON'T YOU, SNOWBÉBÉ?
THE BREEZE SMELLS LIKE SPRING NOW.

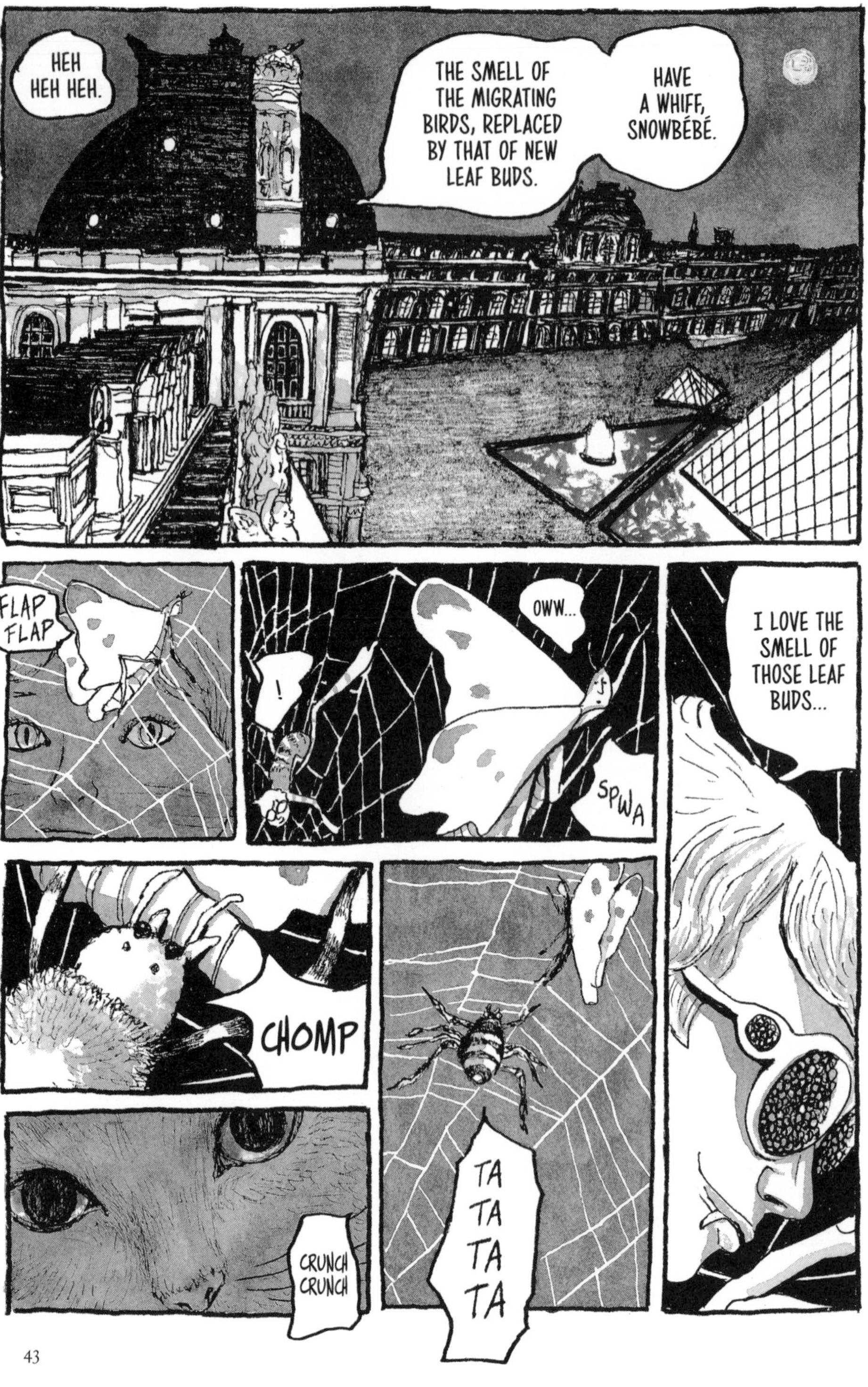
HAVE A WHIFF, SNOWBÉBÉ.
THE SMELL OF THE MIGRATING BIRDS, REPLACED BY THAT OF NEW LEAF BUDS.
HEH HEH HEH.
I LOVE THE SMELL OF THOSE LEAF BUDS...
OWW...
!
SPWA
FLAP FLAP
TA TA TA TA
CHOMP
CRUNCH CRUNCH

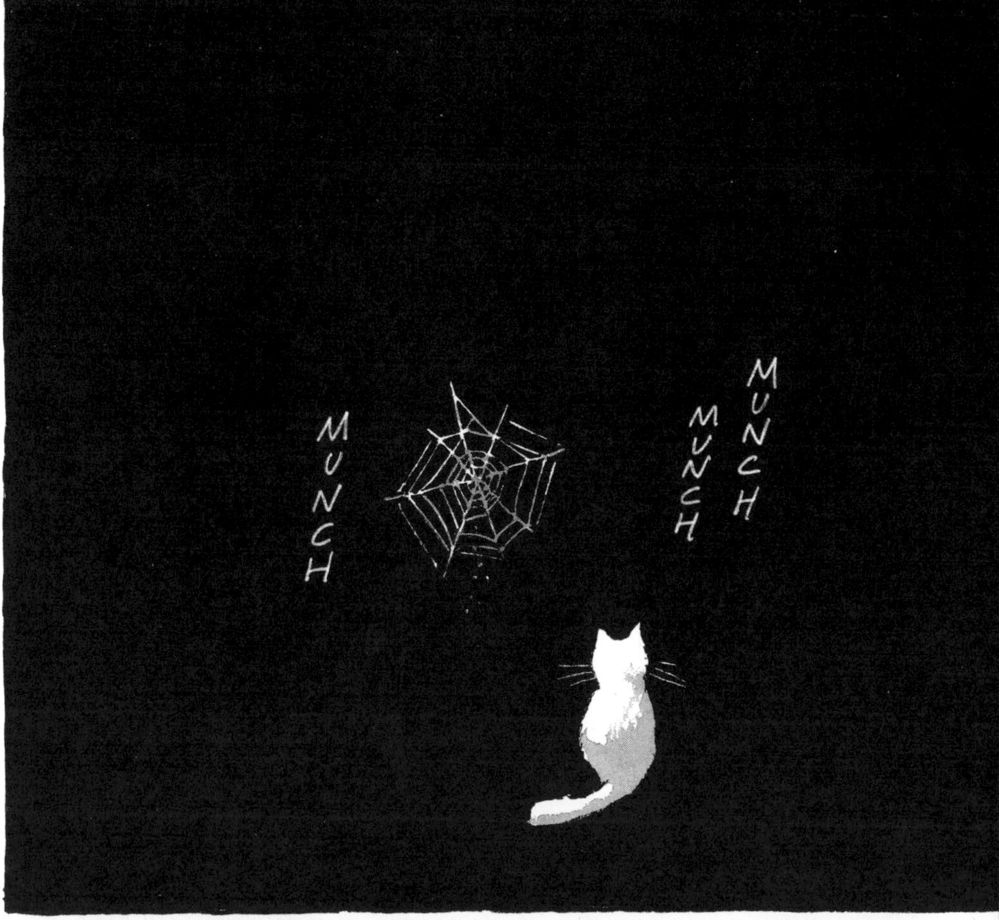
MUNCH
MUNCH
MUNCH

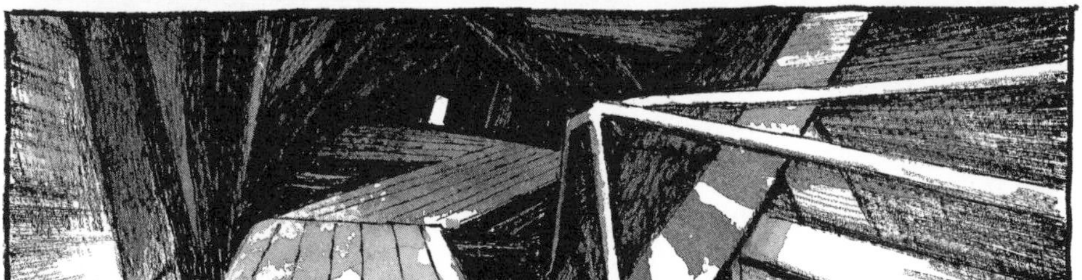

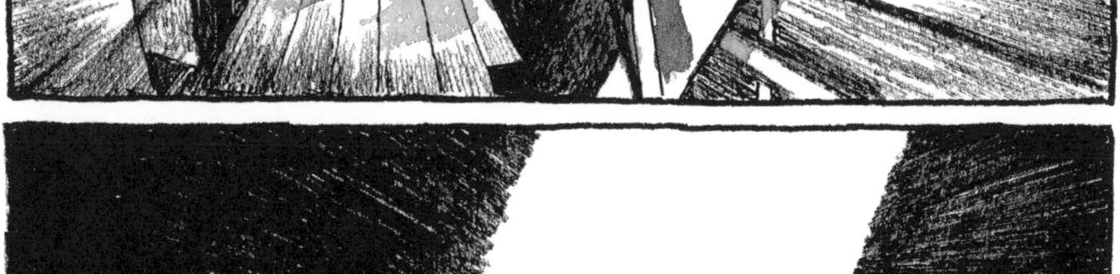

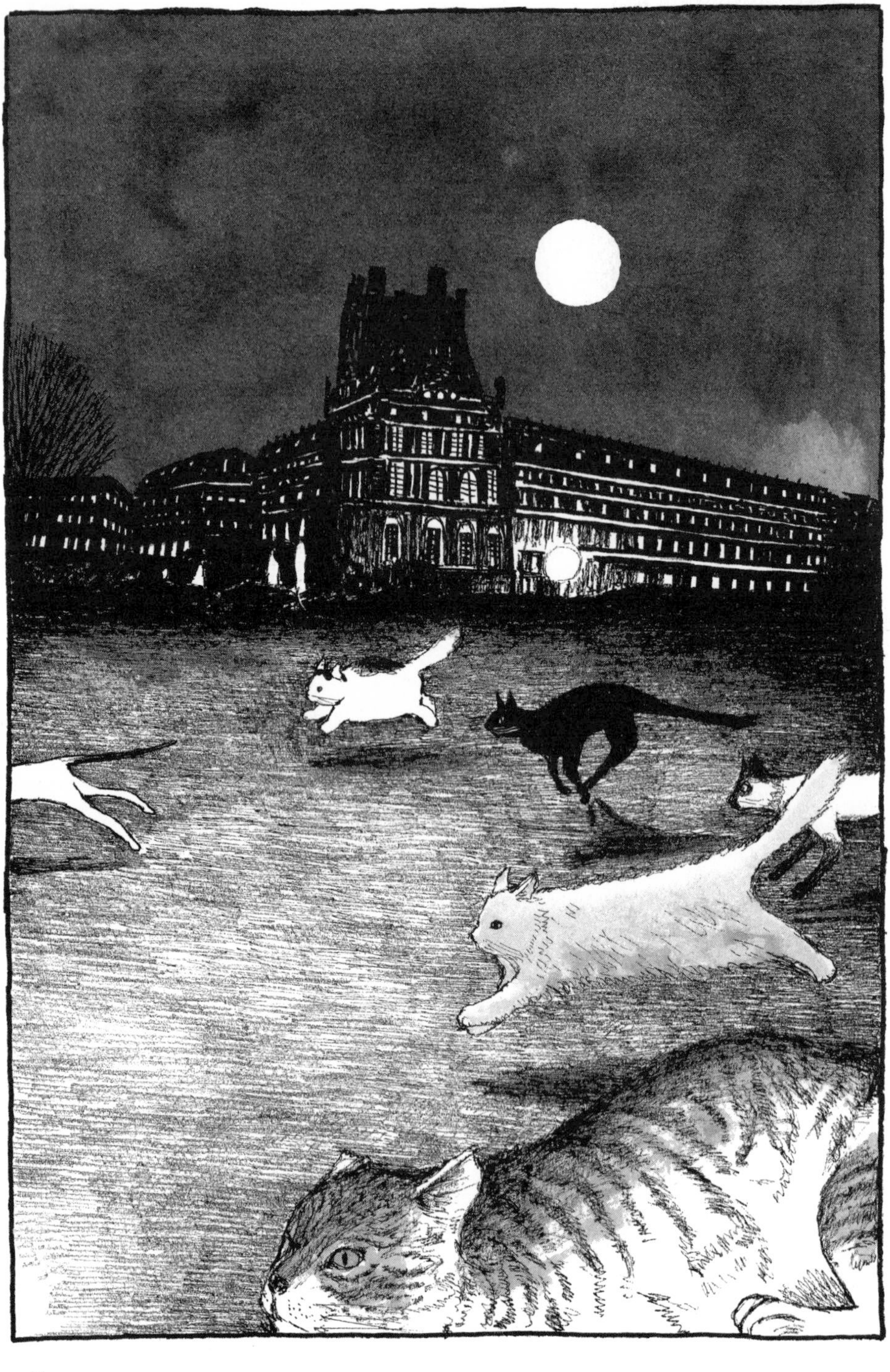

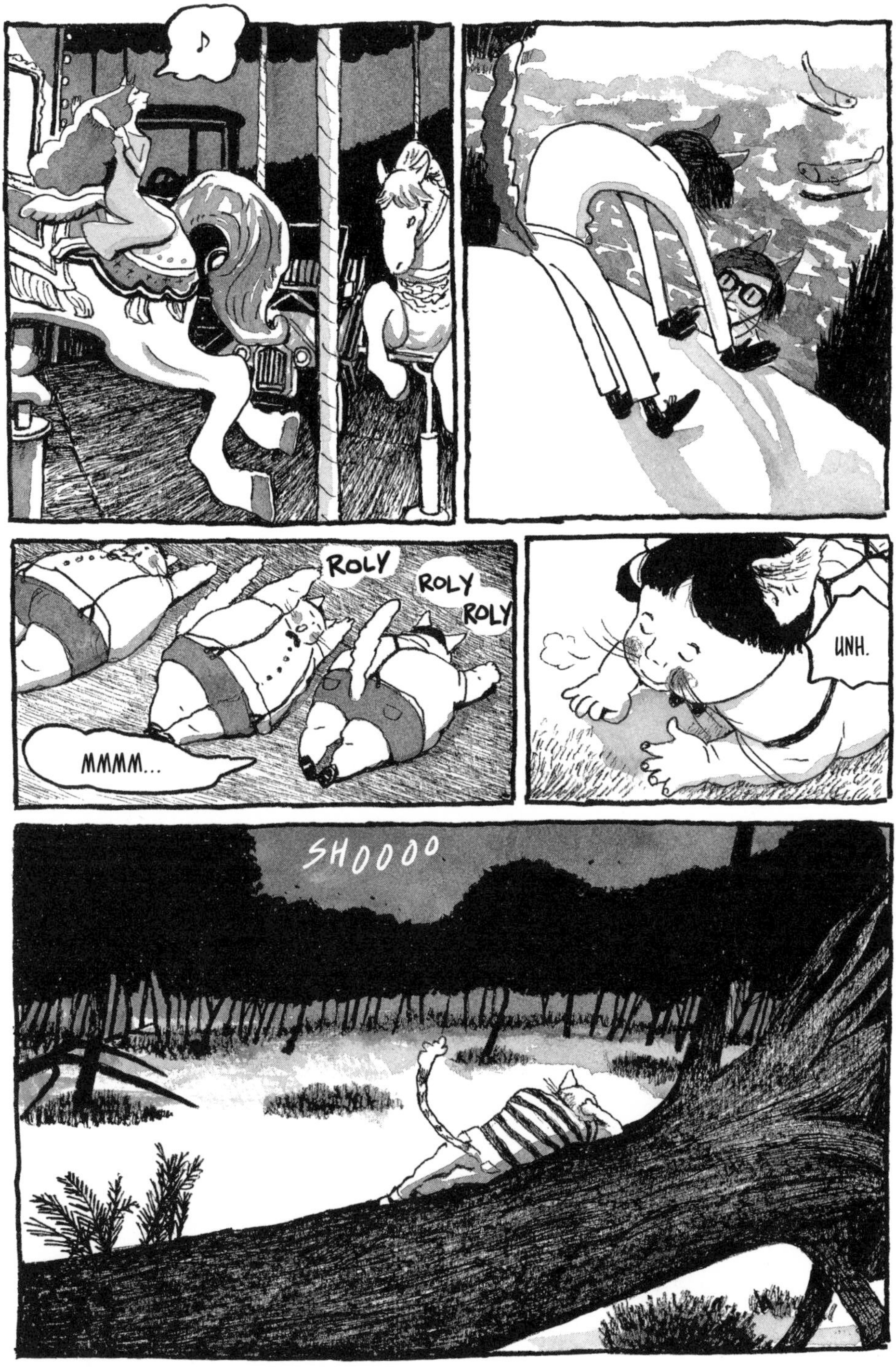
♪
UNH.
ROLY
ROLY
ROLY
MMMM...
SHOOOO

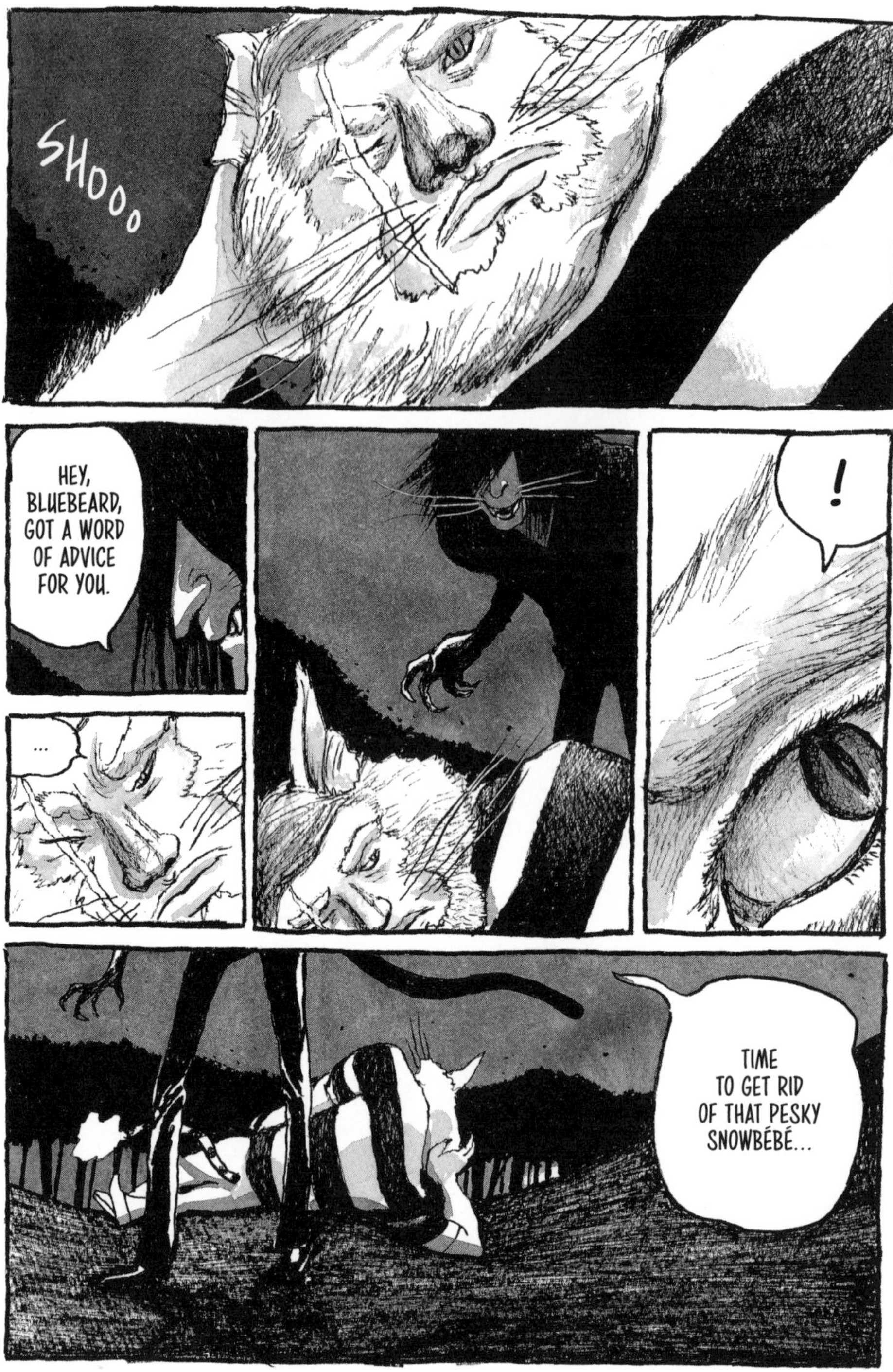
SHOOOO
!
HEY, BLUEBEARD, GOT A WORD OF ADVICE FOR YOU.
...
TIME TO GET RID OF THAT PESKY SNOWBÉBÉ...

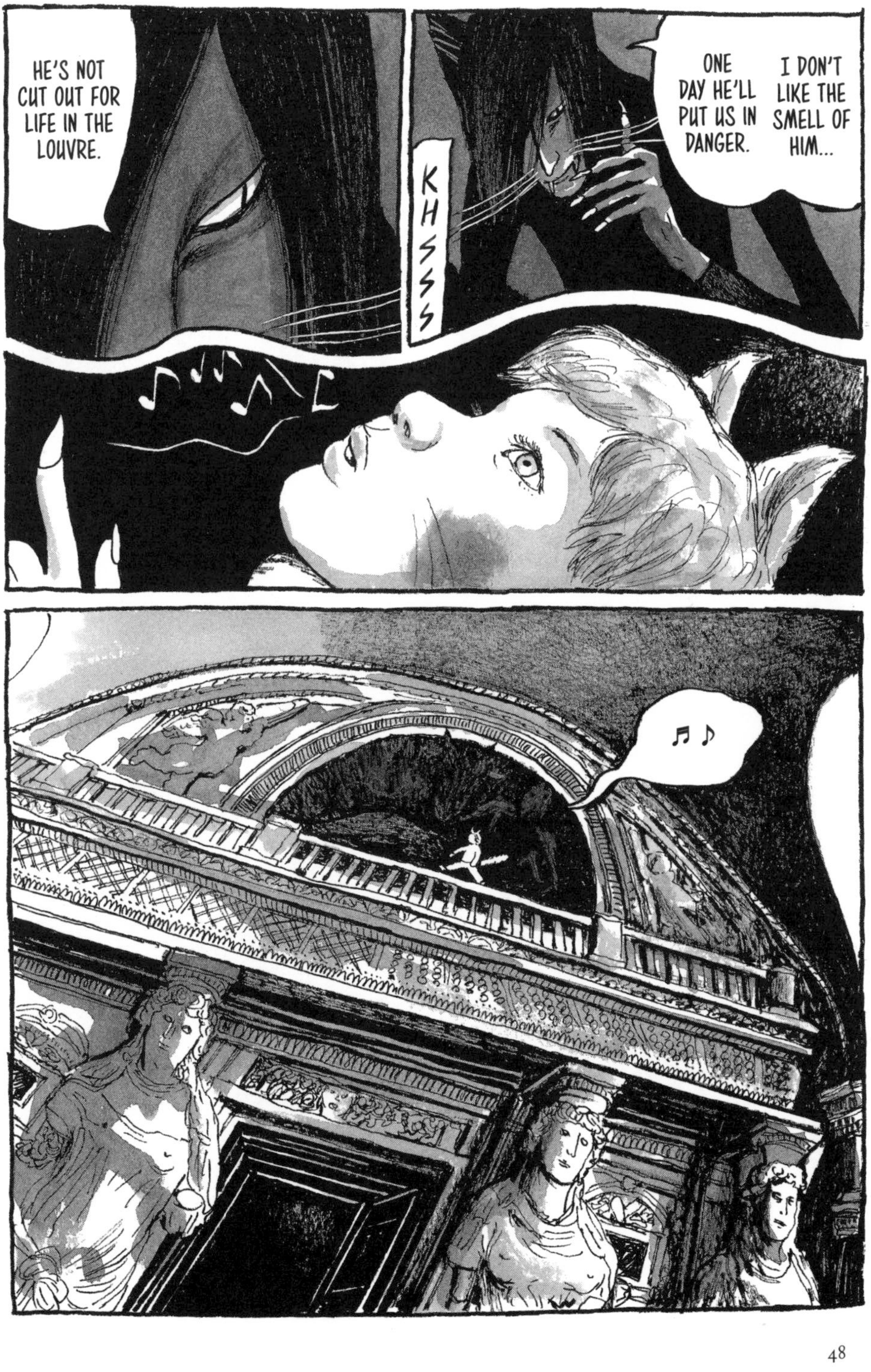

I DON'T LIKE THE SMELL OF HIM...
ONE DAY HE'LL PUT US IN DANGER.
KHSSS
HE'S NOT CUT OUT FOR LIFE IN THE LOUVRE.
♬ ♪

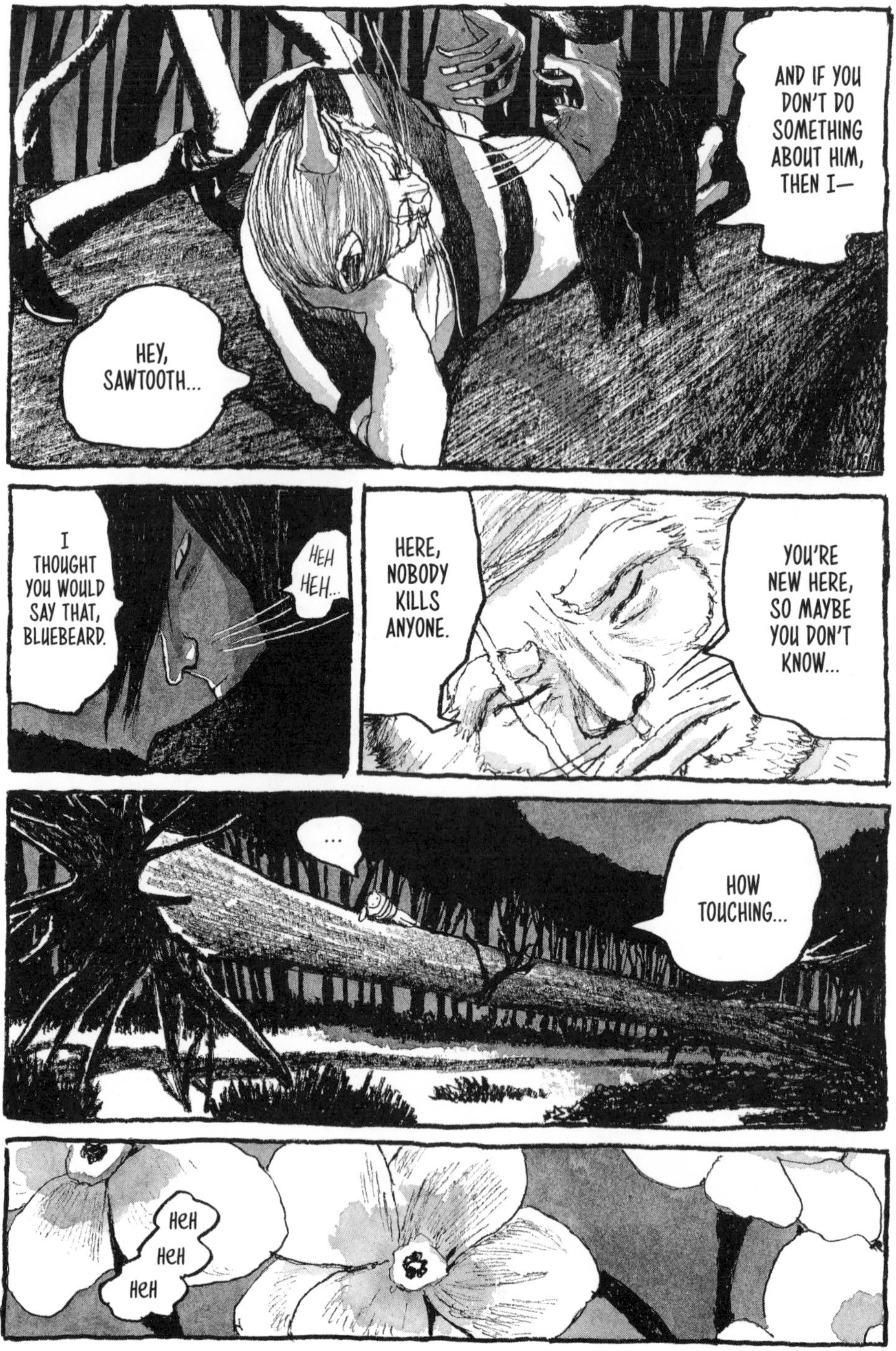
AND IF YOU DON'T DO SOMETHING ABOUT HIM, THEN I—
HEY, SAWTOOTH...
YOU'RE NEW HERE, SO MAYBE YOU DON'T KNOW...
HERE, NOBODY KILLS ANYONE.
HEH HEH...
I THOUGHT YOU WOULD SAY THAT, BLUEBEARD.
HOW TOUCHING...
...
HEH HEH HEH

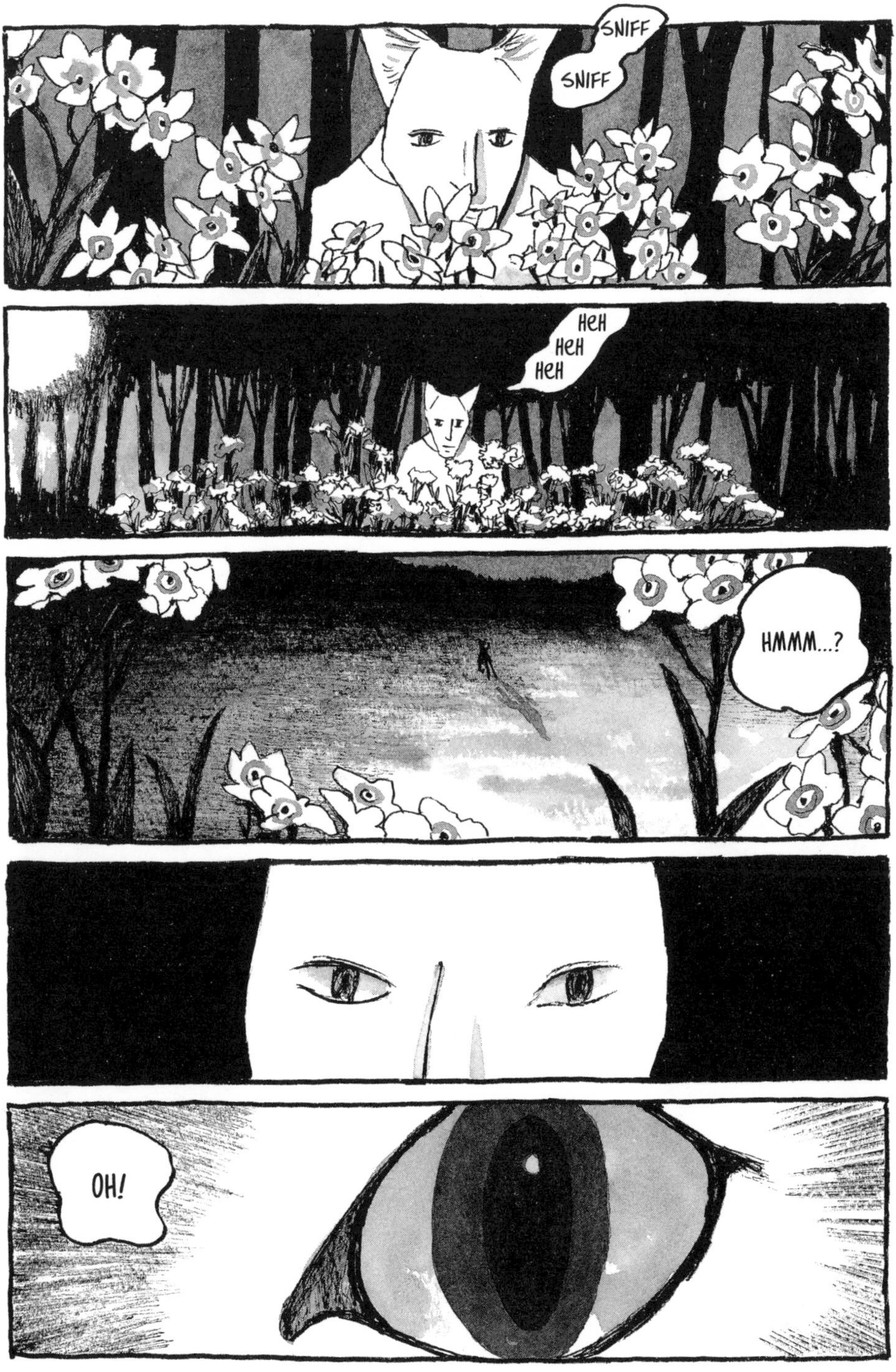
SNIFF
SNIFF
HEH
HEH
HEH
HMMM...?
OH!

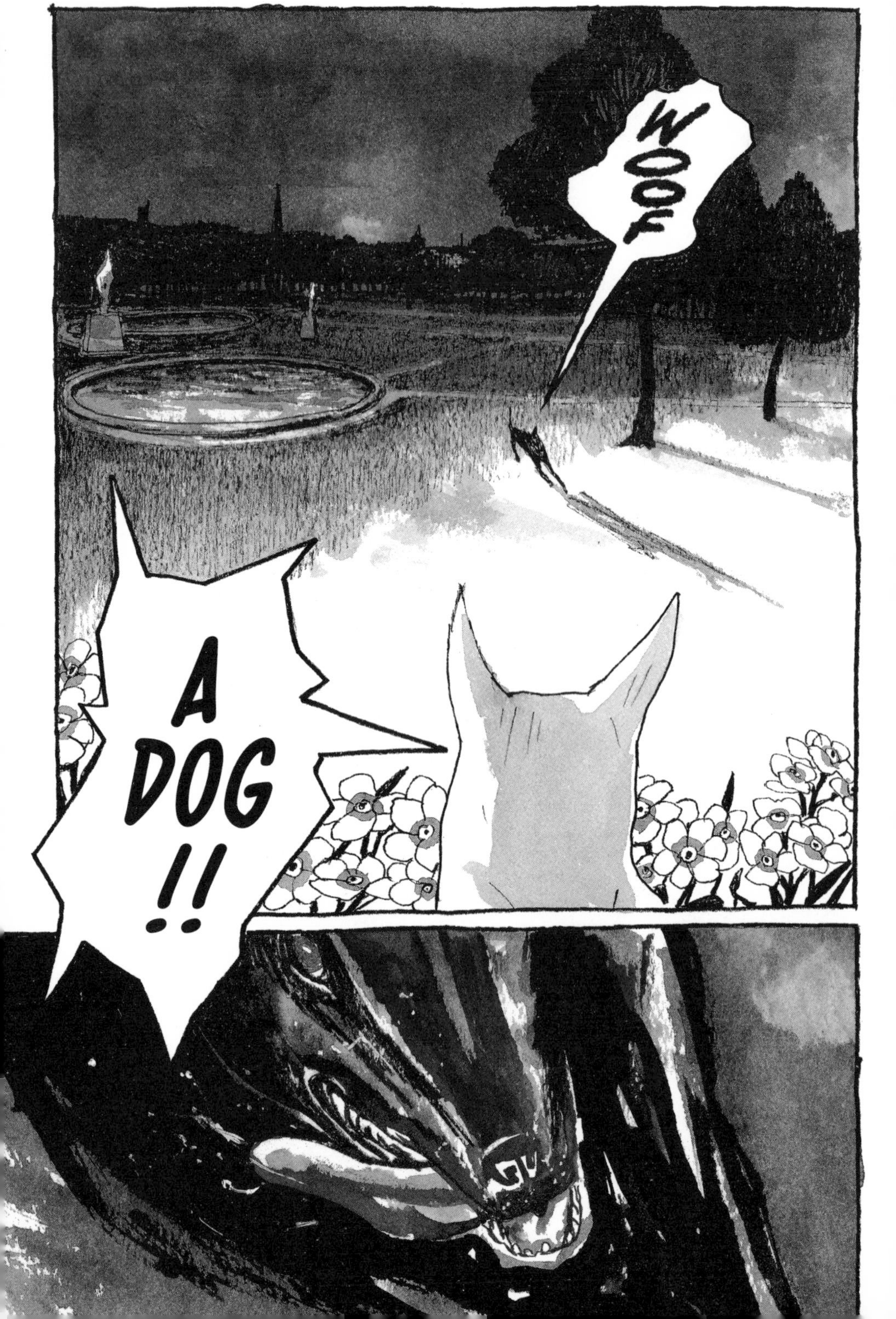
WOOF
A DOG!!

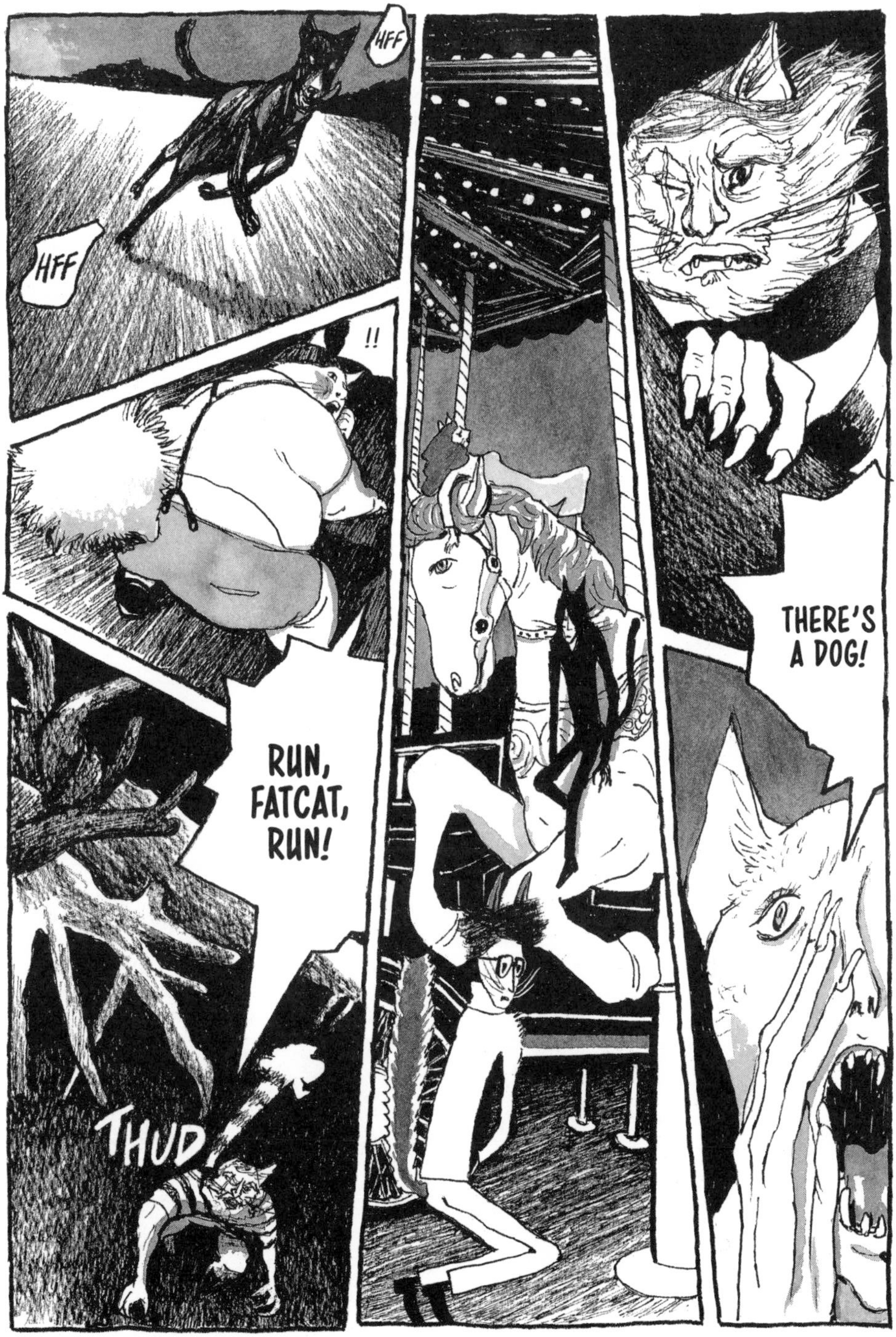
THERE'S A DOG!
HFF
HFF
!!
RUN, FATCAT, RUN!
THUD

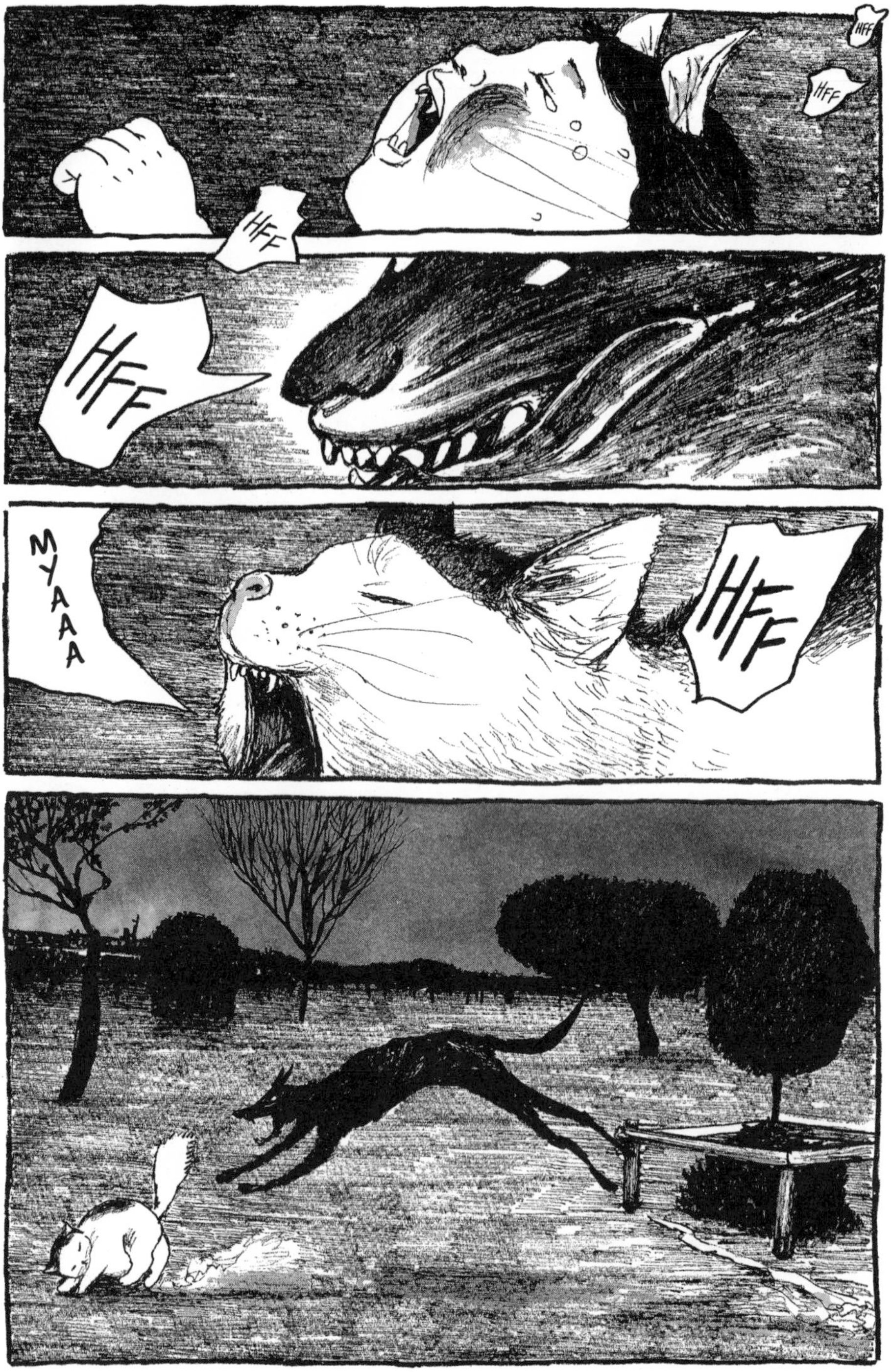
HFF
HFF
HFF
HFF
HFF
MYAAA

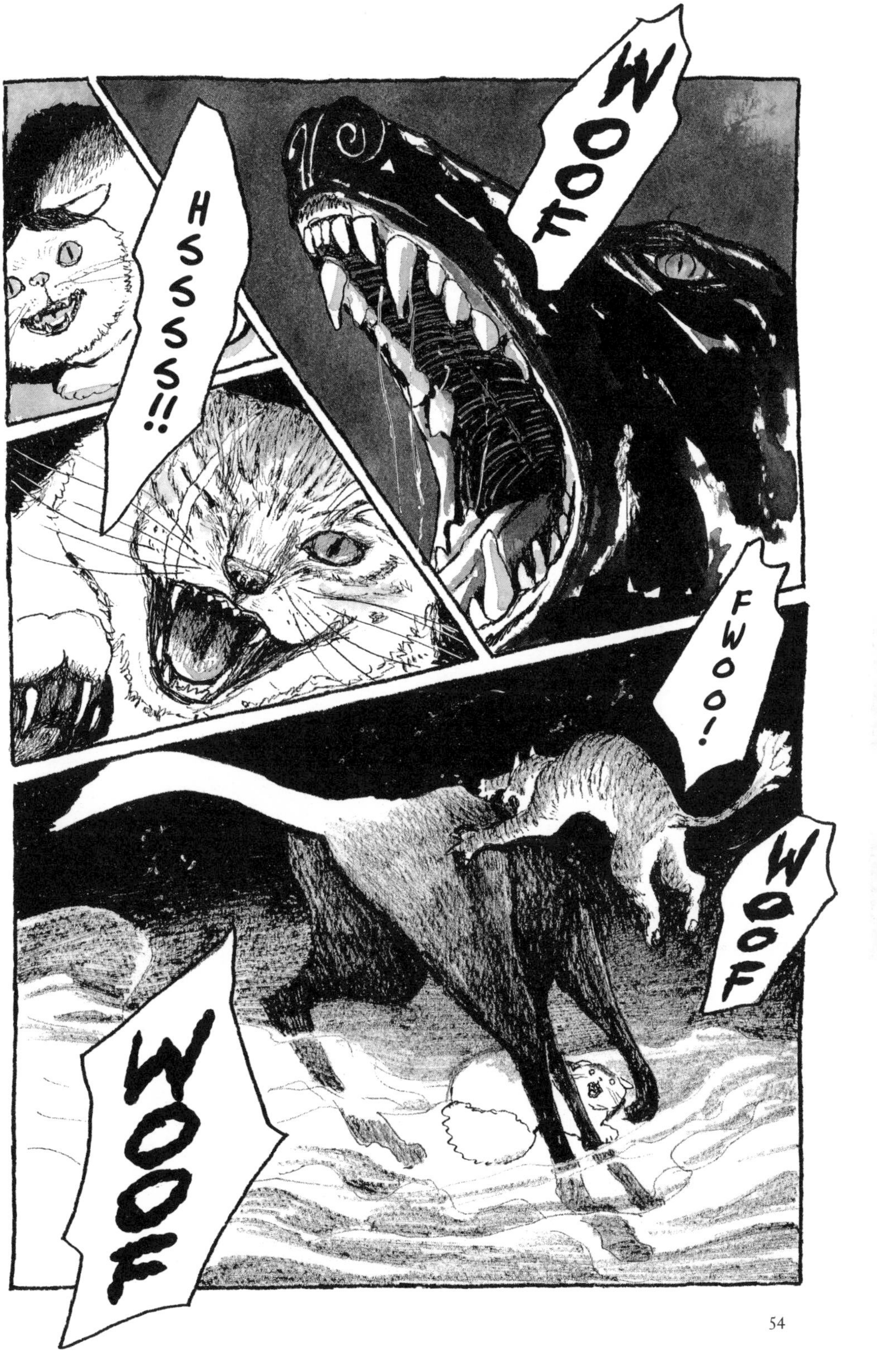
WOOF
HSSSSS!!
FWOOO!
WOOF
WOOF

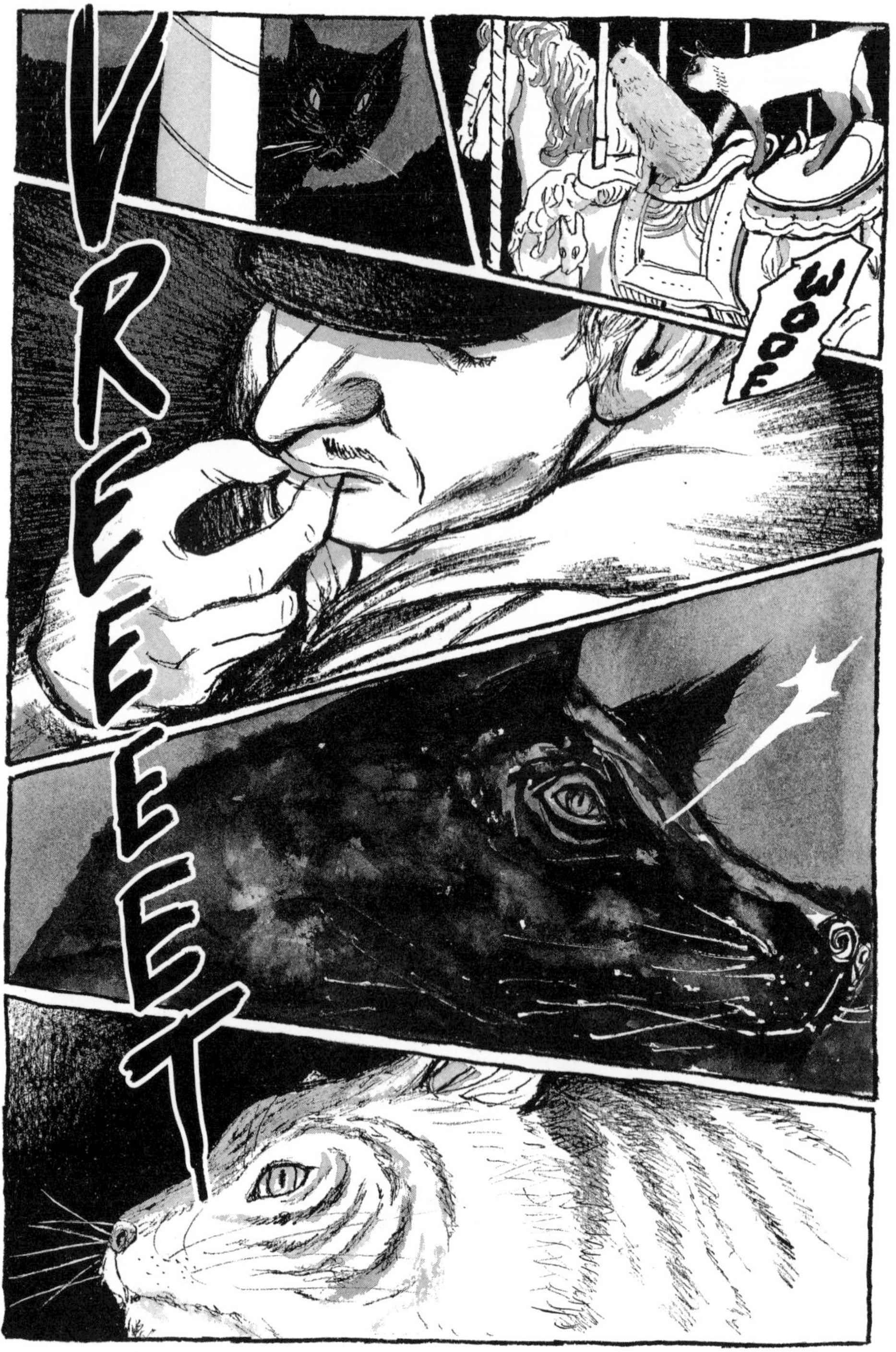
WOOF
VREEEET

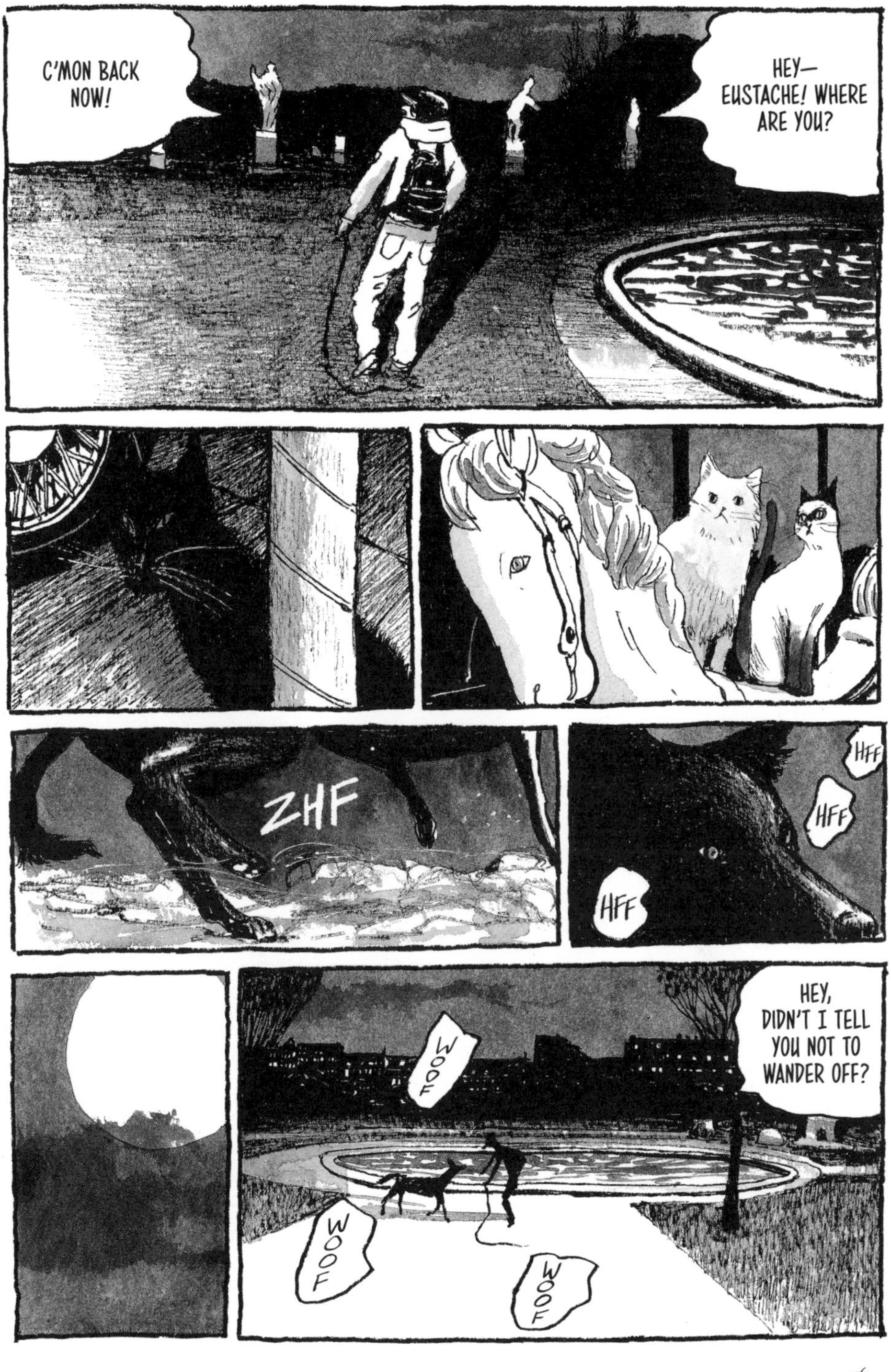
HEY—
EUSTACHE! WHERE ARE YOU?
C'MON BACK NOW!
HFF
HFF
HFF
ZHF
HEY, DIDN'T I TELL YOU NOT TO WANDER OFF?
WOOF
WOOF
WOOF

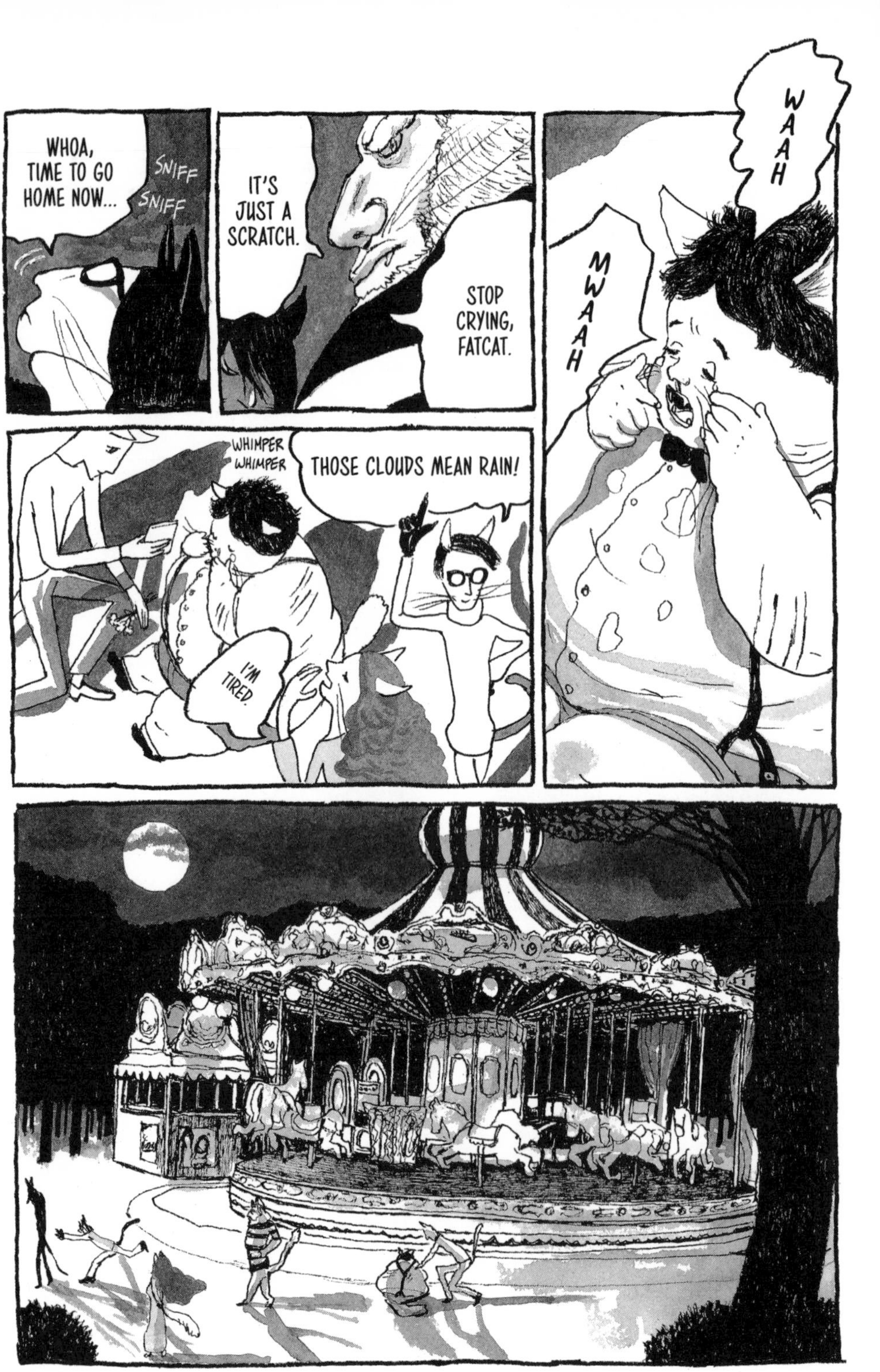
WAAAH
MWAAAH
STOP CRYING, FATCAT.
IT'S JUST A SCRATCH.
SNIFF SNIFF
WHOA, TIME TO GO HOME NOW...
THOSE CLOUDS MEAN RAIN!
WHIMPER WHIMPER
I'M TIRED.

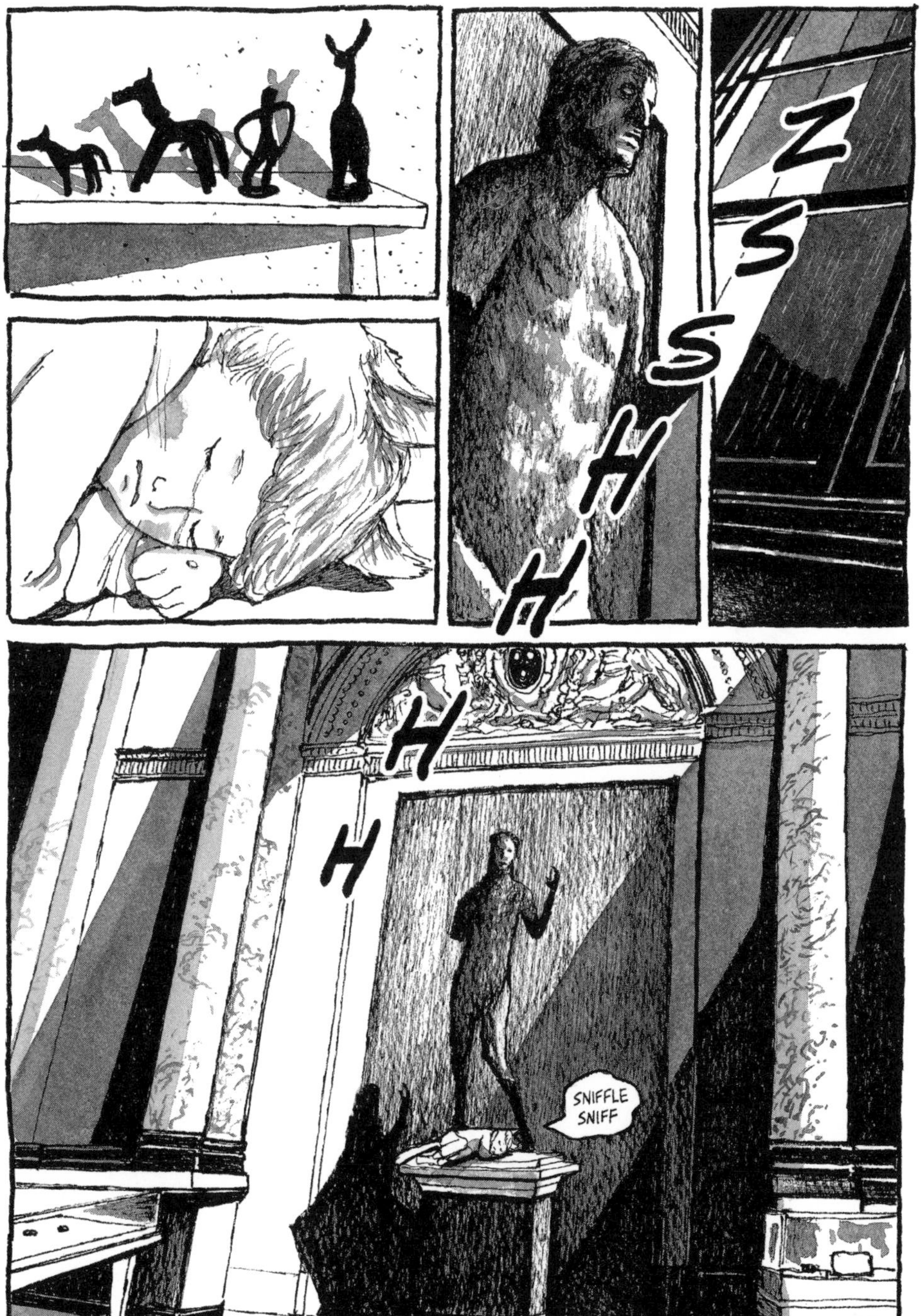
ZSSHHHH
SNIFFLE SNIFF

CHAPTER 3

The Secret of the Children

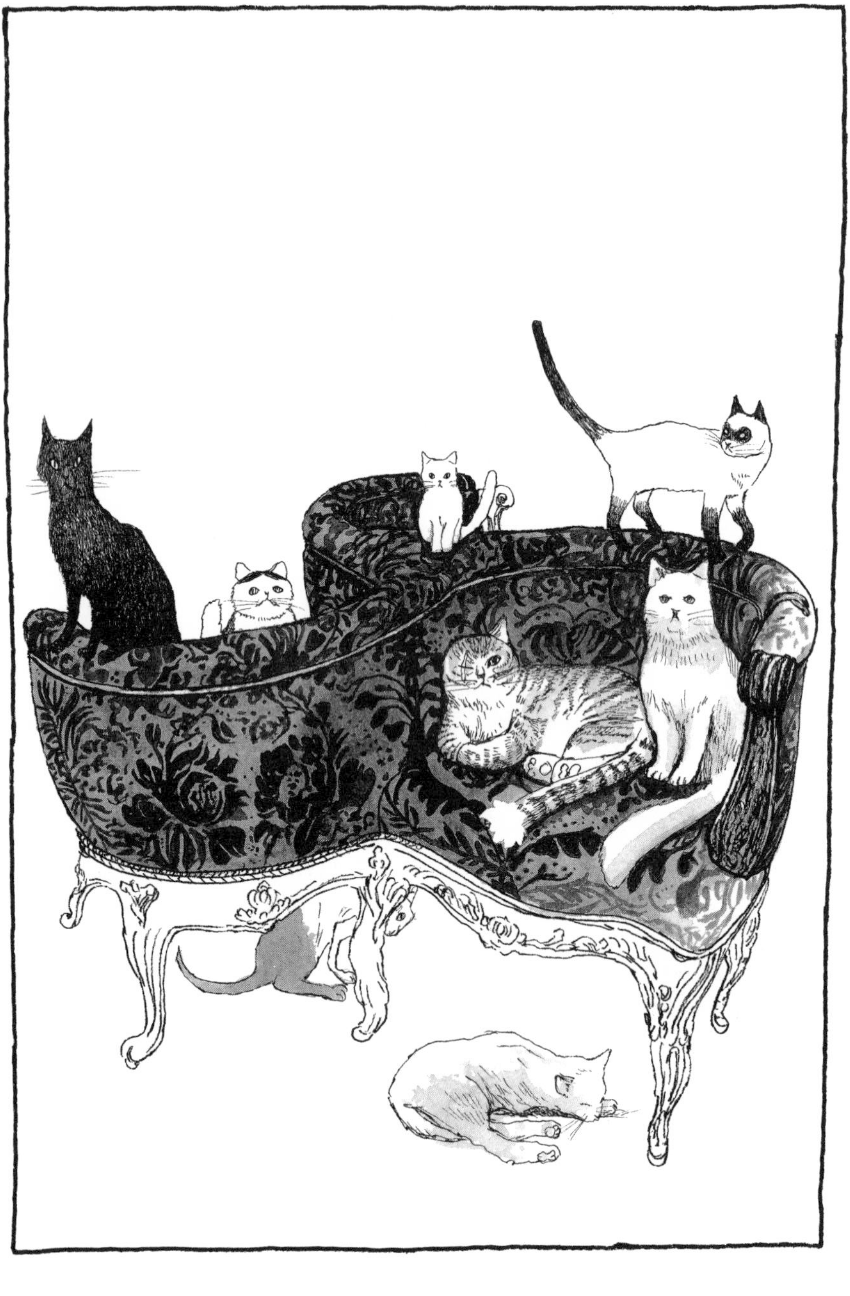

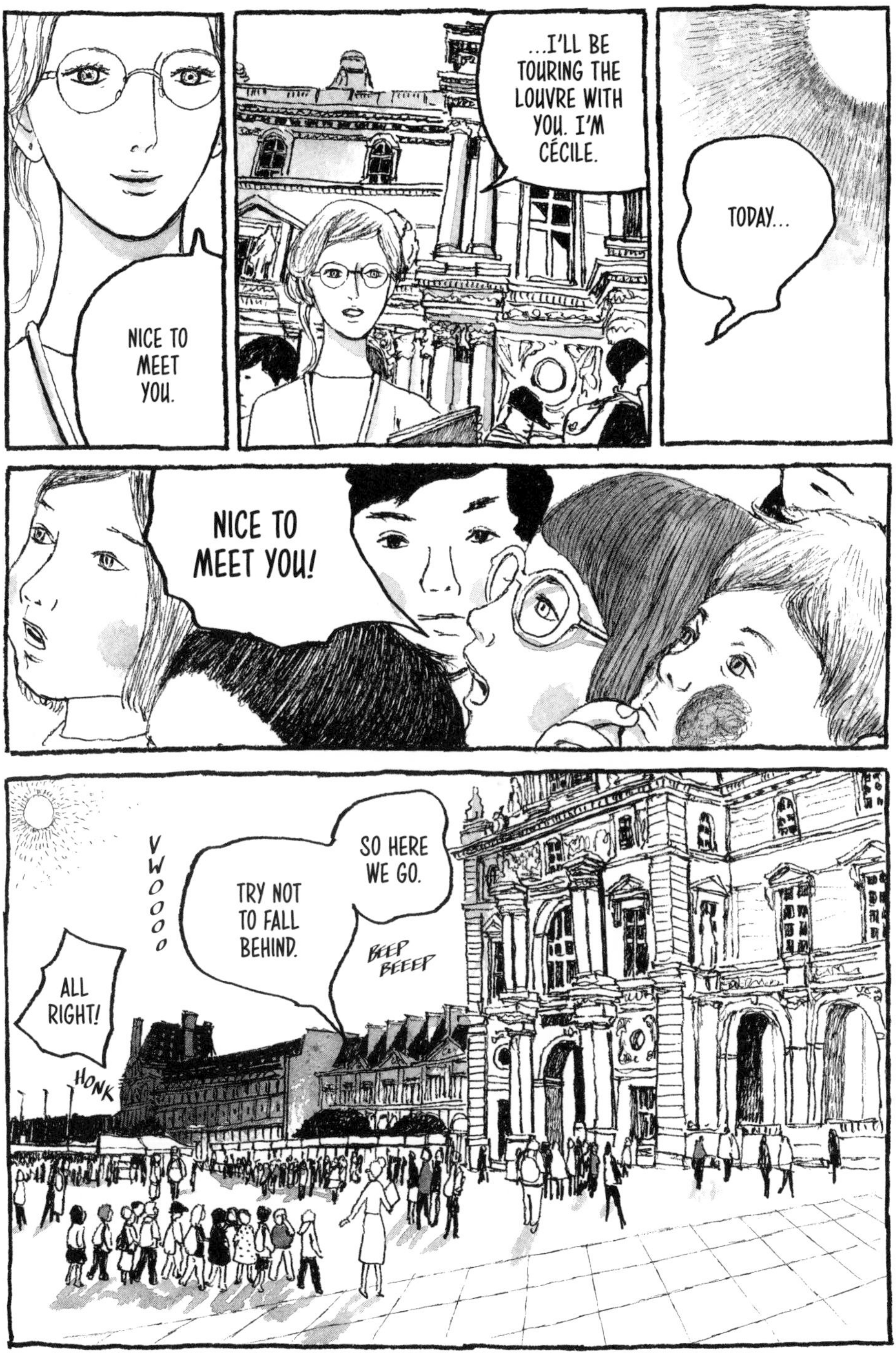
TODAY...
...I'LL BE TOURING THE LOUVRE WITH YOU. I'M CÉCILE.
NICE TO MEET YOU.
NICE TO MEET YOU!
SO HERE WE GO.
TRY NOT TO FALL BEHIND.
BEEP BEEEP
VWOOOO
ALL RIGHT!
HONK

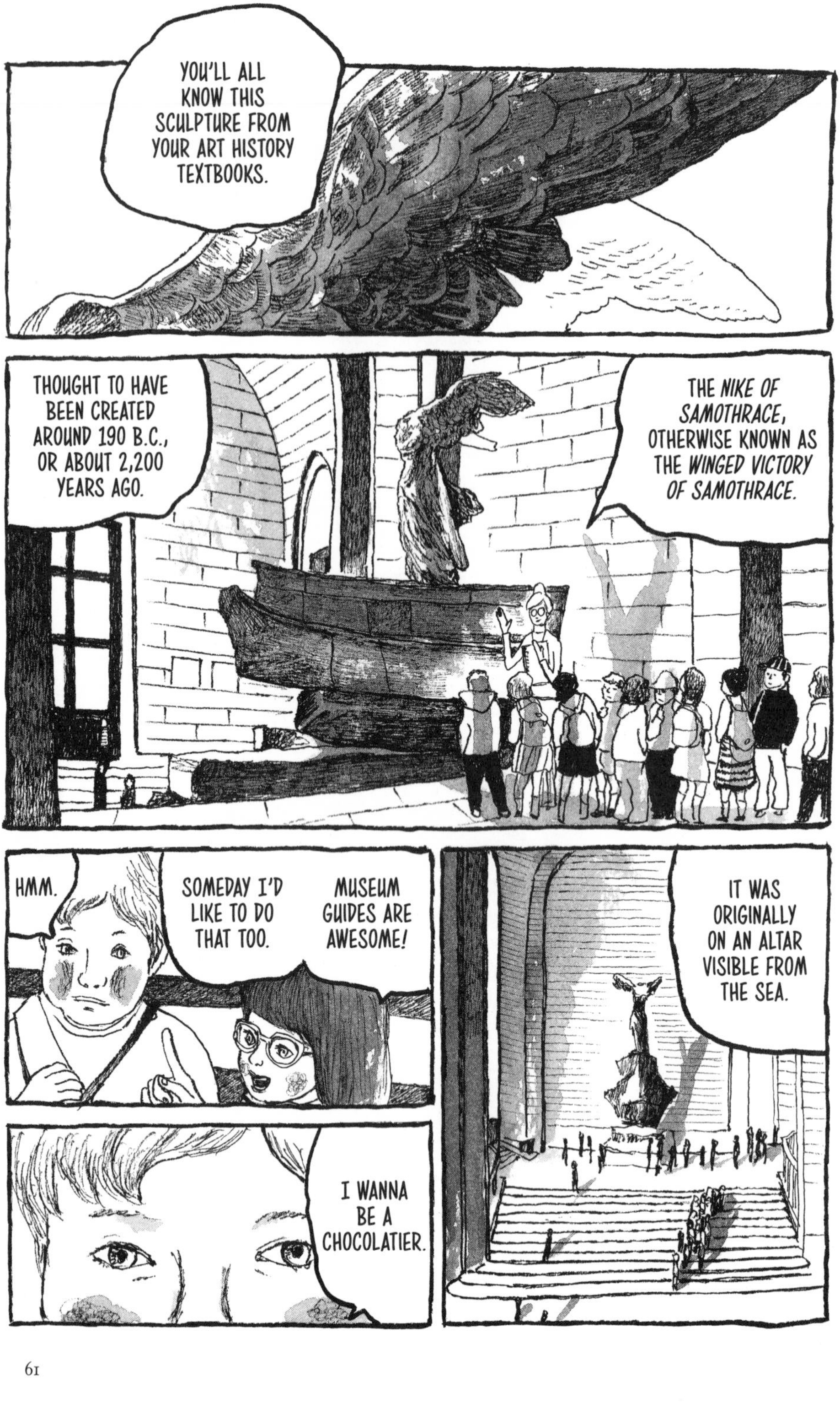
YOU'LL ALL KNOW THIS SCULPTURE FROM YOUR ART HISTORY TEXTBOOKS.
THE NIKE OF SAMOTHRACE, OTHERWISE KNOWN AS THE WINGED VICTORY OF SAMOTHRACE.
THOUGHT TO HAVE BEEN CREATED AROUND 190 B.C., OR ABOUT 2,200 YEARS AGO.
IT WAS ORIGINALLY ON AN ALTAR VISIBLE FROM THE SEA.
MUSEUM GUIDES ARE AWESOME!
SOMEDAY I'D LIKE TO DO THAT TOO.
HMM.
I WANNA BE A CHOCOLATIER.

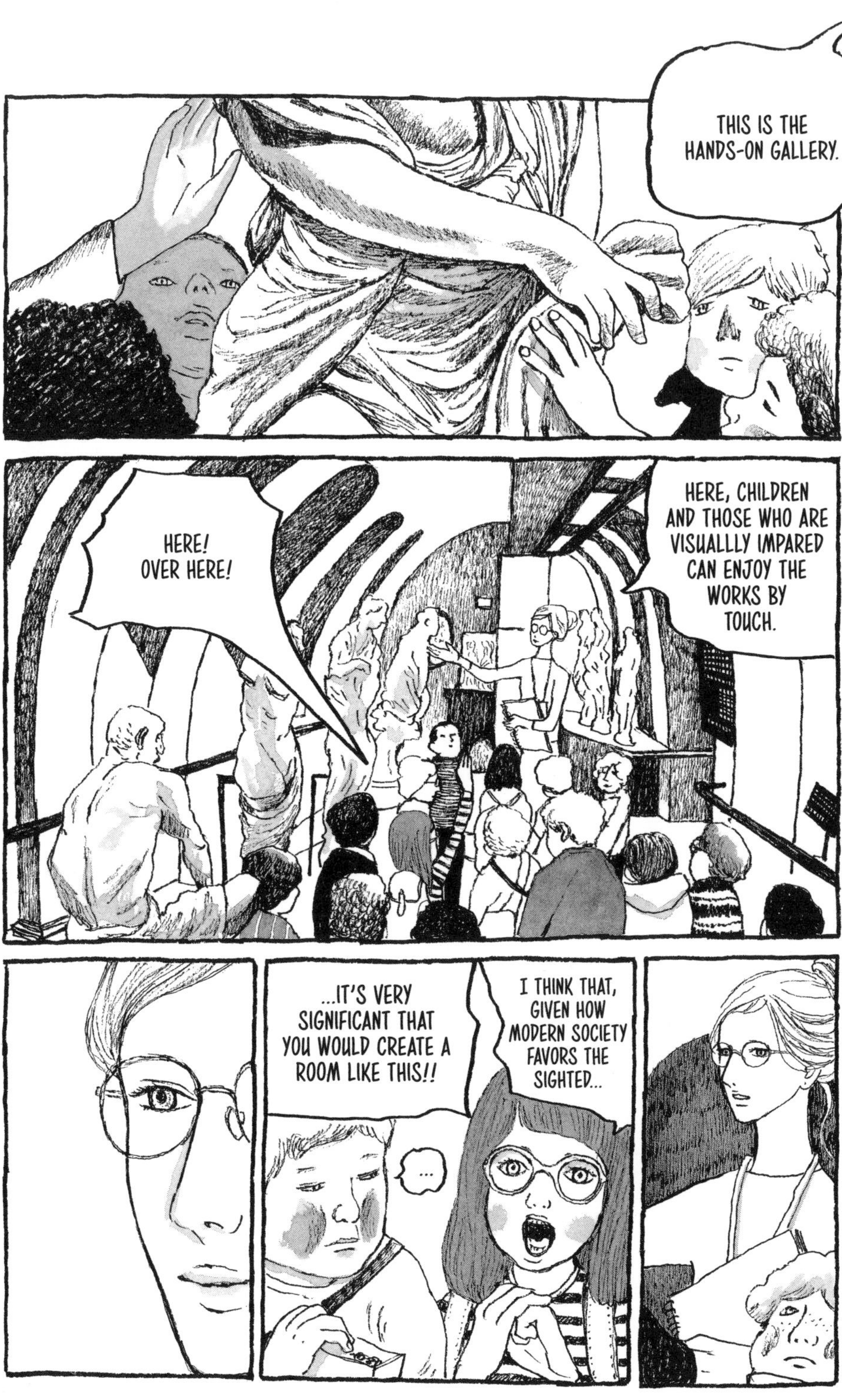
THIS IS THE HANDS-ON GALLERY.
HERE, CHILDREN AND THOSE WHO ARE VISUALLLY IMPARED CAN ENJOY THE WORKS BY TOUCH.
HERE! OVER HERE!
I THINK THAT, GIVEN HOW MODERN SOCIETY FAVORS THE SIGHTED...
...IT'S VERY SIGNIFICANT THAT YOU WOULD CREATE A ROOM LIKE THIS!!
...

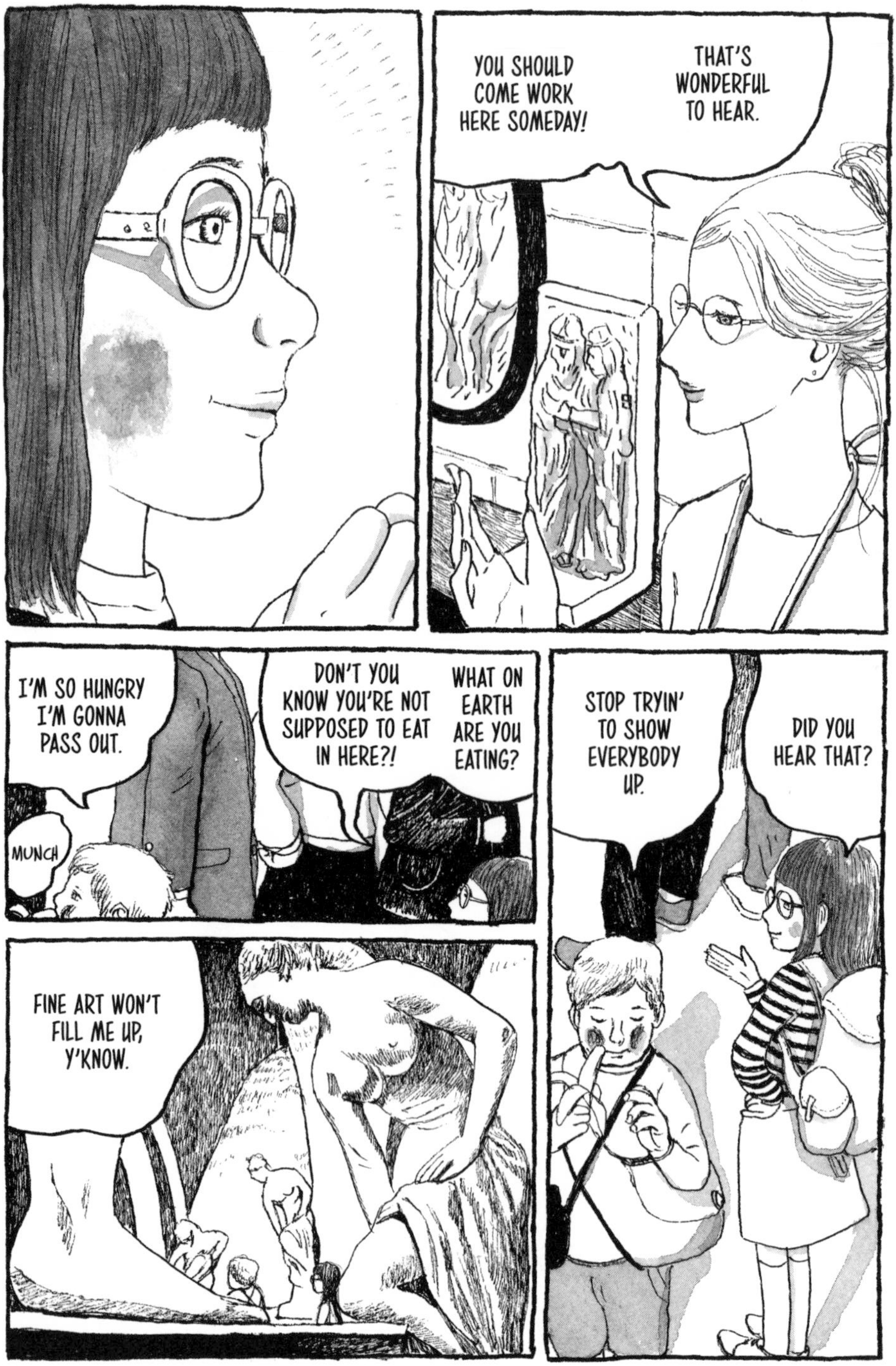
THAT'S WONDERFUL TO HEAR.
YOU SHOULD COME WORK HERE SOMEDAY!
DID YOU HEAR THAT?
STOP TRYIN' TO SHOW EVERYBODY UP.
WHAT ON EARTH ARE YOU EATING?
DON'T YOU KNOW YOU'RE NOT SUPPOSED TO EAT IN HERE?!
I'M SO HUNGRY I'M GONNA PASS OUT.
MUNCH
FINE ART WON'T FILL ME UP, Y'KNOW.

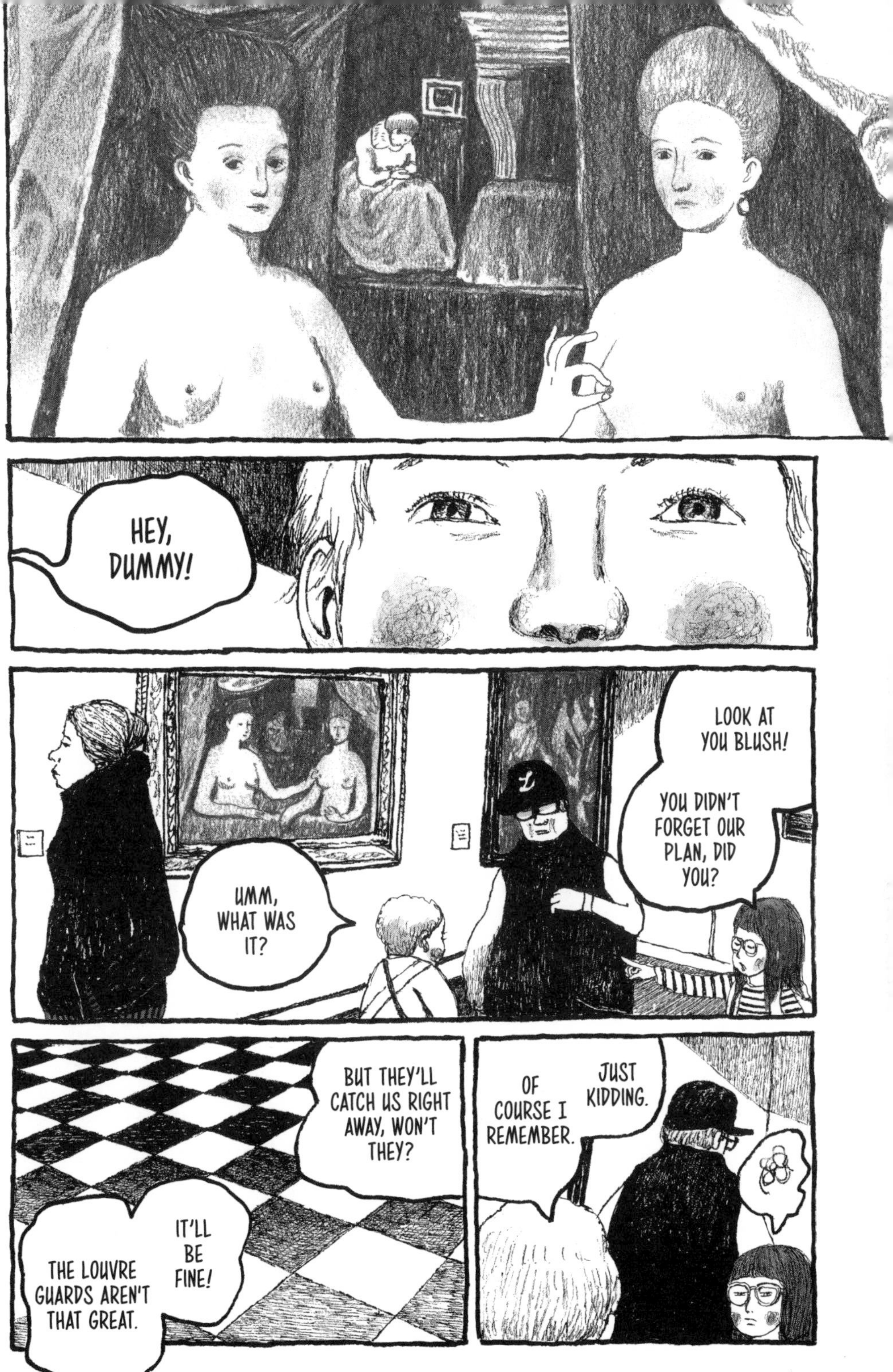
HEY, DUMMY!
LOOK AT YOU BLUSH!
YOU DIDN'T FORGET OUR PLAN, DID YOU?
UMM, WHAT WAS IT?
JUST KIDDING.
OF COURSE I REMEMBER.
BUT THEY'LL CATCH US RIGHT AWAY, WON'T THEY?
IT'LL BE FINE!
THE LOUVRE GUARDS AREN'T THAT GREAT.

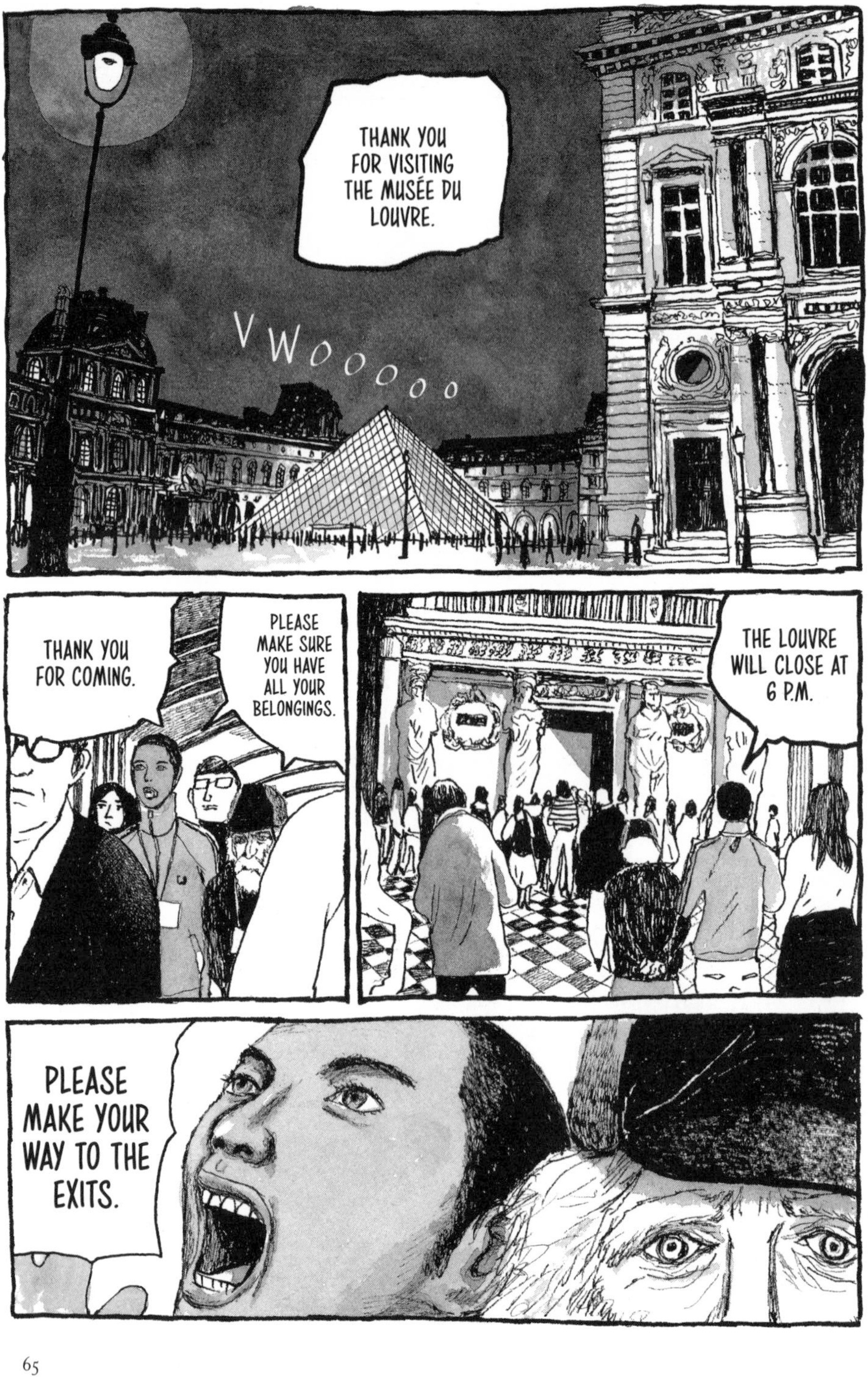
THANK YOU FOR VISITING THE MUSÉE DU LOUVRE.
VWOOOOOO
THE LOUVRE WILL CLOSE AT 6 P.M.
PLEASE MAKE SURE YOU HAVE ALL YOUR BELONGINGS.
THANK YOU FOR COMING.
PLEASE MAKE YOUR WAY TO THE EXITS.

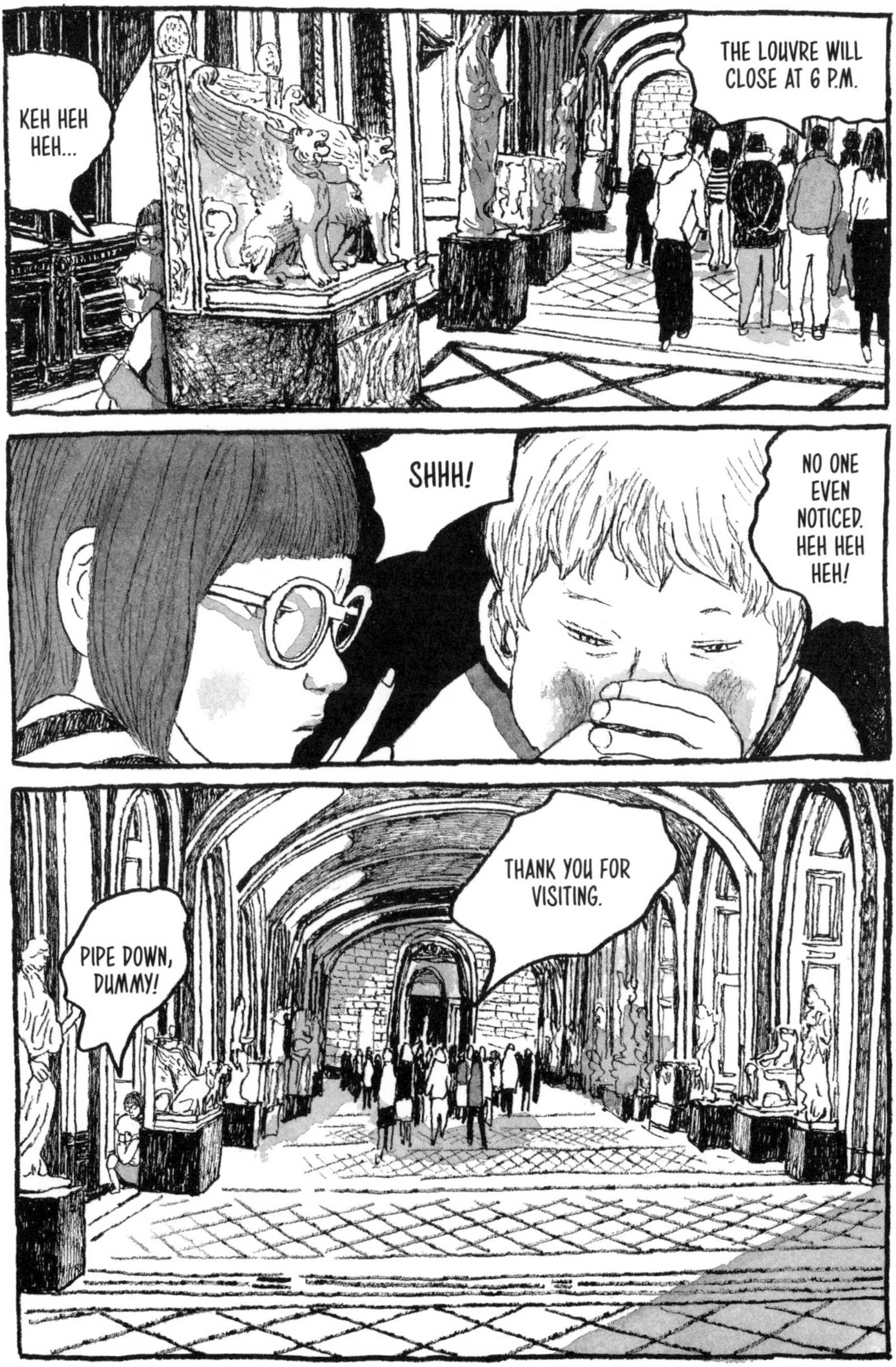
THE LOUVRE WILL CLOSE AT 6 P.M.
KEH HEH HEH...
NO ONE EVEN NOTICED. HEH HEH HEH!
SHHH!
THANK YOU FOR VISITING.
PIPE DOWN, DUMMY!

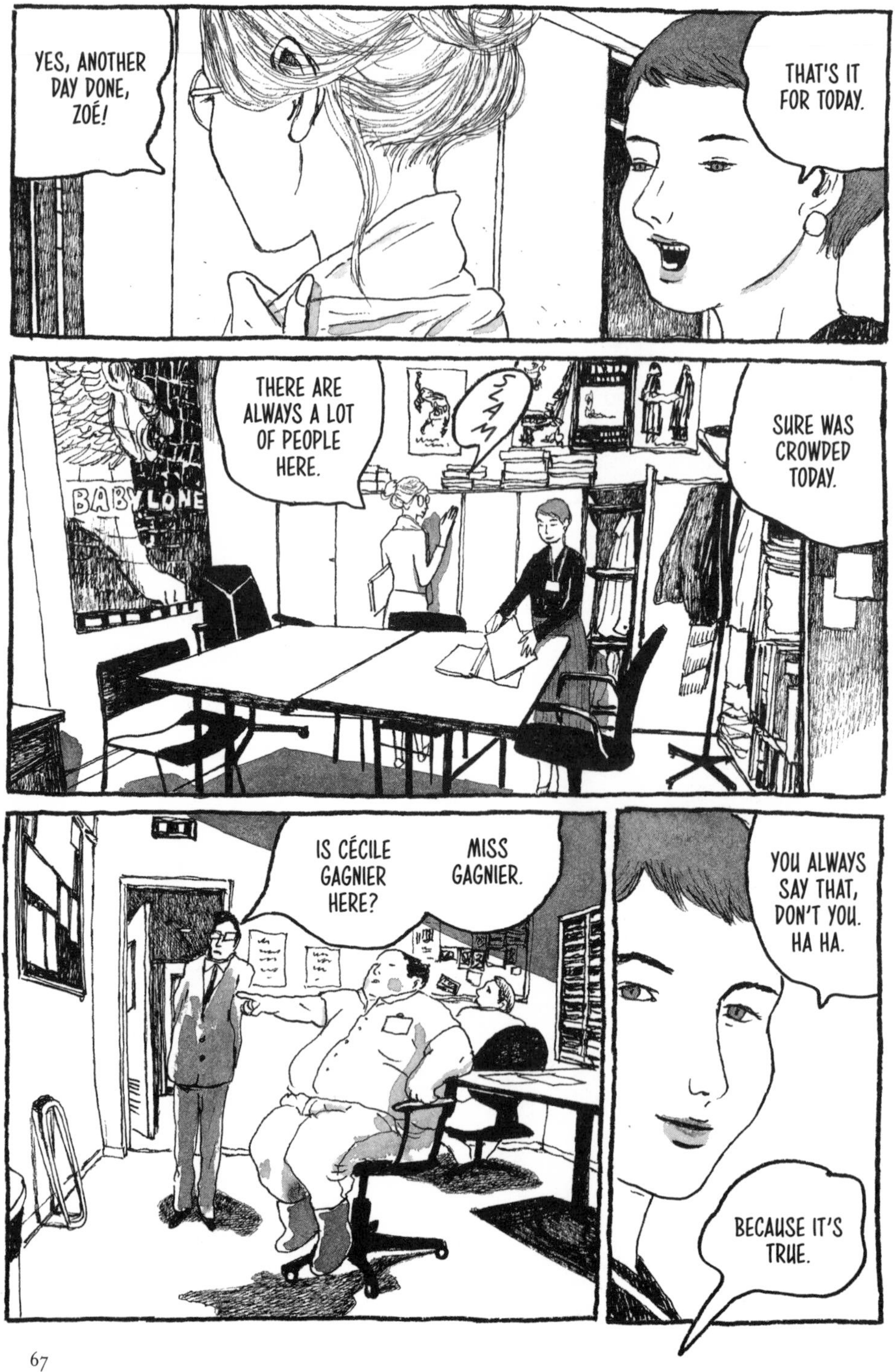
THAT'S IT FOR TODAY.
YES, ANOTHER DAY DONE, ZOÉ!
SURE WAS CROWDED TODAY.
SLAM
THERE ARE ALWAYS A LOT OF PEOPLE HERE.
YOU ALWAYS SAY THAT, DON'T YOU. HA HA.
BECAUSE IT'S TRUE.
MISS GAGNIER.
IS CÉCILE GAGNIER HERE?

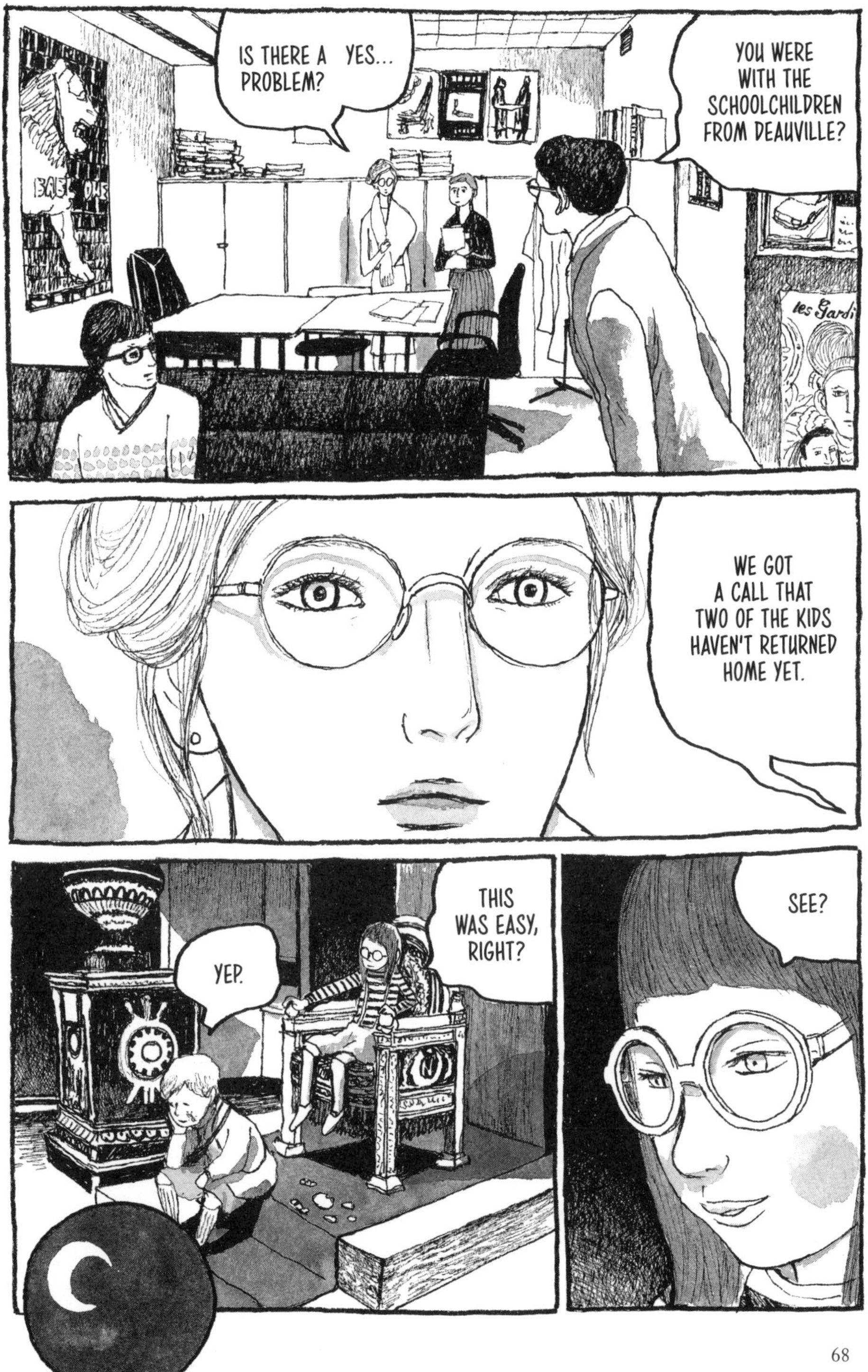
YOU WERE WITH THE SCHOOLCHILDREN FROM DEAUVILLE?
YES...
IS THERE A PROBLEM?
WE GOT A CALL THAT TWO OF THE KIDS HAVEN'T RETURNED HOME YET.
SEE?
THIS WAS EASY, RIGHT?
YEP.

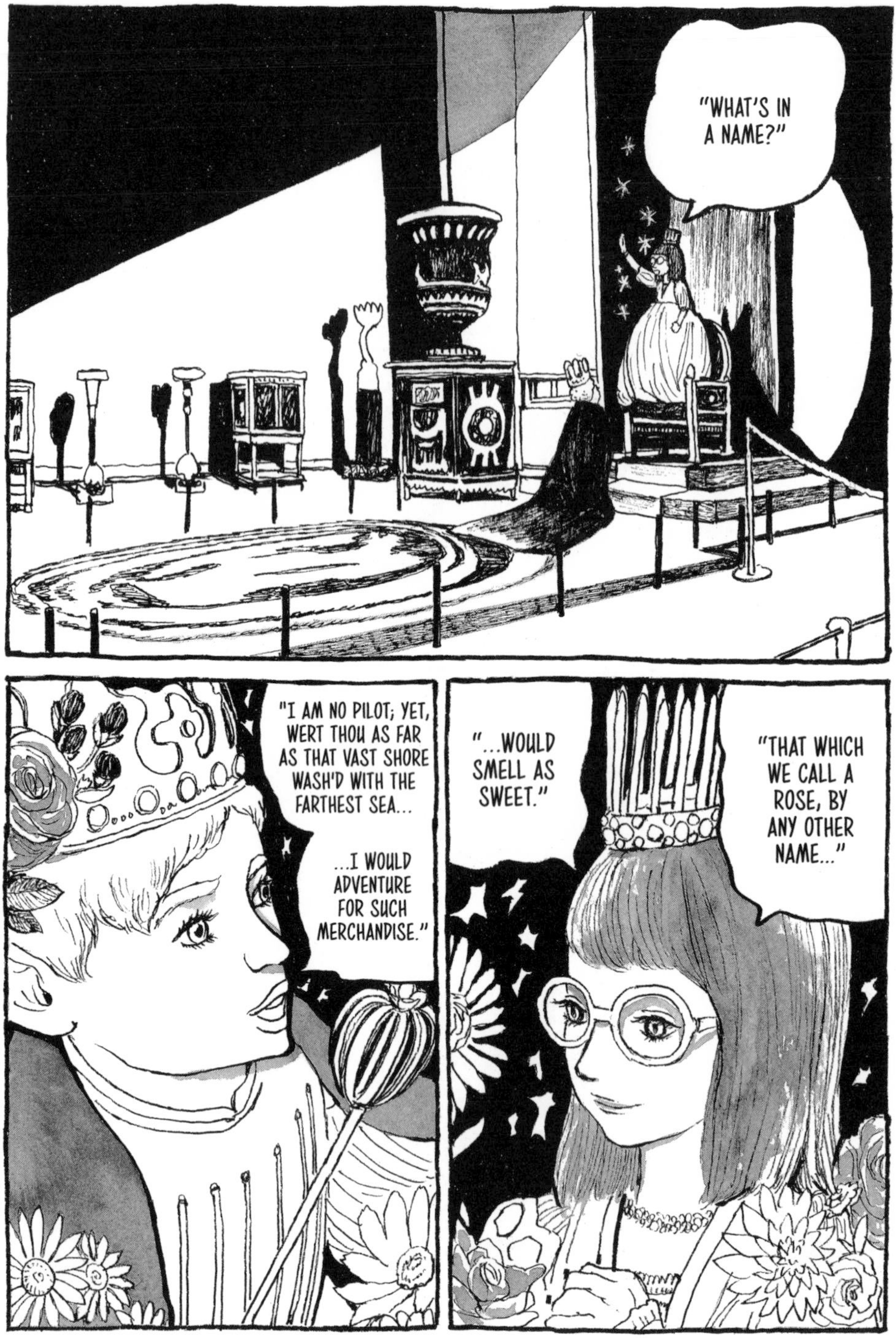
"WHAT'S IN A NAME?"
"THAT WHICH WE CALL A ROSE, BY ANY OTHER NAME..."
"...WOULD SMELL AS SWEET."
"I AM NO PILOT; YET, WERT THOU AS FAR AS THAT VAST SHORE WASH'D WITH THE FARTHEST SEA...
...I WOULD ADVENTURE FOR SUCH MERCHANDISE."

YEAH, SURE.

STILL HAVE THAT CANDY?

GURGLE

THAT'S ALL? THERE'S HARDLY ANY LEFT.

BECAUSE I ATE SOME.

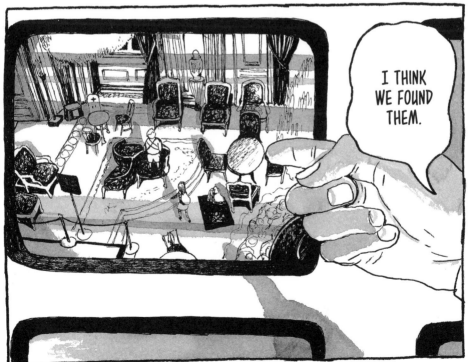

I THINK WE FOUND THEM.

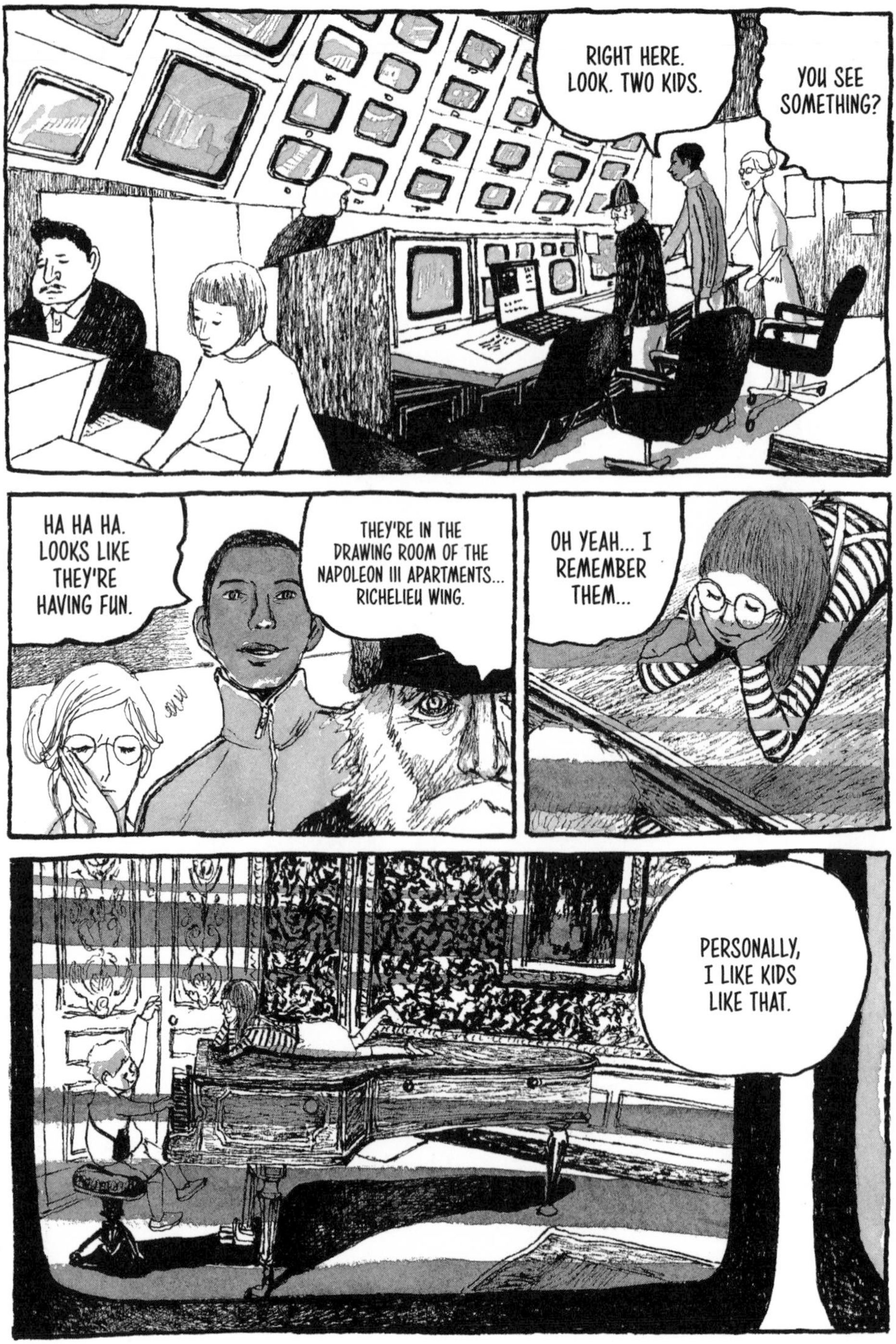
YOU SEE SOMETHING?
RIGHT HERE. LOOK. TWO KIDS.
OH YEAH... I REMEMBER THEM...
THEY'RE IN THE DRAWING ROOM OF THE NAPOLEON III APARTMENTS... RICHELIEU WING.
HA HA HA. LOOKS LIKE THEY'RE HAVING FUN.
PERSONALLY, I LIKE KIDS LIKE THAT.

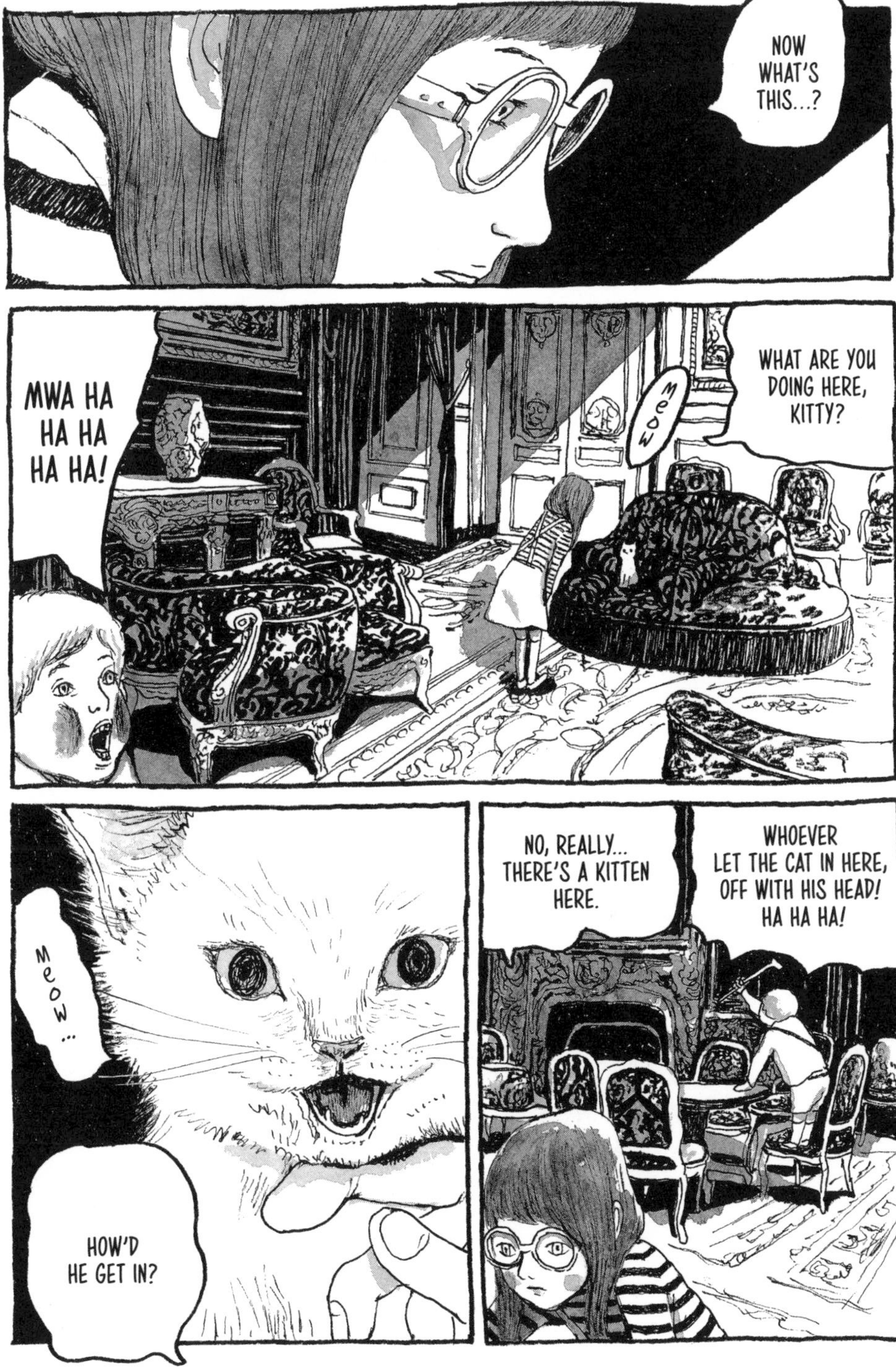
NOW WHAT'S THIS...?
WHAT ARE YOU DOING HERE, KITTY?
Meow
MWA HA HA HA HA HA!
WHOEVER LET THE CAT IN HERE, OFF WITH HIS HEAD! HA HA HA!
NO, REALLY... THERE'S A KITTEN HERE.
Meow...
HOW'D HE GET IN?

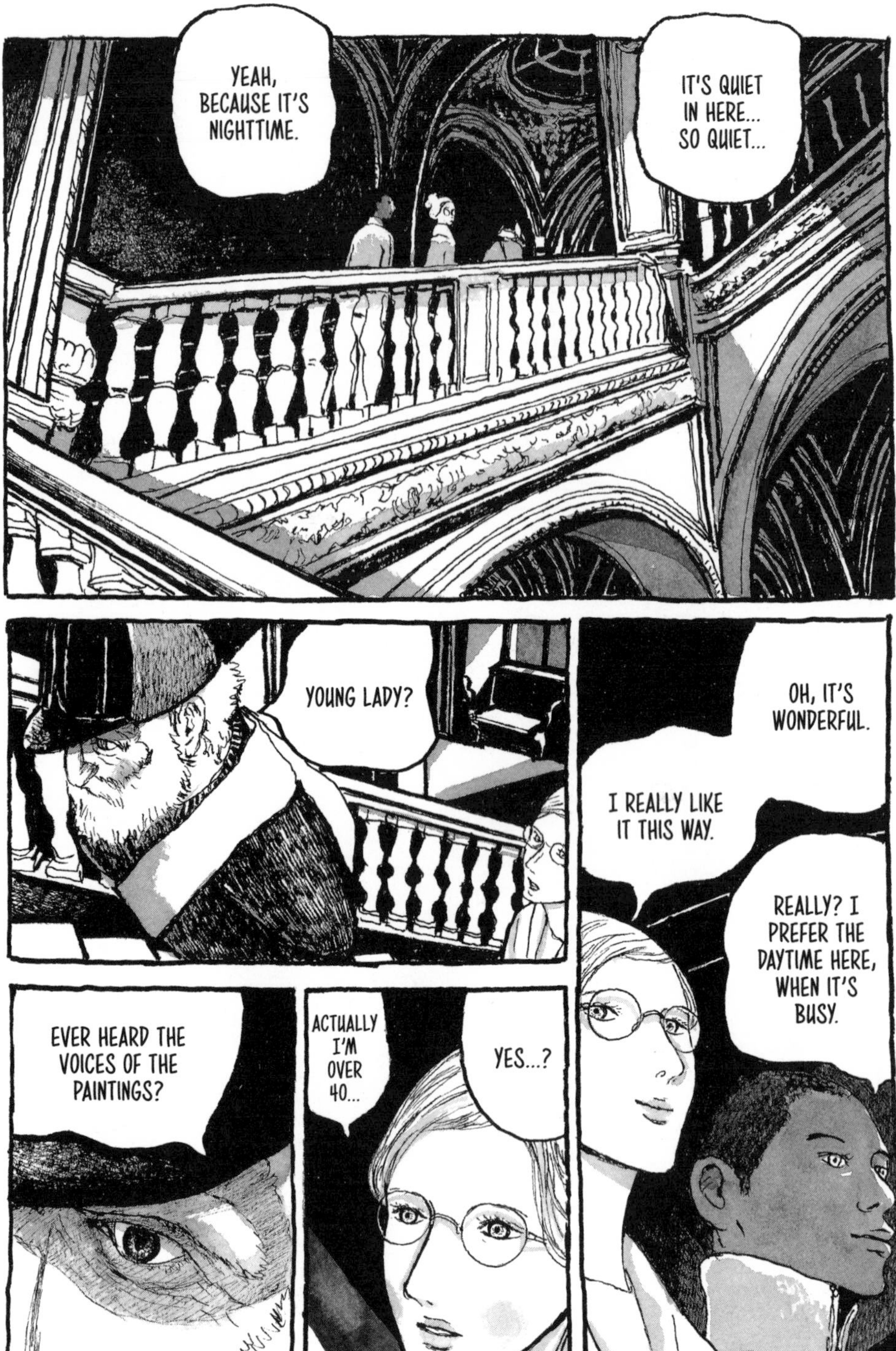
IT'S QUIET IN HERE... SO QUIET...
YEAH, BECAUSE IT'S NIGHTTIME.
OH, IT'S WONDERFUL.
I REALLY LIKE IT THIS WAY.
REALLY? I PREFER THE DAYTIME HERE, WHEN IT'S BUSY.
YOUNG LADY?
YES...?
ACTUALLY I'M OVER 40...
EVER HEARD THE VOICES OF THE PAINTINGS?

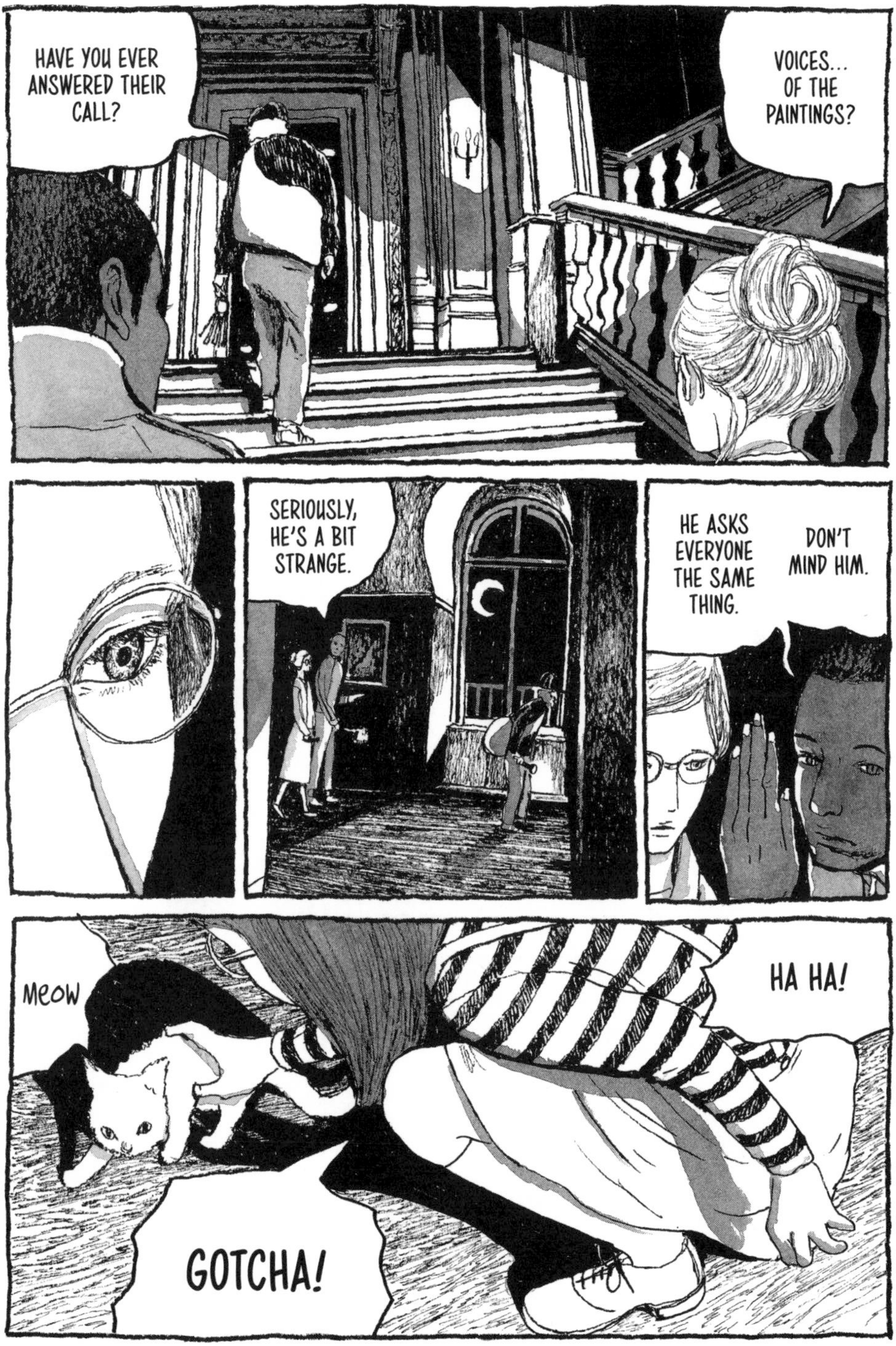
VOICES... OF THE PAINTINGS?
HAVE YOU EVER ANSWERED THEIR CALL?
DON'T MIND HIM.
HE ASKS EVERYONE THE SAME THING.
SERIOUSLY, HE'S A BIT STRANGE.
HA HA!
Meow
GOTCHA!

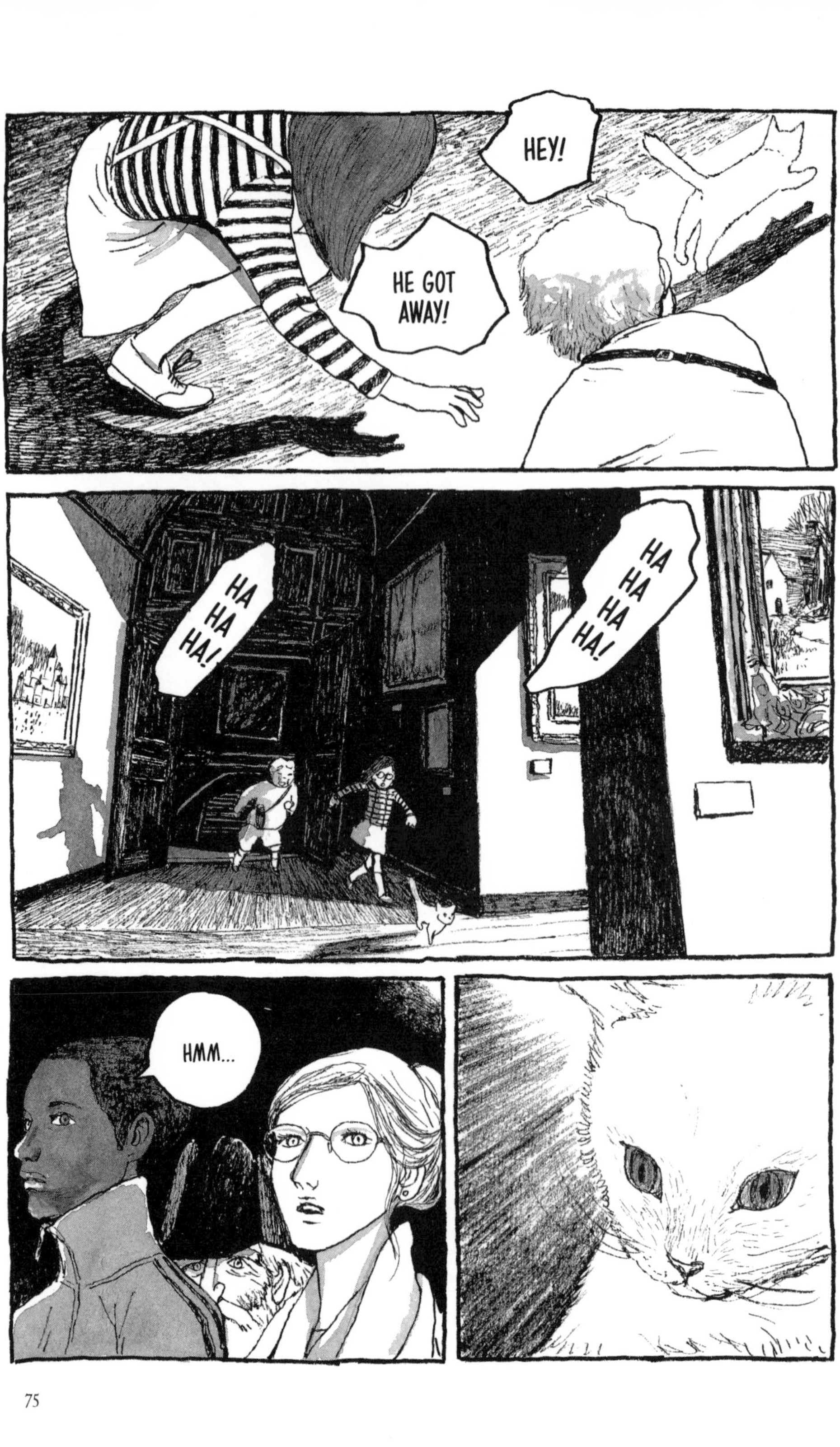
HEY!
HE GOT AWAY!
HA HA HA HA!
HA HA HA!
HMM...

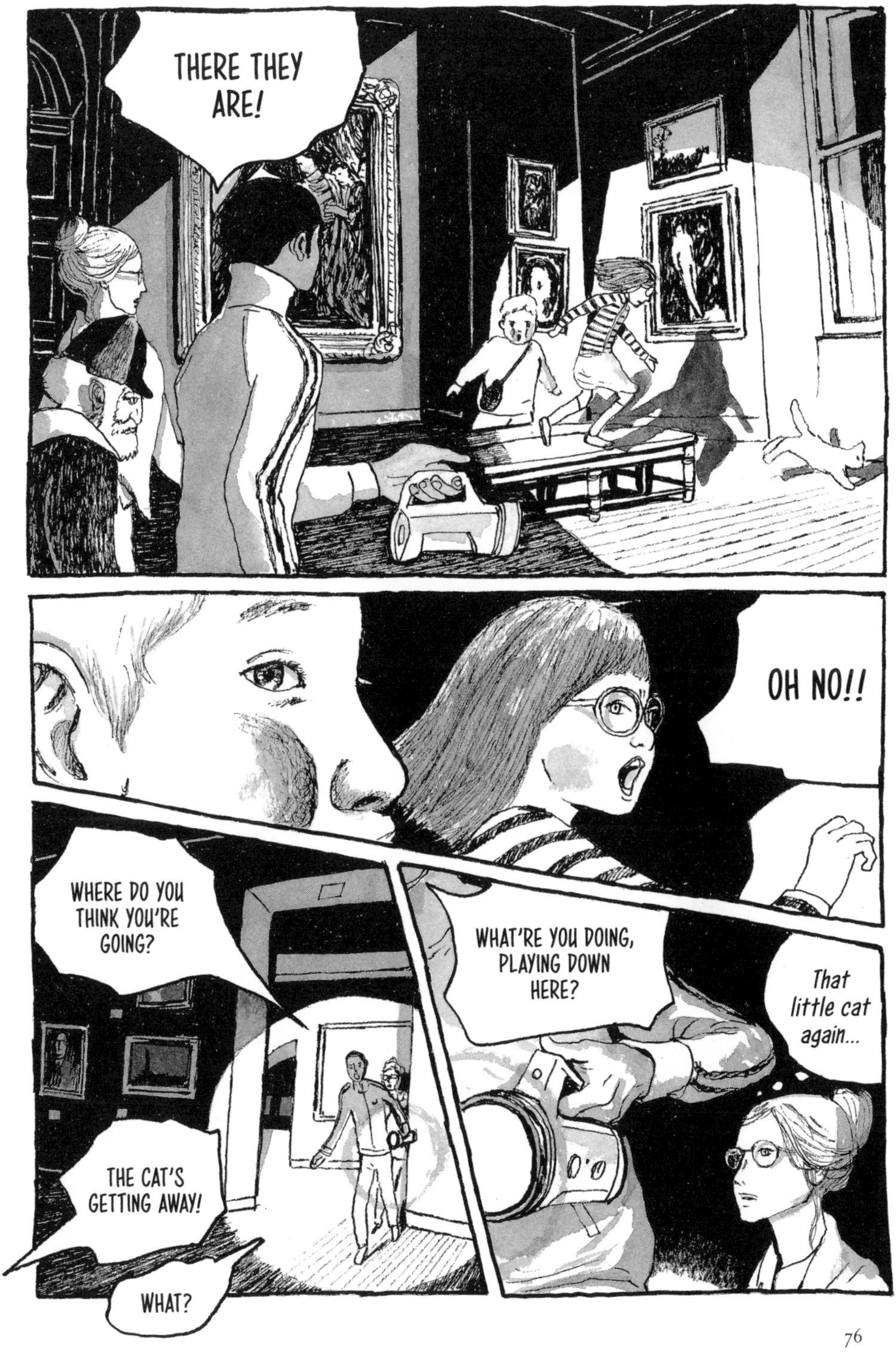
THERE THEY ARE!
OH NO!!
WHAT'RE YOU DOING, PLAYING DOWN HERE?
That little cat again...
WHERE DO YOU THINK YOU'RE GOING?
THE CAT'S GETTING AWAY!
WHAT?

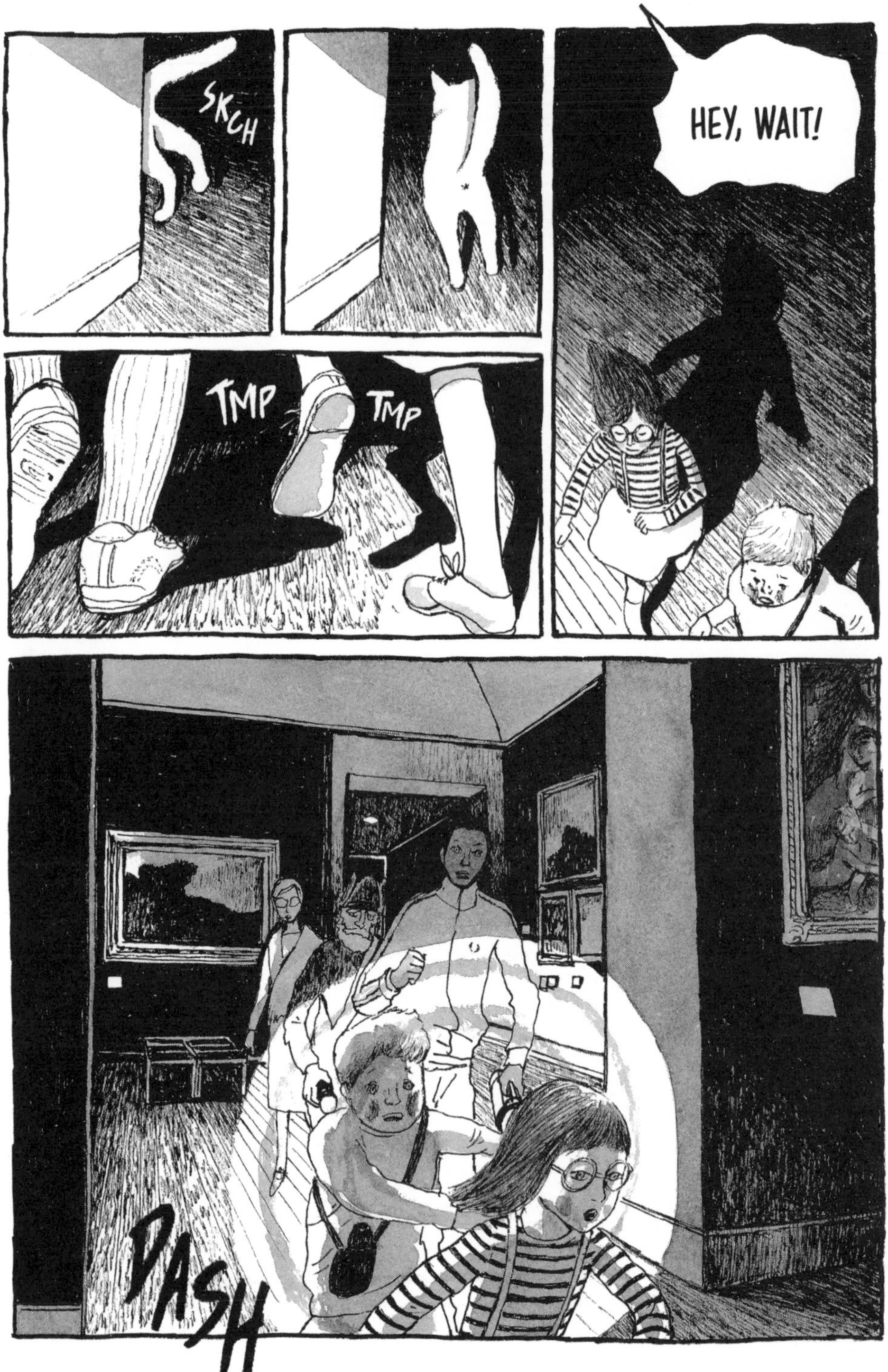
HEY, WAIT!
SKCH
TMP
TMP
DASH

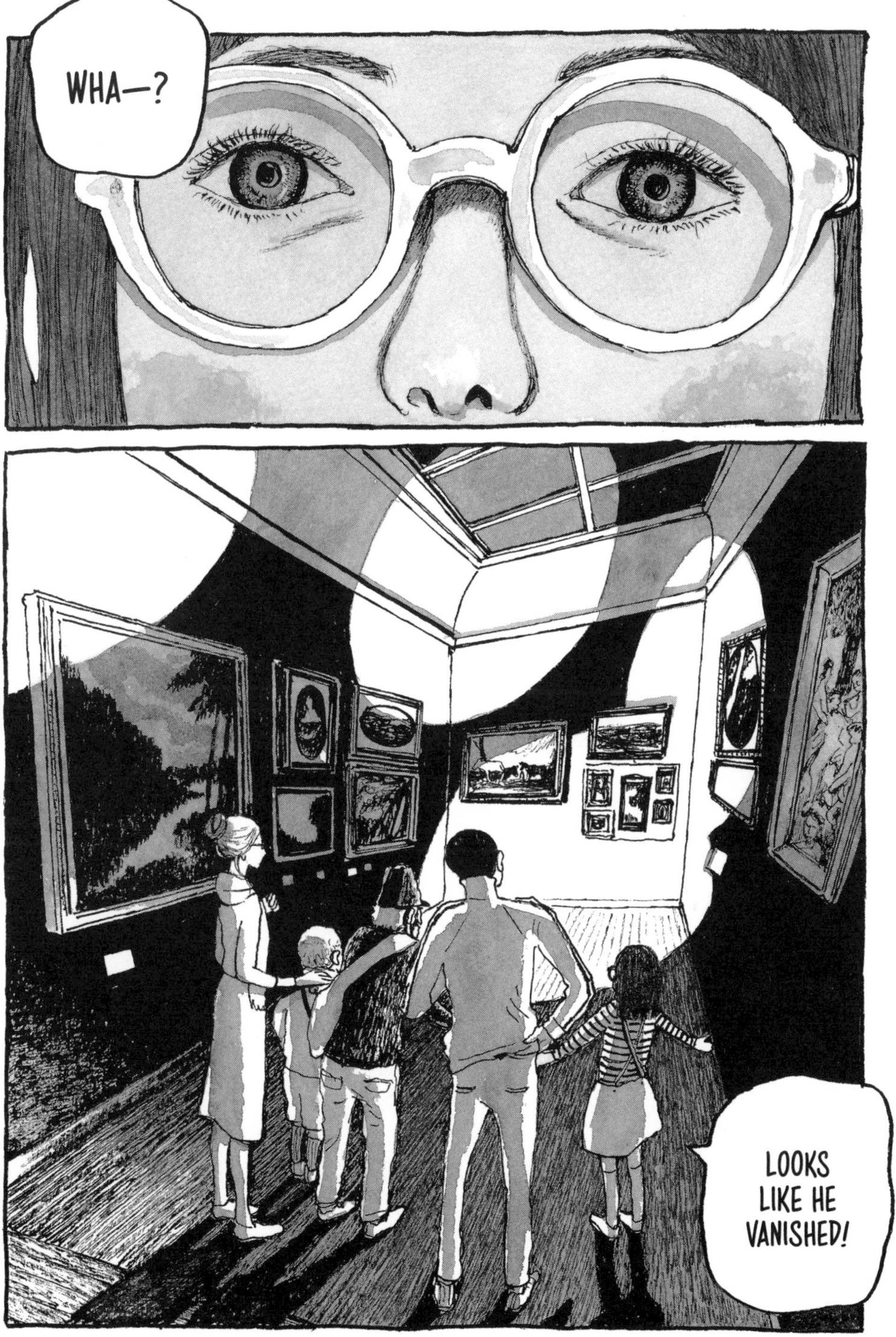
WHA—?
LOOKS LIKE HE VANISHED!

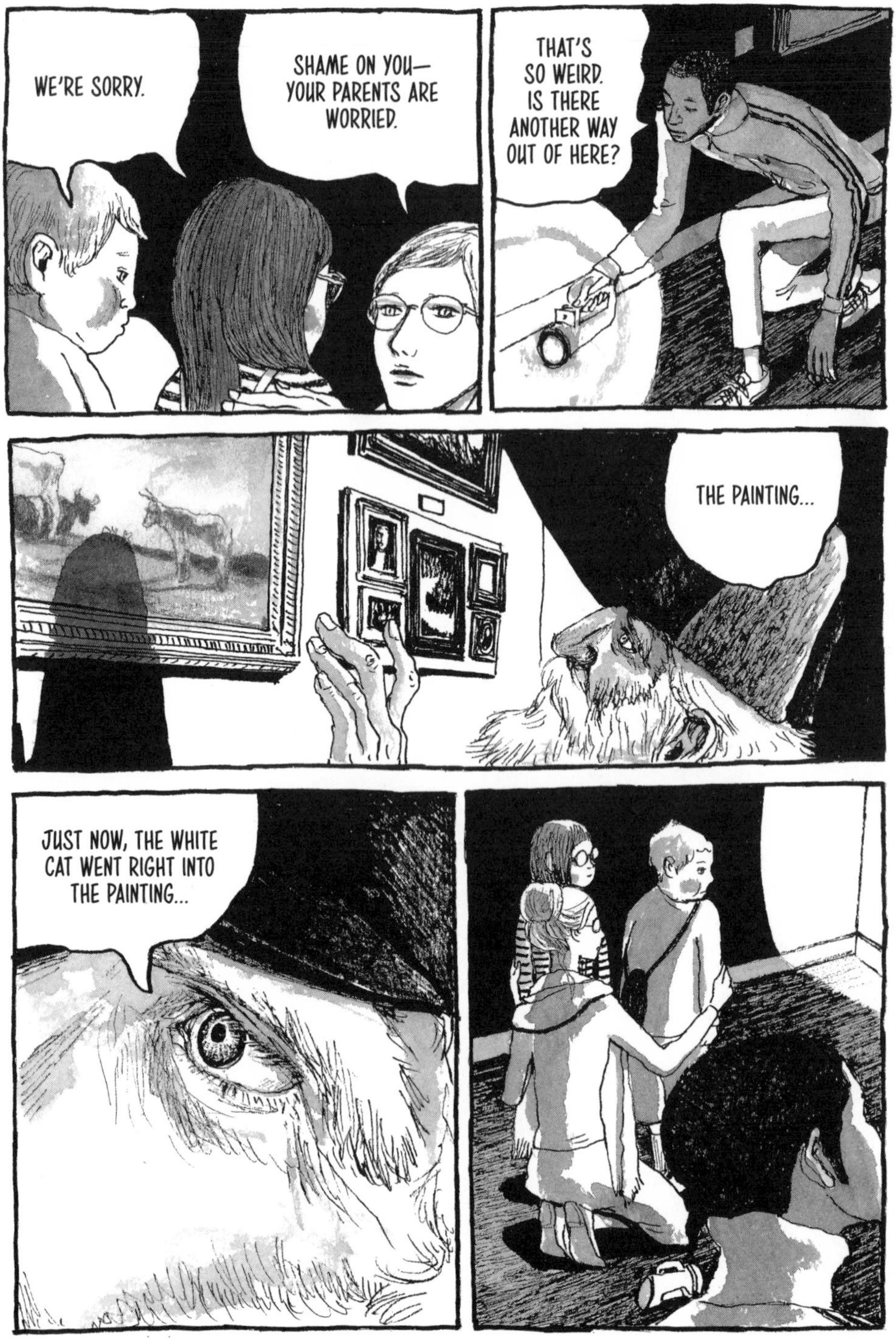
THAT'S SO WEIRD. IS THERE ANOTHER WAY OUT OF HERE?
SHAME ON YOU— YOUR PARENTS ARE WORRIED.
WE'RE SORRY.
THE PAINTING...
JUST NOW, THE WHITE CAT WENT RIGHT INTO THE PAINTING...

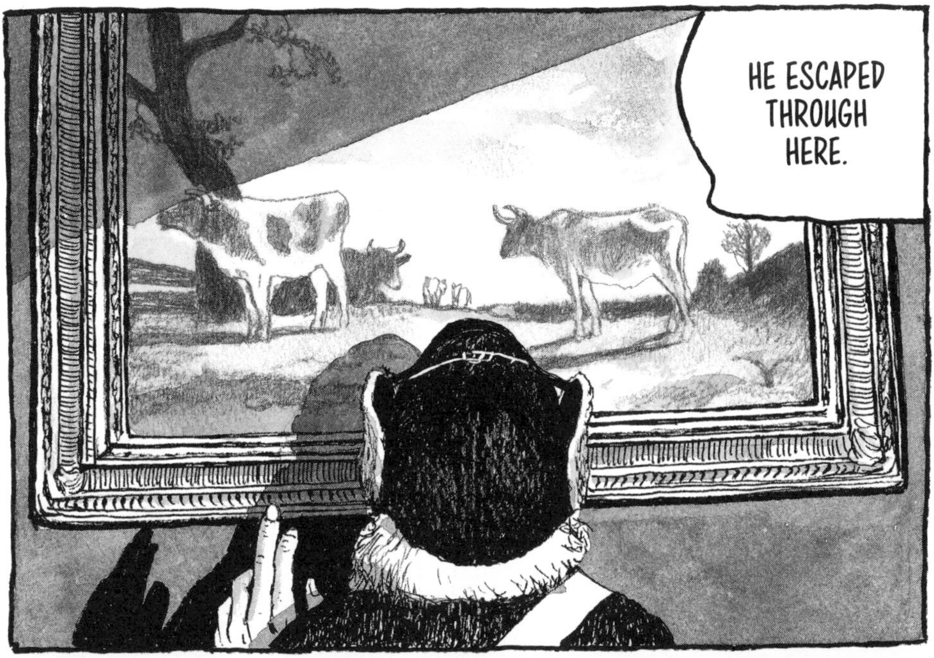
HE ESCAPED THROUGH HERE.

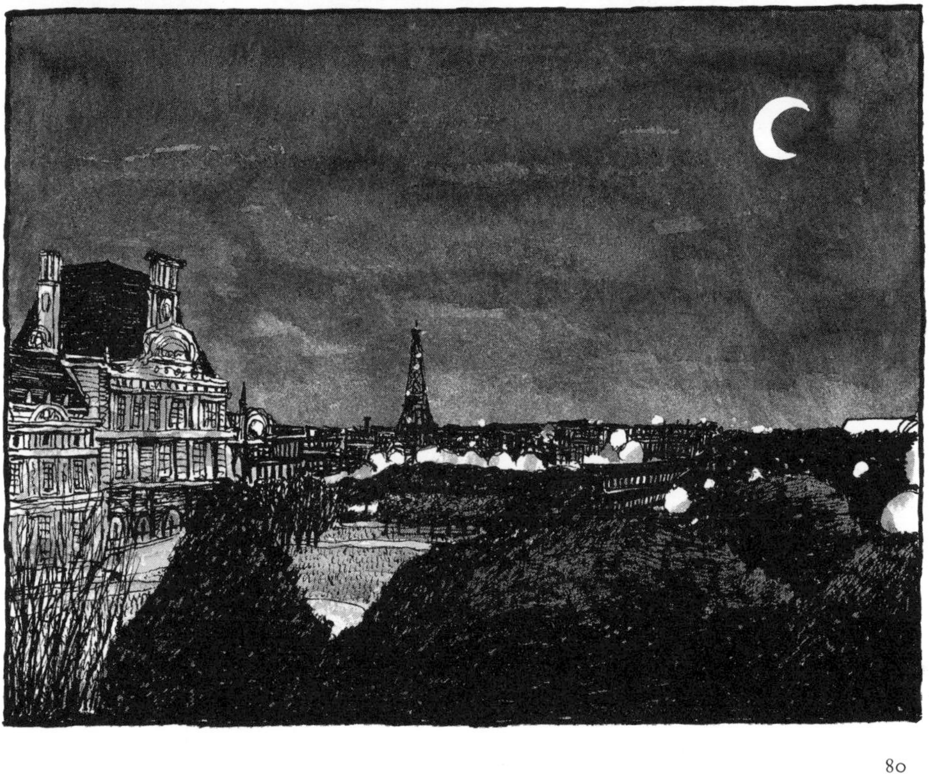

CHAPTER 4

The Secret of Sawtooth

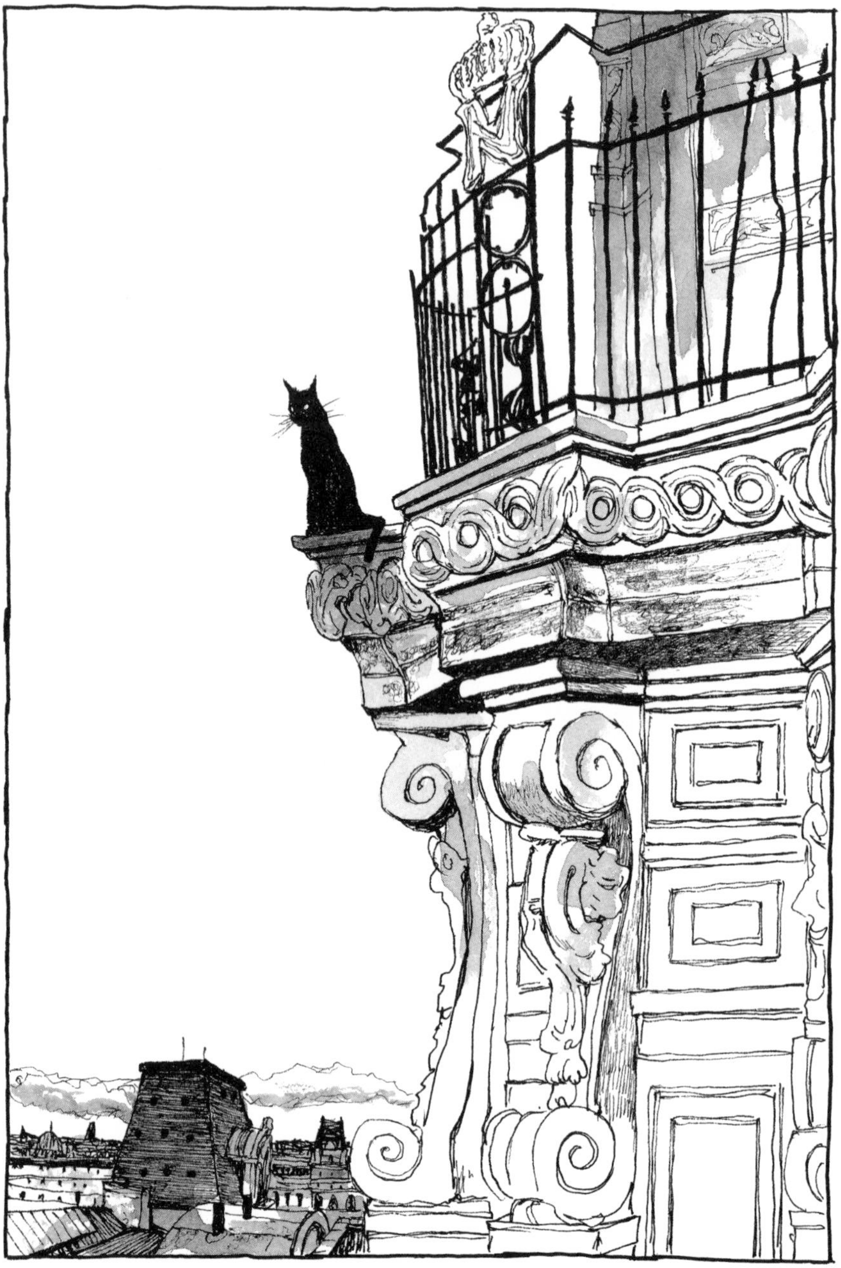

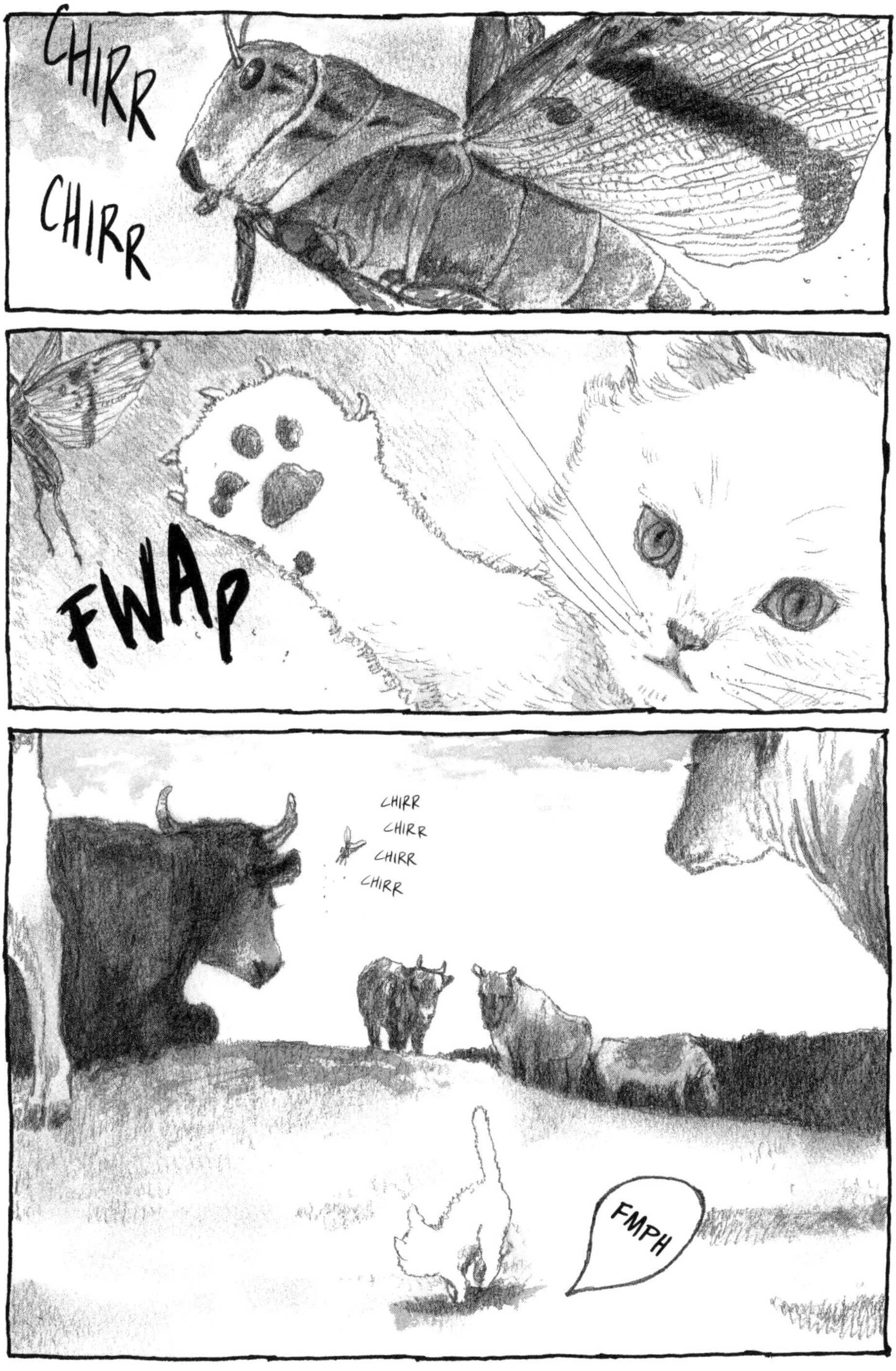
CHIRR
CHIRR
FWAP
CHIRR
CHIRR
CHIRR
CHIRR
FMPH

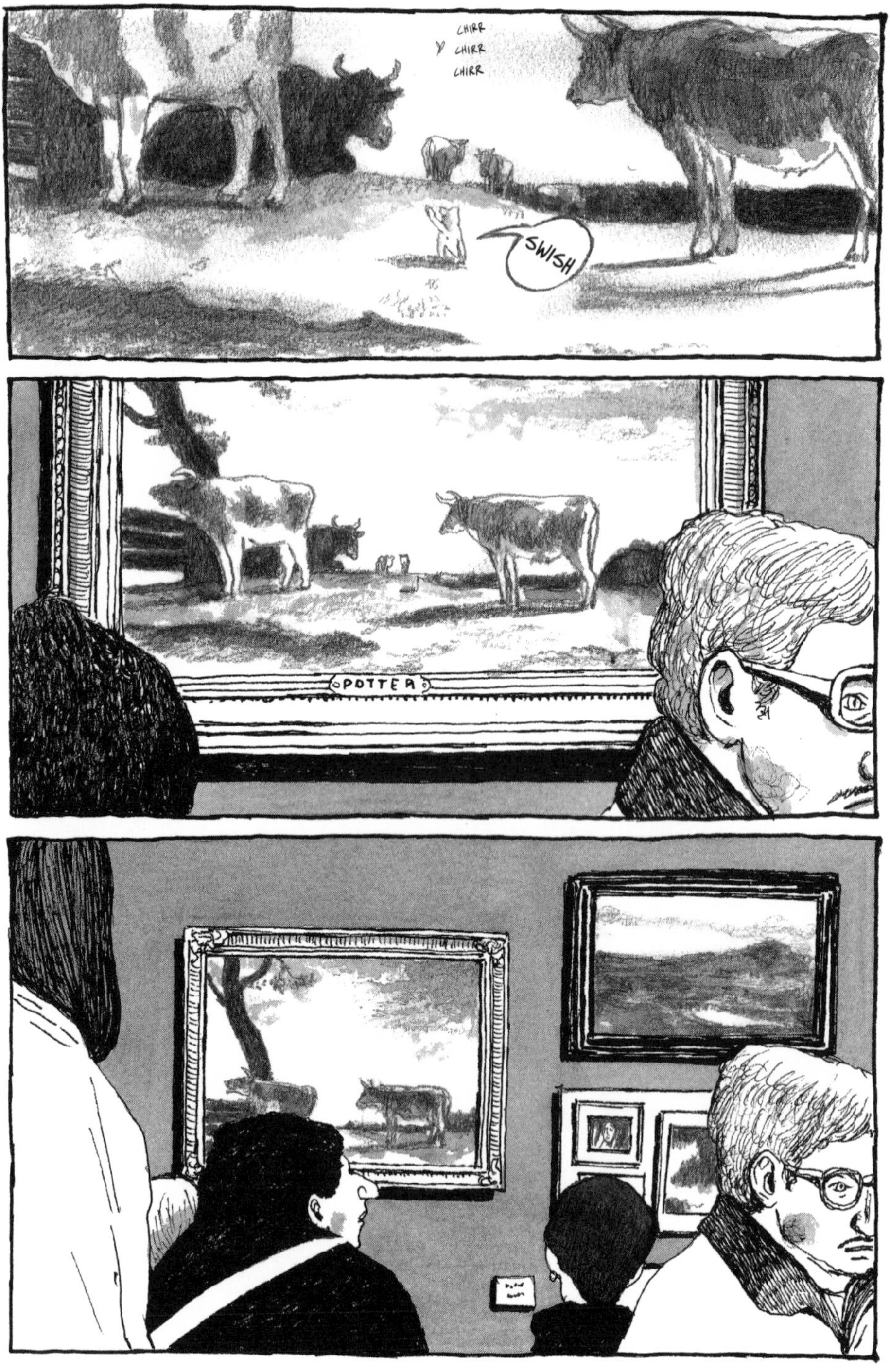
CHIRR
CHIRR
CHIRR
SWISH
POTTER

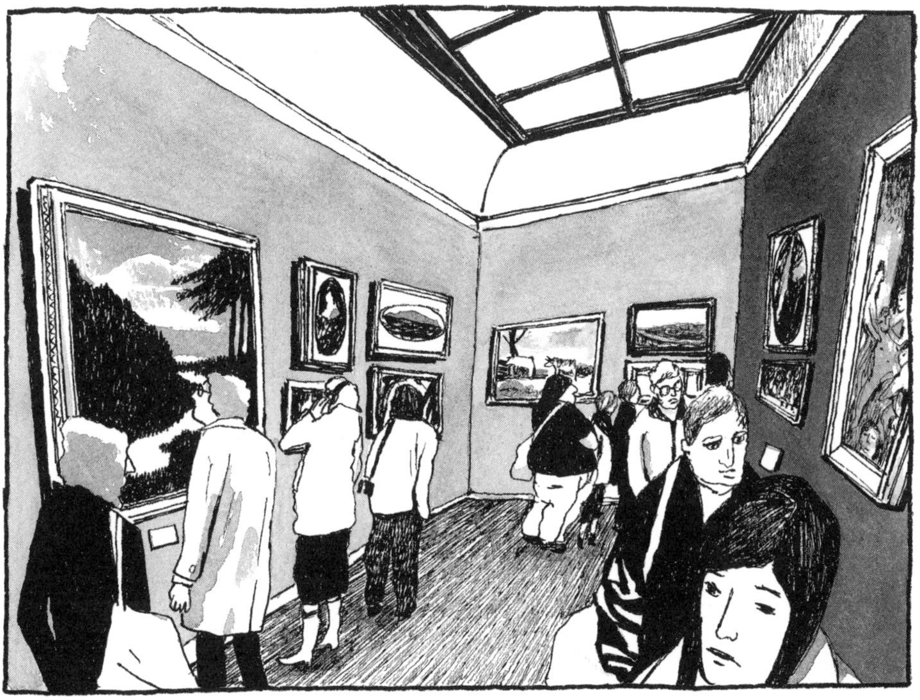

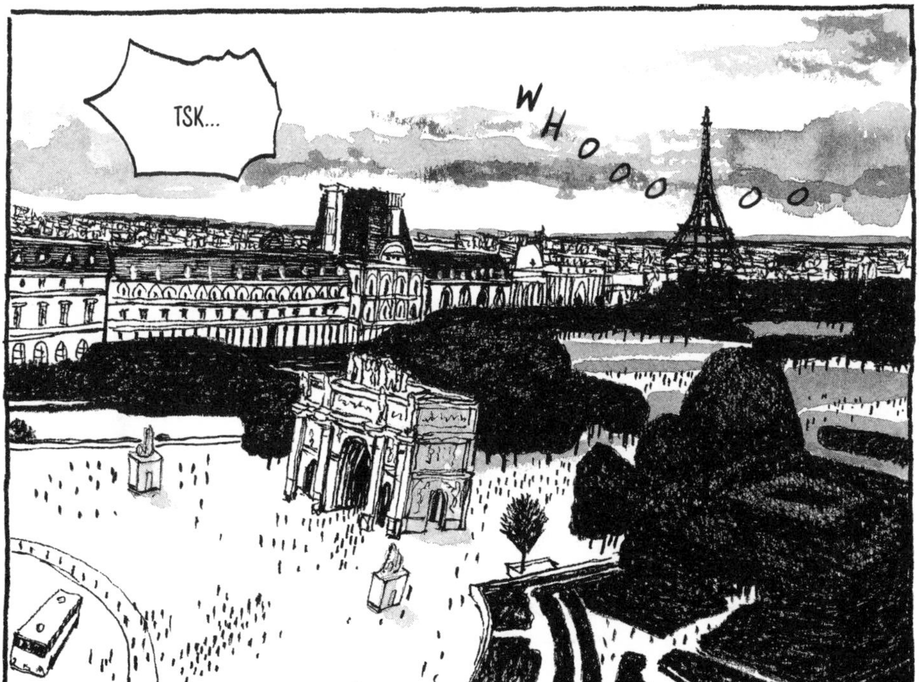
TSK...
WHOOOOOO

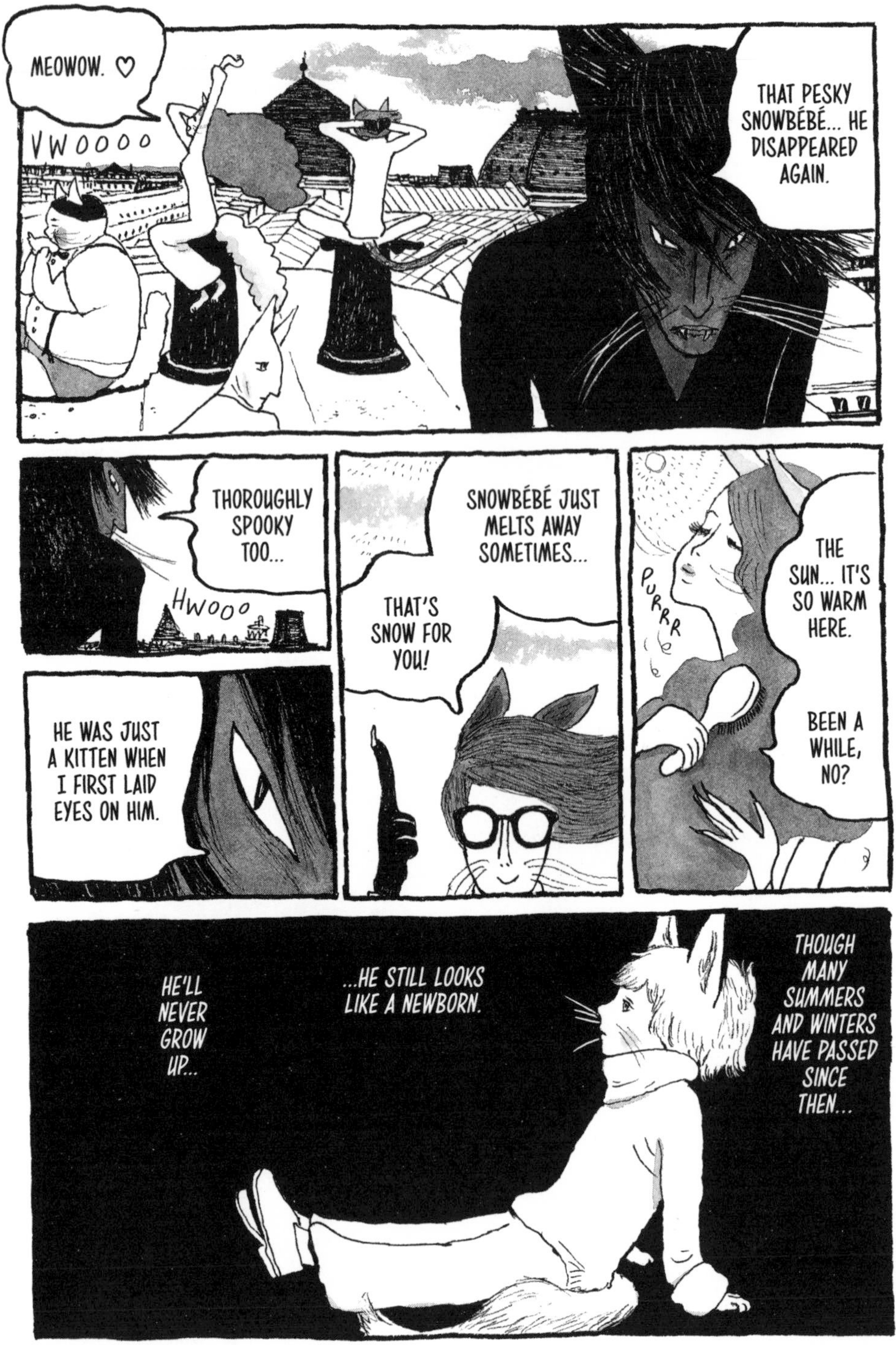
THAT PESKY SNOWBÉBÉ... HE DISAPPEARED AGAIN.
MEOWOW. ♡
VWOOOO
THE SUN... IT'S SO WARM HERE.
PURRR
BEEN A WHILE, NO?
SNOWBÉBÉ JUST MELTS AWAY SOMETIMES...
THAT'S SNOW FOR YOU!
THOROUGHLY SPOOKY TOO...
HWOOO
HE WAS JUST A KITTEN WHEN I FIRST LAID EYES ON HIM.
THOUGH MANY SUMMERS AND WINTERS HAVE PASSED SINCE THEN...
...HE STILL LOOKS LIKE A NEWBORN.
HE'LL NEVER GROW UP...

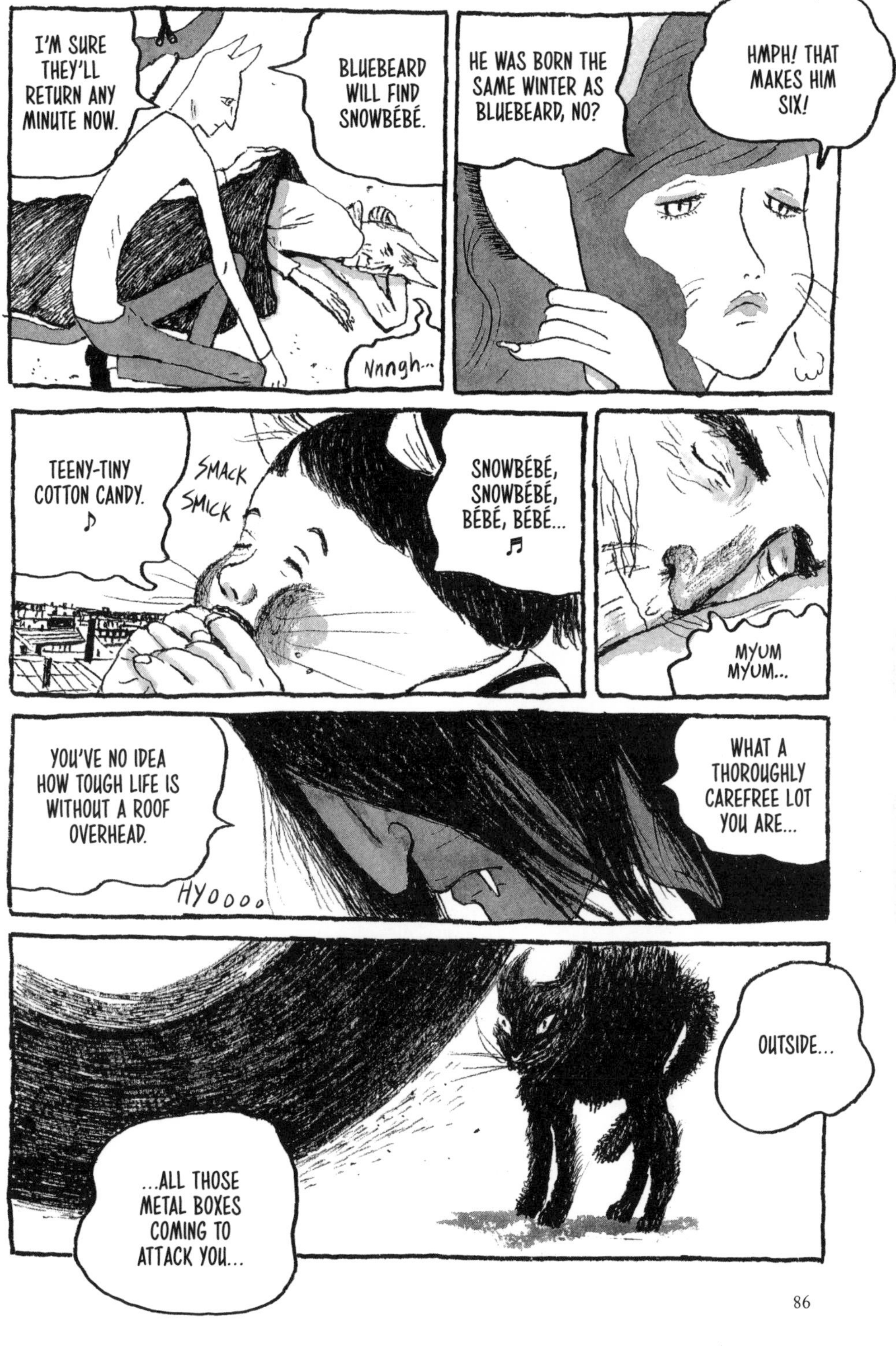
HMPH! THAT MAKES HIM SIX!
HE WAS BORN THE SAME WINTER AS BLUEBEARD, NO?
BLUEBEARD WILL FIND SNOWBÉBÉ.
I'M SURE THEY'LL RETURN ANY MINUTE NOW.
Nnngh...
MYUM MYUM...
SNOWBÉBÉ, SNOWBÉBÉ, BÉBÉ, BÉBÉ... ♬
SMACK SMICK
TEENY-TINY COTTON CANDY. ♪
WHAT A THOROUGHLY CAREFREE LOT YOU ARE...
YOU'VE NO IDEA HOW TOUGH LIFE IS WITHOUT A ROOF OVERHEAD.
HYOOOO
OUTSIDE...
...ALL THOSE METAL BOXES COMING TO ATTACK YOU...

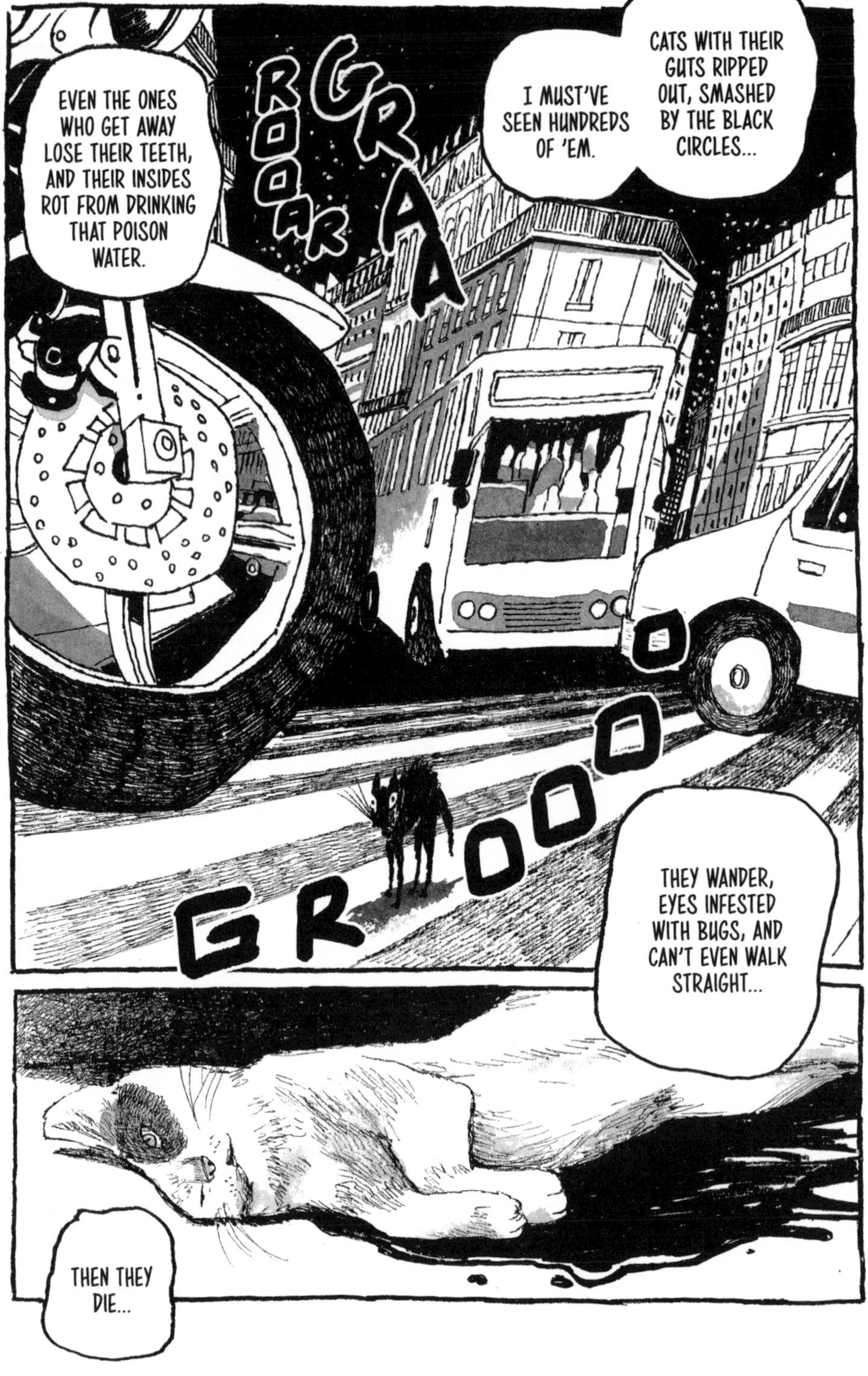
I MUST'VE SEEN HUNDREDS OF 'EM.
CATS WITH THEIR GUTS RIPPED OUT, SMASHED BY THE BLACK CIRCLES...
GRA
ROOAR
EVEN THE ONES WHO GET AWAY LOSE THEIR TEETH, AND THEIR INSIDES ROT FROM DRINKING THAT POISON WATER.
GROOOOO
THEY WANDER, EYES INFESTED WITH BUGS, AND CAN'T EVEN WALK STRAIGHT...
THEN THEY DIE...

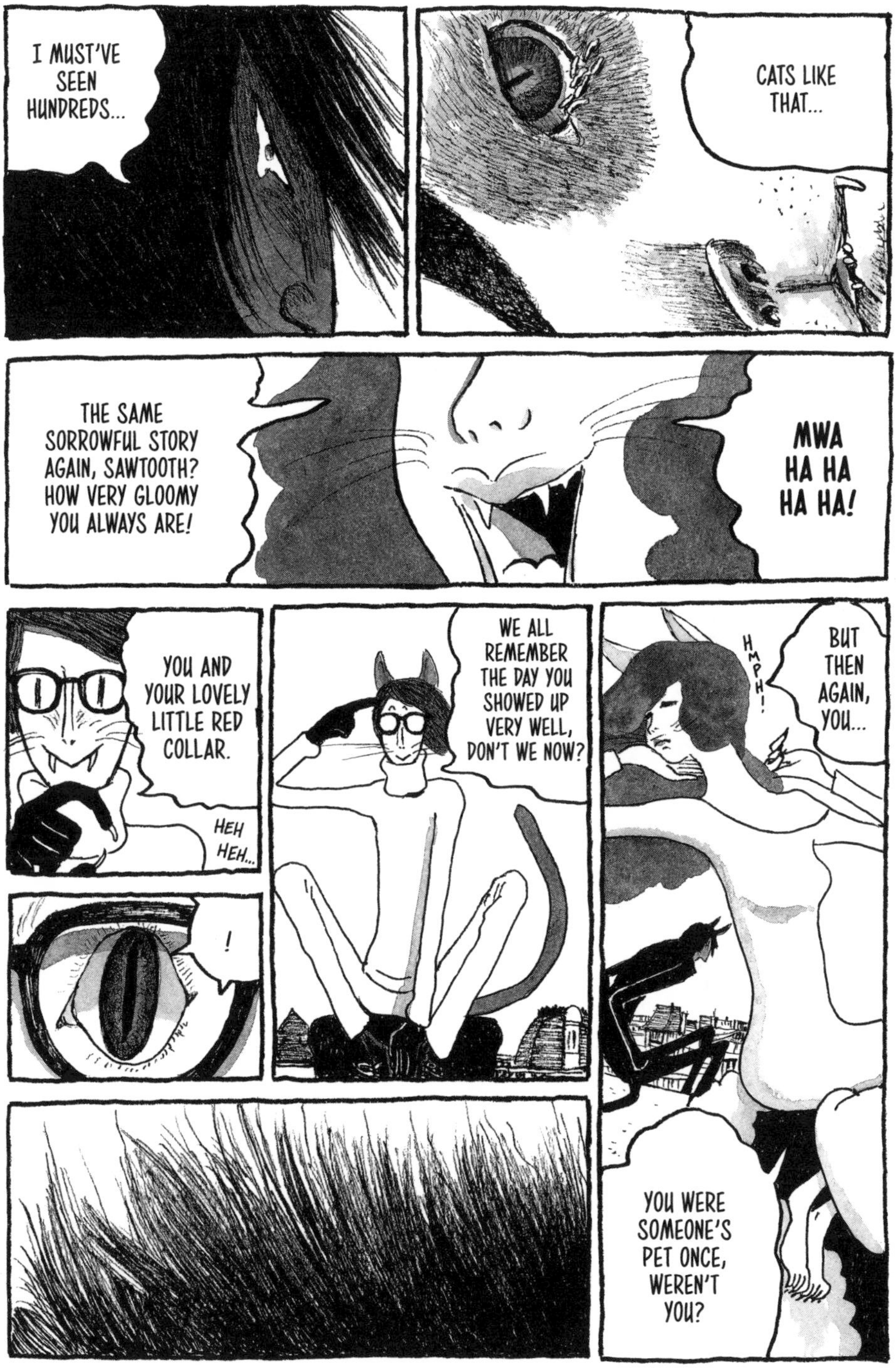
CATS LIKE THAT...
I MUST'VE SEEN HUNDREDS...
MWA HA HA HA HA!
THE SAME SORROWFUL STORY AGAIN, SAWTOOTH? HOW VERY GLOOMY YOU ALWAYS ARE!
BUT THEN AGAIN, YOU...
HMPH!
YOU WERE SOMEONE'S PET ONCE, WEREN'T YOU?
WE ALL REMEMBER THE DAY YOU SHOWED UP VERY WELL, DON'T WE NOW?
YOU AND YOUR LOVELY LITTLE RED COLLAR.
HEH HEH...
!

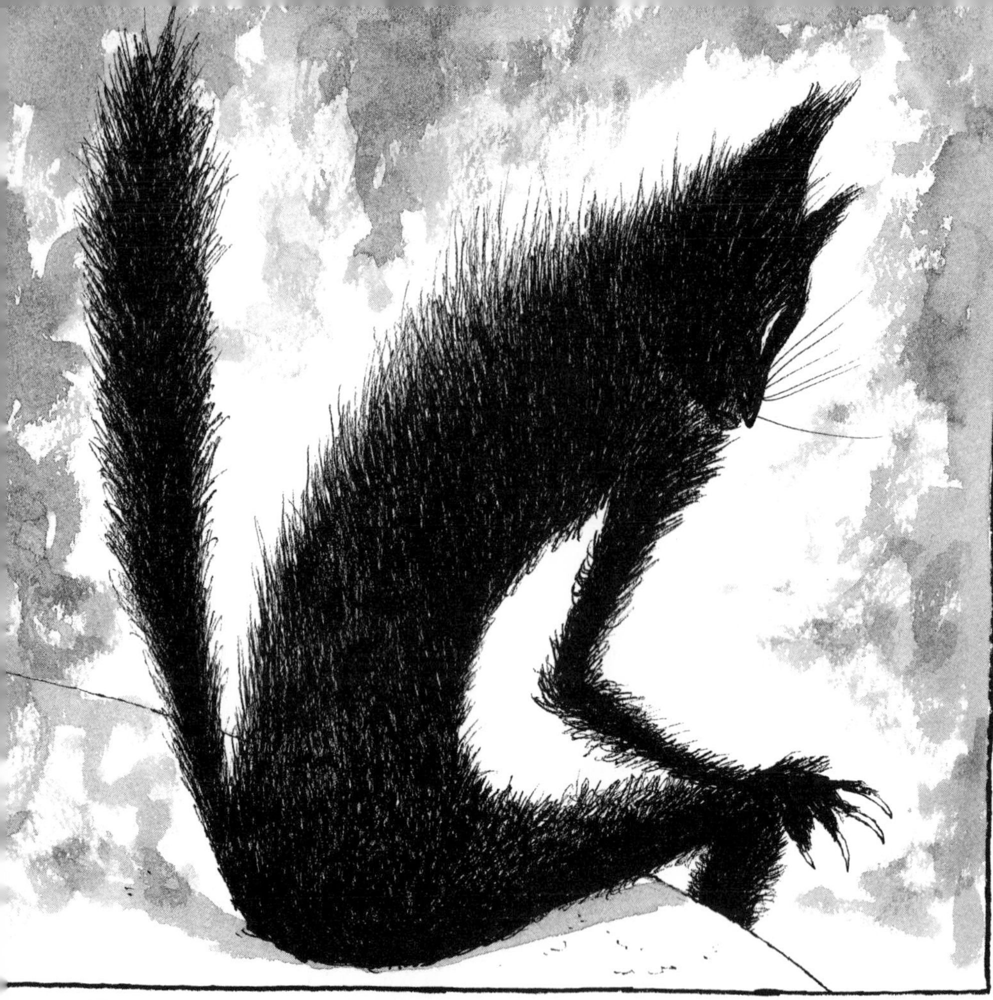

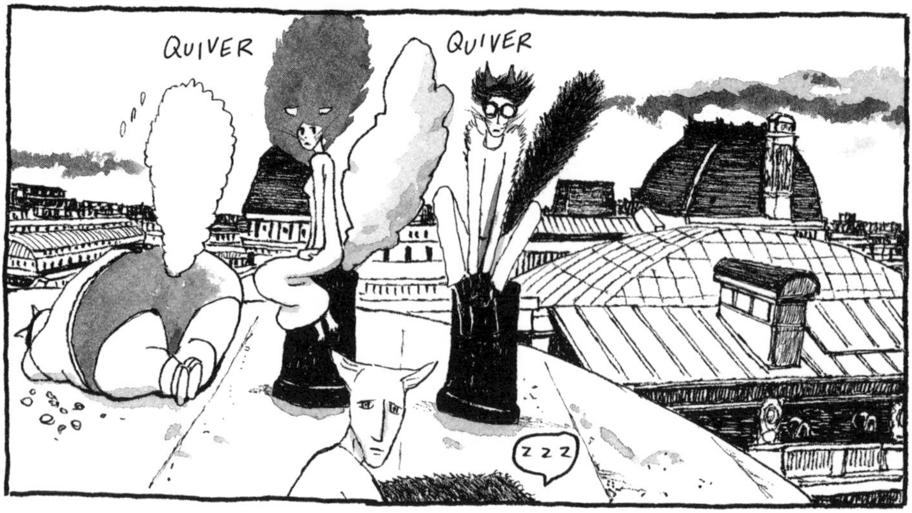
QUIVER
QUIVER
ZZZ

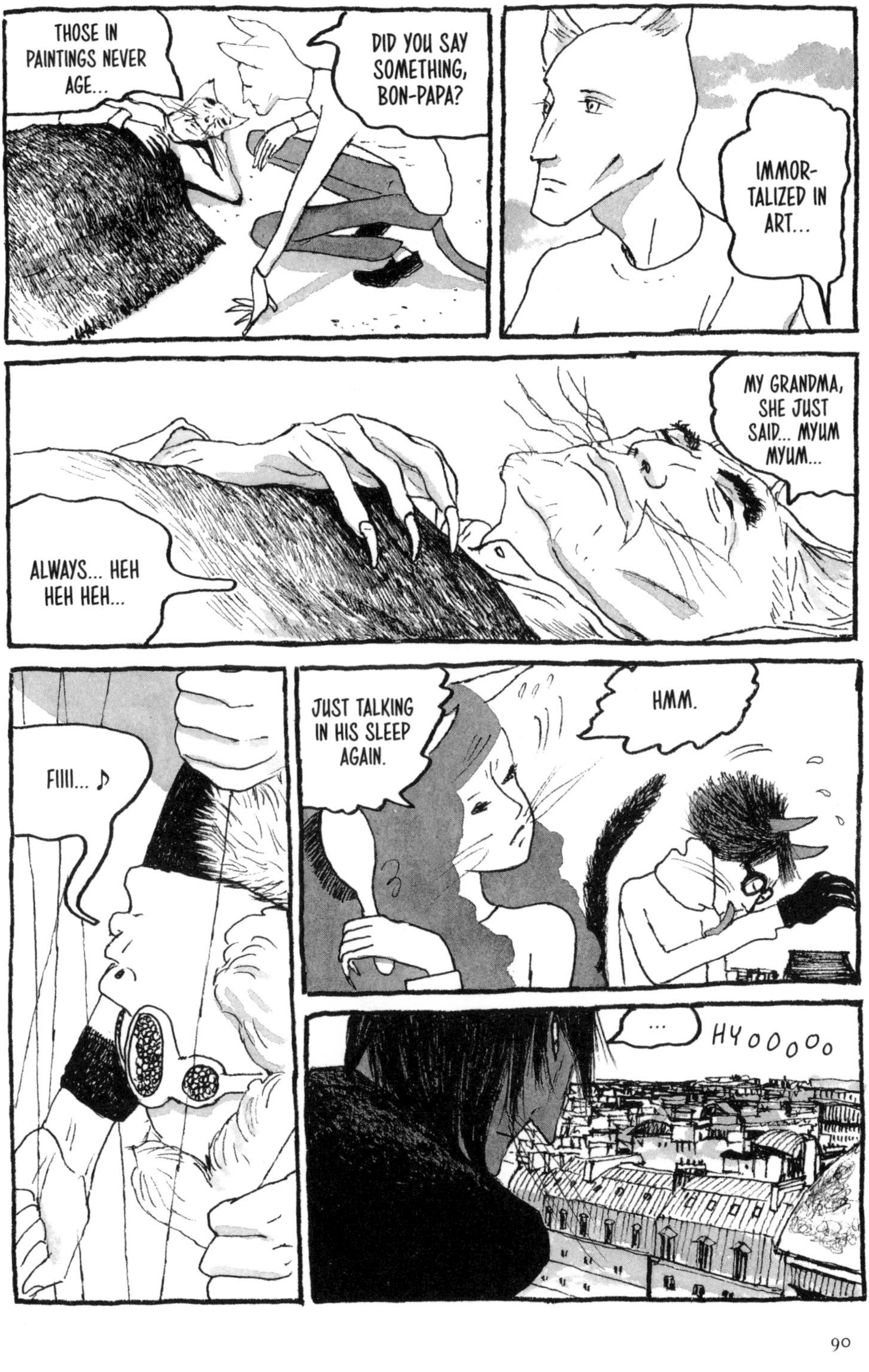
IMMORTALIZED IN ART...
DID YOU SAY SOMETHING, BON-PAPA?
THOSE IN PAINTINGS NEVER AGE...
MY GRANDMA, SHE JUST SAID... MYUM MYUM...
ALWAYS... HEH HEH HEH...
HMM.
JUST TALKING IN HIS SLEEP AGAIN.
...
HYOOOOOO
FIIII... ♪

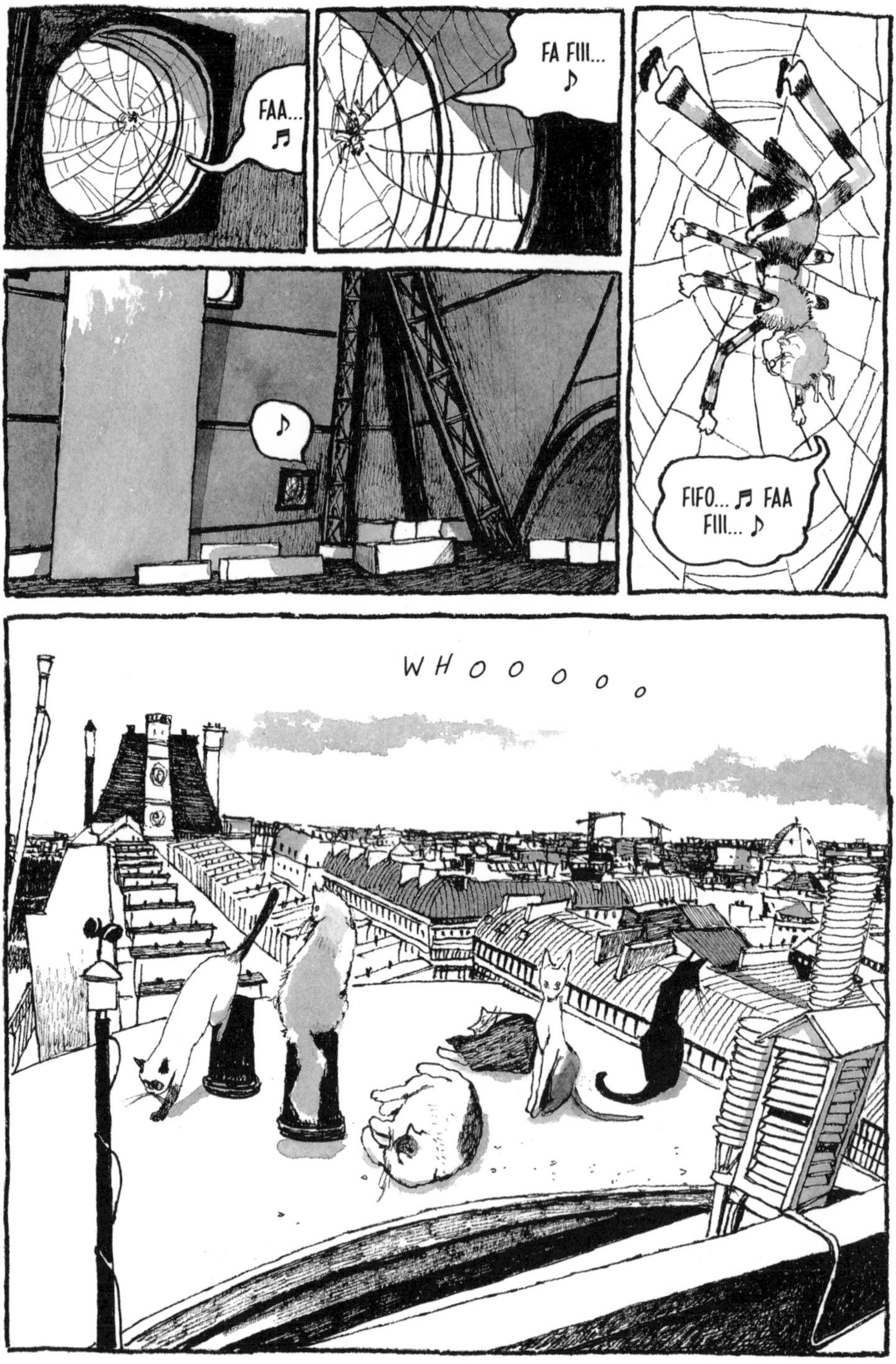
FIFO... ♬ FAA FIII... ♪
FA FIII... ♪
FAA... ♬
♪
WHOOOOO

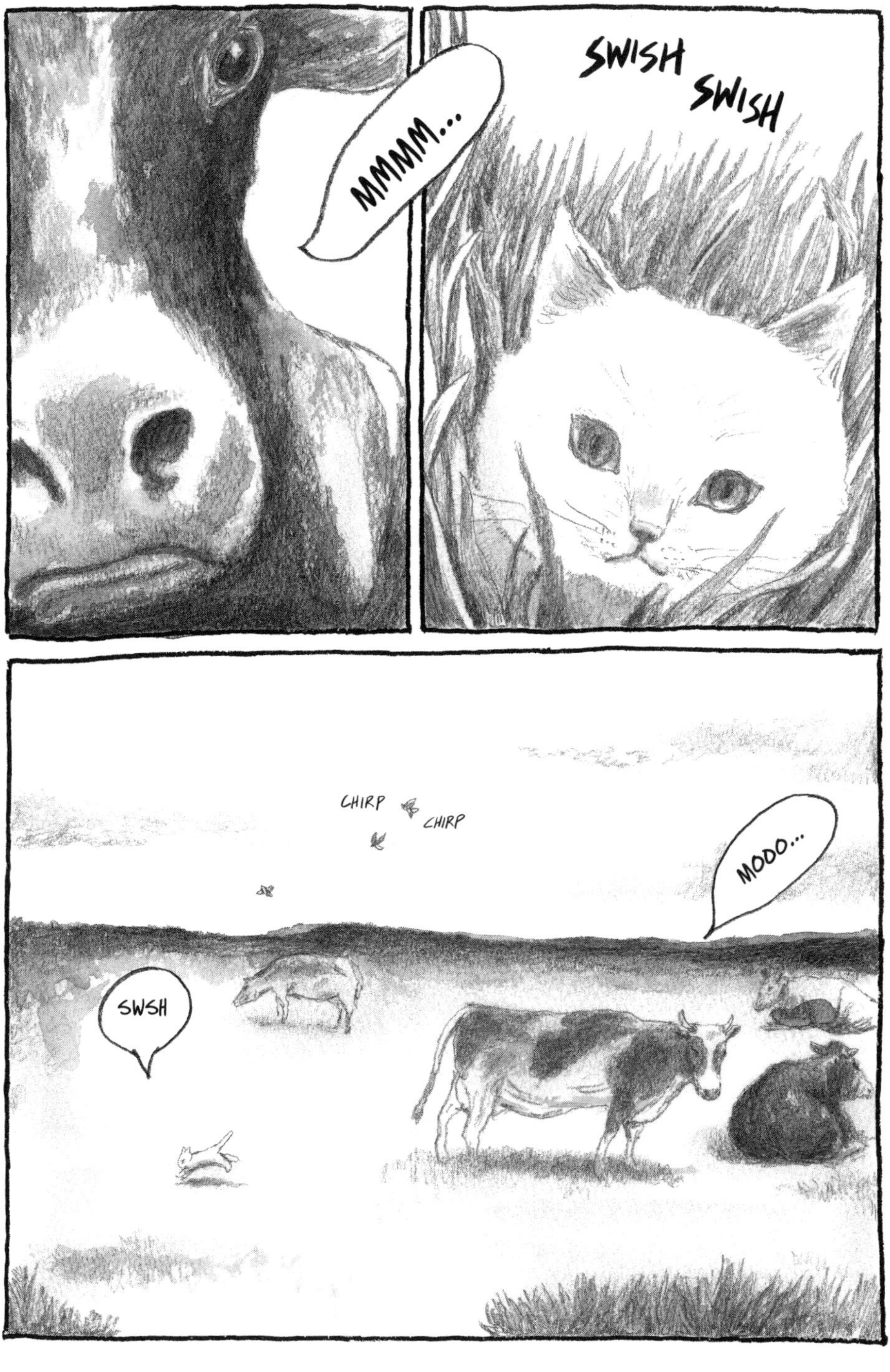
SWISH SWISH
MMMM...
MODO...
CHIRP CHIRP
SWSH

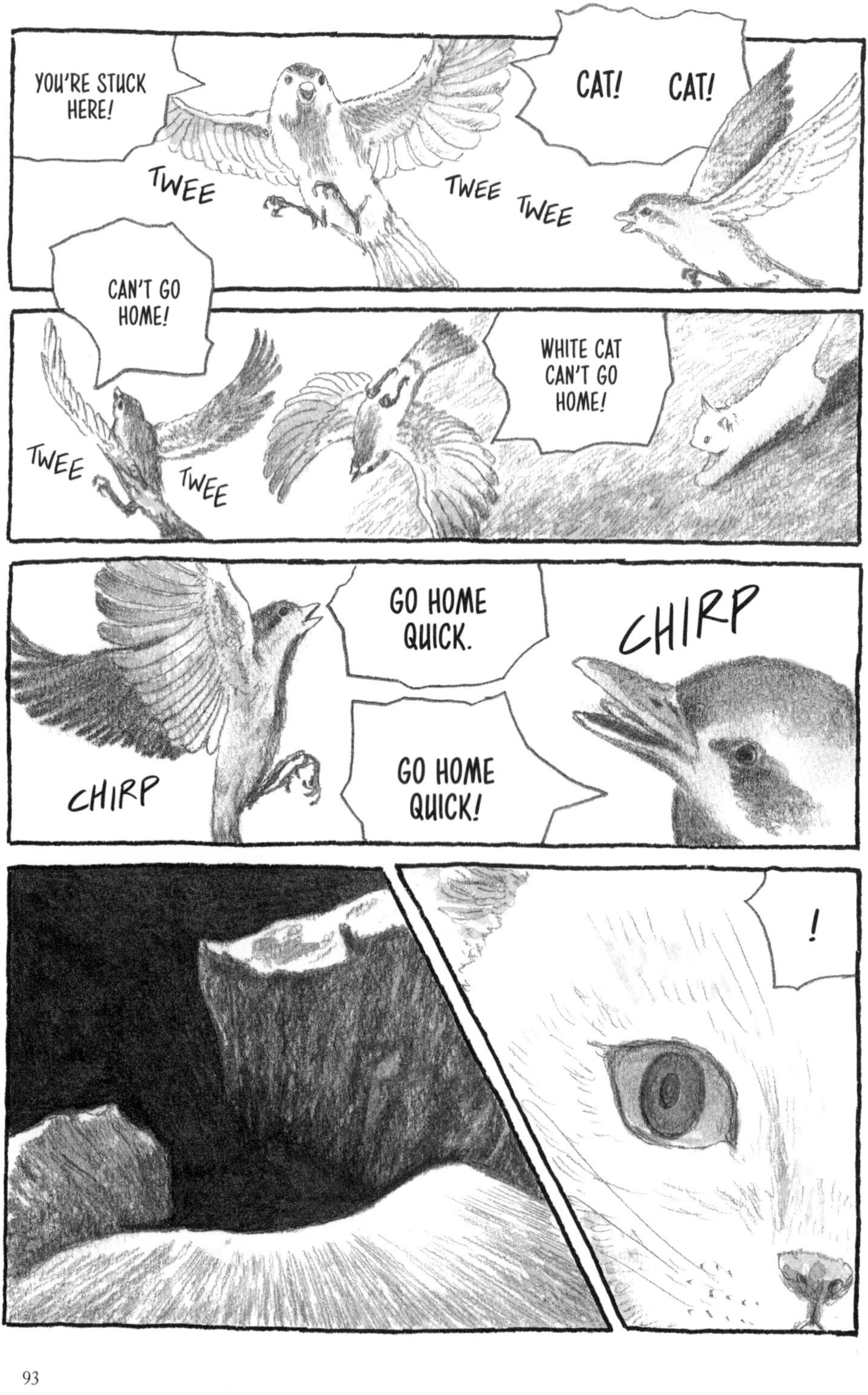
CAT! CAT!
YOU'RE STUCK HERE!
TWEE TWEE
TWEE
WHITE CAT CAN'T GO HOME!
CAN'T GO HOME!
TWEE
TWEE
CHIRP
GO HOME QUICK.
GO HOME QUICK!
CHIRP
!

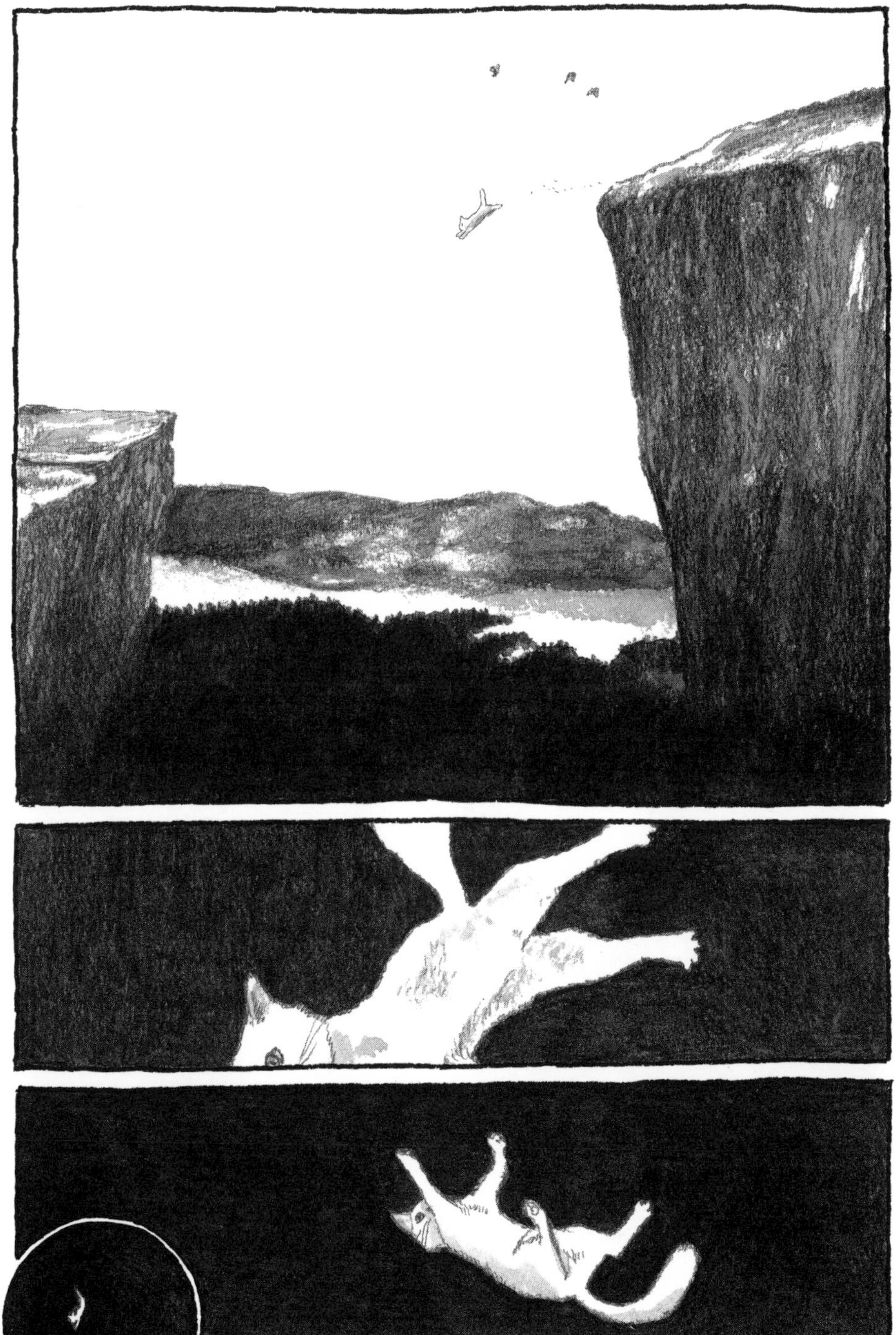

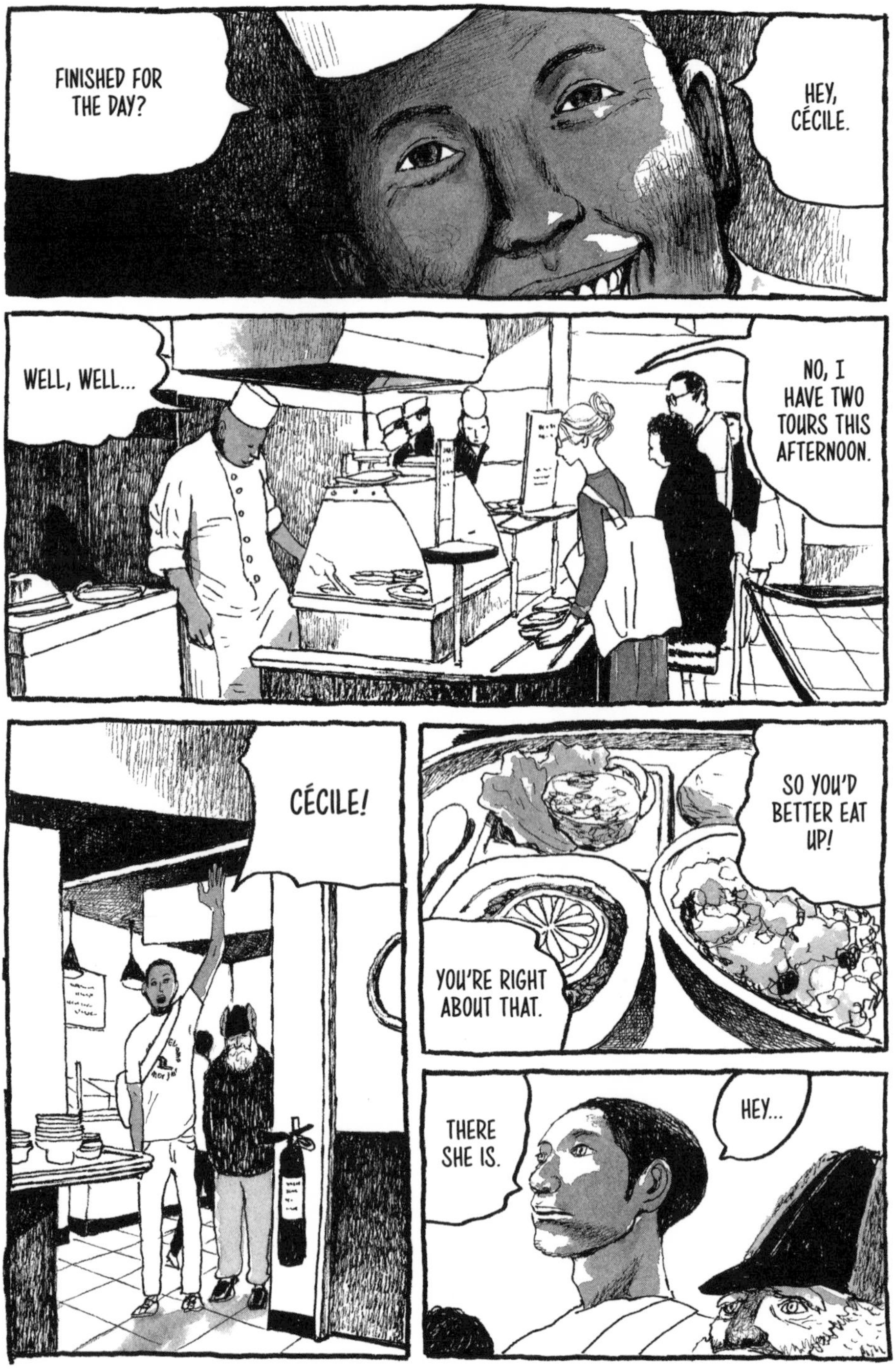
HEY, CÉCILE.
FINISHED FOR THE DAY?
NO, I HAVE TWO TOURS THIS AFTERNOON.
WELL, WELL...
SO YOU'D BETTER EAT UP!
YOU'RE RIGHT ABOUT THAT.
HEY...
THERE SHE IS.
CÉCILE!

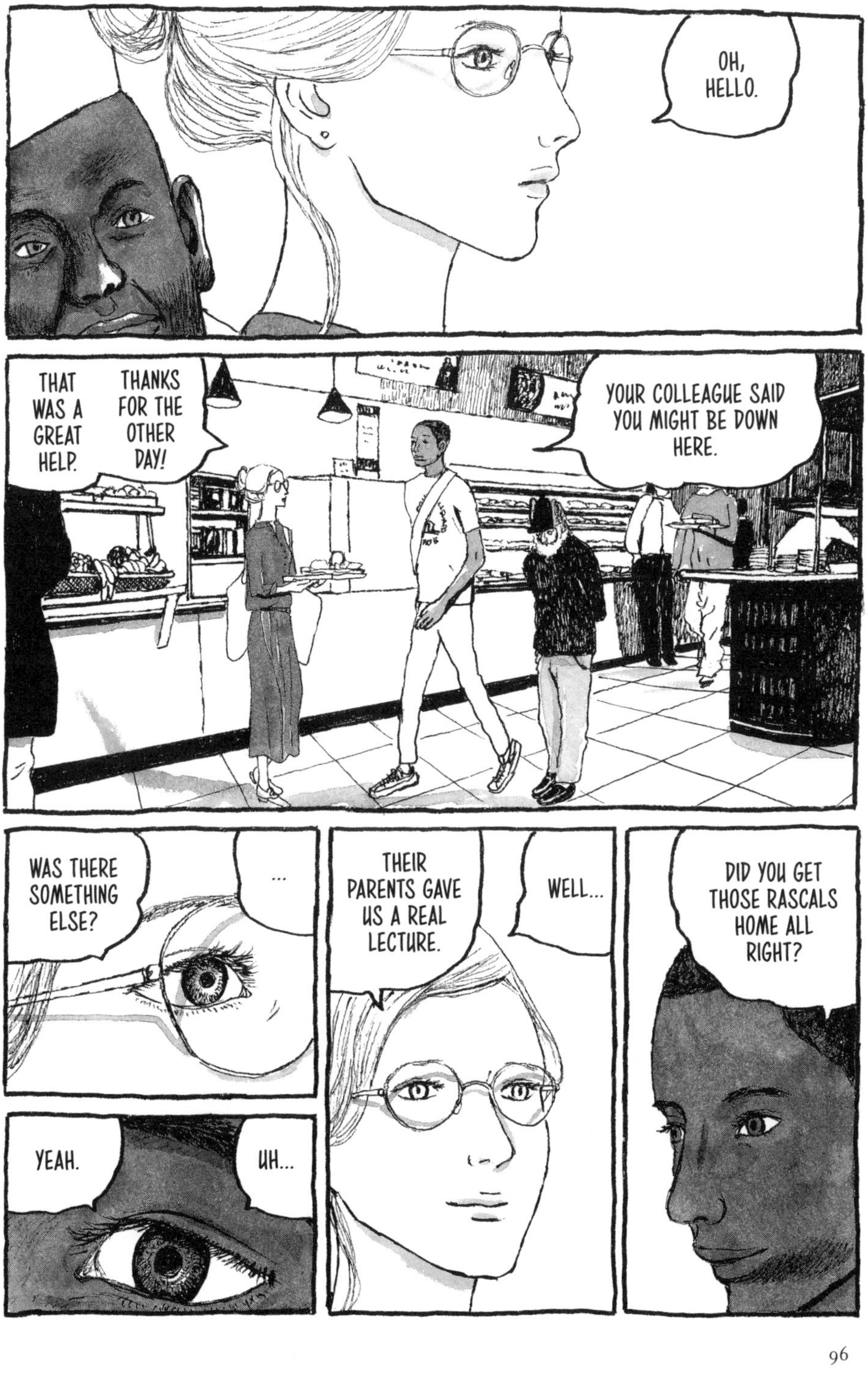
OH, HELLO.
YOUR COLLEAGUE SAID YOU MIGHT BE DOWN HERE.
THANKS FOR THE OTHER DAY!
THAT WAS A GREAT HELP.
DID YOU GET THOSE RASCALS HOME ALL RIGHT?
WELL...
THEIR PARENTS GAVE US A REAL LECTURE.
...
WAS THERE SOMETHING ELSE?
UH...
YEAH.

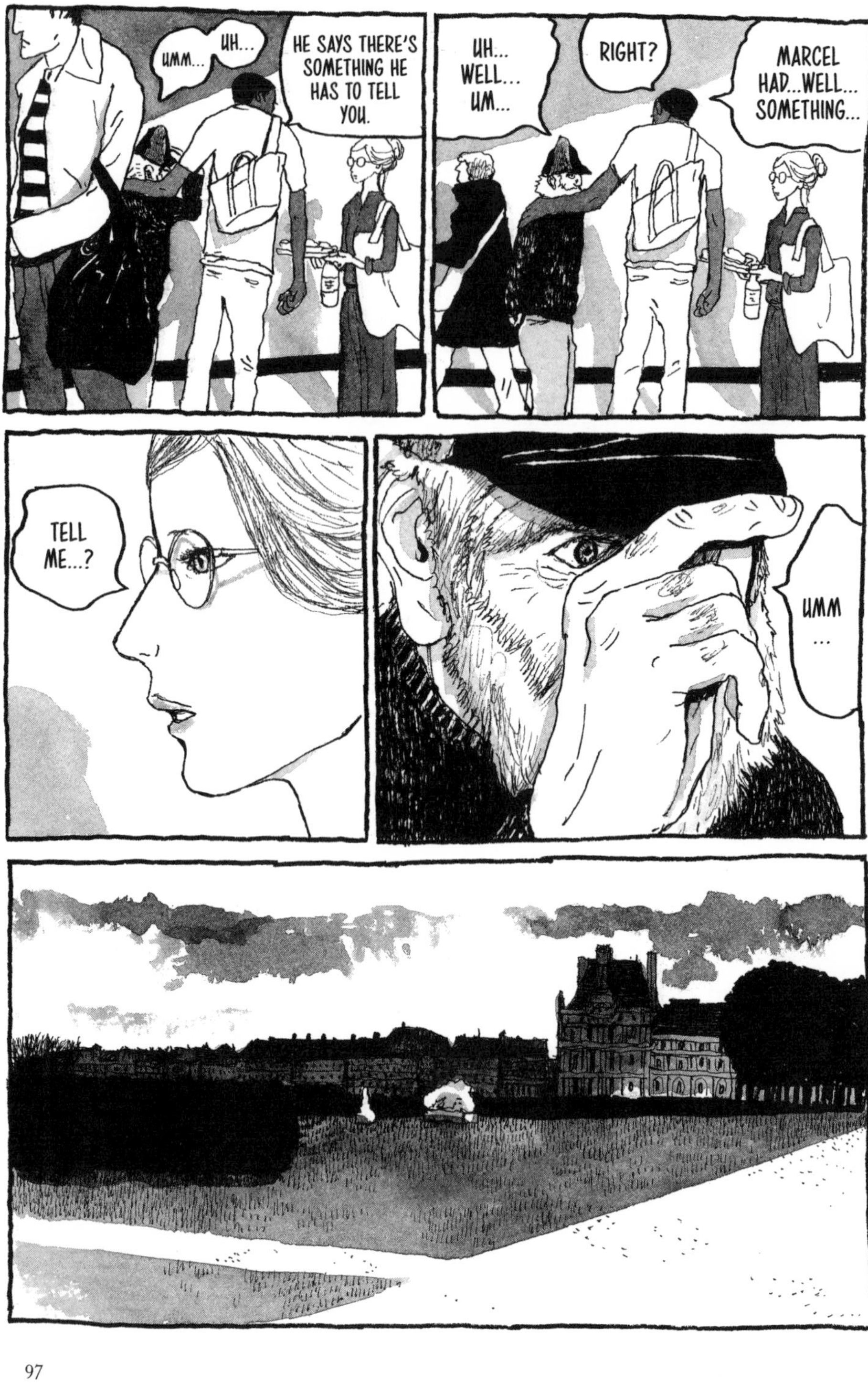
MARCEL HAD...WELL... SOMETHING...
RIGHT?
UH... WELL... UM...
HE SAYS THERE'S SOMETHING HE HAS TO TELL YOU.
UH...
UMM...
UMM ...
TELL ME...?

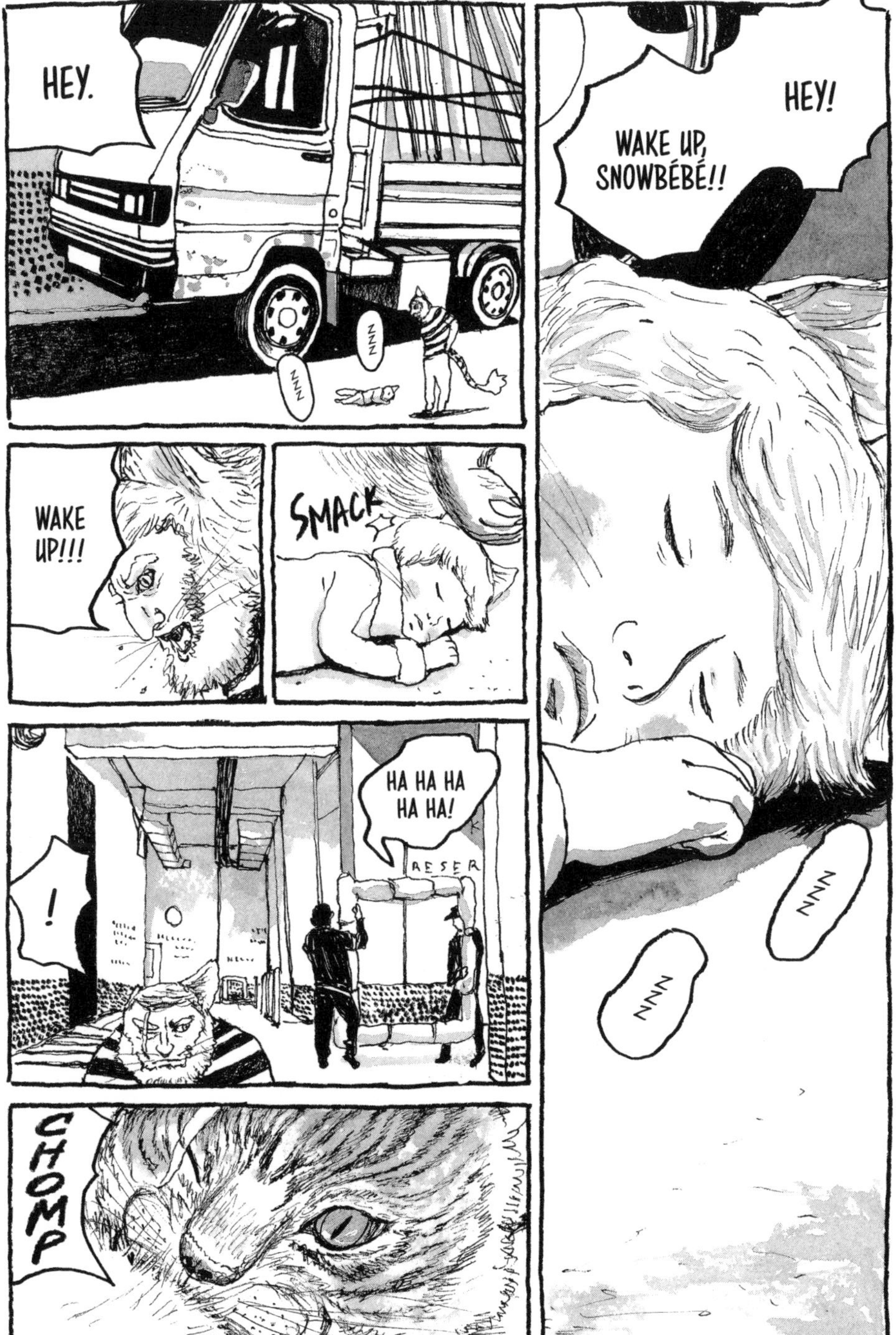
HEY!
WAKE UP, SNOWBÉBÉ!!
NNN
NNN
HEY.
ZZZ
ZZZ
SMACK
WAKE UP!!!
HA HA HA HA!
RESER
!
CHOMP

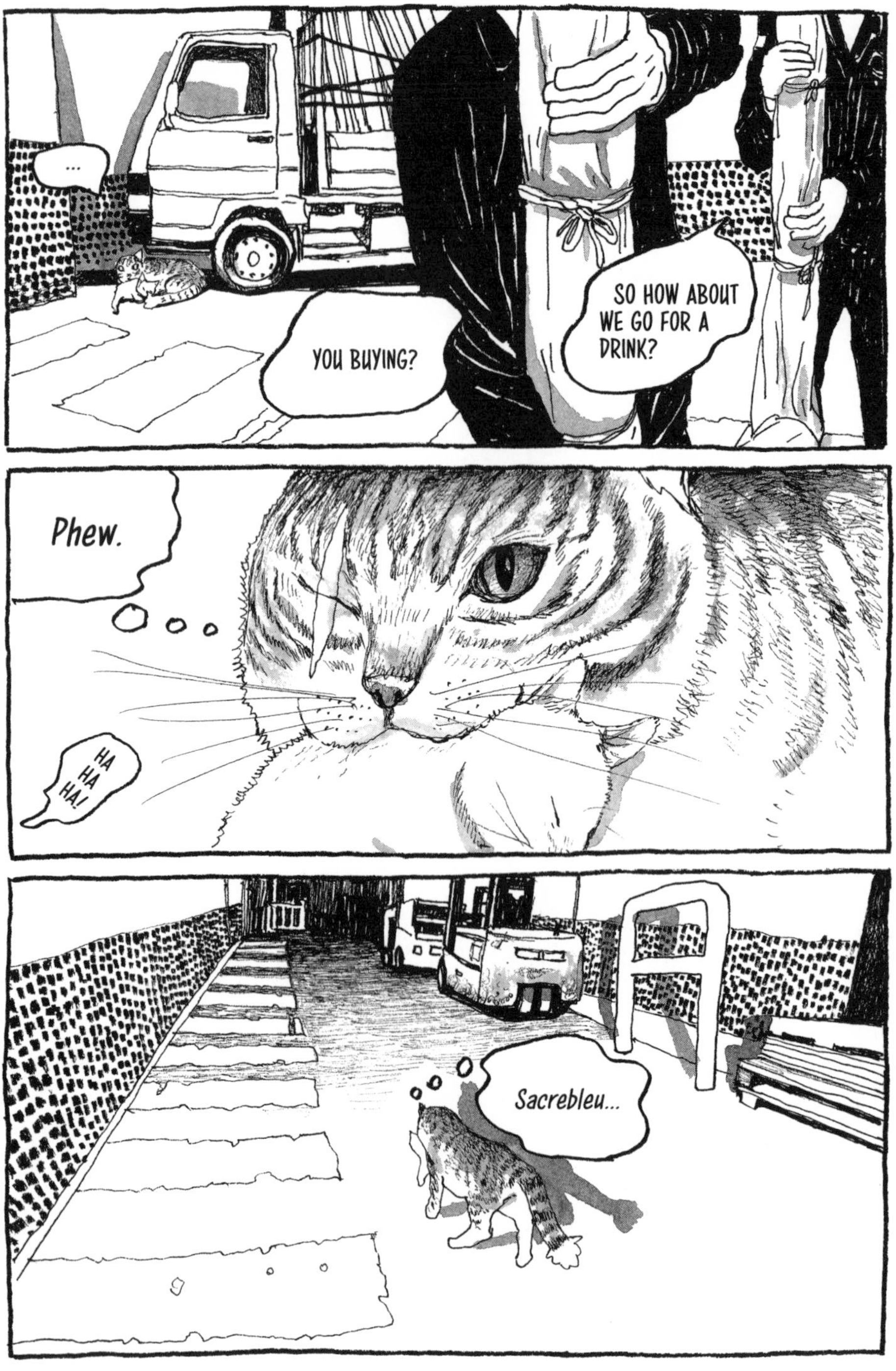
SO HOW ABOUT WE GO FOR A DRINK?
YOU BUYING?
...
Phew.
HA HA HA!
Sacrebleu...

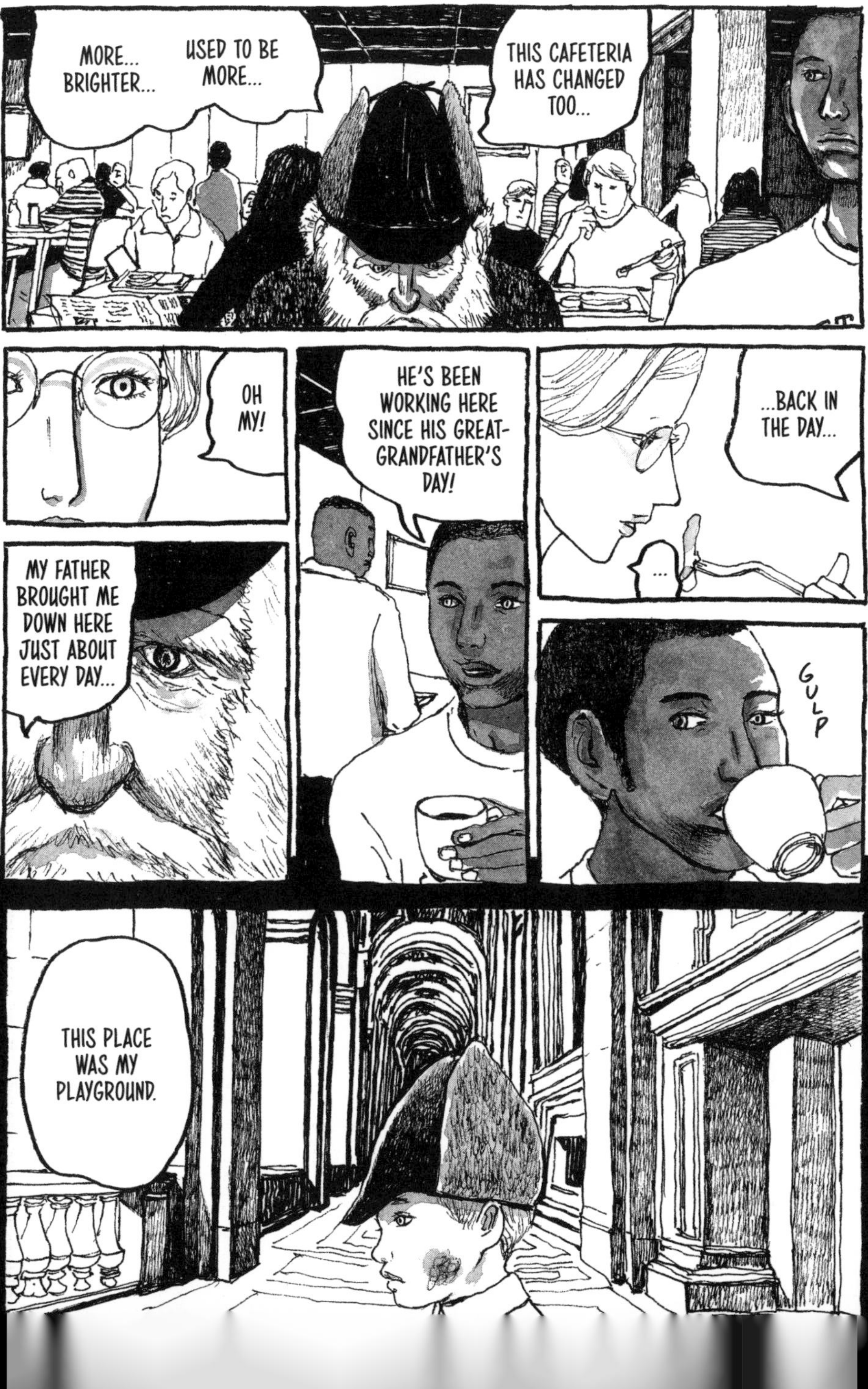
THIS CAFETERIA HAS CHANGED TOO...
USED TO BE MORE...
MORE... BRIGHTER...
...BACK IN THE DAY...
...
GULP
HE'S BEEN WORKING HERE SINCE HIS GREAT-GRANDFATHER'S DAY!
OH MY!
MY FATHER BROUGHT ME DOWN HERE JUST ABOUT EVERY DAY...
THIS PLACE WAS MY PLAYGROUND.

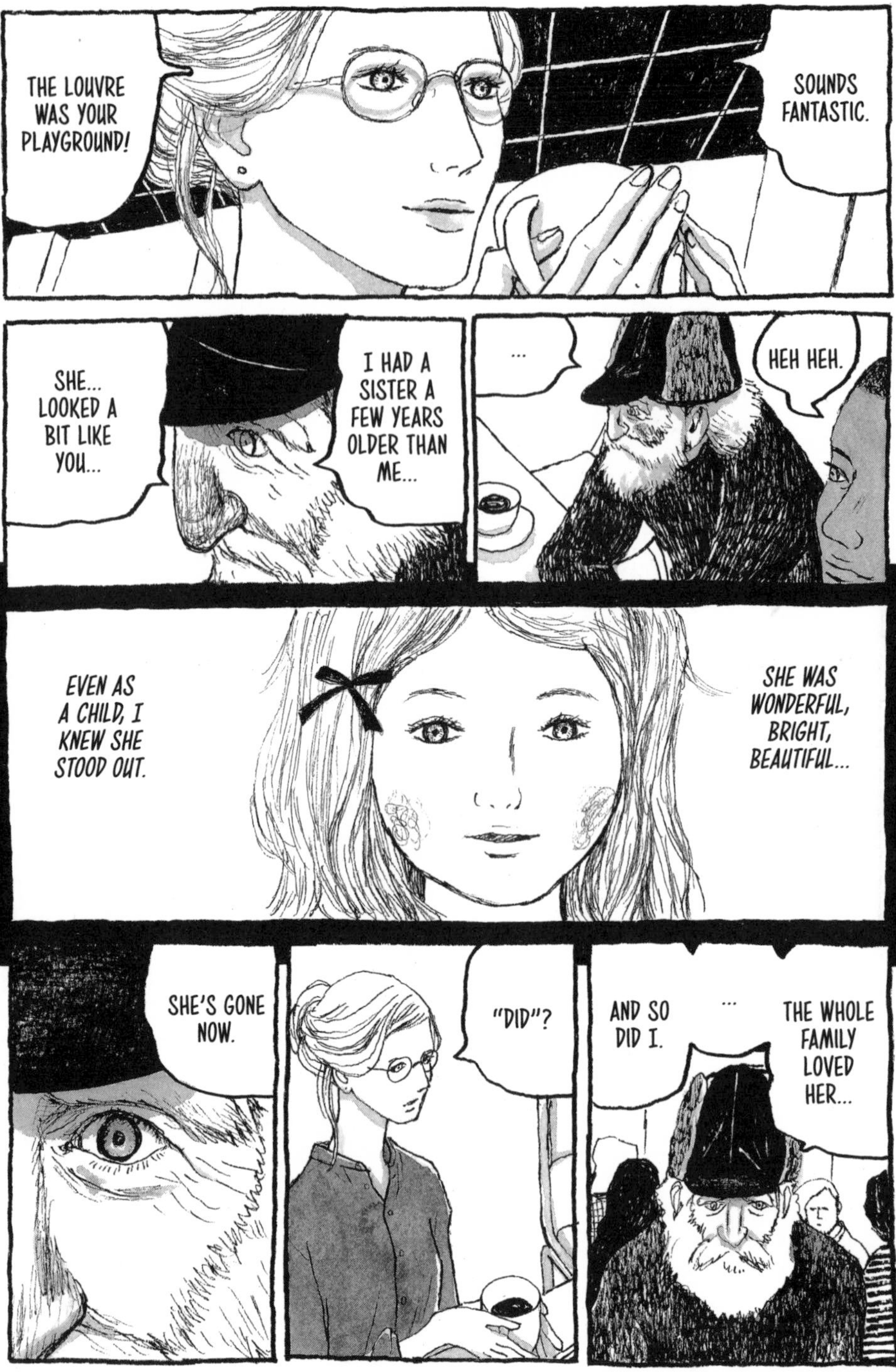
SOUNDS FANTASTIC.
THE LOUVRE WAS YOUR PLAYGROUND!
HEH HEH.
...
I HAD A SISTER A FEW YEARS OLDER THAN ME...
SHE... LOOKED A BIT LIKE YOU...
SHE WAS WONDERFUL, BRIGHT, BEAUTIFUL...
EVEN AS A CHILD, I KNEW SHE STOOD OUT.
THE WHOLE FAMILY LOVED HER...
...
AND SO DID I.
"DID"?
SHE'S GONE NOW.

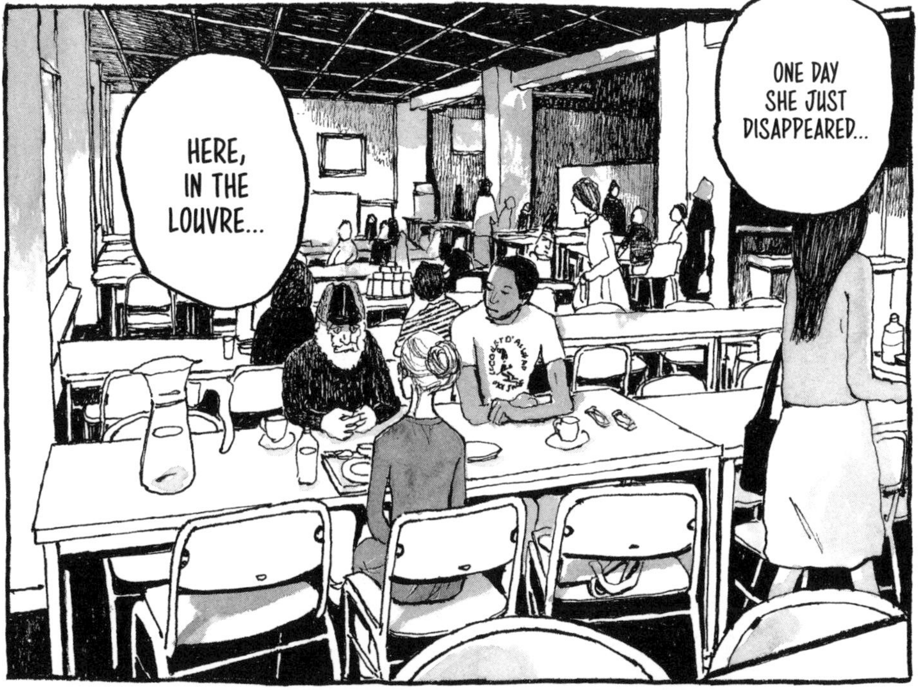
ONE DAY SHE JUST DISAPPEARED...
HERE, IN THE LOUVRE...

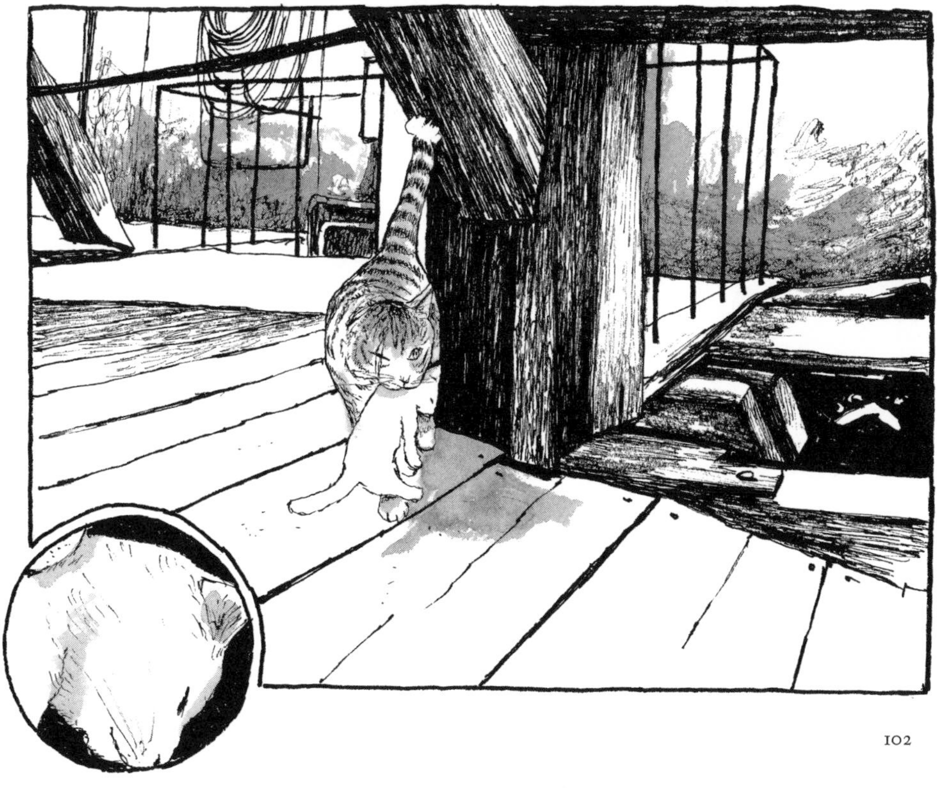

CHAPTER 5
The Secret of Marcel

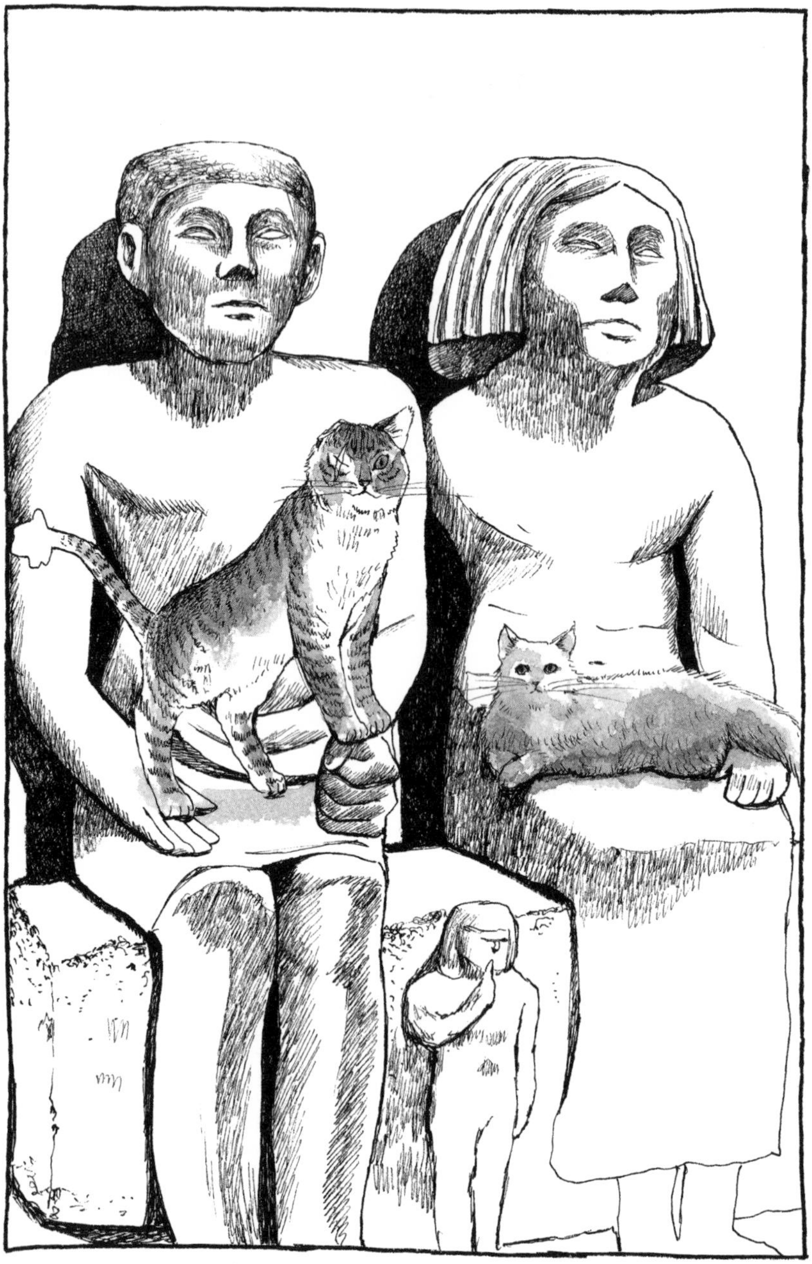

▲ Statue of parents and child (Egyptian Antiquities)

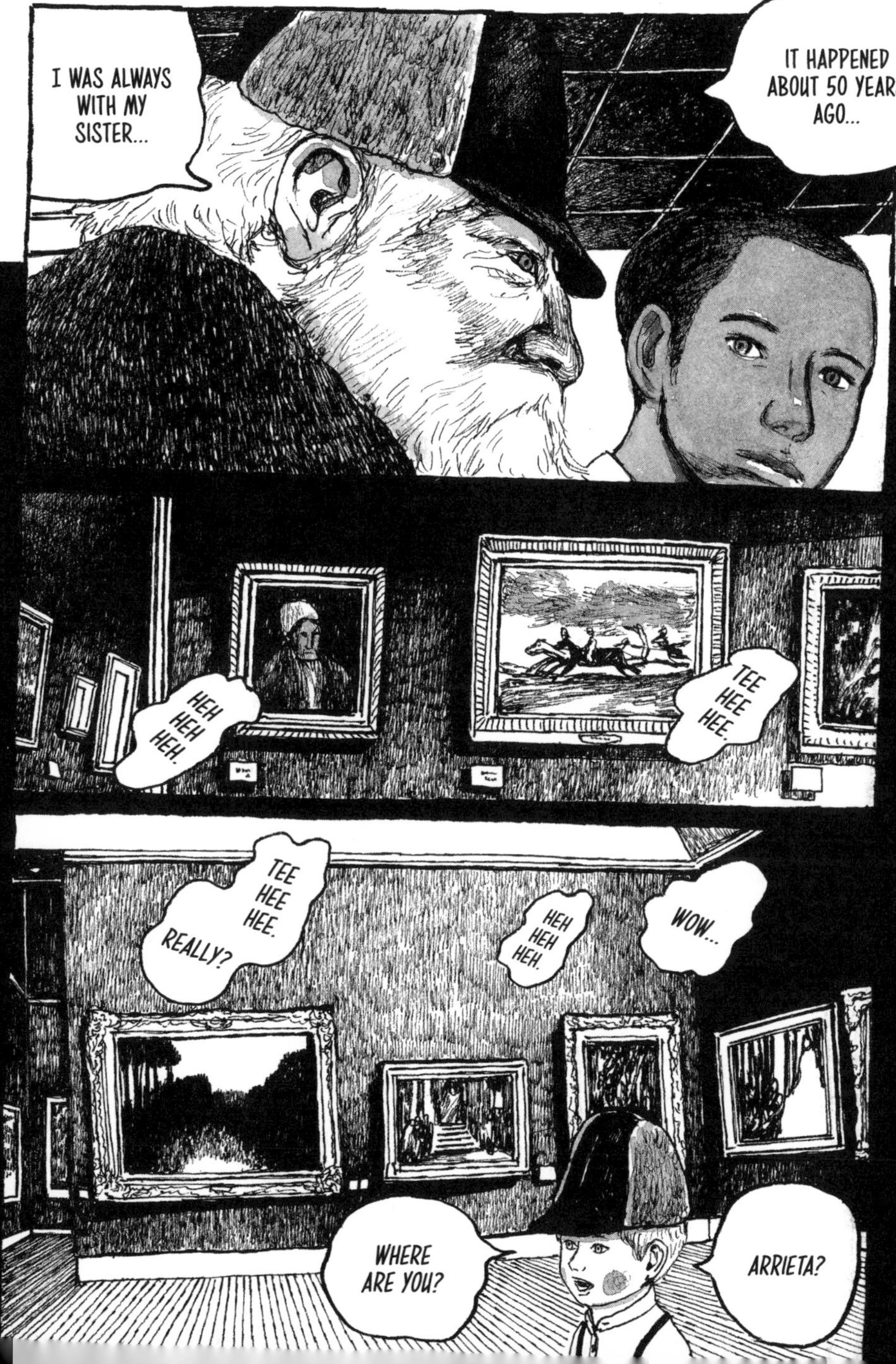
IT HAPPENED ABOUT 50 YEARS AGO...
I WAS ALWAYS WITH MY SISTER...
TEE HEE HEE.
HEH HEH HEH.
WOW...
HEH HEH HEH.
TEE HEE HEE.
REALLY?
ARRIETA?
WHERE ARE YOU?

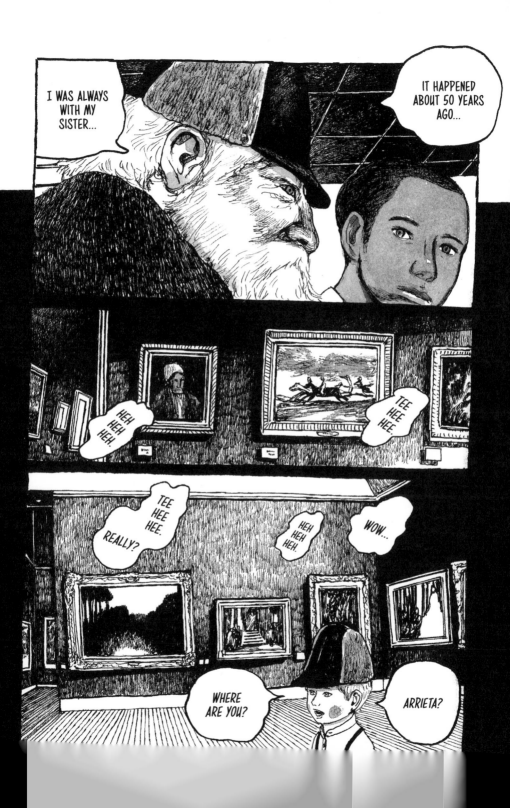

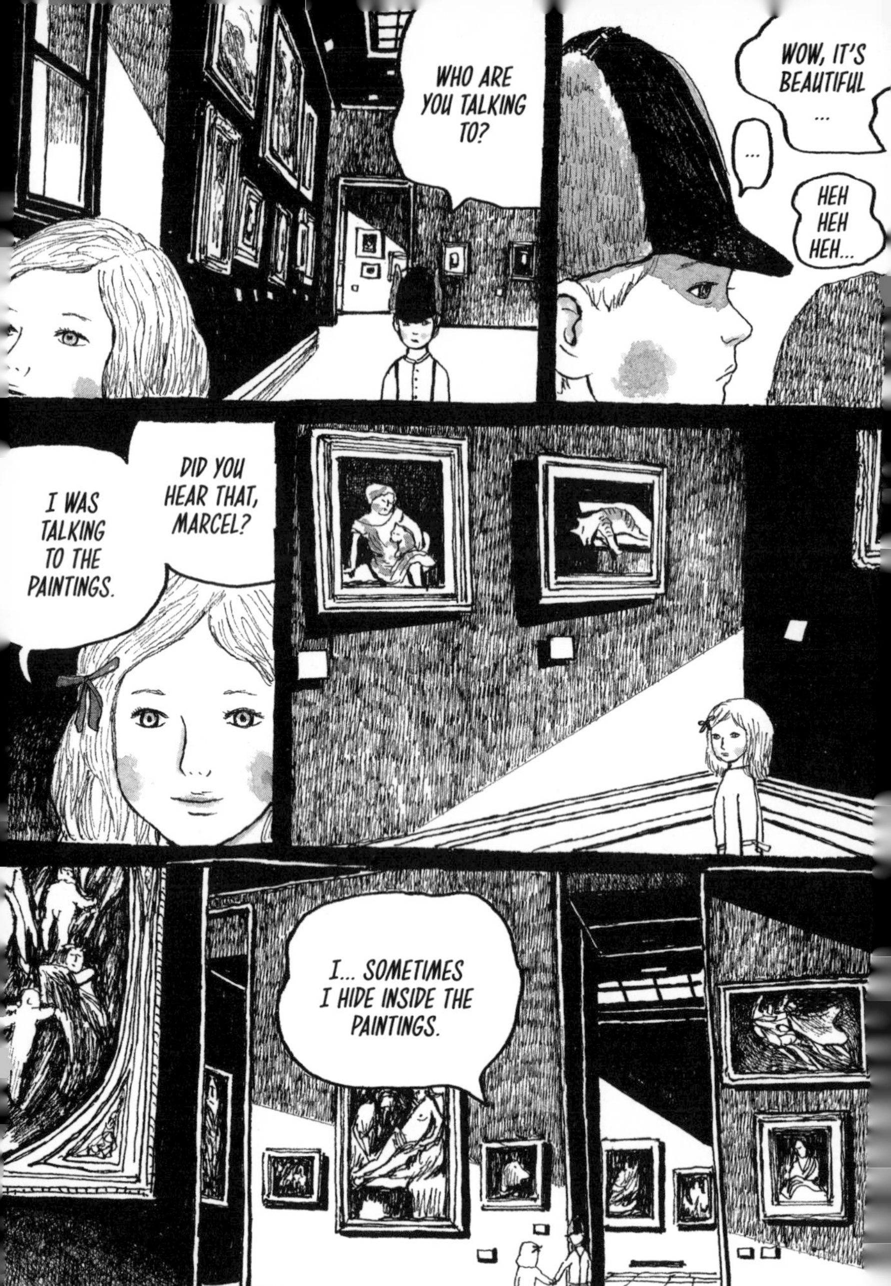
WOW, IT'S BEAUTIFUL ...
...
HEH HEH HEH...
WHO ARE YOU TALKING TO?
DID YOU HEAR THAT, MARCEL?
I WAS TALKING TO THE PAINTINGS.
I... SOMETIMES I HIDE INSIDE THE PAINTINGS.

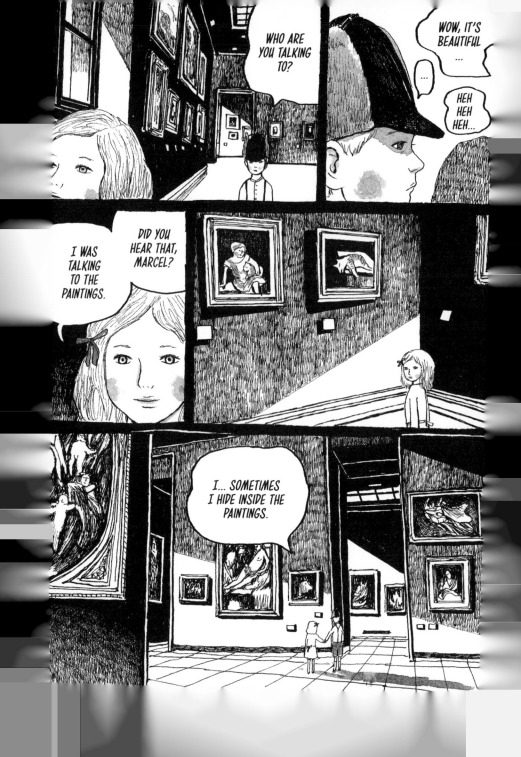

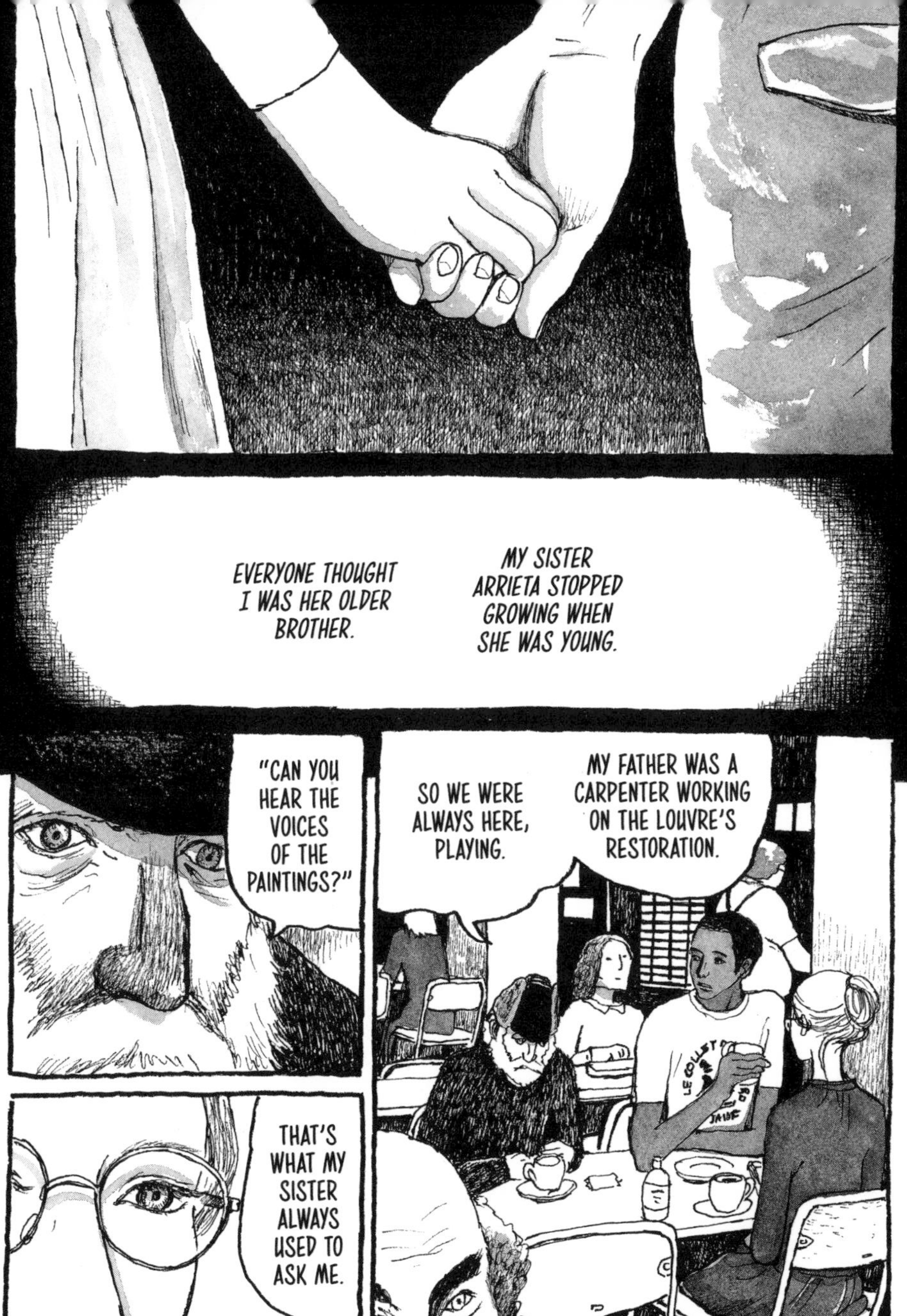
MY SISTER ARRIETA STOPPED GROWING WHEN SHE WAS YOUNG.
EVERYONE THOUGHT I WAS HER OLDER BROTHER.
MY FATHER WAS A CARPENTER WORKING ON THE LOUVRE'S RESTORATION.
SO WE WERE ALWAYS HERE, PLAYING.
"CAN YOU HEAR THE VOICES OF THE PAINTINGS?"
THAT'S WHAT MY SISTER ALWAYS USED TO ASK ME.

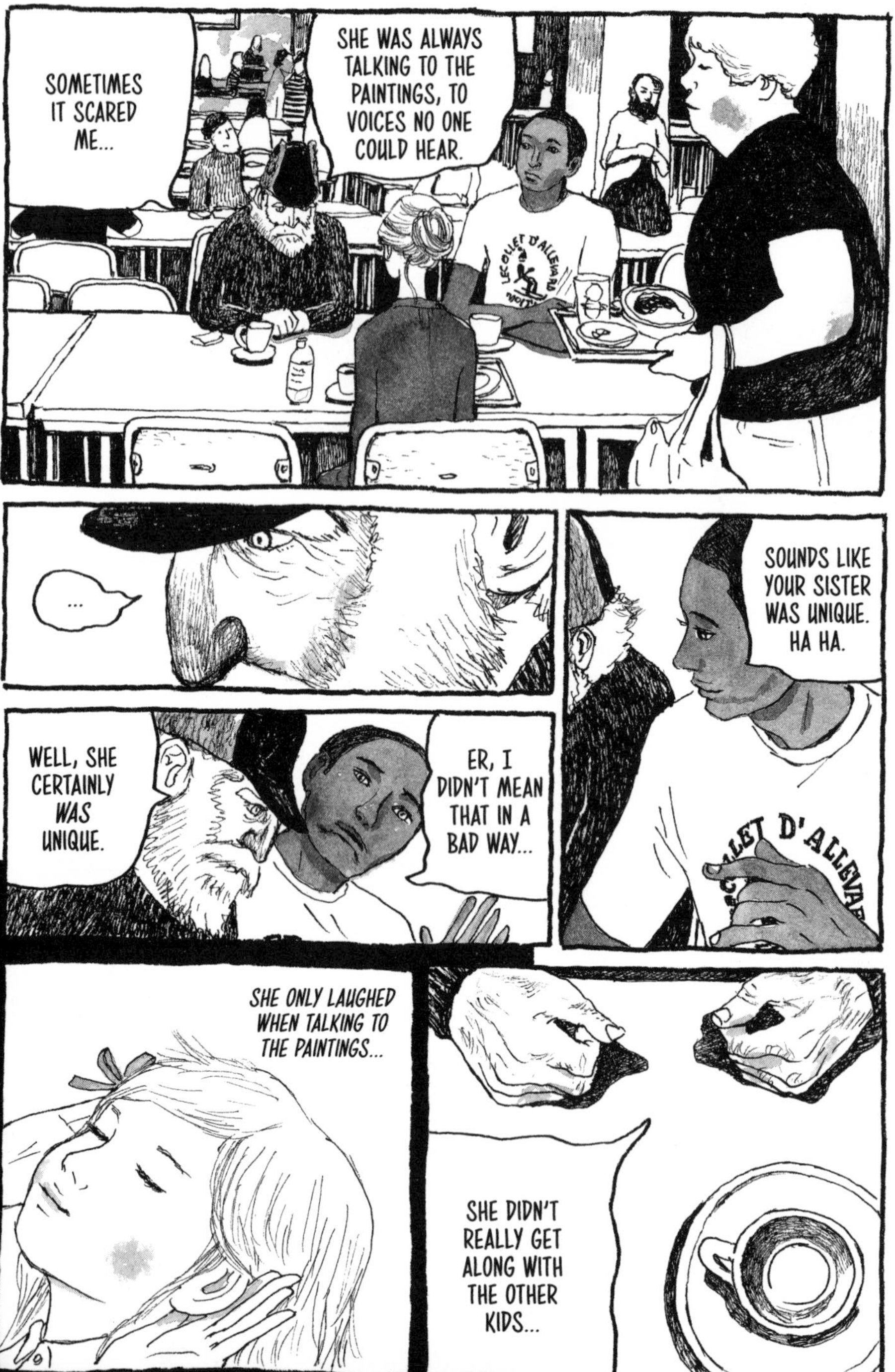
SHE WAS ALWAYS TALKING TO THE PAINTINGS, TO VOICES NO ONE COULD HEAR.
SOMETIMES IT SCARED ME...
SOUNDS LIKE YOUR SISTER WAS UNIQUE. HA HA.
...
ER, I DIDN'T MEAN THAT IN A BAD WAY...
WELL, SHE CERTAINLY *WAS* UNIQUE.
SHE DIDN'T REALLY GET ALONG WITH THE OTHER KIDS...
SHE ONLY LAUGHED WHEN TALKING TO THE PAINTINGS...

I LOVED MY SISTER DEARLY, BUT...
SHE HID HER FEELINGS SOMEWHERE FAR AWAY.
TIK
TOK
TOK
TIK
THIS IS OUR GREAT-GRANDFATHER'S POCKET WATCH, MARCEL.
TIK
WANT IT?

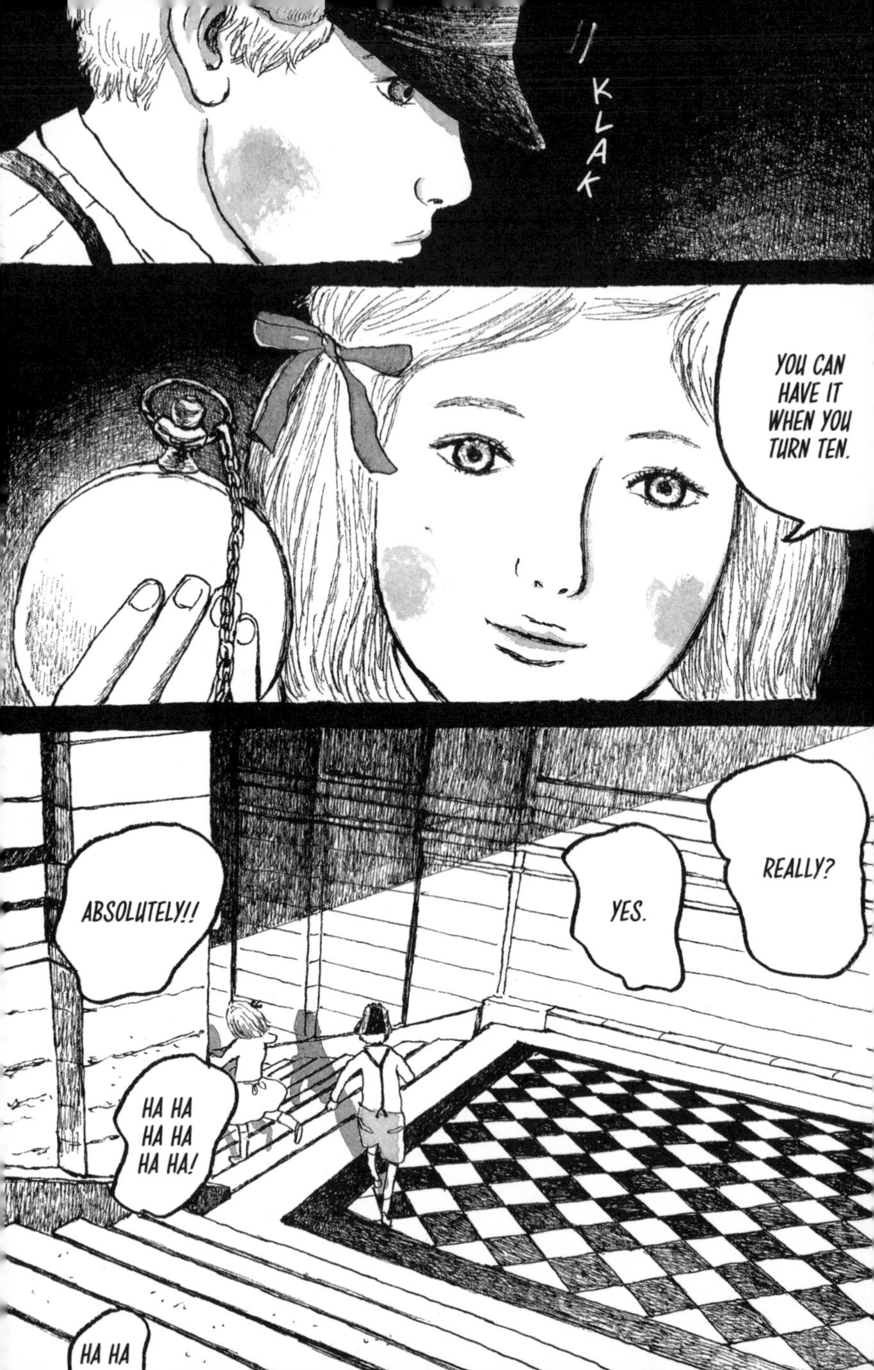
KLAK
YOU CAN HAVE IT WHEN YOU TURN TEN.
REALLY?
YES.
ABSOLUTELY!!
HA HA HA HA HA HA!
HA HA

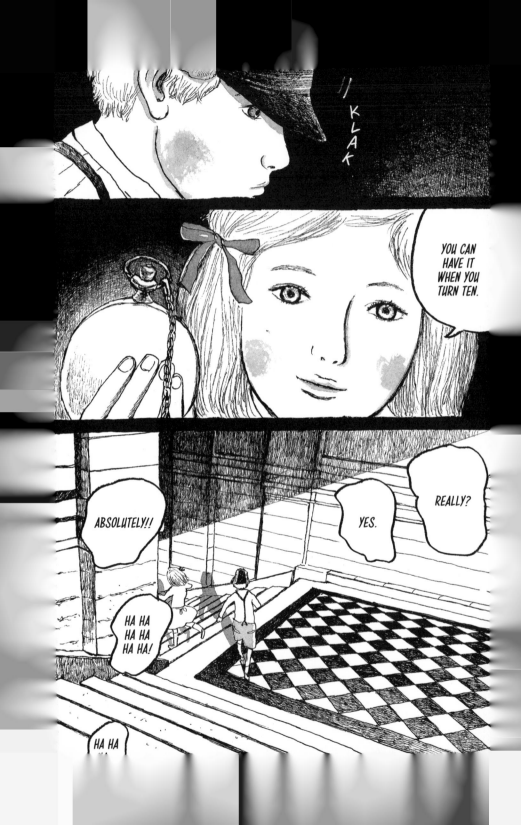

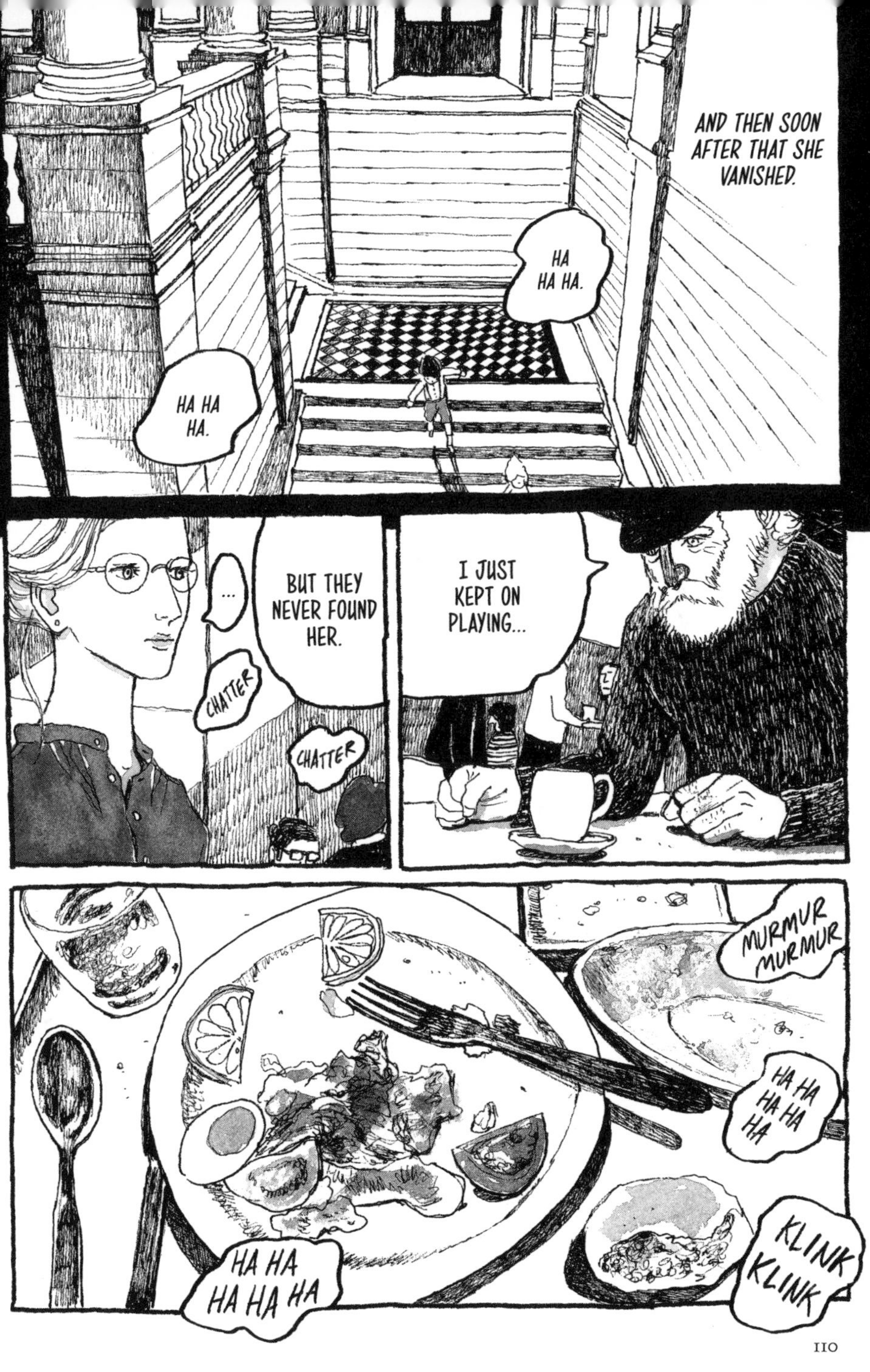
AND THEN SOON AFTER THAT SHE VANISHED.
HA HA HA.
HA HA HA.
I JUST KEPT ON PLAYING...
BUT THEY NEVER FOUND HER.
...
CHATTER
CHATTER
MURMUR MURMUR
HA HA HA HA HA
KLINK KLINK
HA HA HA HA HA

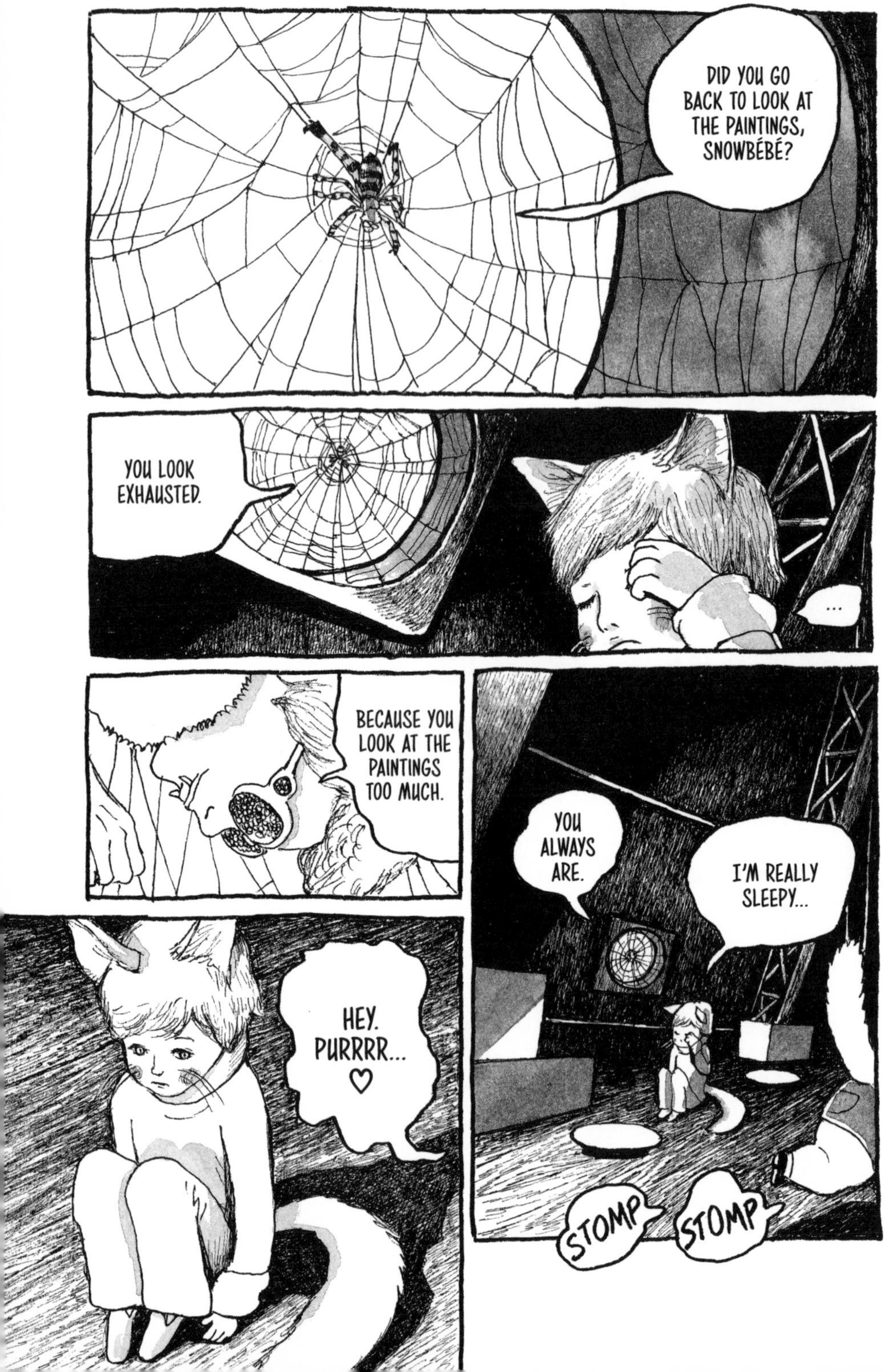
DID YOU GO BACK TO LOOK AT THE PAINTINGS, SNOWBÉBÉ?
YOU LOOK EXHAUSTED.
...
I'M REALLY SLEEPY...
YOU ALWAYS ARE.
STOMP
STOMP
BECAUSE YOU LOOK AT THE PAINTINGS TOO MUCH.
HEY. PURRRR... ♡

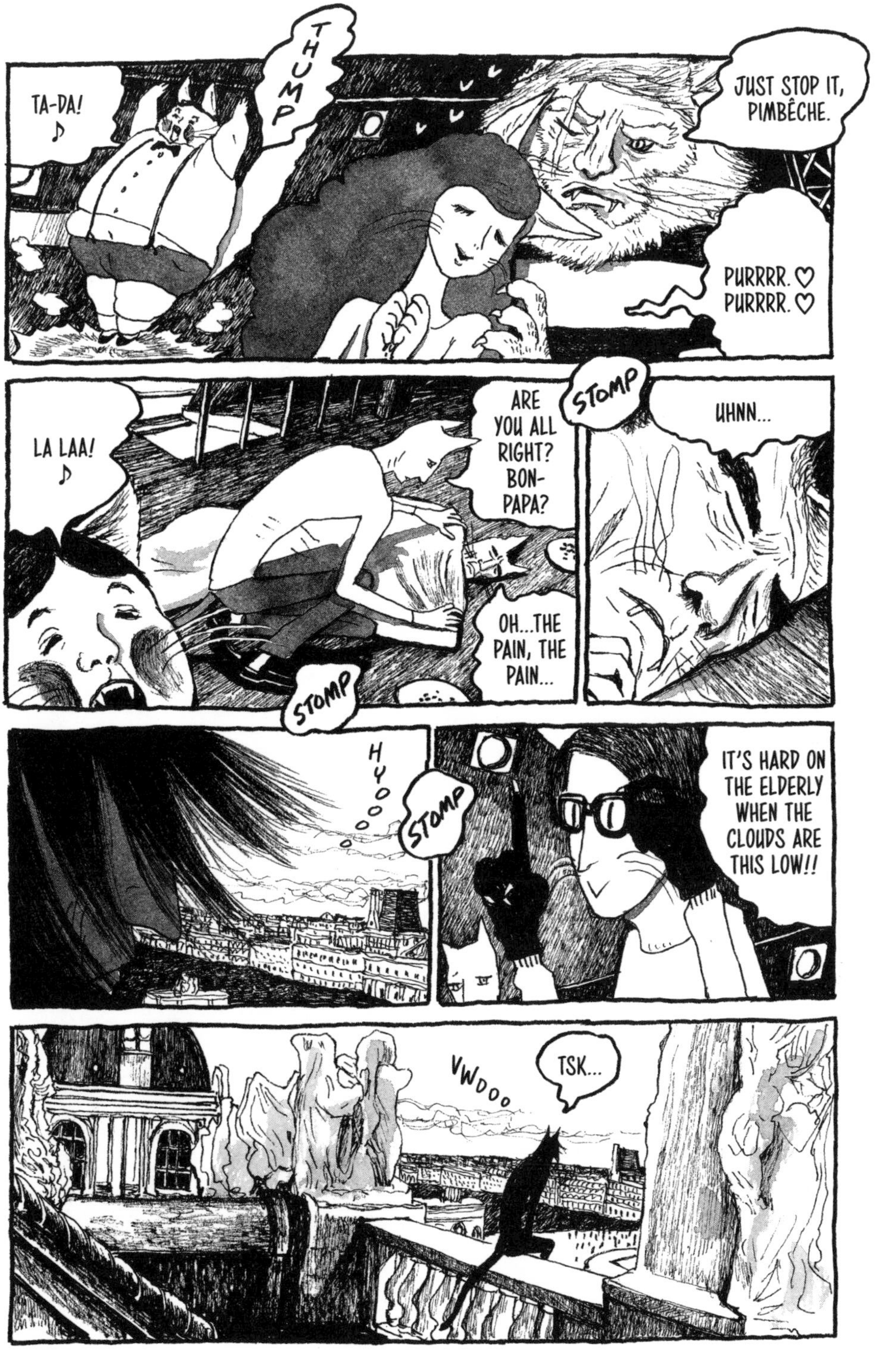
JUST STOP IT, PIMBÊCHE.
PURRRR. ♡ PURRRR. ♡
THUMP
TA-DA! ♪
STOMP
UHNN...
ARE YOU ALL RIGHT? BON-PAPA?
OH...THE PAIN, THE PAIN...
STOMP
LA LAA! ♪
IT'S HARD ON THE ELDERLY WHEN THE CLOUDS ARE THIS LOW!!
STOMP
HYOOOO
TSK...
VWDOOO

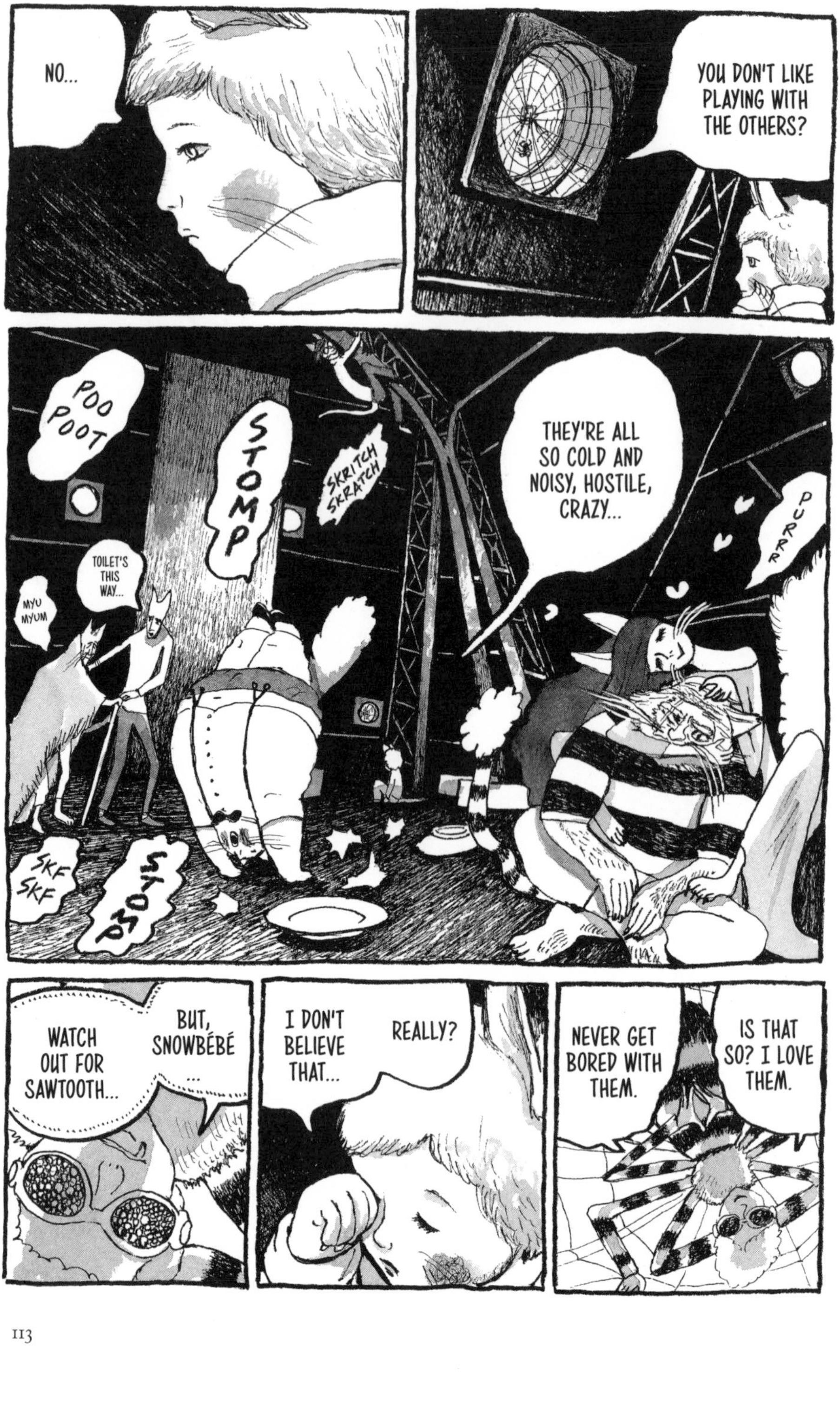
YOU DON'T LIKE PLAYING WITH THE OTHERS?
NO...
PURRR
THEY'RE ALL SO COLD AND NOISY, HOSTILE, CRAZY...
SKRITCH SKRATCH
STOMP
POO POOT
TOILET'S THIS WAY...
MYU MYUM
STOMP
SKF SKF
IS THAT SO? I LOVE THEM.
NEVER GET BORED WITH THEM.
REALLY?
I DON'T BELIEVE THAT...
BUT, SNOWBÉBÉ ...
WATCH OUT FOR SAWTOOTH...

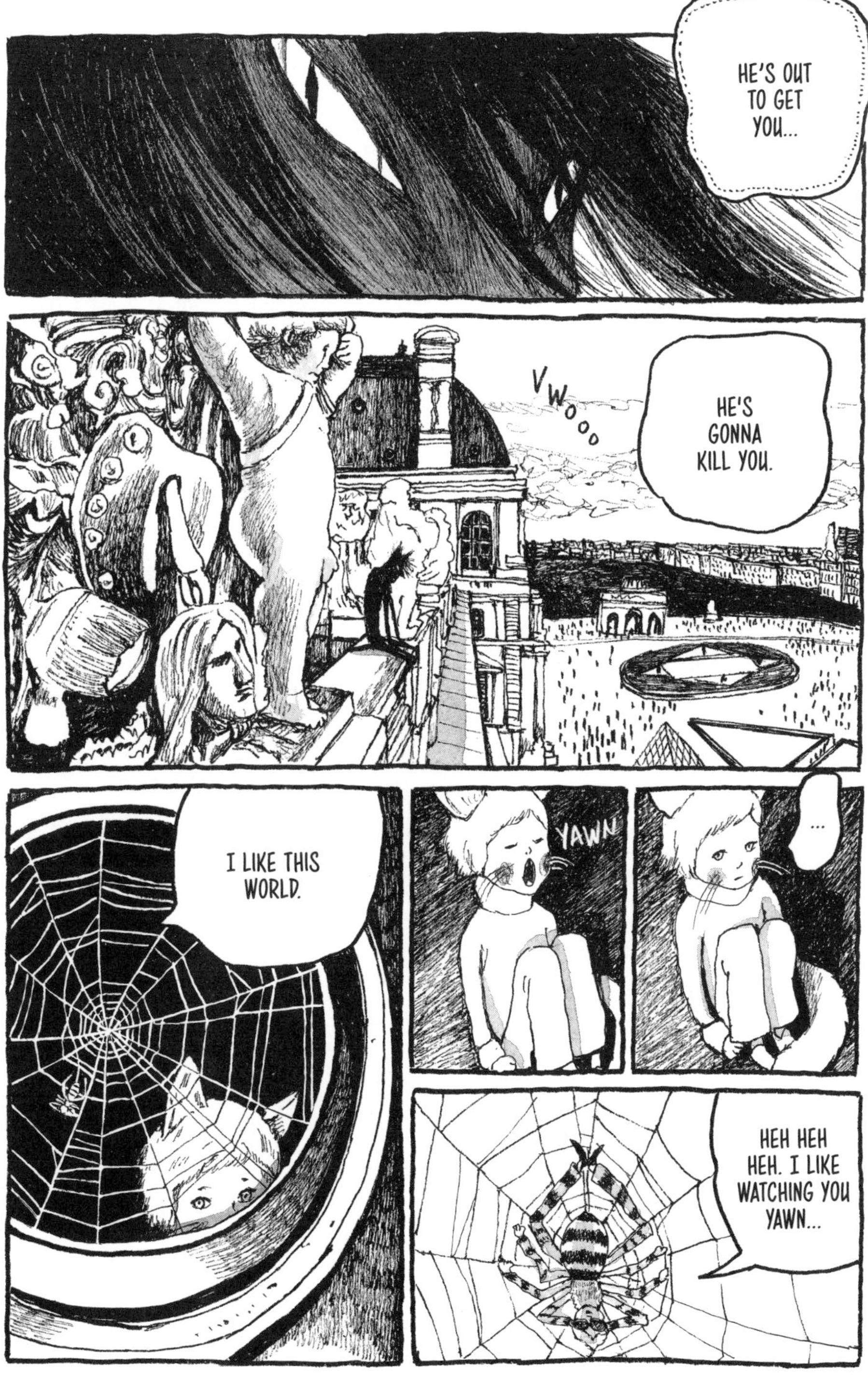
HE'S OUT TO GET YOU...
VWOOO
HE'S GONNA KILL YOU.
...
YAWN
HEH HEH HEH. I LIKE WATCHING YOU YAWN...
I LIKE THIS WORLD.

I LIKE SMELLING THE NEW LEAVES HERE.

WHEN THOSE LEAVES FALL FROM THE BRANCHES...

...MY TIME WILL BE DONE, BUT STILL...

...THE WORLD KEEPS ON GOING.

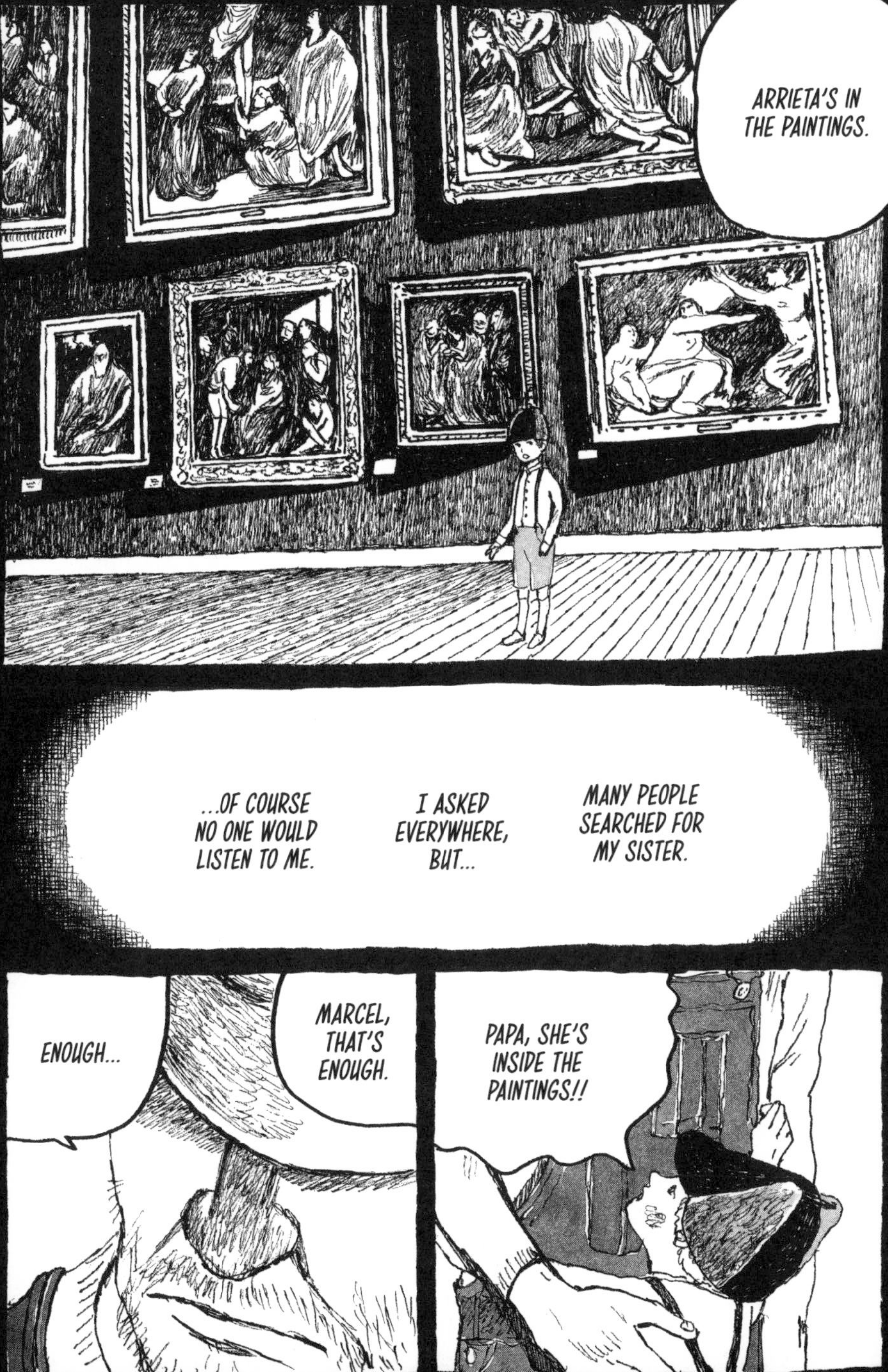
ARRIETA'S IN THE PAINTINGS.
MANY PEOPLE SEARCHED FOR MY SISTER.
I ASKED EVERYWHERE, BUT...
...OF COURSE NO ONE WOULD LISTEN TO ME.
PAPA, SHE'S INSIDE THE PAINTINGS!!
MARCEL, THAT'S ENOUGH.
ENOUGH...

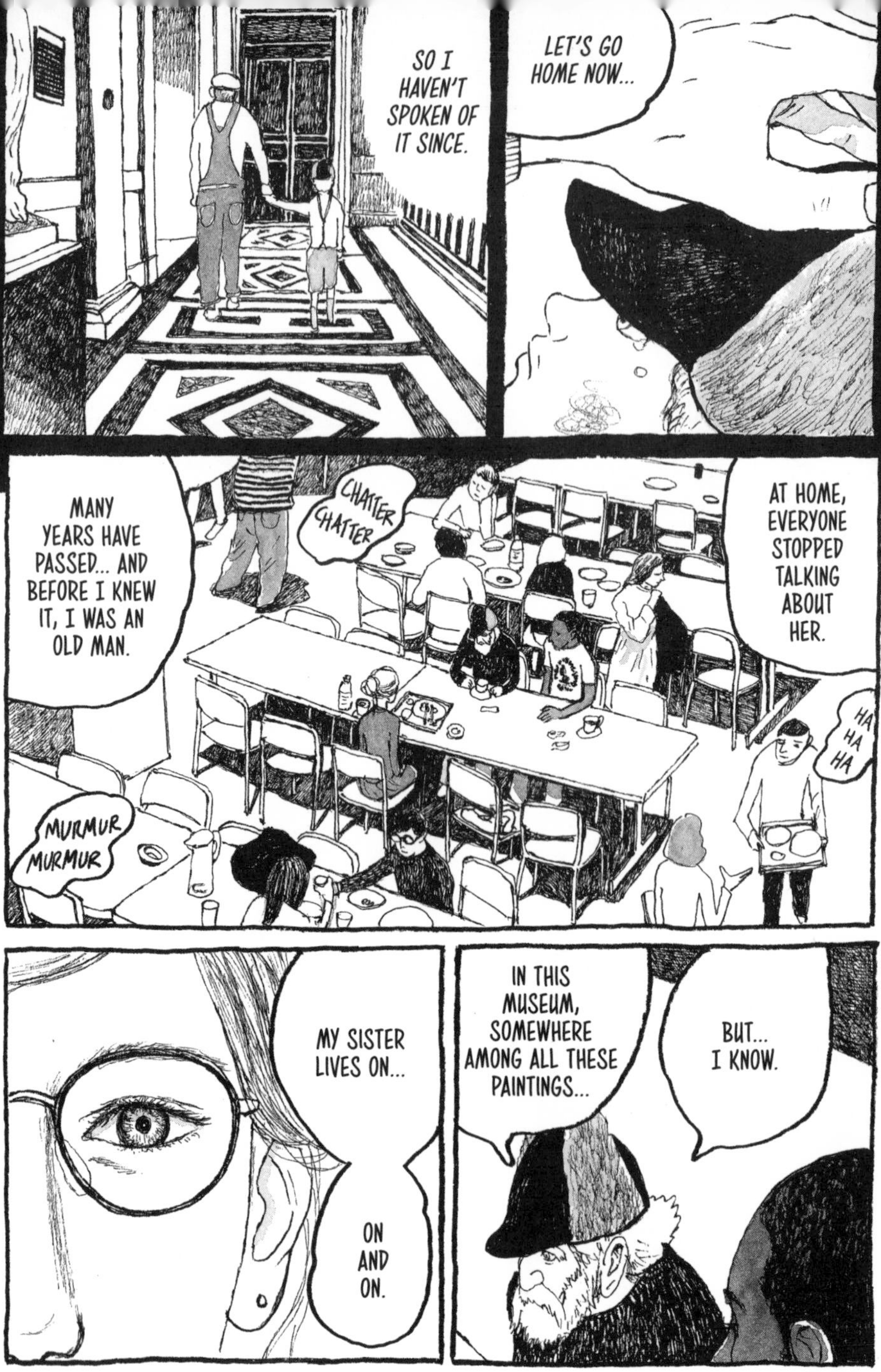
LET'S GO HOME NOW...
SO I HAVEN'T SPOKEN OF IT SINCE.
AT HOME, EVERYONE STOPPED TALKING ABOUT HER.
CHATTER CHATTER
MANY YEARS HAVE PASSED... AND BEFORE I KNEW IT, I WAS AN OLD MAN.
HA HA HA
MURMUR MURMUR
BUT... I KNOW.
IN THIS MUSEUM, SOMEWHERE AMONG ALL THESE PAINTINGS...
MY SISTER LIVES ON...
ON AND ON.

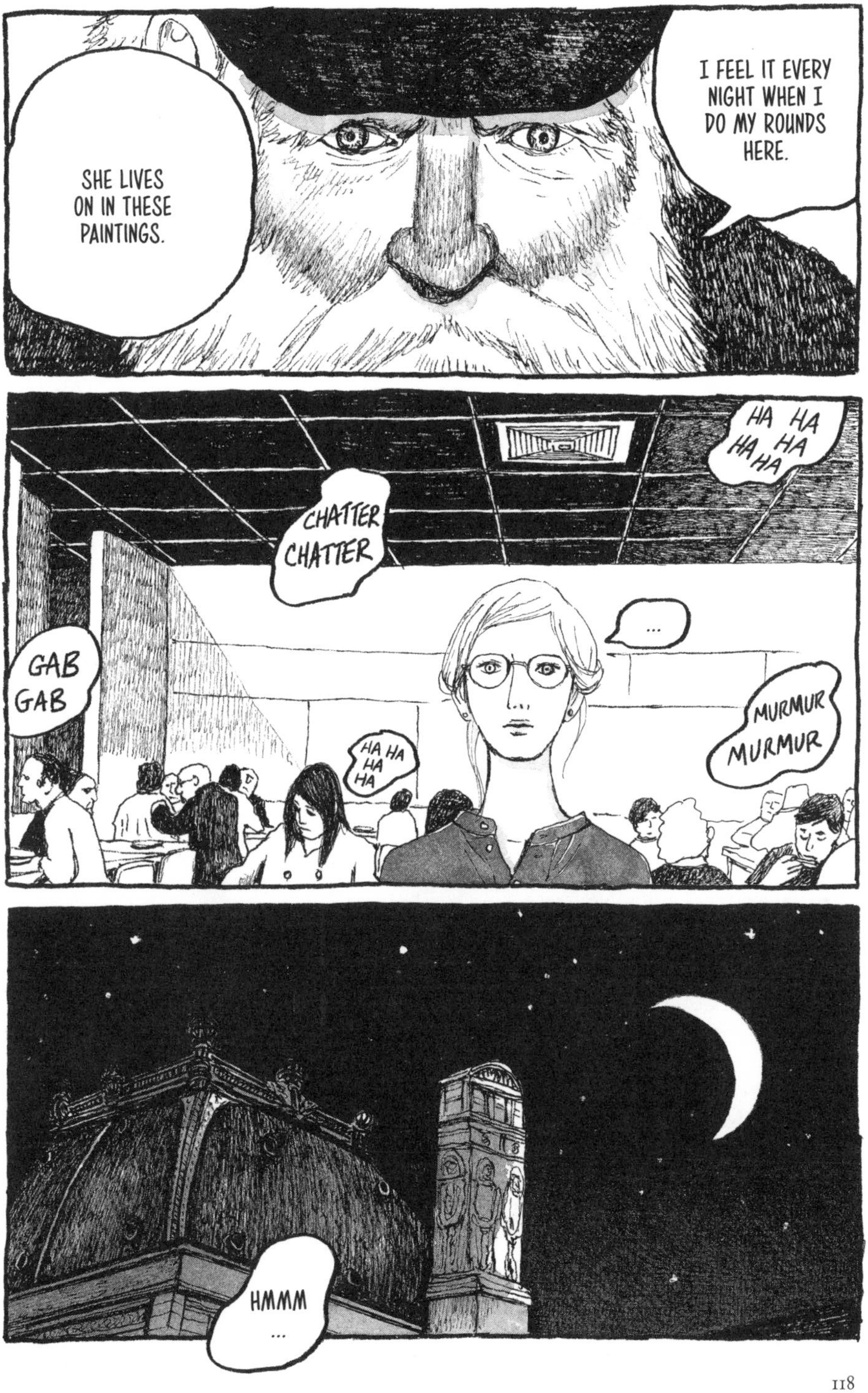
I FEEL IT EVERY NIGHT WHEN I DO MY ROUNDS HERE.
SHE LIVES ON IN THESE PAINTINGS.
HA HA HA HA HA
CHATTER CHATTER
...
MURMUR MURMUR
GAB GAB
HA HA HA HA
HMMM ...

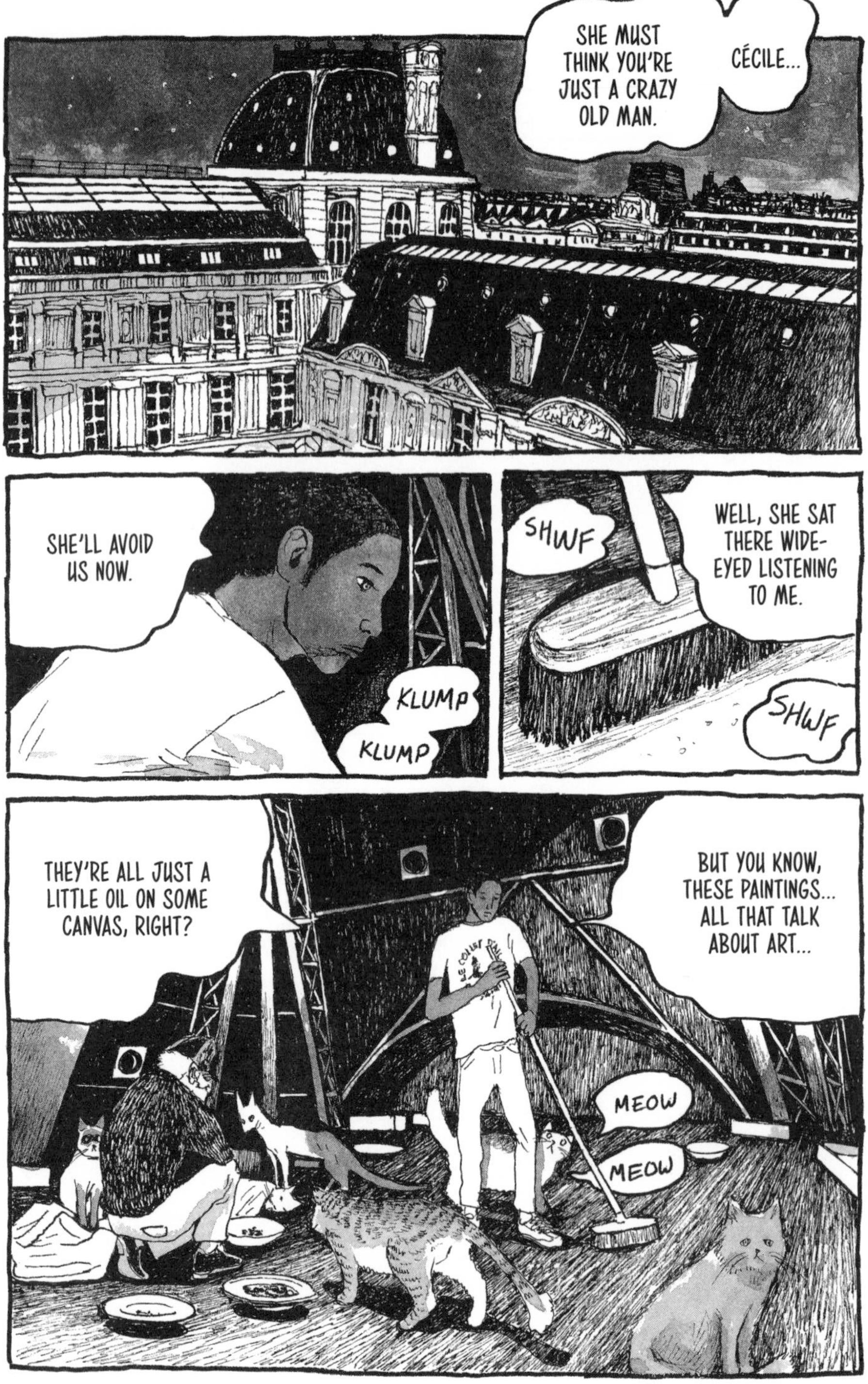
CÉCILE...
SHE MUST THINK YOU'RE JUST A CRAZY OLD MAN.
SHWF
WELL, SHE SAT THERE WIDE-EYED LISTENING TO ME.
SHWF
SHE'LL AVOID US NOW.
KLUMP
KLUMP
BUT YOU KNOW, THESE PAINTINGS... ALL THAT TALK ABOUT ART...
THEY'RE ALL JUST A LITTLE OIL ON SOME CANVAS, RIGHT?
MEOW
MEOW

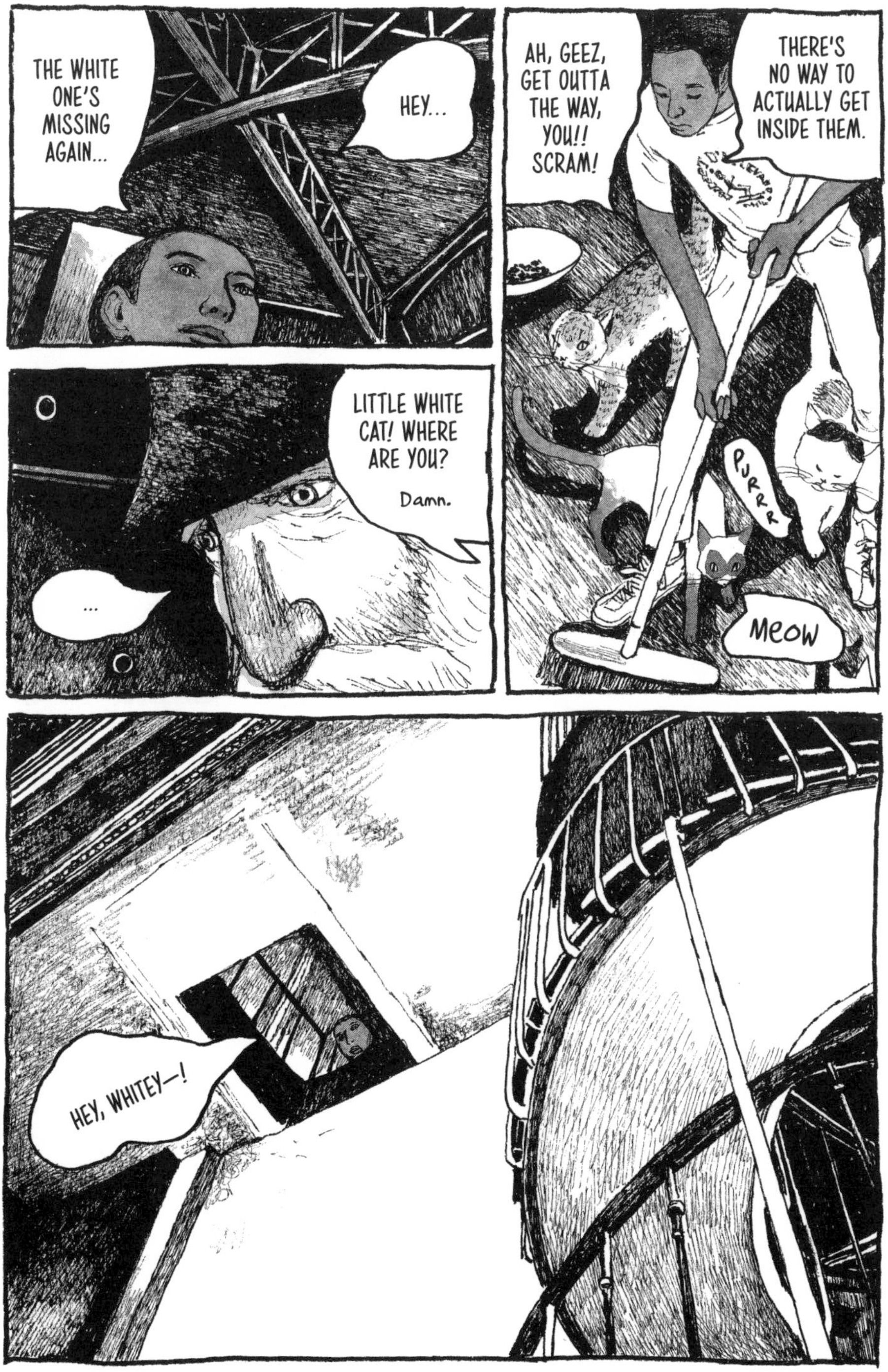
THERE'S NO WAY TO ACTUALLY GET INSIDE THEM.
AH, GEEZ, GET OUTTA THE WAY, YOU!! SCRAM!
PURRR
MEOW
HEY...
THE WHITE ONE'S MISSING AGAIN...
LITTLE WHITE CAT! WHERE ARE YOU?
Damn.
...
HEY, WHITEY—!

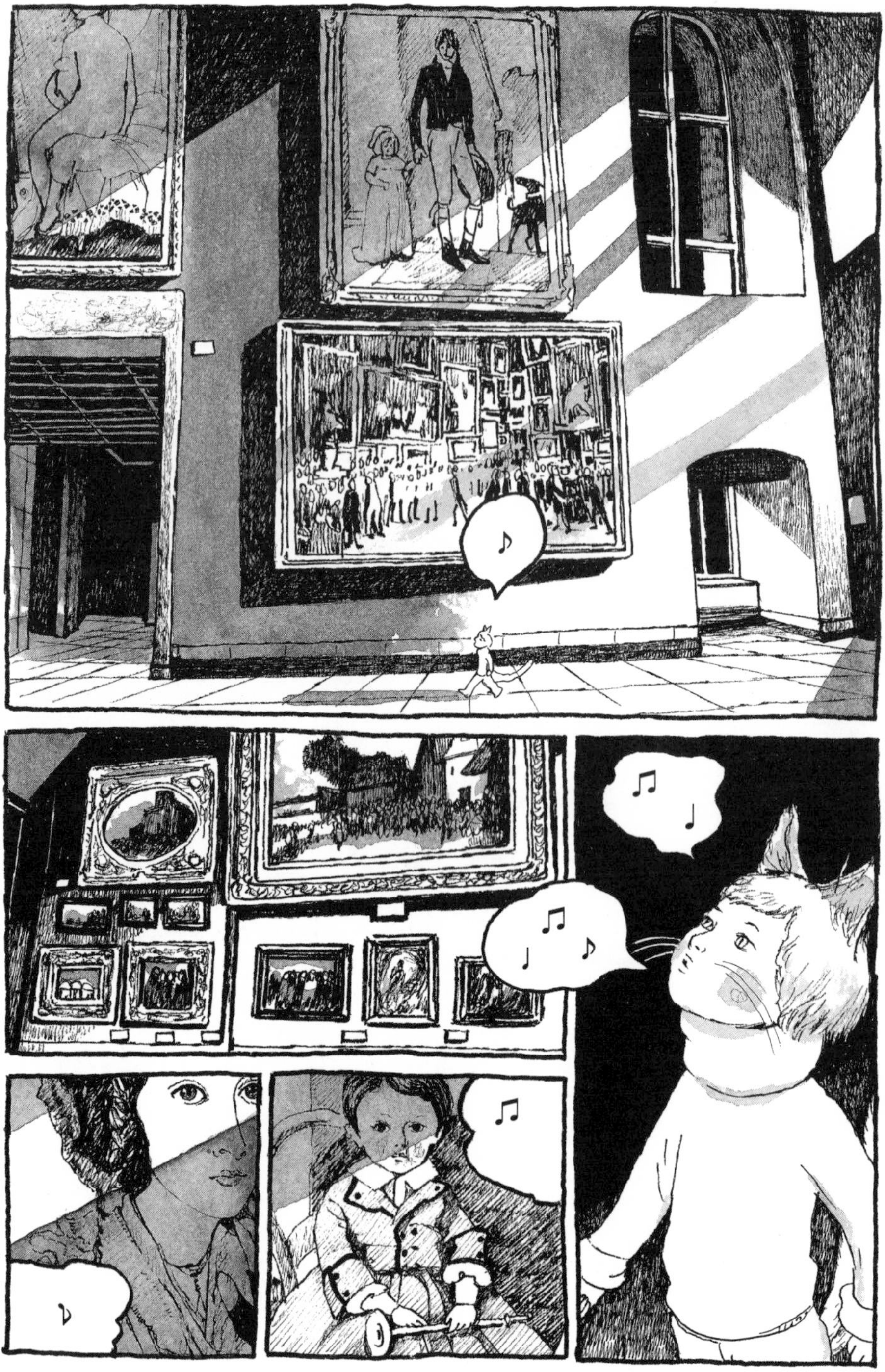

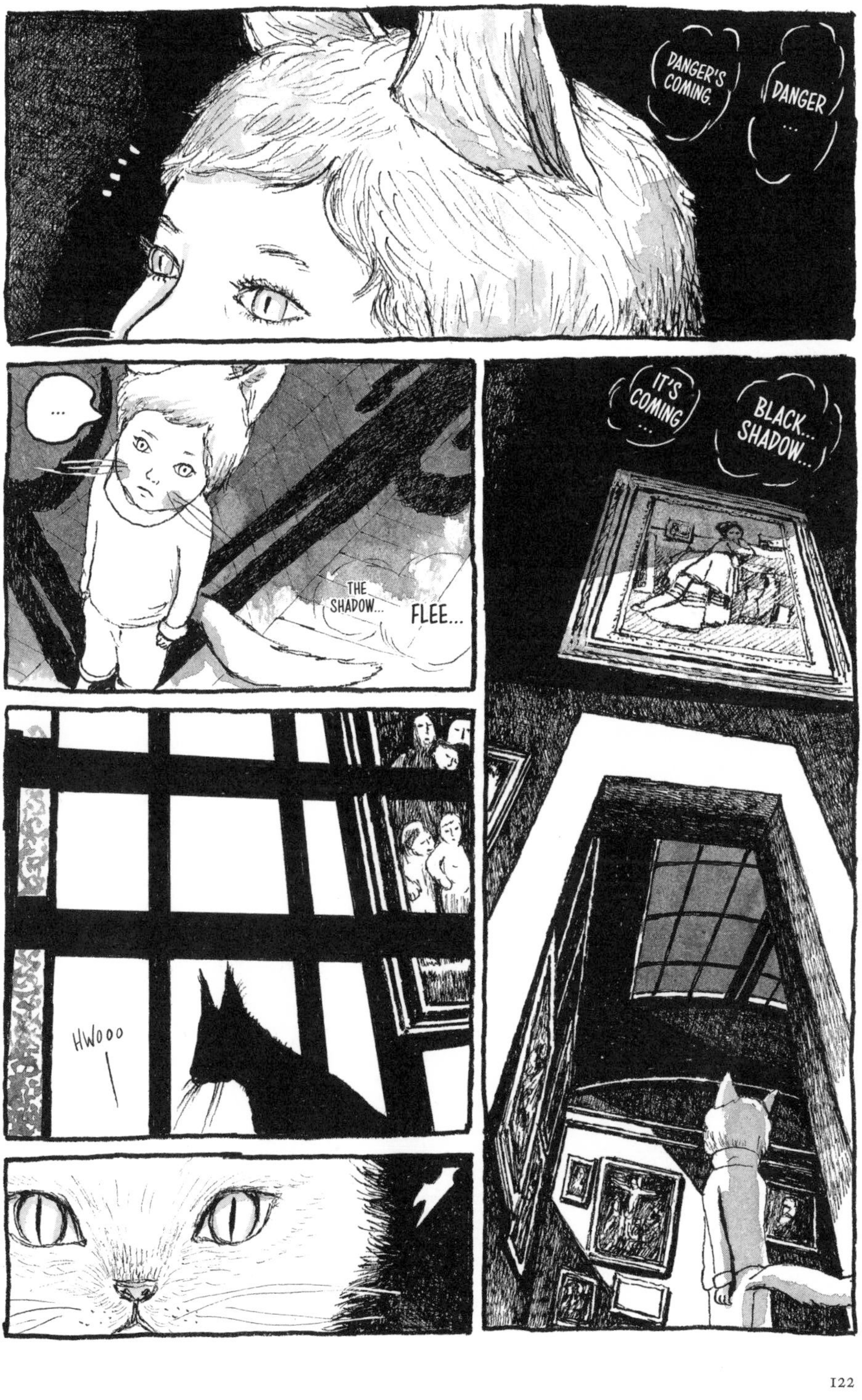
DANGER ...
DANGER'S COMING.
BLACK... SHADOW...
IT'S COMING ...
...
THE SHADOW...
FLEE...
HWOOO

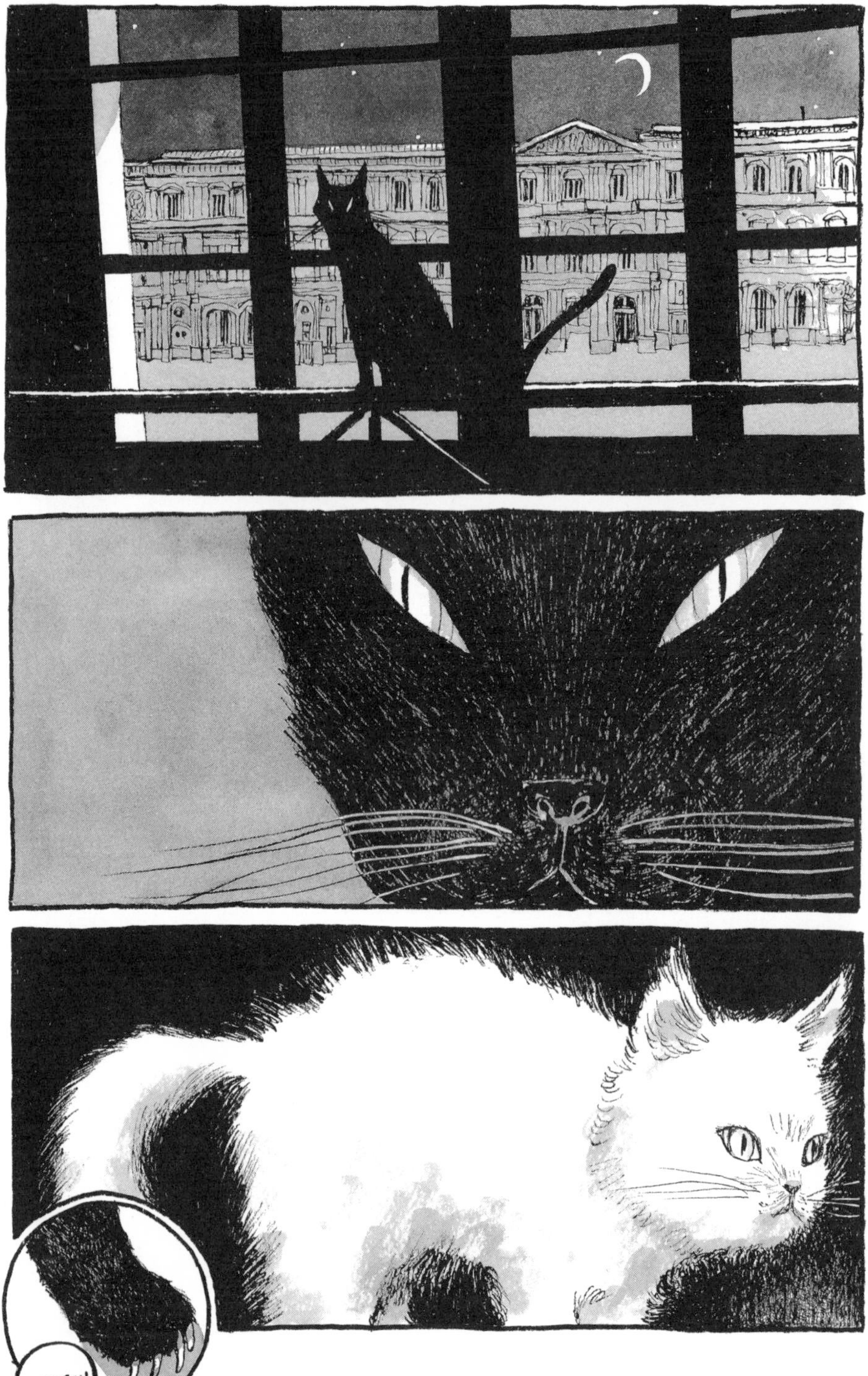
SKRITCH

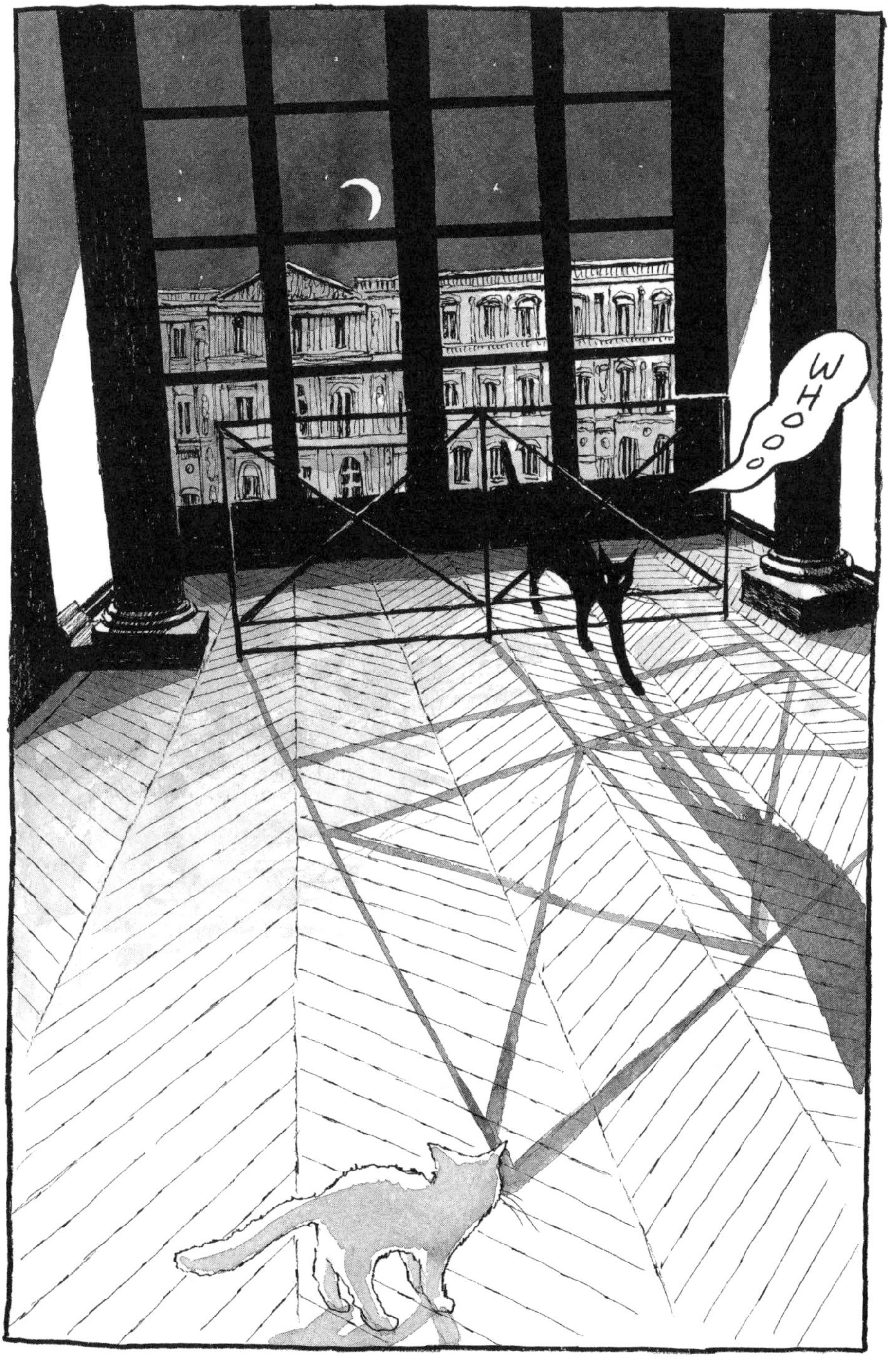
WHOOOO

CHAPTER 6

The Secret of the Night of the Crescent Moon

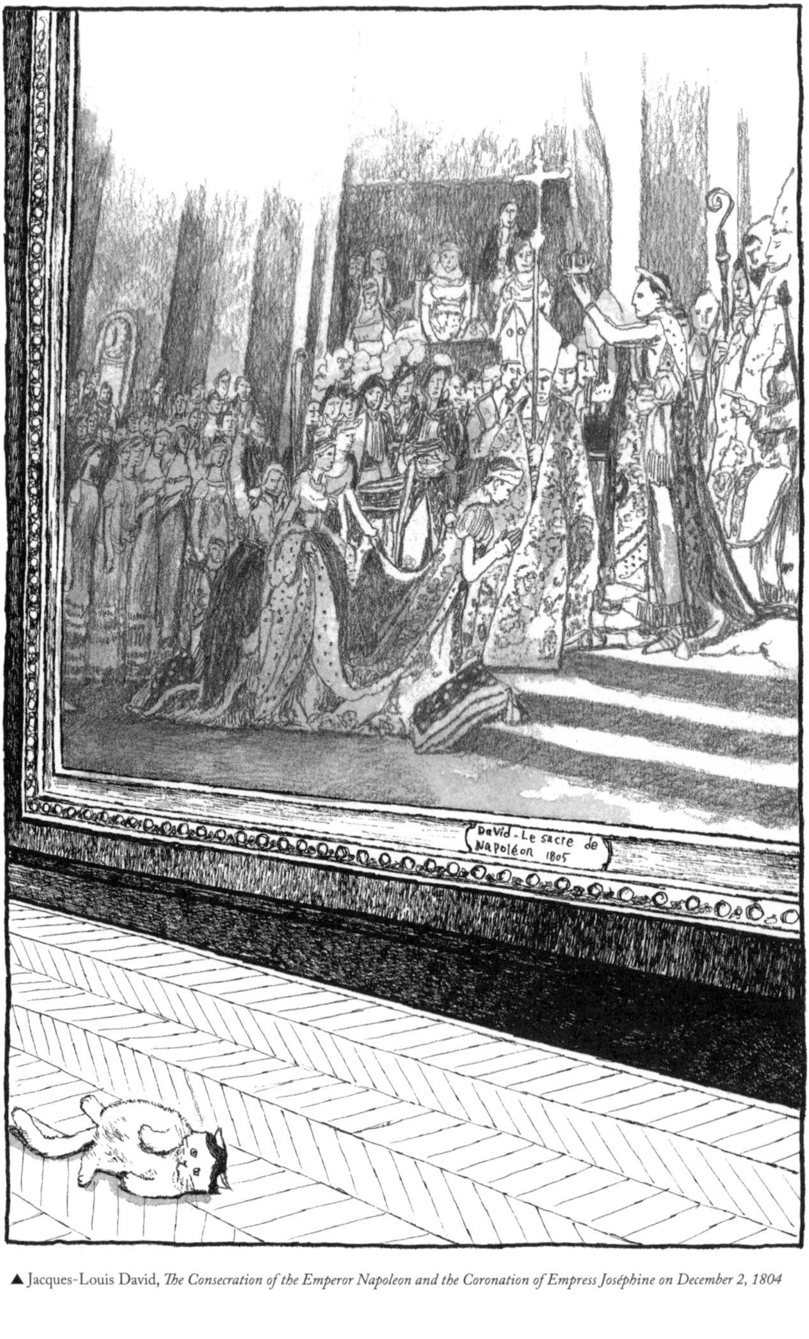
David - Le sacre de Napoléon 1805

▲ Jacques-Louis David, *The Consecration of the Emperor Napoleon and the Coronation of Empress Joséphine on December 2, 1804*

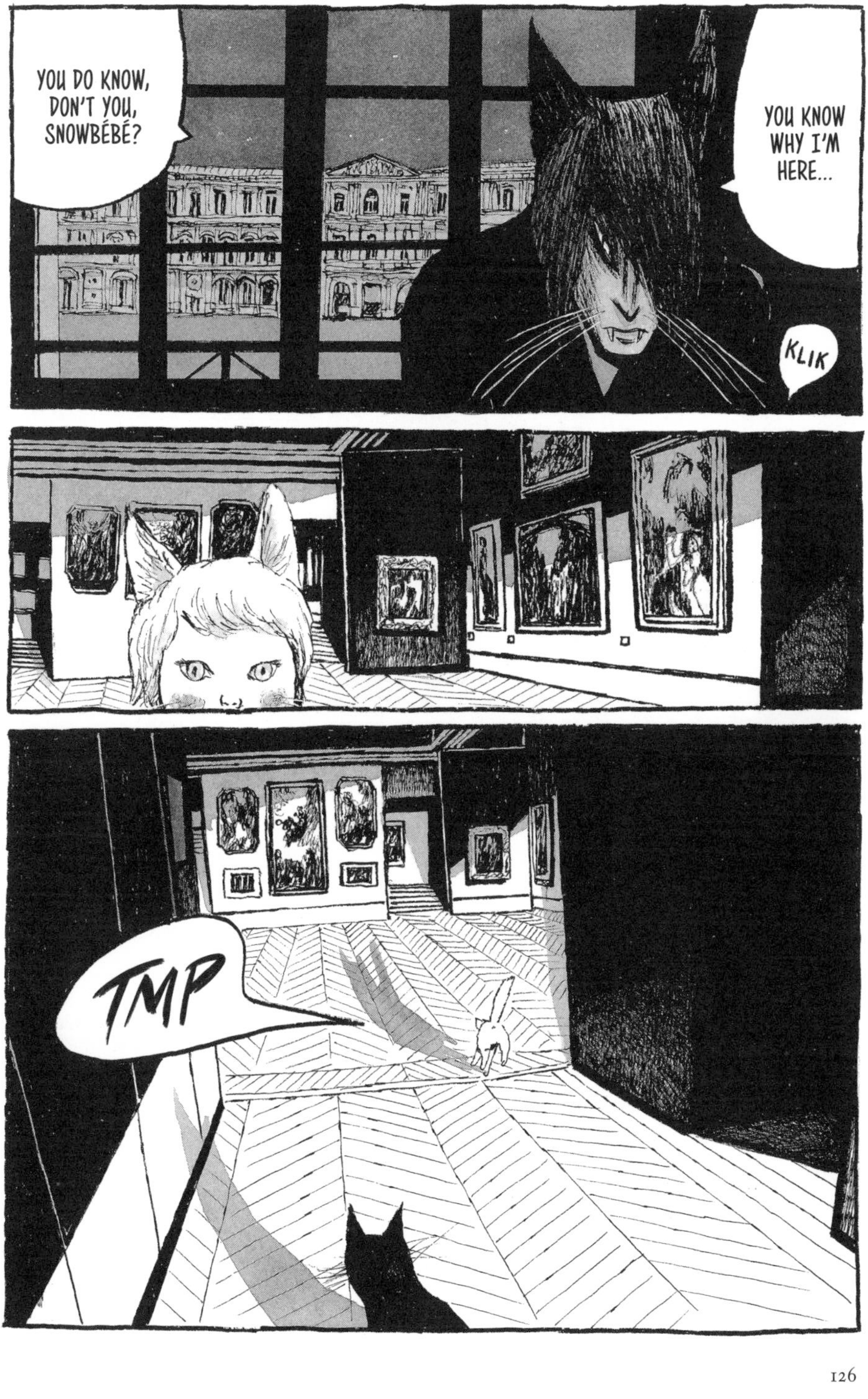
YOU KNOW WHY I'M HERE...
YOU DO KNOW, DON'T YOU, SNOWBÉBÉ?
KLIK
TMP

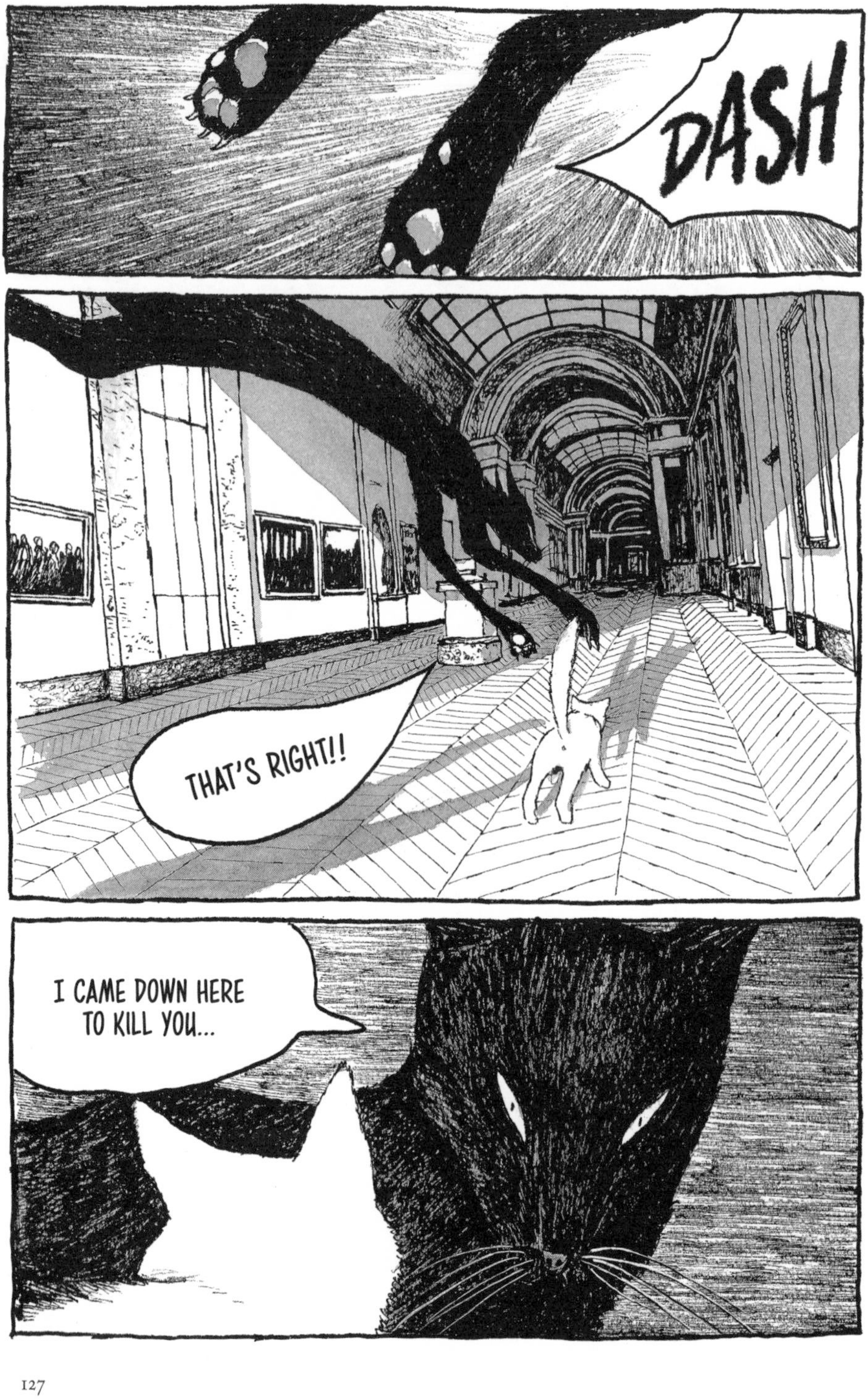
DASH
THAT'S RIGHT!!
I CAME DOWN HERE TO KILL YOU...

FWSH

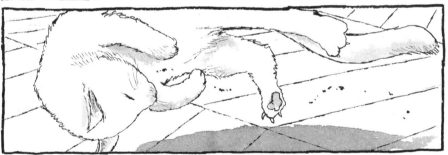

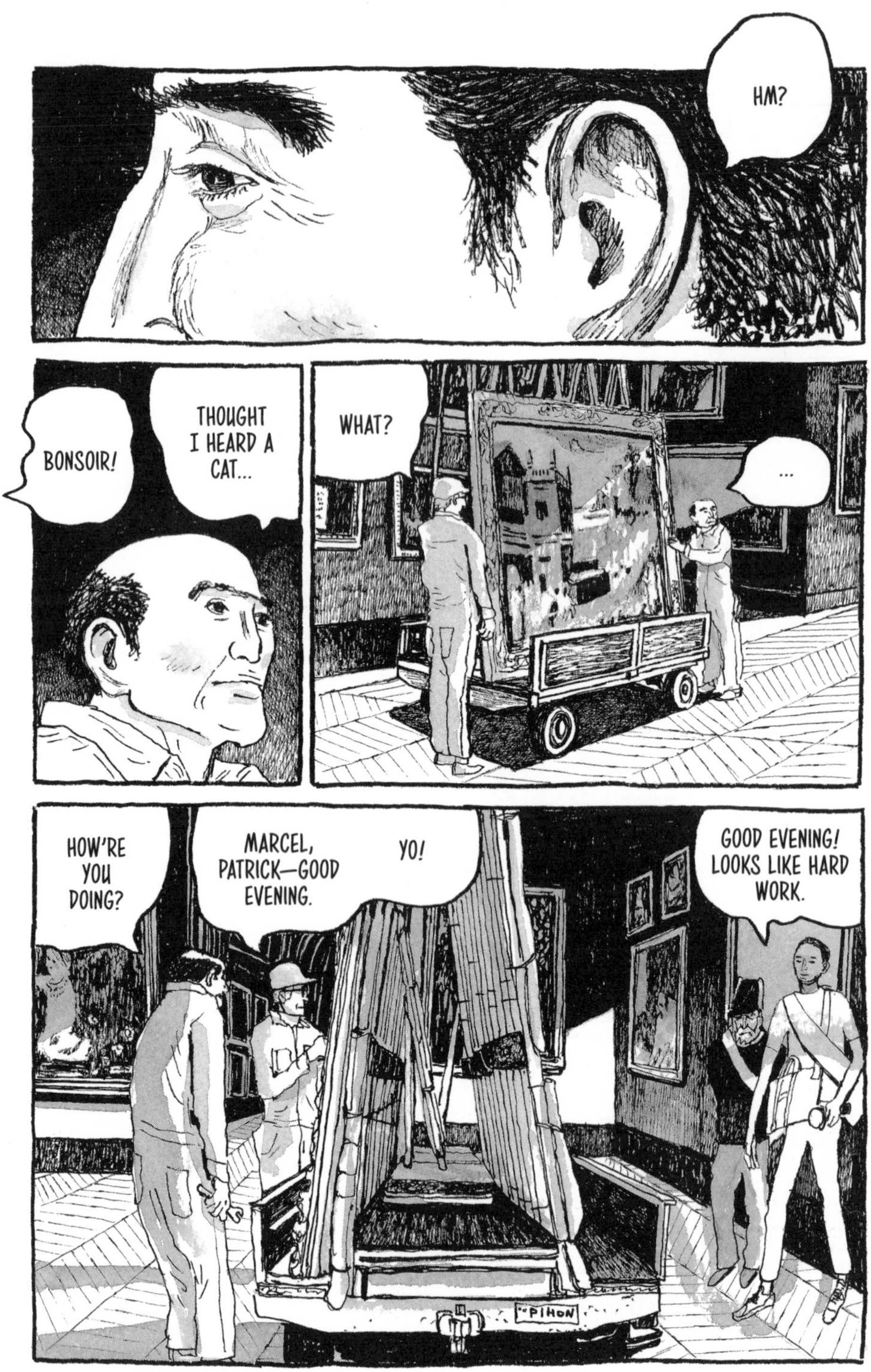
HM?
...
WHAT?
THOUGHT I HEARD A CAT...
BONSOIR!
GOOD EVENING! LOOKS LIKE HARD WORK.
YO!
MARCEL, PATRICK—GOOD EVENING.
HOW'RE YOU DOING?

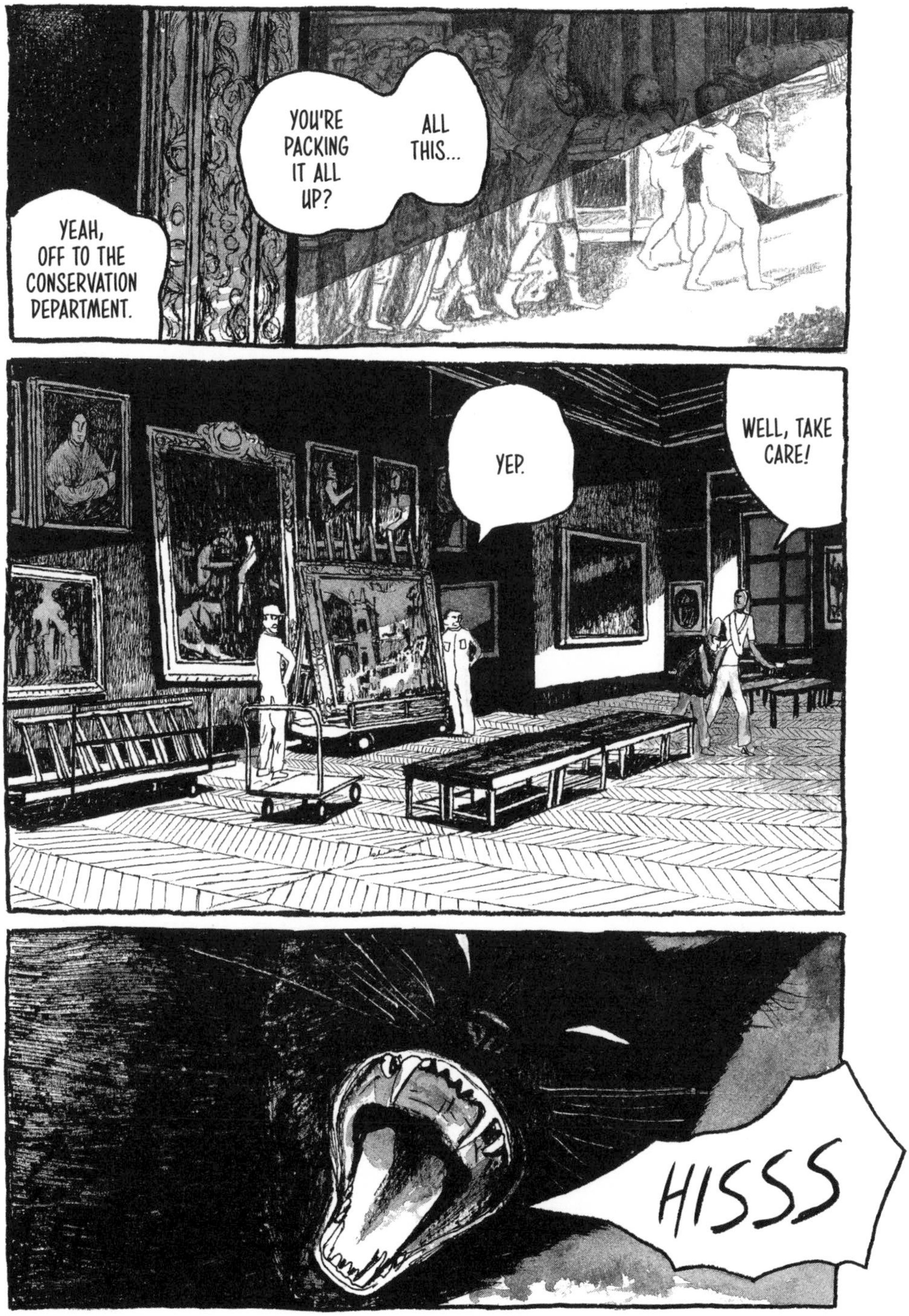
ALL THIS...
YOU'RE PACKING IT ALL UP?
YEAH, OFF TO THE CONSERVATION DEPARTMENT.
WELL, TAKE CARE!
YEP.
HISSS

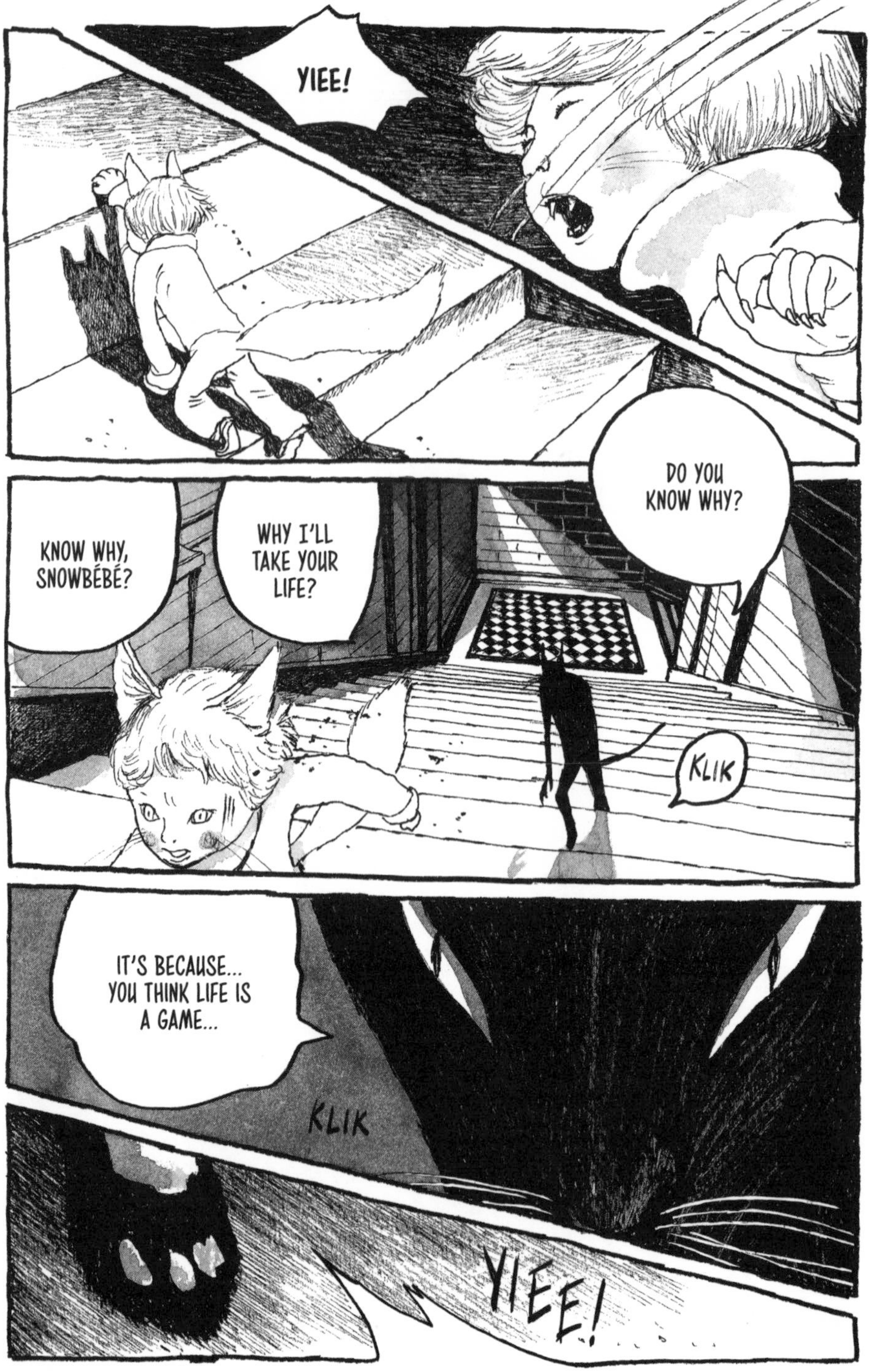
YIEE!
DO YOU KNOW WHY?
WHY I'LL TAKE YOUR LIFE?
KNOW WHY, SNOWBÉBÉ?
KLIK
IT'S BECAUSE... YOU THINK LIFE IS A GAME...
KLIK
YIEE!

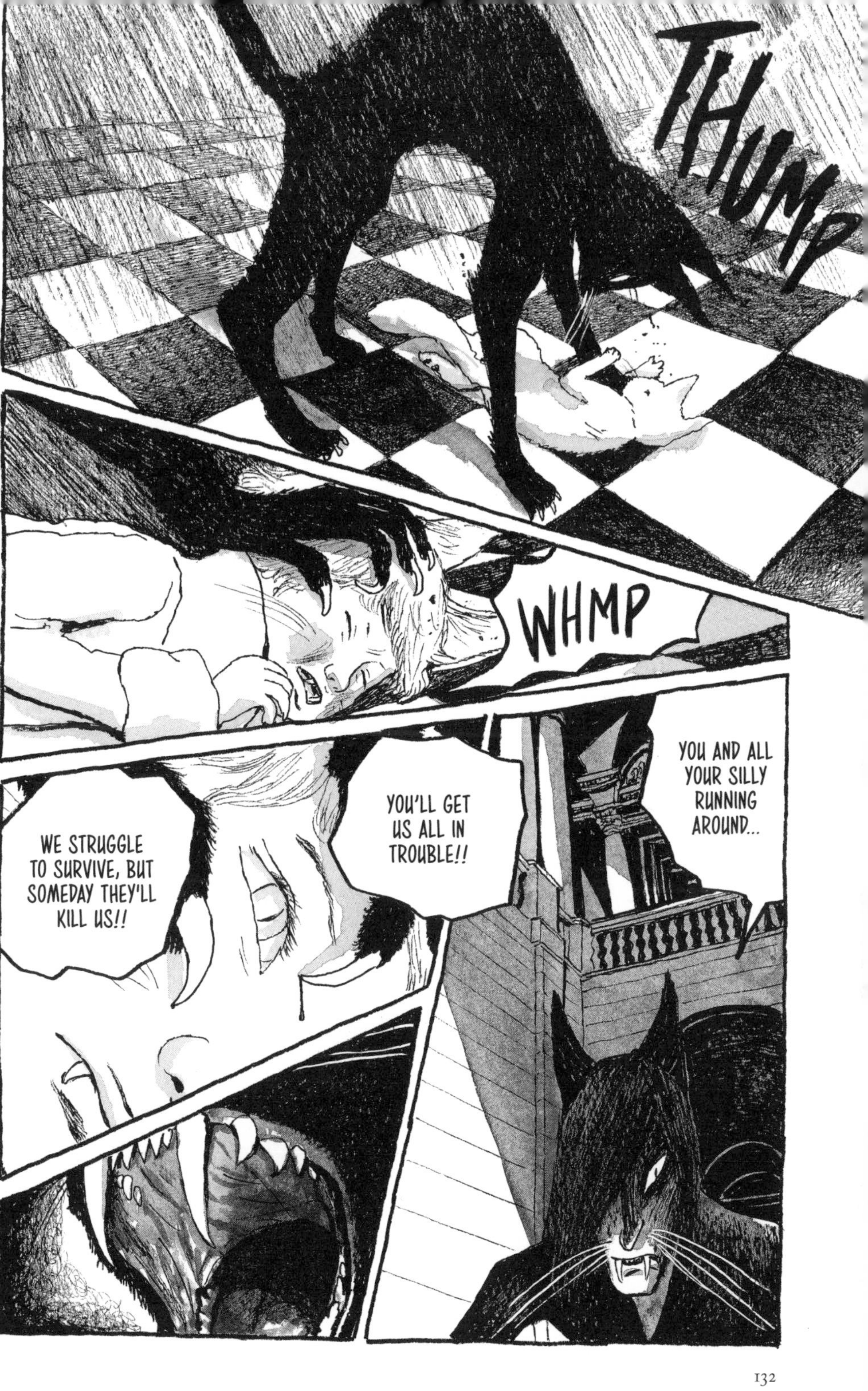
THUMP
WHMP
YOU AND ALL YOUR SILLY RUNNING AROUND...
YOU'LL GET US ALL IN TROUBLE!!
WE STRUGGLE TO SURVIVE, BUT SOMEDAY THEY'LL KILL US!!

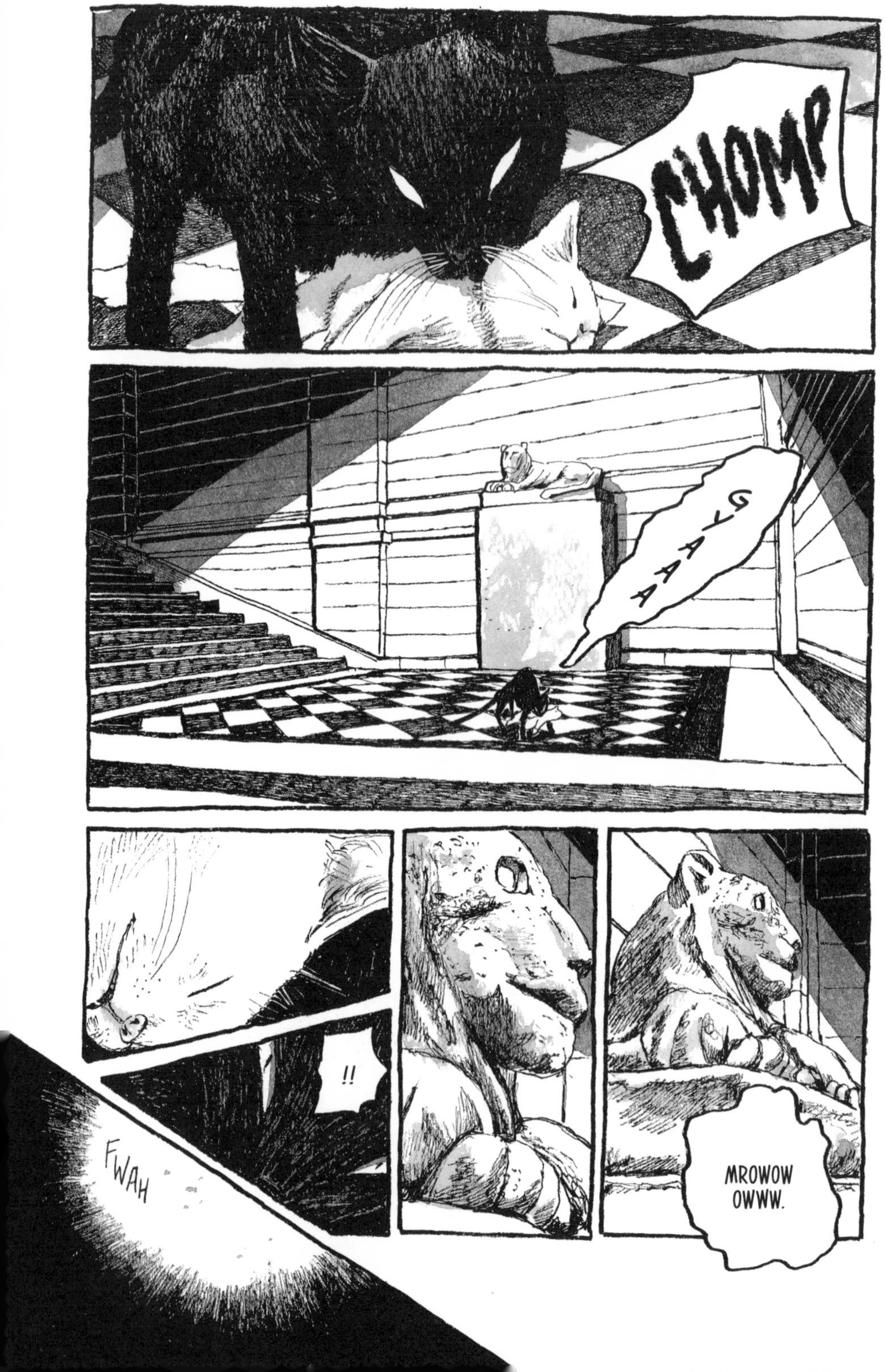
CHOMP
GYAAAA
MROWOW OWWW.
!!
FWAH

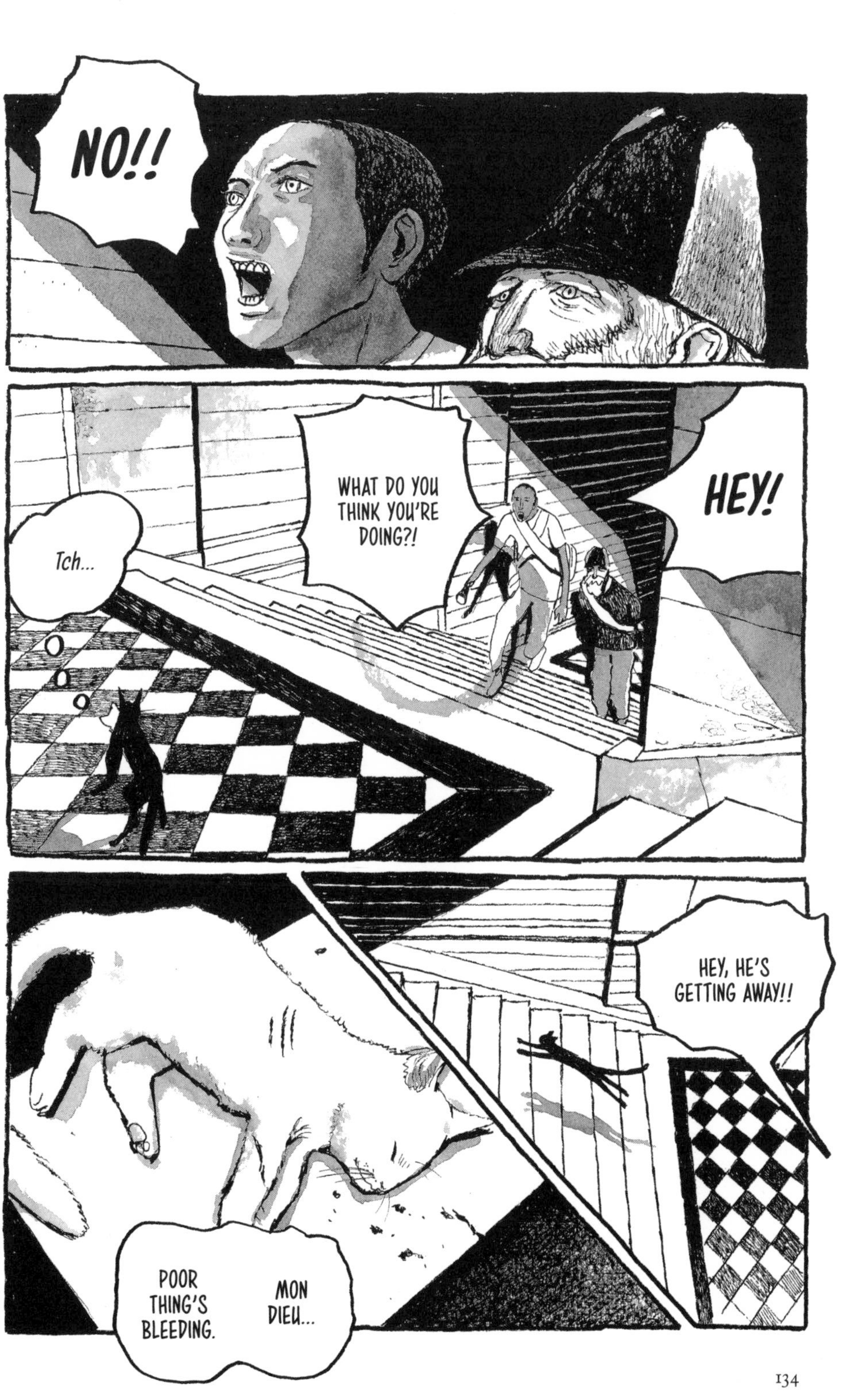
NO!!
HEY!
WHAT DO YOU THINK YOU'RE DOING?!
Tch...
HEY, HE'S GETTING AWAY!!
POOR THING'S BLEEDING.
MON DIEU...

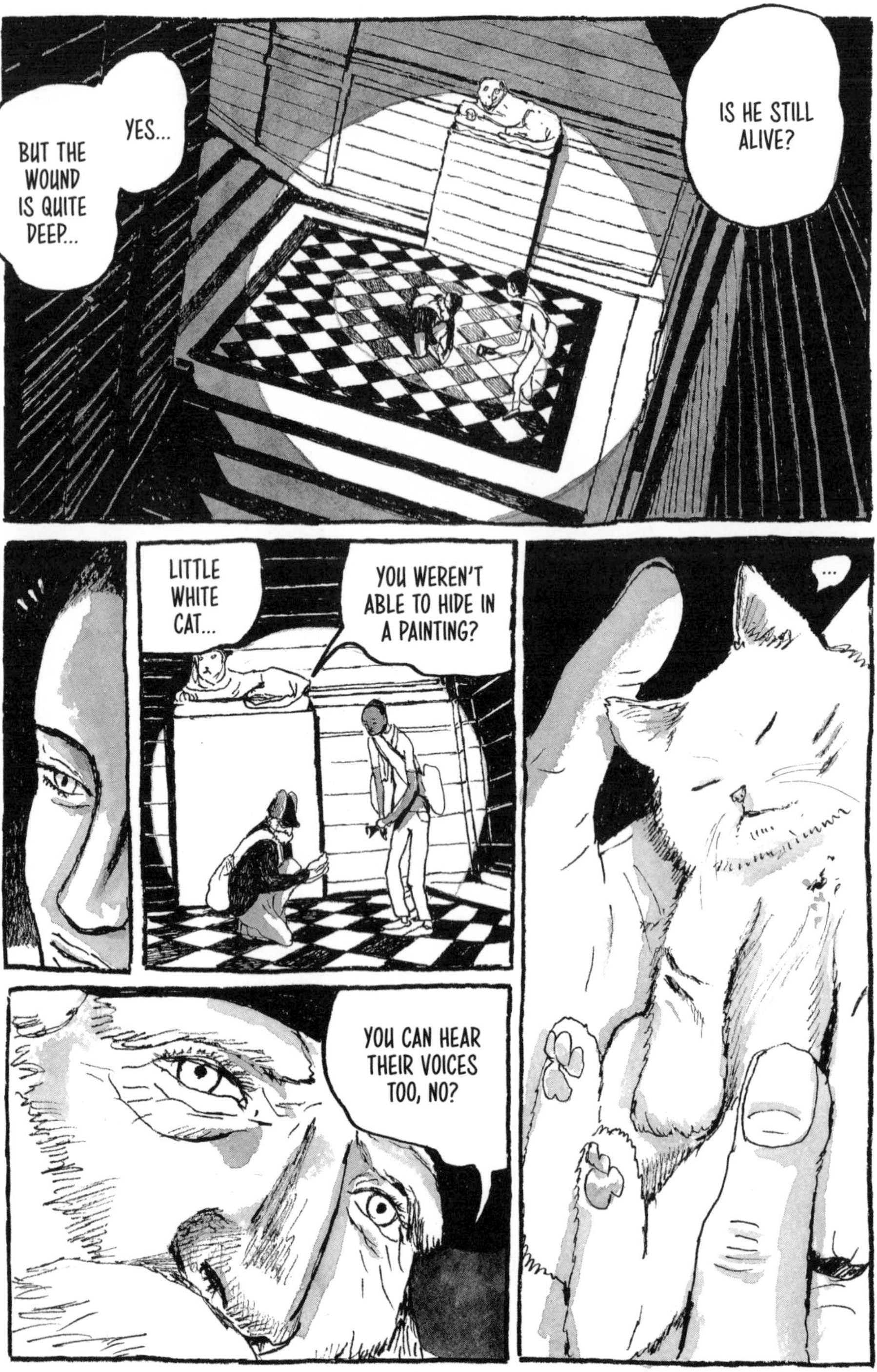
IS HE STILL ALIVE?
YES...
BUT THE WOUND IS QUITE DEEP...
...
YOU WEREN'T ABLE TO HIDE IN A PAINTING?
LITTLE WHITE CAT...
YOU CAN HEAR THEIR VOICES TOO, NO?

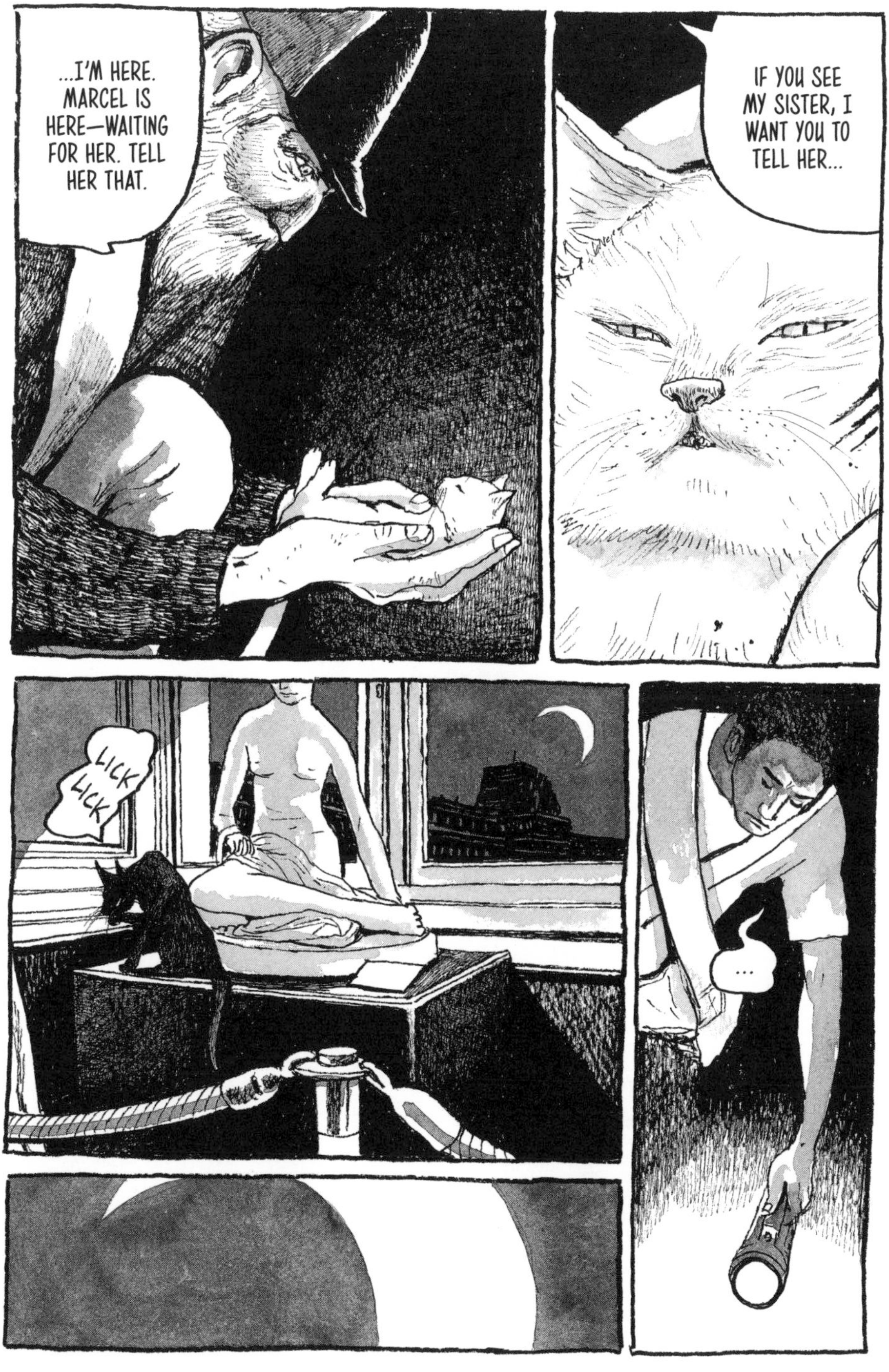
IF YOU SEE MY SISTER, I WANT YOU TO TELL HER...
...I'M HERE. MARCEL IS HERE—WAITING FOR HER. TELL HER THAT.
...
LICK LICK

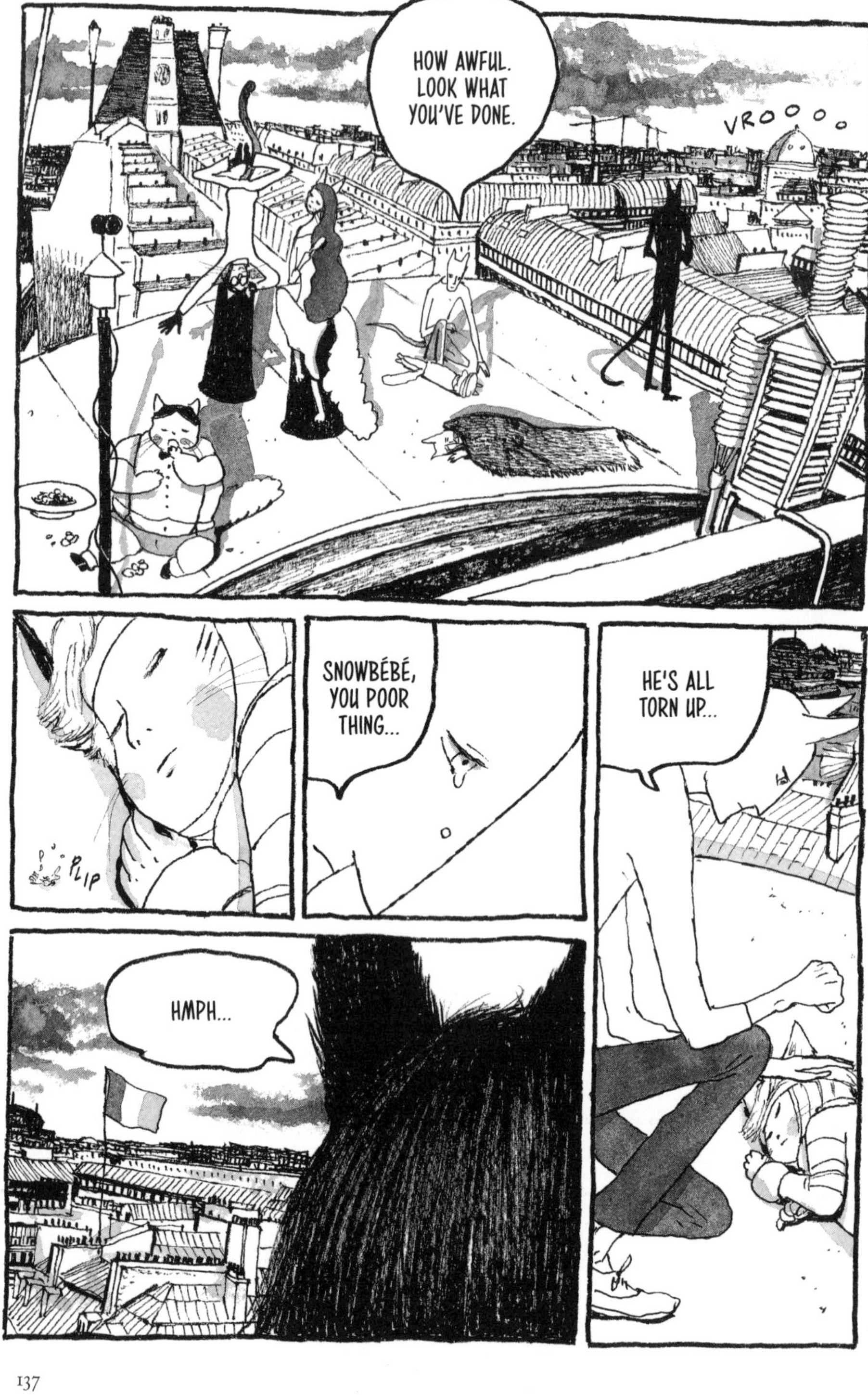
HOW AWFUL. LOOK WHAT YOU'VE DONE.
VROOOOO
HE'S ALL TORN UP...
SNOWBÉBÉ, YOU POOR THING...
PLIP
HMPH...

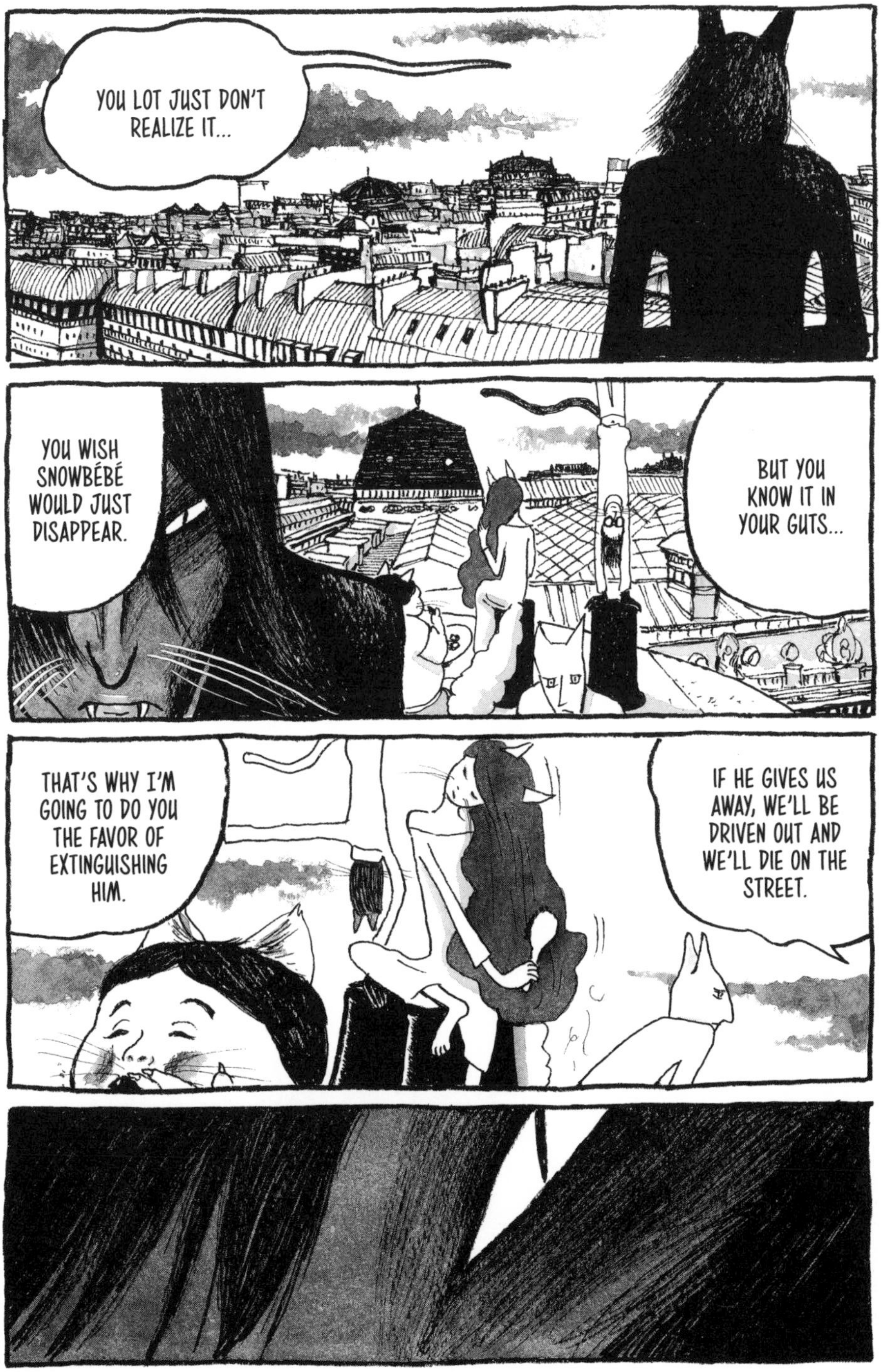
YOU LOT JUST DON'T REALIZE IT...
BUT YOU KNOW IT IN YOUR GUTS...
YOU WISH SNOWBÉBÉ WOULD JUST DISAPPEAR.
IF HE GIVES US AWAY, WE'LL BE DRIVEN OUT AND WE'LL DIE ON THE STREET.
THAT'S WHY I'M GOING TO DO YOU THE FAVOR OF EXTINGUISHING HIM.

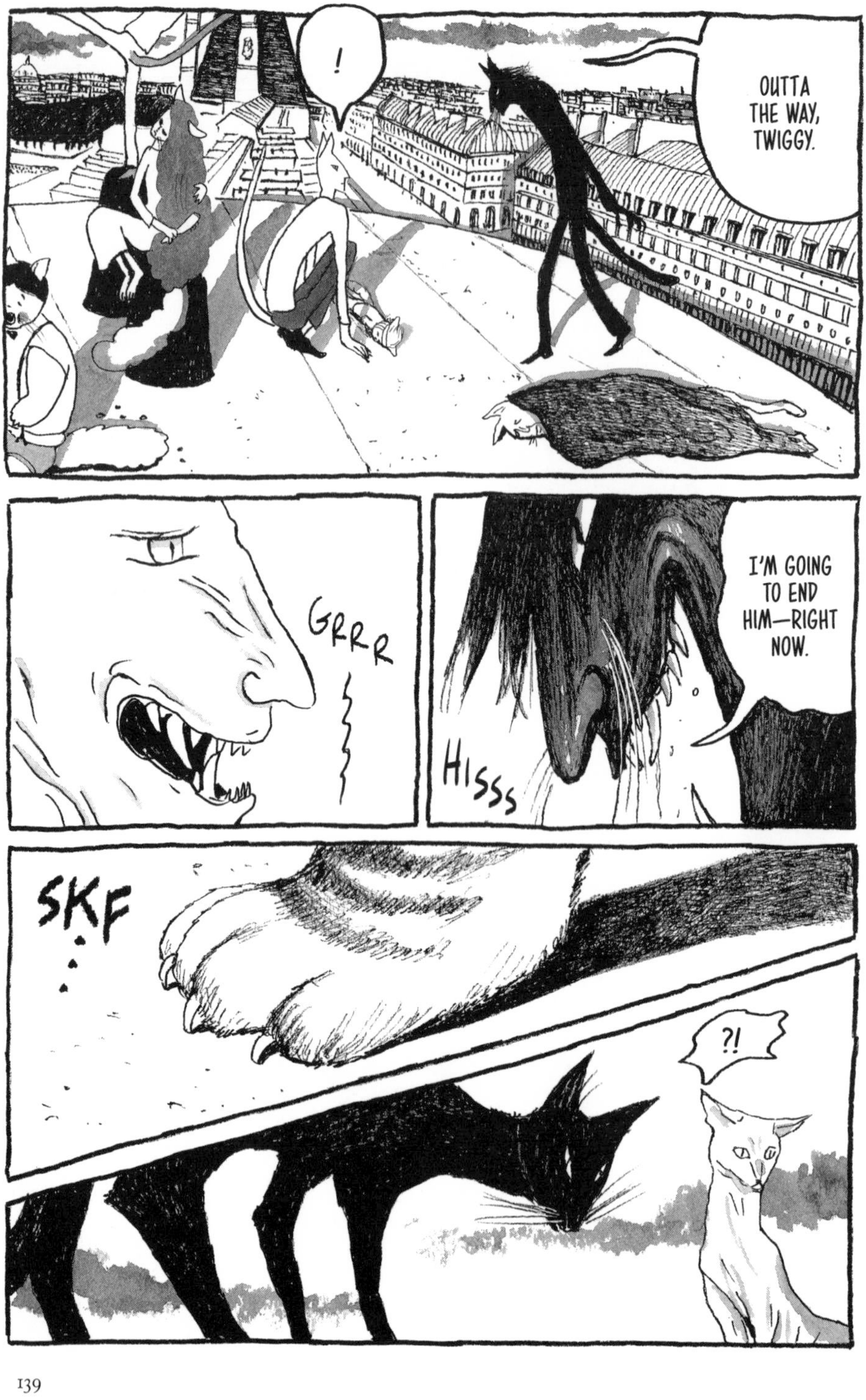
OUTTA THE WAY, TWIGGY.
!
I'M GOING TO END HIM—RIGHT NOW.
HISSS
GRRRR
SKF
?!

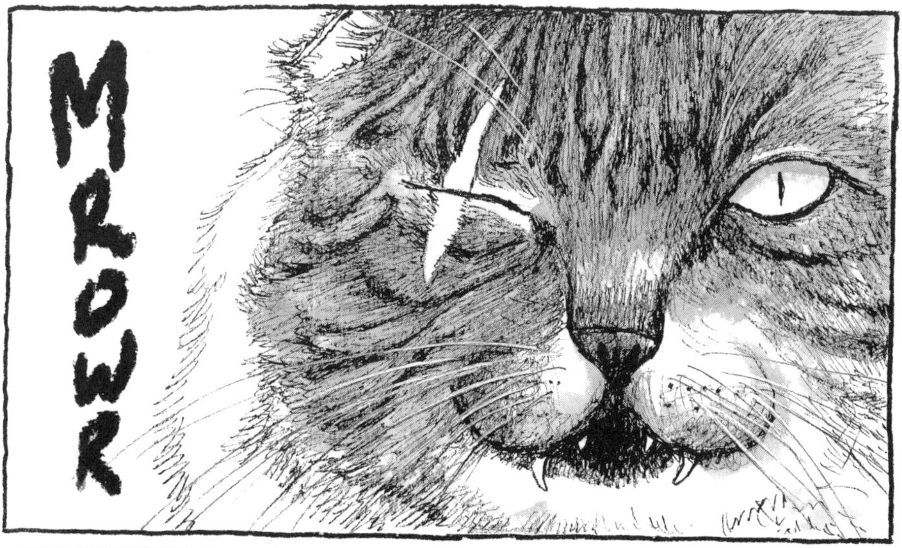
MROWR

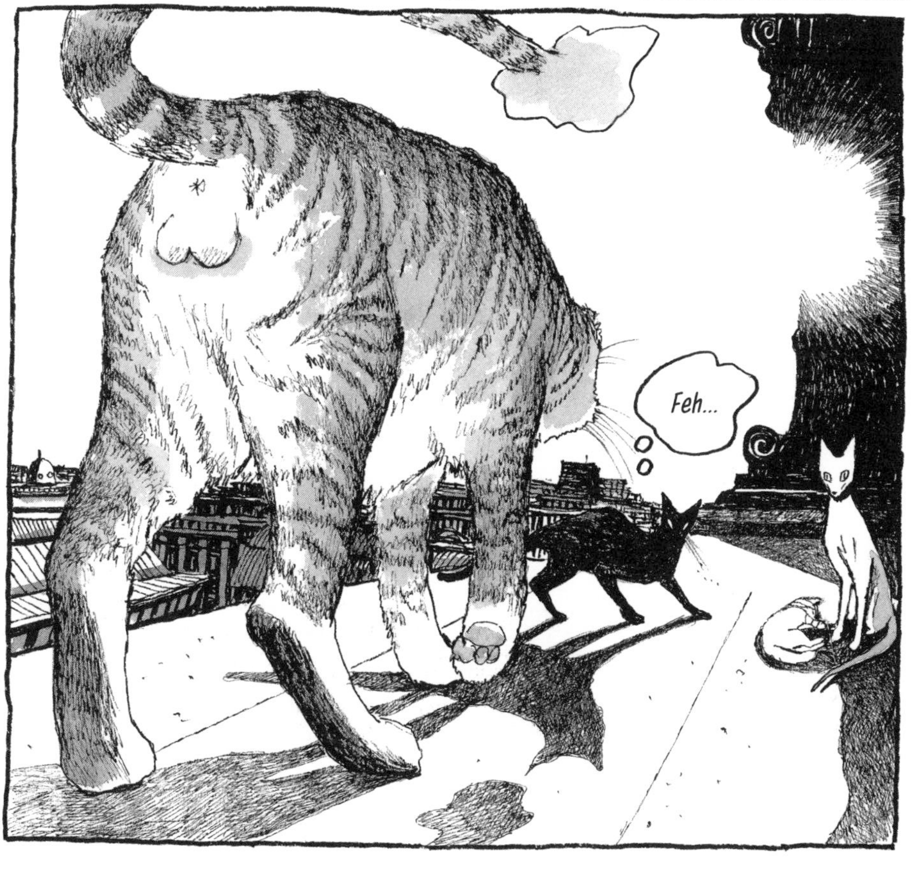
Feh...

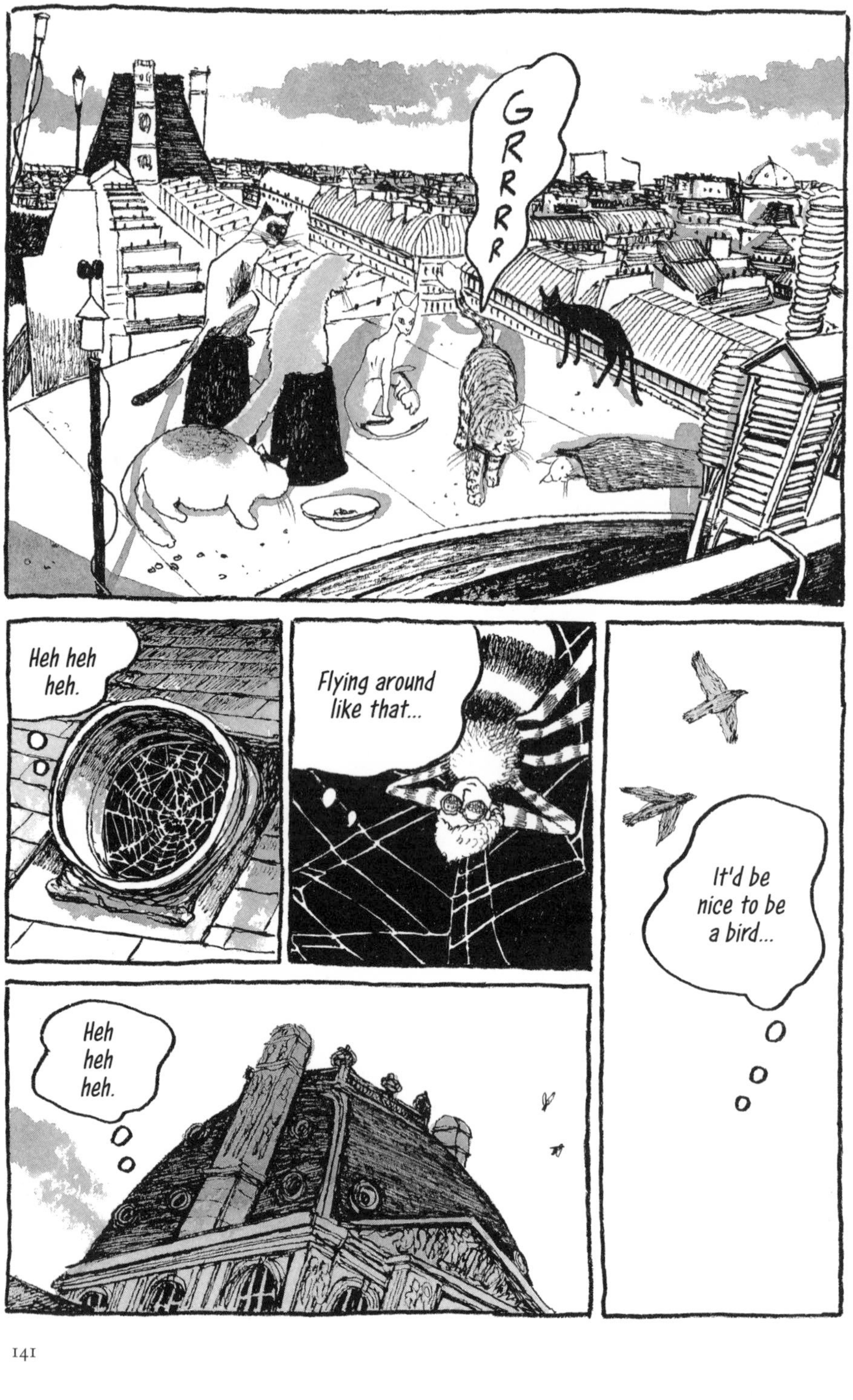
GRRRR
It'd be nice to be a bird...
Flying around like that...
Heh heh heh.
Heh heh heh.

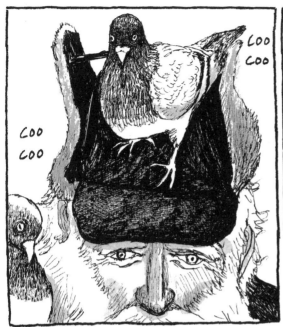

COO
COO

COO
COO

FLAP
FLAP
FLAP

...

BWA HA
HA HA
HA!

142

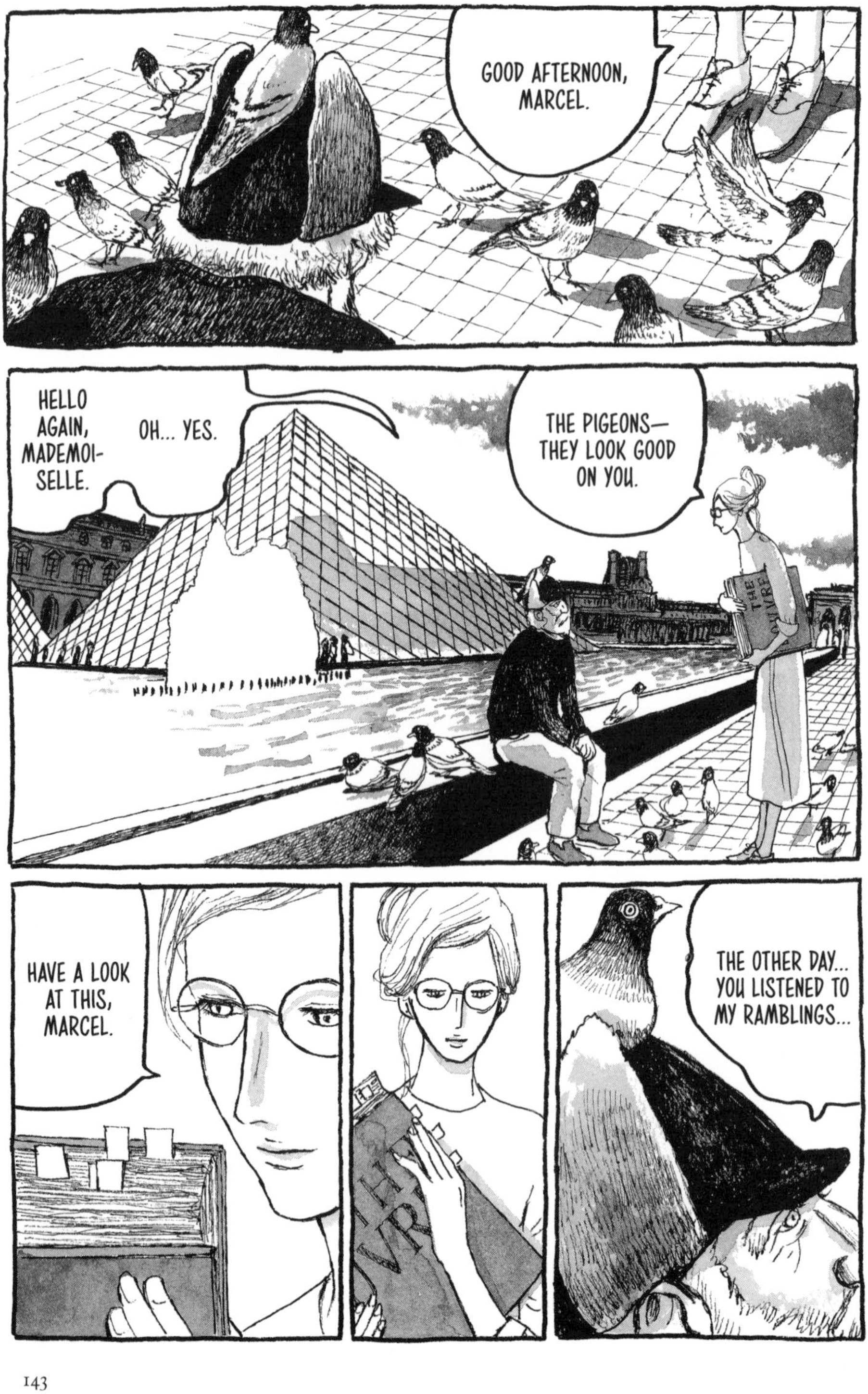
GOOD AFTERNOON, MARCEL.
THE PIGEONS— THEY LOOK GOOD ON YOU.
OH... YES.
HELLO AGAIN, MADEMOI-SELLE.
THE OTHER DAY... YOU LISTENED TO MY RAMBLINGS...
HAVE A LOOK AT THIS, MARCEL.

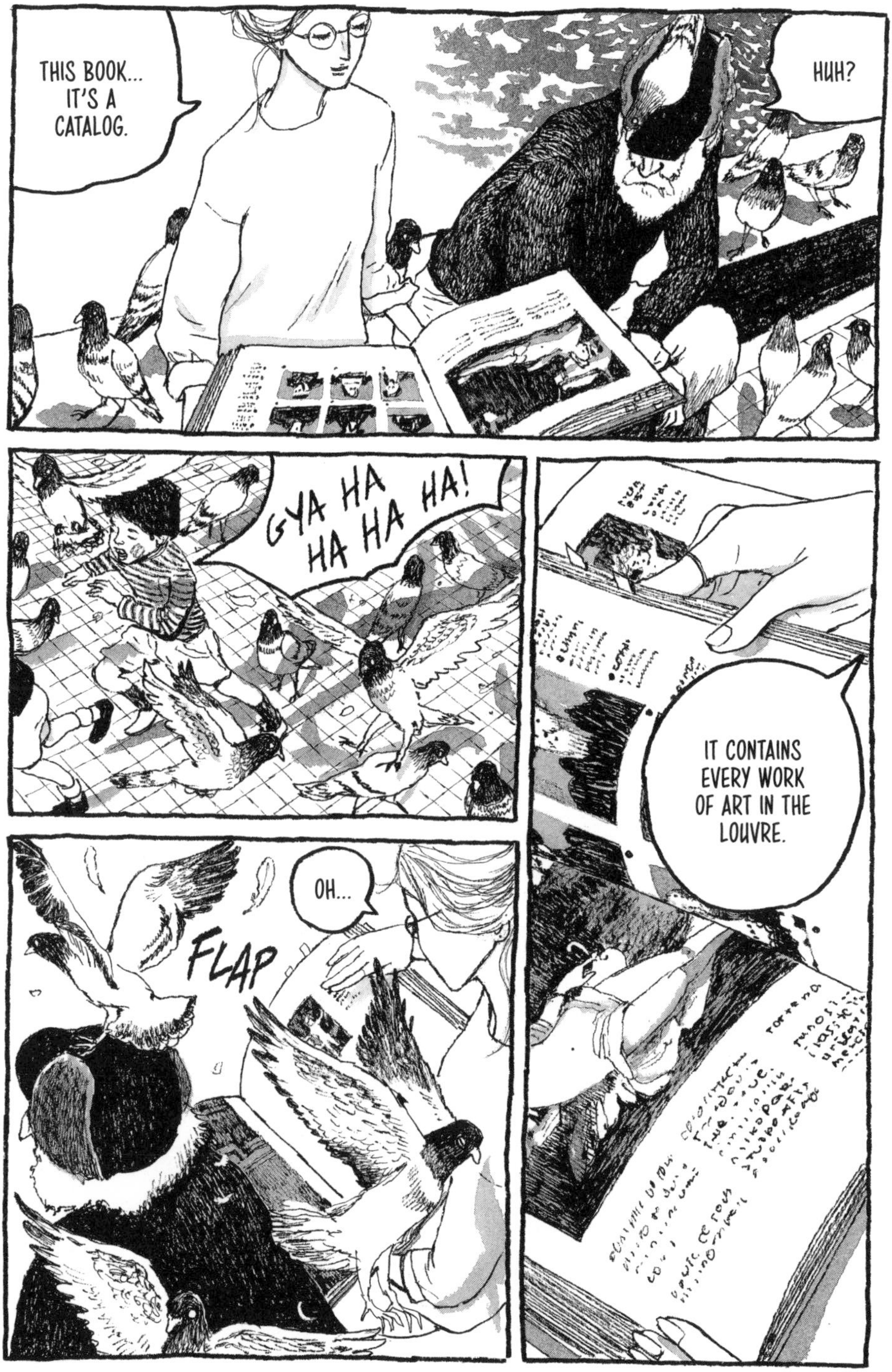
THIS BOOK... IT'S A CATALOG.
HUH?
IT CONTAINS EVERY WORK OF ART IN THE LOUVRE.
GYA HA HA HA HA!
OH...
FLAP

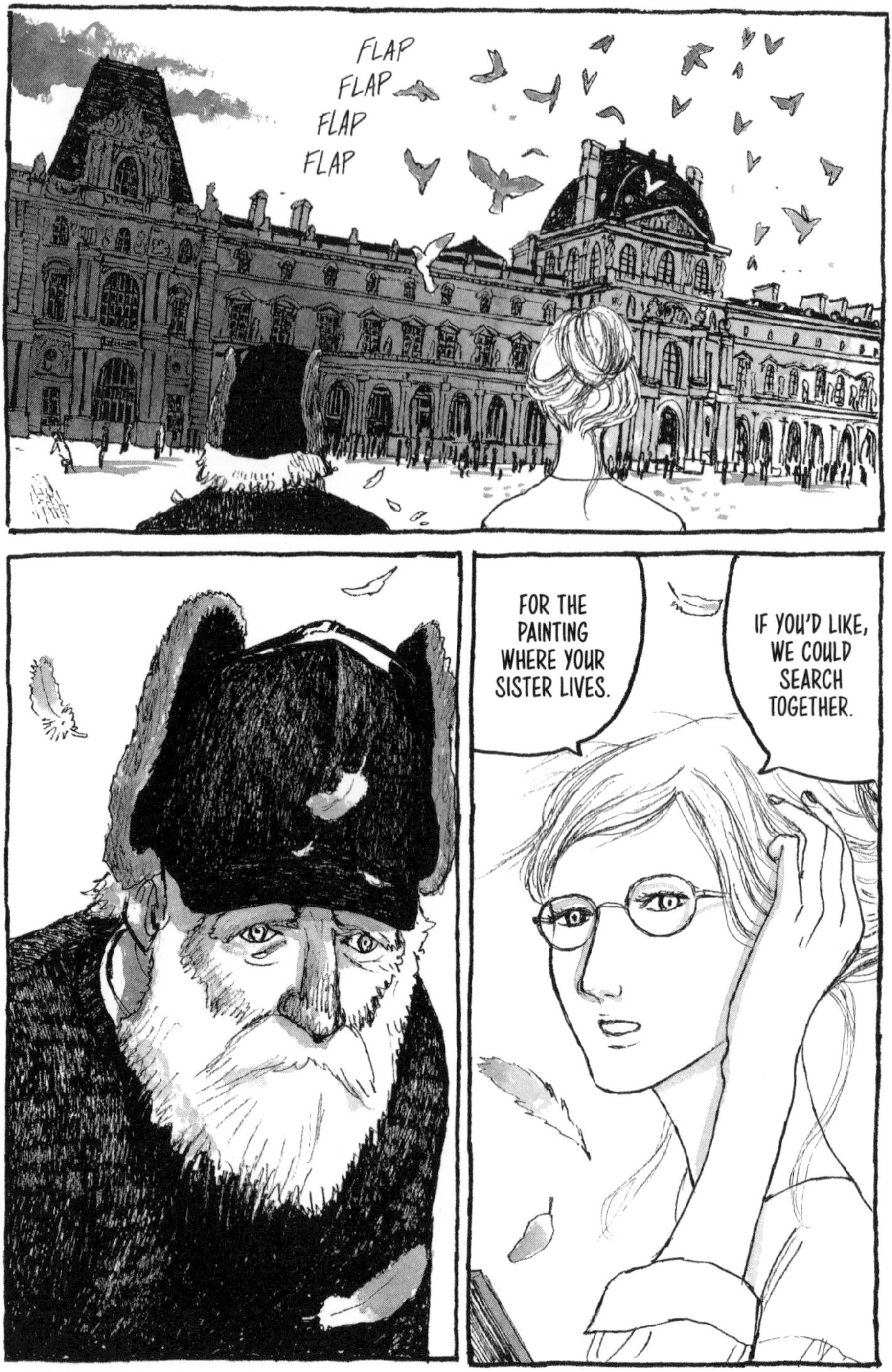
FLAP
FLAP
FLAP
FLAP
IF YOU'D LIKE, WE COULD SEARCH TOGETHER.
FOR THE PAINTING WHERE YOUR SISTER LIVES.

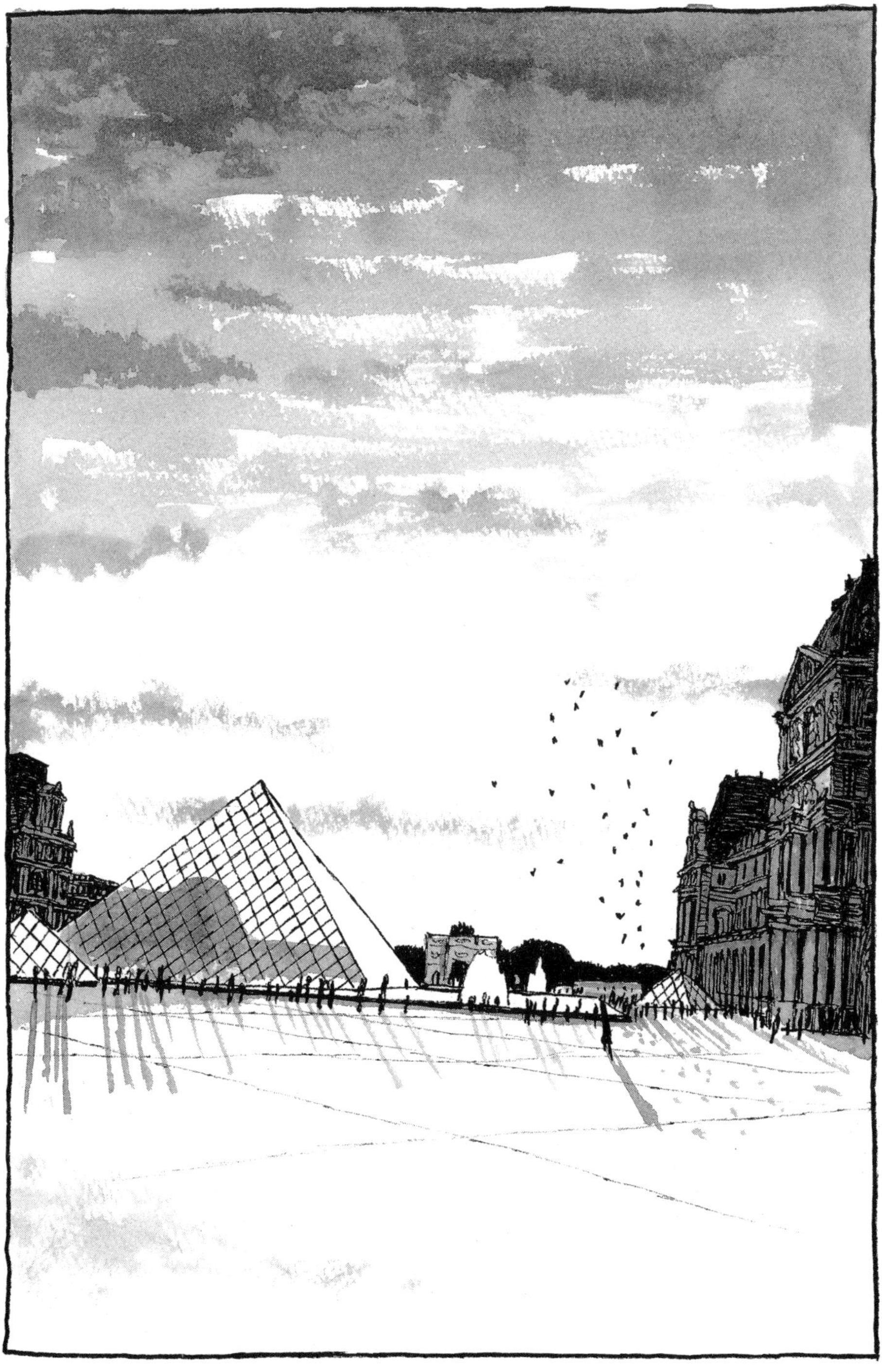

CHAPTER 7

The Secret of Twiggy

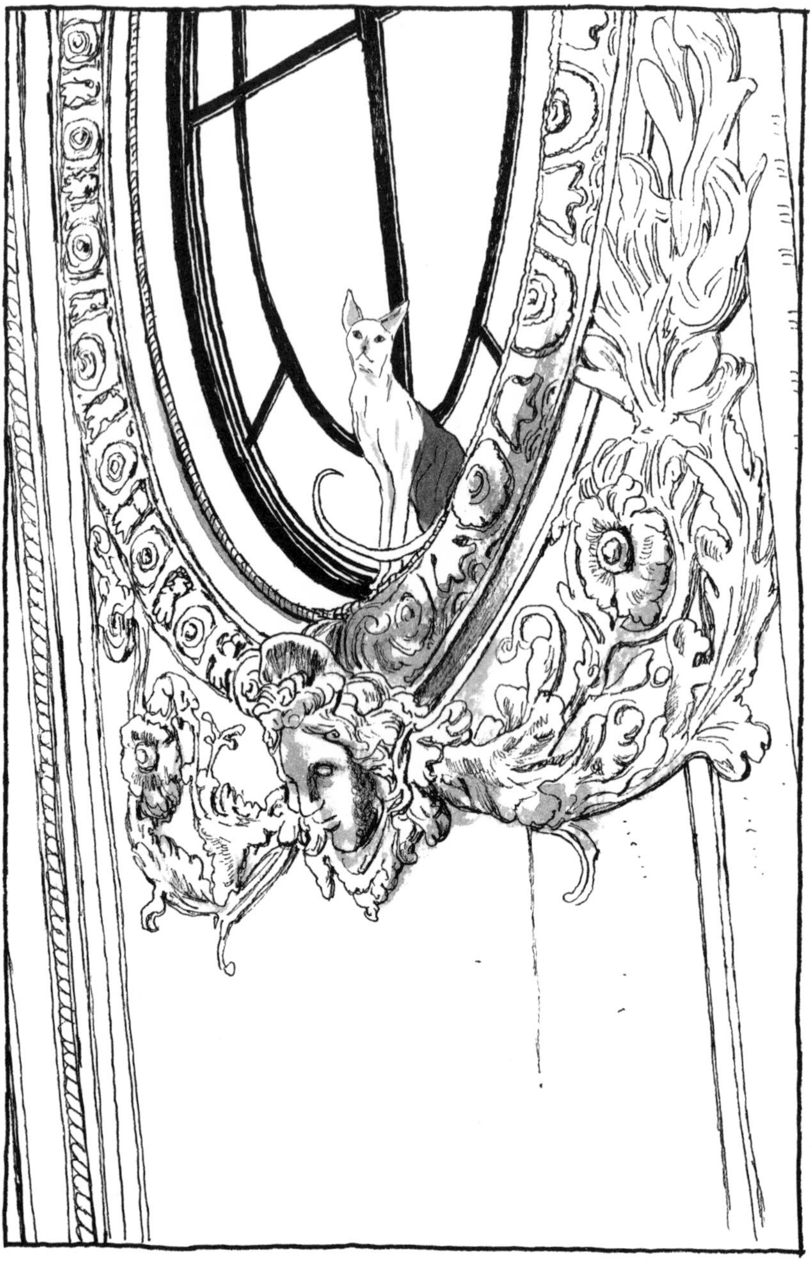

SNOWBÉBÉ,
SNOWBÉBÉ...

I WONDER IF
YOU'RE WELL...

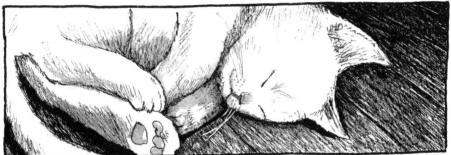

YOU HAVEN'T
COME TO
SEE THE
PAINTINGS
LATELY.

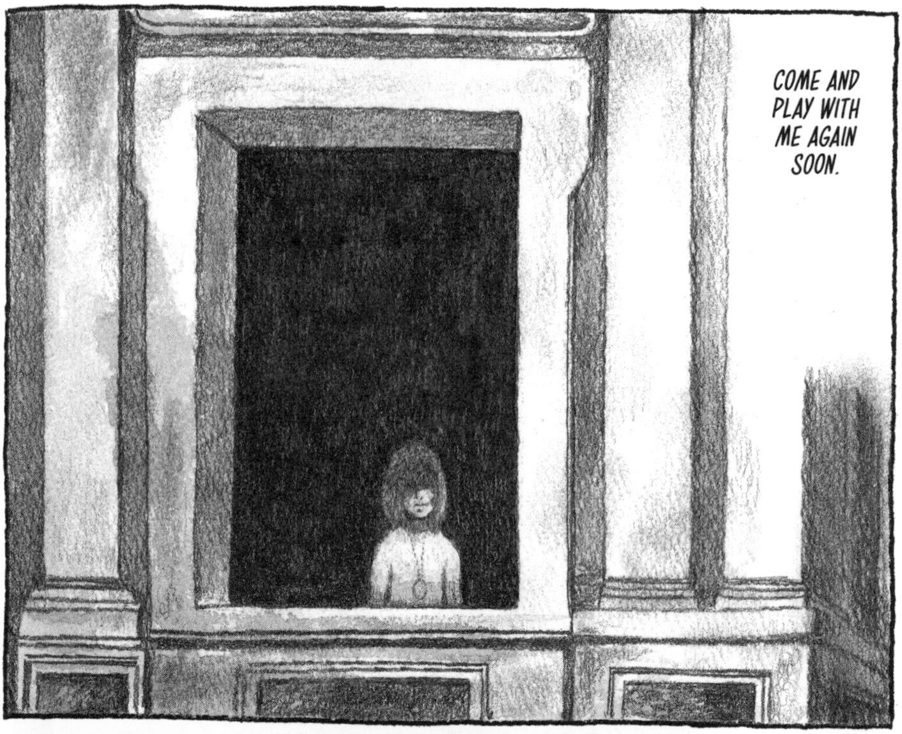
COME AND PLAY WITH ME AGAIN SOON.
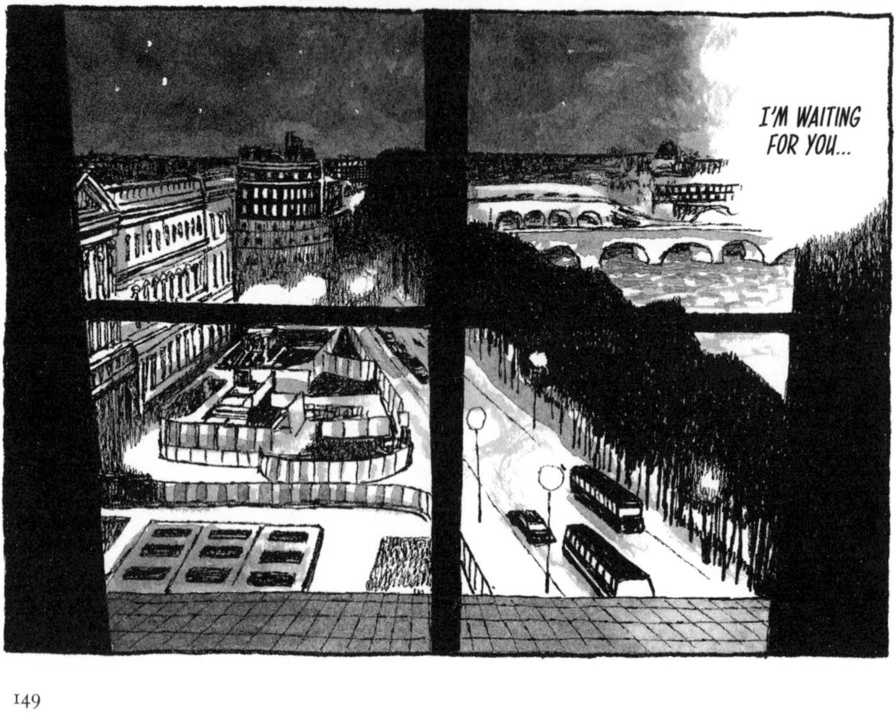
I'M WAITING FOR YOU...

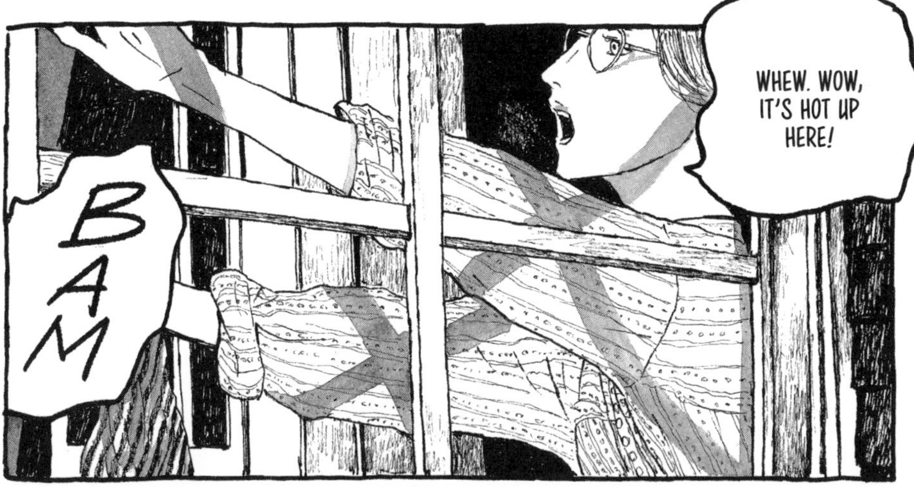
WHEW. WOW, IT'S HOT UP HERE!
BAM

SUMMER

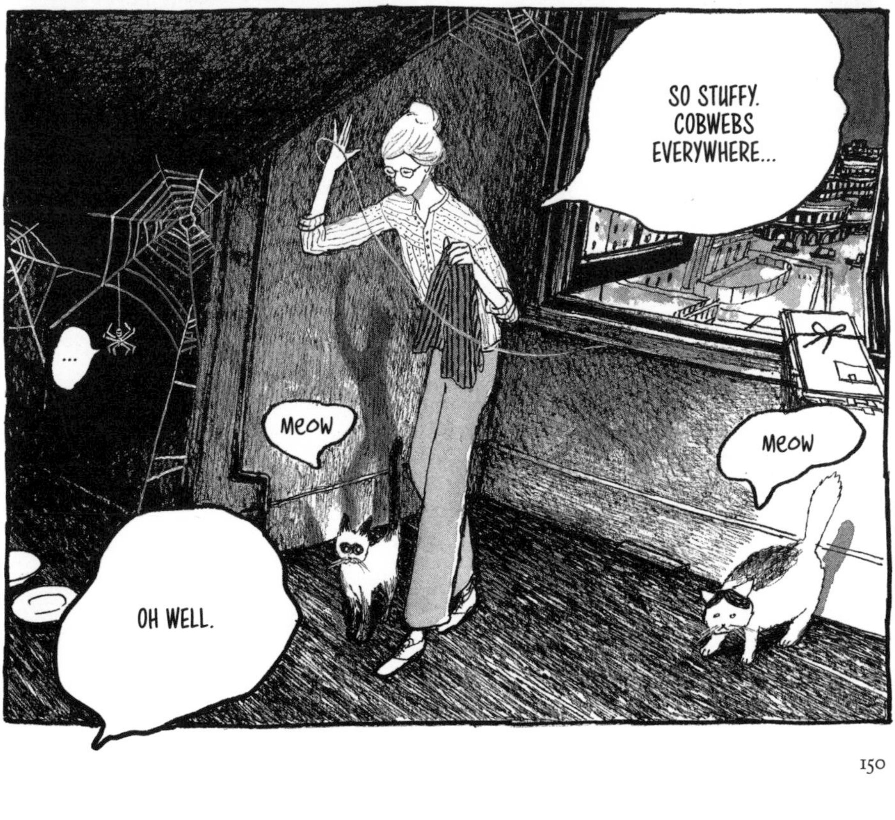
SO STUFFY. COBWEBS EVERYWHERE...
Meow
...
Meow
OH WELL.

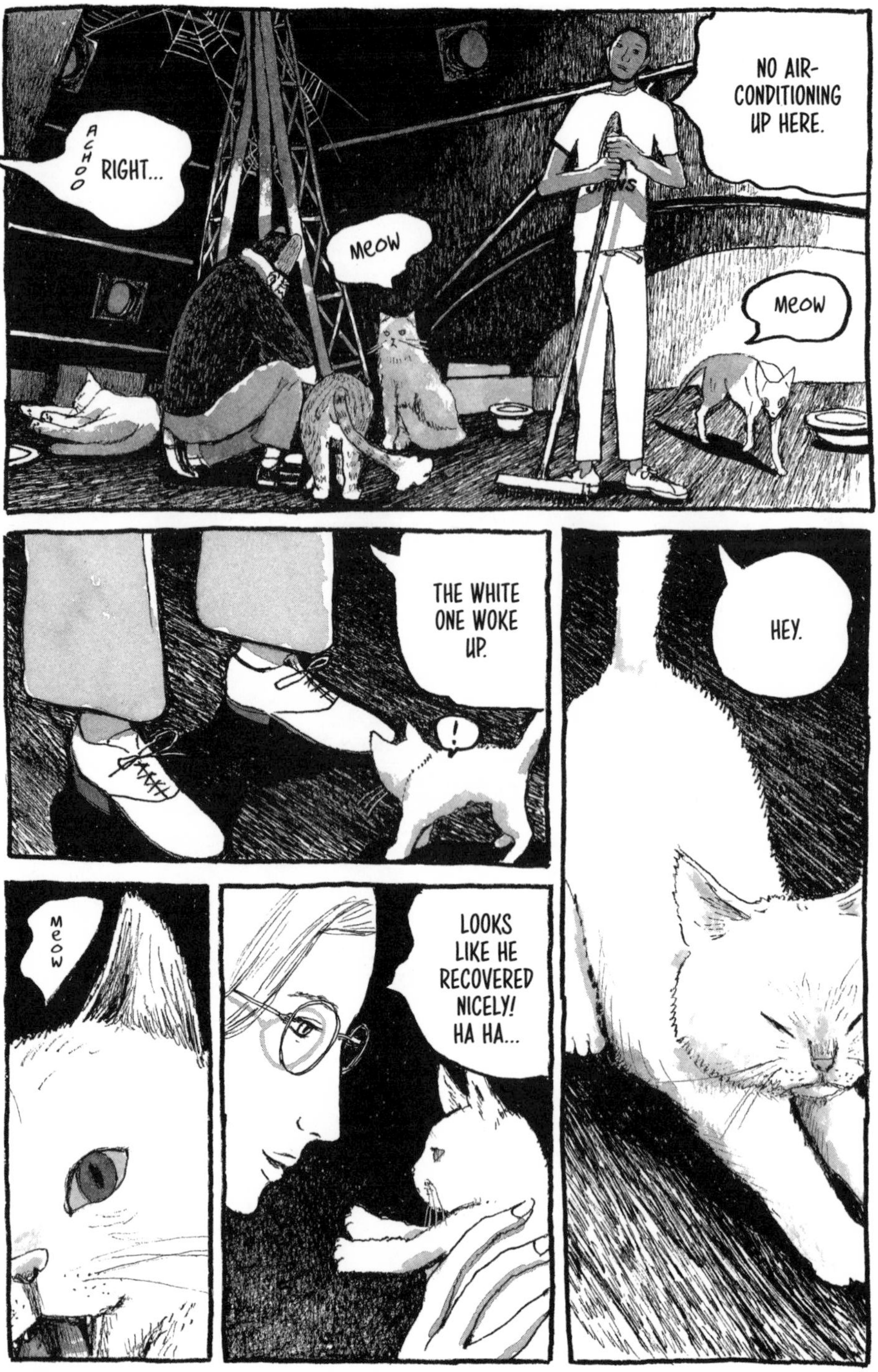
NO AIR-CONDITIONING UP HERE.
ACHOO
RIGHT...
MEOW
MEOW
HEY.
THE WHITE ONE WOKE UP.
!
LOOKS LIKE HE RECOVERED NICELY! HA HA...
MEOW

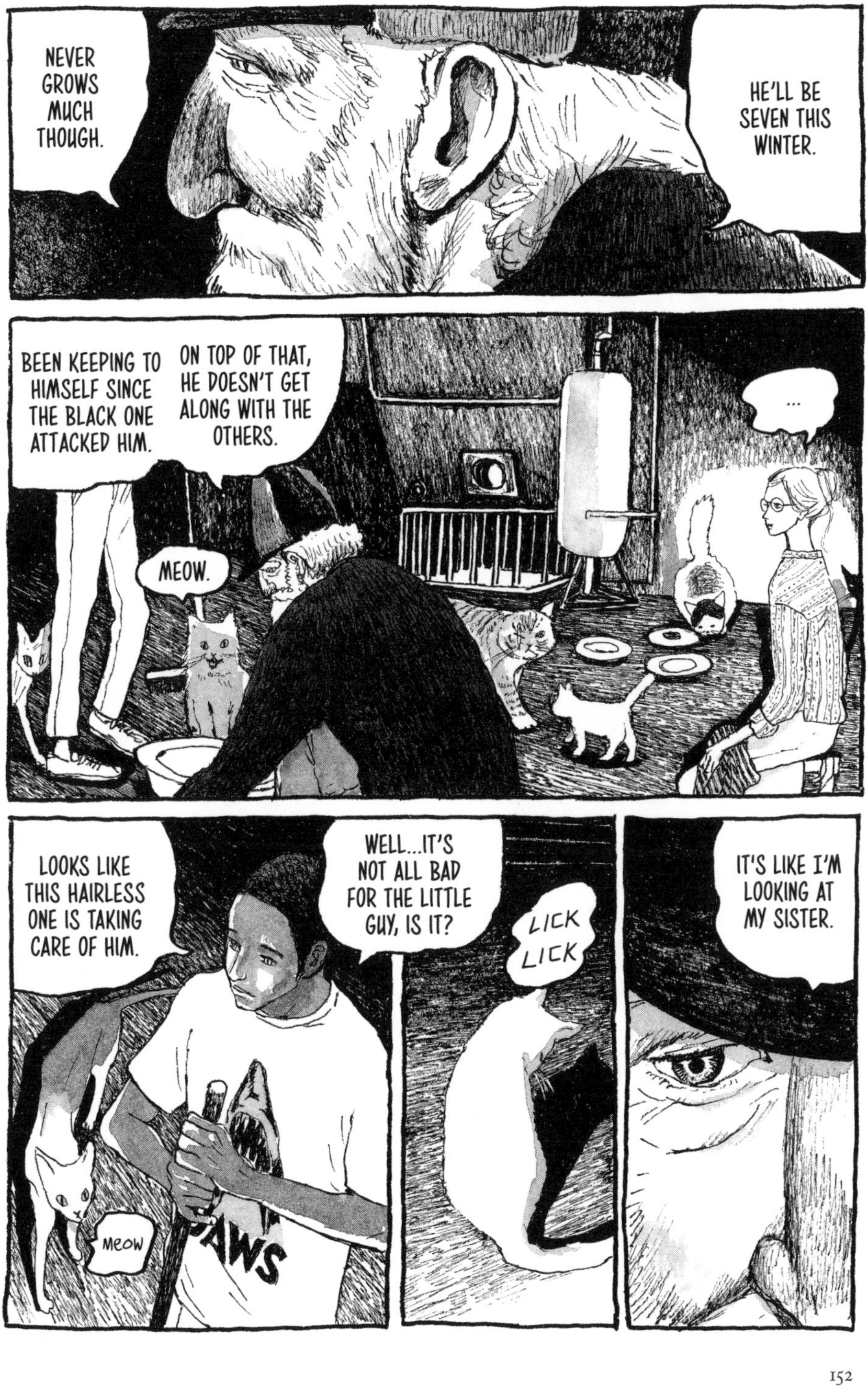
HE'LL BE SEVEN THIS WINTER.
NEVER GROWS MUCH THOUGH.
...
ON TOP OF THAT, HE DOESN'T GET ALONG WITH THE OTHERS.
BEEN KEEPING TO HIMSELF SINCE THE BLACK ONE ATTACKED HIM.
MEOW.
IT'S LIKE I'M LOOKING AT MY SISTER.
LICK LICK
WELL...IT'S NOT ALL BAD FOR THE LITTLE GUY, IS IT?
LOOKS LIKE THIS HAIRLESS ONE IS TAKING CARE OF HIM.
JAWS
Meow

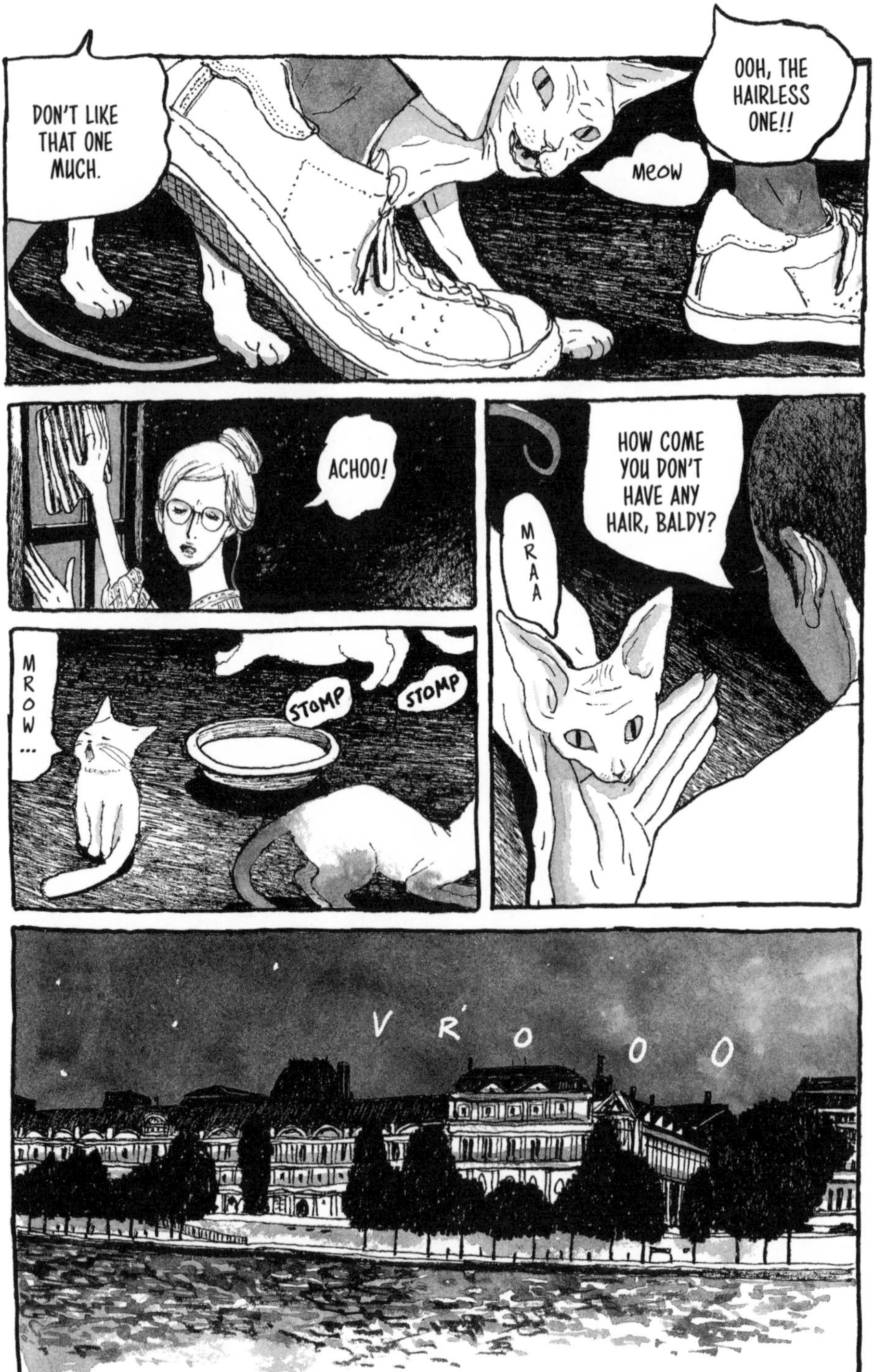
OOH, THE HAIRLESS ONE!!
MEOW
DON'T LIKE THAT ONE MUCH.
HOW COME YOU DON'T HAVE ANY HAIR, BALDY?
MRAA
ACHOO!
STOMP
STOMP
MROW...
VROOO

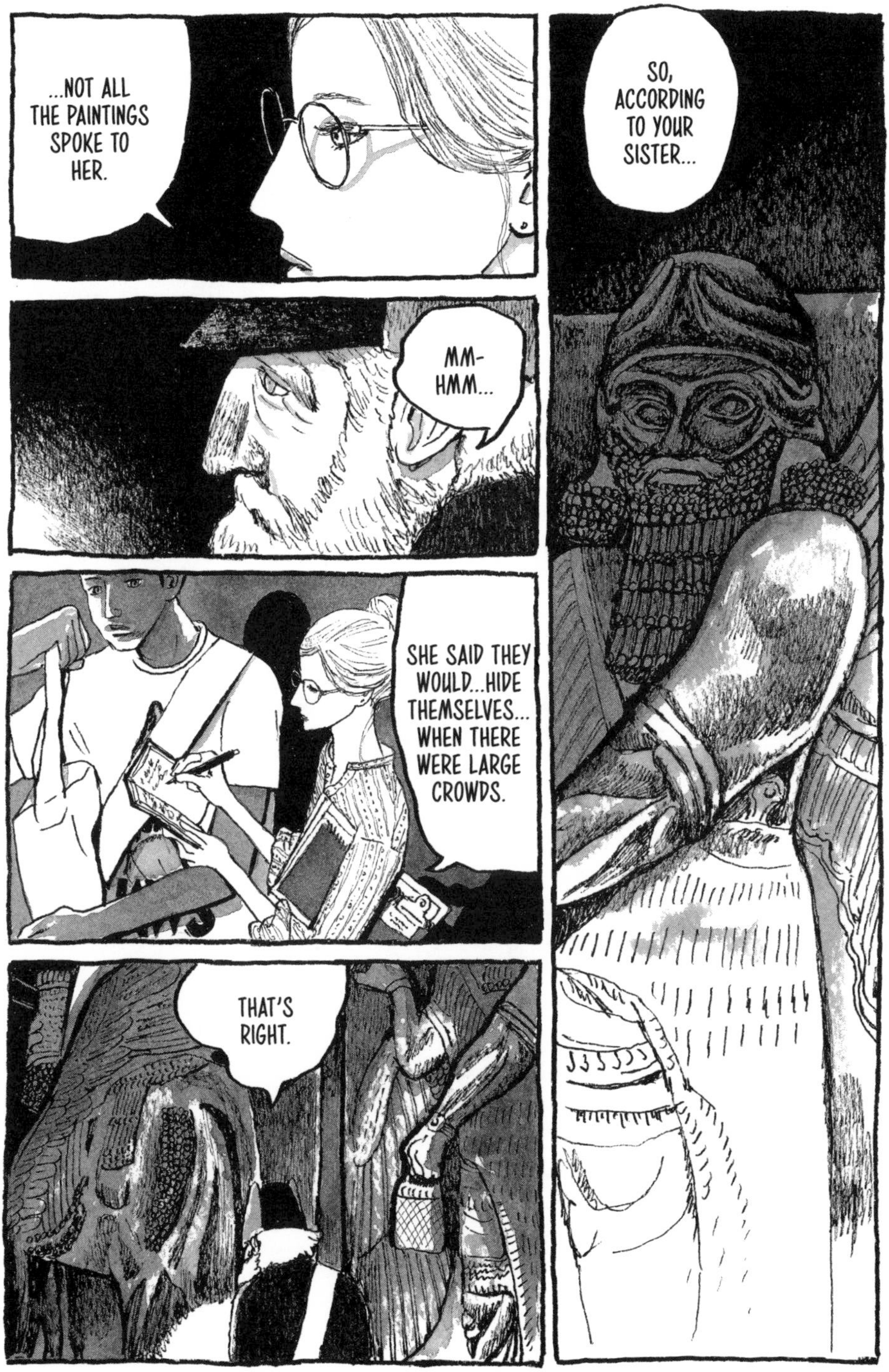
SO, ACCORDING TO YOUR SISTER...
...NOT ALL THE PAINTINGS SPOKE TO HER.
MM-HMM...
SHE SAID THEY WOULD...HIDE THEMSELVES... WHEN THERE WERE LARGE CROWDS.
THAT'S RIGHT.

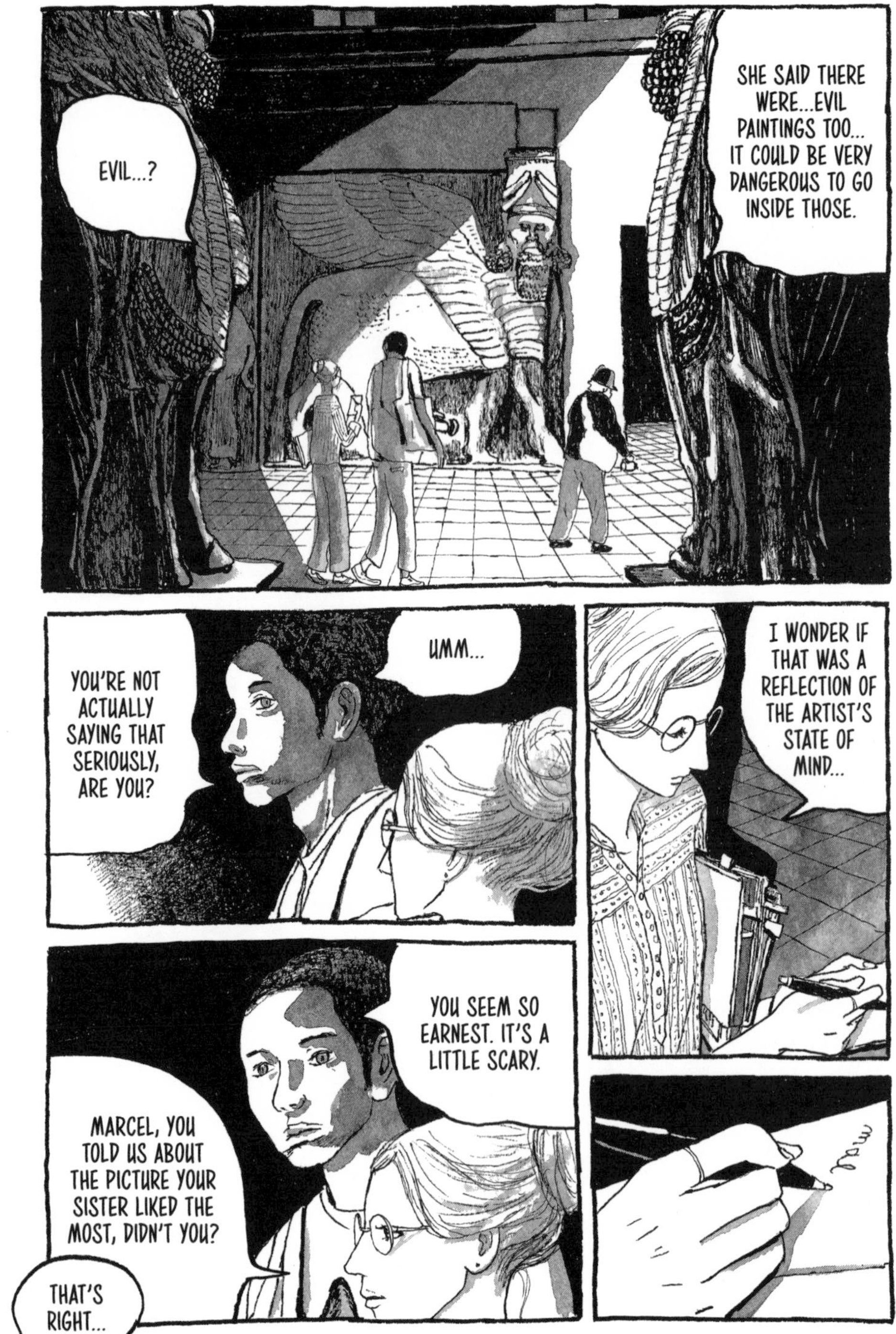
SHE SAID THERE WERE...EVIL PAINTINGS TOO... IT COULD BE VERY DANGEROUS TO GO INSIDE THOSE.
EVIL...?
I WONDER IF THAT WAS A REFLECTION OF THE ARTIST'S STATE OF MIND...
UMM...
YOU'RE NOT ACTUALLY SAYING THAT SERIOUSLY, ARE YOU?
YOU SEEM SO EARNEST. IT'S A LITTLE SCARY.
MARCEL, YOU TOLD US ABOUT THE PICTURE YOUR SISTER LIKED THE MOST, DIDN'T YOU?
THAT'S RIGHT...

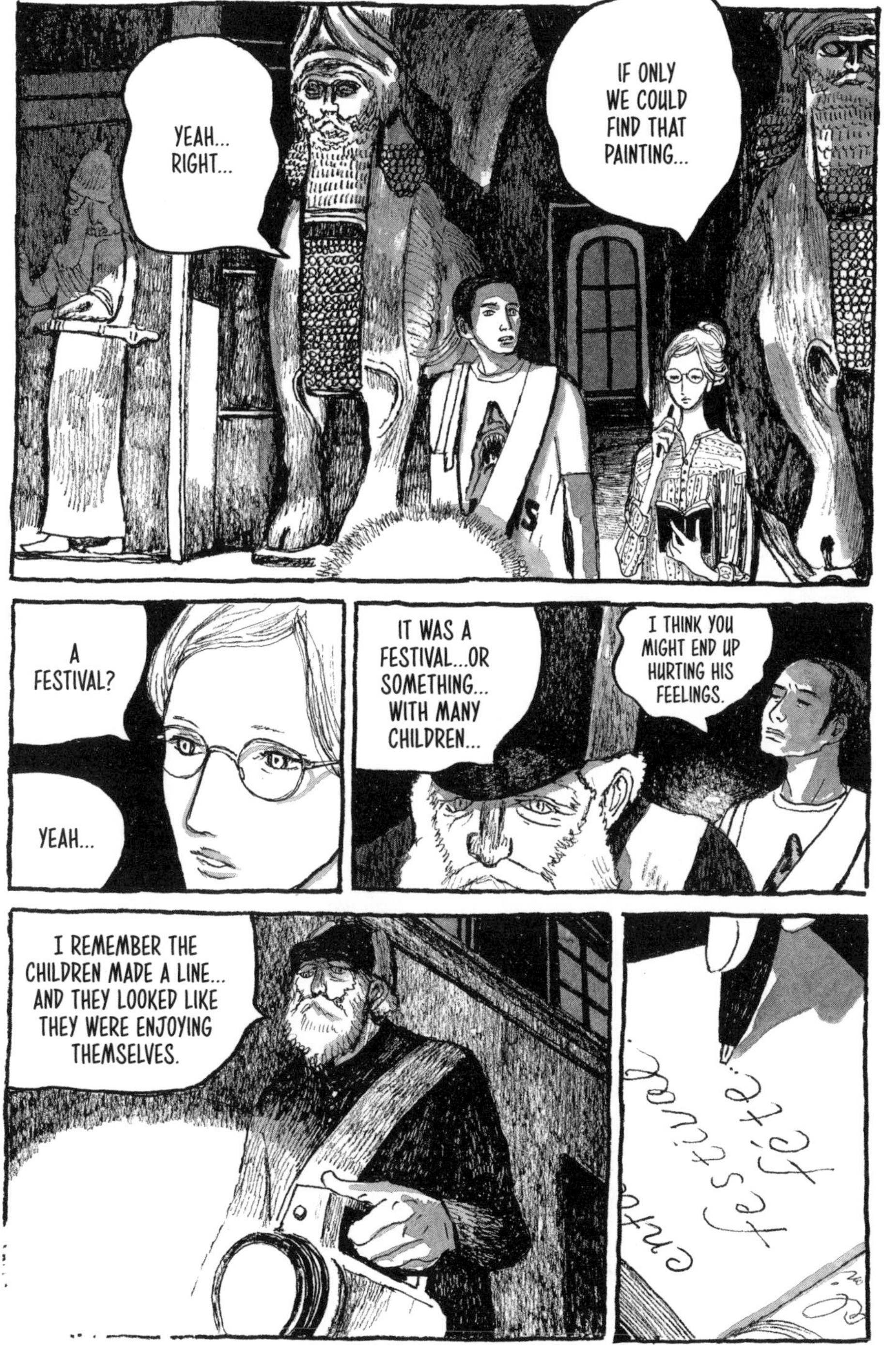
IF ONLY WE COULD FIND THAT PAINTING...
YEAH... RIGHT...
I THINK YOU MIGHT END UP HURTING HIS FEELINGS.
IT WAS A FESTIVAL...OR SOMETHING... WITH MANY CHILDREN...
A FESTIVAL?
YEAH...
I REMEMBER THE CHILDREN MADE A LINE... AND THEY LOOKED LIKE THEY WERE ENJOYING THEMSELVES.

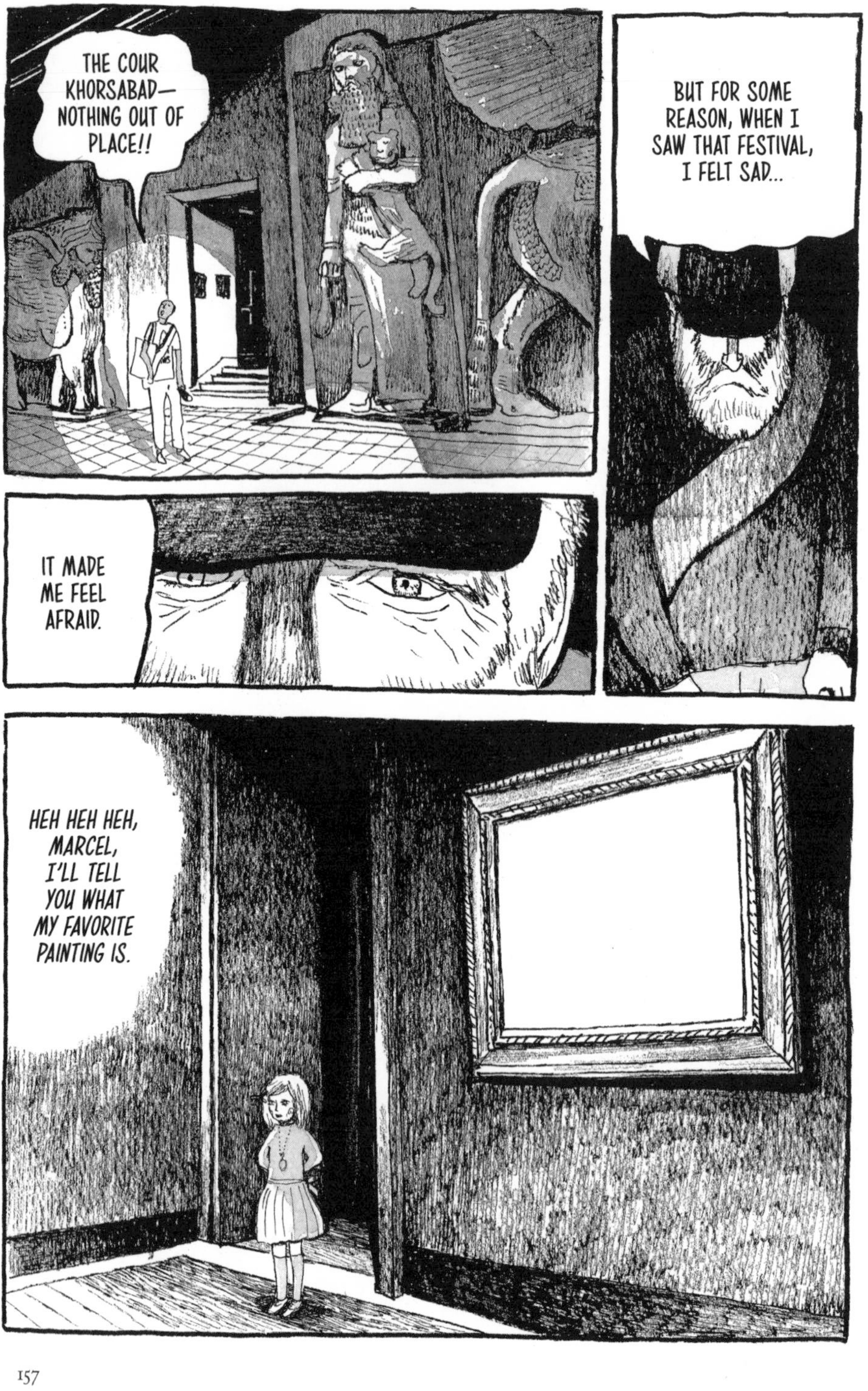
BUT FOR SOME REASON, WHEN I SAW THAT FESTIVAL, I FELT SAD...
THE COUR KHORSABAD— NOTHING OUT OF PLACE!!
IT MADE ME FEEL AFRAID.
HEH HEH HEH, MARCEL, I'LL TELL YOU WHAT MY FAVORITE PAINTING IS.

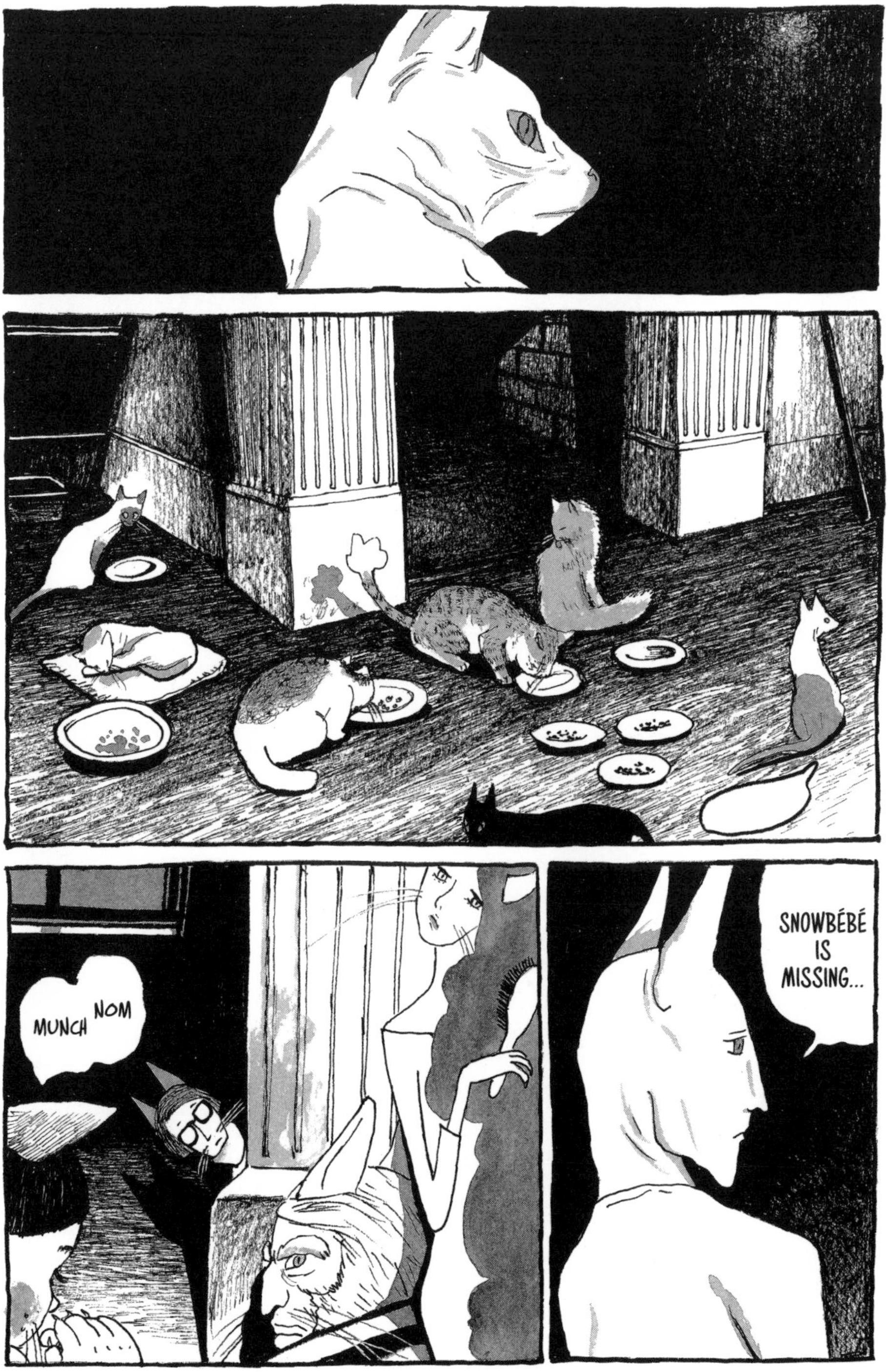
SNOWBÉBÉ IS MISSING...
MUNCH NOM

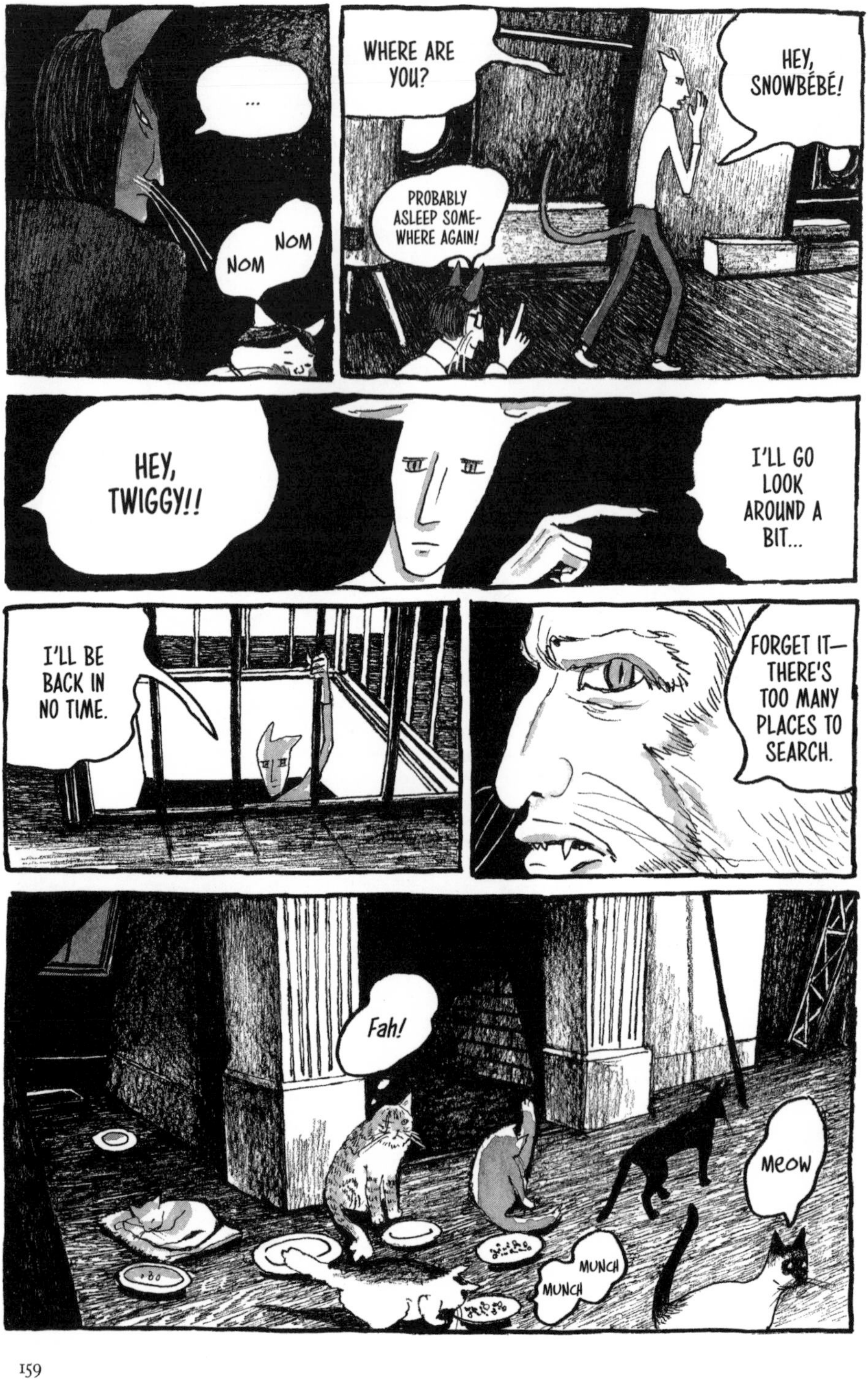
HEY, SNOWBÉBÉ!
WHERE ARE YOU?
PROBABLY ASLEEP SOME-WHERE AGAIN!
...
NOM NOM
I'LL GO LOOK AROUND A BIT...
HEY, TWIGGY!!
FORGET IT—THERE'S TOO MANY PLACES TO SEARCH.
I'LL BE BACK IN NO TIME.
Meow
Fah!
MUNCH MUNCH

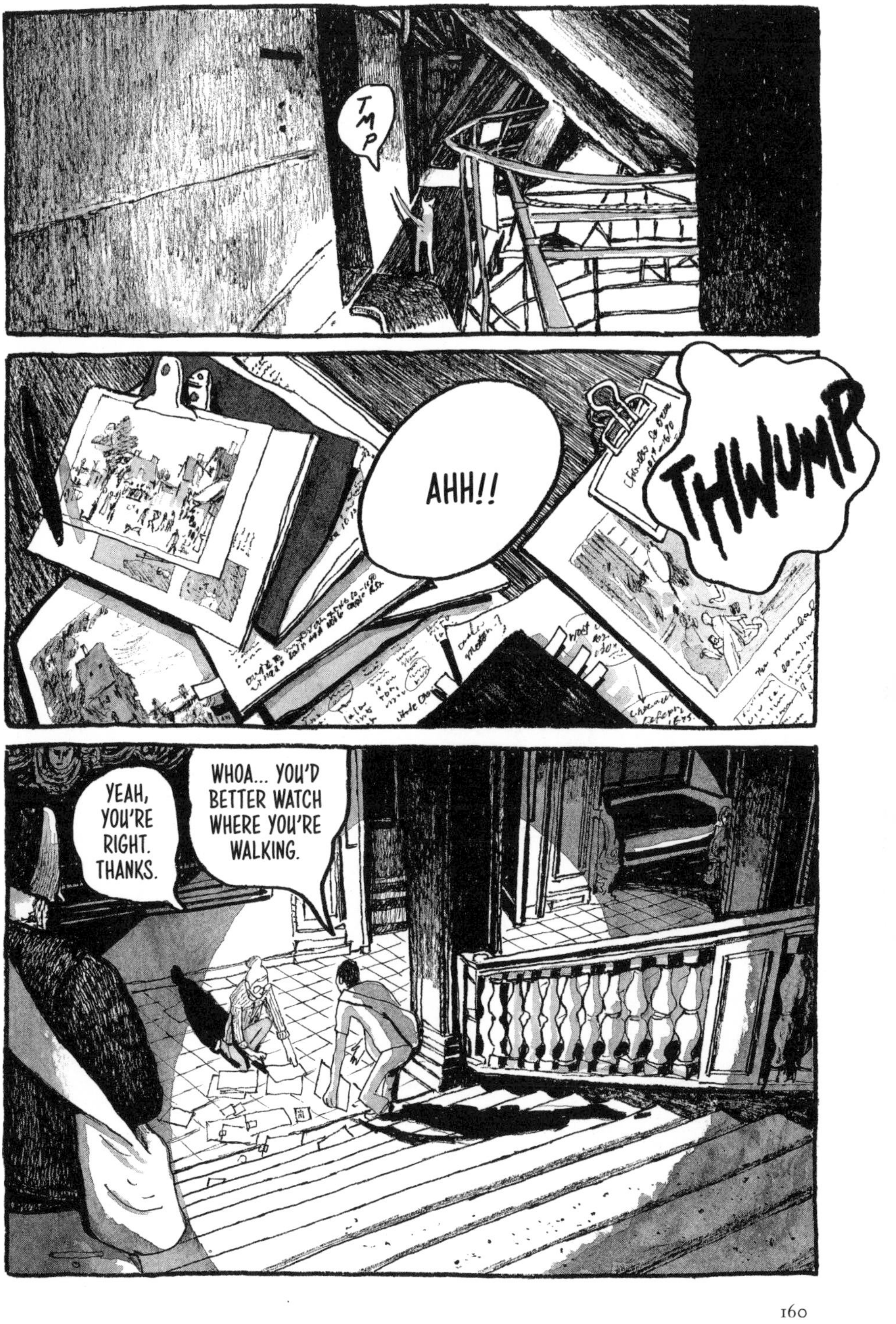
TMP
THWUMP
AHH!!
WHOA... YOU'D BETTER WATCH WHERE YOU'RE WALKING.
YEAH, YOU'RE RIGHT. THANKS.

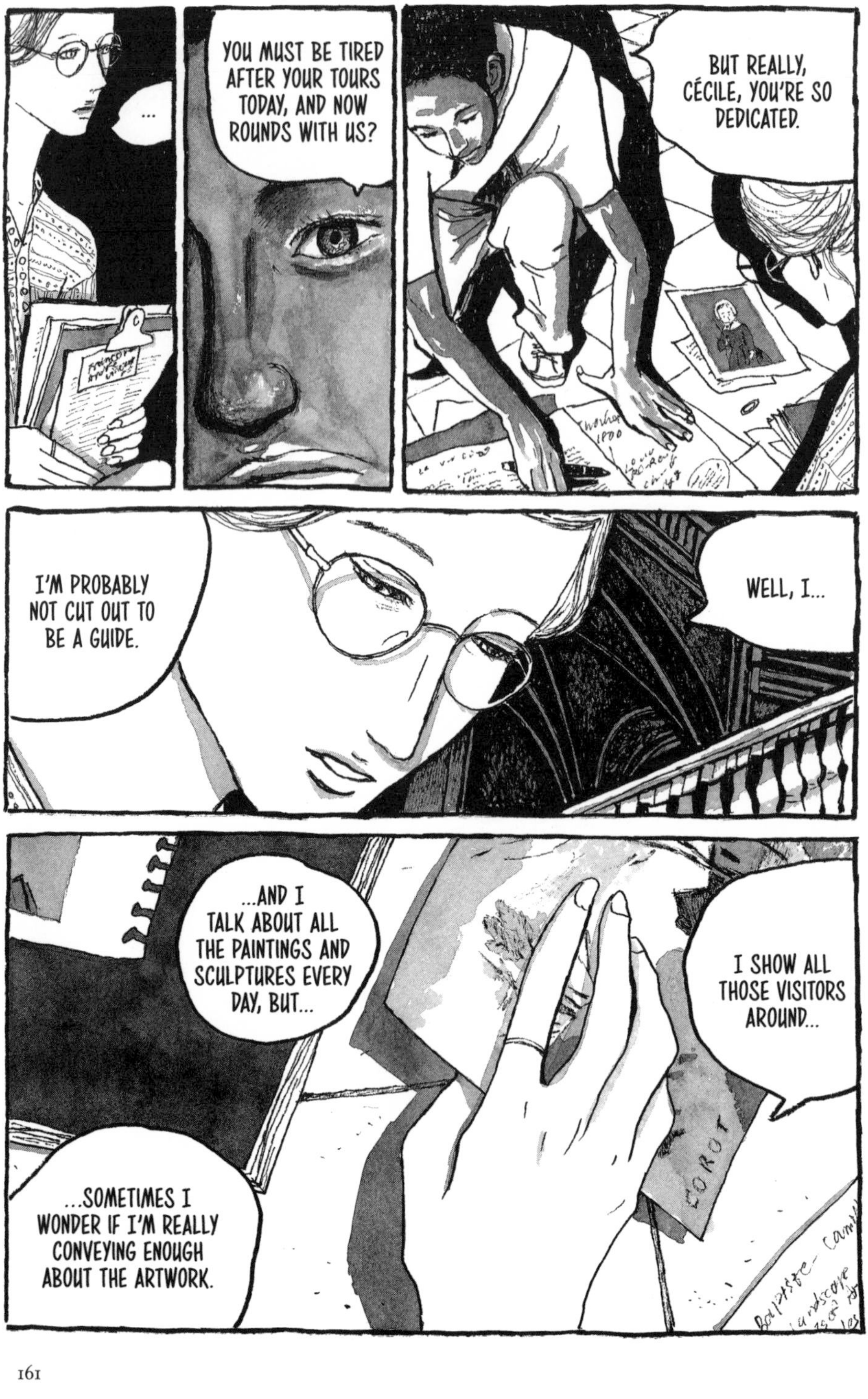

BUT REALLY, CÉCILE, YOU'RE SO DEDICATED.
YOU MUST BE TIRED AFTER YOUR TOURS TODAY, AND NOW ROUNDS WITH US?
...
WELL, I...
I'M PROBABLY NOT CUT OUT TO BE A GUIDE.
I SHOW ALL THOSE VISITORS AROUND...
...AND I TALK ABOUT ALL THE PAINTINGS AND SCULPTURES EVERY DAY, BUT...
...SOMETIMES I WONDER IF I'M REALLY CONVEYING ENOUGH ABOUT THE ARTWORK.
COROT

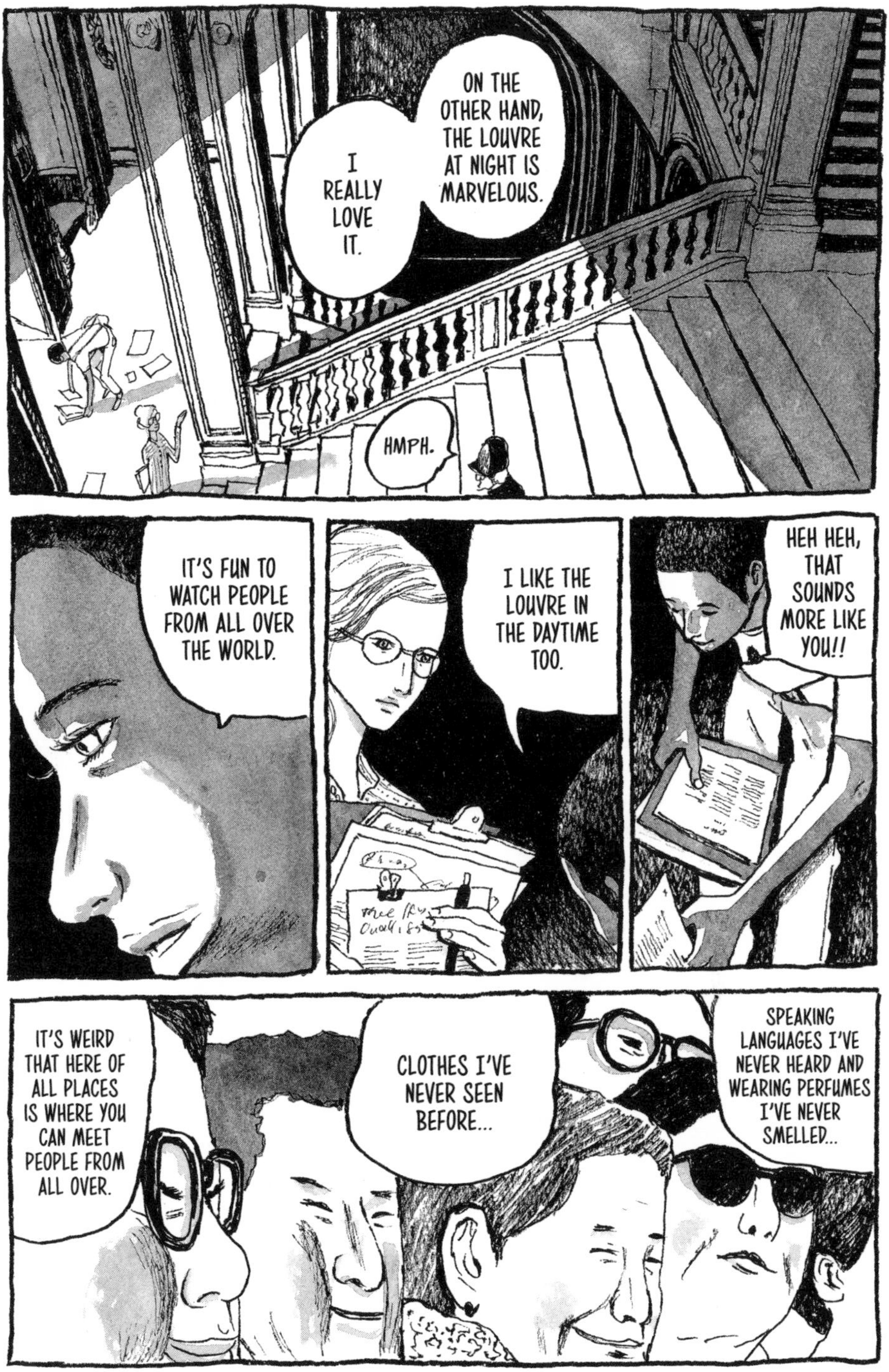
ON THE OTHER HAND, THE LOUVRE AT NIGHT IS MARVELOUS.
I REALLY LOVE IT.
HMPH.
HEH HEH, THAT SOUNDS MORE LIKE YOU!!
I LIKE THE LOUVRE IN THE DAYTIME TOO.
IT'S FUN TO WATCH PEOPLE FROM ALL OVER THE WORLD.
SPEAKING LANGUAGES I'VE NEVER HEARD AND WEARING PERFUMES I'VE NEVER SMELLED...
CLOTHES I'VE NEVER SEEN BEFORE...
IT'S WEIRD THAT HERE OF ALL PLACES IS WHERE YOU CAN MEET PEOPLE FROM ALL OVER.

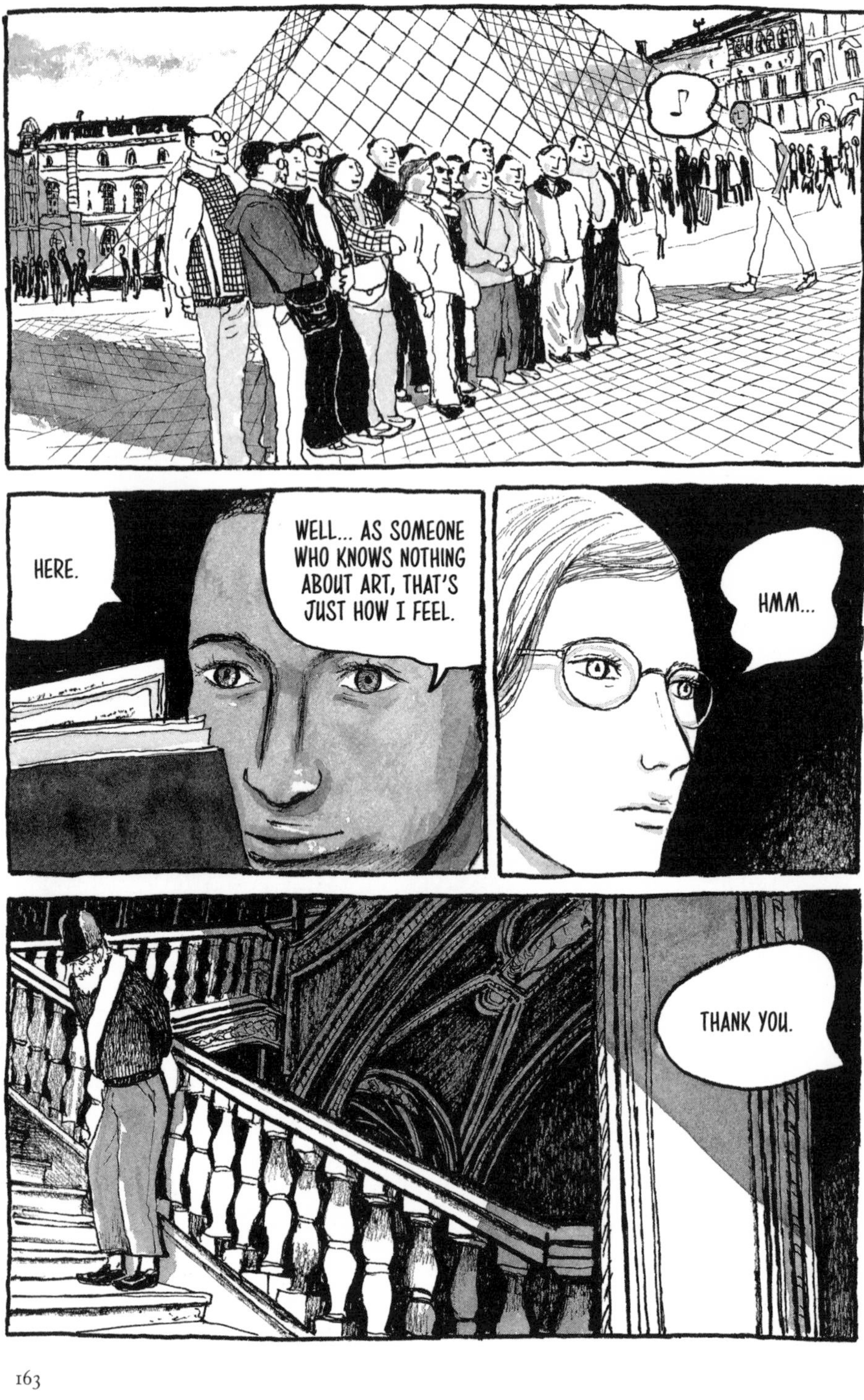
♪
HMM...
WELL... AS SOMEONE WHO KNOWS NOTHING ABOUT ART, THAT'S JUST HOW I FEEL.
HERE.
THANK YOU.

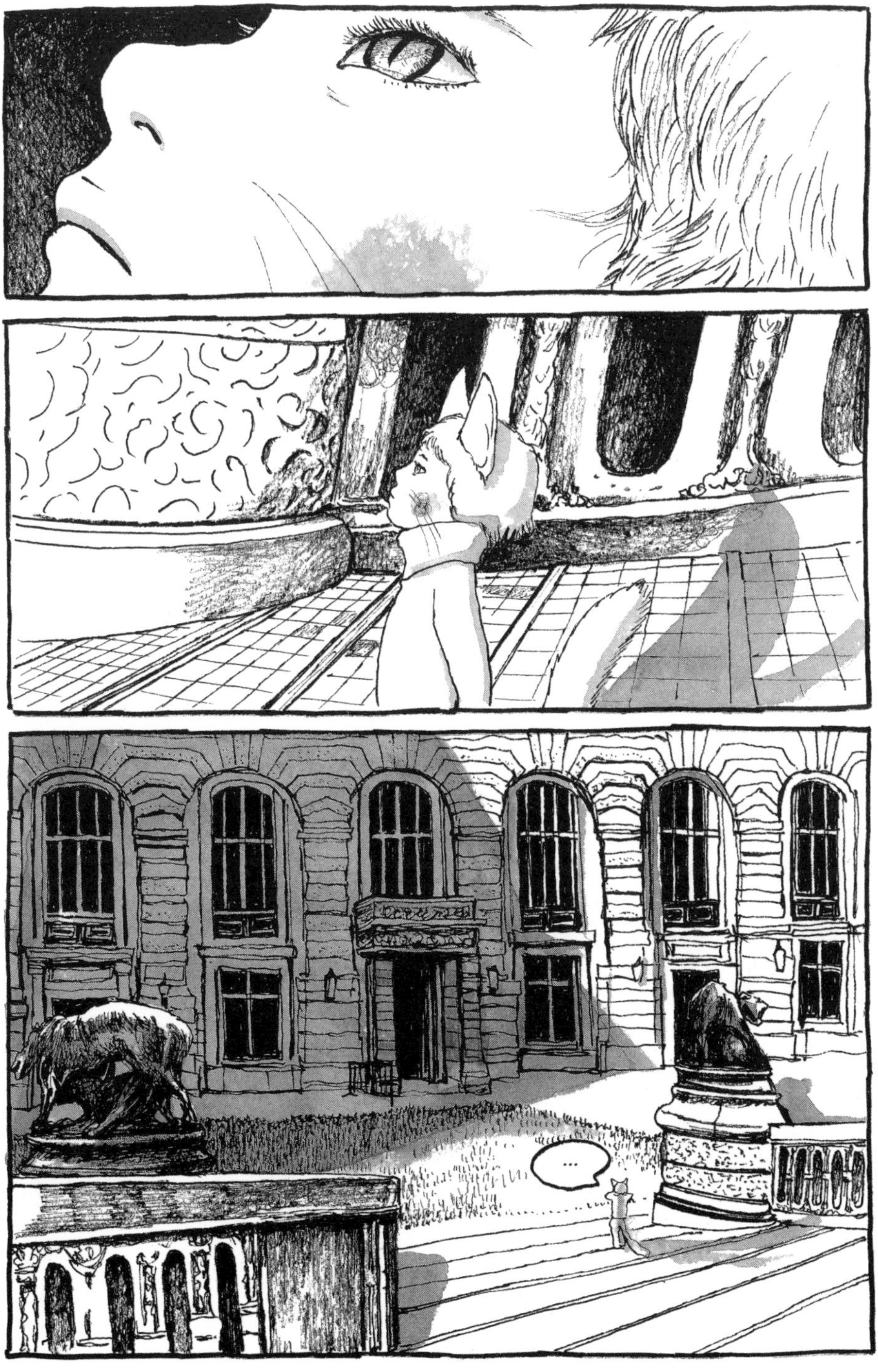
...

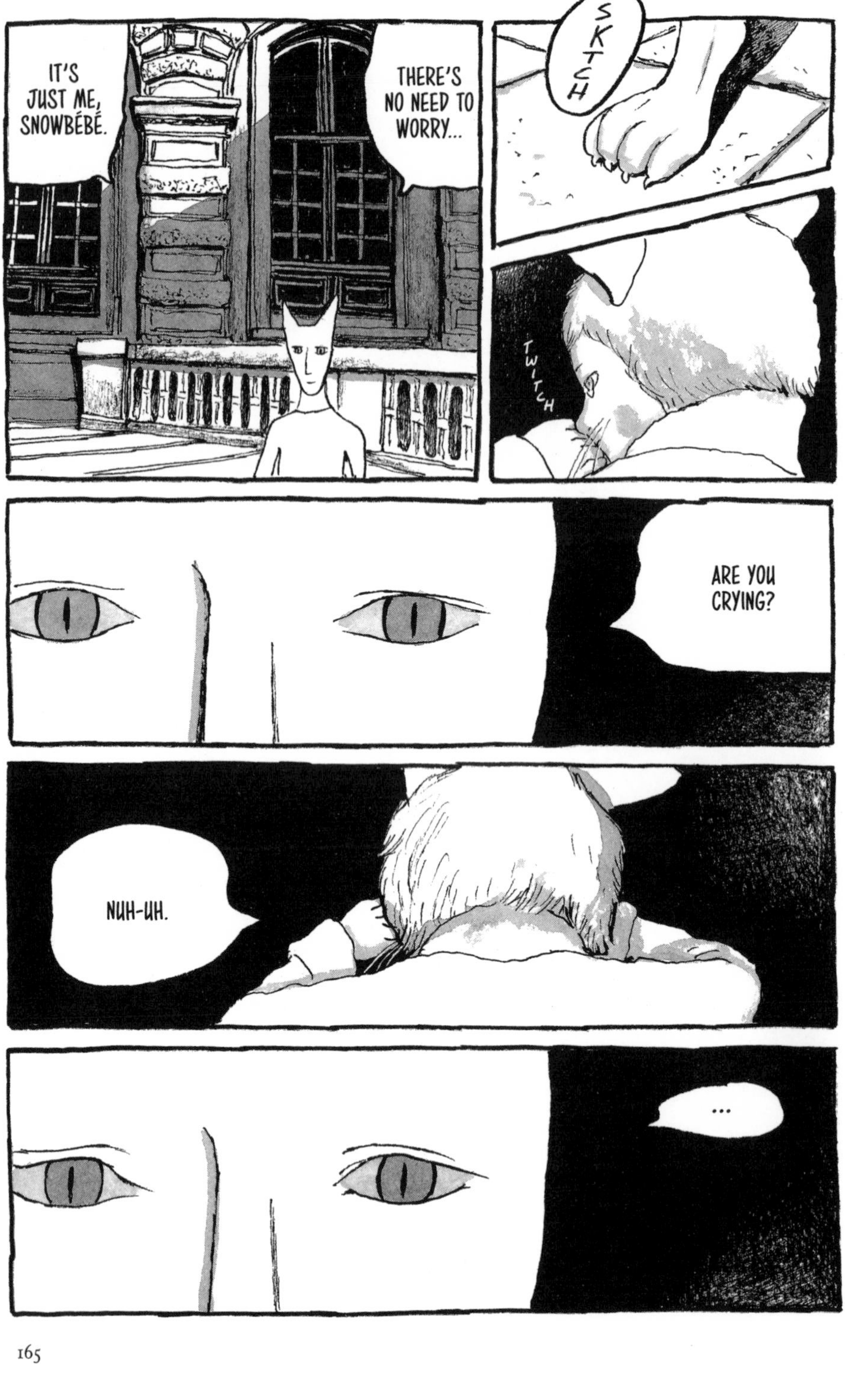
SKTCH
TWITCH
THERE'S NO NEED TO WORRY...
IT'S JUST ME, SNOWBÉBÉ.
ARE YOU CRYING?
NUH-UH.
...

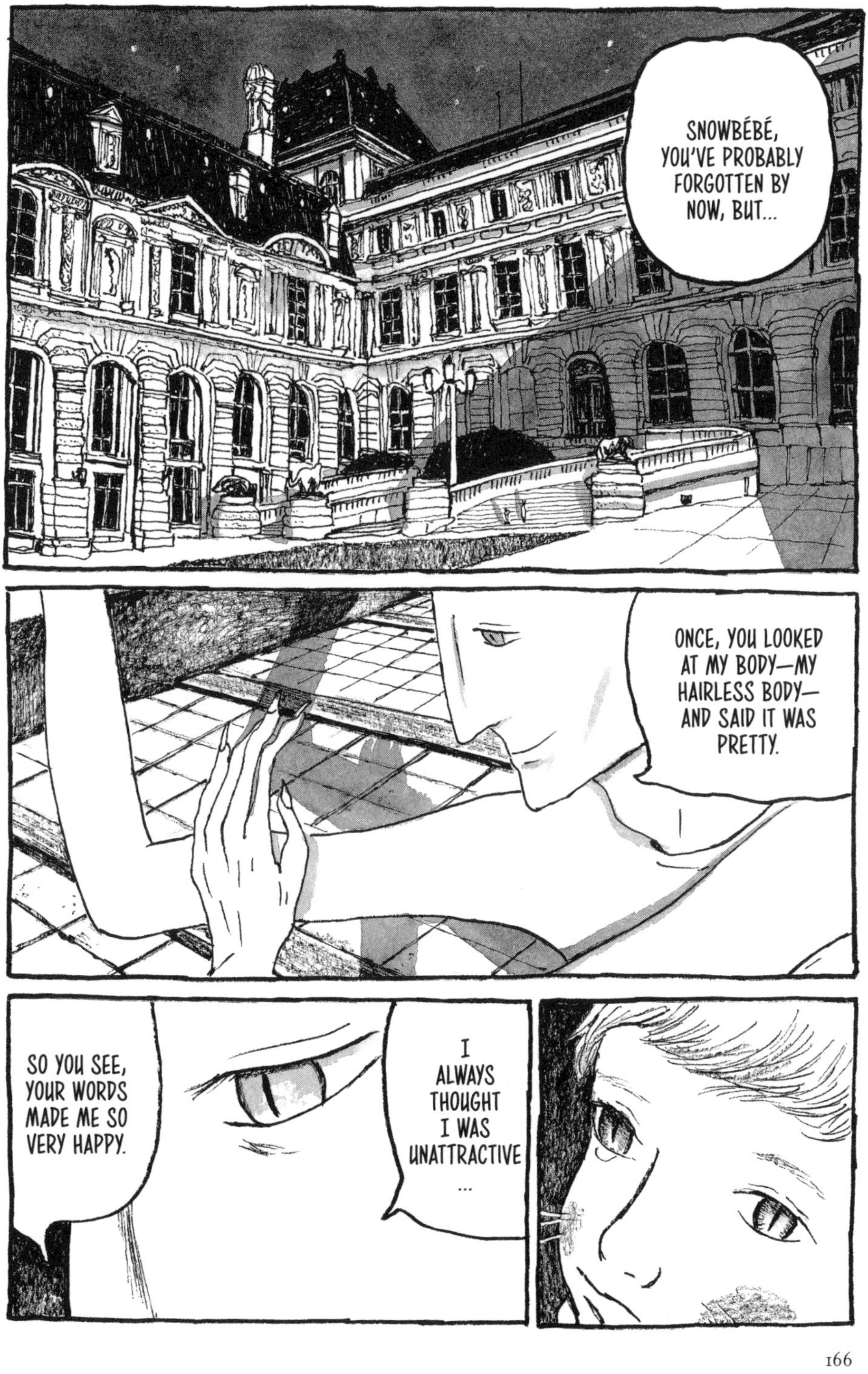
SNOWBÉBÉ, YOU'VE PROBABLY FORGOTTEN BY NOW, BUT...
ONCE, YOU LOOKED AT MY BODY—MY HAIRLESS BODY—AND SAID IT WAS PRETTY.
I ALWAYS THOUGHT I WAS UNATTRACTIVE...
SO YOU SEE, YOUR WORDS MADE ME SO VERY HAPPY.

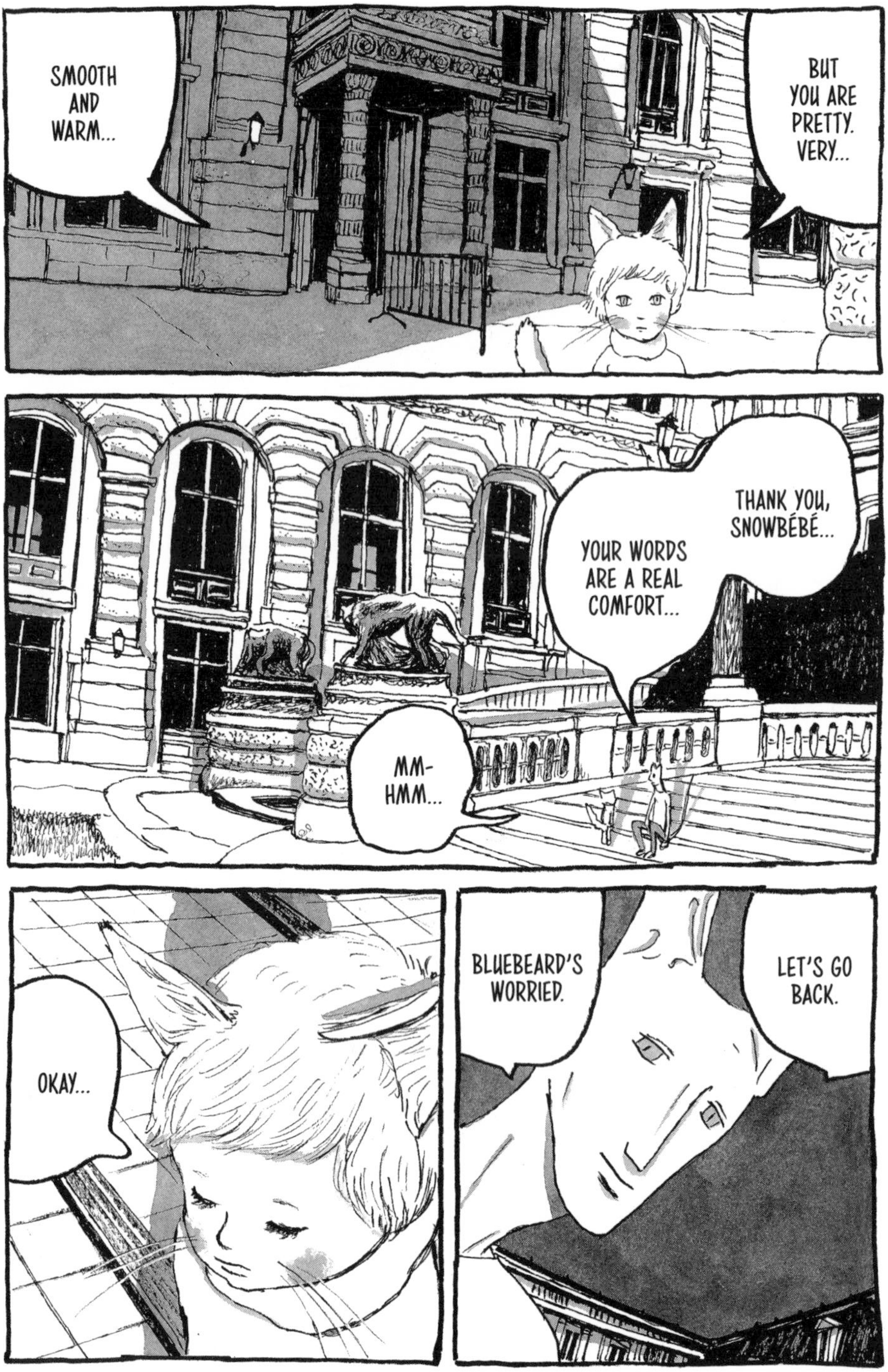
BUT YOU ARE PRETTY. VERY...
SMOOTH AND WARM...
THANK YOU, SNOWBÉBÉ...
YOUR WORDS ARE A REAL COMFORT...
MM-HMM...
LET'S GO BACK.
BLUEBEARD'S WORRIED.
OKAY...

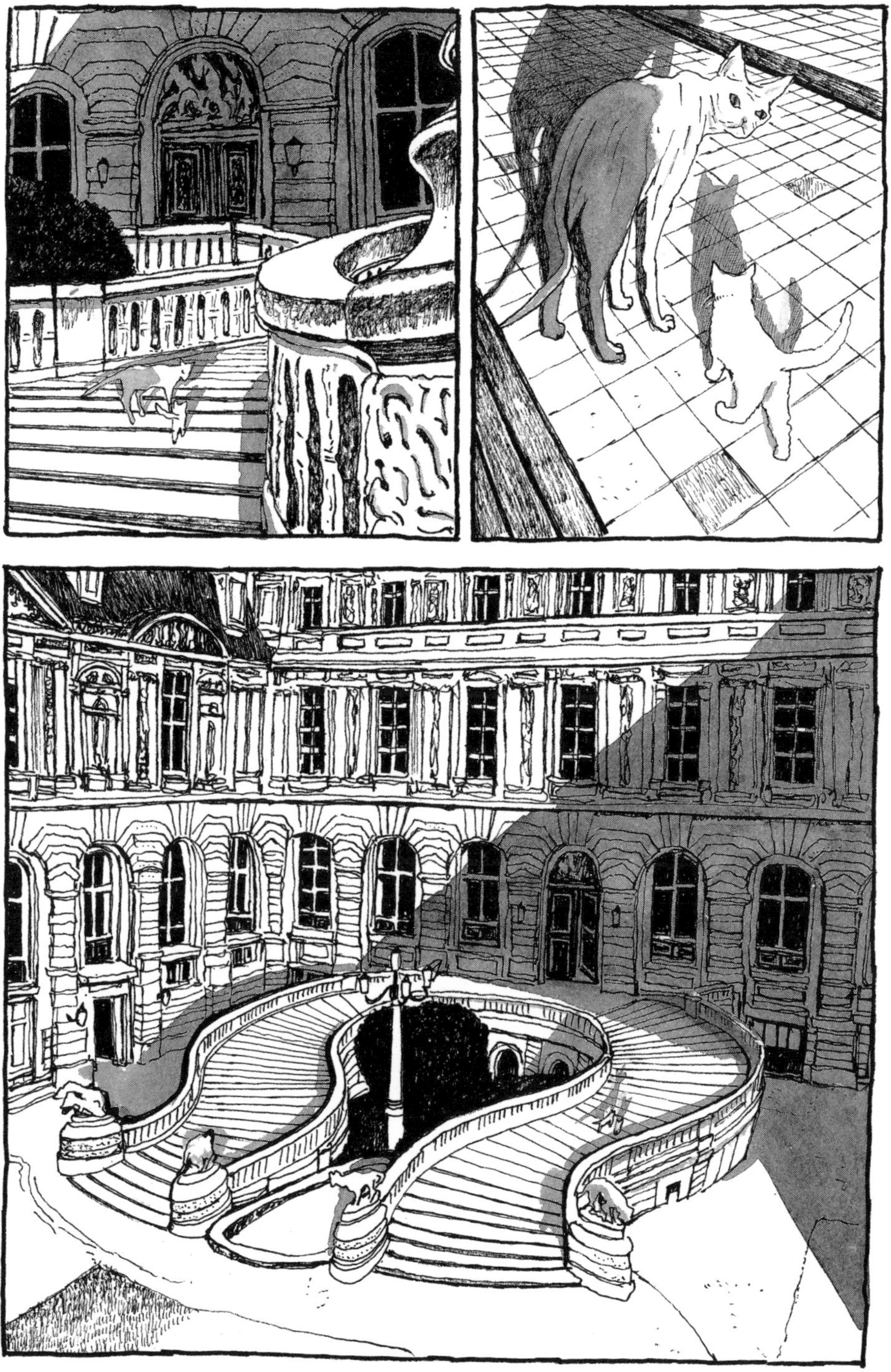

CHAPTER 8

The Secret of the Little Spider

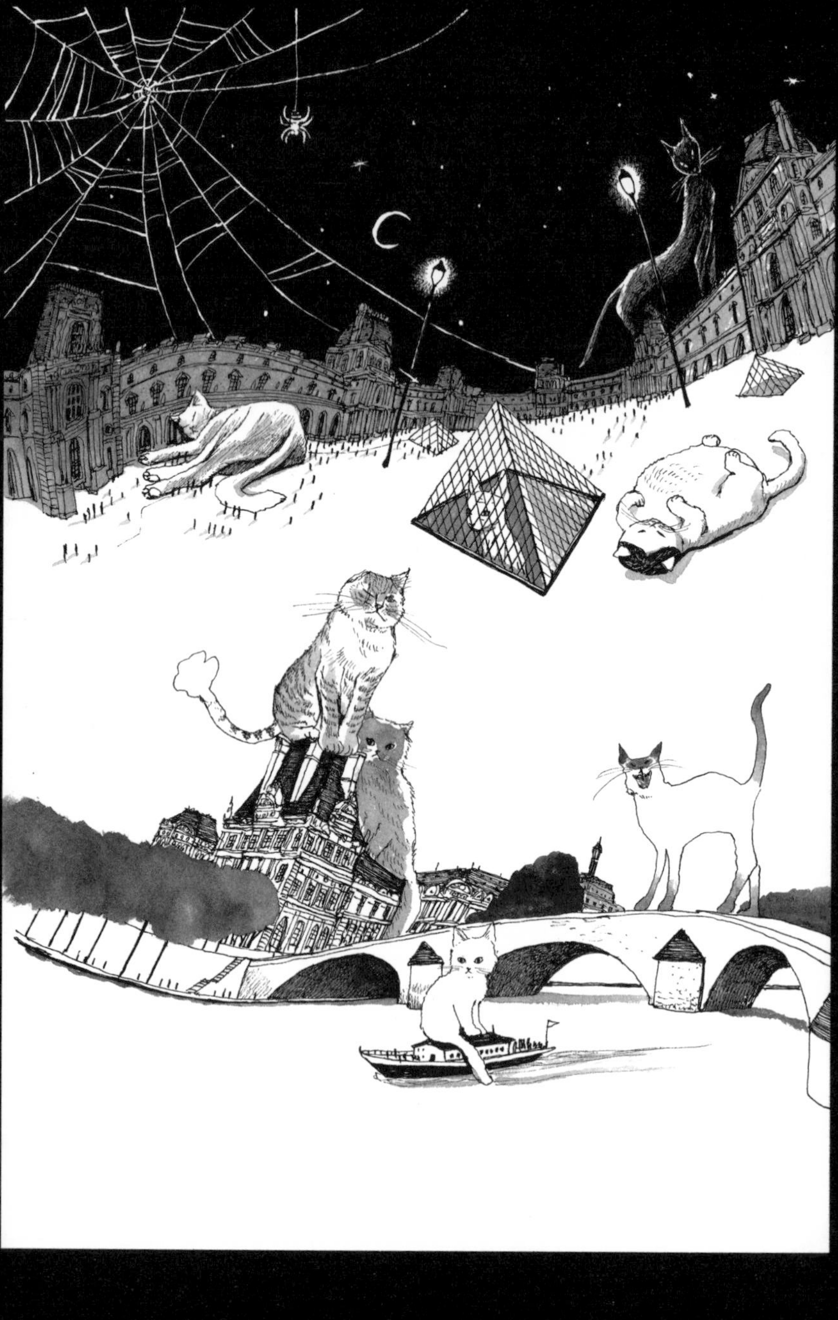

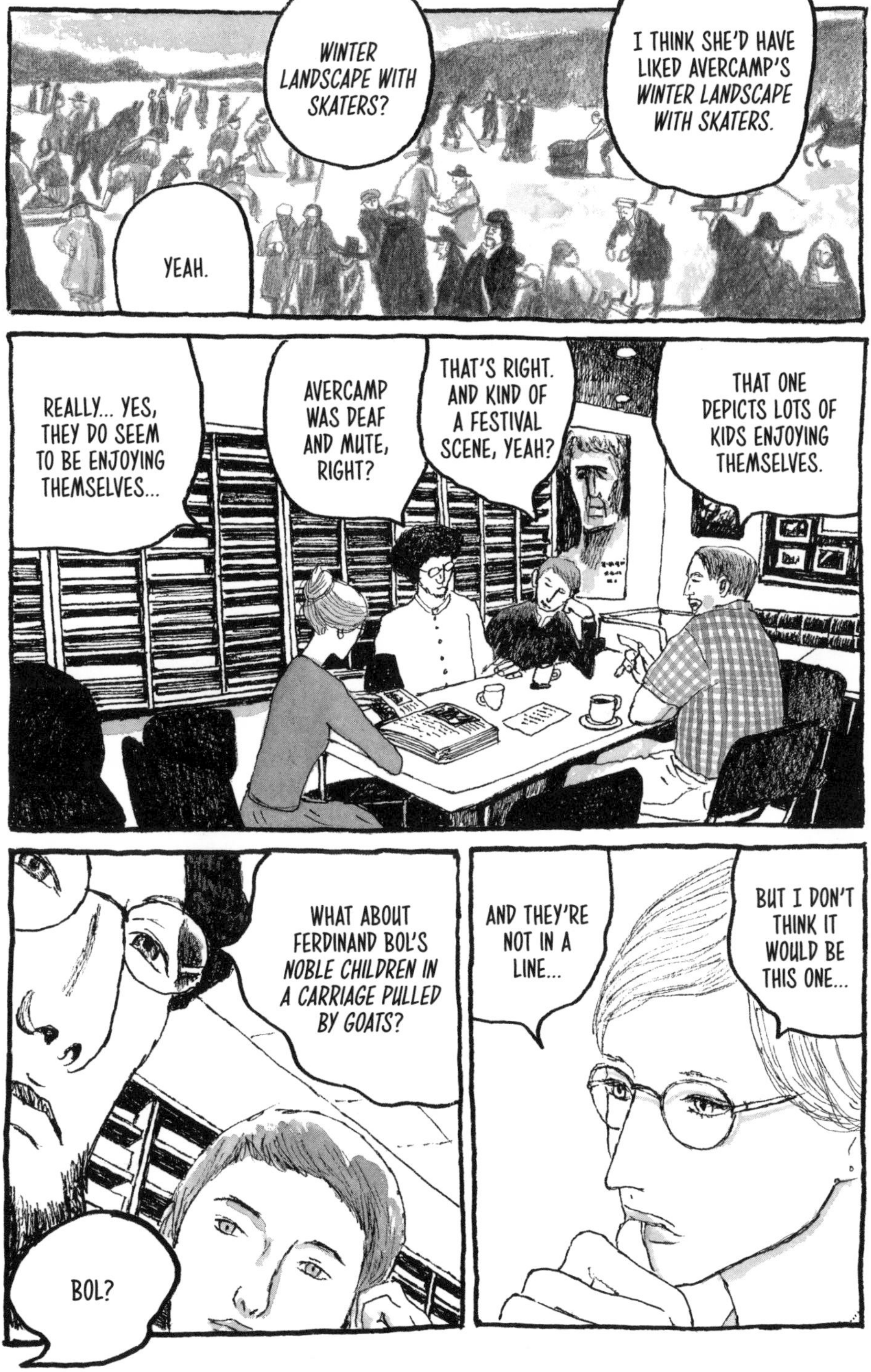
I THINK SHE'D HAVE LIKED AVERCAMP'S *WINTER LANDSCAPE WITH SKATERS.*
WINTER LANDSCAPE WITH SKATERS?
YEAH.
THAT ONE DEPICTS LOTS OF KIDS ENJOYING THEMSELVES.
THAT'S RIGHT. AND KIND OF A FESTIVAL SCENE, YEAH?
AVERCAMP WAS DEAF AND MUTE, RIGHT?
REALLY... YES, THEY DO SEEM TO BE ENJOYING THEMSELVES...
BUT I DON'T THINK IT WOULD BE THIS ONE...
AND THEY'RE NOT IN A LINE...
WHAT ABOUT FERDINAND BOL'S *NOBLE CHILDREN IN A CARRIAGE PULLED BY GOATS?*
BOL?

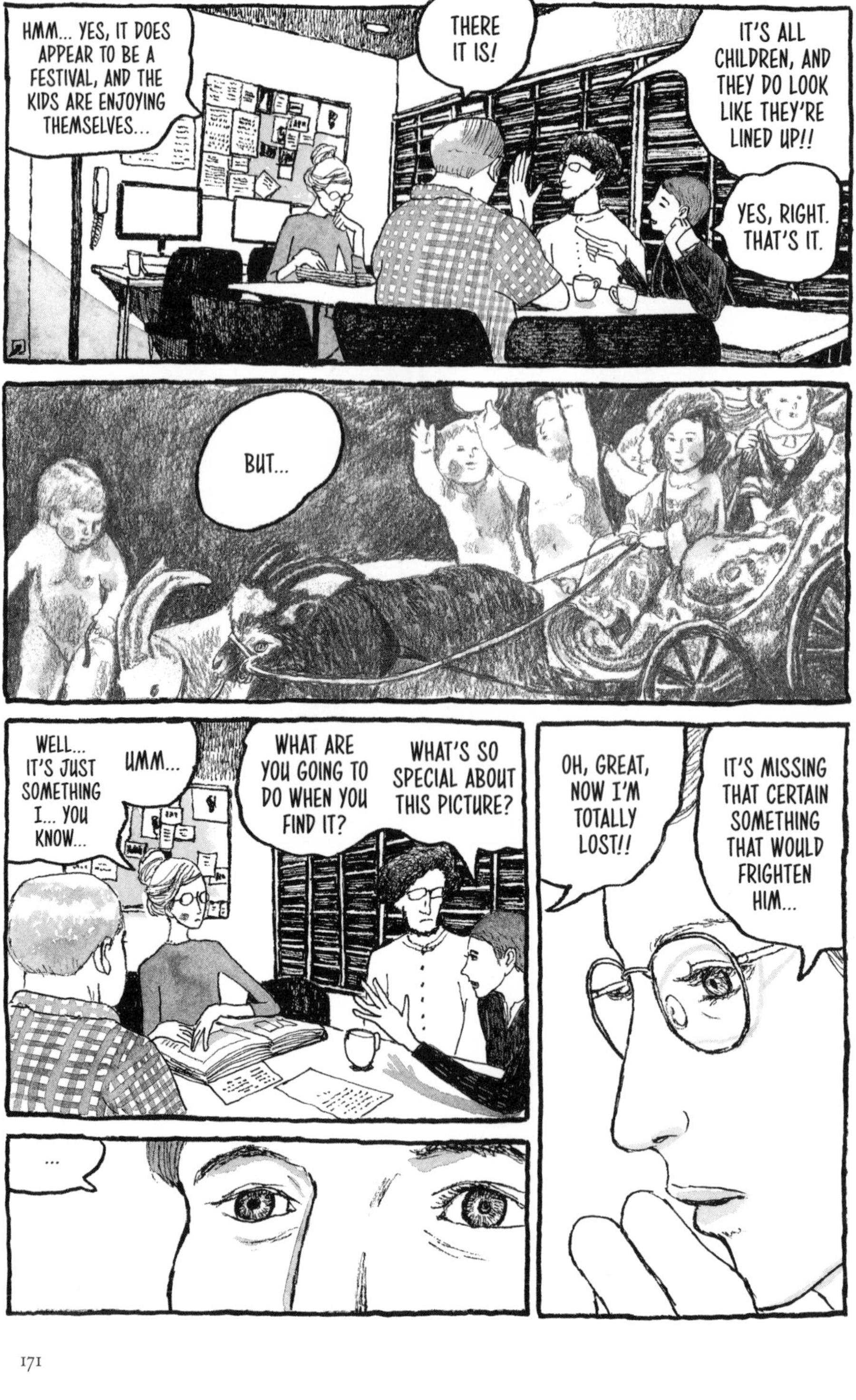
IT'S ALL CHILDREN, AND THEY DO LOOK LIKE THEY'RE LINED UP!!
YES, RIGHT. THAT'S IT.
THERE IT IS!
HMM... YES, IT DOES APPEAR TO BE A FESTIVAL, AND THE KIDS ARE ENJOYING THEMSELVES...
BUT...
IT'S MISSING THAT CERTAIN SOMETHING THAT WOULD FRIGHTEN HIM...
OH, GREAT, NOW I'M TOTALLY LOST!!
WHAT'S SO SPECIAL ABOUT THIS PICTURE?
WHAT ARE YOU GOING TO DO WHEN YOU FIND IT?
UMM...
WELL... IT'S JUST SOMETHING I... YOU KNOW...
...

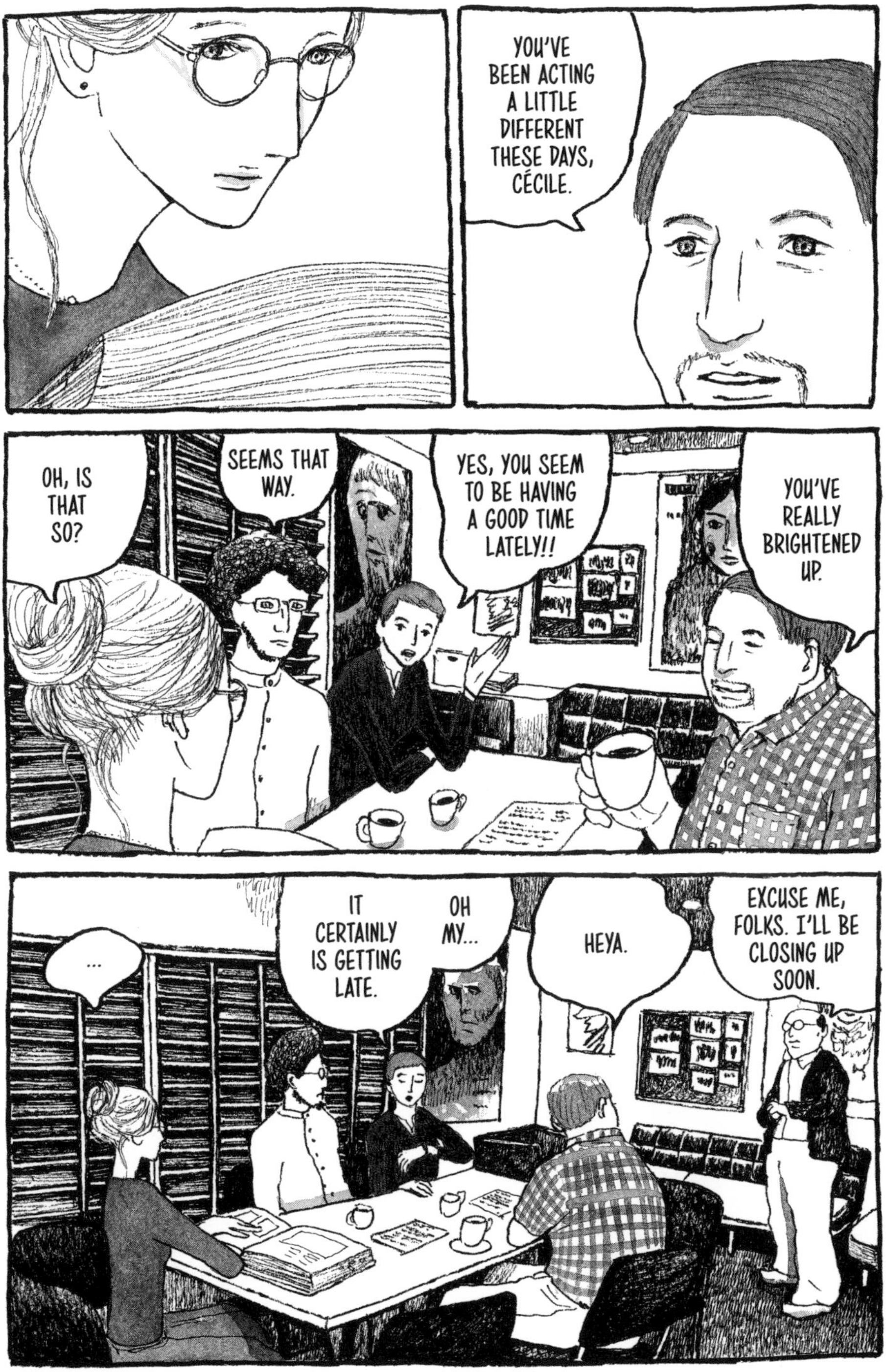
YOU'VE BEEN ACTING A LITTLE DIFFERENT THESE DAYS, CÉCILE.
YOU'VE REALLY BRIGHTENED UP.
YES, YOU SEEM TO BE HAVING A GOOD TIME LATELY!!
SEEMS THAT WAY.
OH, IS THAT SO?
EXCUSE ME, FOLKS. I'LL BE CLOSING UP SOON.
HEYA.
OH MY...
IT CERTAINLY IS GETTING LATE.
...

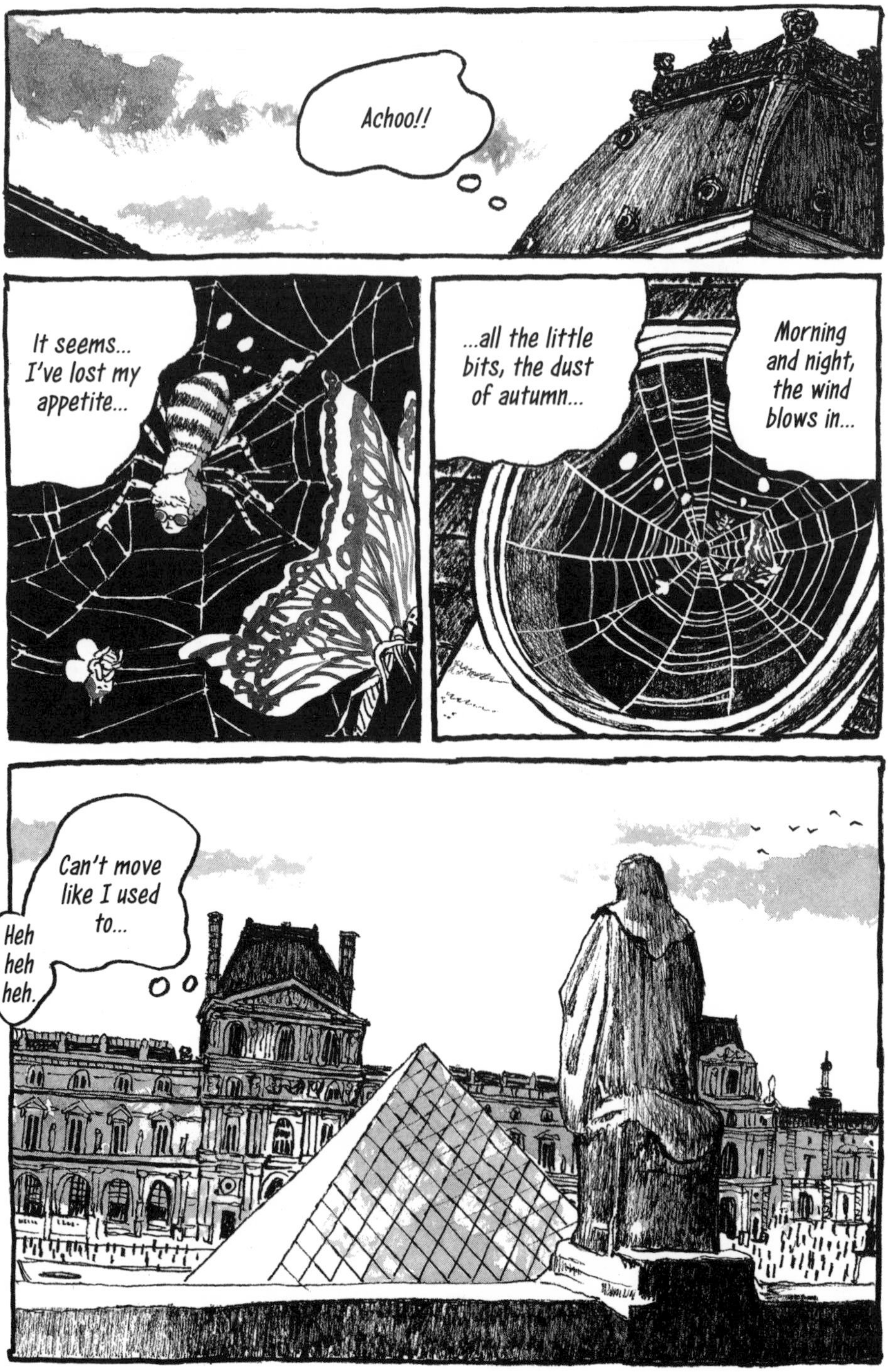
Achoo!!
Morning and night, the wind blows in...
...all the little bits, the dust of autumn...
It seems... I've lost my appetite...
Can't move like I used to...
Heh heh heh.

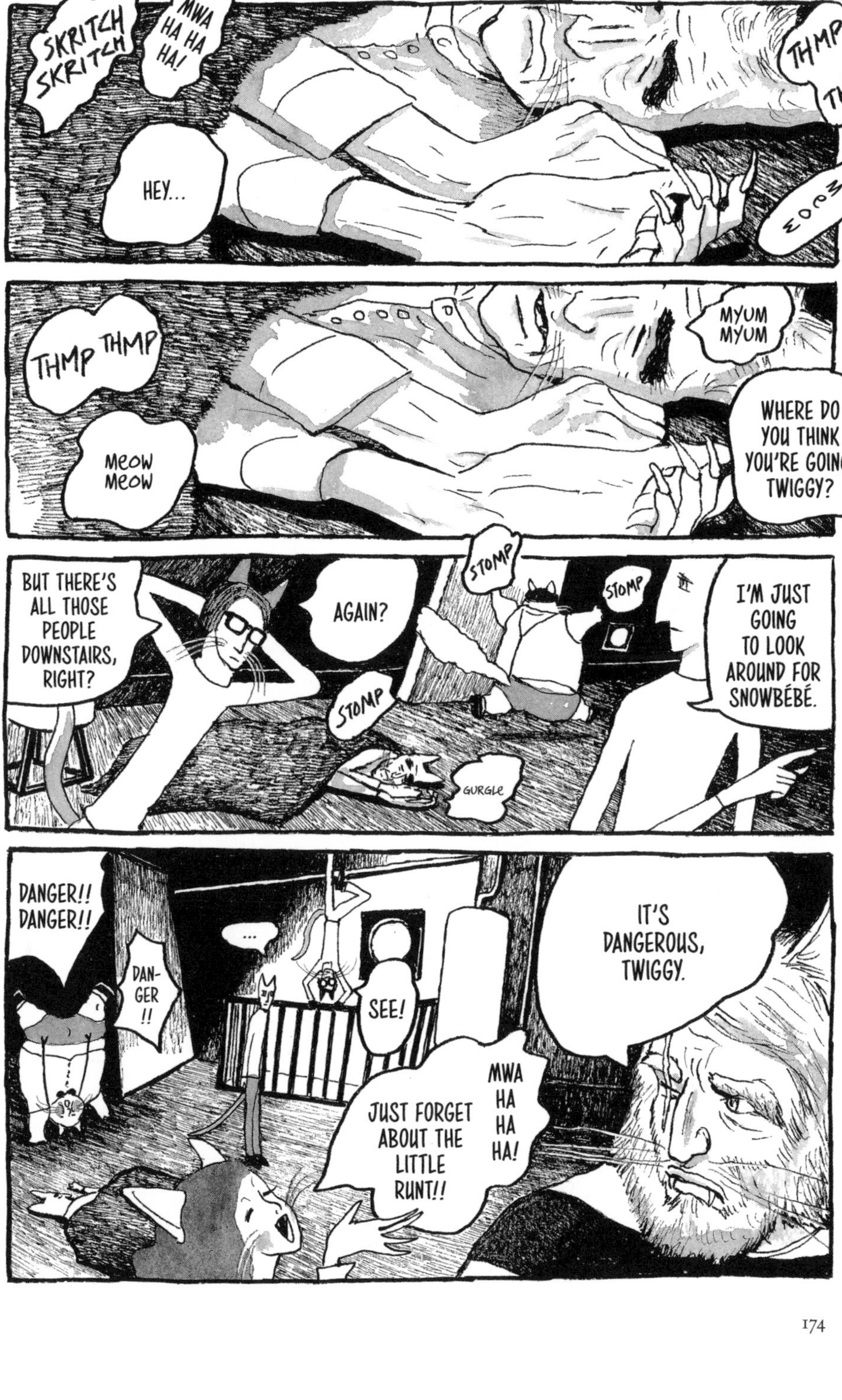
THMP THMP
MWA HA HA HA!
SKRITCH SKRITCH
HEY...
MYUM MYUM
WHERE DO YOU THINK YOU'RE GOING, TWIGGY?
THMP THMP
MEOW MEOW
I'M JUST GOING TO LOOK AROUND FOR SNOWBÉBÉ.
STOMP
STOMP
AGAIN?
BUT THERE'S ALL THOSE PEOPLE DOWNSTAIRS, RIGHT?
STOMP
GURGLE
IT'S DANGEROUS, TWIGGY.
SEE!
MWA HA HA HA!
JUST FORGET ABOUT THE LITTLE RUNT!!
...
DAN-GER!!
DANGER!! DANGER!!

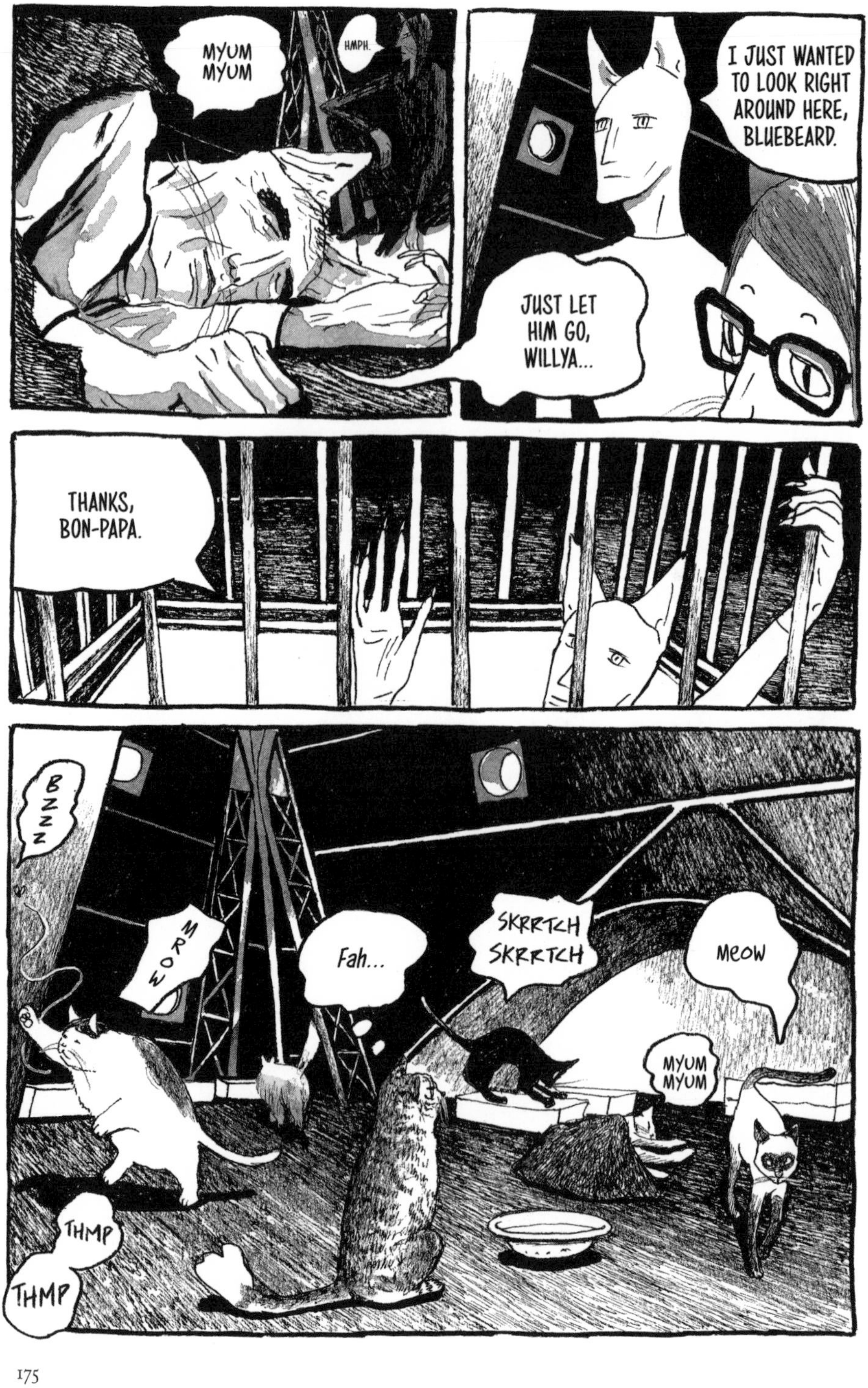
I JUST WANTED TO LOOK RIGHT AROUND HERE, BLUEBEARD.
JUST LET HIM GO, WILLYA...
MYUM MYUM
HMPH.
THANKS, BON-PAPA.
Meow
SKRRTCH SKRRTCH
MYUM MYUM
Fah...
MROW
BZZZ
THMP
THMP

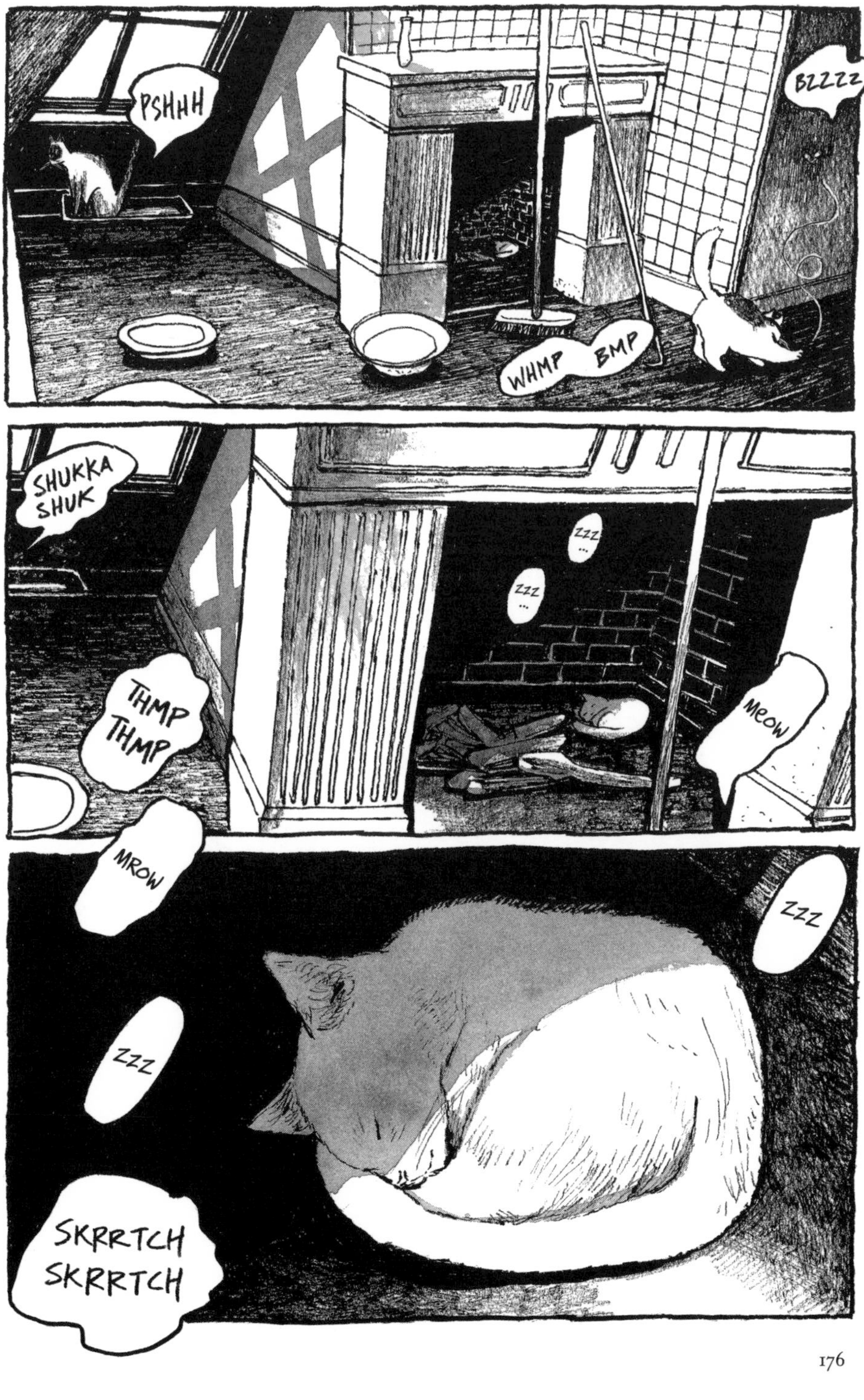
BZZZZ
PSHHH
BMP
WHMP
ZZZ...
ZZZ...
SHUKKA SHUK
MEOW
THMP THMP
ZZZ
MROW
ZZZ
SKRRTCH SKRRTCH

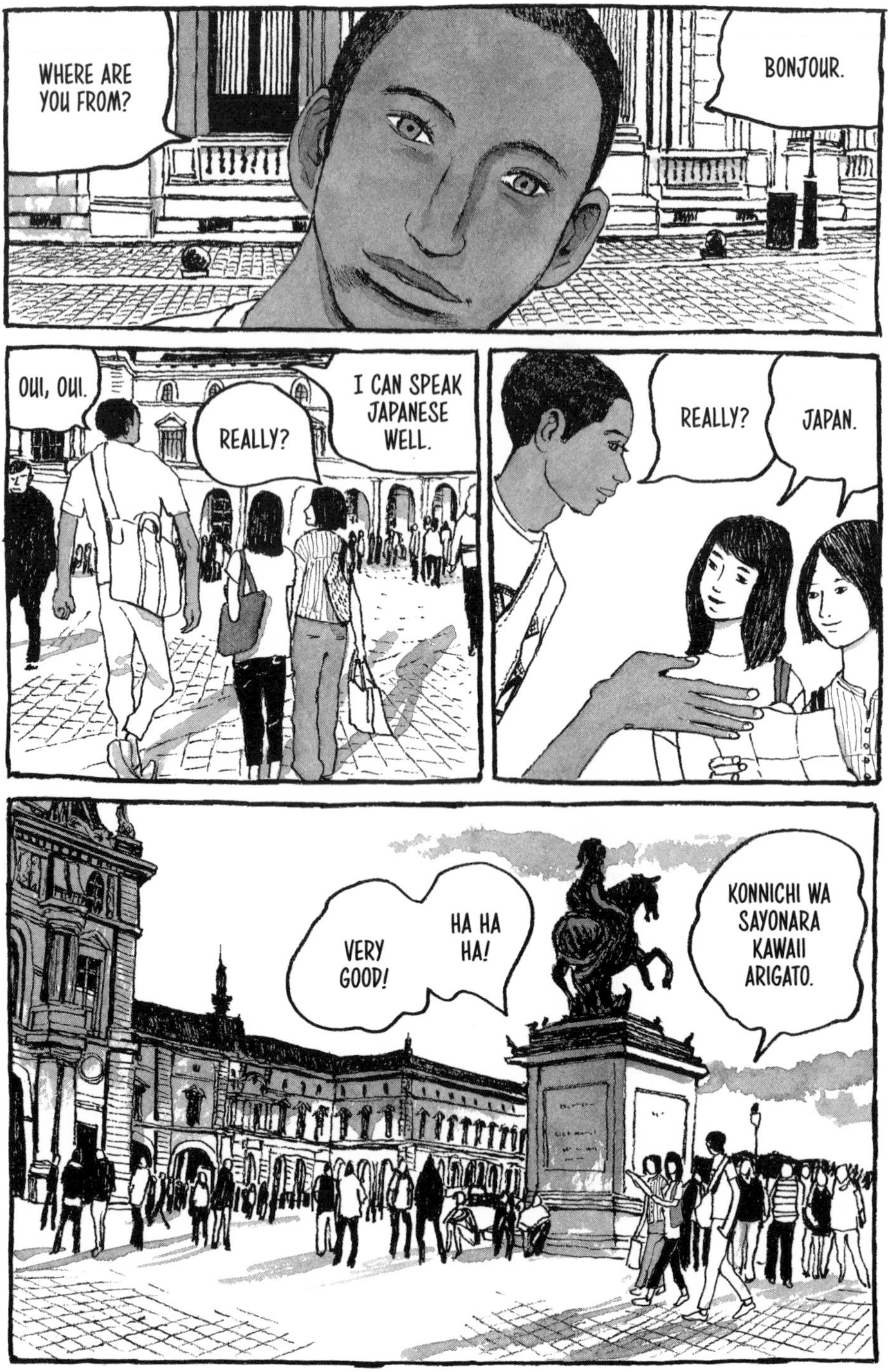
BONJOUR.
WHERE ARE YOU FROM?
JAPAN.
REALLY?
I CAN SPEAK JAPANESE WELL.
REALLY?
OUI, OUI.
KONNICHI WA SAYONARA KAWAII ARIGATO.
HA HA HA!
VERY GOOD!

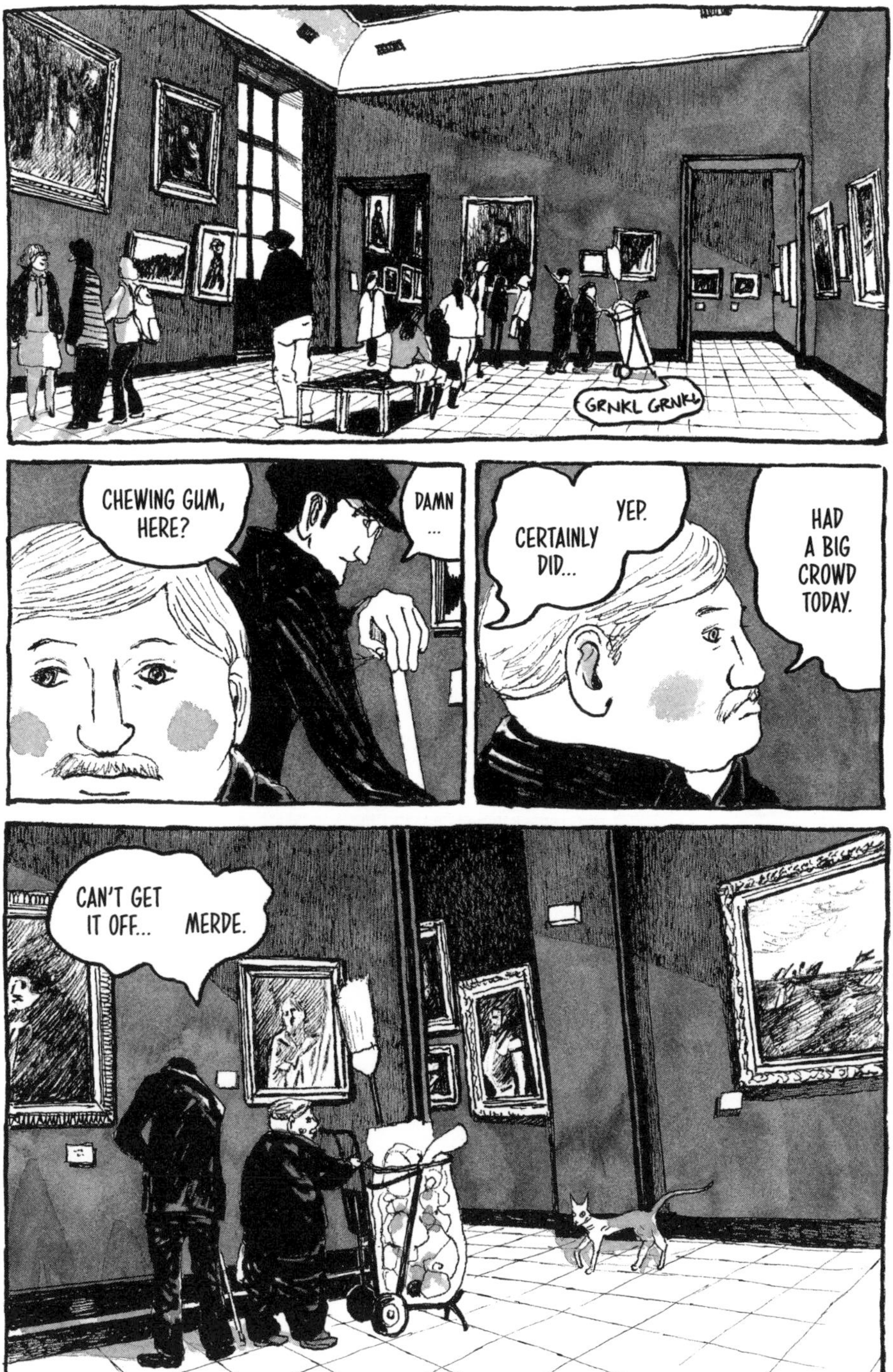
GRNKL GRNKL
HAD A BIG CROWD TODAY.
CERTAINLY DID... YEP.
DAMN ...
CHEWING GUM, HERE?
CAN'T GET IT OFF... MERDE.

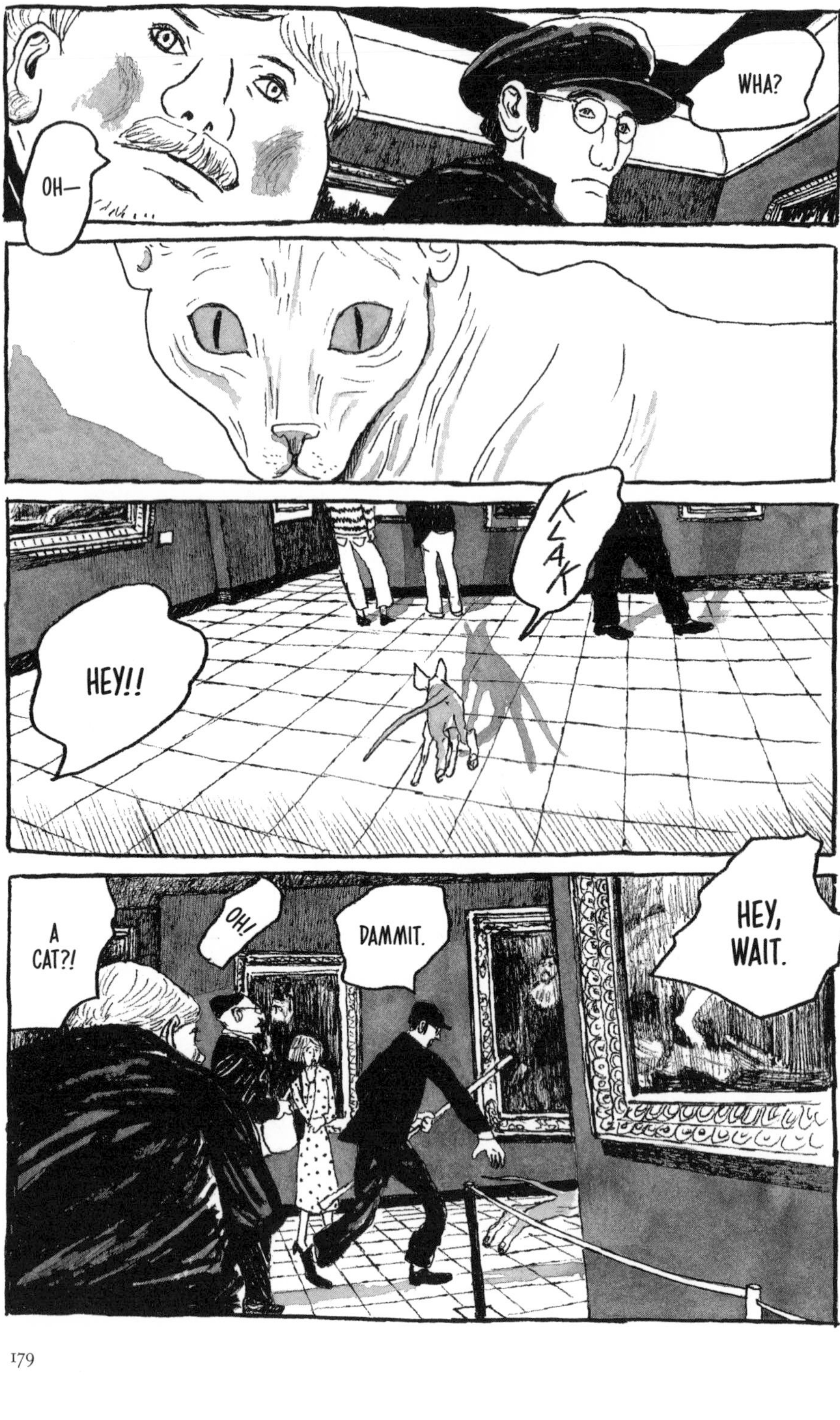
WHA?
OH—
KLAK
HEY!!
HEY, WAIT.
DAMMIT.
OH!
A CAT?!

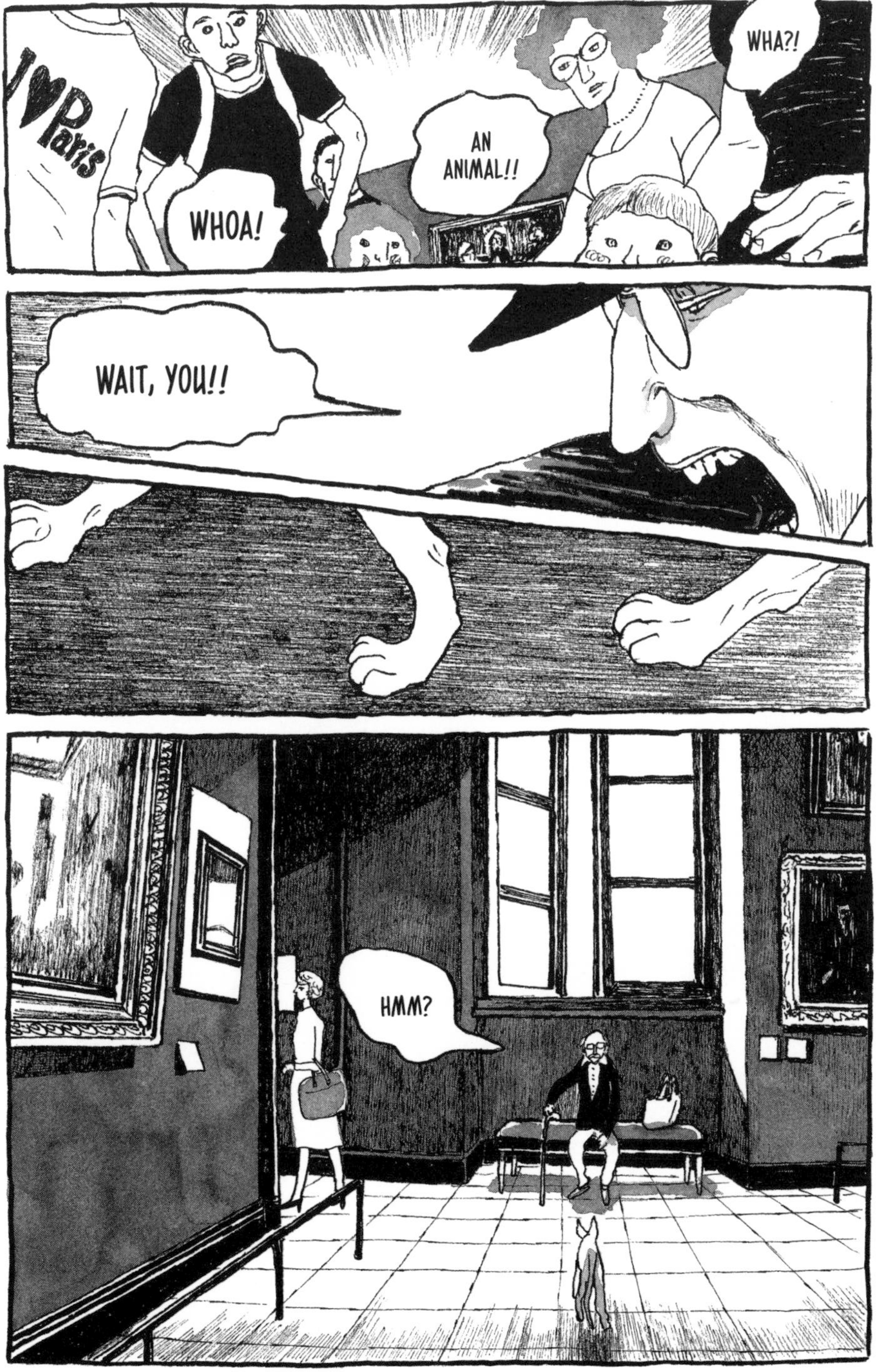
WHA?!
AN ANIMAL!!
WHOA!
Paris
WAIT, YOU!!
HMM?

GAH!
WHAP
HEY!
HE'S GOING OUTSIDE!!
HE WENT OUT THE WINDOW!!
HFF
HFF
HFF
MEOW...

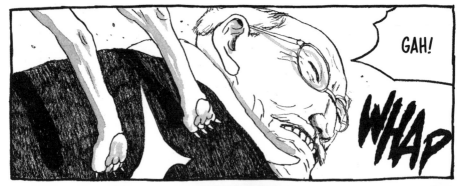

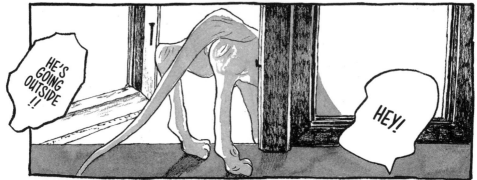

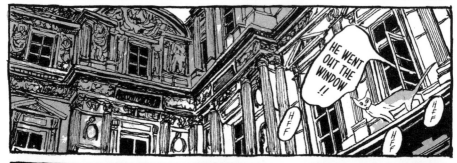

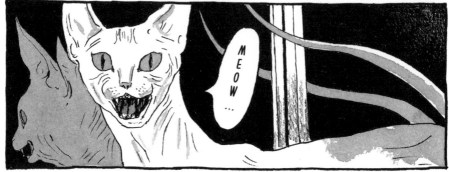

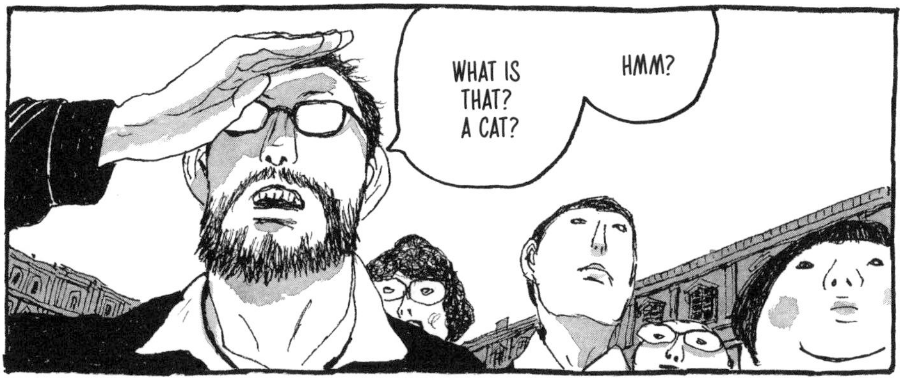
HMM?
WHAT IS THAT? A CAT?

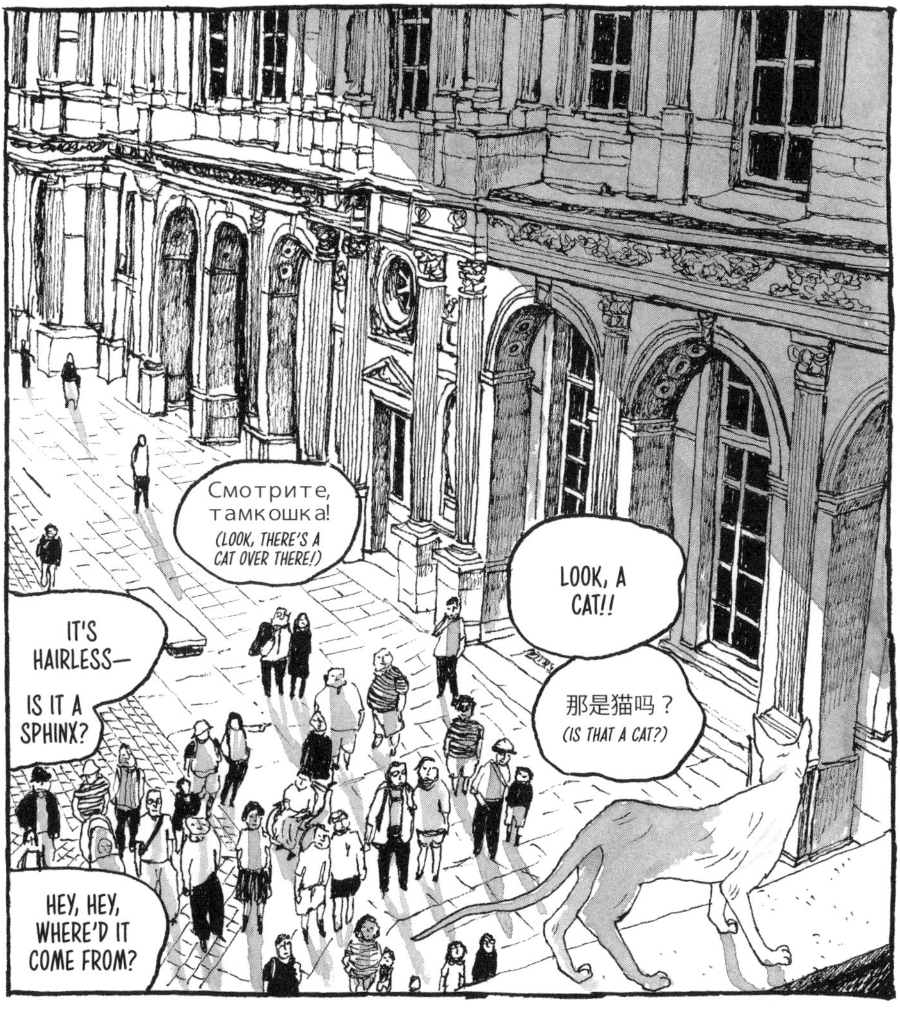
LOOK, A CAT!!
那是猫吗？
(IS THAT A CAT?)
Смотрите, тамкошка!
(LOOK, THERE'S A CAT OVER THERE!)
IT'S HAIRLESS— IS IT A SPHINX?
HEY, HEY, WHERE'D IT COME FROM?

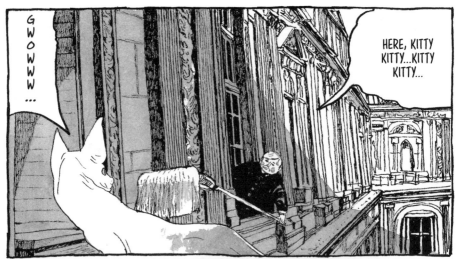

GWOWWW...

HERE, KITTY KITTY...KITTY KITTY...

BE CAREFUL, JAKOB. DON'T DROP IT.

HEY!!

HISSS!

SLIP SLIP

HERE, HERE, LITTLE HAIRLESS KITTY...

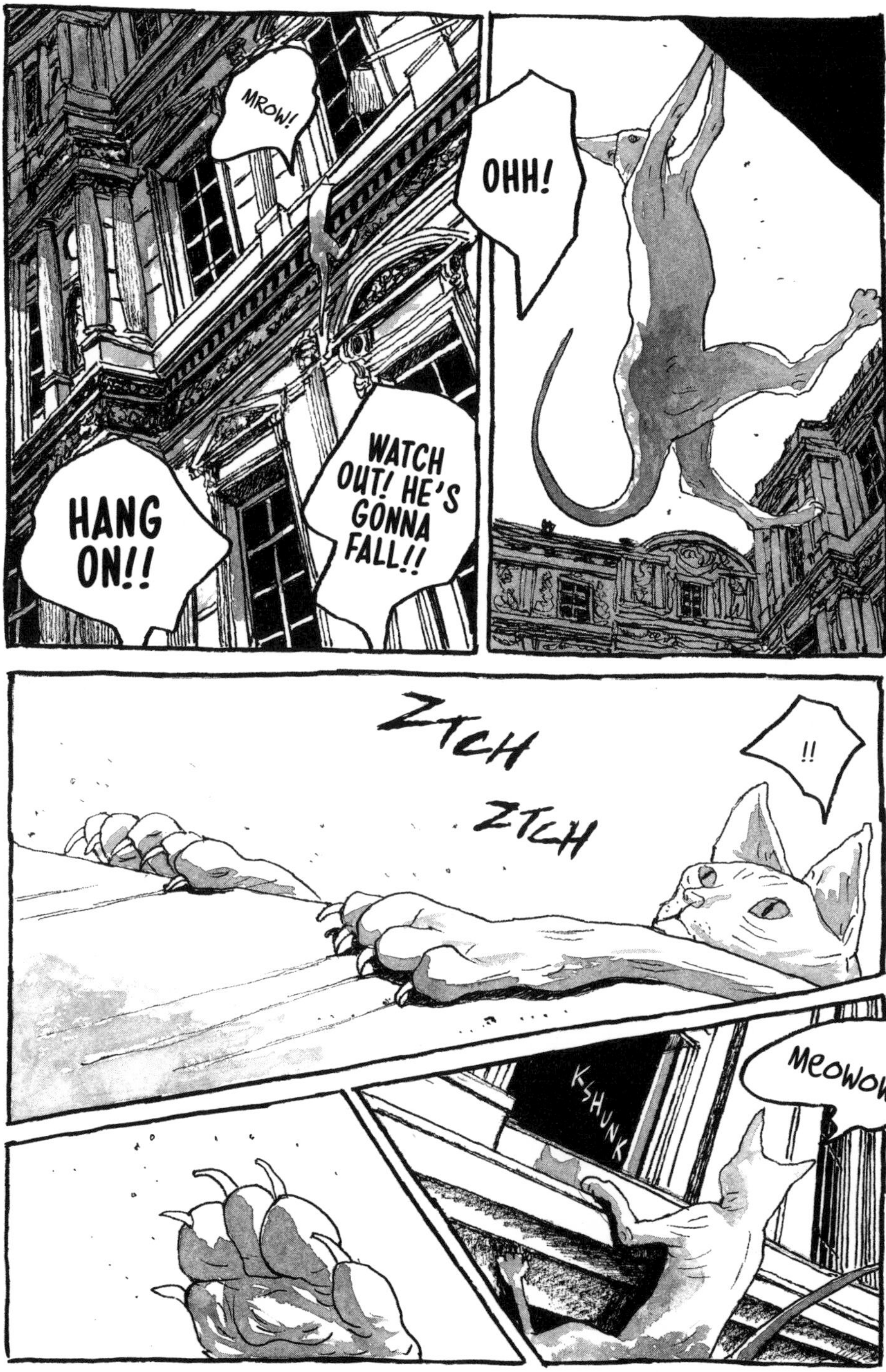
OHH!
MROW!
WATCH OUT! HE'S GONNA FALL!!
HANG ON!!
!!
ZTCH
ZTCH
MEOWOW!
KSHUNK

AHHH!

WHAT'S THE COMMOTION?

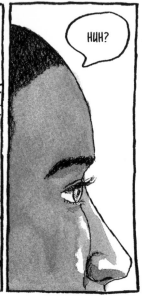

HUH?

HSSSHAA!
WAH!
OH... HIS LEG'S BROKEN...
WE SHOULD CALL THE INFIRMARY.
WHAT'S HAPPENING?
THERE'S A CAT RUNNING LOOSE...
WHAT?
?!
WHAT KINDA CAT IS THAT?
CAN'T BELIEVE IT SURVIVED A FALL LIKE THAT.
I CAN'T SEEEE!
SUCH A RUCKUS...
EXCUSE ME...
LET ME THROUGH!
OH.

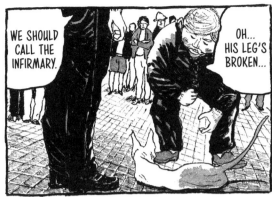

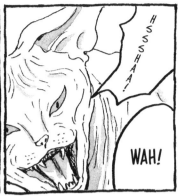

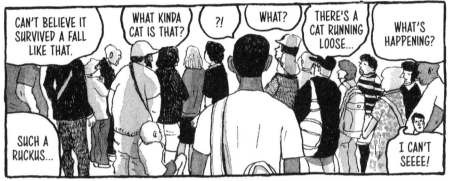

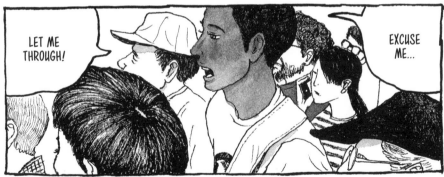

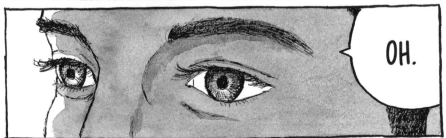

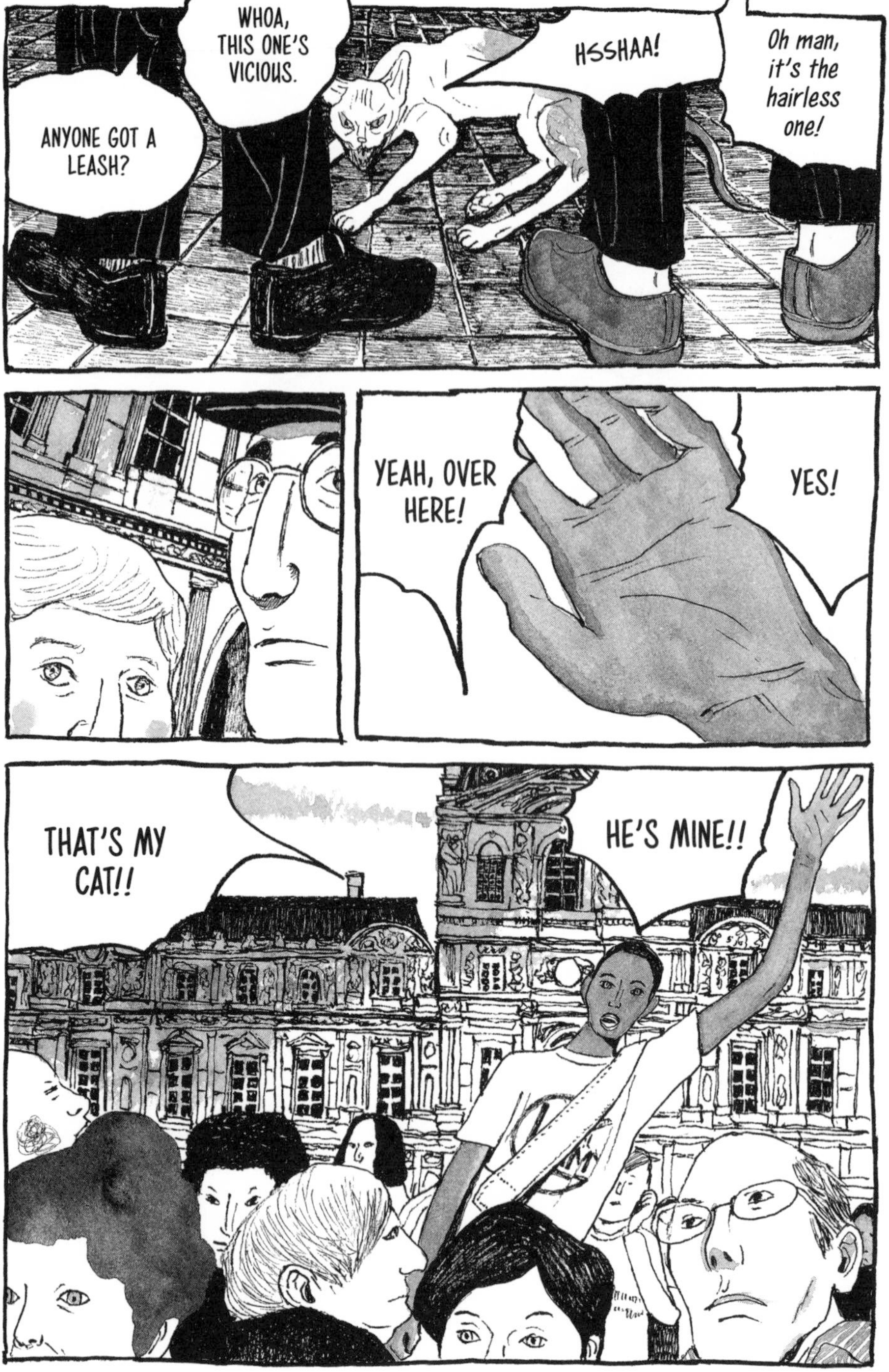
Oh man, it's the hairless one!
HSSHAA!
WHOA, THIS ONE'S VICIOUS.
ANYONE GOT A LEASH?
YES!
YEAH, OVER HERE!
HE'S MINE!!
THAT'S MY CAT!!

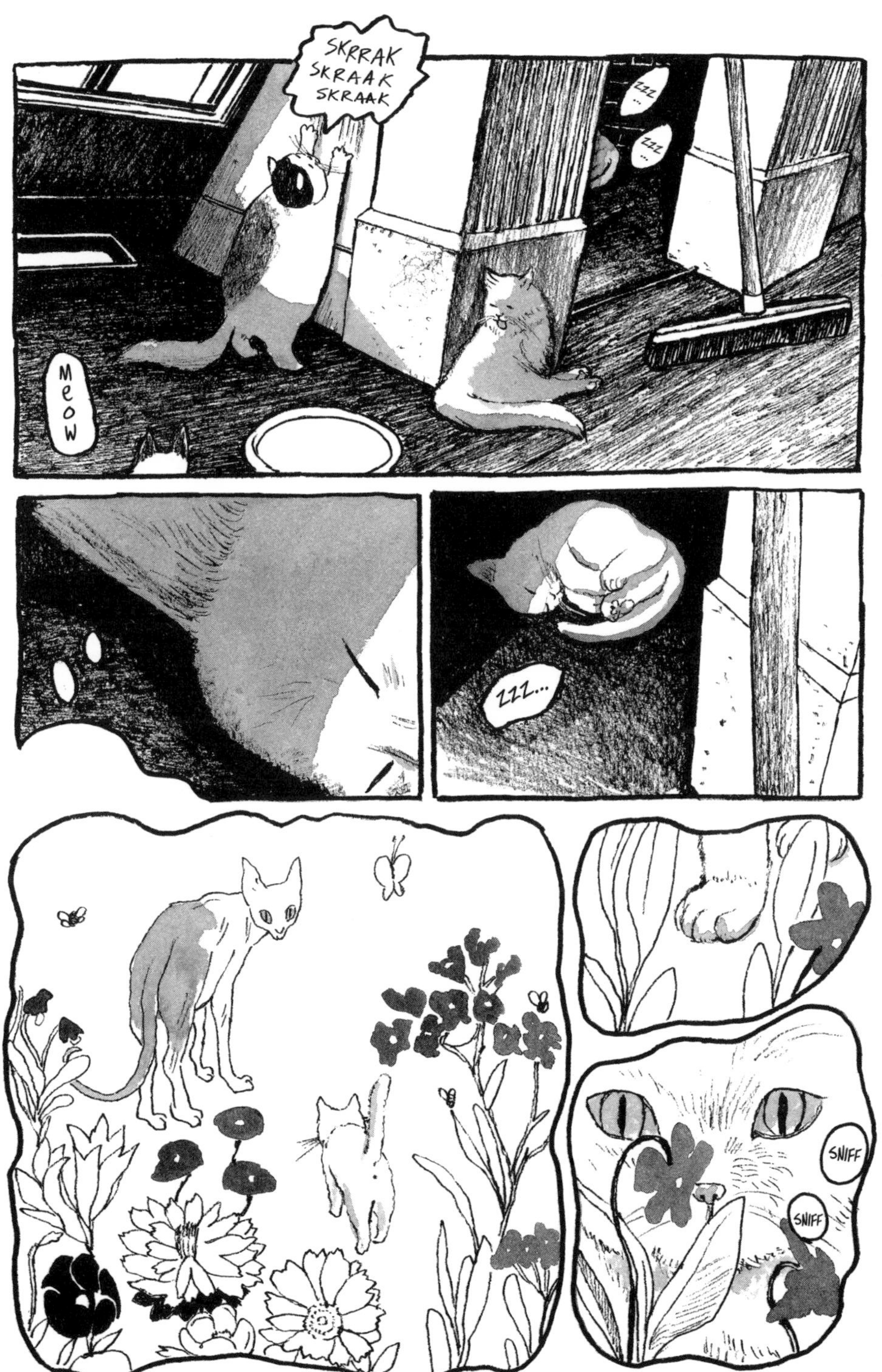
Zzz...
Zzz...
SKRRAK SKRAAK SKRAAK
MEOW
ZZZ...
SNIFF
SNIFF

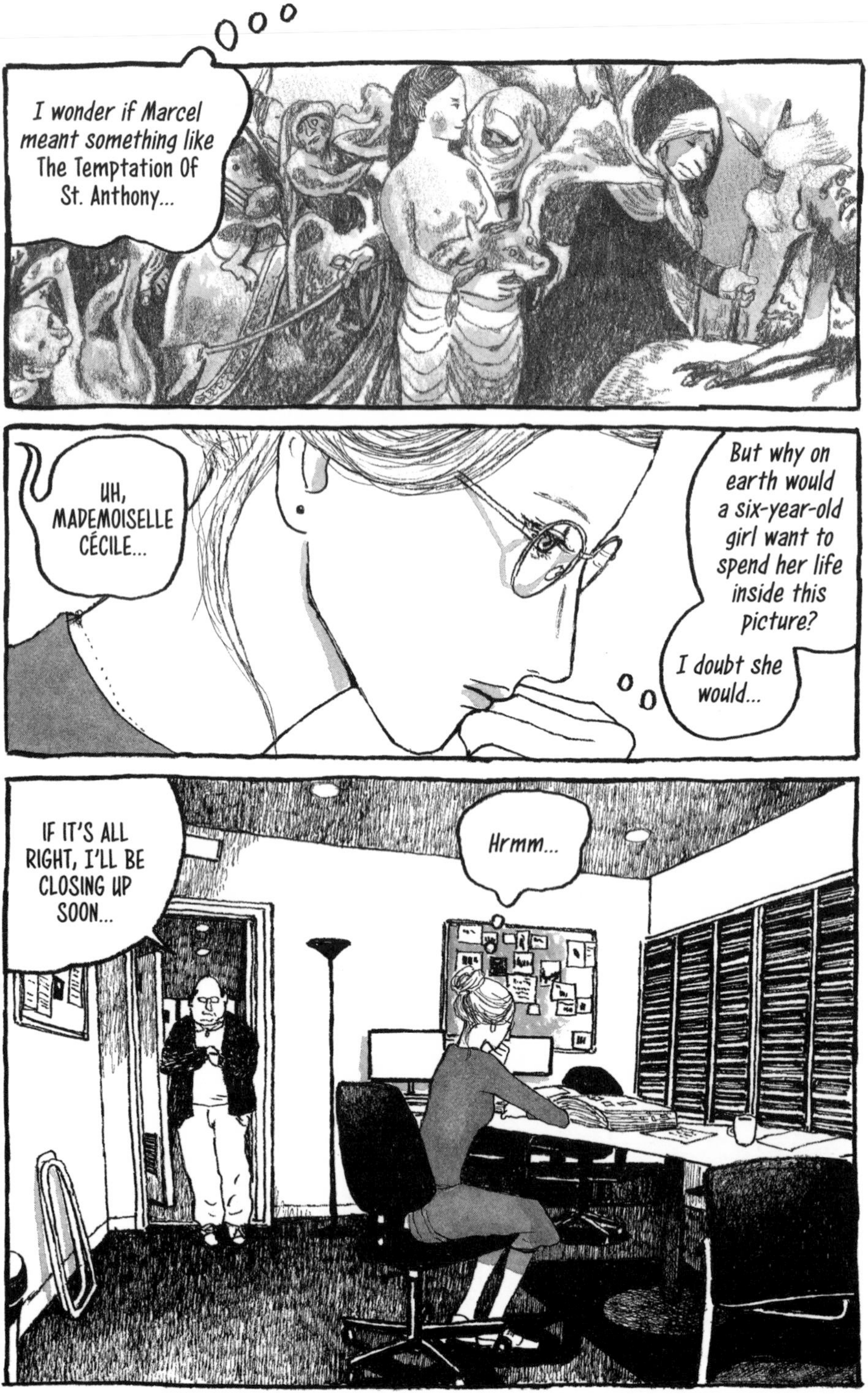
I wonder if Marcel meant something like The Temptation Of St. Anthony...
But why on earth would a six-year-old girl want to spend her life inside this picture?
I doubt she would...
UH, MADEMOISELLE CÉCILE...
Hrmm...
IF IT'S ALL RIGHT, I'LL BE CLOSING UP SOON...

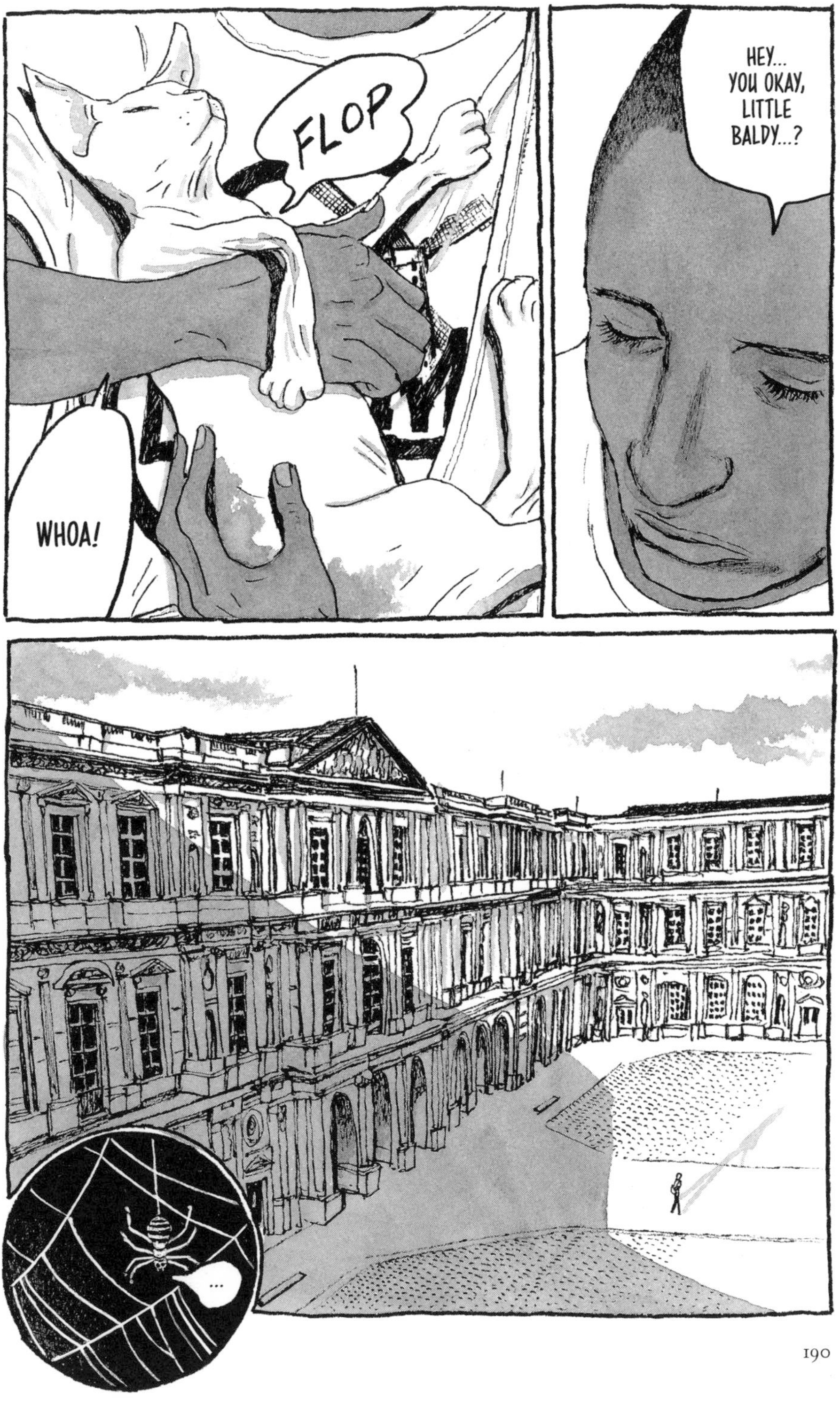
HEY... YOU OKAY, LITTLE BALDY...?
FLOP
WHOA!
...

CHAPTER 9

The Secret on the Roof

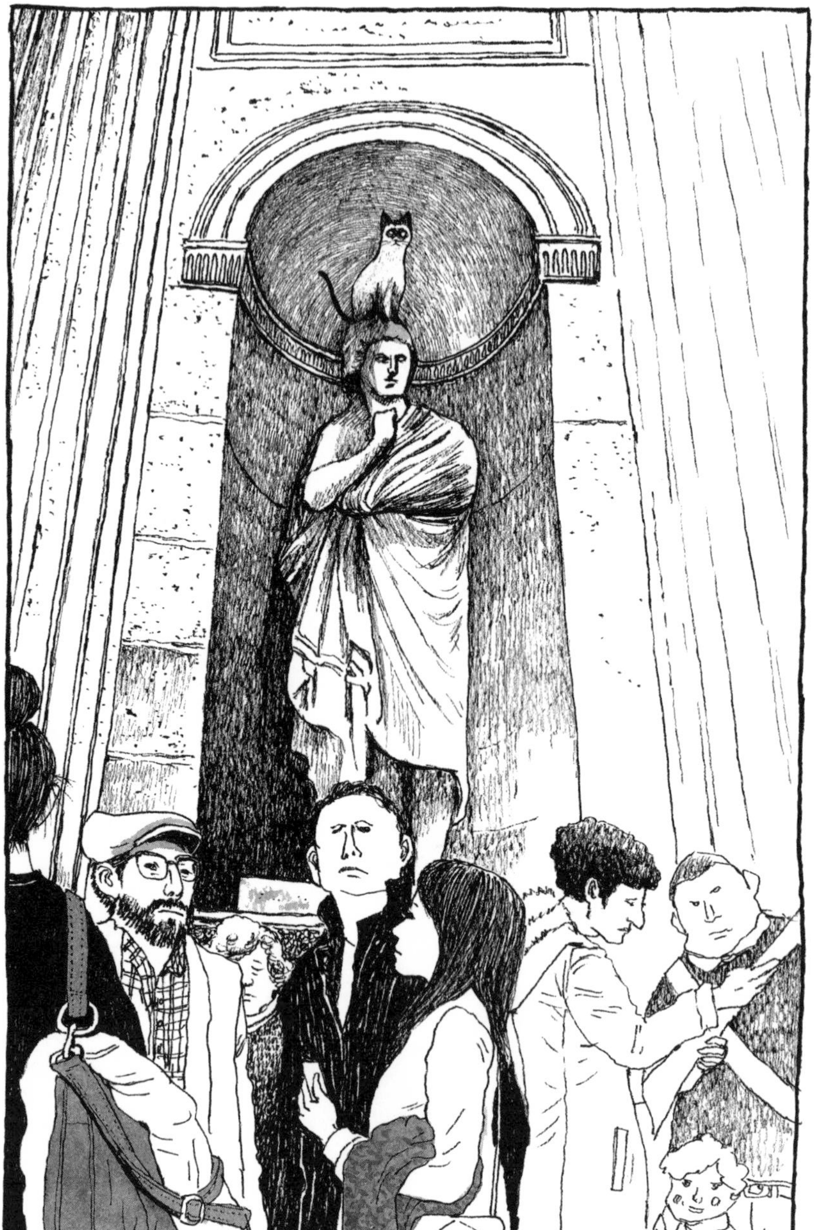

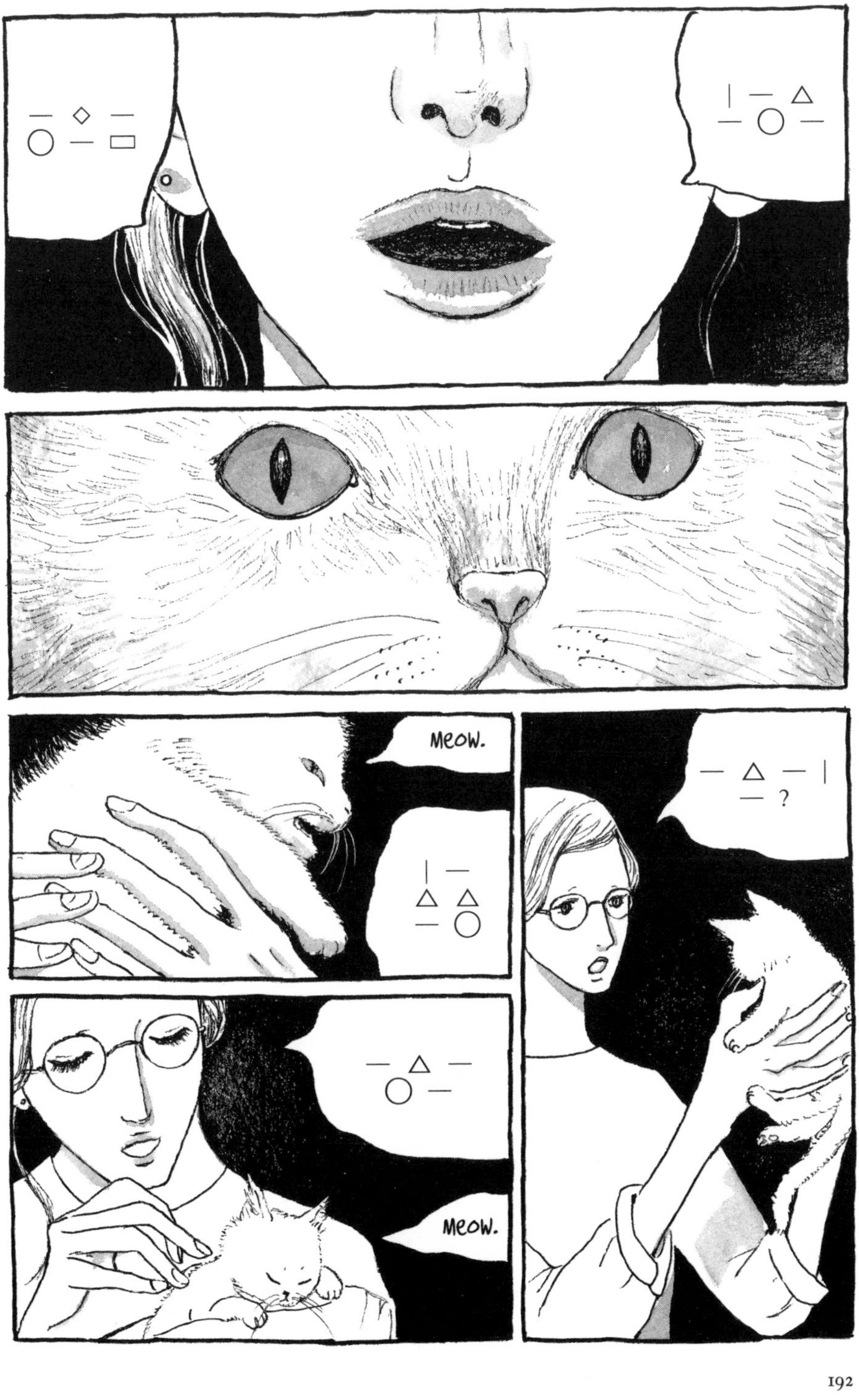
Meow.
Meow.

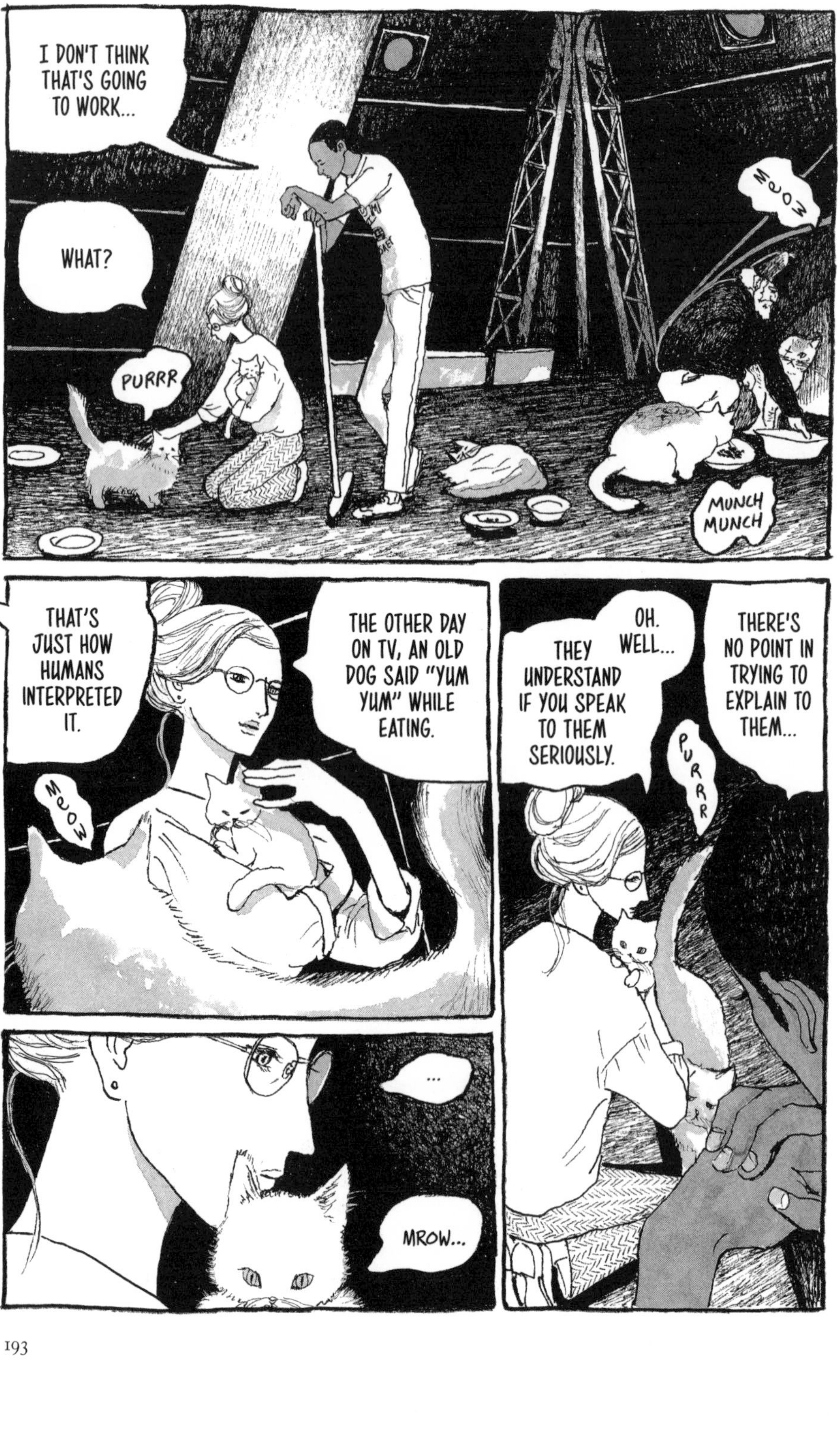
MEOW
I DON'T THINK THAT'S GOING TO WORK...
WHAT?
PURRR
MUNCH MUNCH
THERE'S NO POINT IN TRYING TO EXPLAIN TO THEM...
OH. WELL...
THEY UNDERSTAND IF YOU SPEAK TO THEM SERIOUSLY.
PURRR
THE OTHER DAY ON TV, AN OLD DOG SAID "YUM YUM" WHILE EATING.
THAT'S JUST HOW HUMANS INTERPRETED IT.
MEOW
...
MROW...

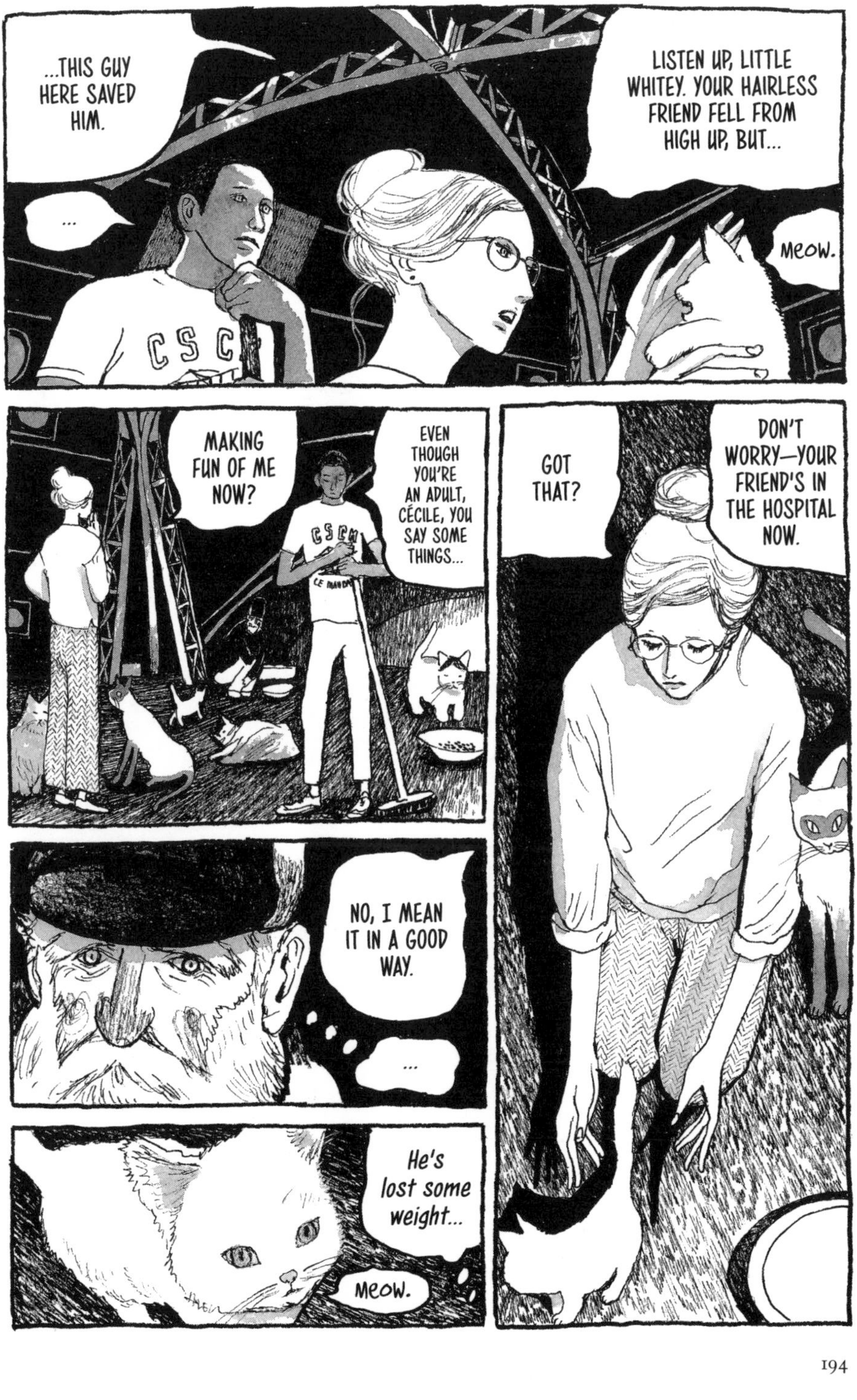
LISTEN UP, LITTLE WHITEY. YOUR HAIRLESS FRIEND FELL FROM HIGH UP, BUT...
...THIS GUY HERE SAVED HIM.
Meow.
...
DON'T WORRY—YOUR FRIEND'S IN THE HOSPITAL NOW.
GOT THAT?
EVEN THOUGH YOU'RE AN ADULT, CÉCILE, YOU SAY SOME THINGS...
MAKING FUN OF ME NOW?
NO, I MEAN IT IN A GOOD WAY.
...
He's lost some weight...
Meow.

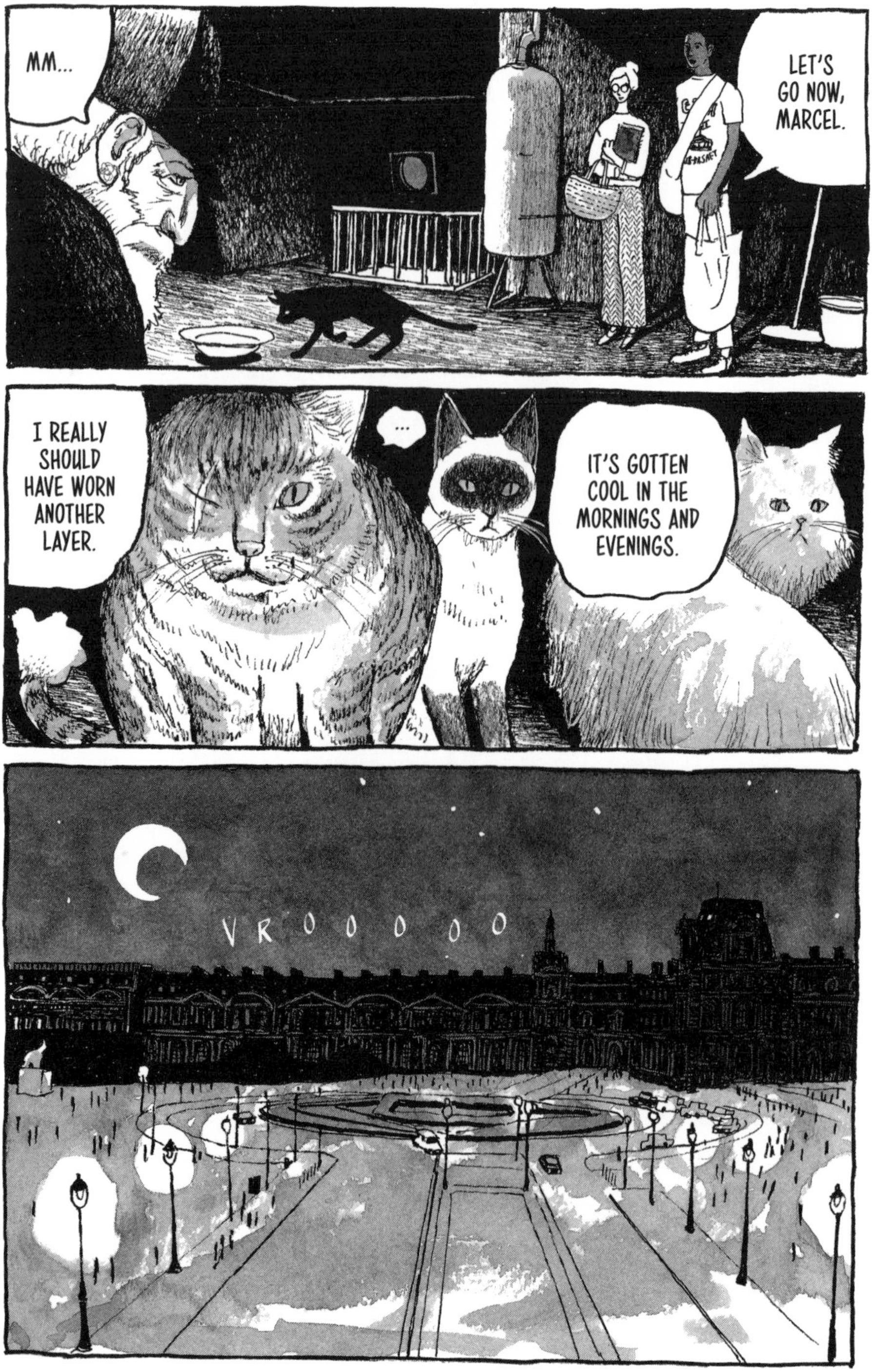
LET'S GO NOW, MARCEL.
MM...
IT'S GOTTEN COOL IN THE MORNINGS AND EVENINGS.
...
I REALLY SHOULD HAVE WORN ANOTHER LAYER.
VROOOOO

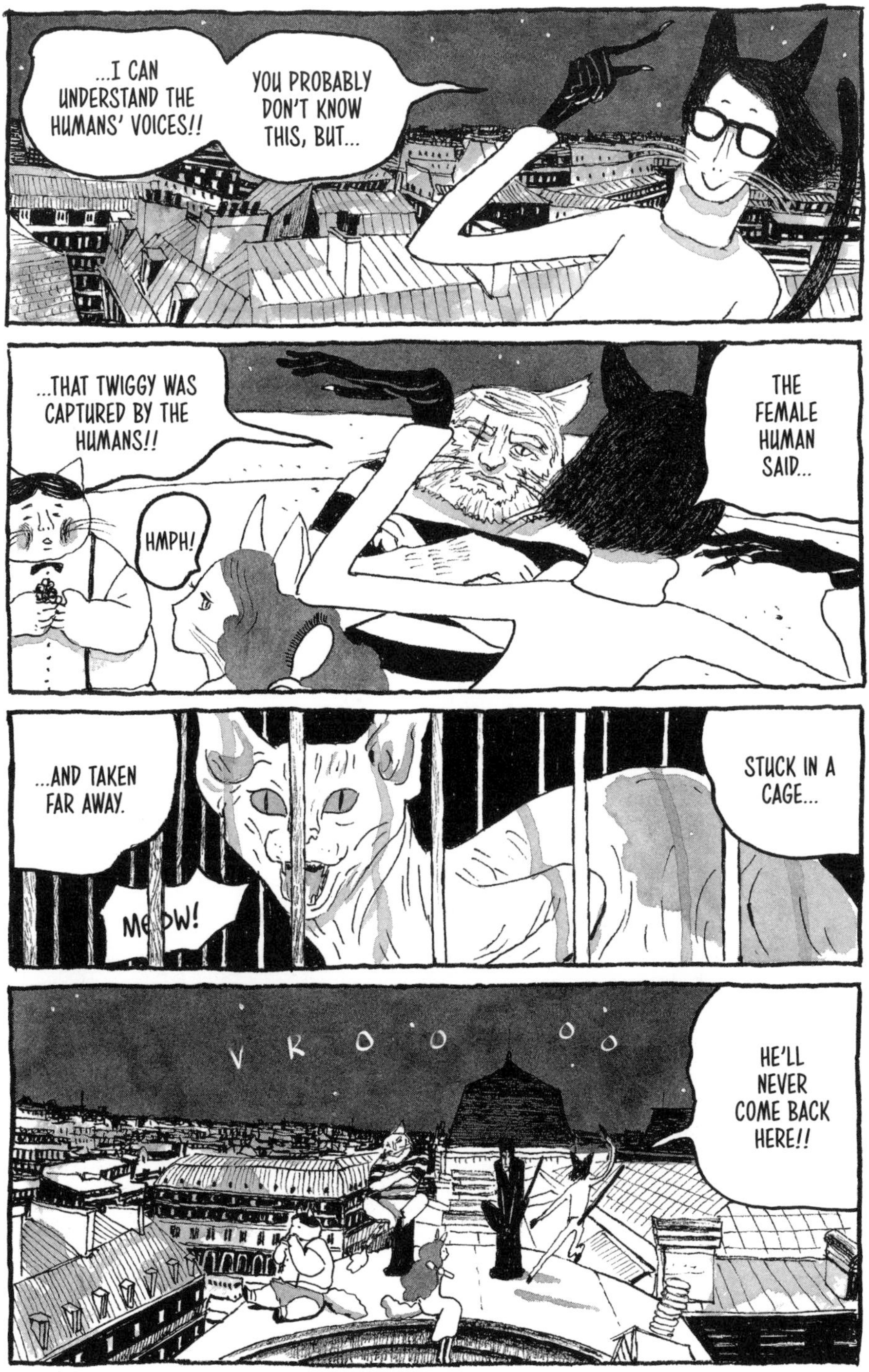
YOU PROBABLY DON'T KNOW THIS, BUT...
...I CAN UNDERSTAND THE HUMANS' VOICES!!
THE FEMALE HUMAN SAID...
...THAT TWIGGY WAS CAPTURED BY THE HUMANS!!
HMPH!
STUCK IN A CAGE...
...AND TAKEN FAR AWAY.
HE'LL NEVER COME BACK HERE!!
VROOOOO

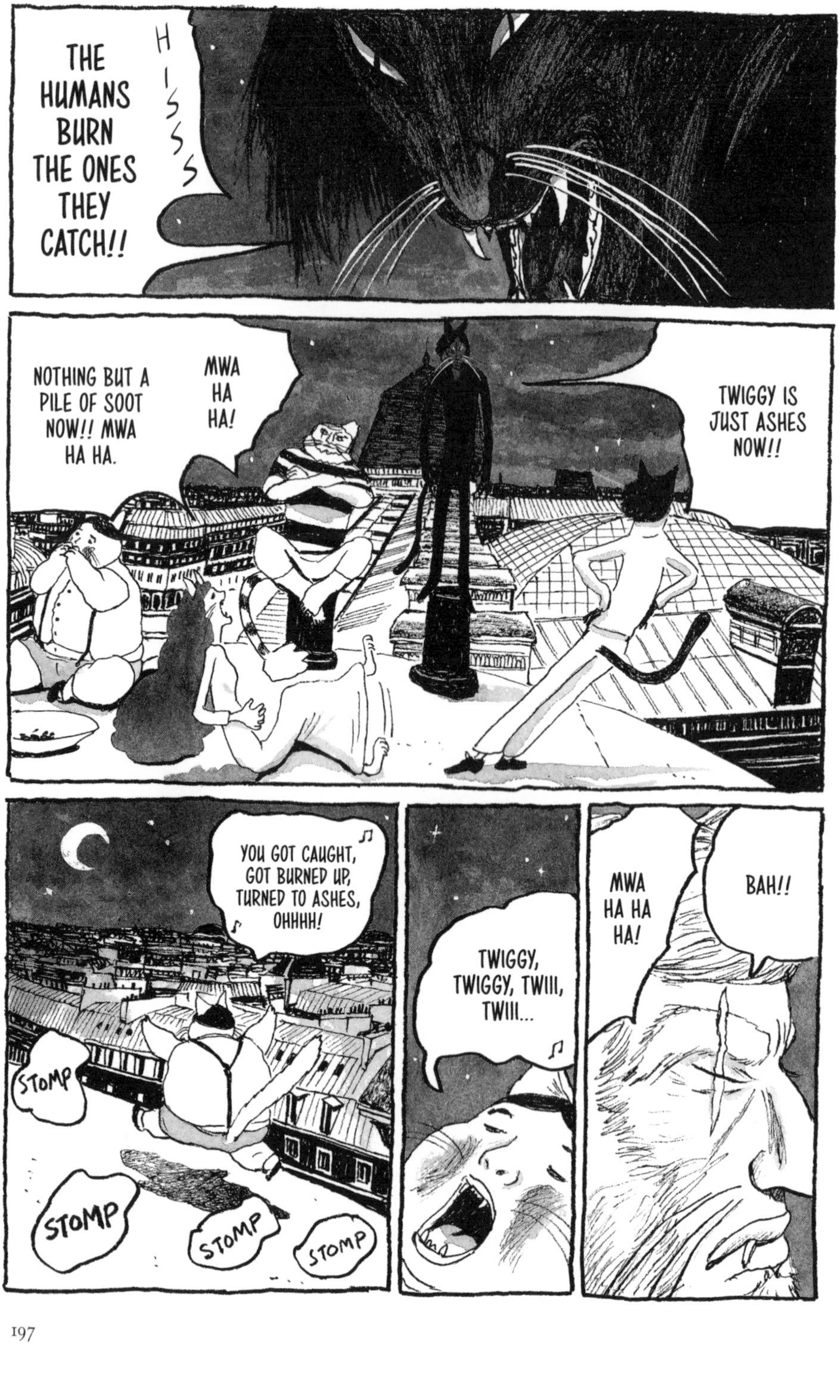
HISSS
THE HUMANS BURN THE ONES THEY CATCH!!
TWIGGY IS JUST ASHES NOW!!
MWA HA HA!
NOTHING BUT A PILE OF SOOT NOW!! MWA HA HA.
BAH!!
MWA HA HA HA!
TWIGGY, TWIGGY, TWIII, TWIII...
YOU GOT CAUGHT, GOT BURNED UP, TURNED TO ASHES, OHHHH!
STOMP
STOMP
STOMP
STOMP

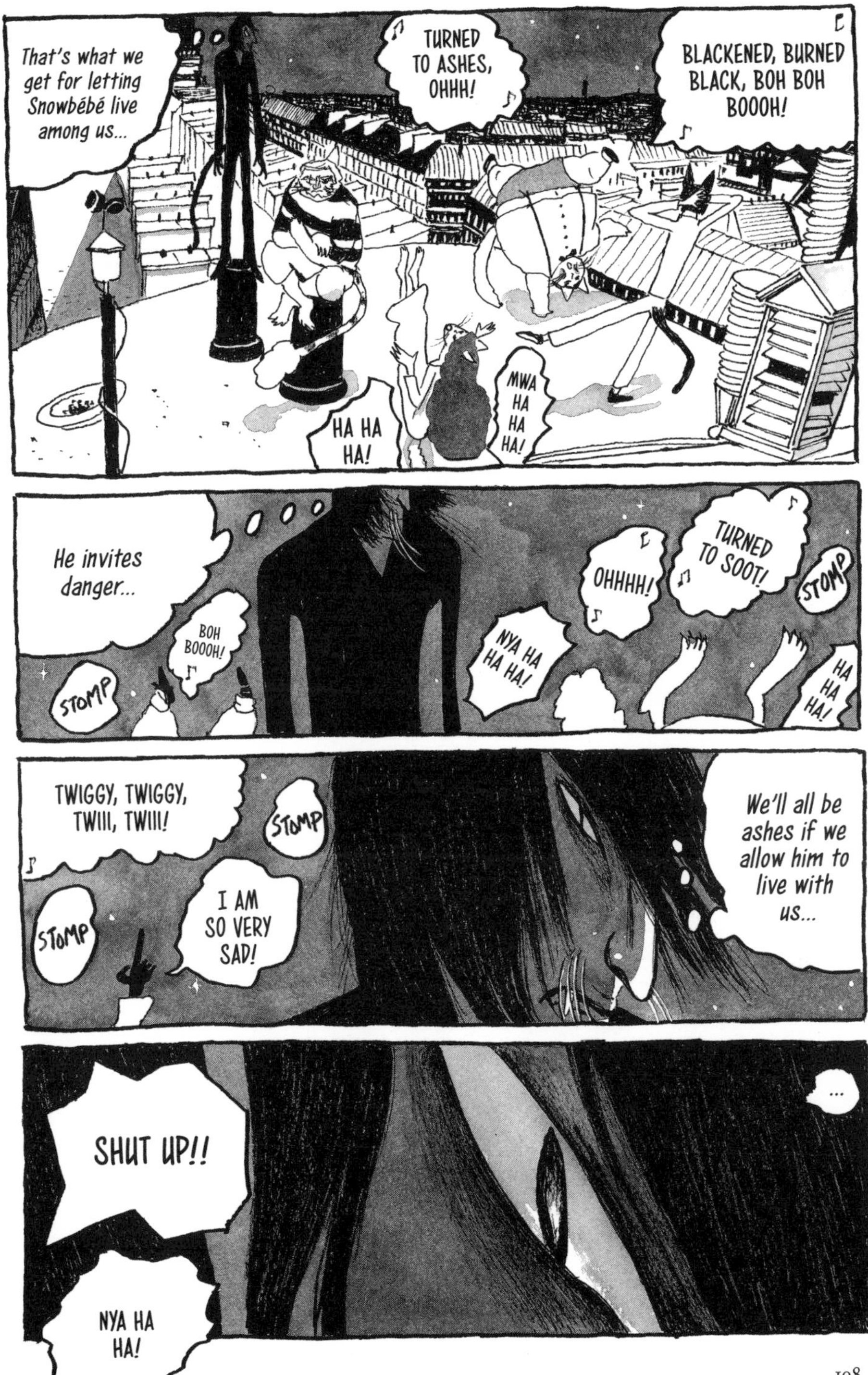
BLACKENED, BURNED BLACK, BOH BOH BOOOH!
MWA HA HA HA!
TURNED TO ASHES, OHHH!
HA HA HA!
That's what we get for letting Snowbébé live among us...
HA HA HA!
STOMP
TURNED TO SOOT!
OHHHH!
NYA HA HA HA!
BOH BOOOH!
He invites danger...
STOMP
We'll all be ashes if we allow him to live with us...
STOMP
TWIGGY, TWIGGY, TWIII, TWIII!
I AM SO VERY SAD!
STOMP
...
SHUT UP!!
NYA HA HA!

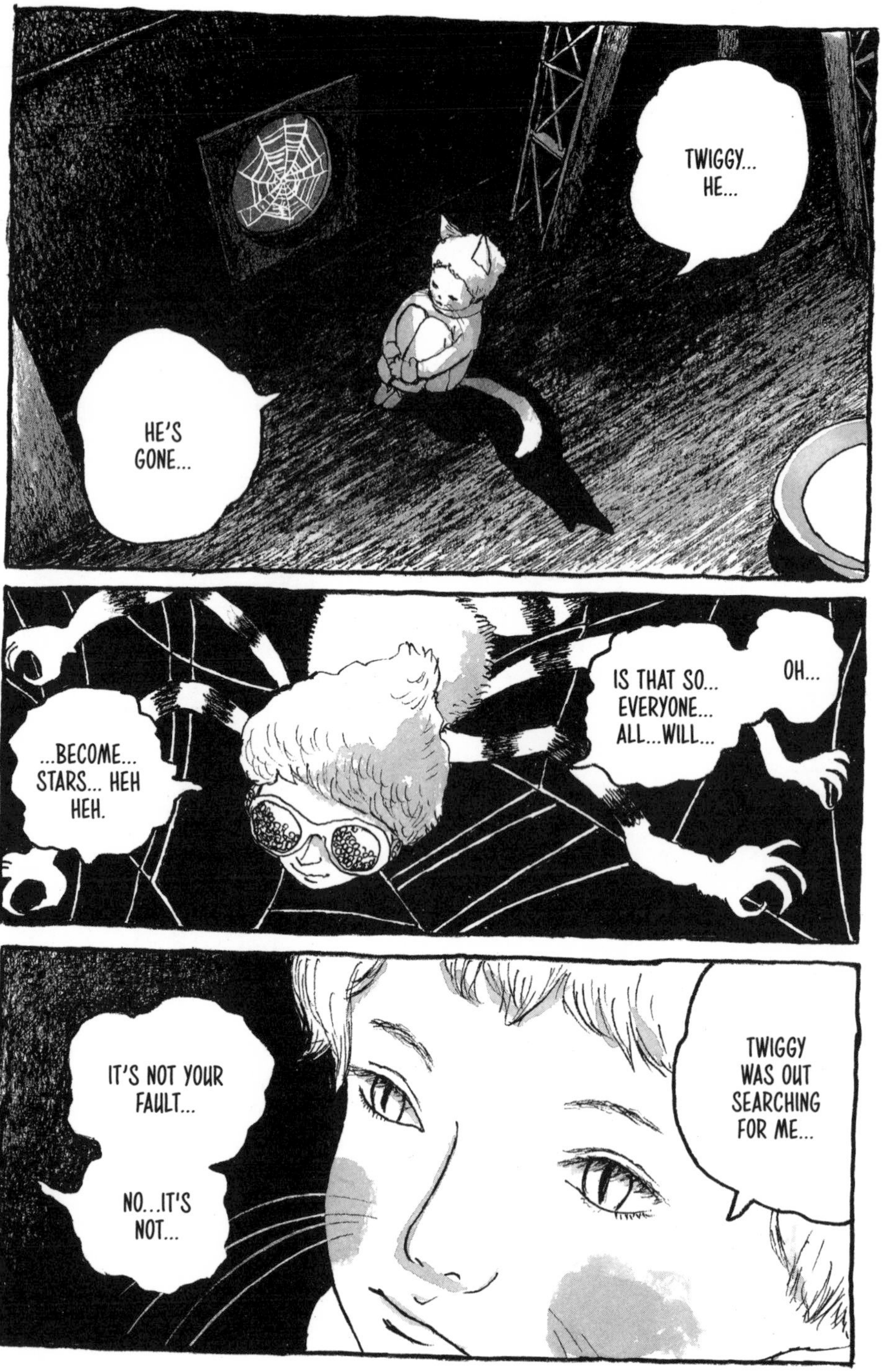
TWIGGY... HE...
HE'S GONE...
OH...
IS THAT SO... EVERYONE... ALL...WILL...
...BECOME... STARS... HEH HEH.
TWIGGY WAS OUT SEARCHING FOR ME...
IT'S NOT YOUR FAULT...
NO...IT'S NOT...

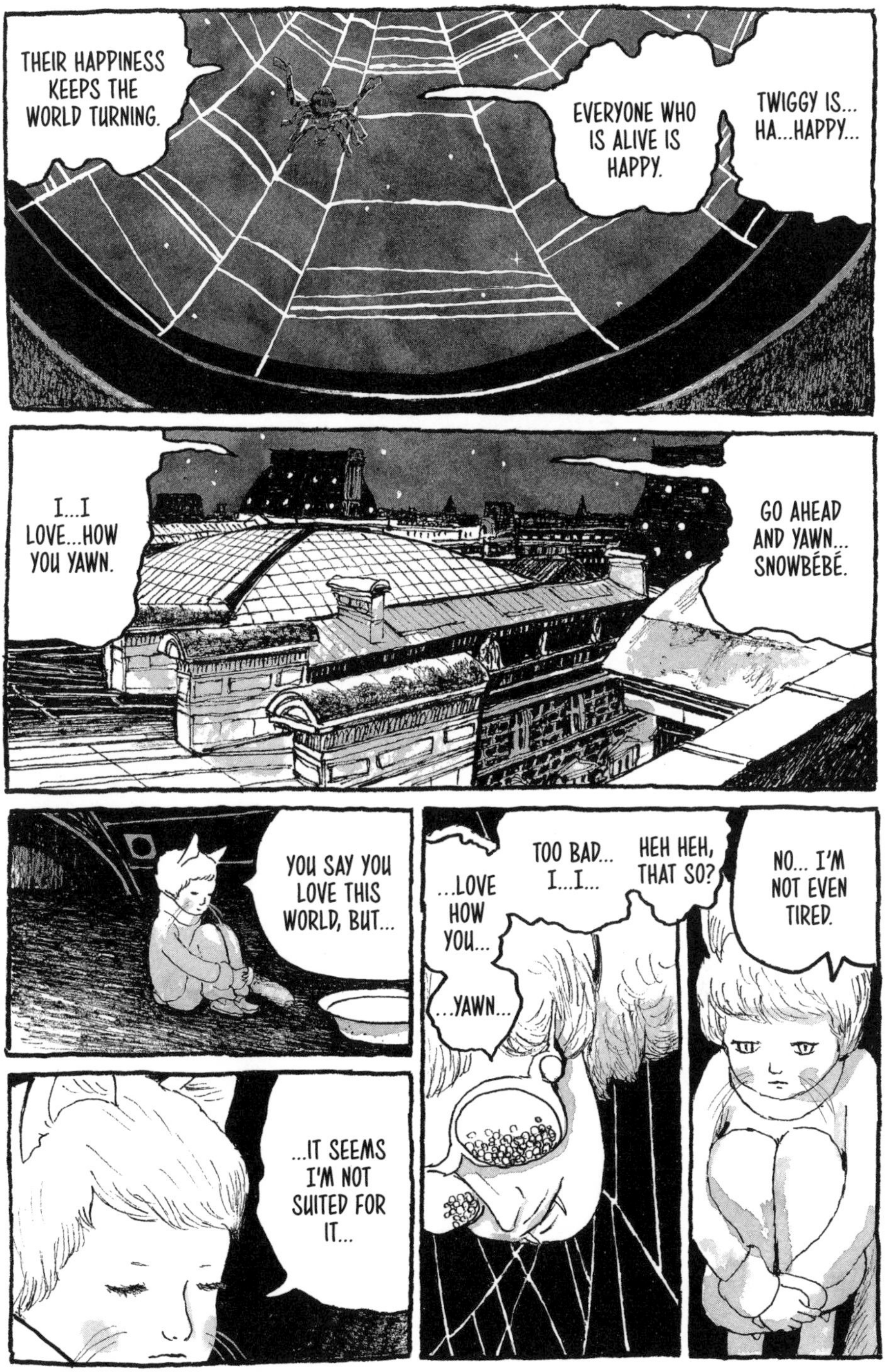
TWIGGY IS... HA...HAPPY...
EVERYONE WHO IS ALIVE IS HAPPY.
THEIR HAPPINESS KEEPS THE WORLD TURNING.
GO AHEAD AND YAWN... SNOWBÉBÉ.
I...I LOVE...HOW YOU YAWN.
NO... I'M NOT EVEN TIRED.
HEH HEH, THAT SO?
TOO BAD... I...I...
...LOVE HOW YOU...
...YAWN...
YOU SAY YOU LOVE THIS WORLD, BUT...
...IT SEEMS I'M NOT SUITED FOR IT...

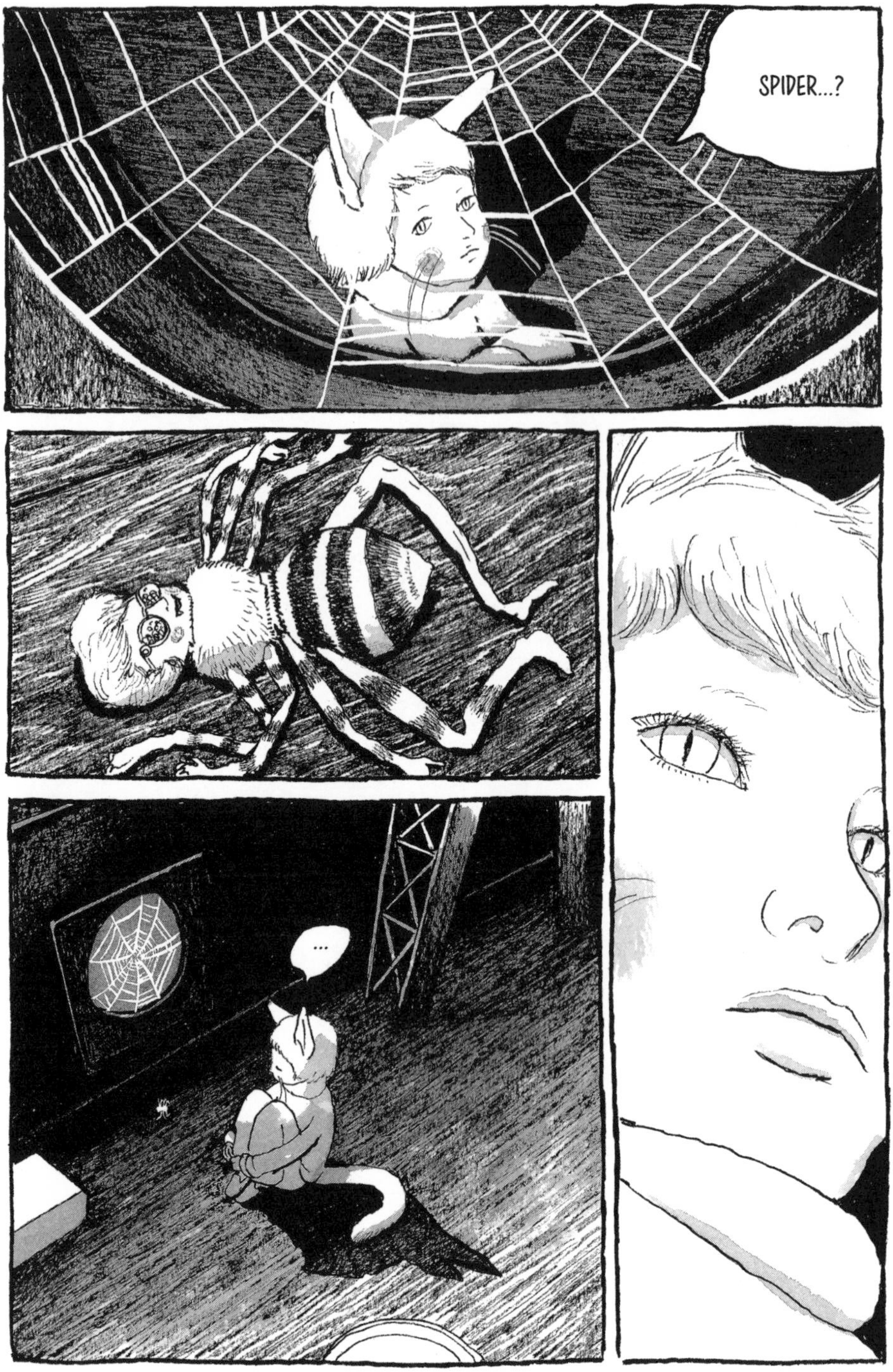
SPIDER...?
...

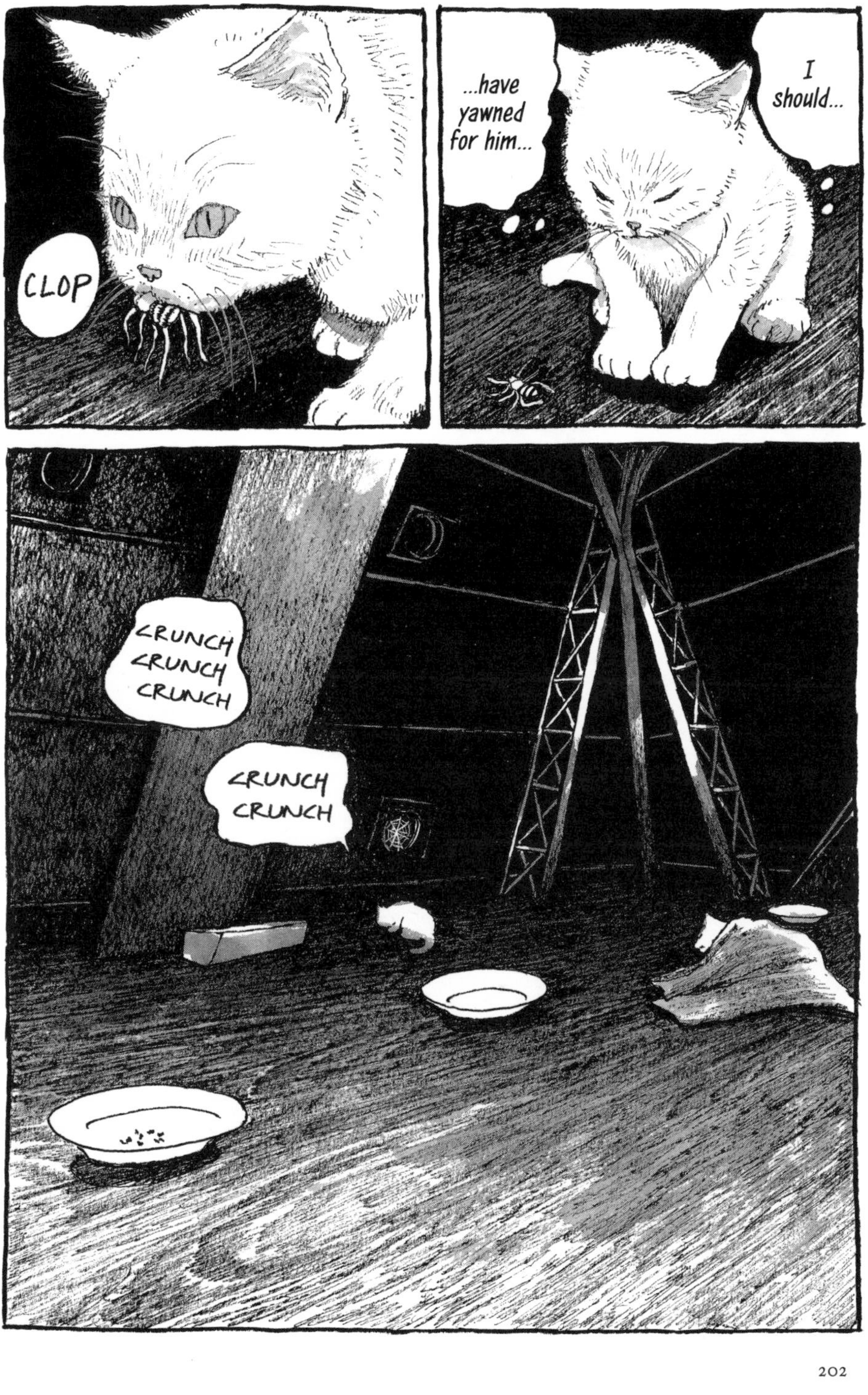
I should...
...have yawned for him...
CLOP
CRUNCH CRUNCH CRUNCH
CRUNCH CRUNCH

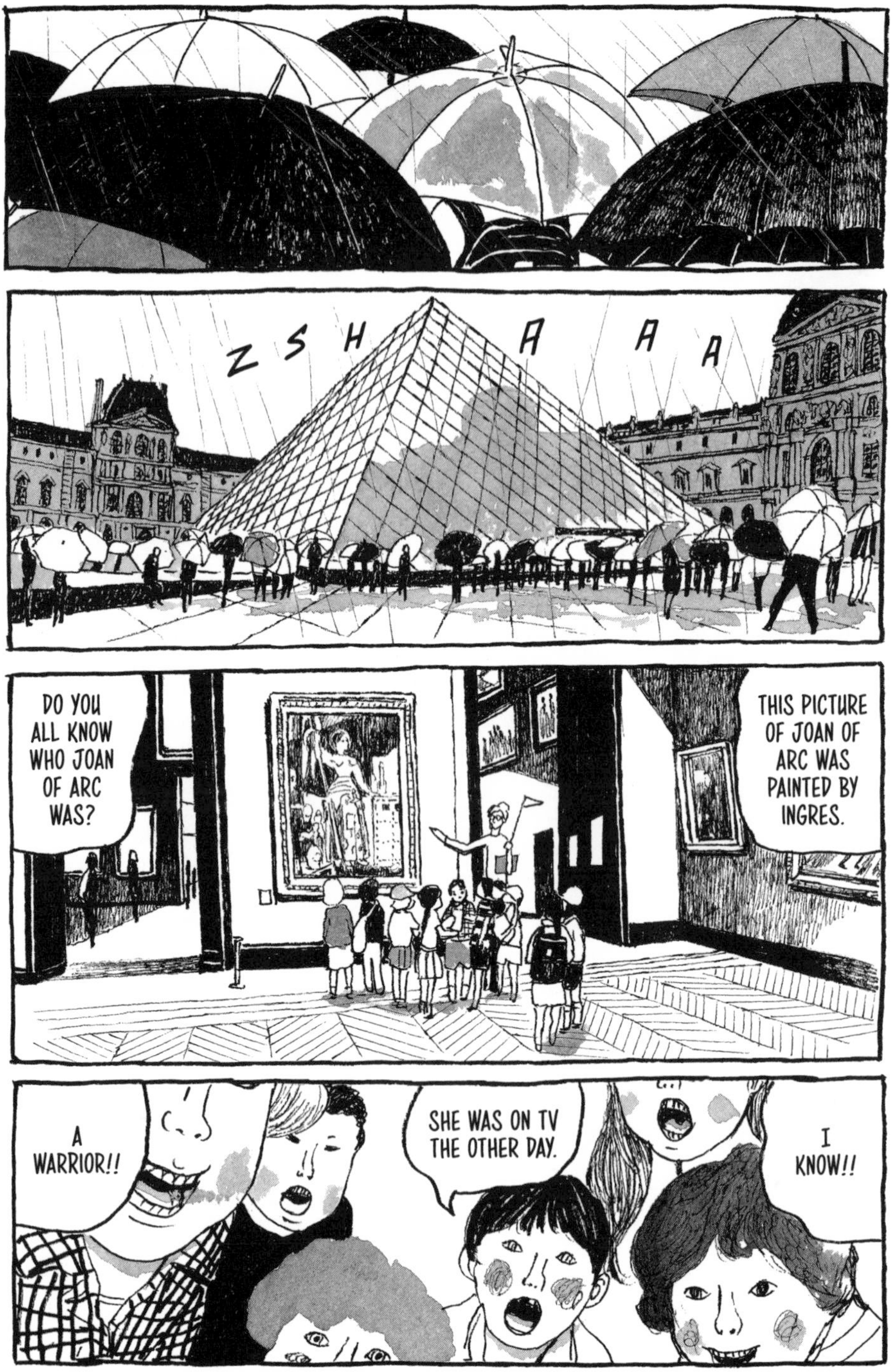
ZSHAAA
THIS PICTURE OF JOAN OF ARC WAS PAINTED BY INGRES.
DO YOU ALL KNOW WHO JOAN OF ARC WAS?
I KNOW!!
SHE WAS ON TV THE OTHER DAY.
A WARRIOR!!

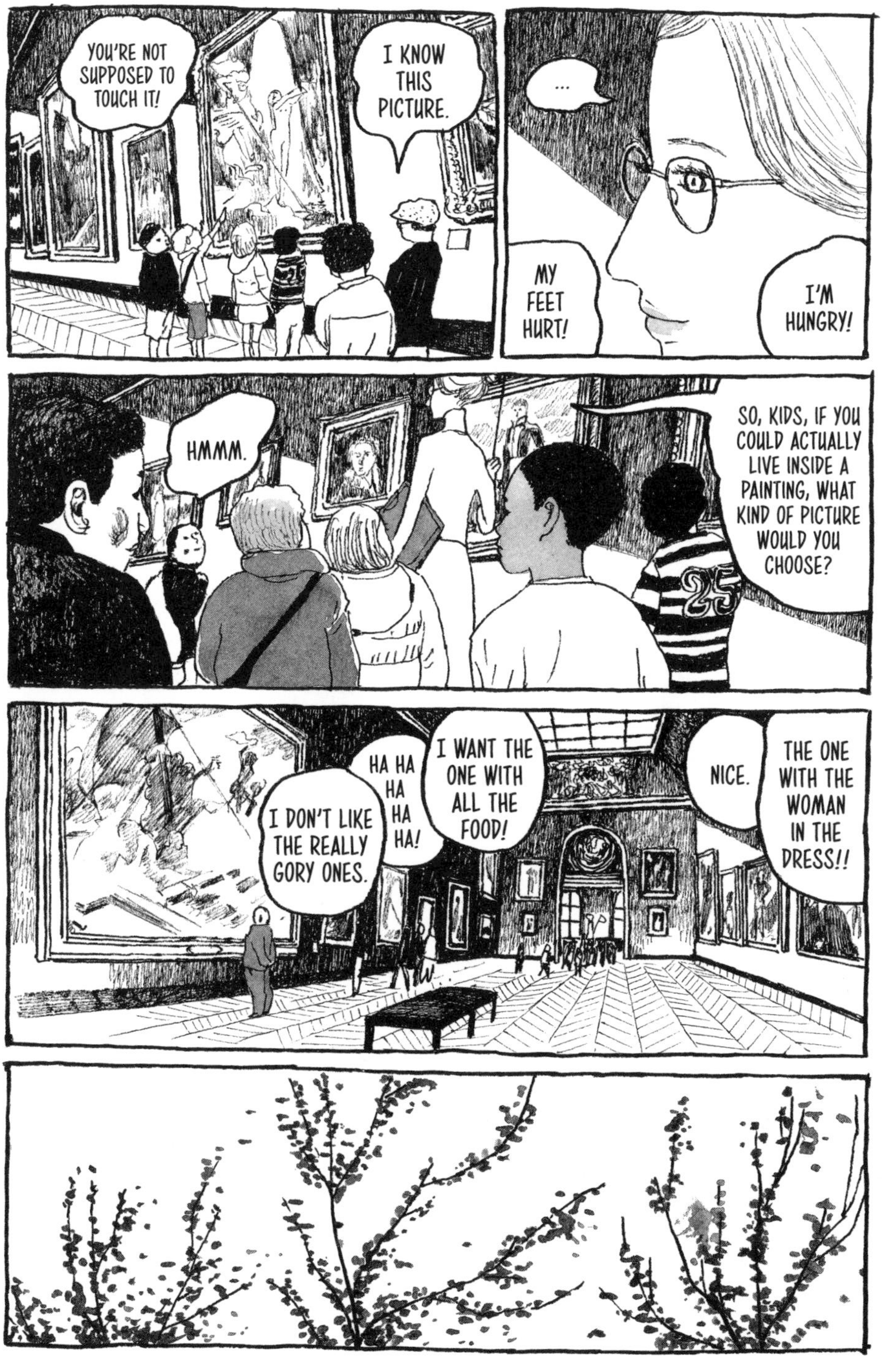
...
I'M HUNGRY!
MY FEET HURT!
I KNOW THIS PICTURE.
YOU'RE NOT SUPPOSED TO TOUCH IT!
SO, KIDS, IF YOU COULD ACTUALLY LIVE INSIDE A PAINTING, WHAT KIND OF PICTURE WOULD YOU CHOOSE?
HMMM.
THE ONE WITH THE WOMAN IN THE DRESS!!
NICE.
I WANT THE ONE WITH ALL THE FOOD!
HA HA HA HA HA!
I DON'T LIKE THE REALLY GORY ONES.

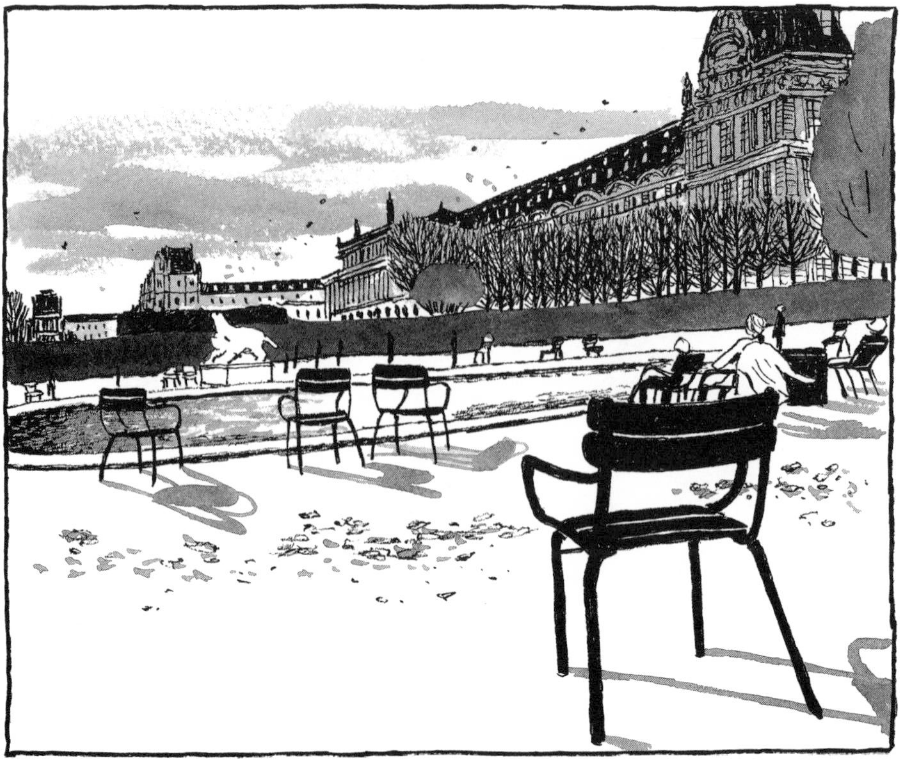

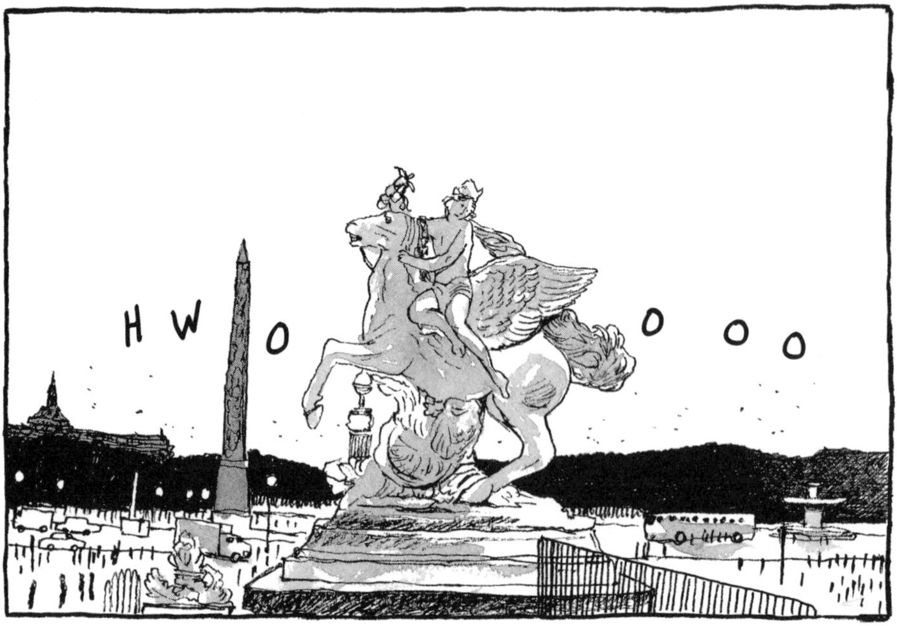
HWOOOO

AUTUMN

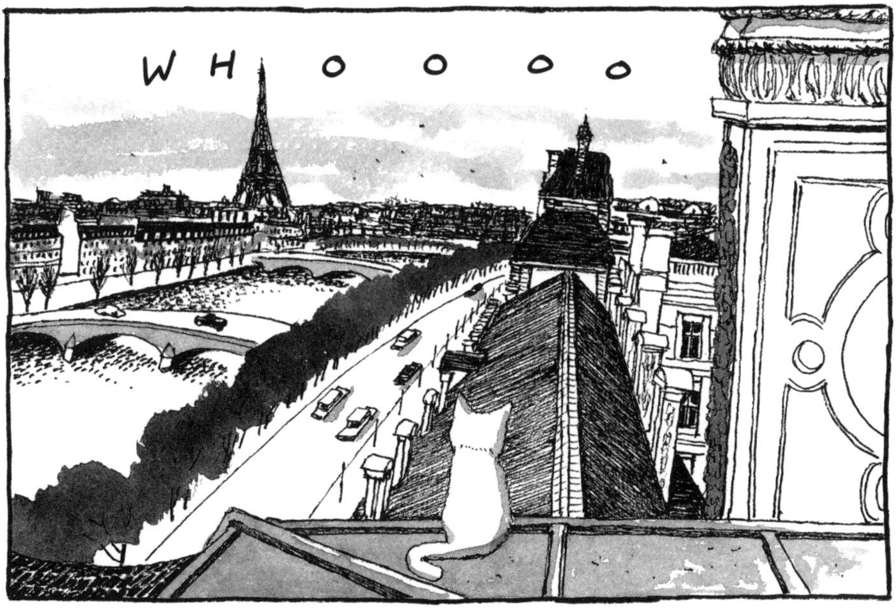
WHOOOO

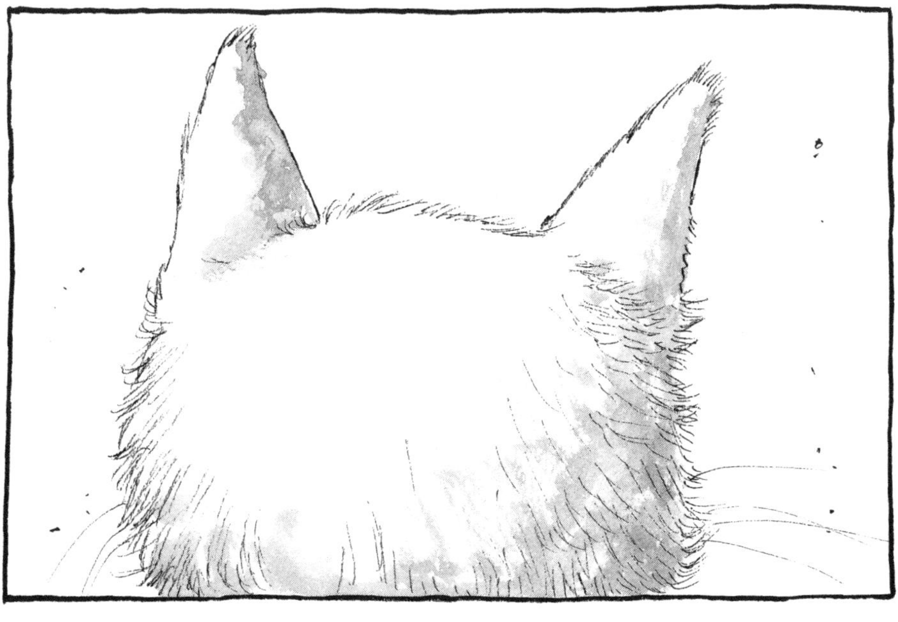

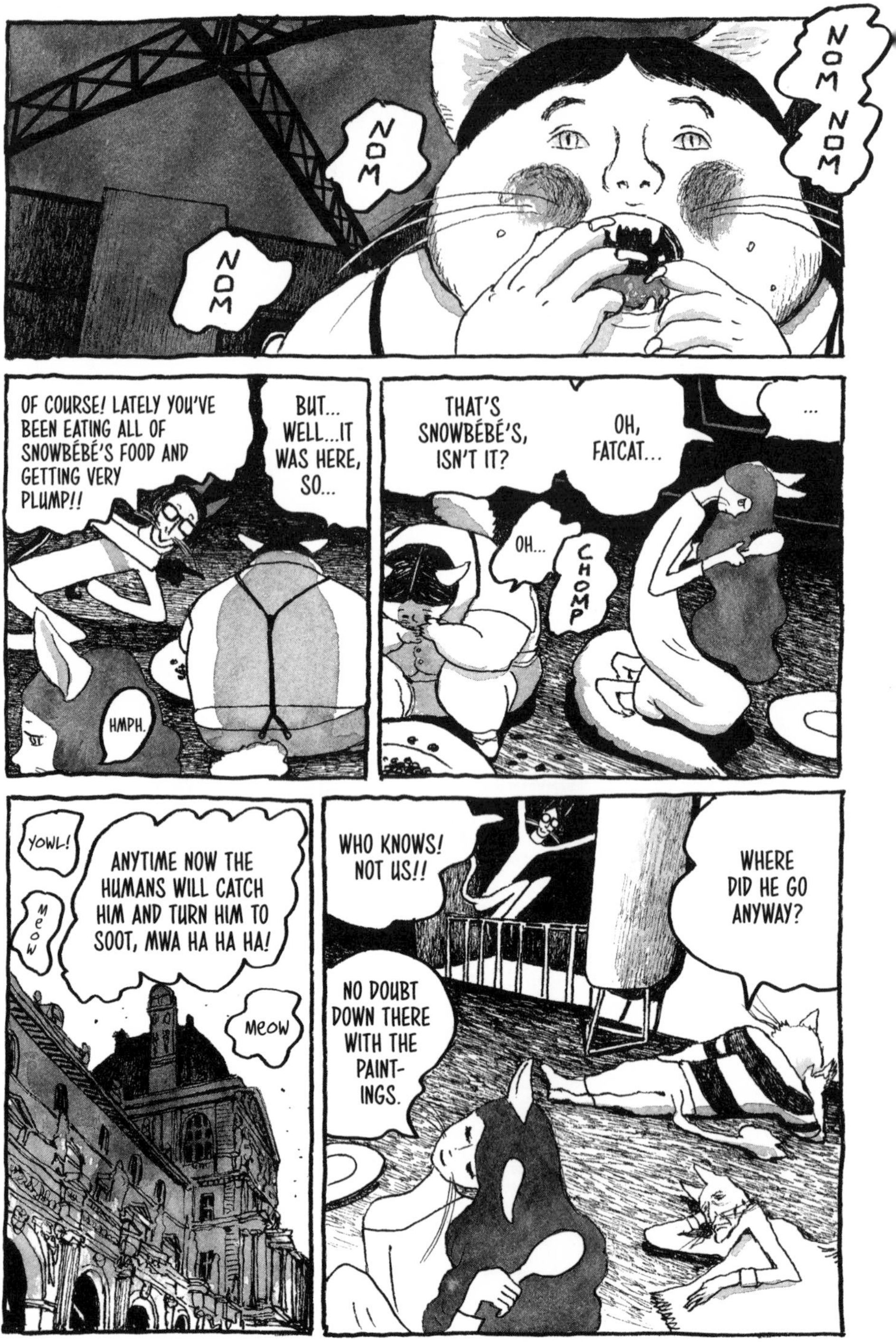
NOM NOM NOM
NOM
NOM
...
OH, FATCAT...
THAT'S SNOWBÉBÉ'S, ISN'T IT?
CHOMP
OH...
BUT... WELL...IT WAS HERE, SO...
OF COURSE! LATELY YOU'VE BEEN EATING ALL OF SNOWBÉBÉ'S FOOD AND GETTING VERY PLUMP!!
HMPH.
WHERE DID HE GO ANYWAY?
WHO KNOWS! NOT US!!
NO DOUBT DOWN THERE WITH THE PAINT-INGS.
ANYTIME NOW THE HUMANS WILL CATCH HIM AND TURN HIM TO SOOT, MWA HA HA HA!
YOWL!
MEOW
MEOW

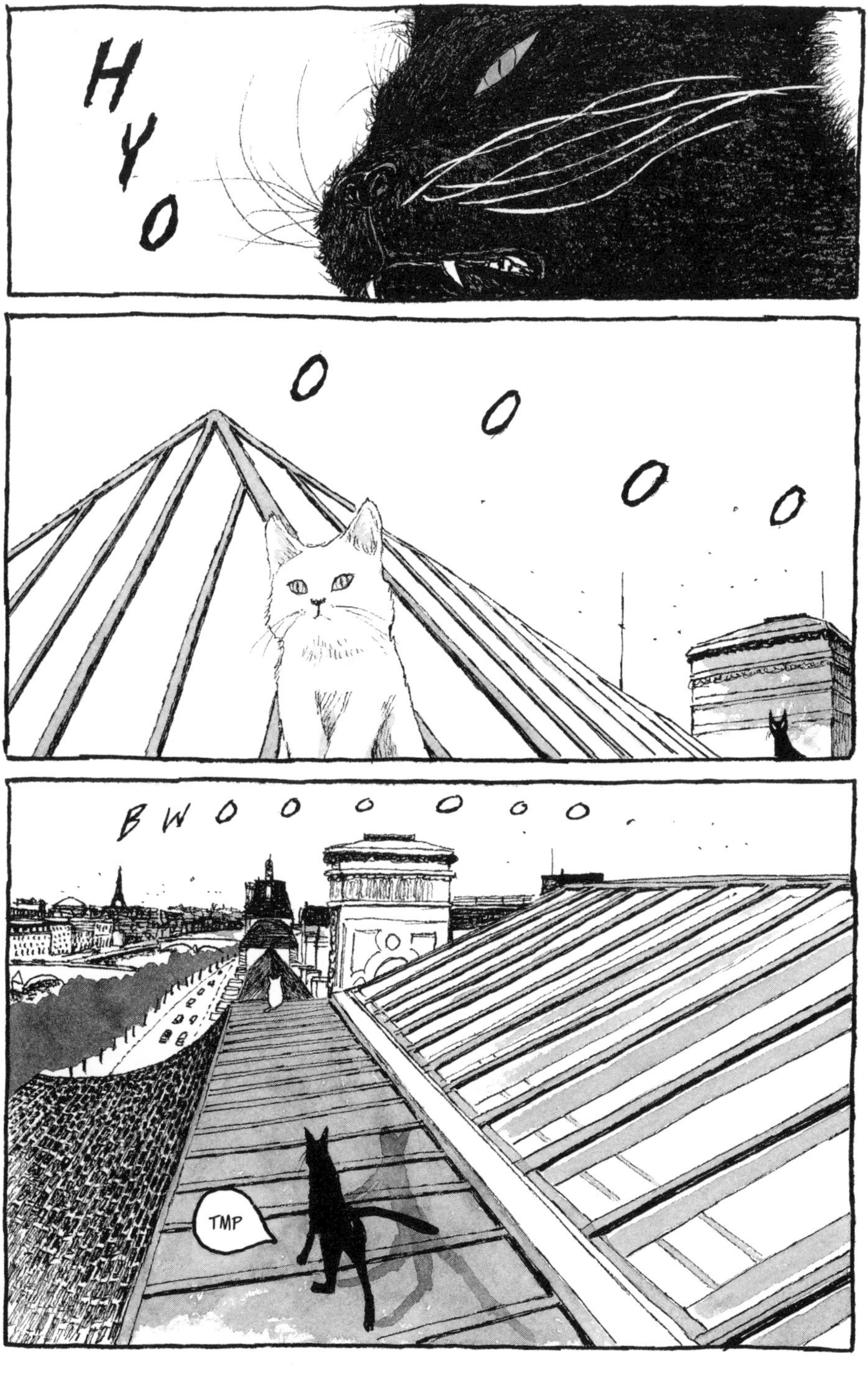
HYO
OOOO
BWOOOOOOO
TMP

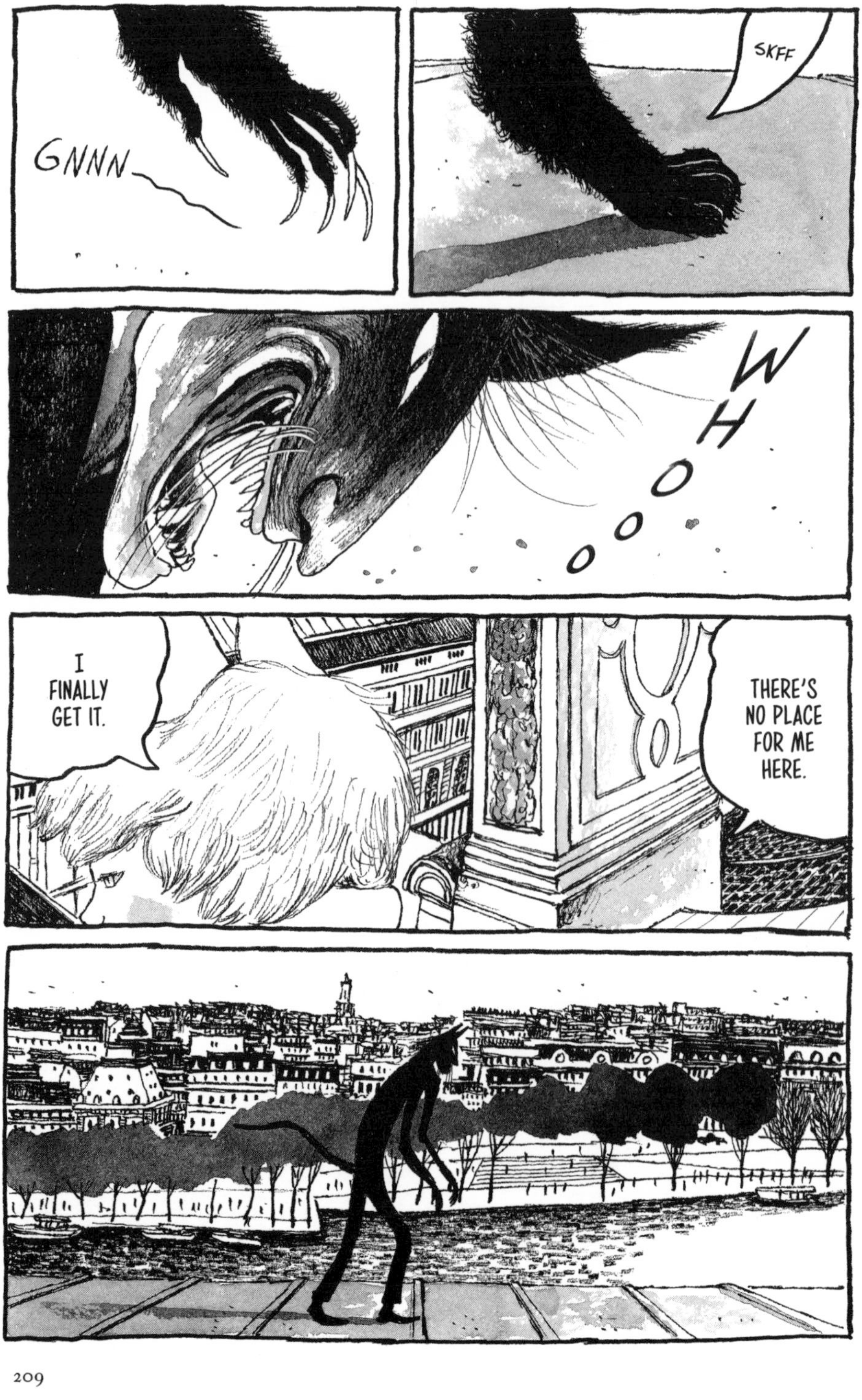
SKFF
GNNN
WHOOOO
THERE'S NO PLACE FOR ME HERE.
I FINALLY GET IT.

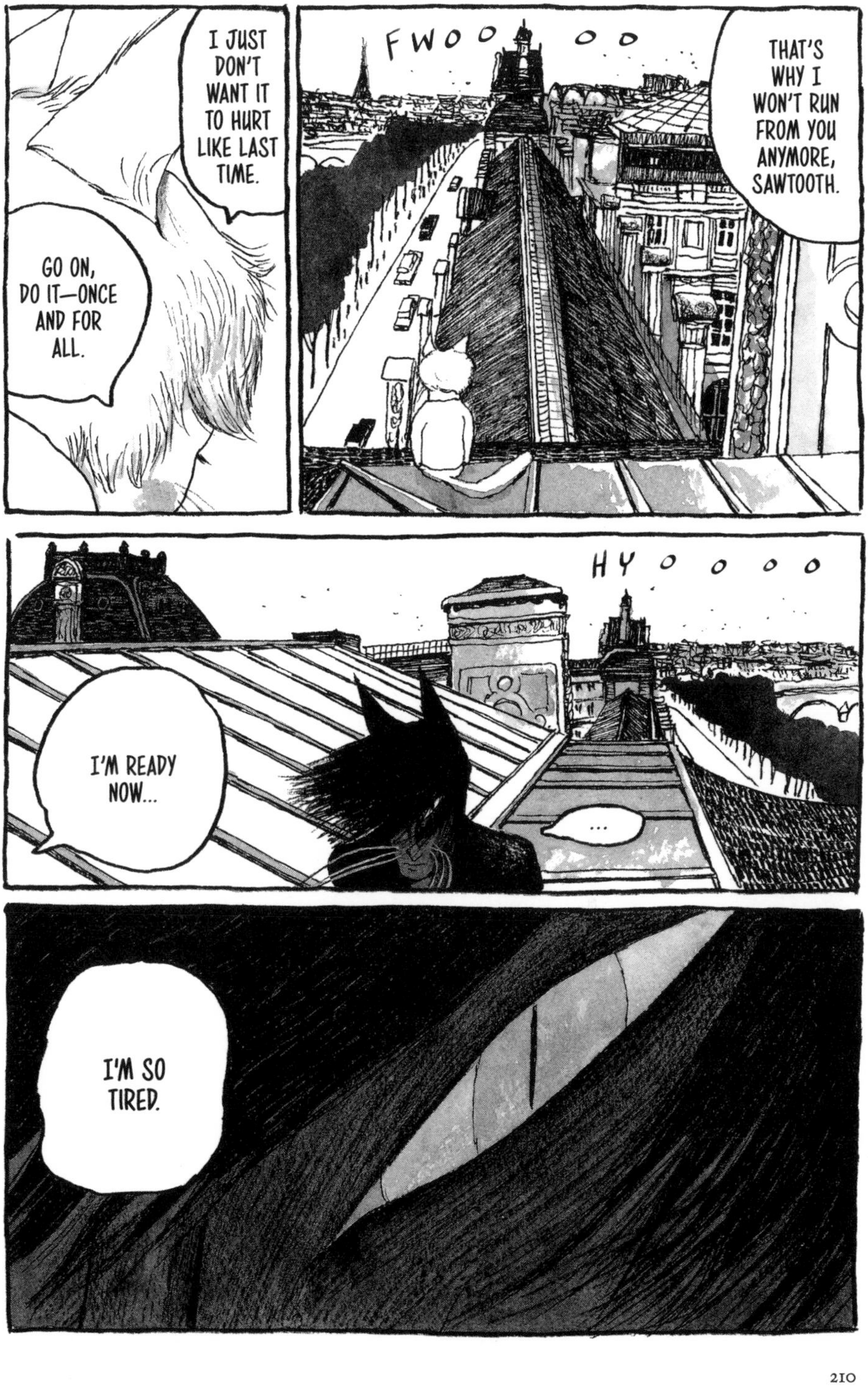
FWOO OO
THAT'S WHY I WON'T RUN FROM YOU ANYMORE, SAWTOOTH.
I JUST DON'T WANT IT TO HURT LIKE LAST TIME.
GO ON, DO IT—ONCE AND FOR ALL.
HYOOOO
I'M READY NOW...
...
I'M SO TIRED.

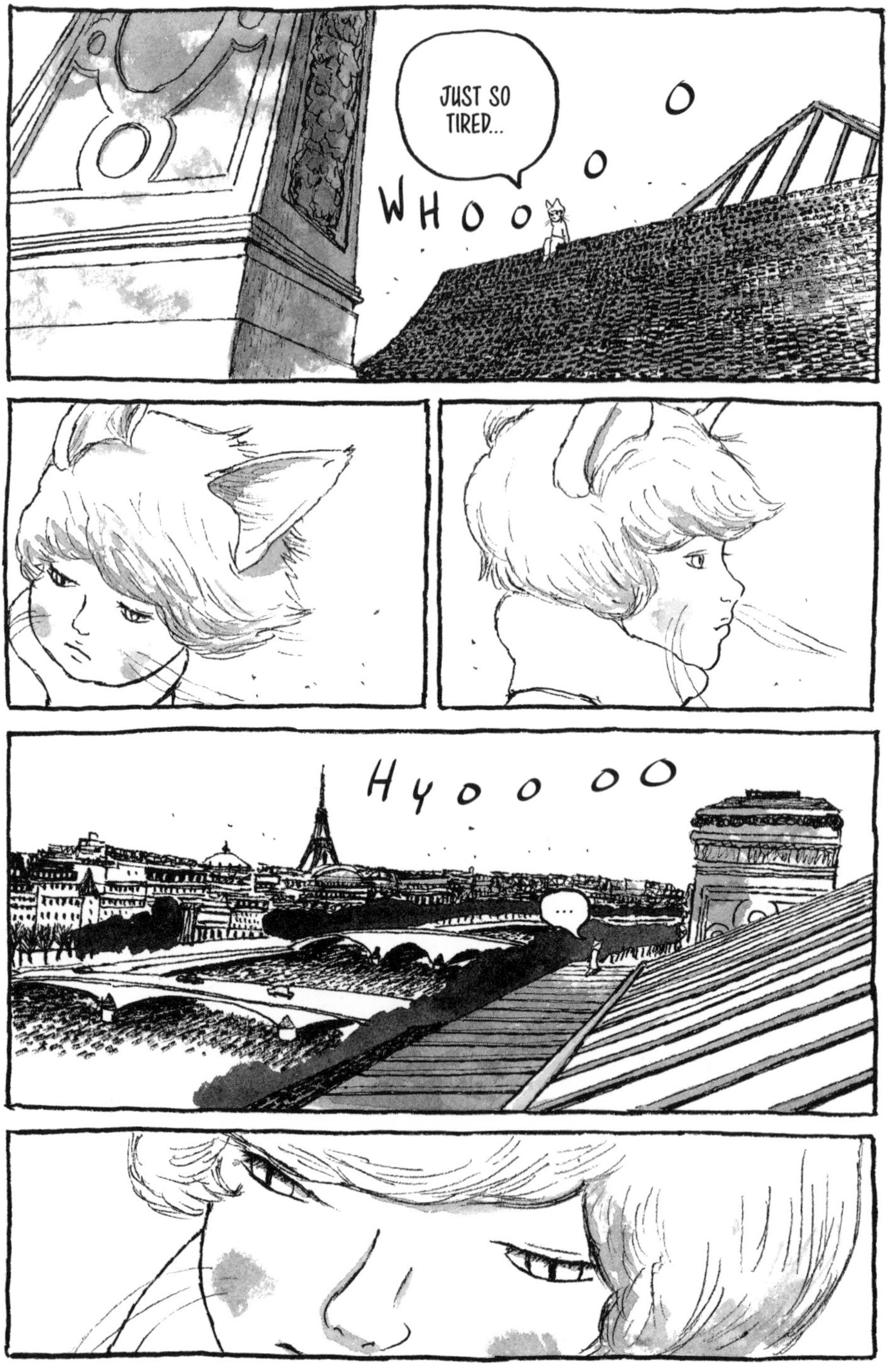
JUST SO TIRED...
WHOOO O O
HYOOOO
...

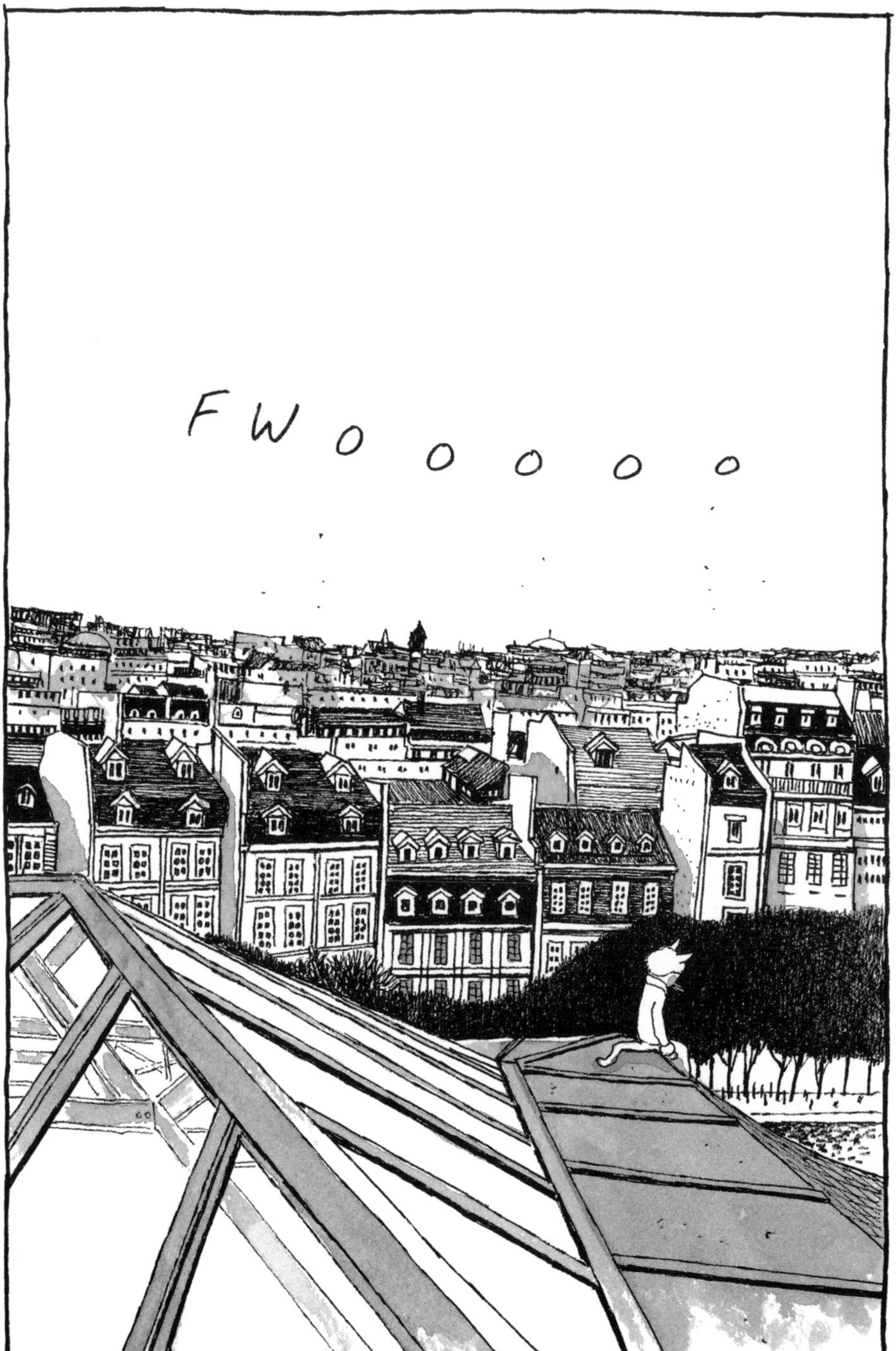
FWOOOOO

CHAPTER 10

The Secret of the Night Watchman's Coffee

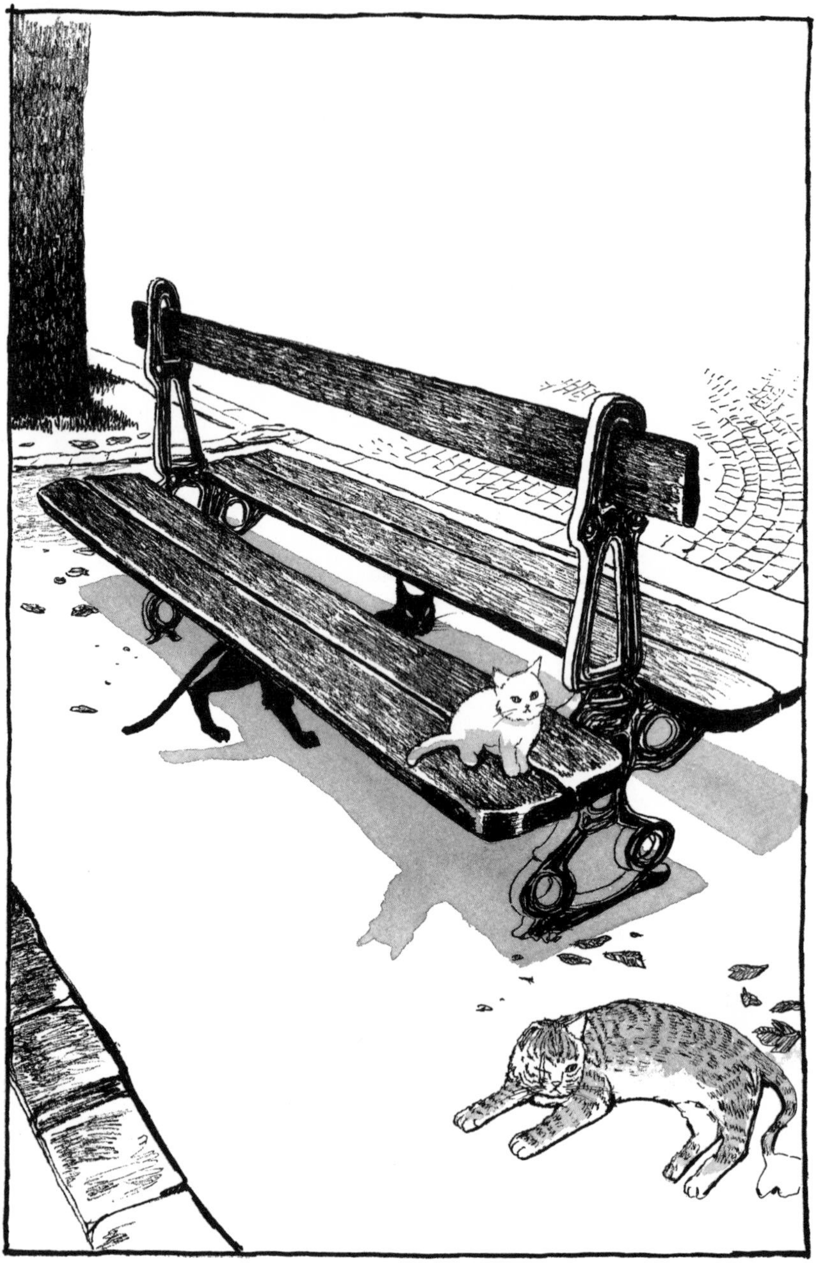

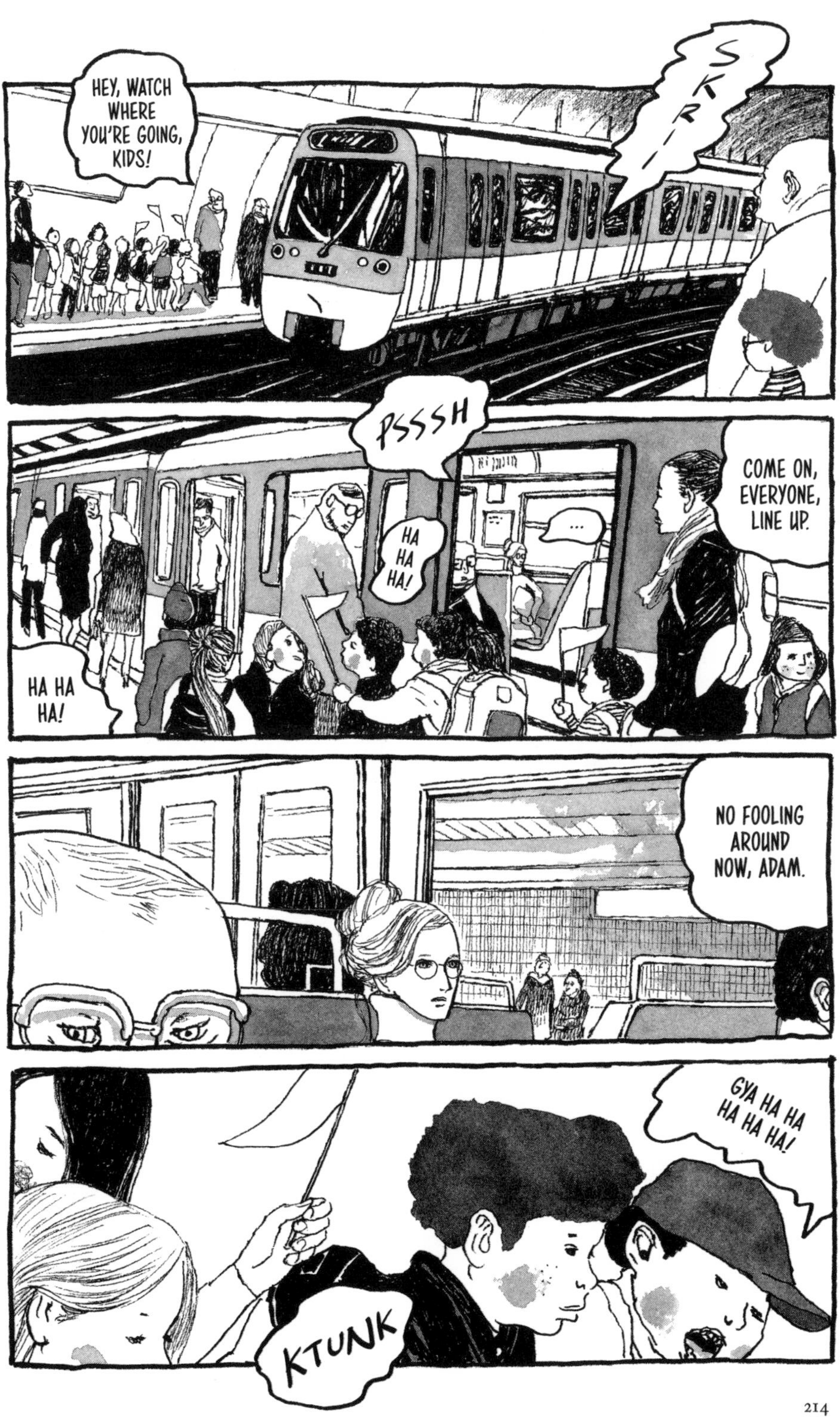
SKRI
HEY, WATCH WHERE YOU'RE GOING, KIDS!
COME ON, EVERYONE, LINE UP.
PSSSH
...
HA HA HA!
HA HA HA!
NO FOOLING AROUND NOW, ADAM.
GYA HA HA HA HA HA!
KTUNK

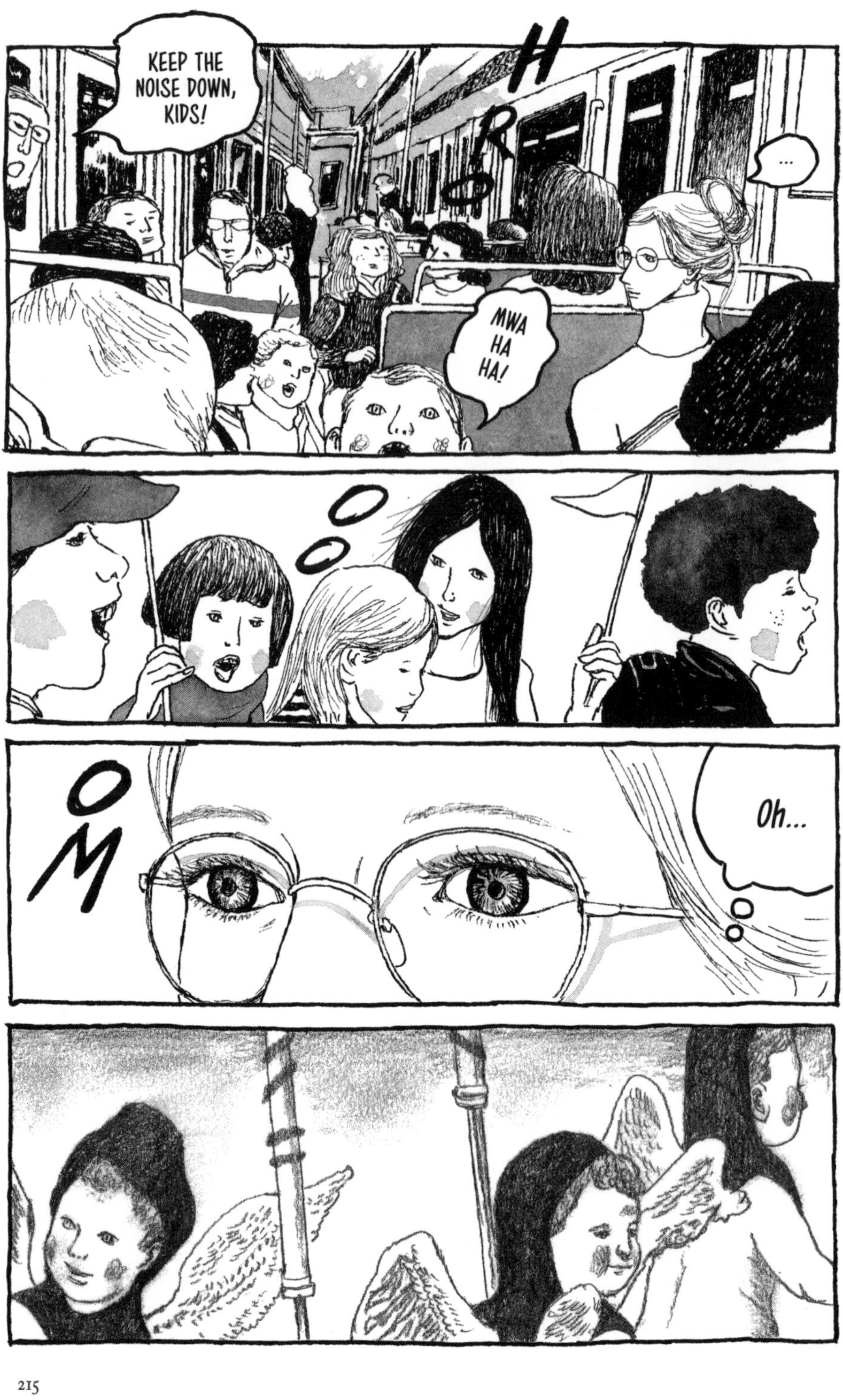
HRO
...
KEEP THE NOISE DOWN, KIDS!
MWA HA HA!
Oh...
OM

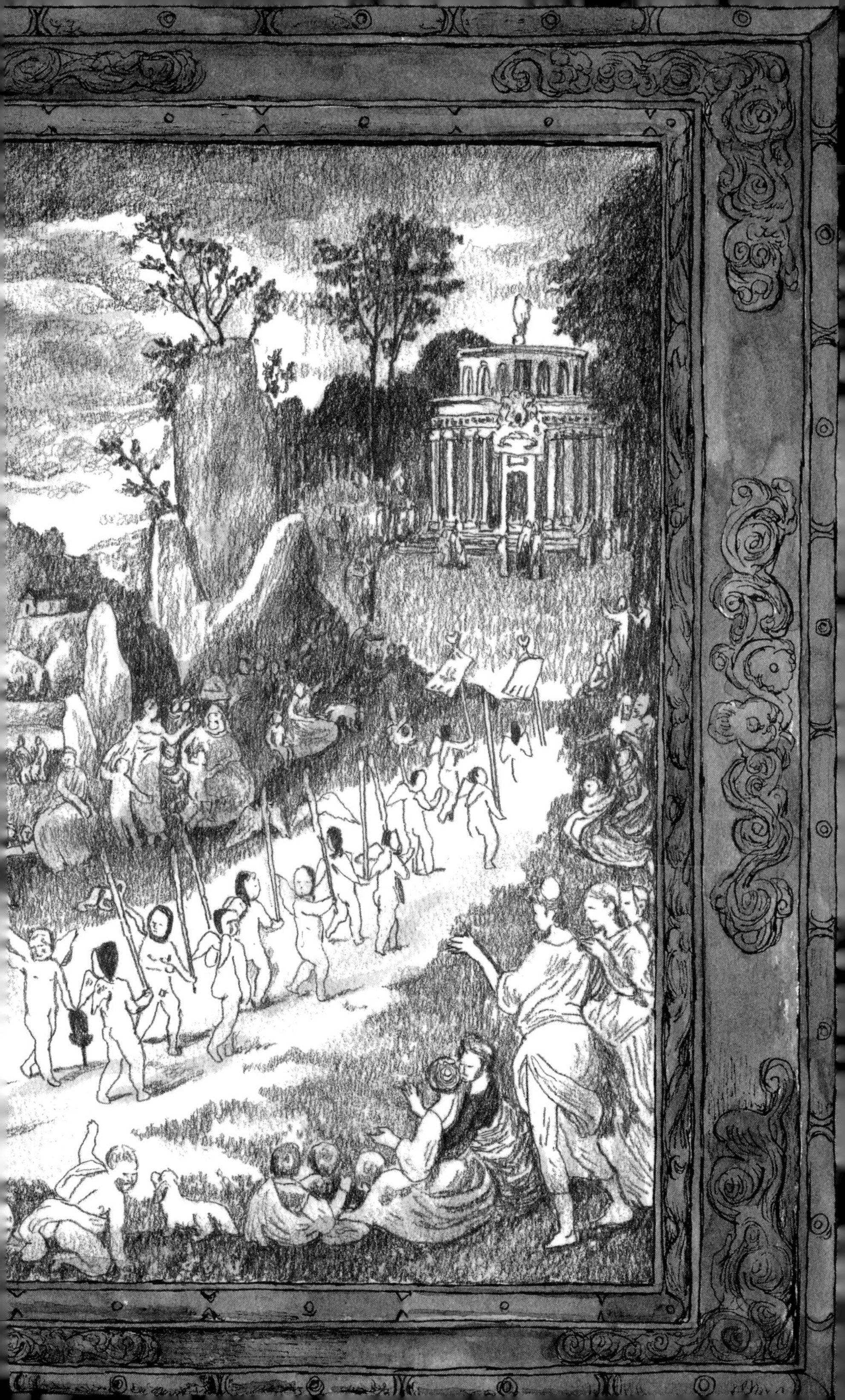

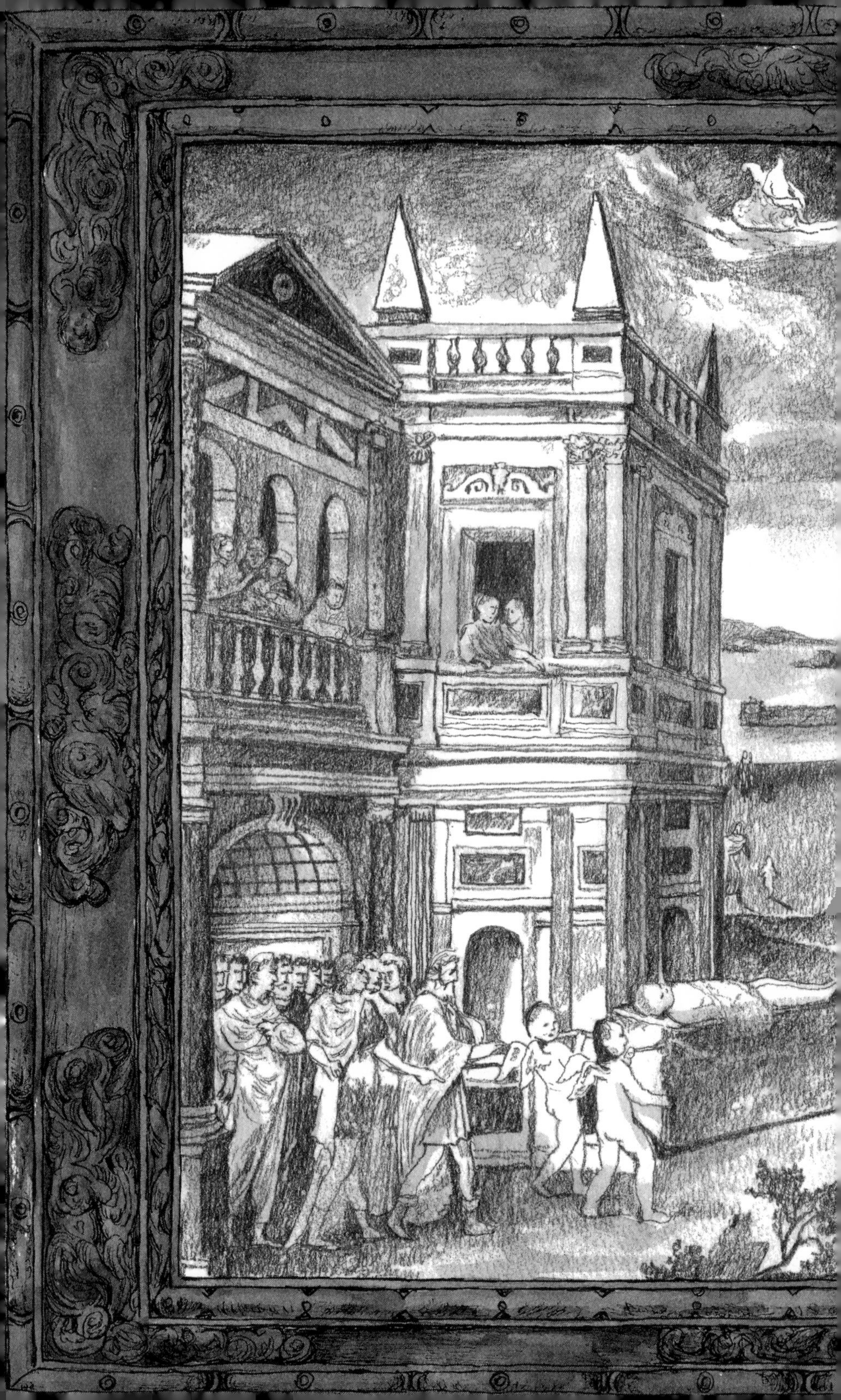

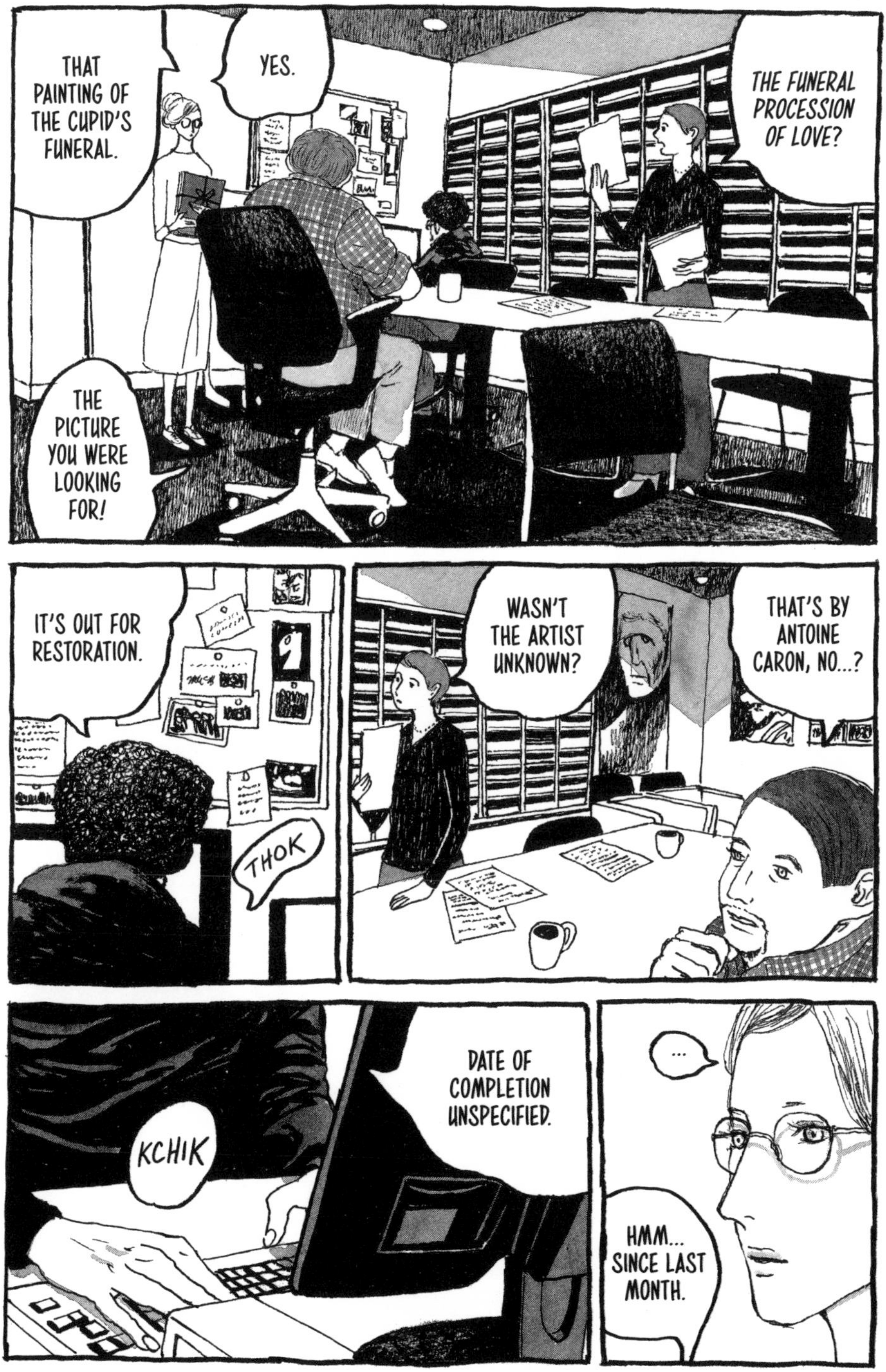
THE FUNERAL PROCESSION OF LOVE?
YES.
THAT PAINTING OF THE CUPID'S FUNERAL.
THE PICTURE YOU WERE LOOKING FOR!
THAT'S BY ANTOINE CARON, NO...?
WASN'T THE ARTIST UNKNOWN?
IT'S OUT FOR RESTORATION.
THOK
...
HMM... SINCE LAST MONTH.
DATE OF COMPLETION UNSPECIFIED.
KCHIK

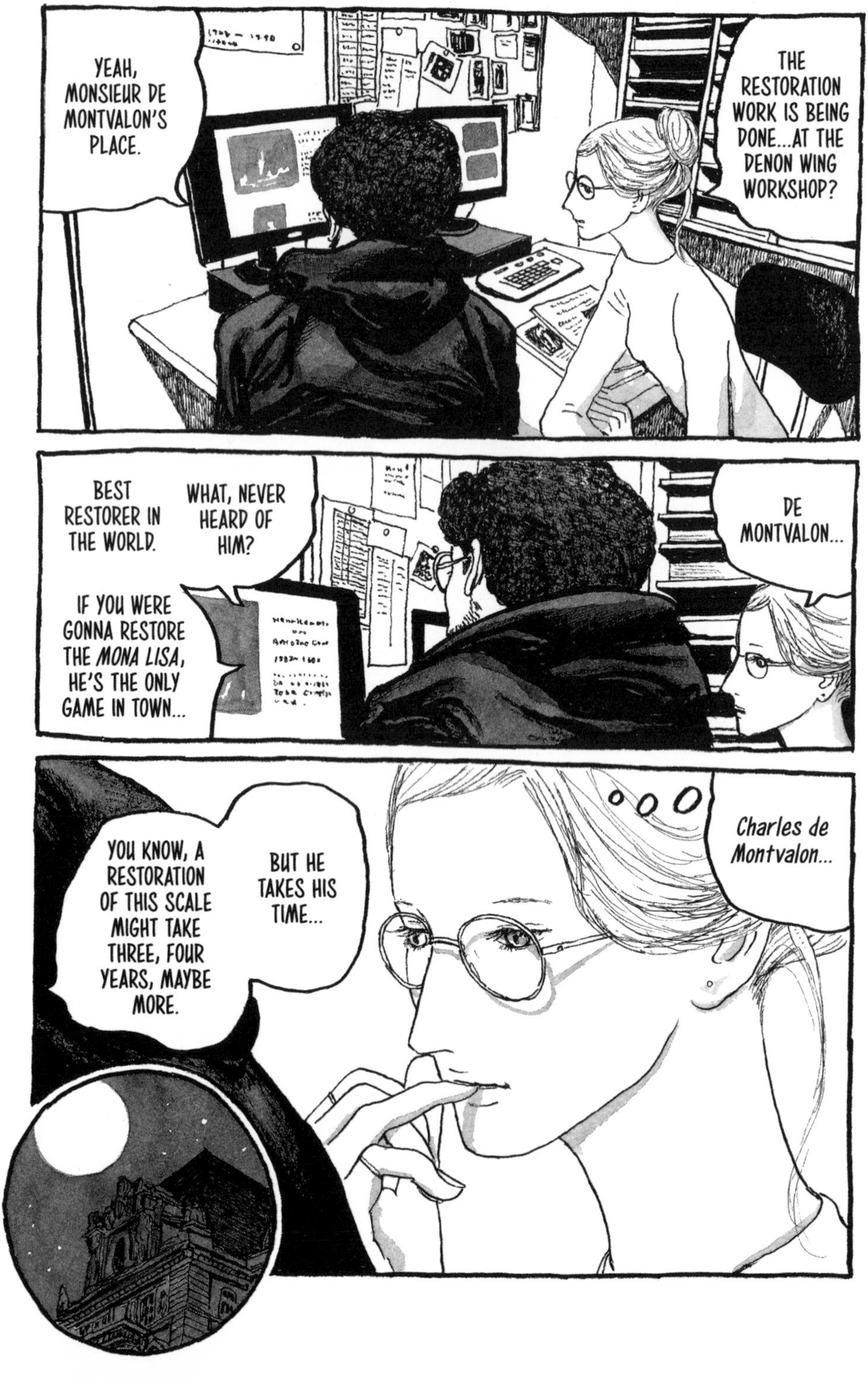
THE RESTORATION WORK IS BEING DONE...AT THE DENON WING WORKSHOP?
YEAH, MONSIEUR DE MONTVALON'S PLACE.
DE MONTVALON...
WHAT, NEVER HEARD OF HIM?
BEST RESTORER IN THE WORLD.
IF YOU WERE GONNA RESTORE THE *MONA LISA*, HE'S THE ONLY GAME IN TOWN...
Charles de Montvalon...
BUT HE TAKES HIS TIME...
YOU KNOW, A RESTORATION OF THIS SCALE MIGHT TAKE THREE, FOUR YEARS, MAYBE MORE.

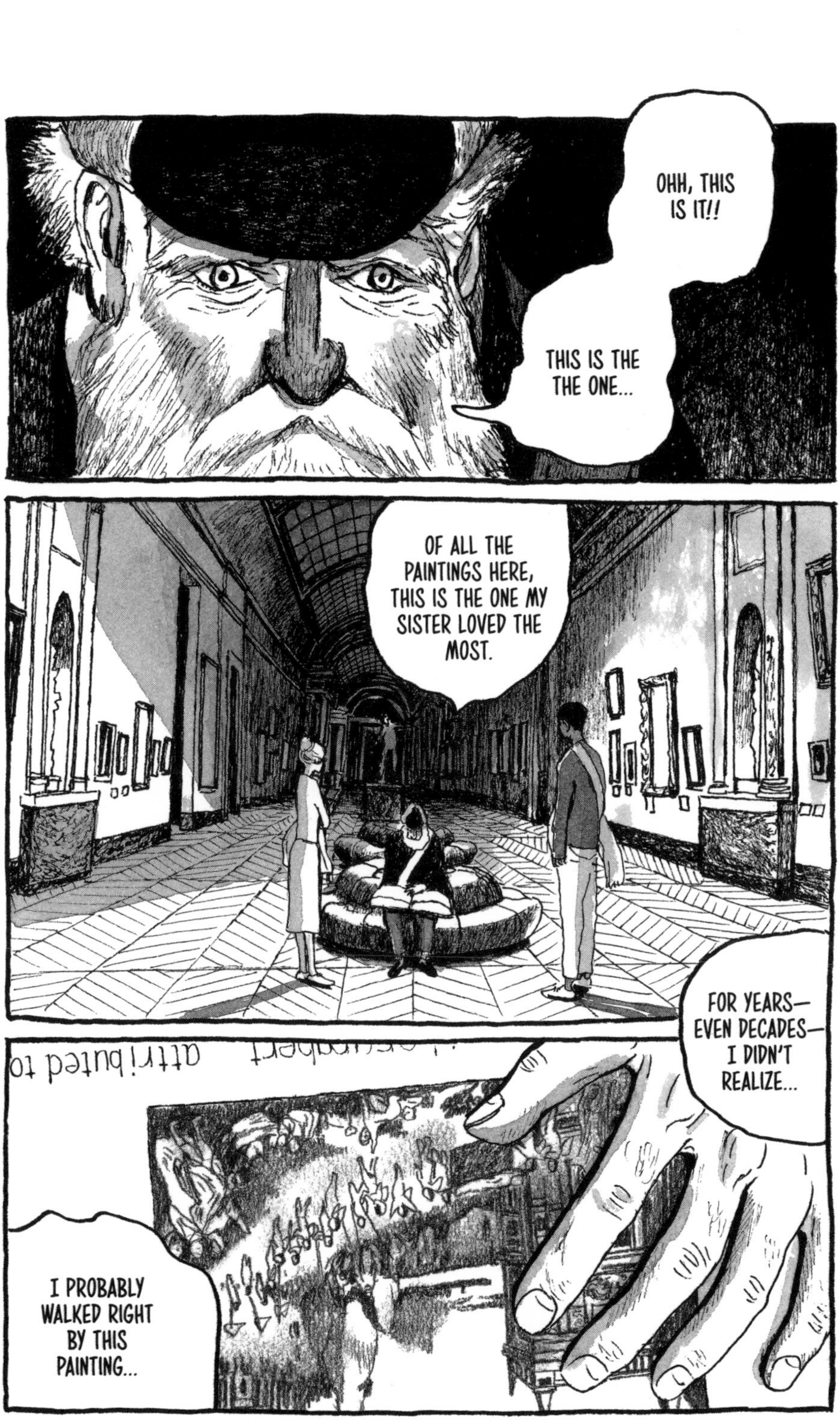
OHH, THIS IS IT!!
THIS IS THE THE ONE...
OF ALL THE PAINTINGS HERE, THIS IS THE ONE MY SISTER LOVED THE MOST.
FOR YEARS—EVEN DECADES—I DIDN'T REALIZE...
I PROBABLY WALKED RIGHT BY THIS PAINTING...

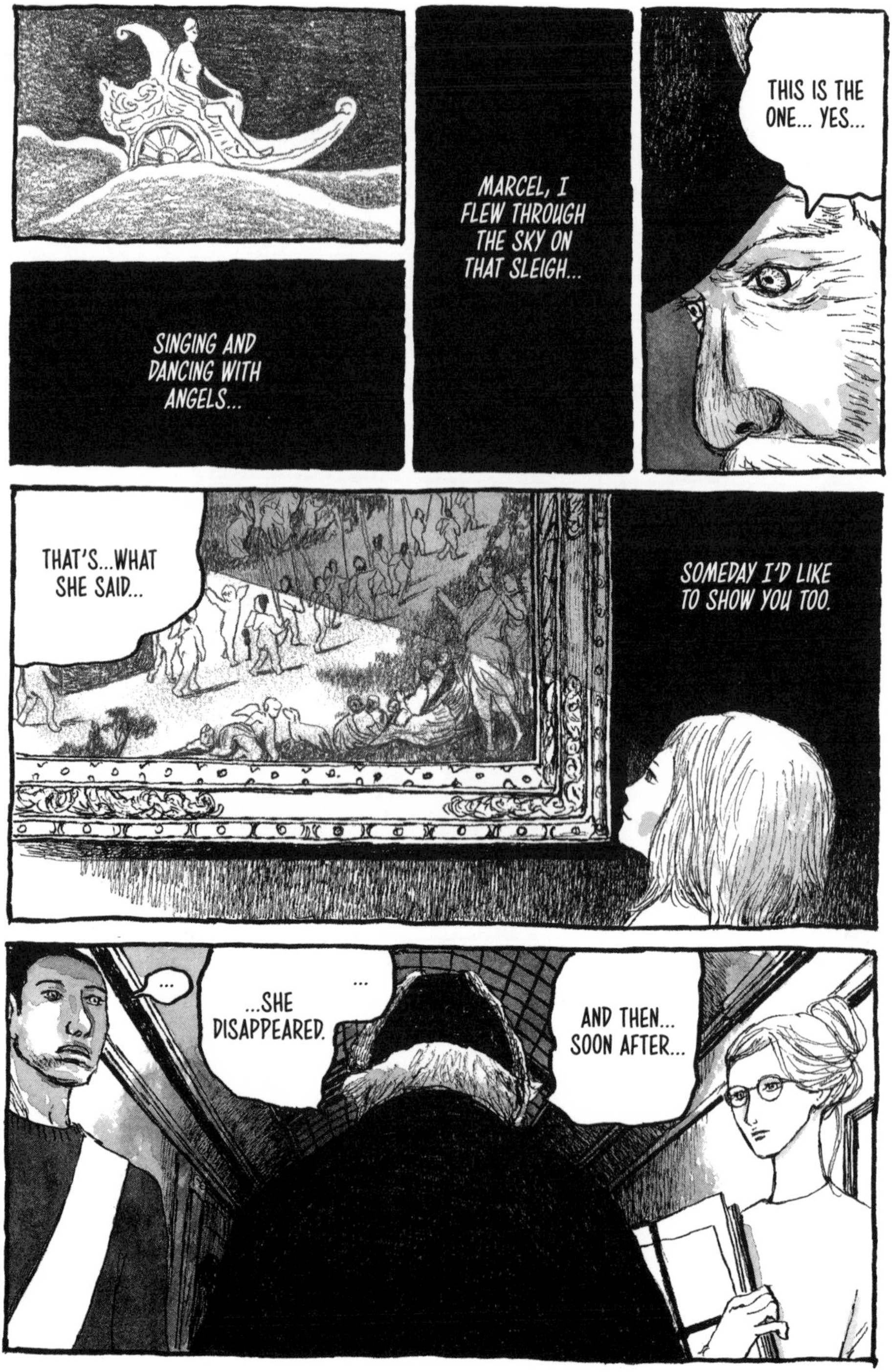
THIS IS THE ONE... YES...
MARCEL, I FLEW THROUGH THE SKY ON THAT SLEIGH...
SINGING AND DANCING WITH ANGELS...
SOMEDAY I'D LIKE TO SHOW YOU TOO.
THAT'S...WHAT SHE SAID...
AND THEN... SOON AFTER...
...
...SHE DISAPPEARED.
...

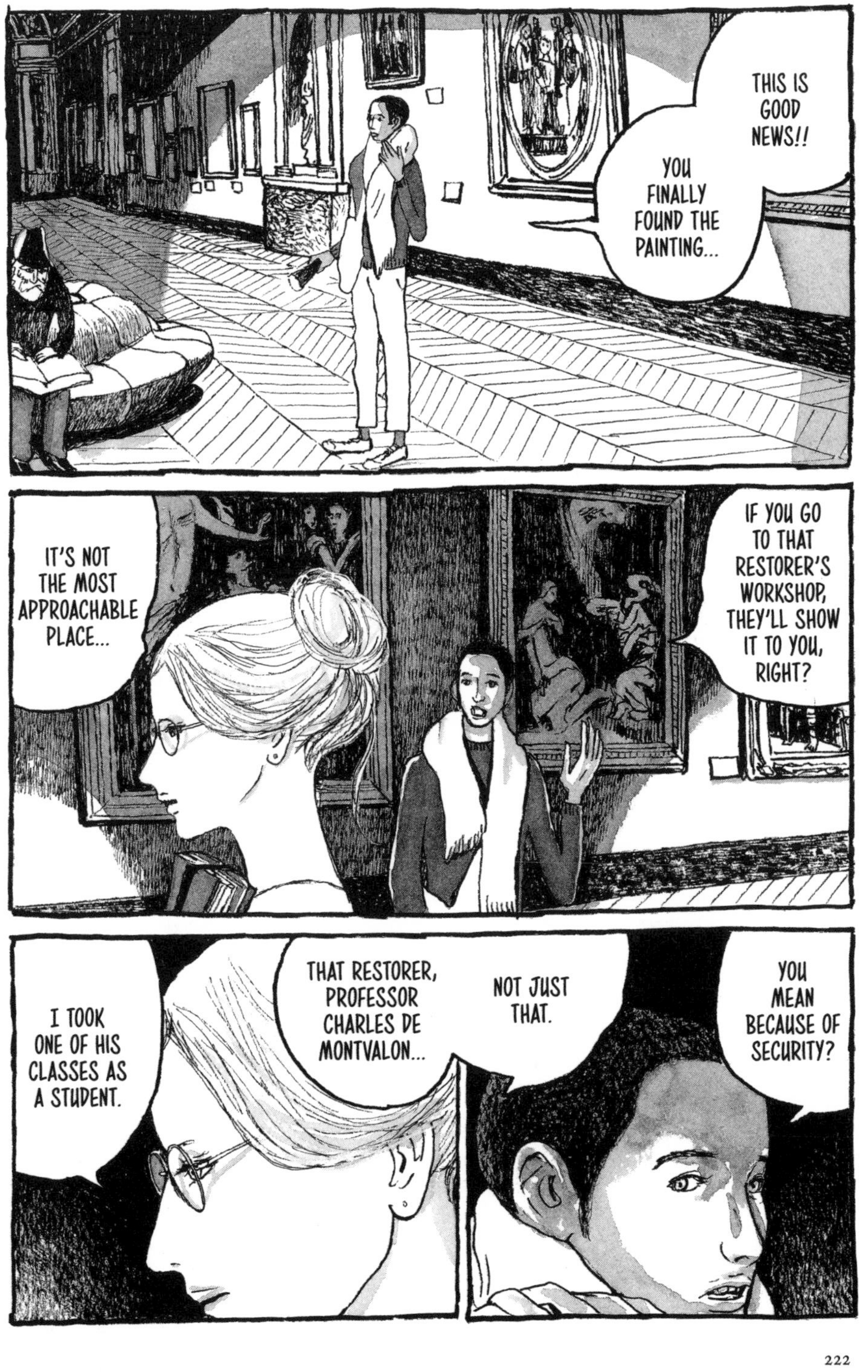
THIS IS GOOD NEWS!!
YOU FINALLY FOUND THE PAINTING...
IF YOU GO TO THAT RESTORER'S WORKSHOP, THEY'LL SHOW IT TO YOU, RIGHT?
IT'S NOT THE MOST APPROACHABLE PLACE...
YOU MEAN BECAUSE OF SECURITY?
NOT JUST THAT.
THAT RESTORER, PROFESSOR CHARLES DE MONTVALON...
I TOOK ONE OF HIS CLASSES AS A STUDENT.

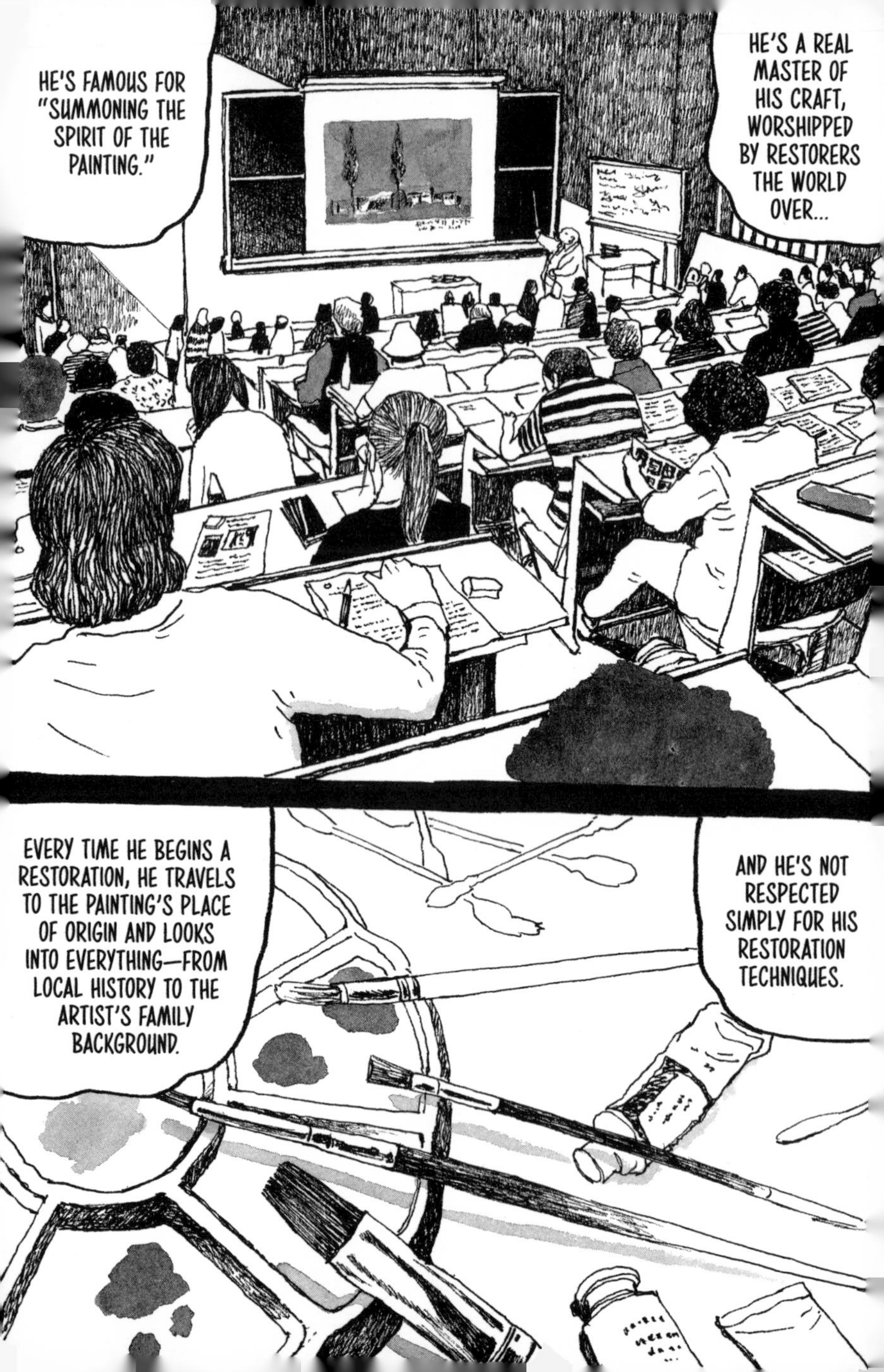
HE'S A REAL MASTER OF HIS CRAFT, WORSHIPPED BY RESTORERS THE WORLD OVER...
HE'S FAMOUS FOR "SUMMONING THE SPIRIT OF THE PAINTING."
AND HE'S NOT RESPECTED SIMPLY FOR HIS RESTORATION TECHNIQUES.
EVERY TIME HE BEGINS A RESTORATION, HE TRAVELS TO THE PAINTING'S PLACE OF ORIGIN AND LOOKS INTO EVERYTHING—FROM LOCAL HISTORY TO THE ARTIST'S FAMILY BACKGROUND.

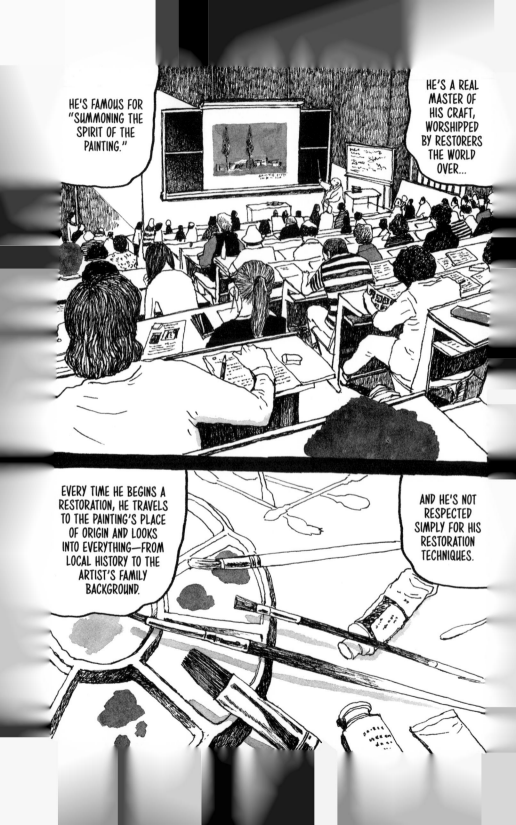

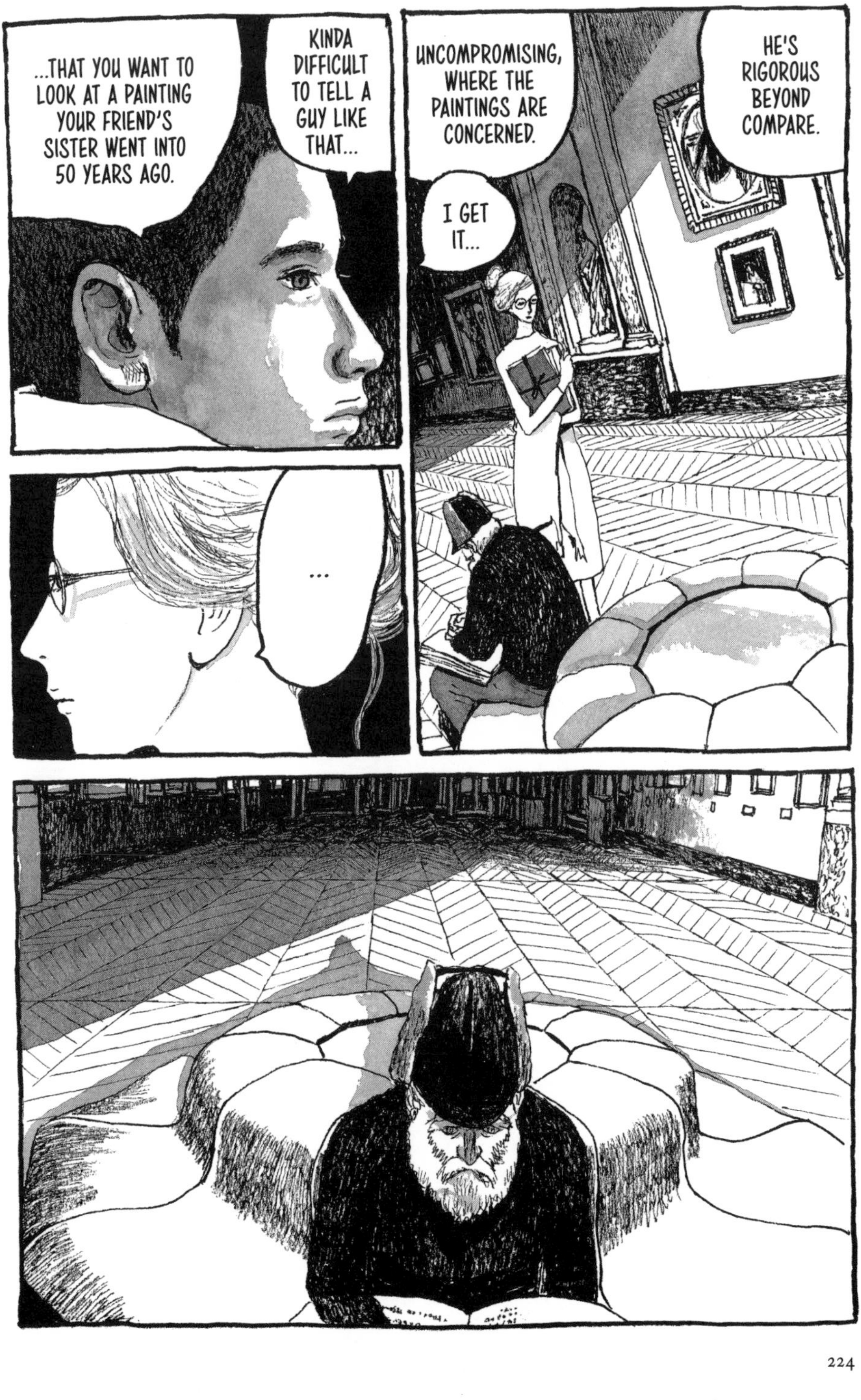
HE'S RIGOROUS BEYOND COMPARE.
UNCOMPROMISING, WHERE THE PAINTINGS ARE CONCERNED.
I GET IT...
KINDA DIFFICULT TO TELL A GUY LIKE THAT...
...THAT YOU WANT TO LOOK AT A PAINTING YOUR FRIEND'S SISTER WENT INTO 50 YEARS AGO.
...

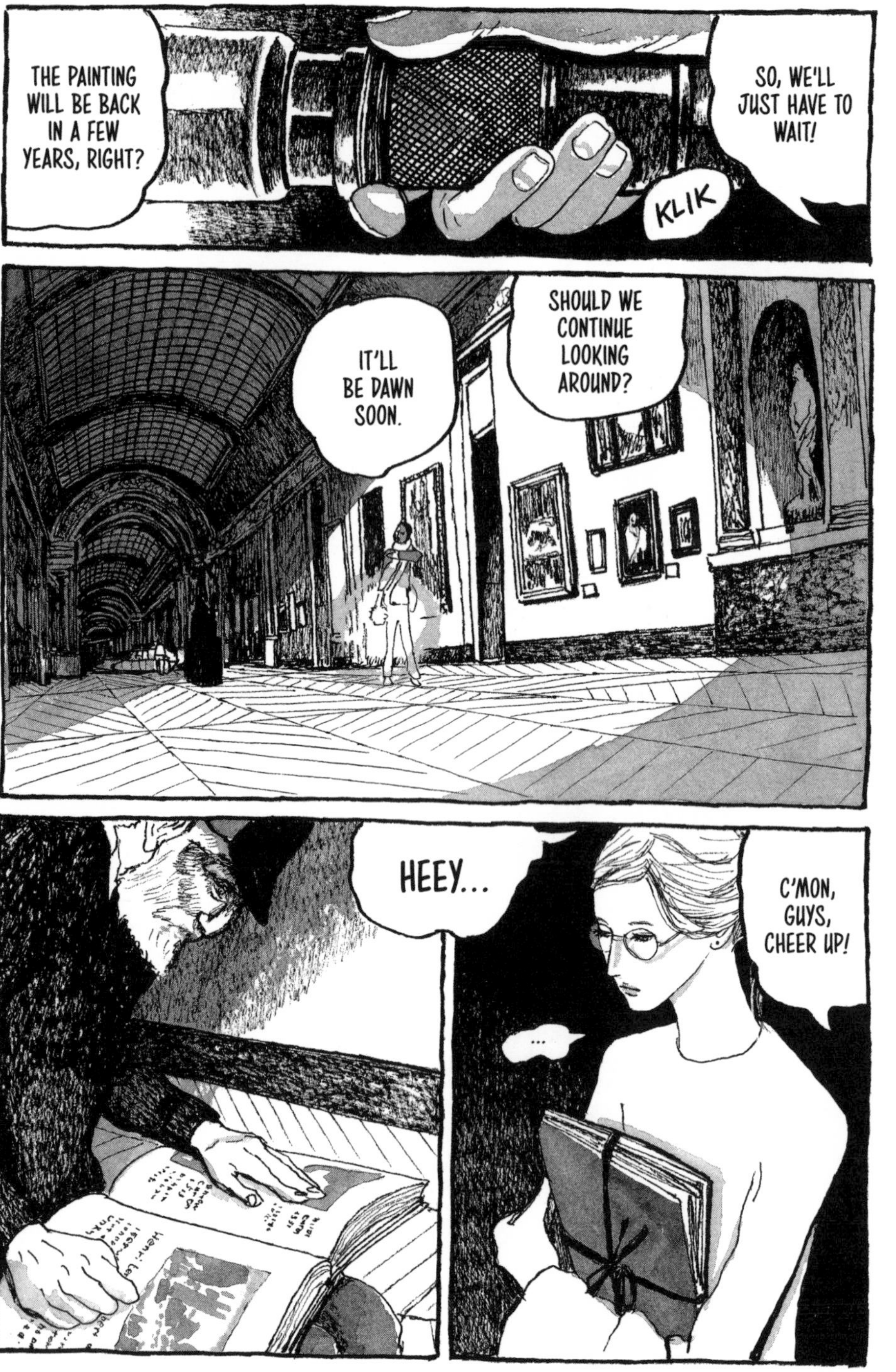
SO, WE'LL JUST HAVE TO WAIT!
THE PAINTING WILL BE BACK IN A FEW YEARS, RIGHT?
KLIK
SHOULD WE CONTINUE LOOKING AROUND?
IT'LL BE DAWN SOON.
C'MON, GUYS, CHEER UP!
HEEY...
...

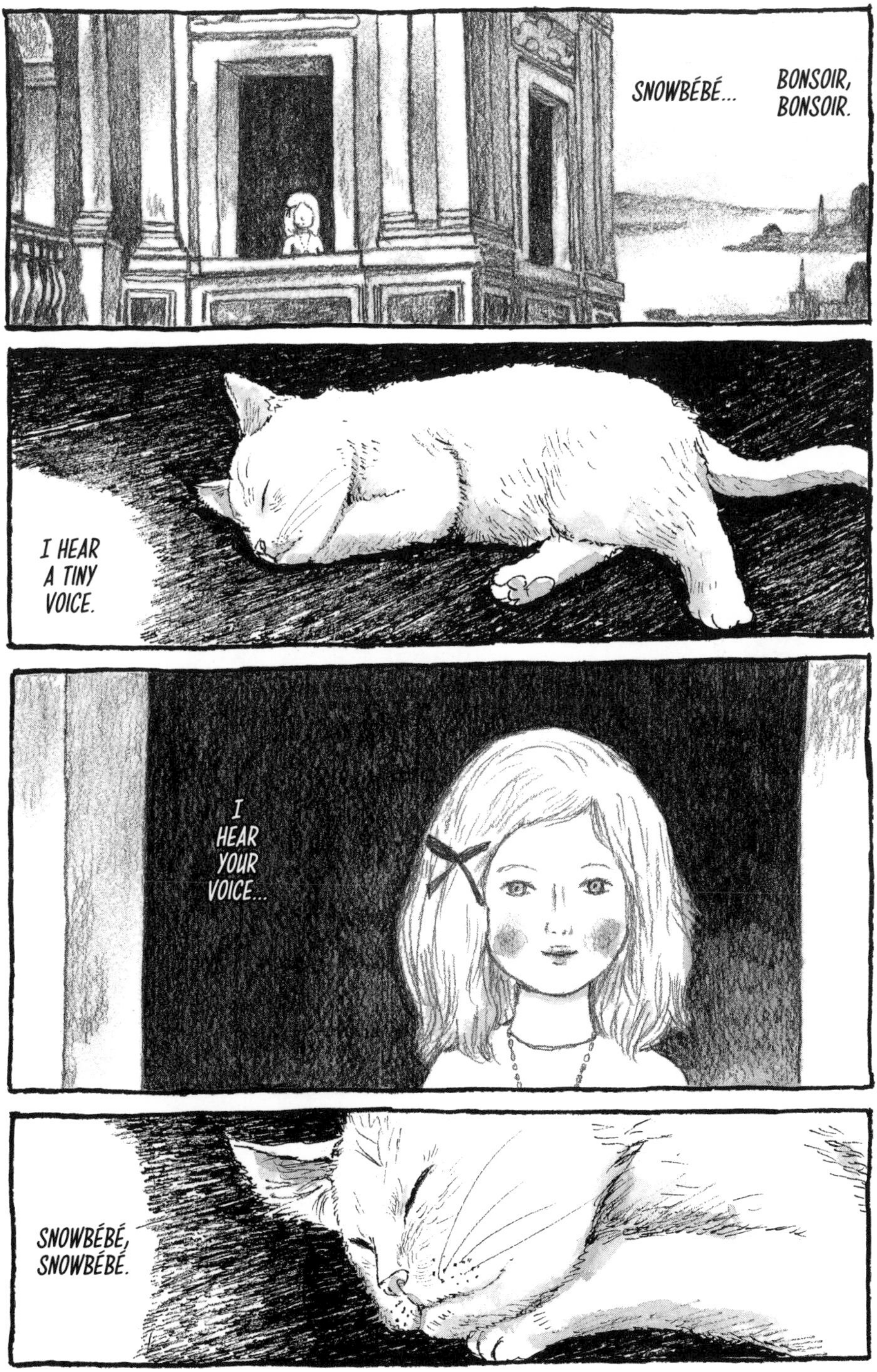
BONSOIR, BONSOIR.
SNOWBÉBÉ...
I HEAR A TINY VOICE.
I HEAR YOUR VOICE...
SNOWBÉBÉ, SNOWBÉBÉ.

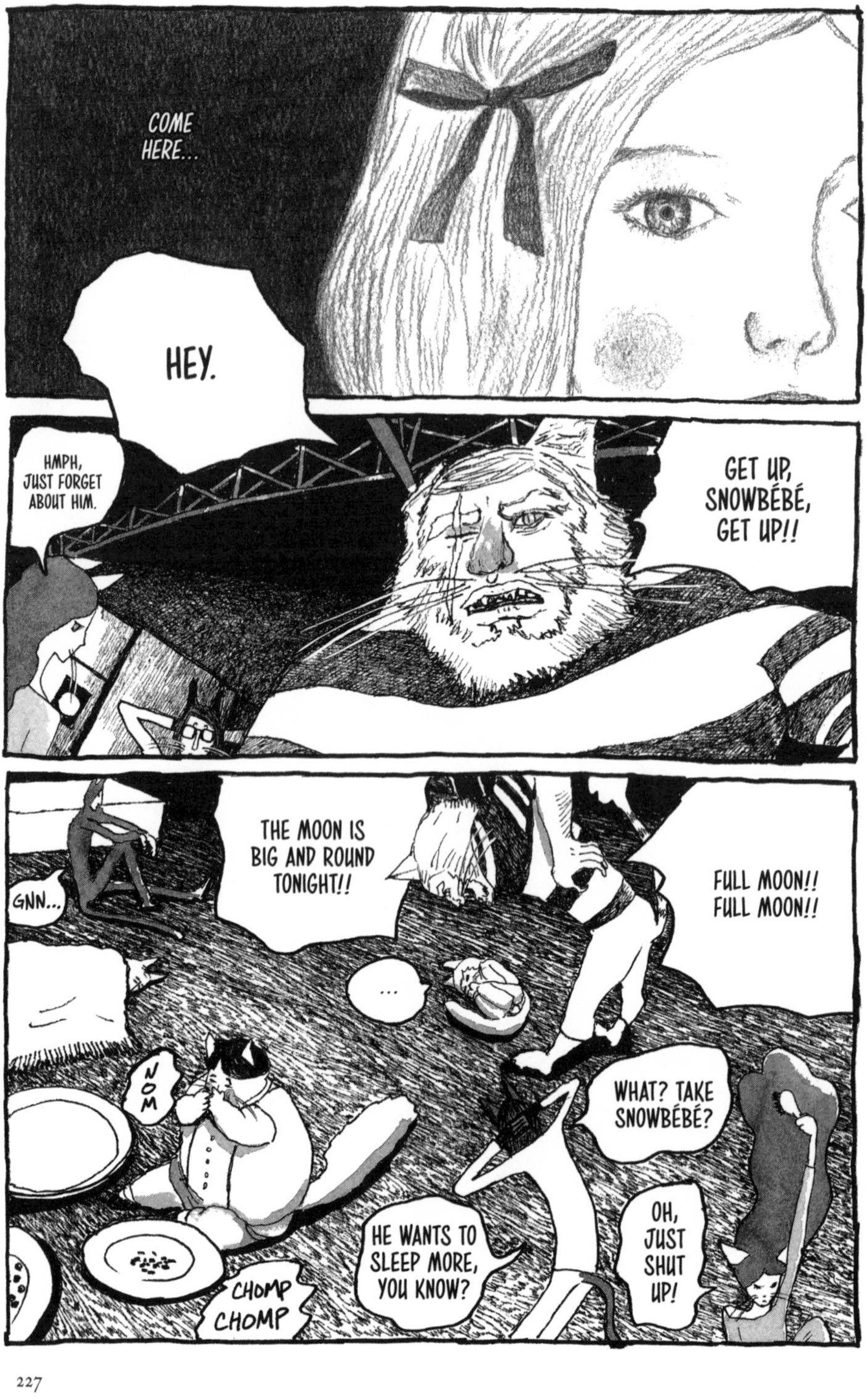
COME HERE...
HEY.
GET UP, SNOWBÉBÉ, GET UP!!
HMPH, JUST FORGET ABOUT HIM.
FULL MOON!! FULL MOON!!
THE MOON IS BIG AND ROUND TONIGHT!!
GNN...
...
WHAT? TAKE SNOWBÉBÉ?
OH, JUST SHUT UP!
HE WANTS TO SLEEP MORE, YOU KNOW?
NOM
CHOMP CHOMP

GET UP, SNOWBÉBÉ.
BIG AND ROUND.
BAM BAM BAM
TO THE PARK WE GO, CATS OF THE LOUVRE!!
MROWW
STOMP
BIG AND ROUND!!
MROWW
THUMP
...
MEOW-WOW.

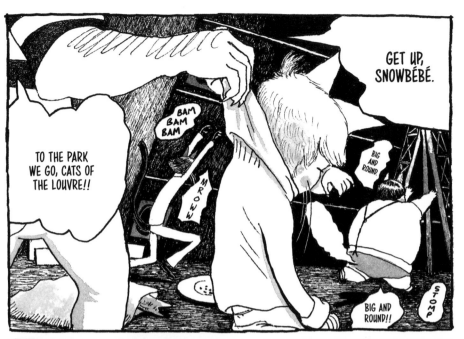

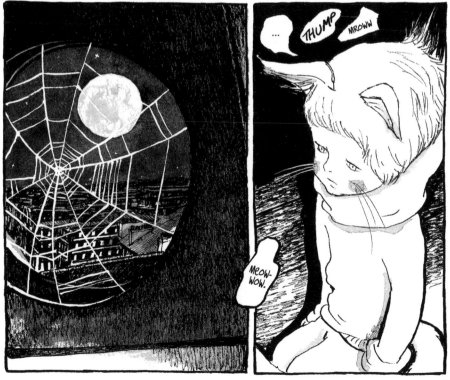

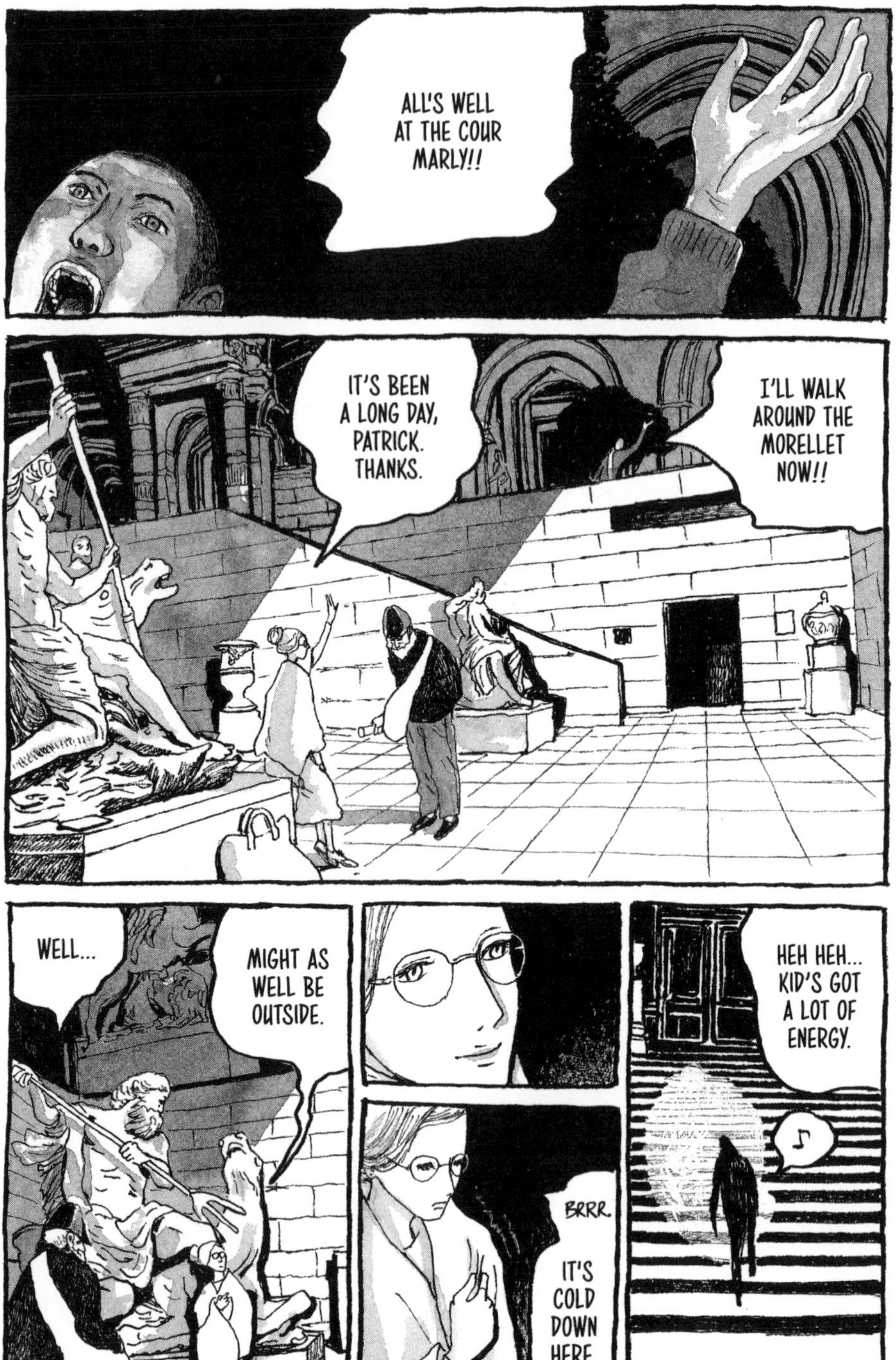
ALL'S WELL AT THE COUR MARLY!!
I'LL WALK AROUND THE MORELLET NOW!!
IT'S BEEN A LONG DAY, PATRICK. THANKS.
HEH HEH... KID'S GOT A LOT OF ENERGY.
BRRR.
IT'S COLD DOWN HERE.
WELL...
MIGHT AS WELL BE OUTSIDE.

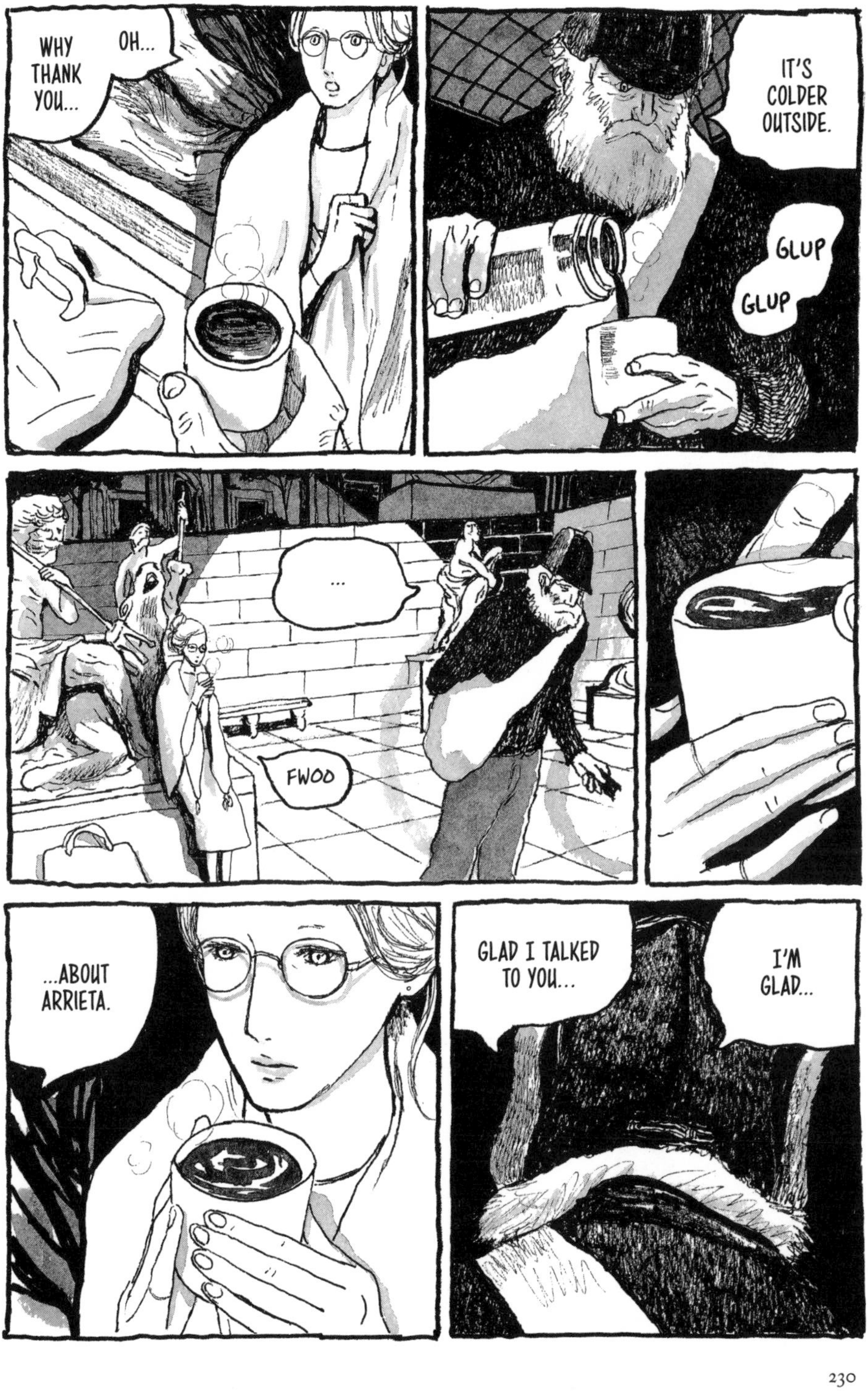
IT'S COLDER OUTSIDE.
GLUP
GLUP
OH...
WHY THANK YOU...
...
FWOO
I'M GLAD...
GLAD I TALKED TO YOU...
...ABOUT ARRIETA.

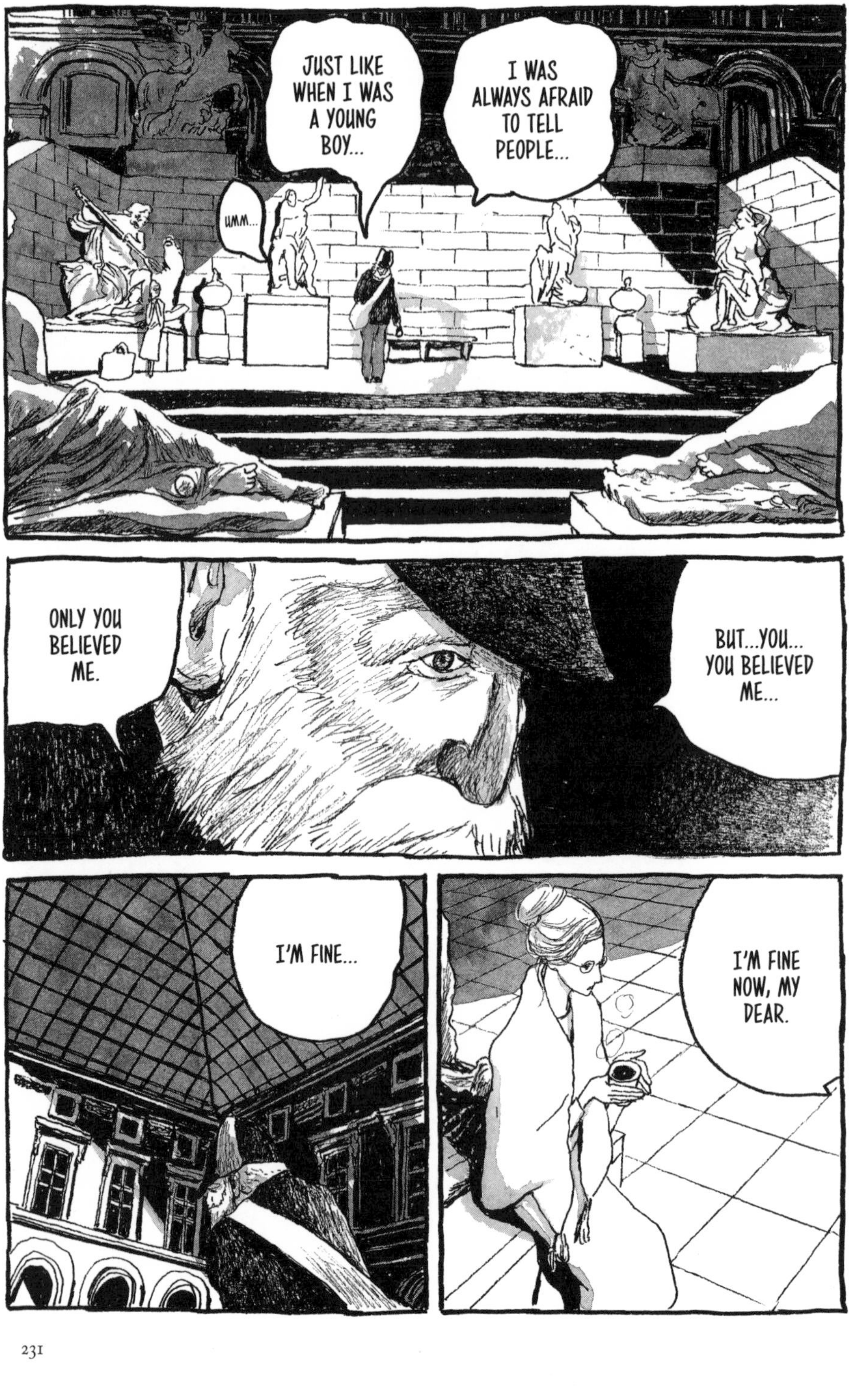
I WAS ALWAYS AFRAID TO TELL PEOPLE...
JUST LIKE WHEN I WAS A YOUNG BOY...
UMM...
BUT...YOU... YOU BELIEVED ME...
ONLY YOU BELIEVED ME.
I'M FINE NOW, MY DEAR.
I'M FINE...

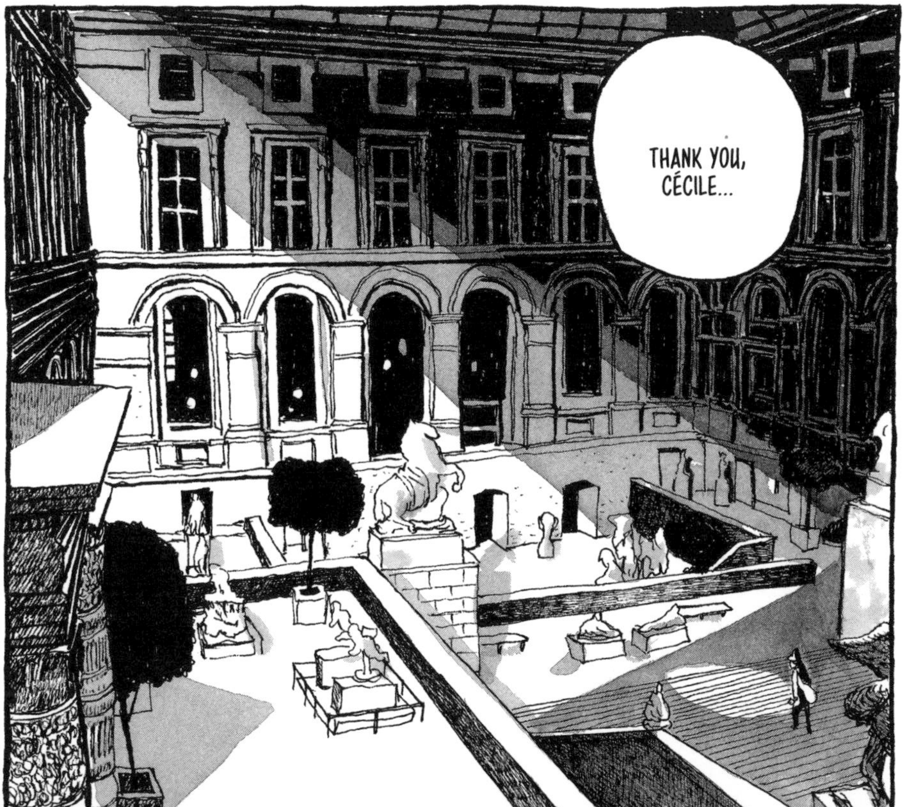
THANK YOU, CÉCILE...
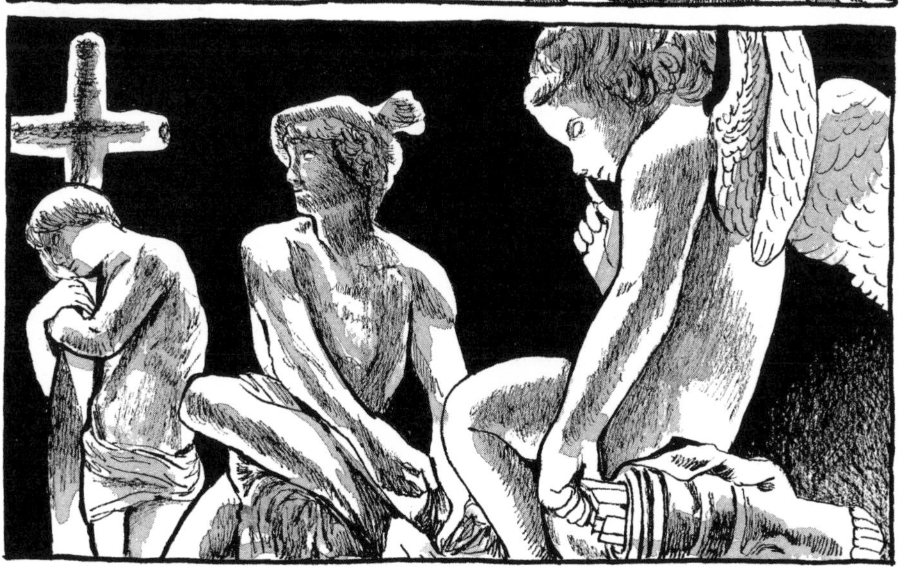

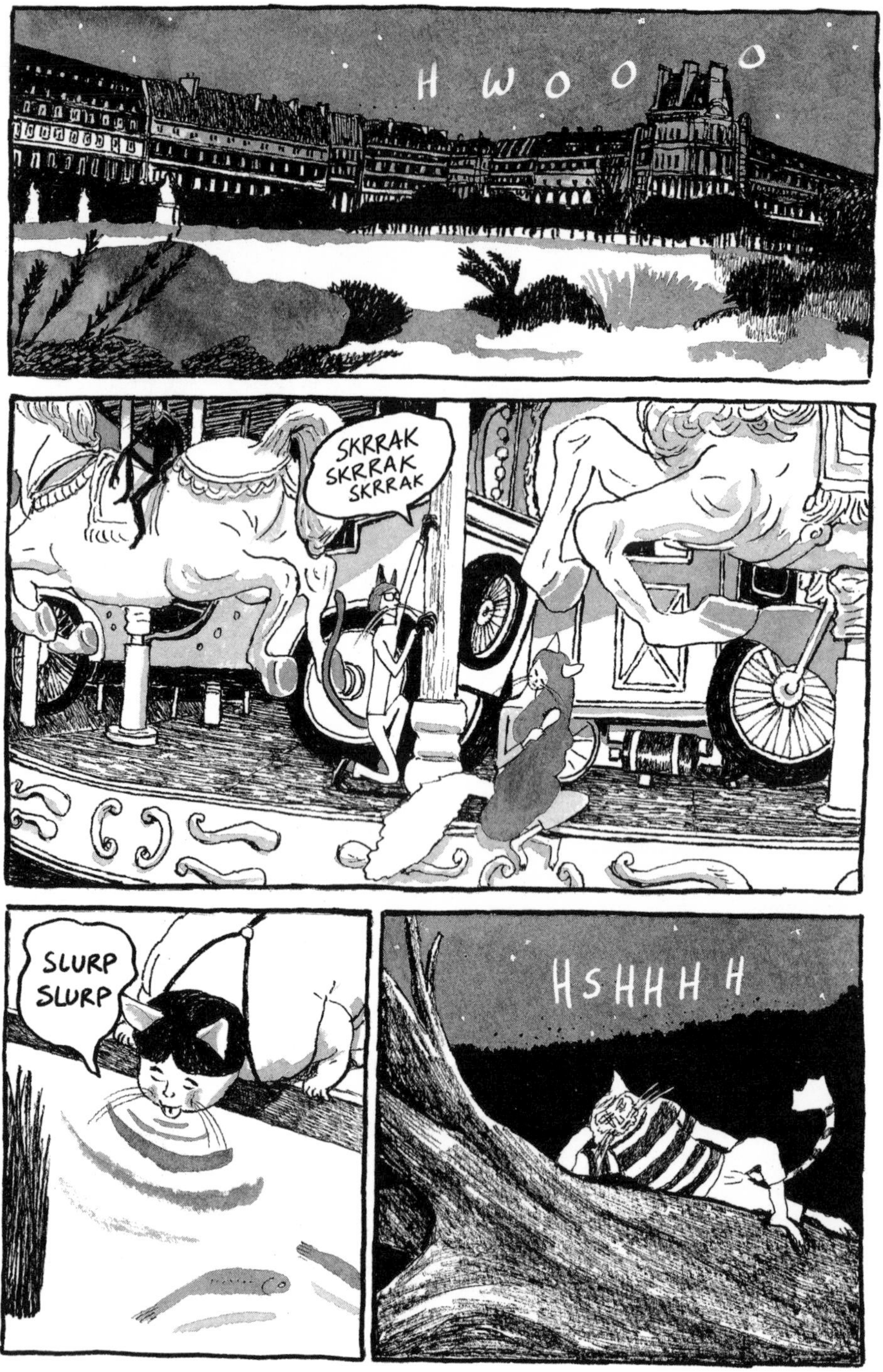
HWOOO
SKRRAK SKRRAK SKRRAK
HSHHHH
SLURP SLURP

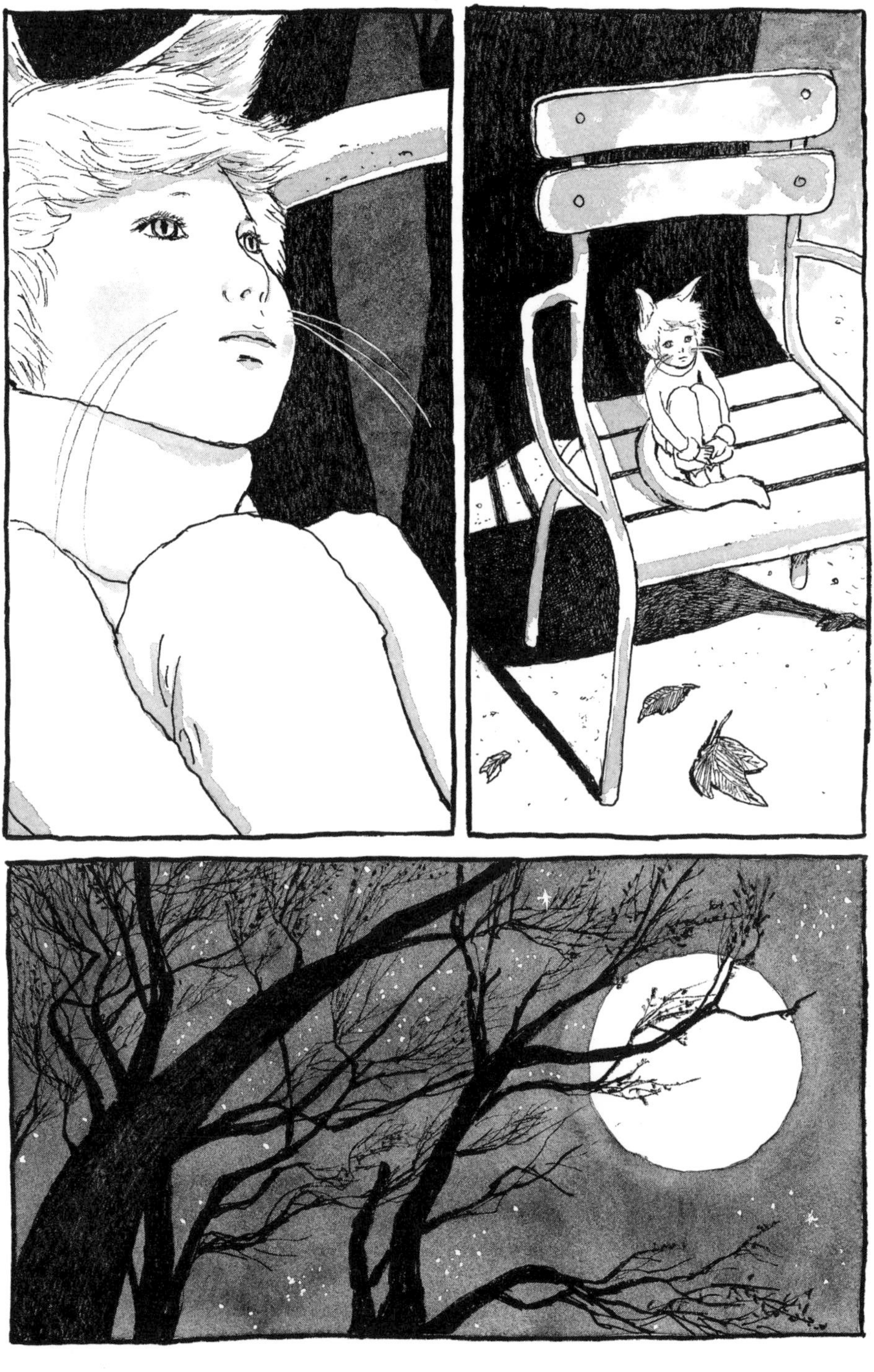

PART ONE
—END—

PART TWO

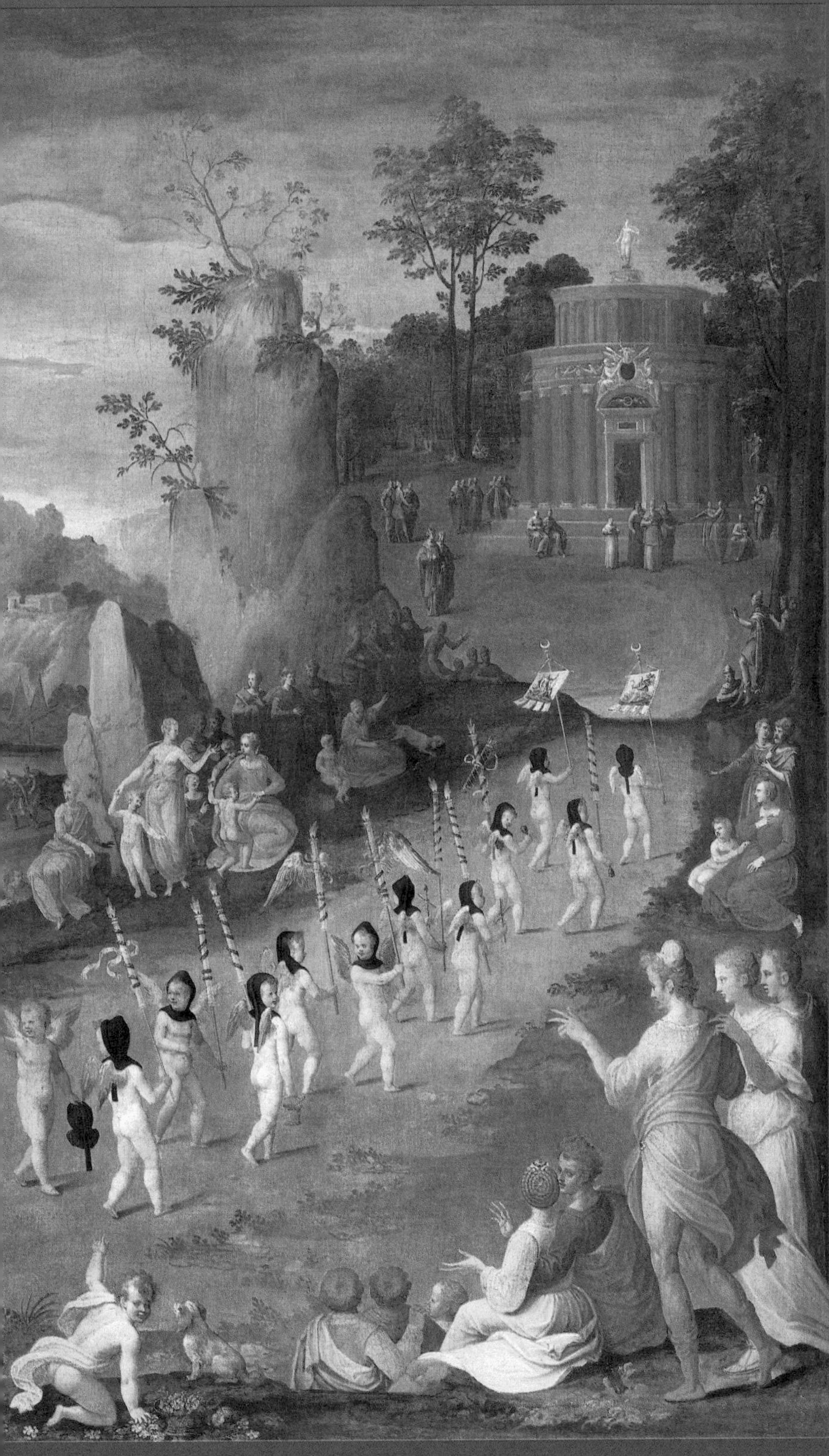

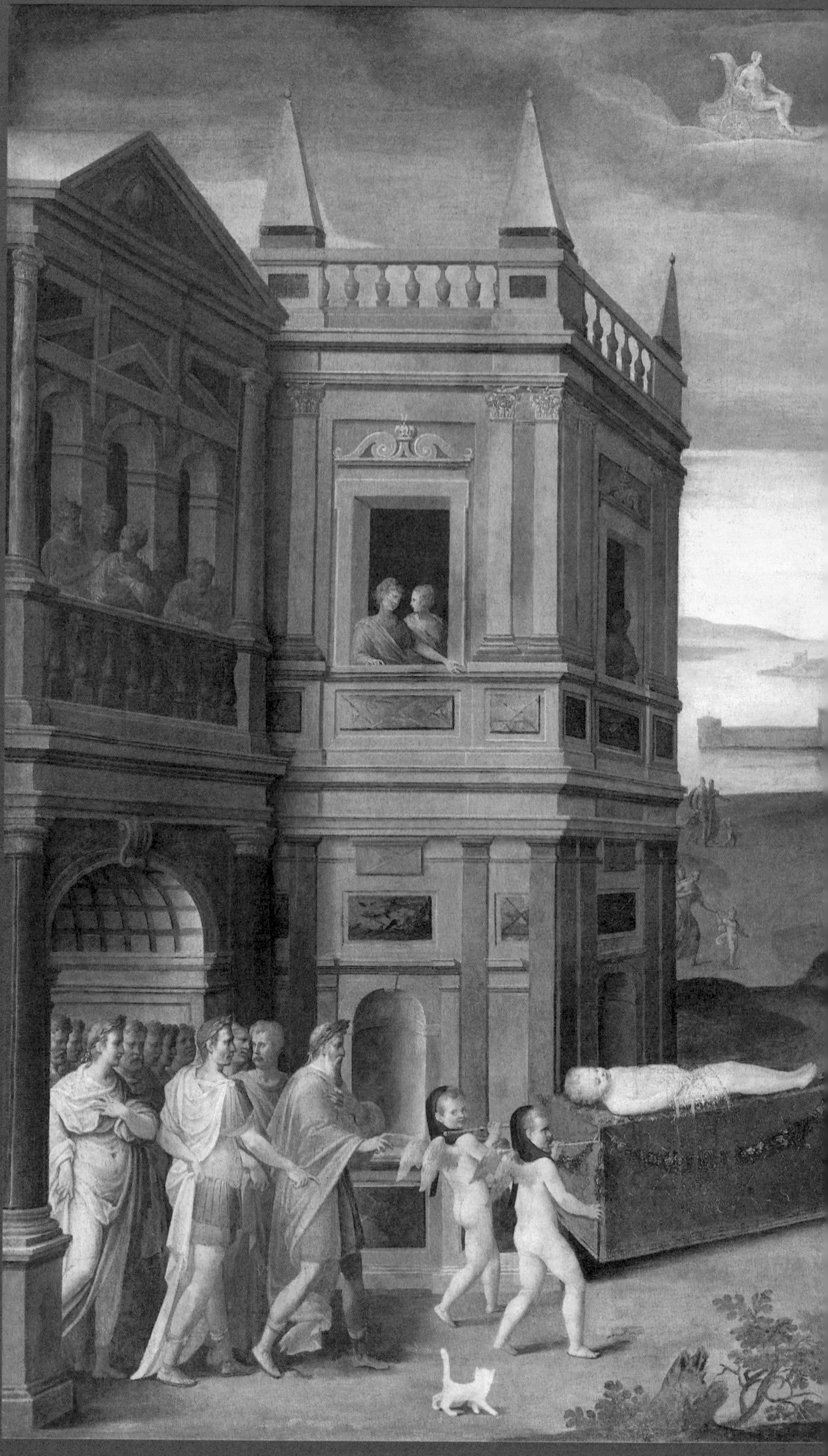

CHAPTER 11

The Secret of the Tuileries Garden

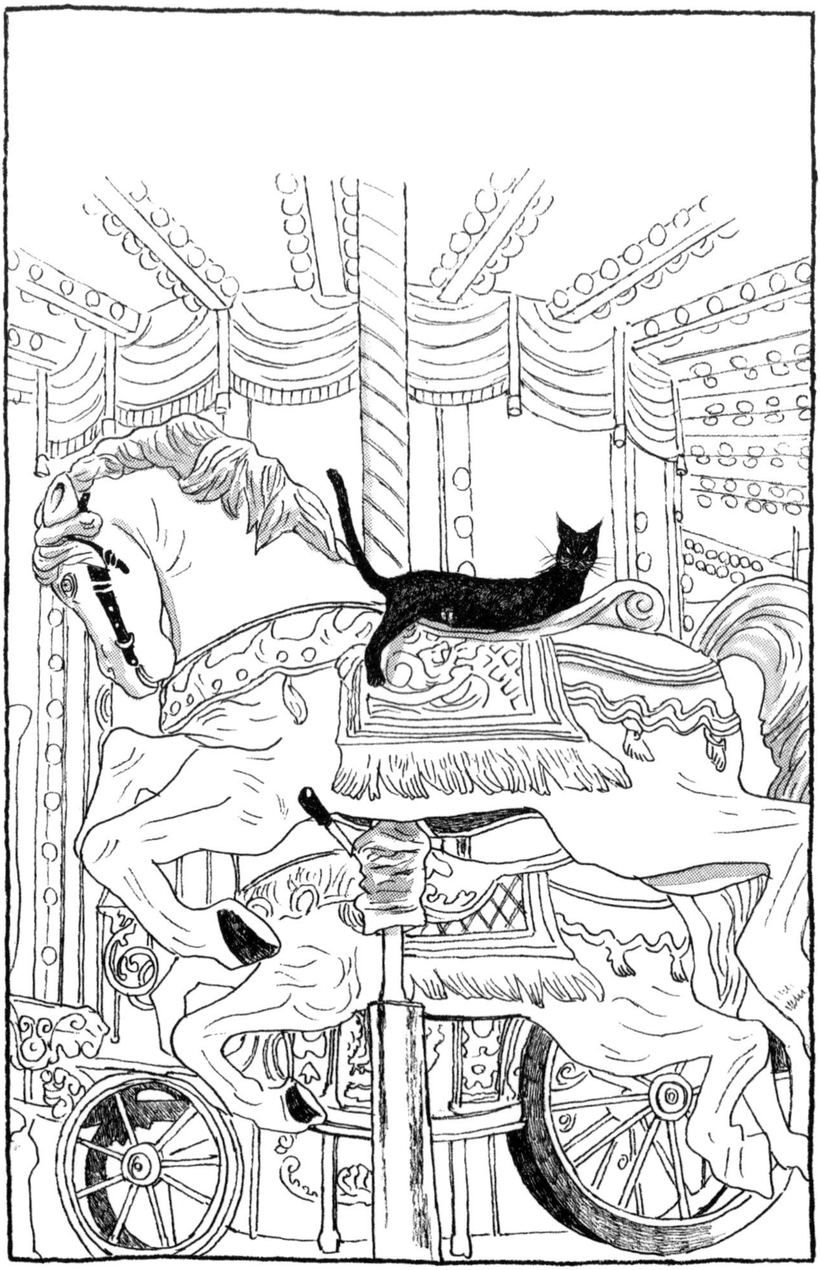

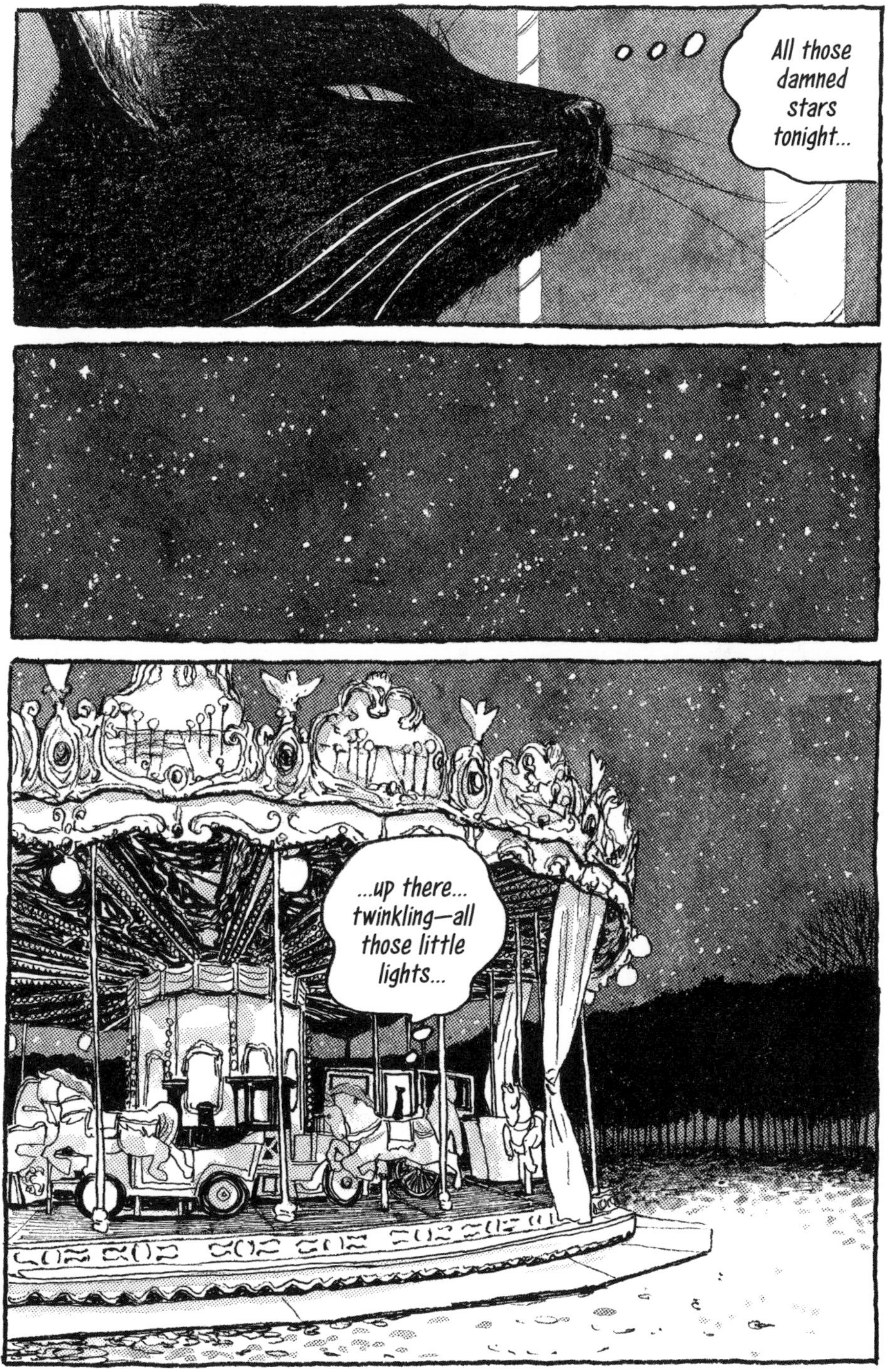
All those damned stars tonight...
...up there... twinkling—all those little lights...

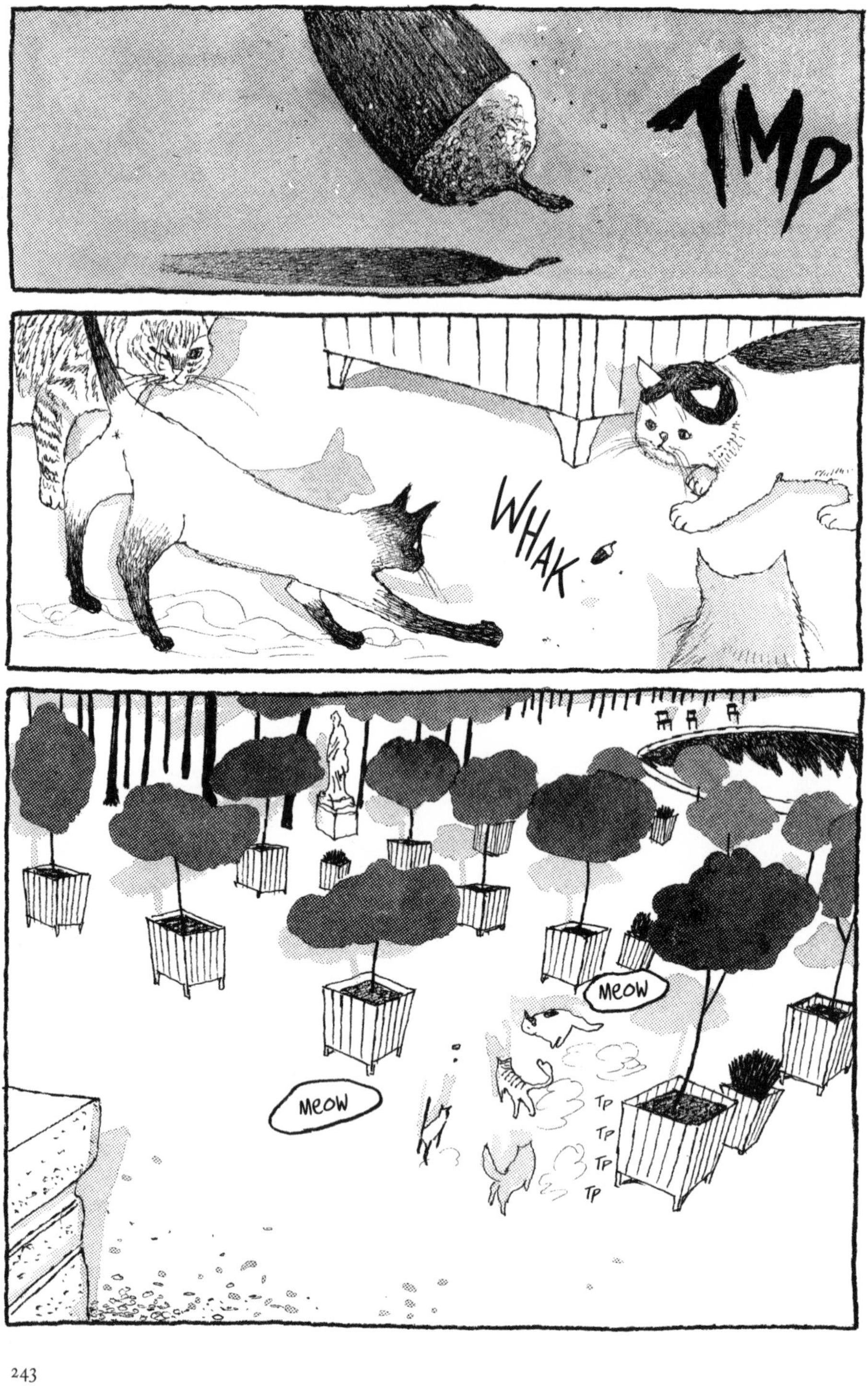

TMP
WHAK
MEOW
MEOW
TP
TP
TP
TP

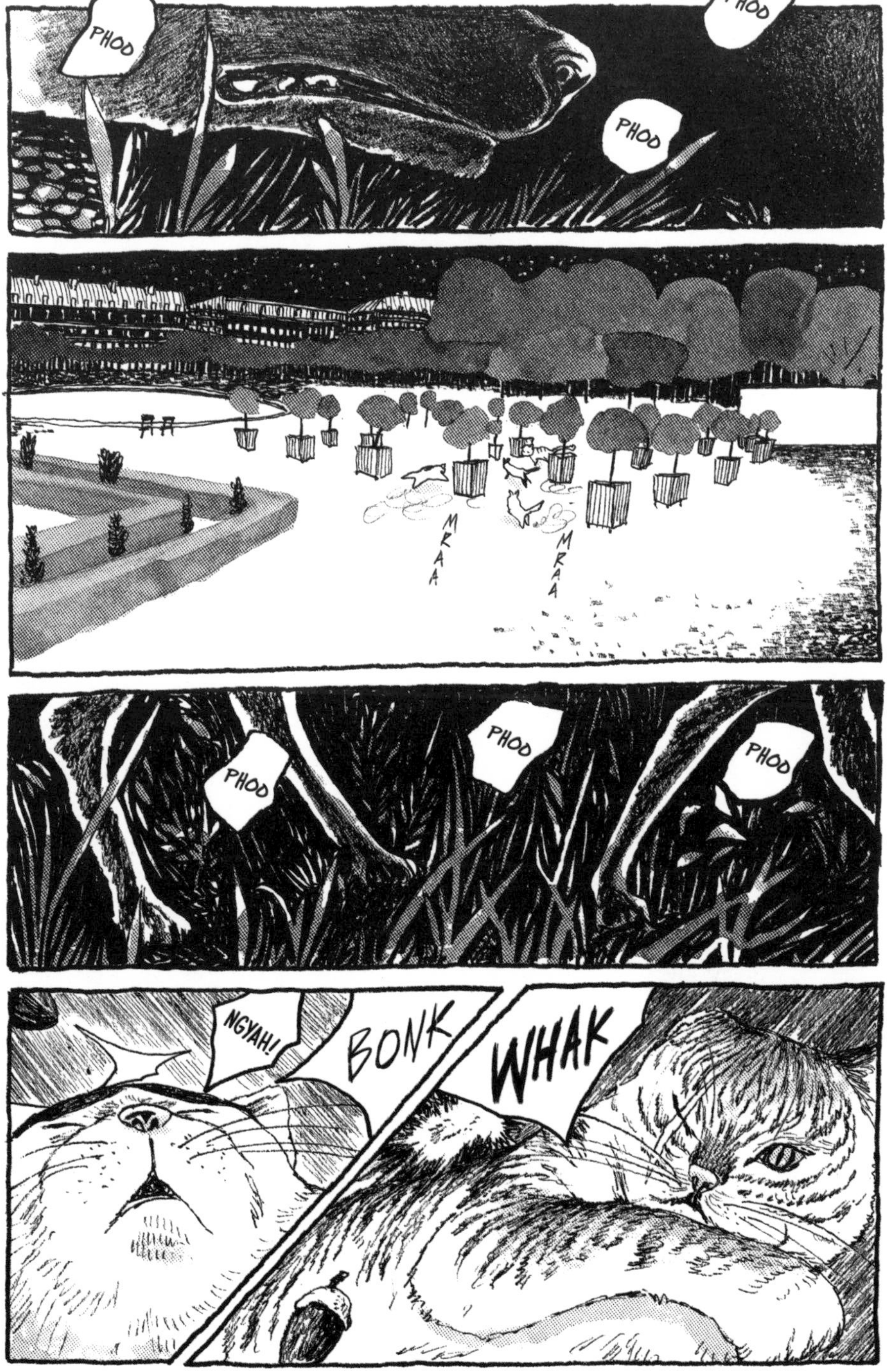
PHOD
PHOD
PHOD
MRAA
MRAA
PHOD
PHOD
PHOD
WHAK
BONK
NGYAH!

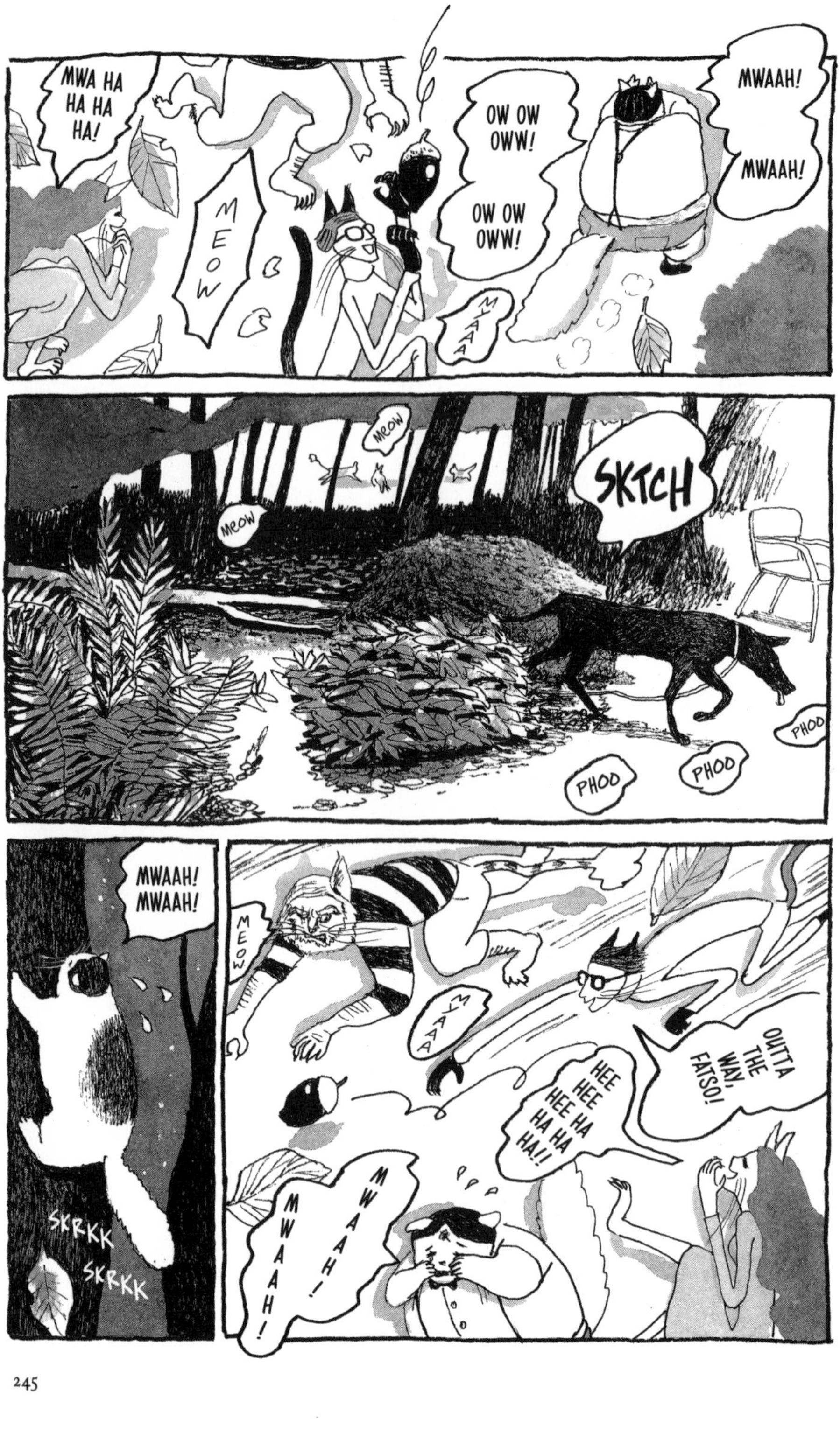
MWAAH!
MWAAH!
OW OW OWW!
OW OW OWW!
MWA HA HA HA HA!
MEOW
MYAAA
SKTCH
MEOW
MEOW
PHOO
PHOO
PHOO
OUTTA THE WAY, FATSO!
HEE HEE HEE HA HA HA!!
MEOW
MYAAA
MWAAH!
MWAAH!
MWAAH! MWAAH!
SKRKK
SKRKK

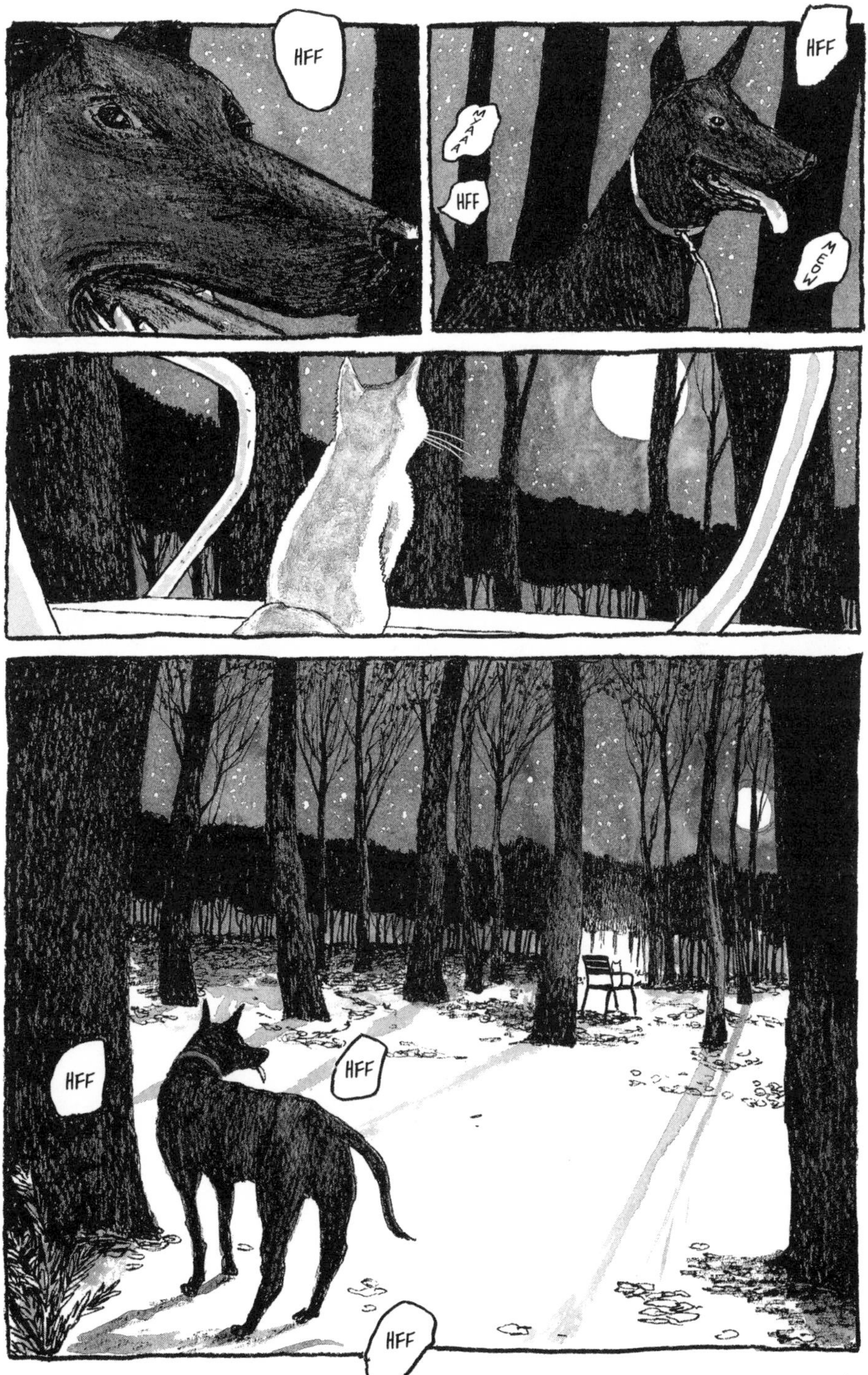
HFF
MYAAAA
HFF
MEOW
HFF
HFF
HFF
HFF

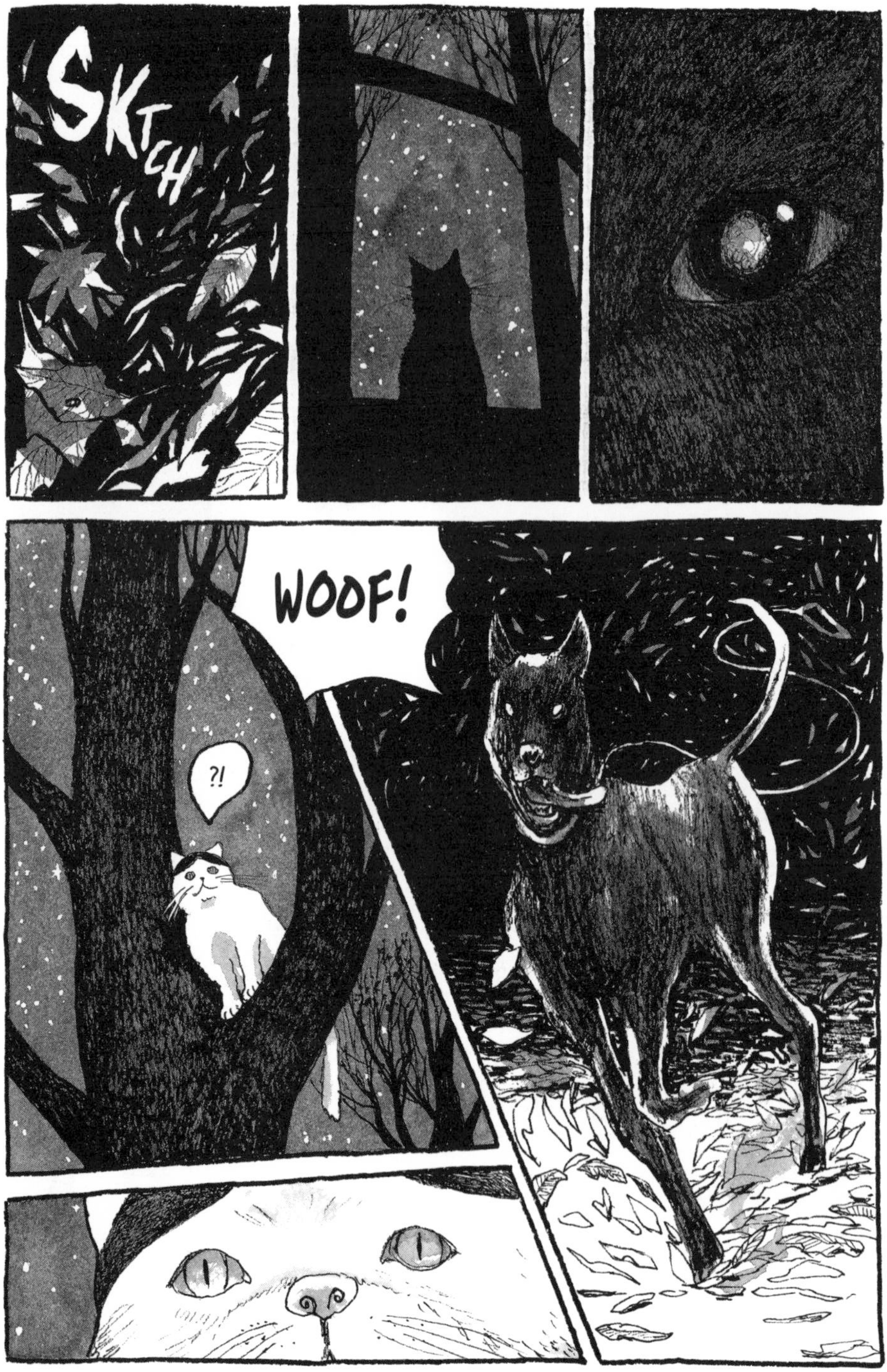
SKTCH
WOOF!
?!

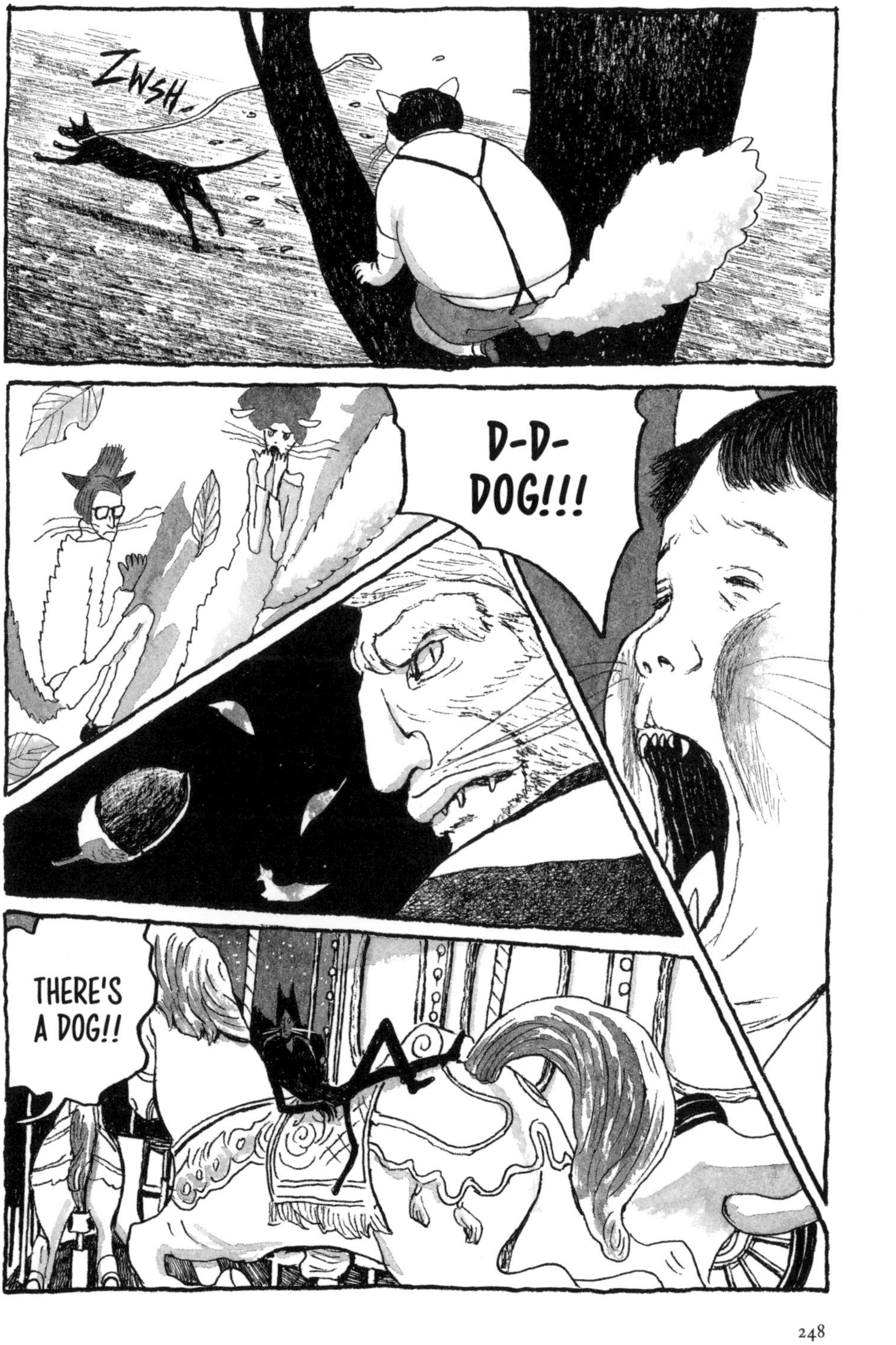
ZWSH
D-D-DOG!!!
THERE'S A DOG!!

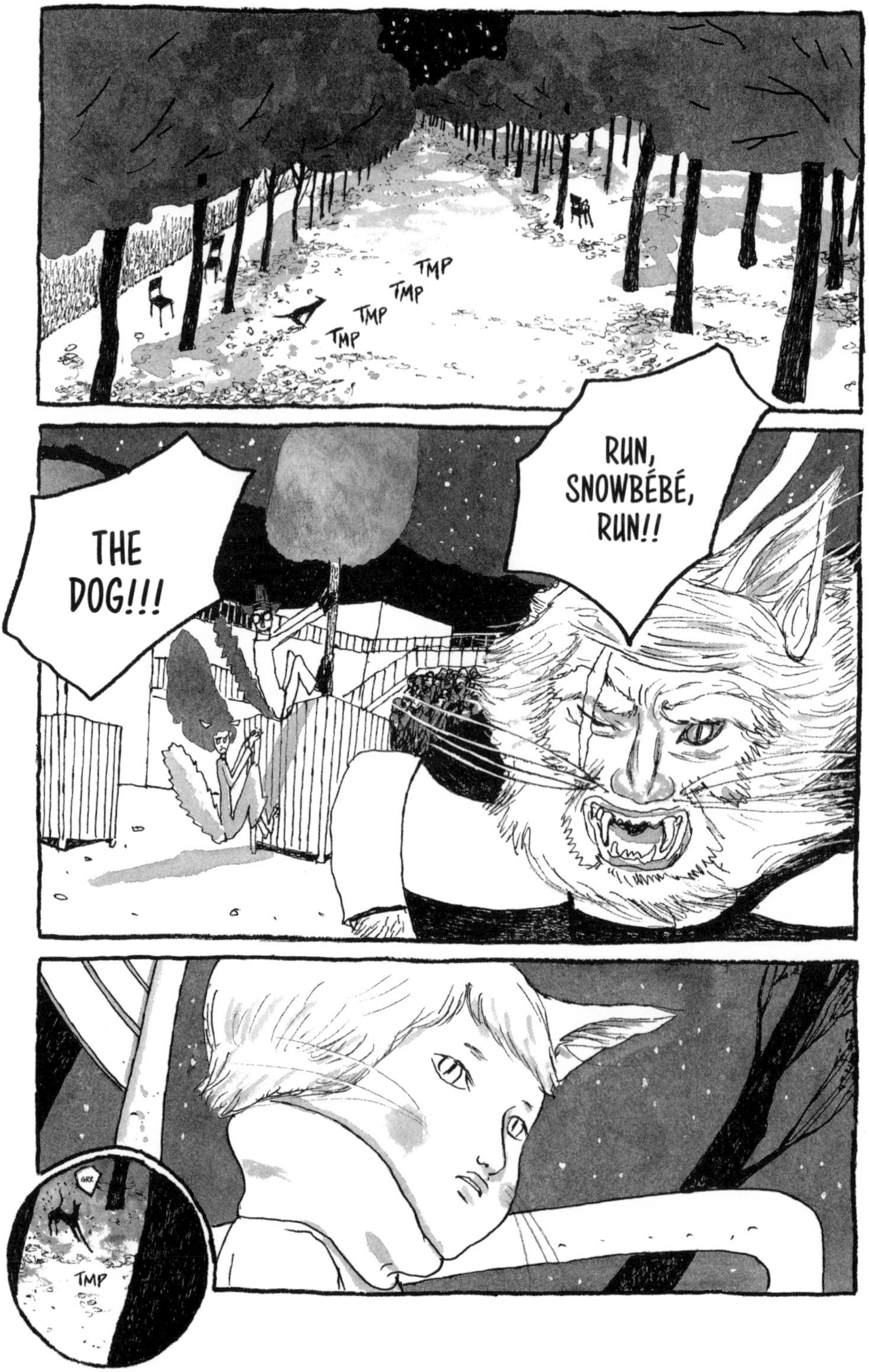
TMP
TMP
TMP
TMP
RUN, SNOWBÉBÉ, RUN!!
THE DOG!!!
GRR
TMP

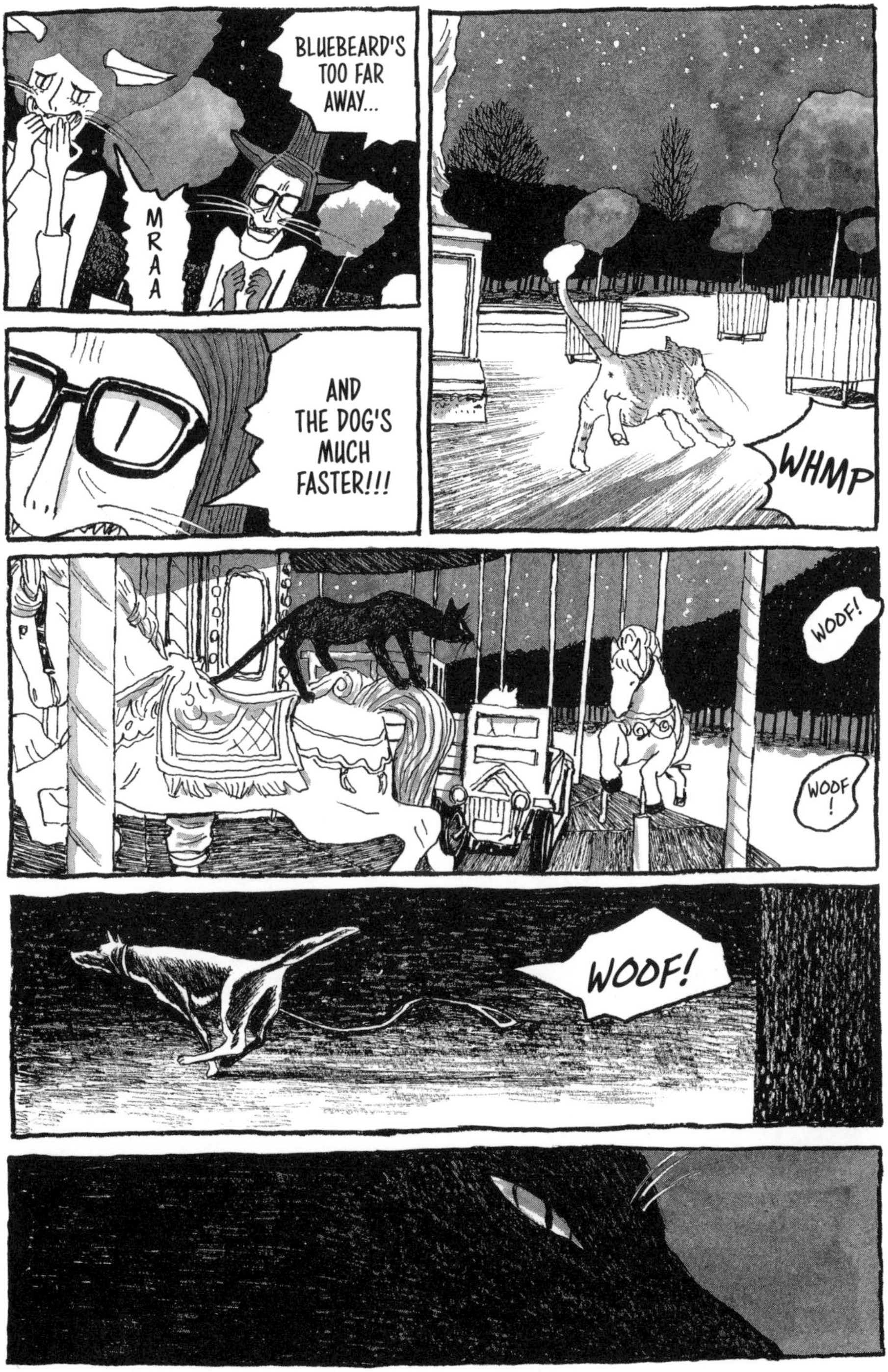
WHMP
BLUEBEARD'S TOO FAR AWAY...
MRAA
AND THE DOG'S MUCH FASTER!!!
WOOF!
WOOF!
WOOF!

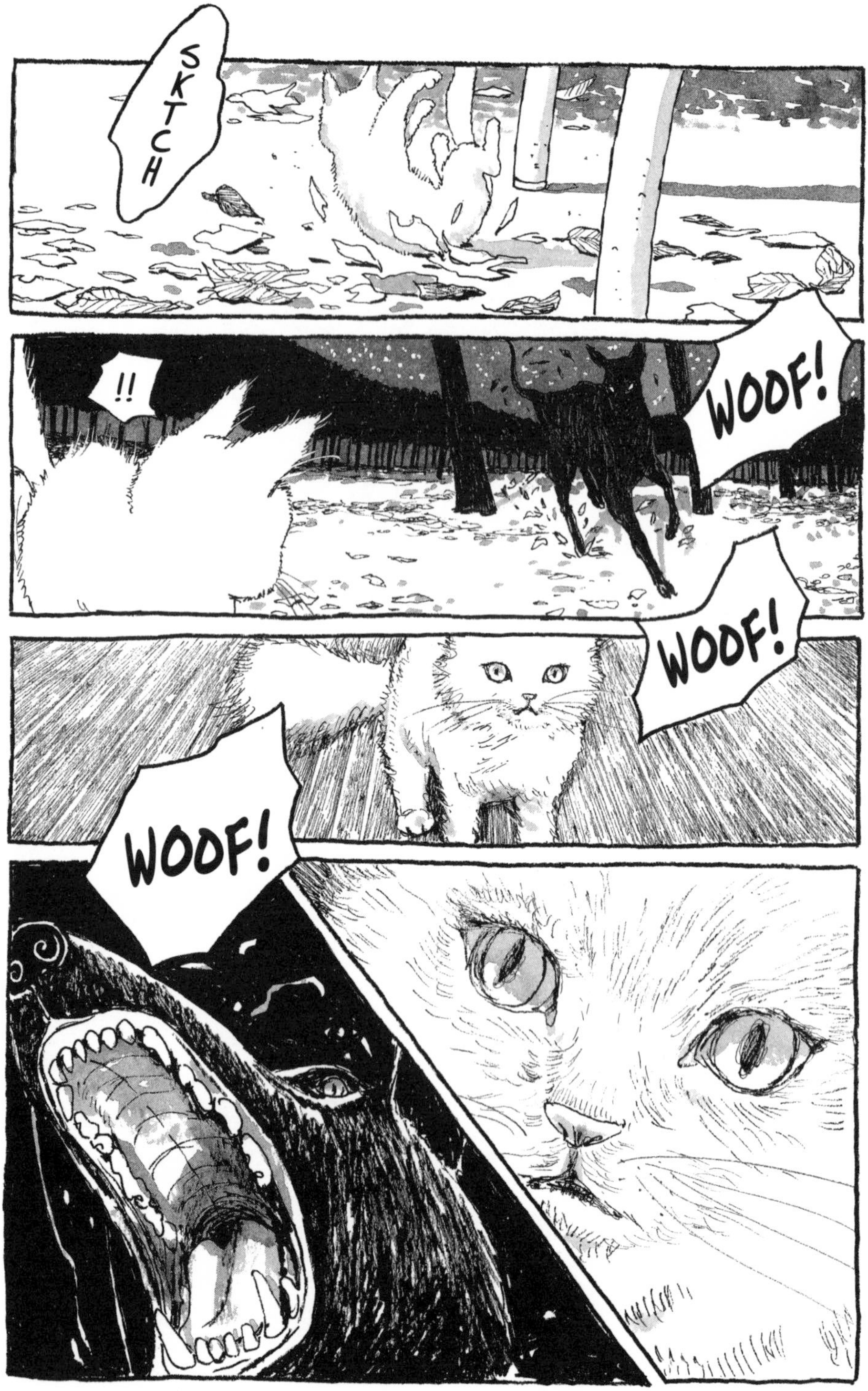
SKTCH
WOOF!
!!
WOOF!
WOOF!

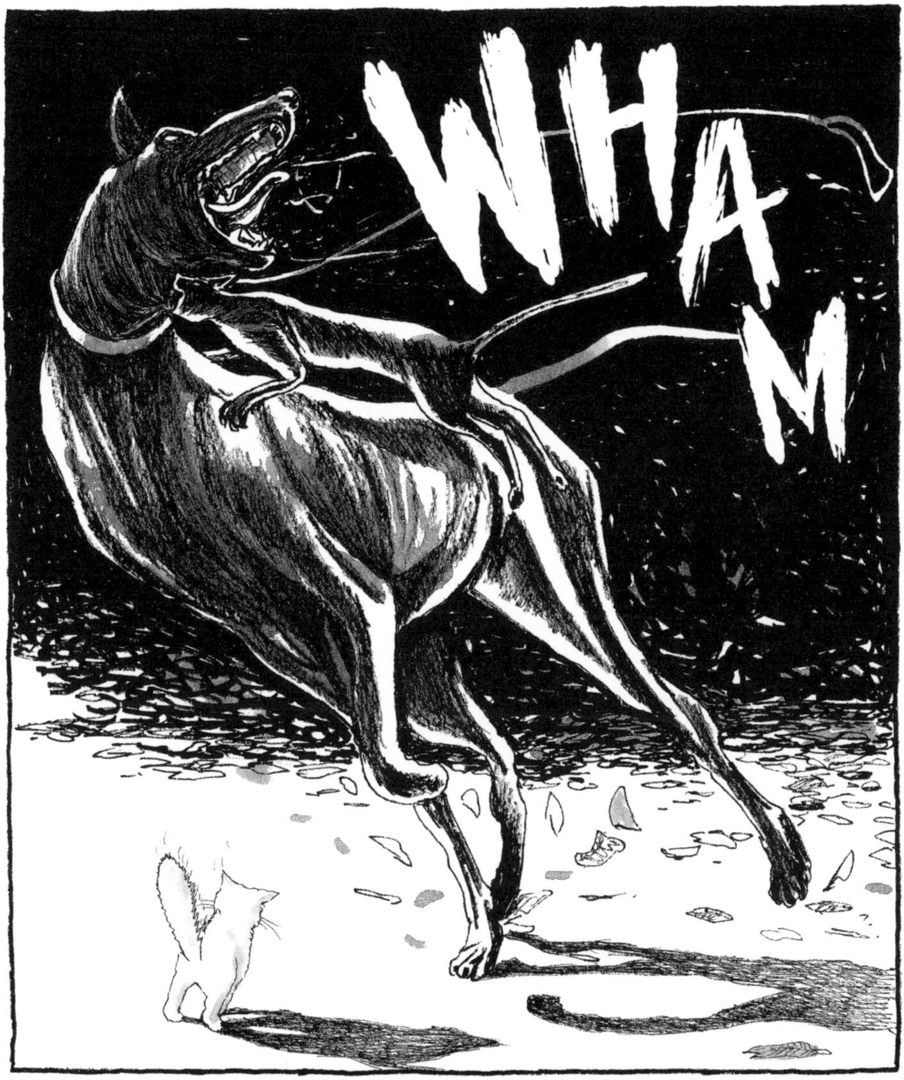
WHAM
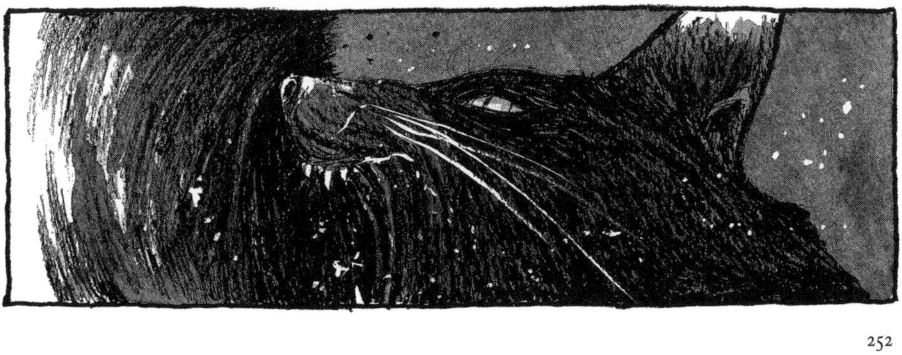

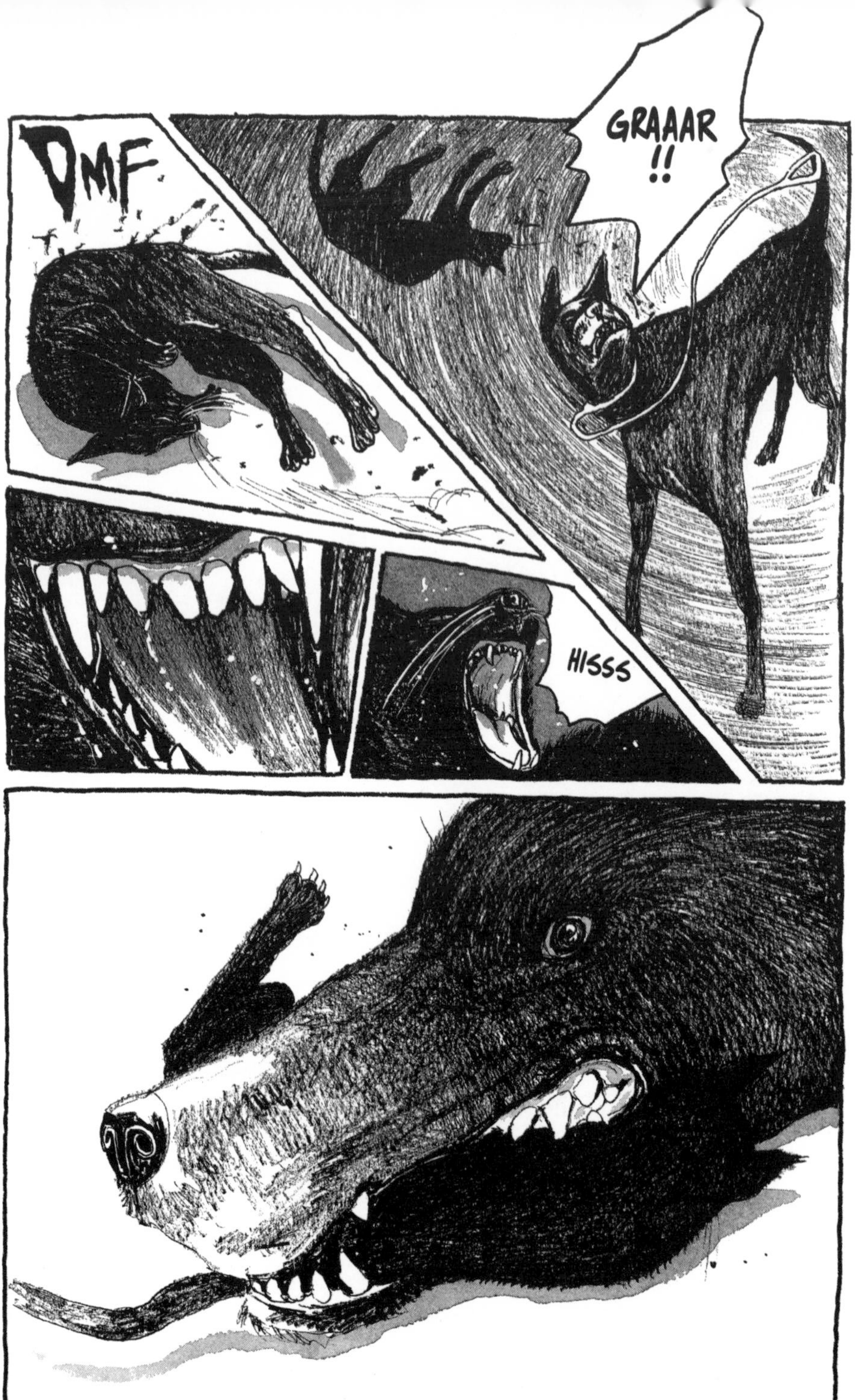
GRAAAR !!
DMF
HISSS

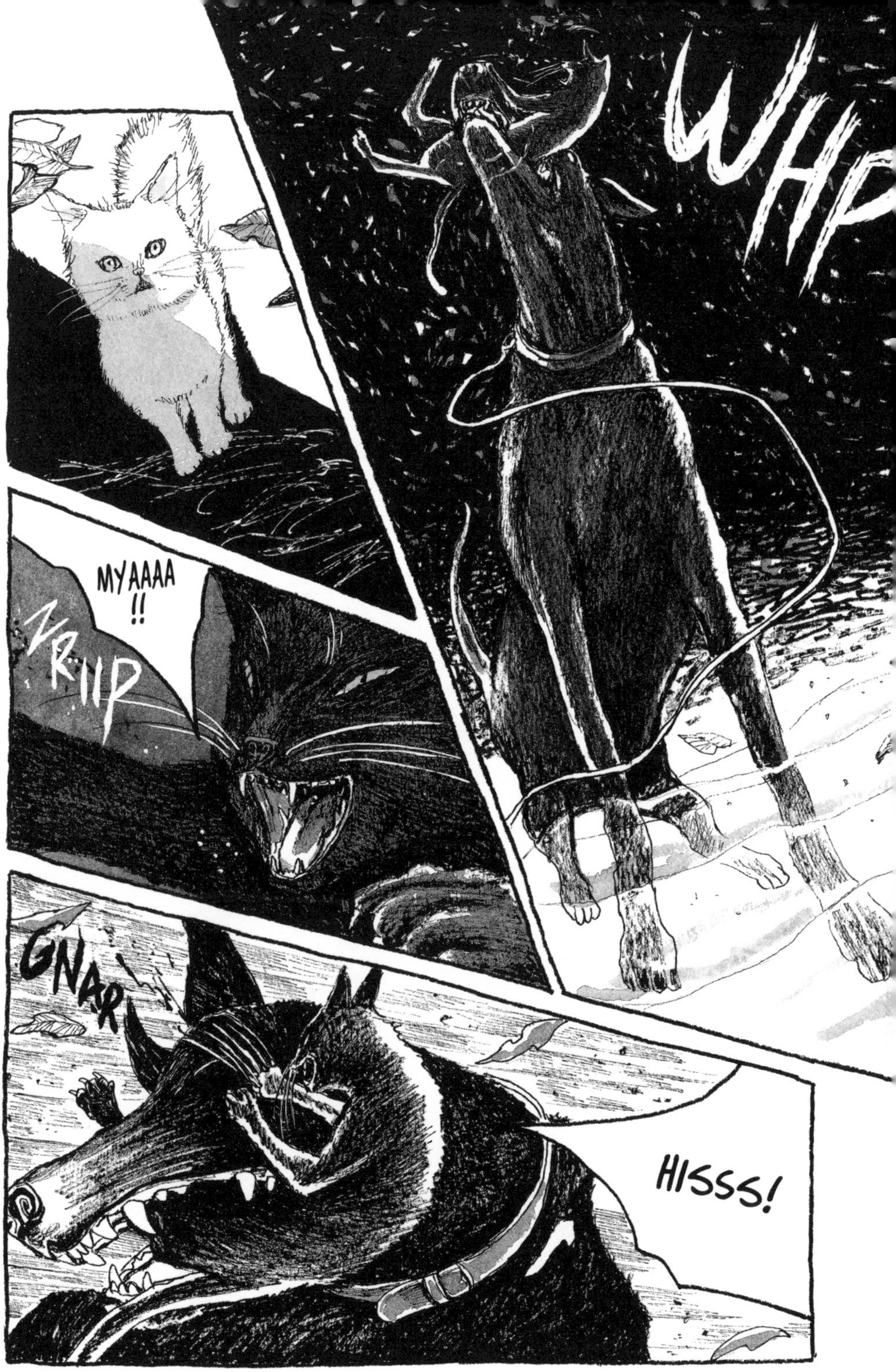
WHP
MYAAAA !!
ZRIIP
HISSS!
GNAR

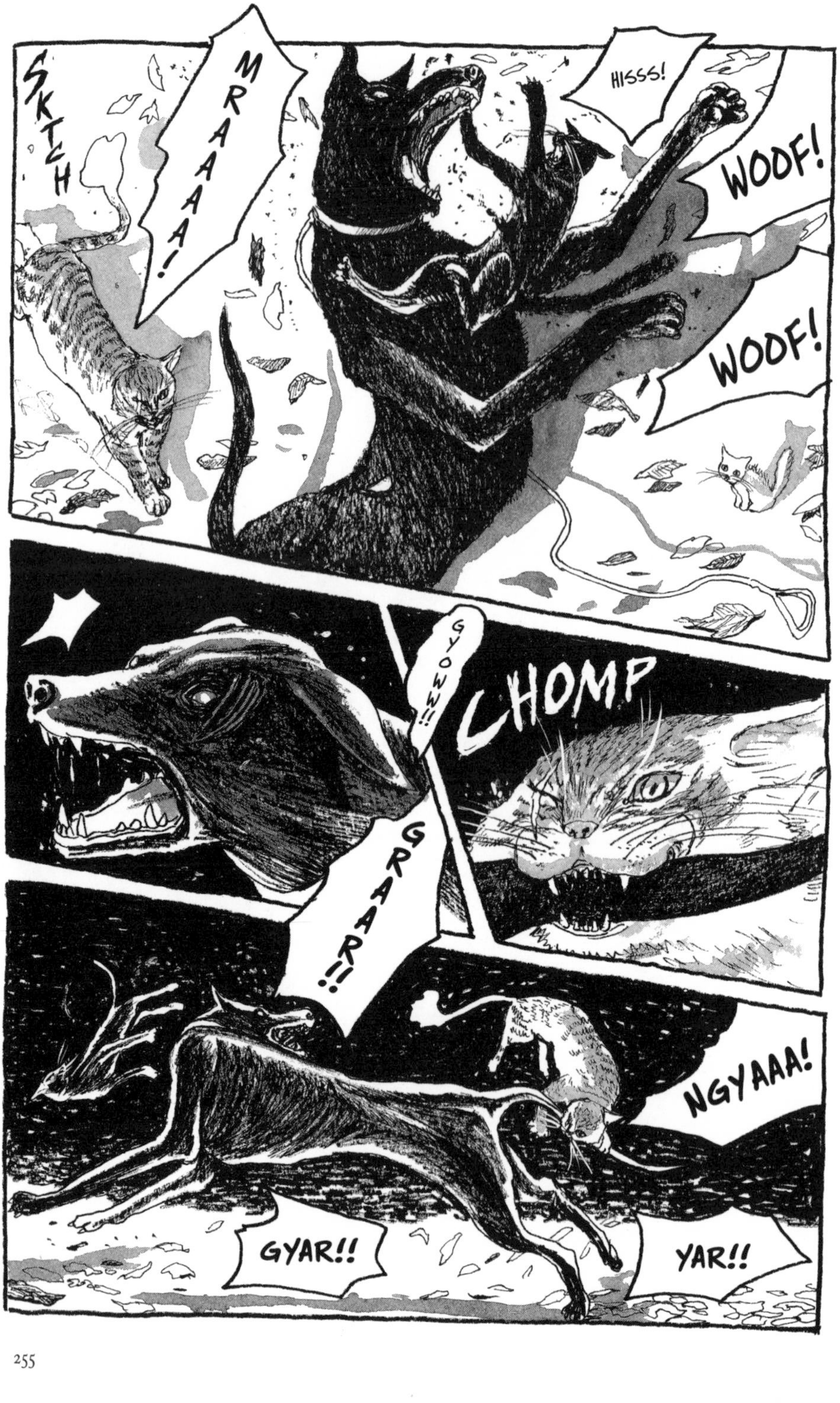
HISSS!
WOOF!
WOOF!
MRAAAAA!
SKTCH
GYOWW!!
CHOMP
GRAAAR!!
NGYAAA!
YAR!!
GYAR!!

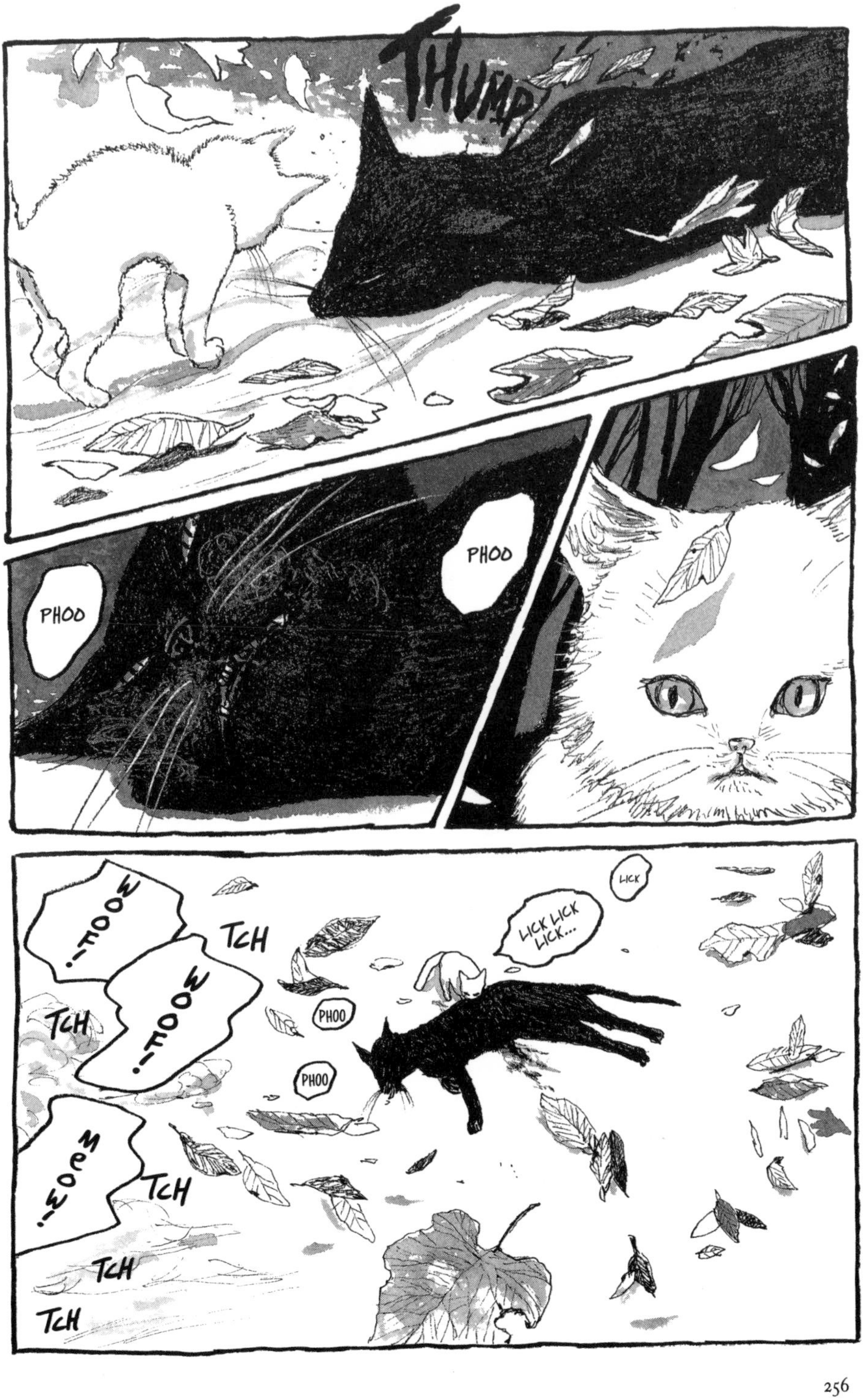
THUMP
PHOO
PHOO
LICK
LICK LICK LICK...
PHOO
PHOO
TCH
WOOF!
WOOF!
TCH
MEOW!
TCH
TCH
TCH

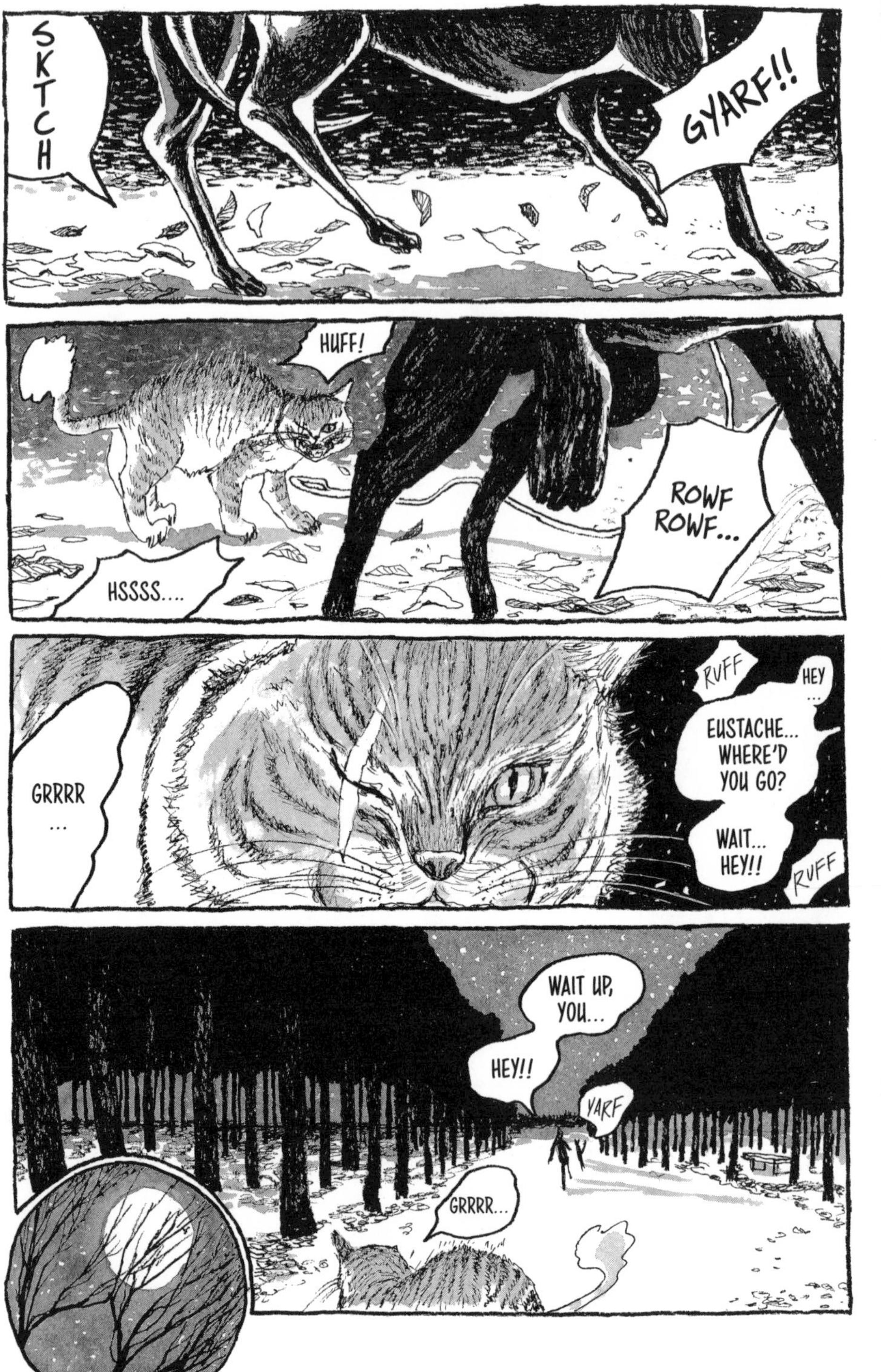
GYARF!!
SKTCH
ROWF ROWF...
HUFF!
HSSSS....
RUFF
HEY ...
EUSTACHE... WHERE'D YOU GO?
WAIT... HEY!!
RUFF
GRRRR ...
WAIT UP, YOU...
HEY!!
YARF
GRRRR...

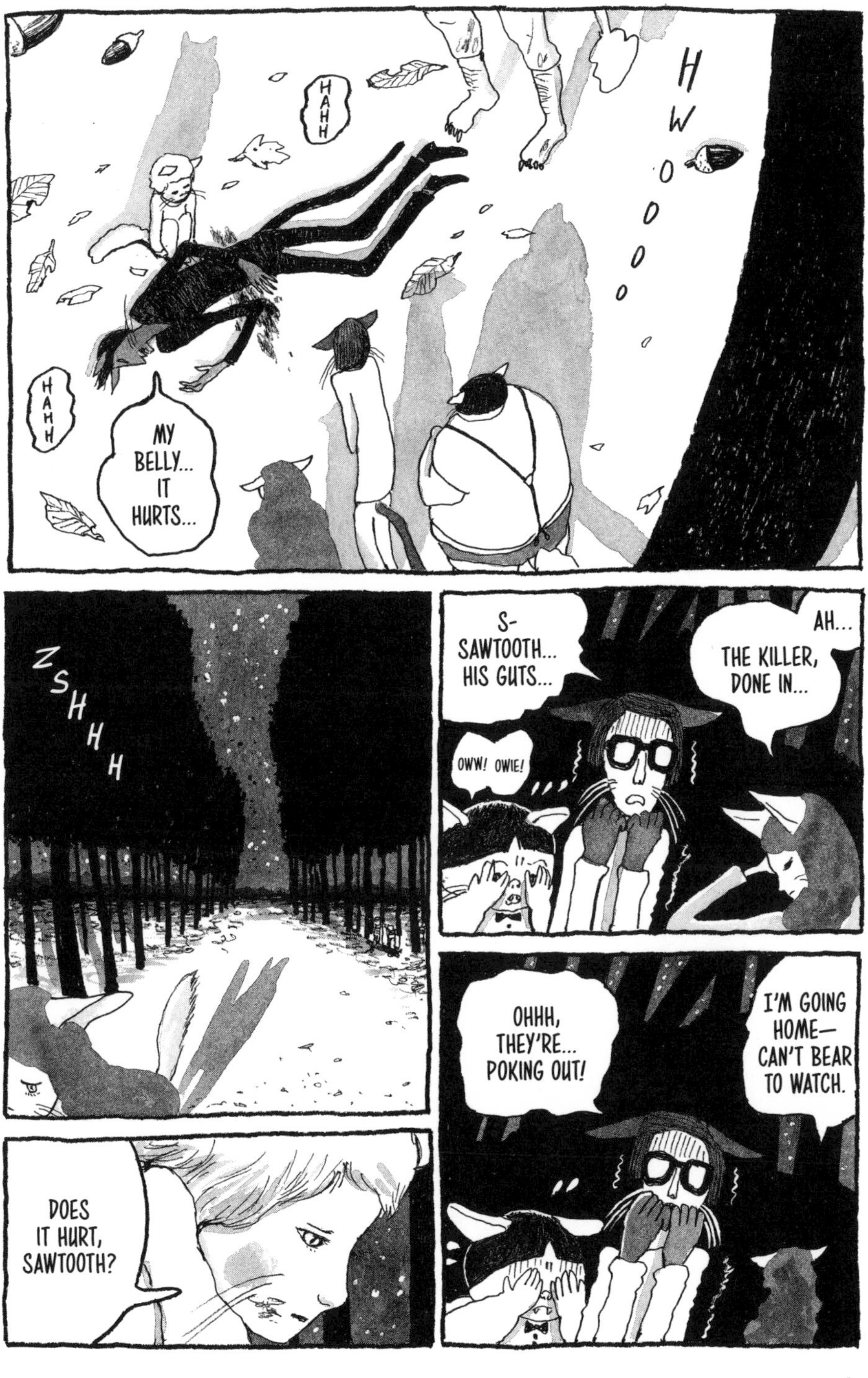
HWOOOOOO
HAHH
HAHH
MY BELLY... IT HURTS...
AH... THE KILLER, DONE IN...
S-SAWTOOTH... HIS GUTS...
OWW! OWIE!
I'M GOING HOME— CAN'T BEAR TO WATCH.
OHHH, THEY'RE... POKING OUT!
ZSHHHH
DOES IT HURT, SAWTOOTH?

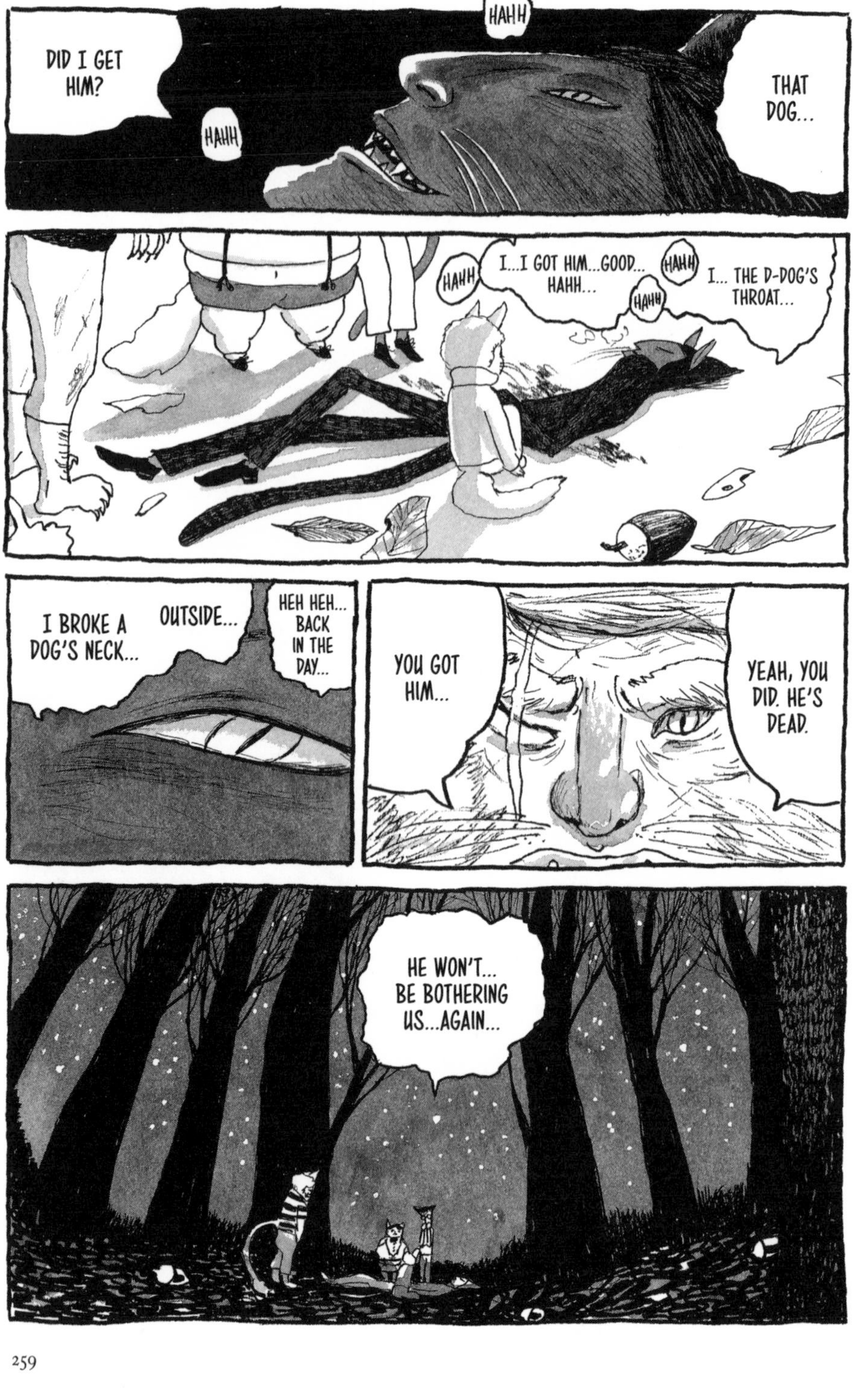
THAT DOG...
HAHH
HAHH
DID I GET HIM?
I... THE D-DOG'S THROAT...
HAHH
HAHH
I...I GOT HIM...GOOD... HAHH...
HAHH
YEAH, YOU DID. HE'S DEAD.
YOU GOT HIM...
HEH HEH... BACK IN THE DAY...
OUTSIDE...
I BROKE A DOG'S NECK...
HE WON'T... BE BOTHERING US...AGAIN...

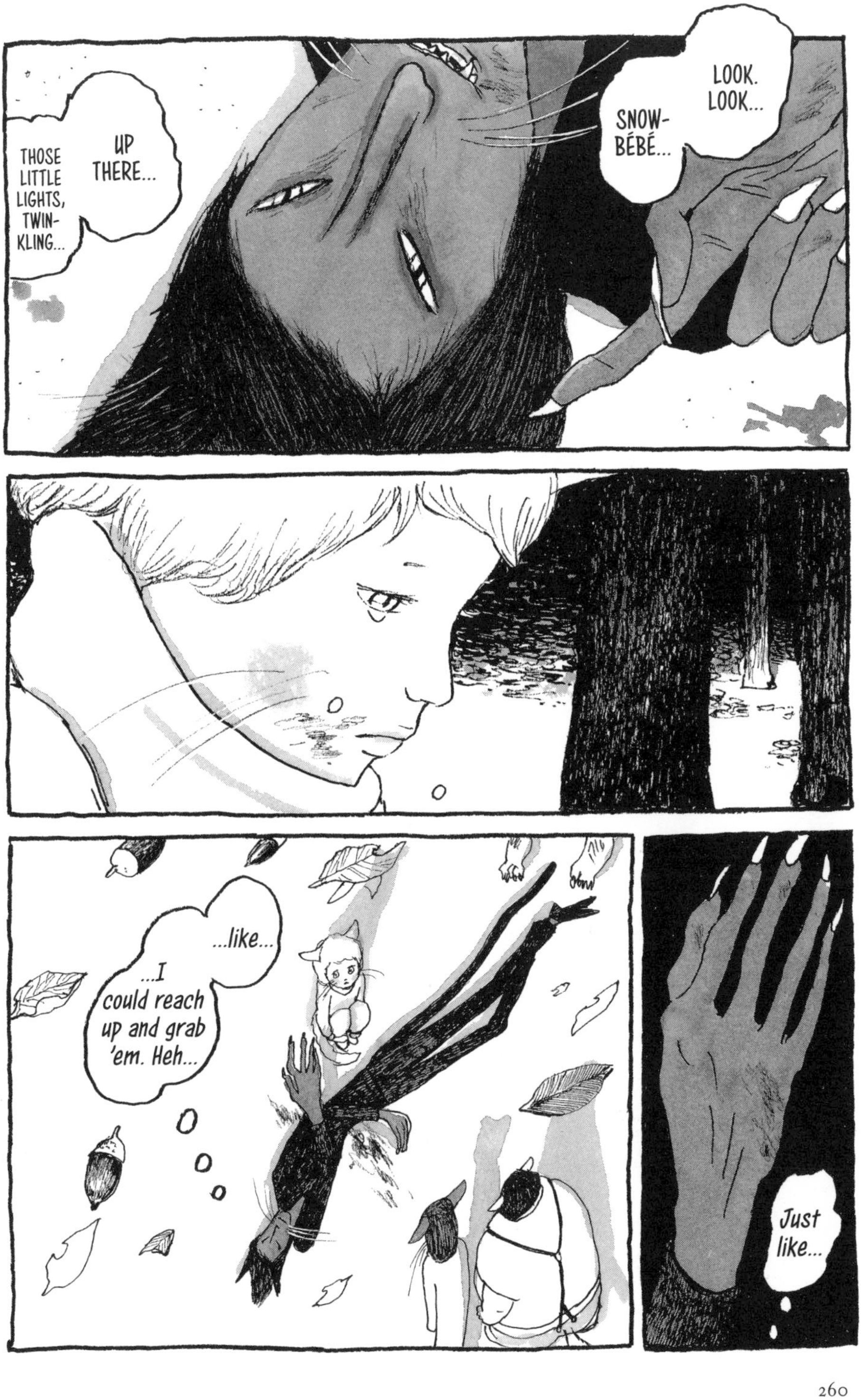
LOOK. LOOK...
SNOW-BÉBÉ...
UP THERE...
THOSE LITTLE LIGHTS, TWINKLING...
Just like...
...like...
...I could reach up and grab 'em. Heh...

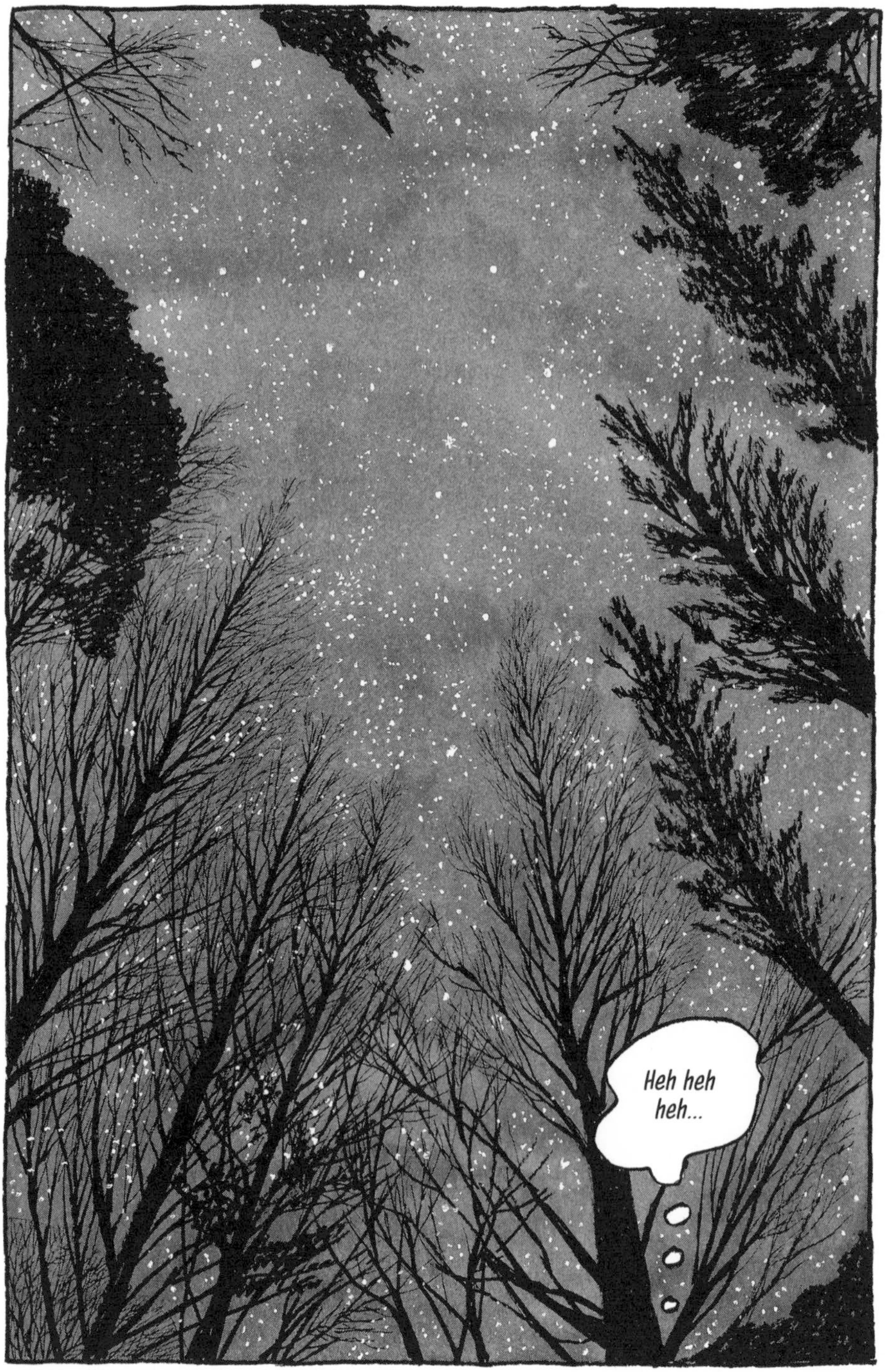
Heh heh heh...

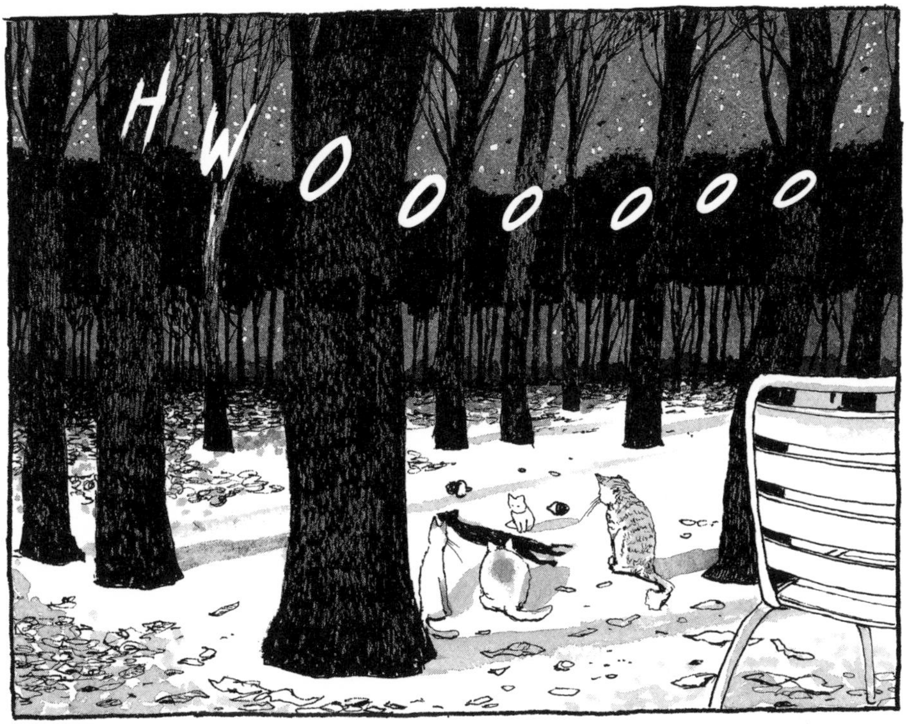
HWOOOOOO

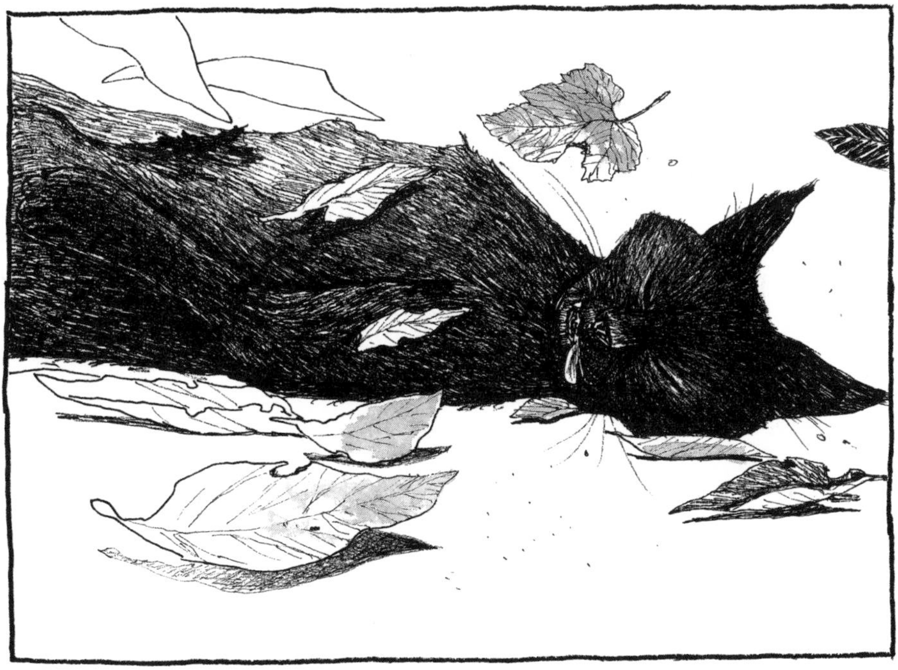

CHAPTER 12

The Secret of the Snowy Morning

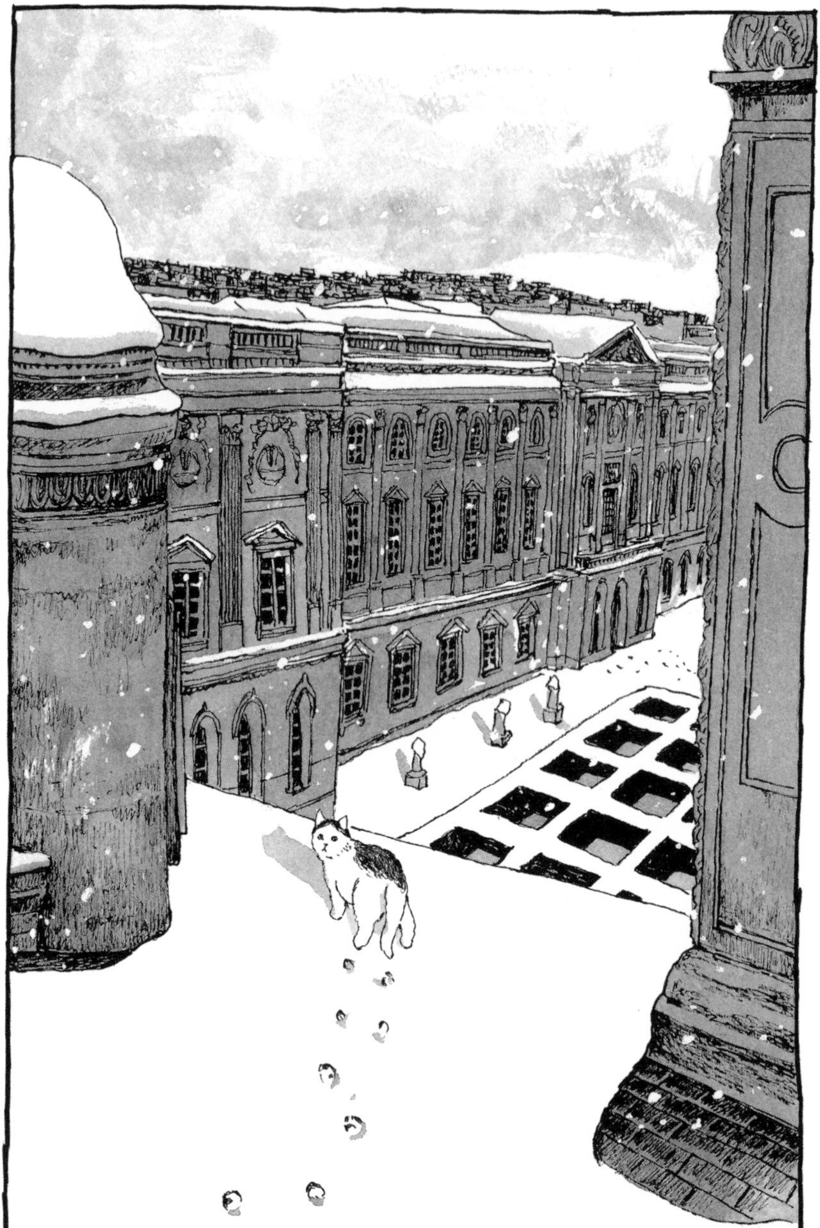

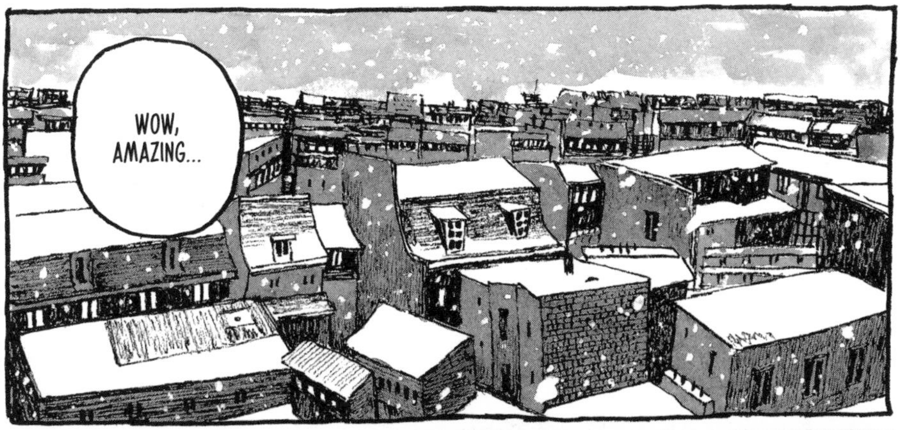
WOW, AMAZING...

WINTER

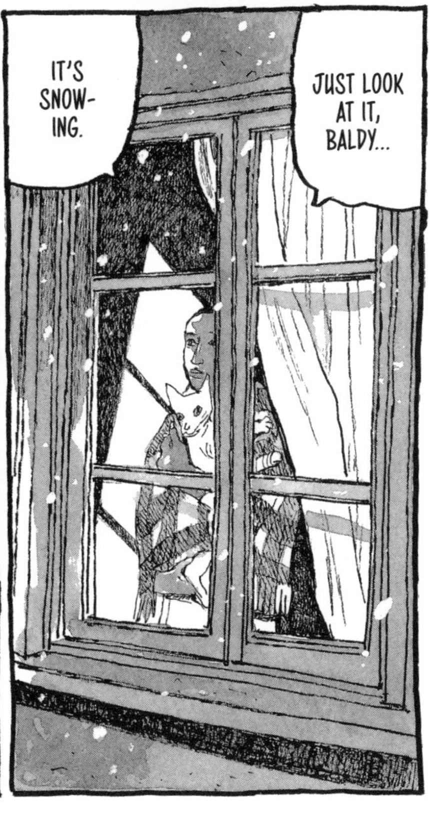
JUST LOOK AT IT, BALDY...
IT'S SNOW-ING.

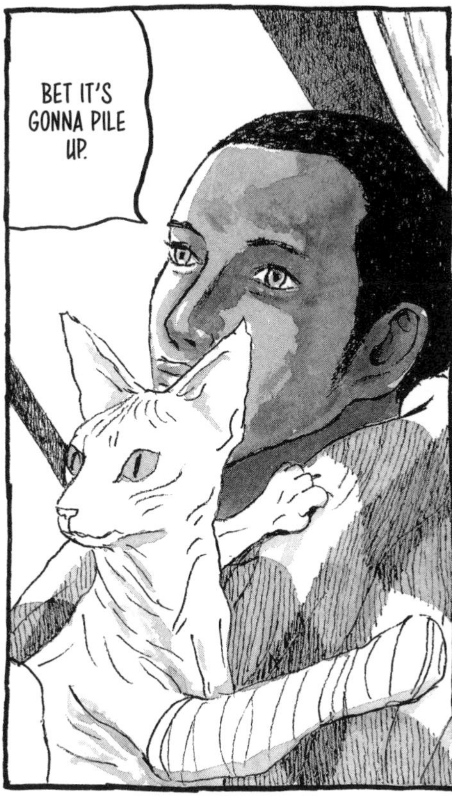
BET IT'S GONNA PILE UP.

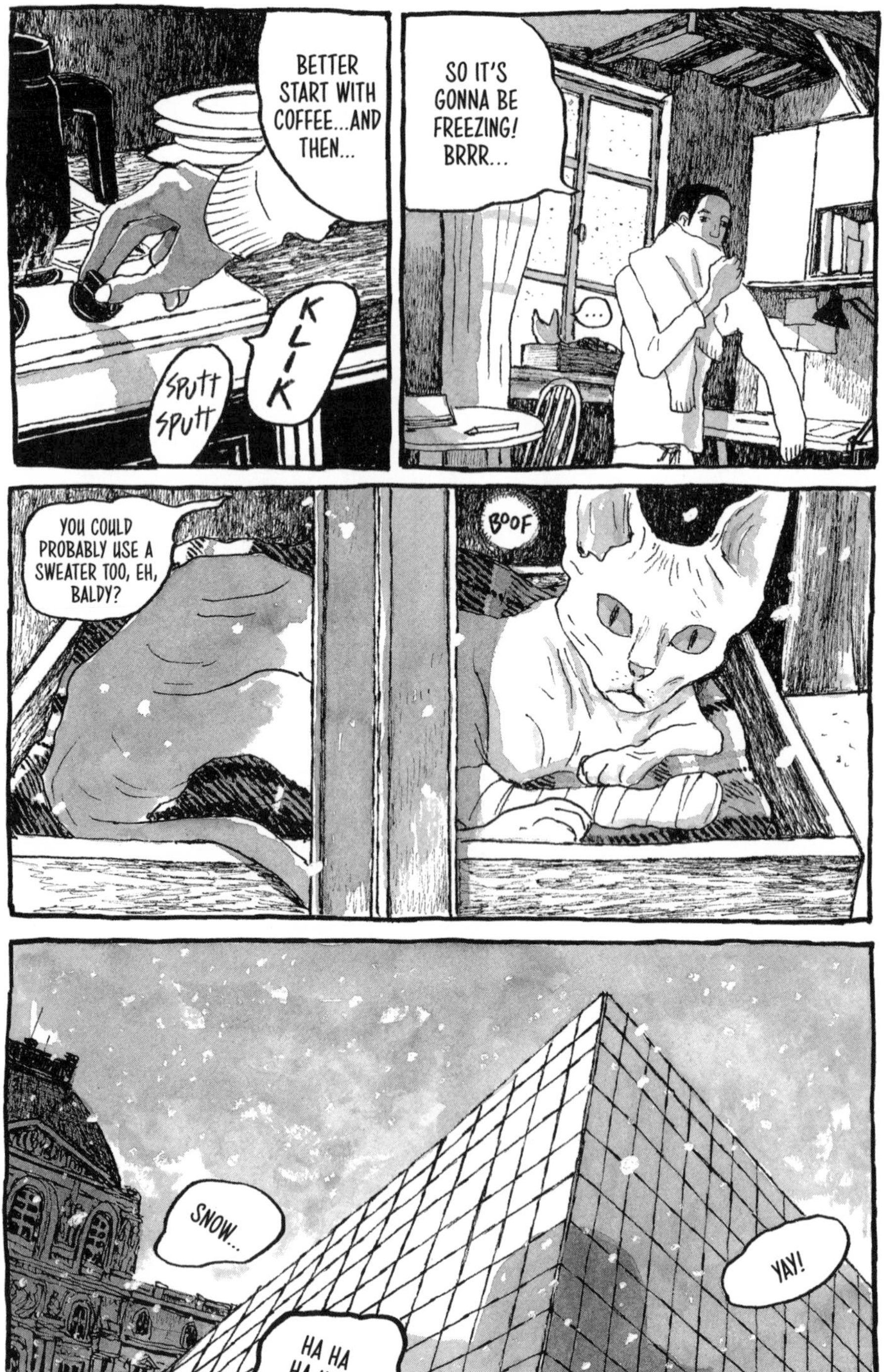
SO IT'S GONNA BE FREEZING! BRRR...
...
BETTER START WITH COFFEE...AND THEN...
KLIK
SPUTT SPUTT
BOOF
YOU COULD PROBABLY USE A SWEATER TOO, EH, BALDY?
SNOW...
YAY!
HA HA HA HA!

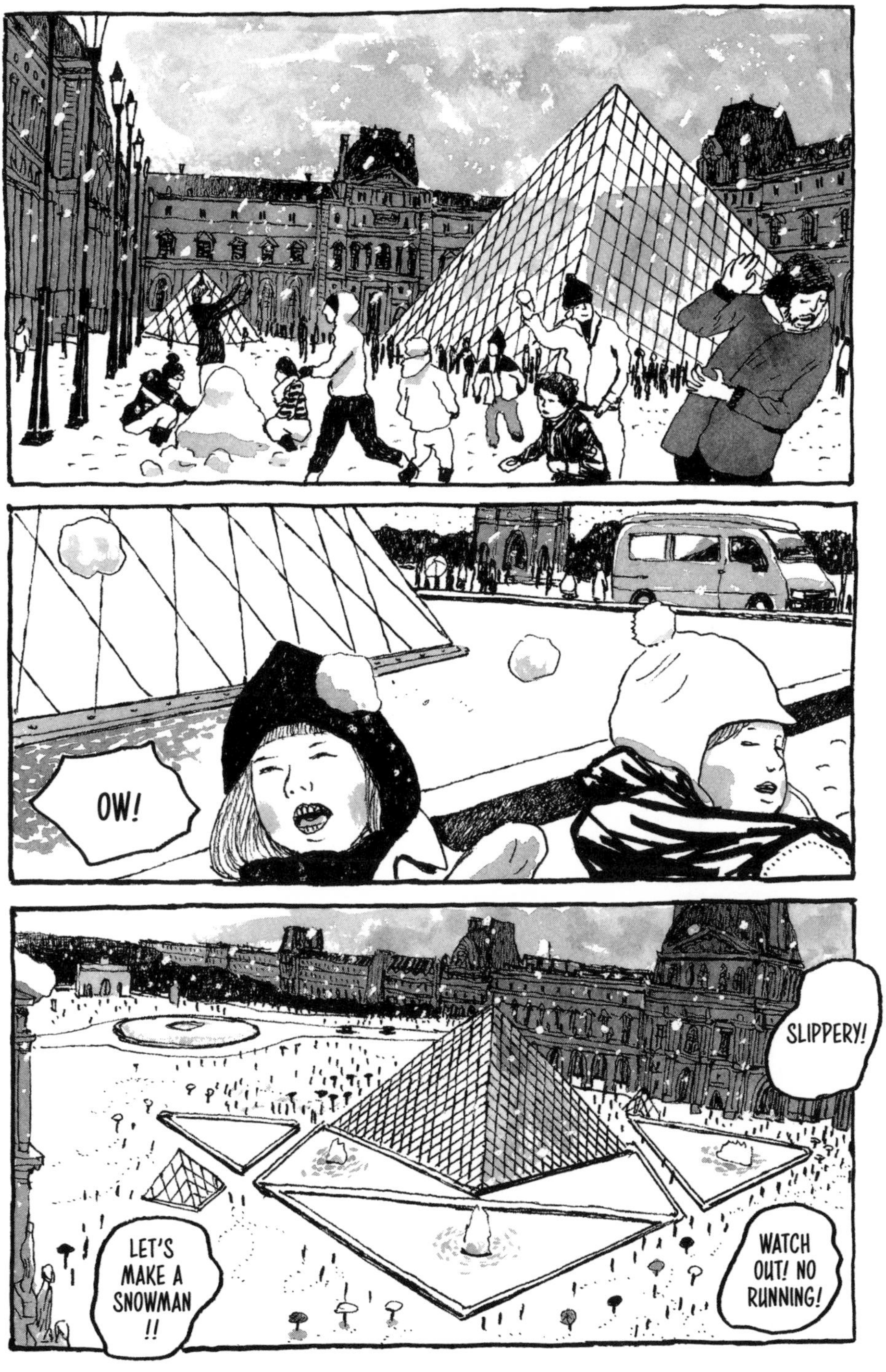
OW!
SLIPPERY!
WATCH OUT! NO RUNNING!
LET'S MAKE A SNOWMAN !!

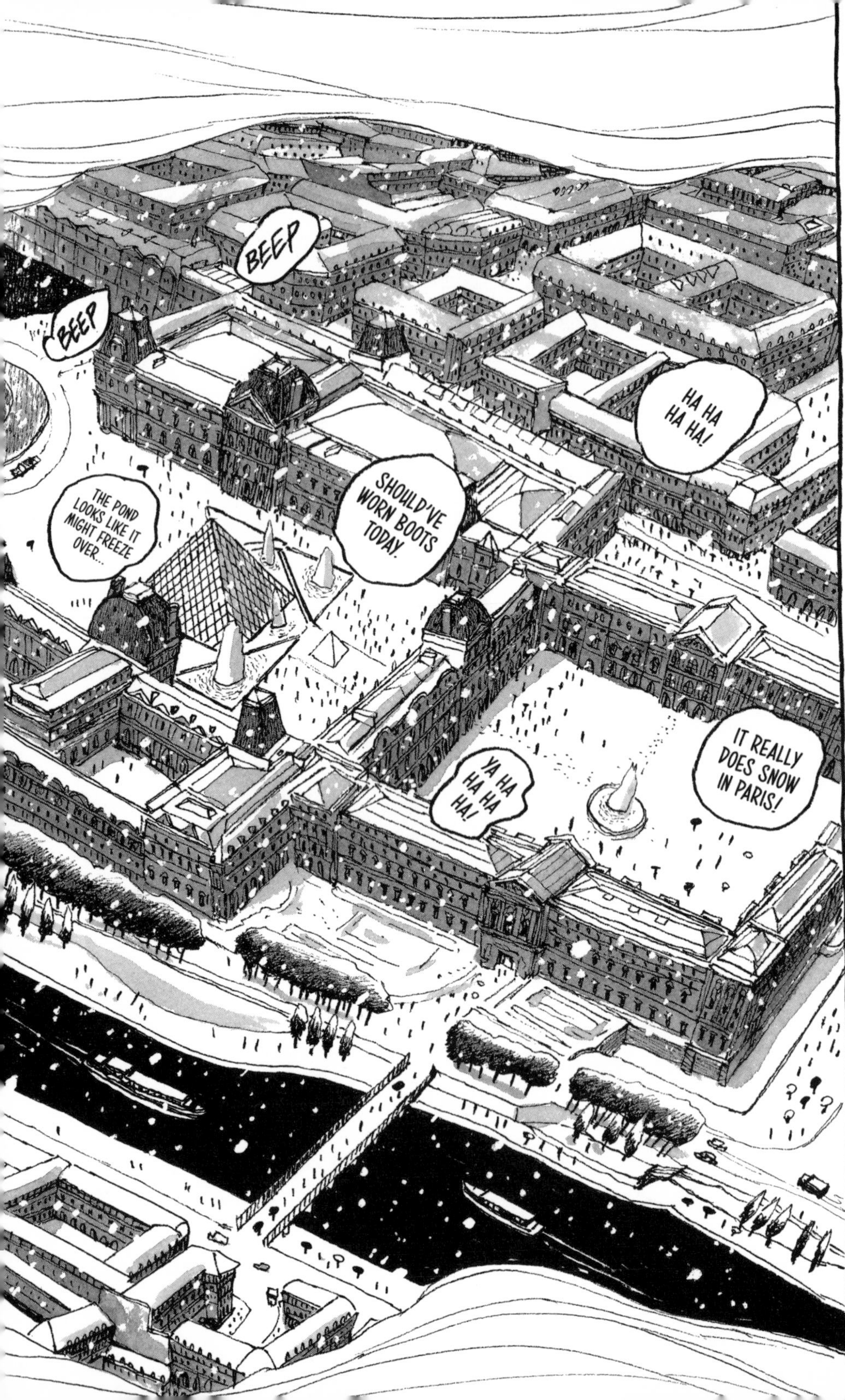
BEEP
BEEP
HA HA HA HA!
SHOULD'VE WORN BOOTS TODAY.
THE POND LOOKS LIKE IT MIGHT FREEZE OVER...
IT REALLY DOES SNOW IN PARIS!
YA HA HA HA HA!

WHMP

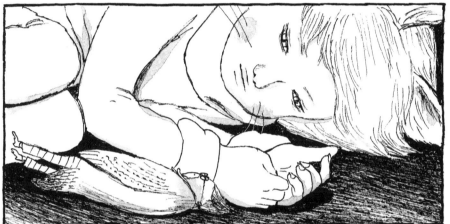

YOU'LL STARVE!!

EAT SOMETHING, SNOWBÉBÉ!

BLUE-BEARD...

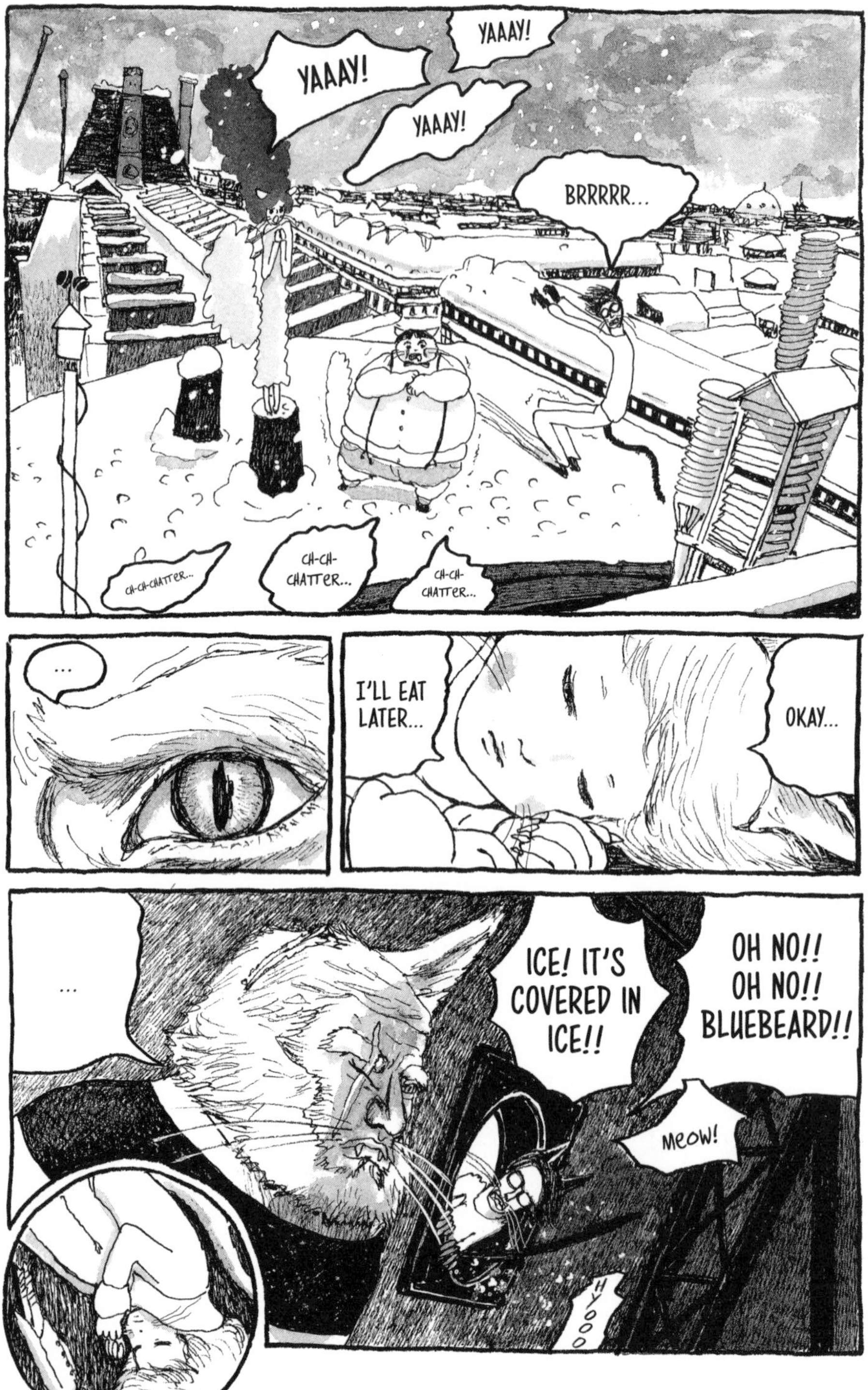
YAAAY!
YAAAY!
YAAAY!
BRRRRR...
CH-CH-CHATTER...
CH-CH-CHATTER...
CH-CH-CHATTER...
OKAY...
I'LL EAT LATER...
...
OH NO!! OH NO!! BLUEBEARD!!
ICE! IT'S COVERED IN ICE!!
...
MEOW!
HYOOO

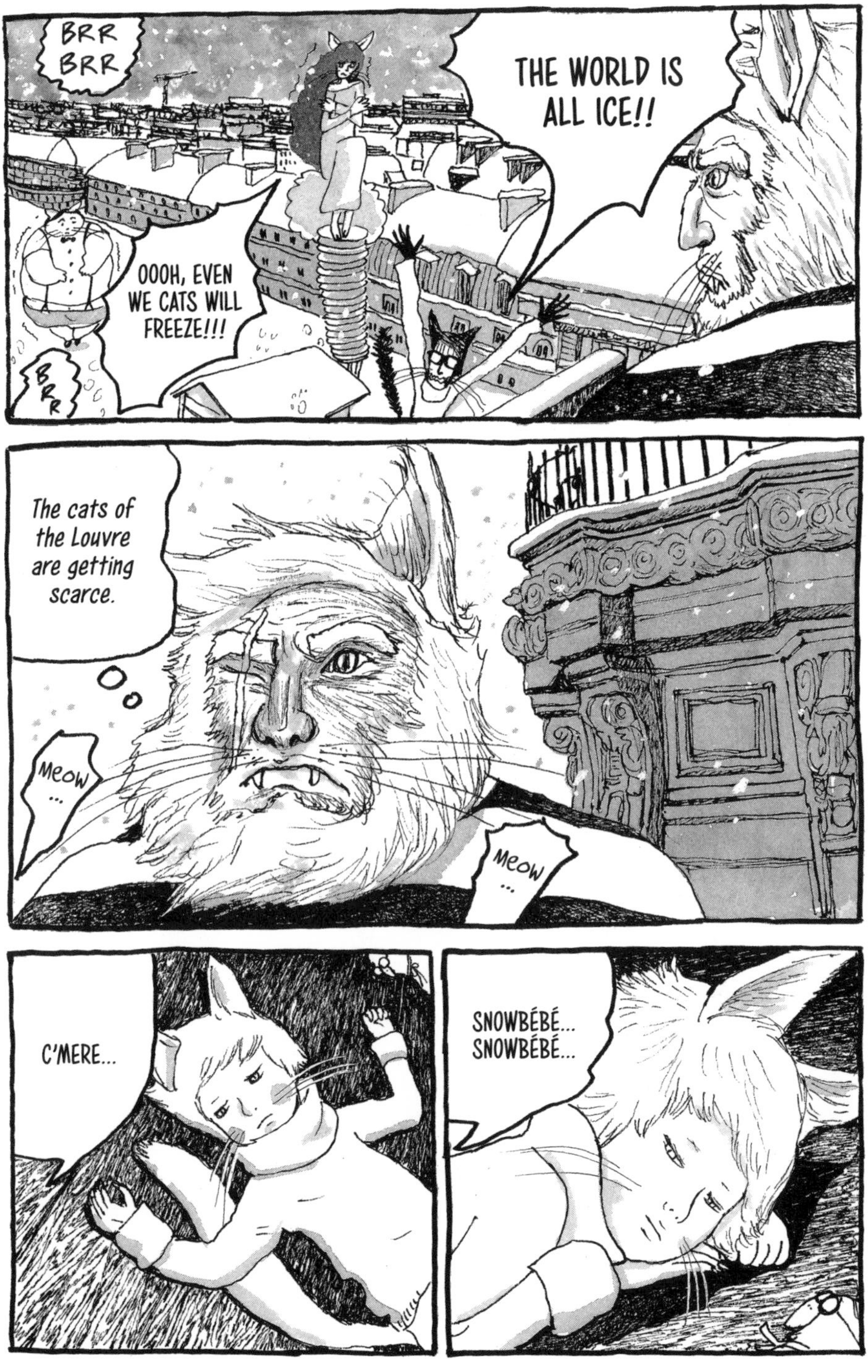
THE WORLD IS ALL ICE!!
BRR BRR
OOOH, EVEN WE CATS WILL FREEZE!!!
BRR
The cats of the Louvre are getting scarce.
Meow ...
Meow ...
SNOWBÉBÉ... SNOWBÉBÉ...
C'MERE...

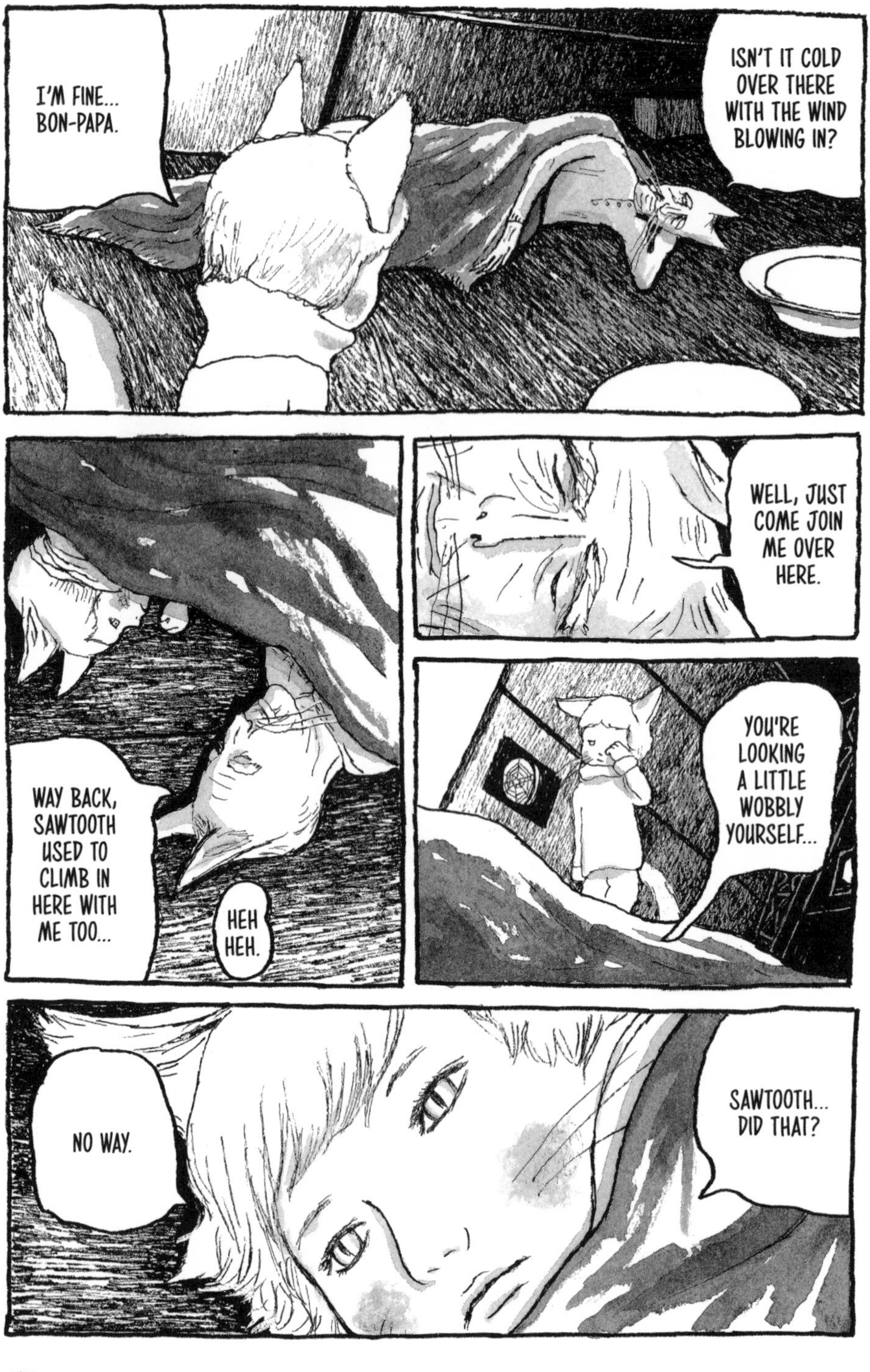
ISN'T IT COLD OVER THERE WITH THE WIND BLOWING IN?
I'M FINE... BON-PAPA.
WELL, JUST COME JOIN ME OVER HERE.
YOU'RE LOOKING A LITTLE WOBBLY YOURSELF...
WAY BACK, SAWTOOTH USED TO CLIMB IN HERE WITH ME TOO...
HEH HEH.
SAWTOOTH... DID THAT?
NO WAY.

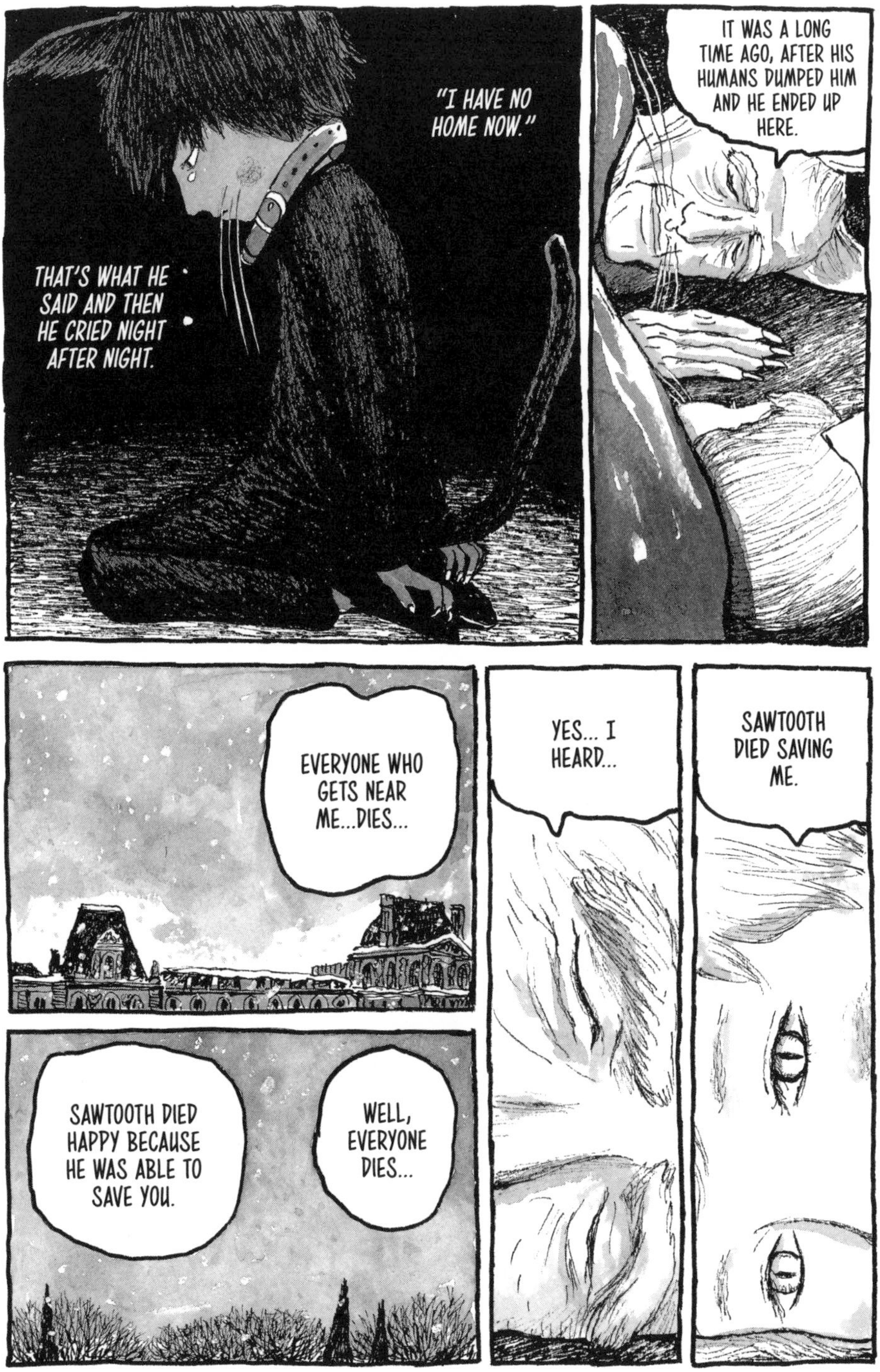
IT WAS A LONG TIME AGO, AFTER HIS HUMANS DUMPED HIM AND HE ENDED UP HERE.
"I HAVE NO HOME NOW."
THAT'S WHAT HE SAID AND THEN HE CRIED NIGHT AFTER NIGHT.
SAWTOOTH DIED SAVING ME.
YES... I HEARD...
EVERYONE WHO GETS NEAR ME...DIES...
WELL, EVERYONE DIES...
SAWTOOTH DIED HAPPY BECAUSE HE WAS ABLE TO SAVE YOU.

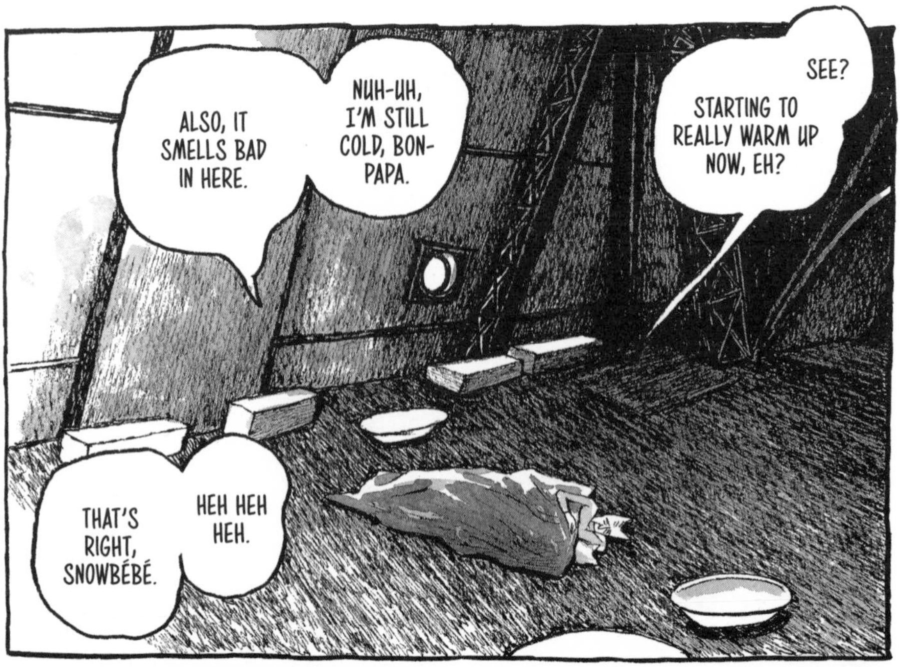
SEE?
STARTING TO REALLY WARM UP NOW, EH?
NUH-UH, I'M STILL COLD, BON-PAPA.
ALSO, IT SMELLS BAD IN HERE.
HEH HEH HEH.
THAT'S RIGHT, SNOWBÉBÉ.

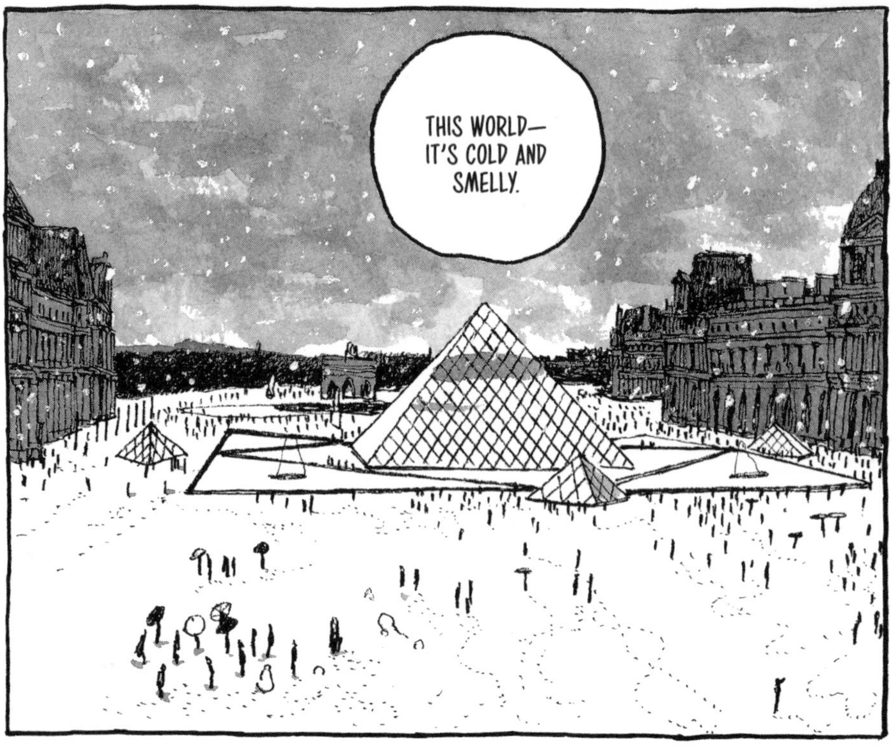
THIS WORLD—IT'S COLD AND SMELLY.

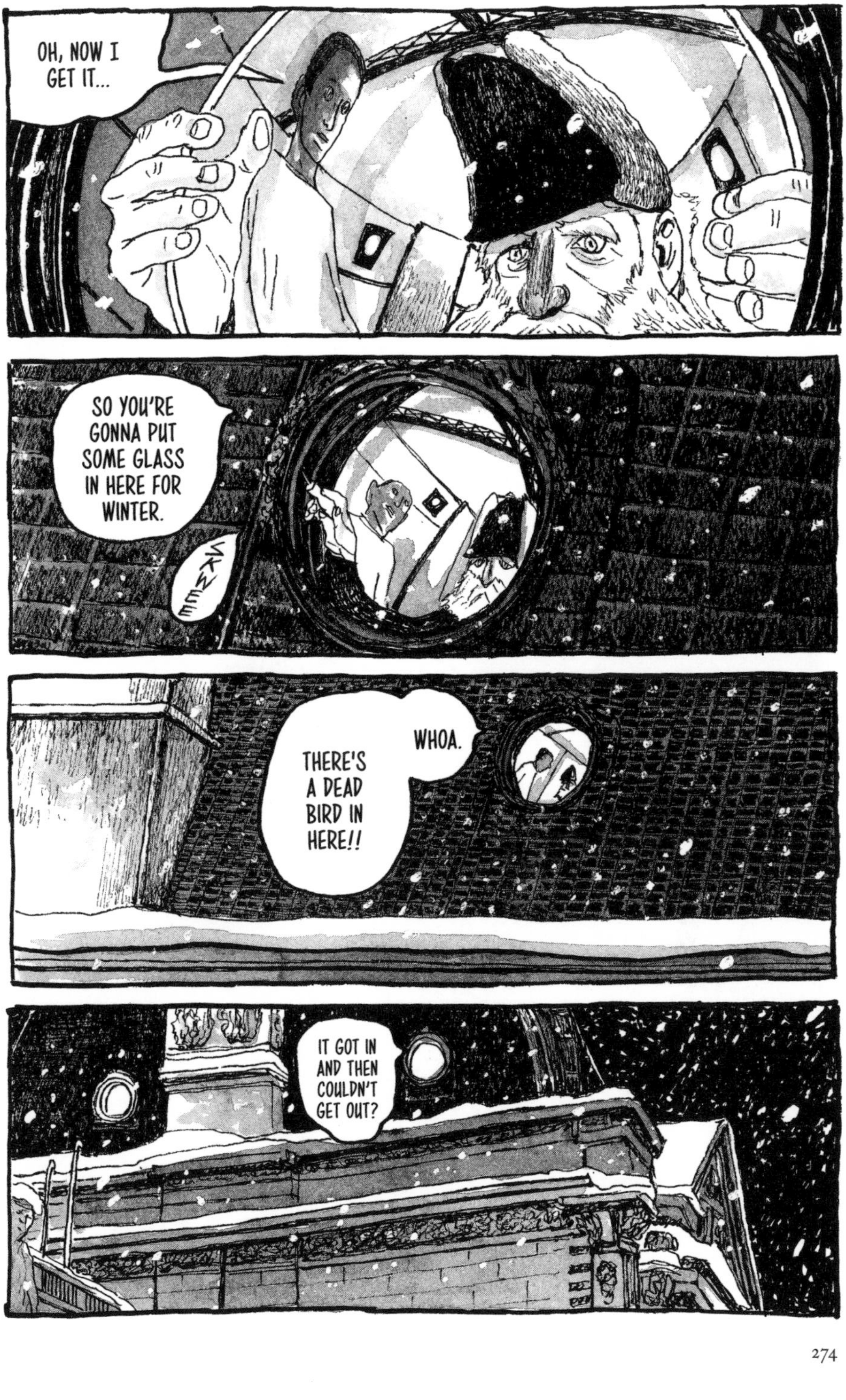
OH, NOW I GET IT...
SO YOU'RE GONNA PUT SOME GLASS IN HERE FOR WINTER.
SKWEE
WHOA.
THERE'S A DEAD BIRD IN HERE!!
IT GOT IN AND THEN COULDN'T GET OUT?

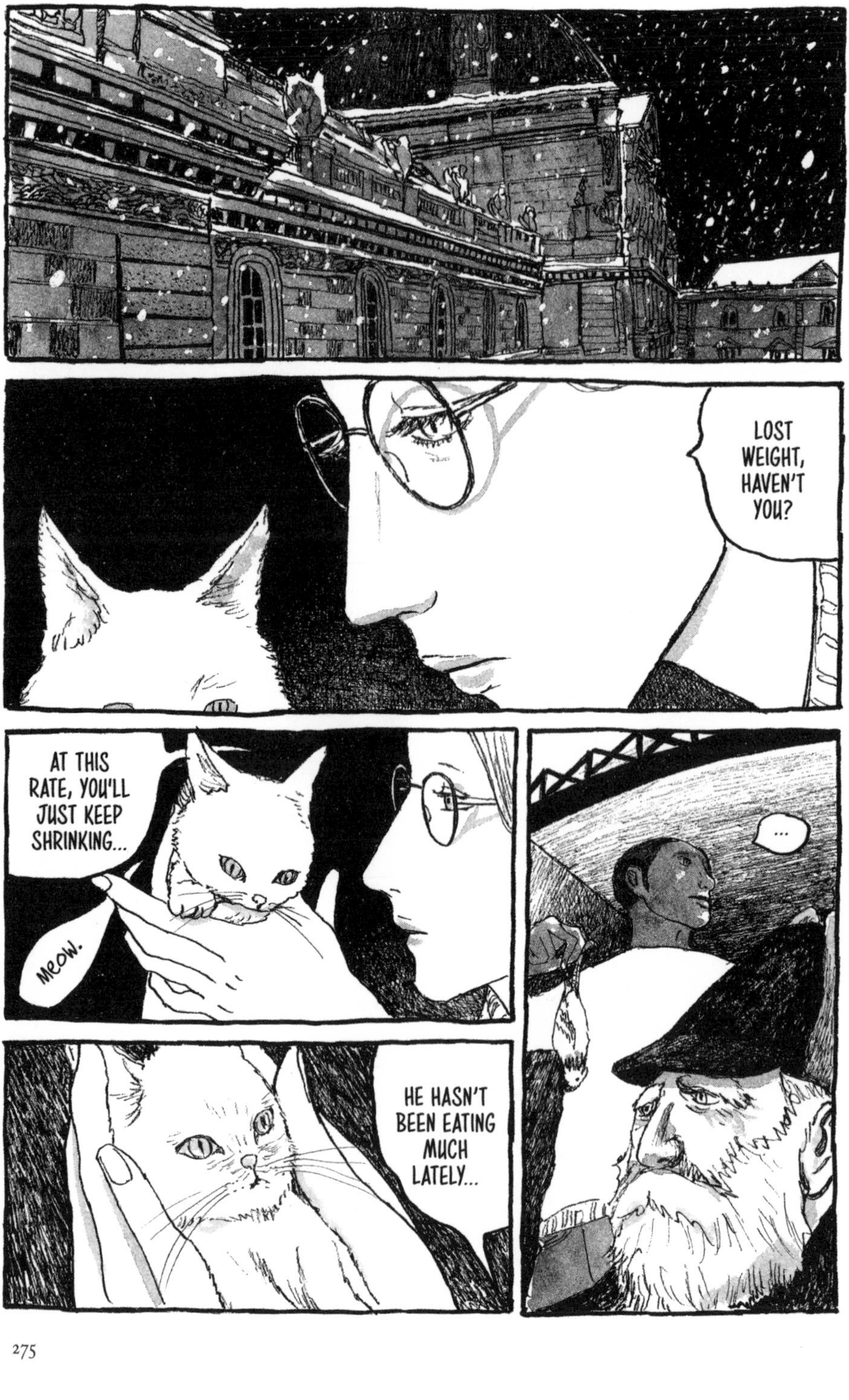
LOST WEIGHT, HAVEN'T YOU?
...
AT THIS RATE, YOU'LL JUST KEEP SHRINKING...
MEOW.
HE HASN'T BEEN EATING MUCH LATELY...

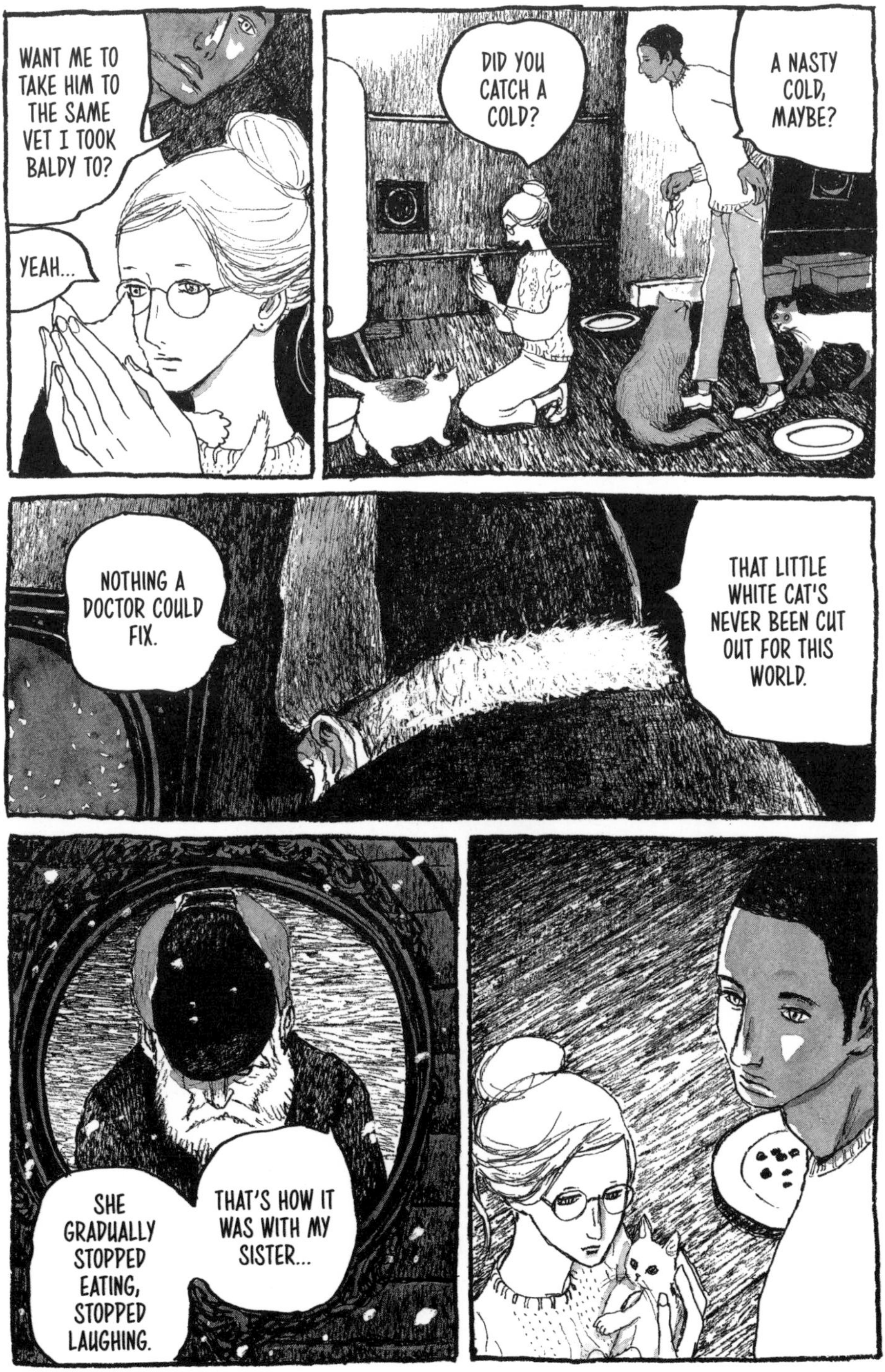
A NASTY COLD, MAYBE?
DID YOU CATCH A COLD?
WANT ME TO TAKE HIM TO THE SAME VET I TOOK BALDY TO?
YEAH...
THAT LITTLE WHITE CAT'S NEVER BEEN CUT OUT FOR THIS WORLD.
NOTHING A DOCTOR COULD FIX.
THAT'S HOW IT WAS WITH MY SISTER...
SHE GRADUALLY STOPPED EATING, STOPPED LAUGHING.

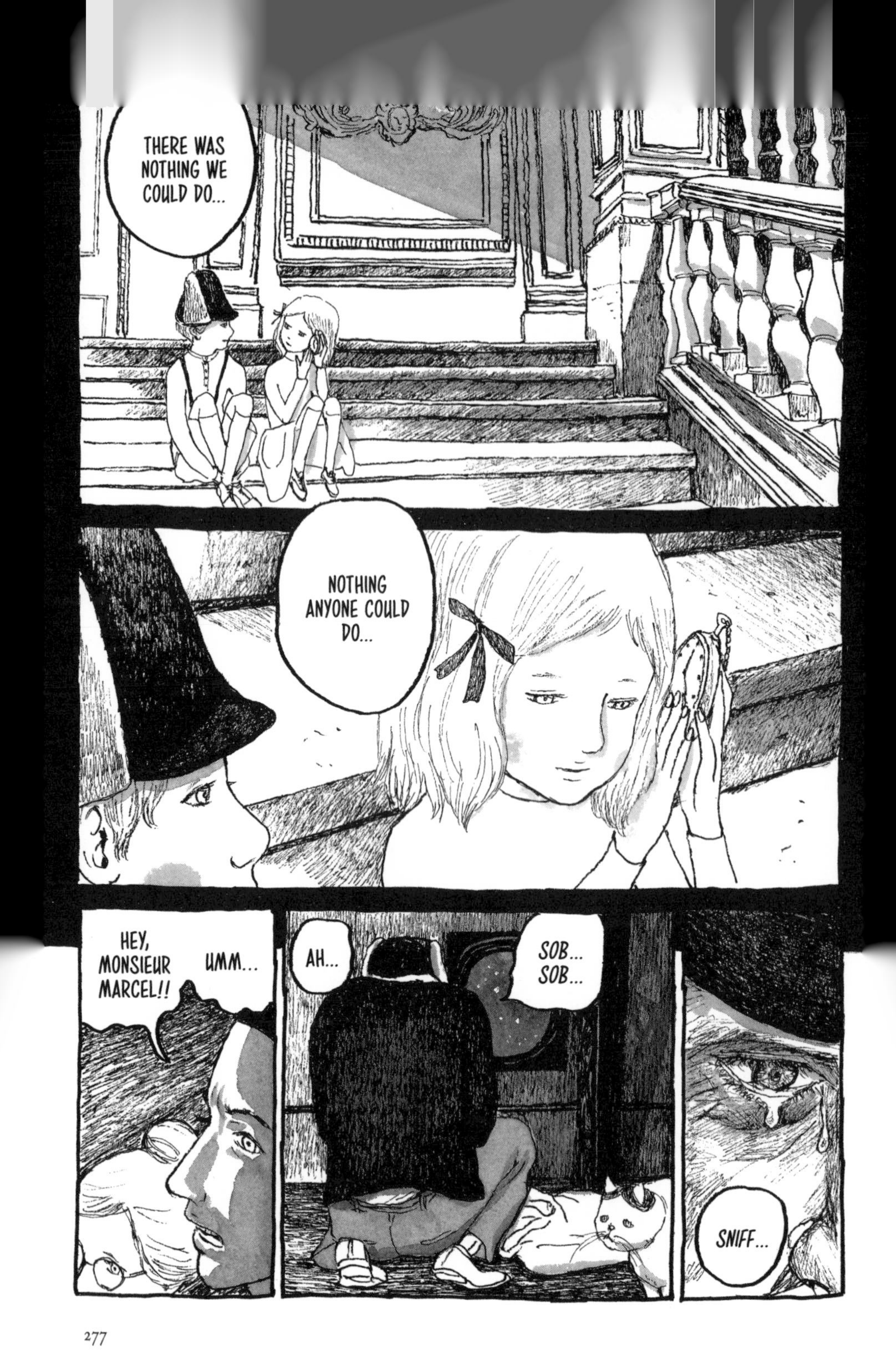
THERE WAS NOTHING WE COULD DO...
NOTHING ANYONE COULD DO...
SNIFF...
SOB... SOB...
AH...
UMM...
HEY, MONSIEUR MARCEL!!

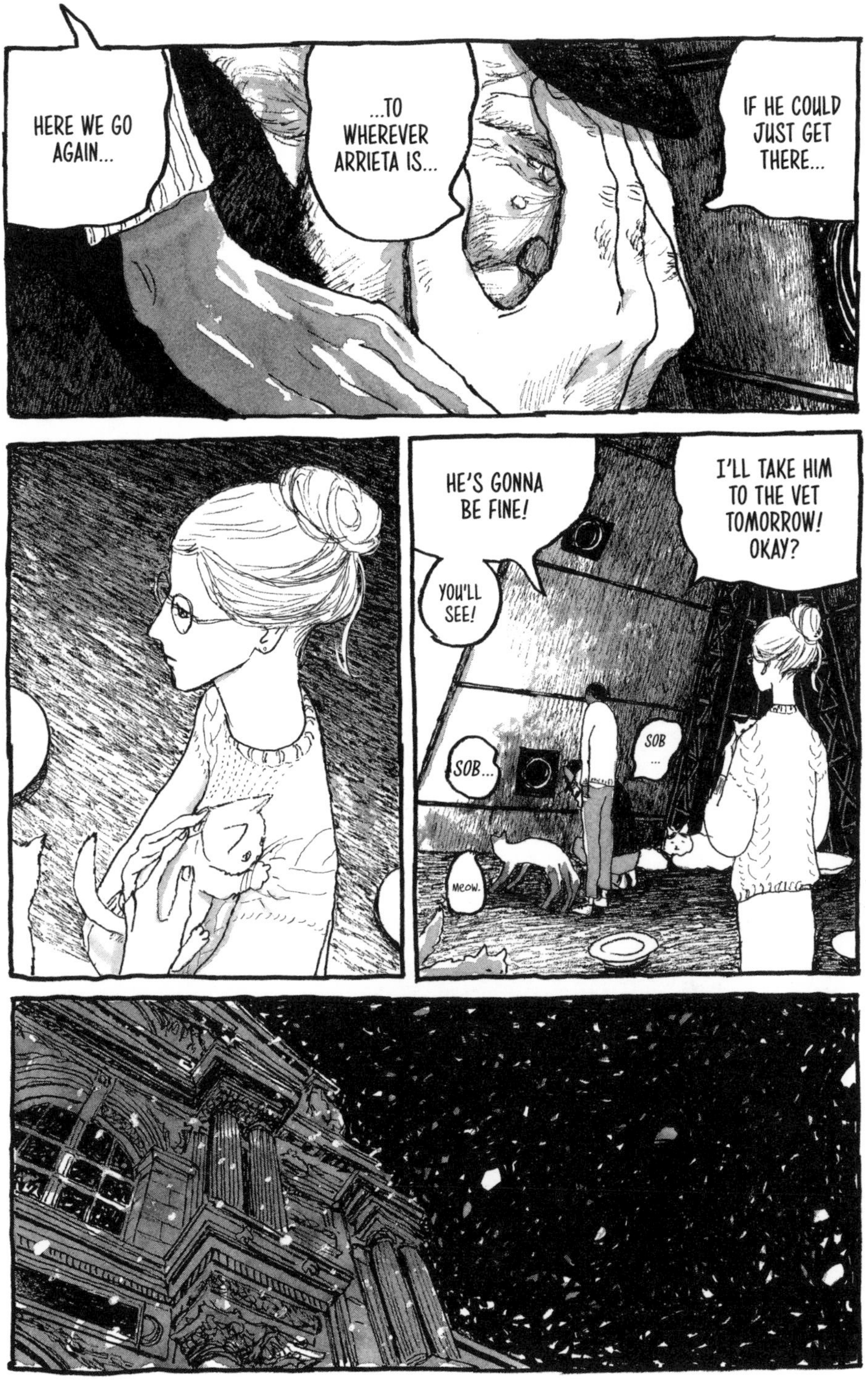
IF HE COULD JUST GET THERE...
...TO WHEREVER ARRIETA IS...
HERE WE GO AGAIN...
I'LL TAKE HIM TO THE VET TOMORROW! OKAY?
HE'S GONNA BE FINE!
YOU'LL SEE!
SOB ...
SOB...
Meow.

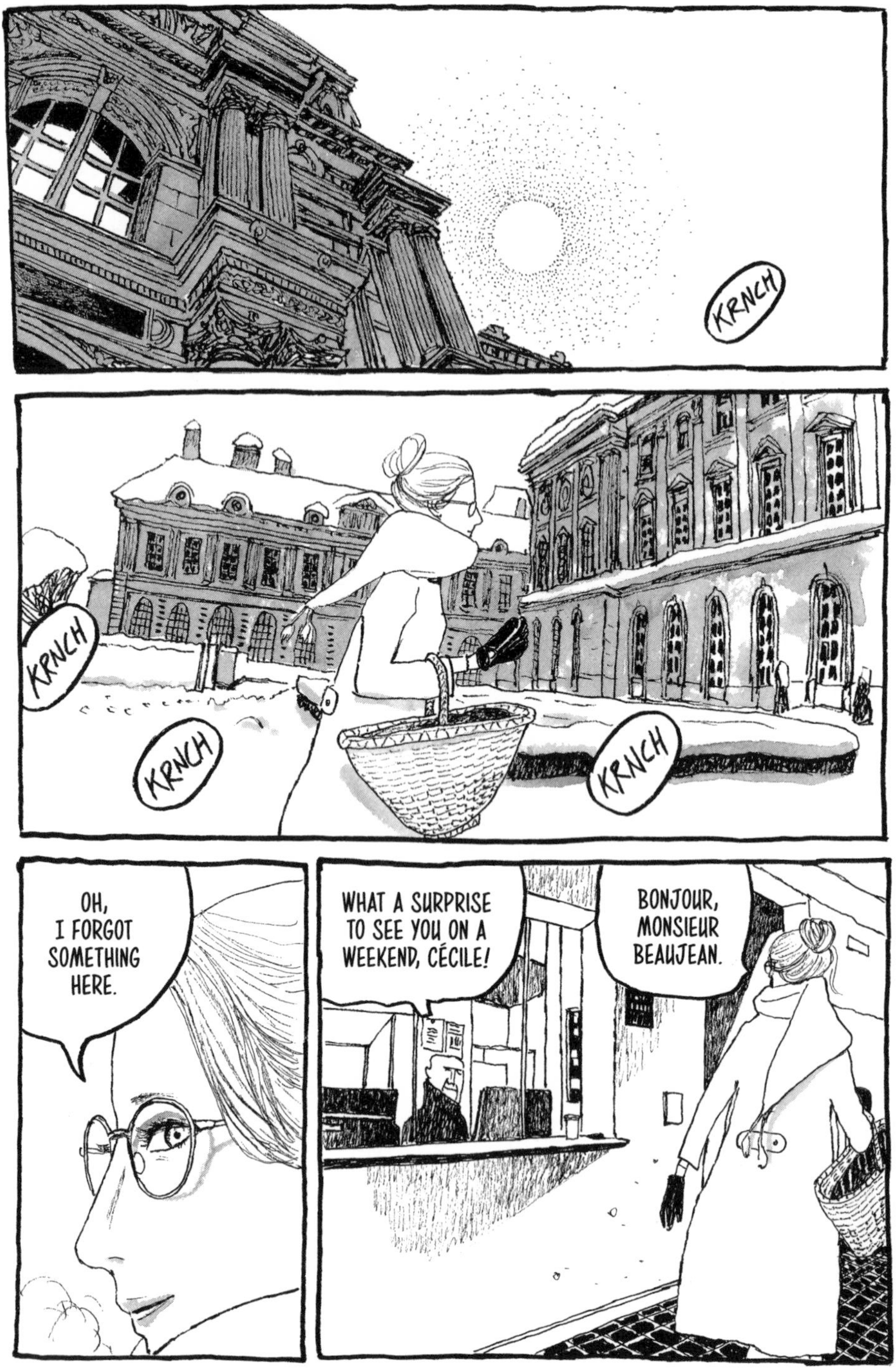
KRNCH
KRNCH
KRNCH
KRNCH
BONJOUR, MONSIEUR BEAUJEAN.
WHAT A SURPRISE TO SEE YOU ON A WEEKEND, CÉCILE!
OH, I FORGOT SOMETHING HERE.

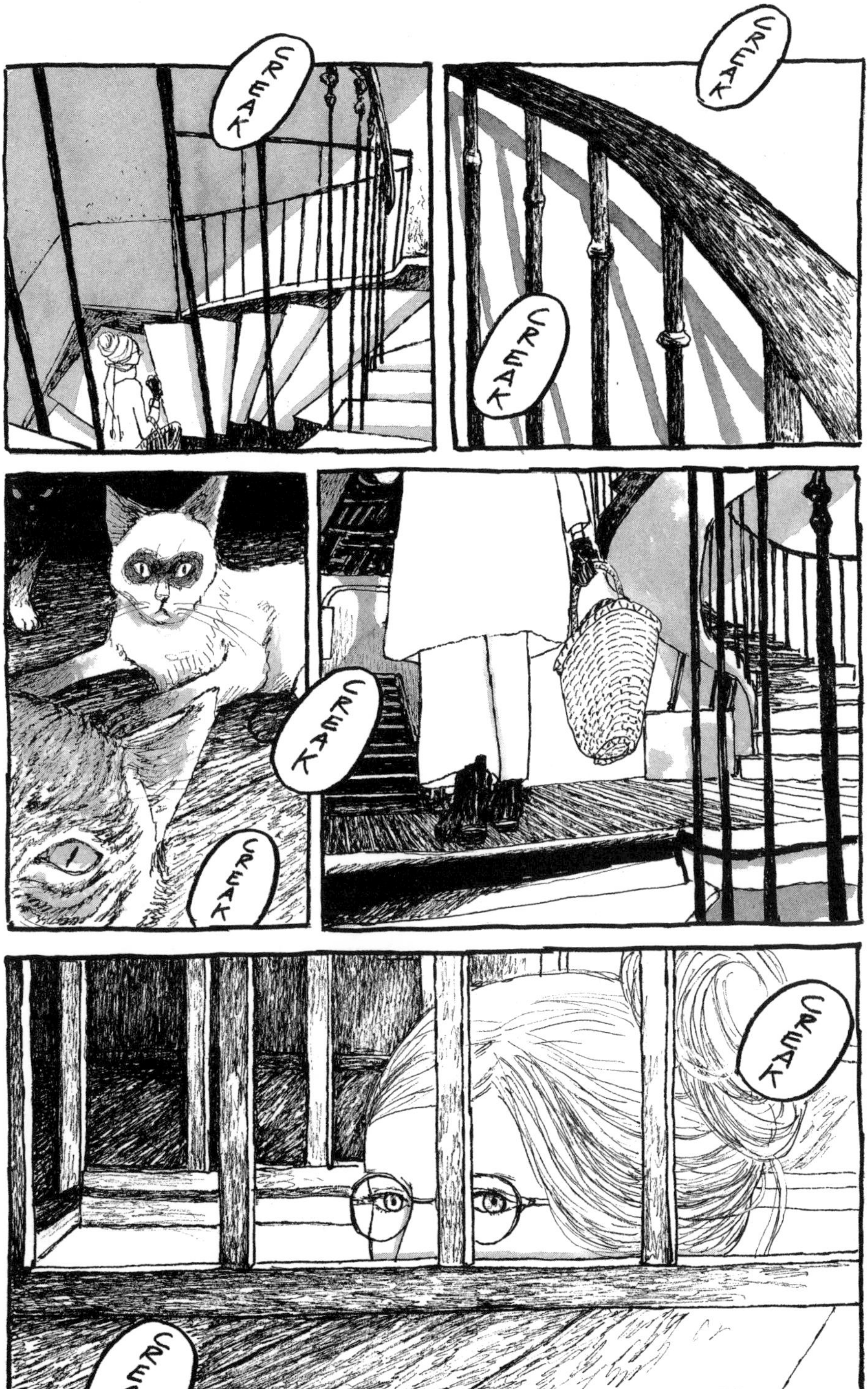
CREAK
CREAK
CREAK
CREAK
CREAK
CREAK
CREAK

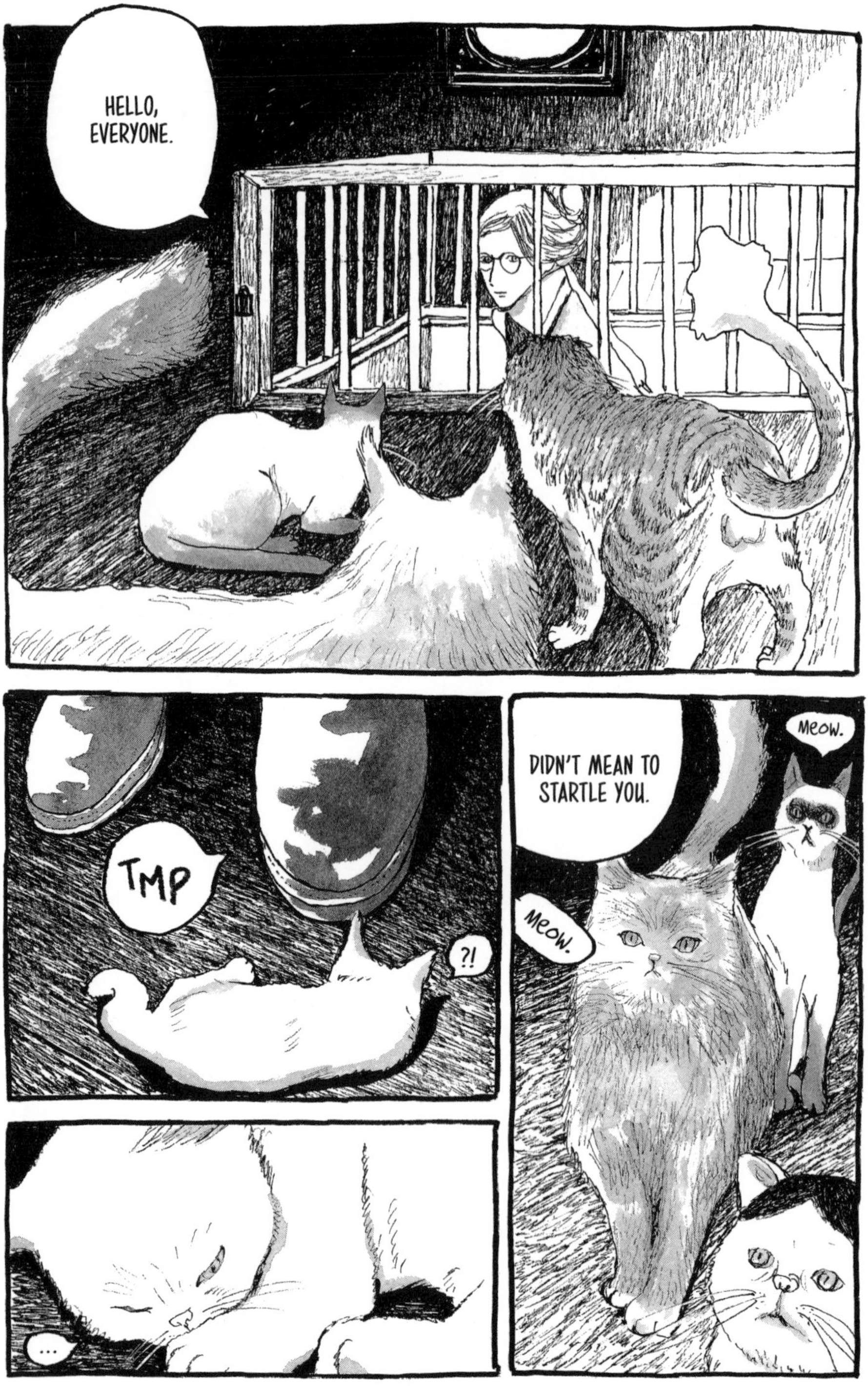

HELLO, EVERYONE.
Meow.
DIDN'T MEAN TO STARTLE YOU.
Meow.
TMP
?!
...

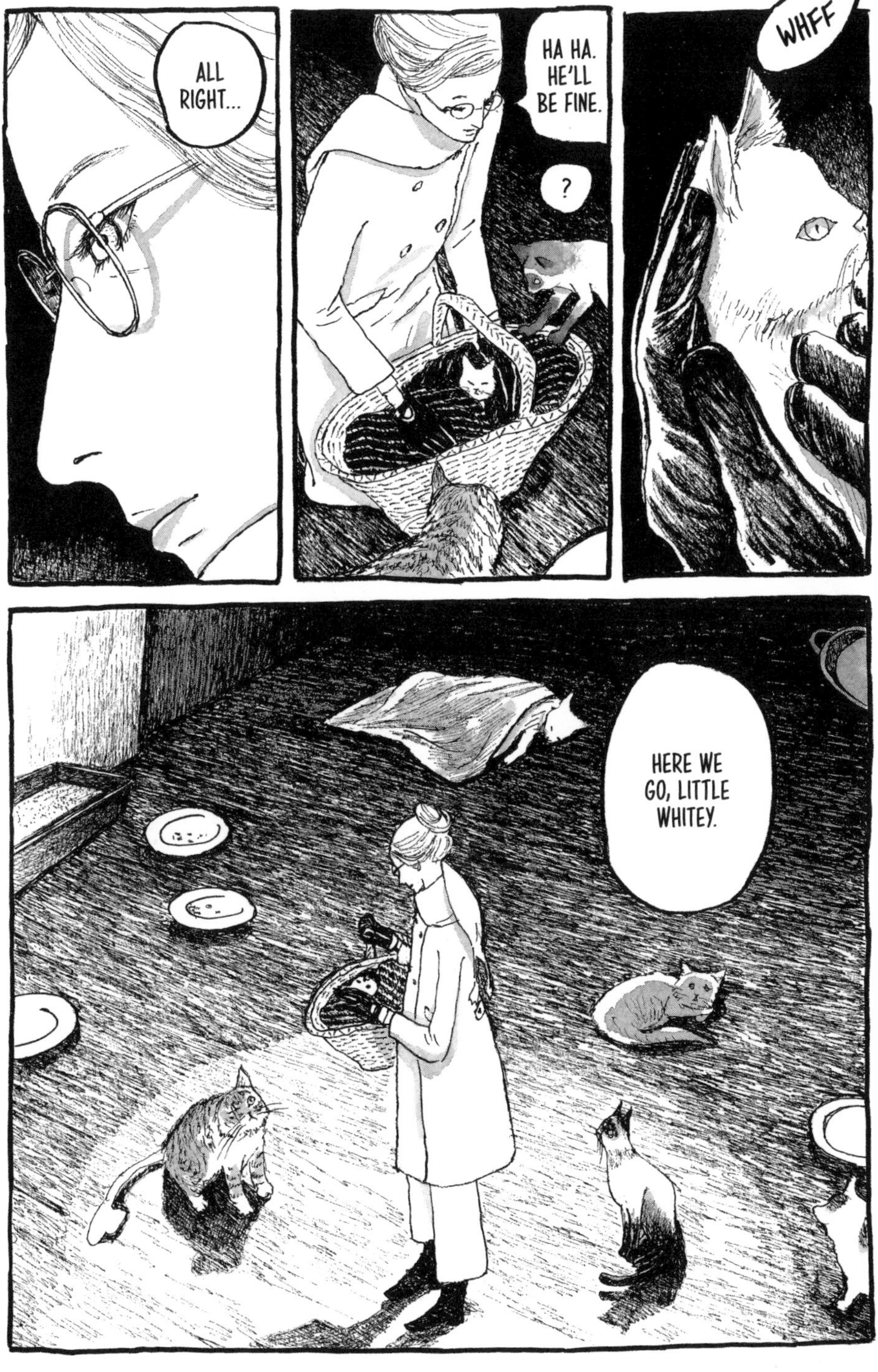
WHFF
HA HA. HE'LL BE FINE.
?
ALL RIGHT...
HERE WE GO, LITTLE WHITEY.

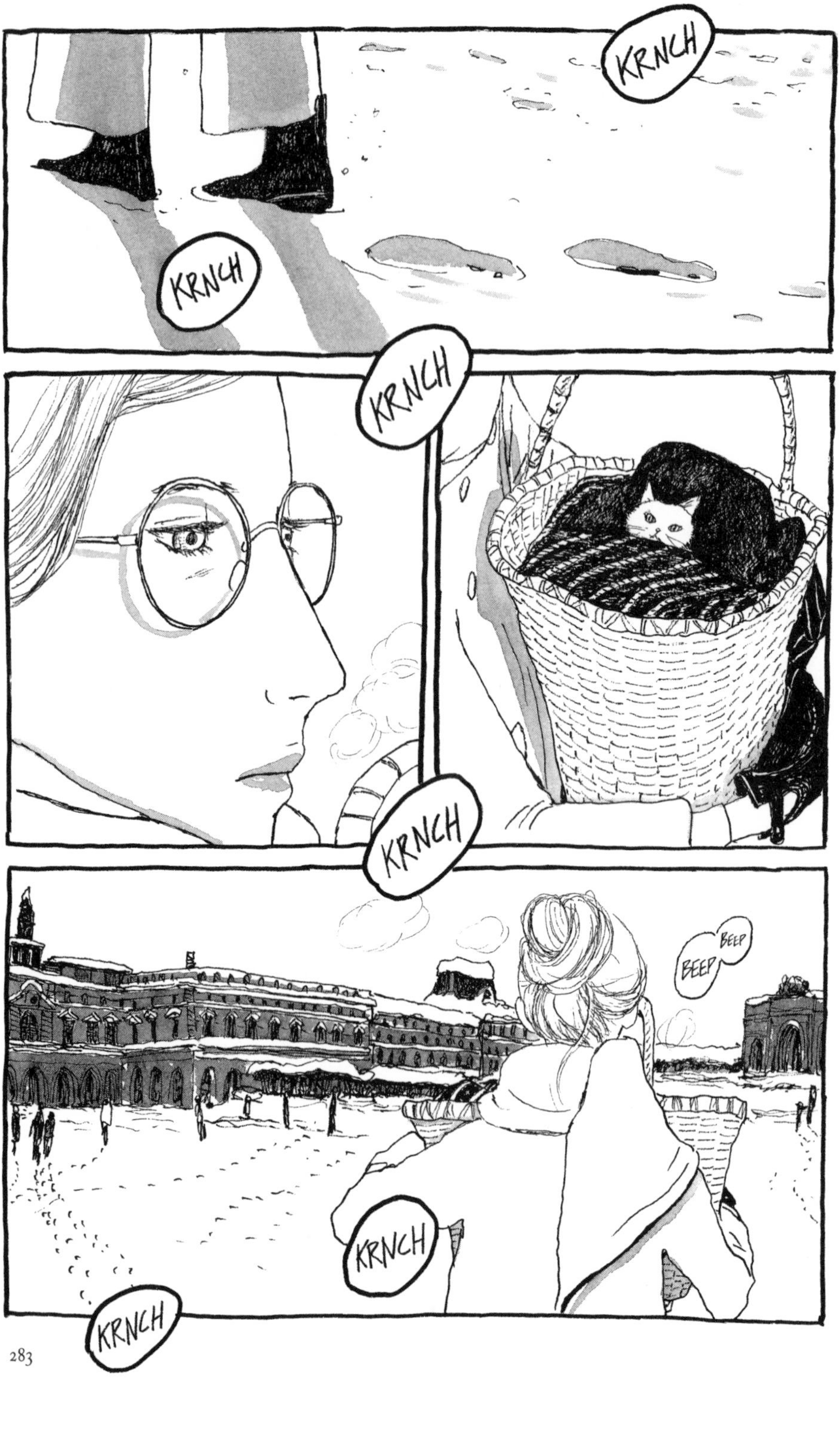
KRNCH
KRNCH
KRNCH
KRNCH
BEEP
BEEP
KRNCH
KRNCH

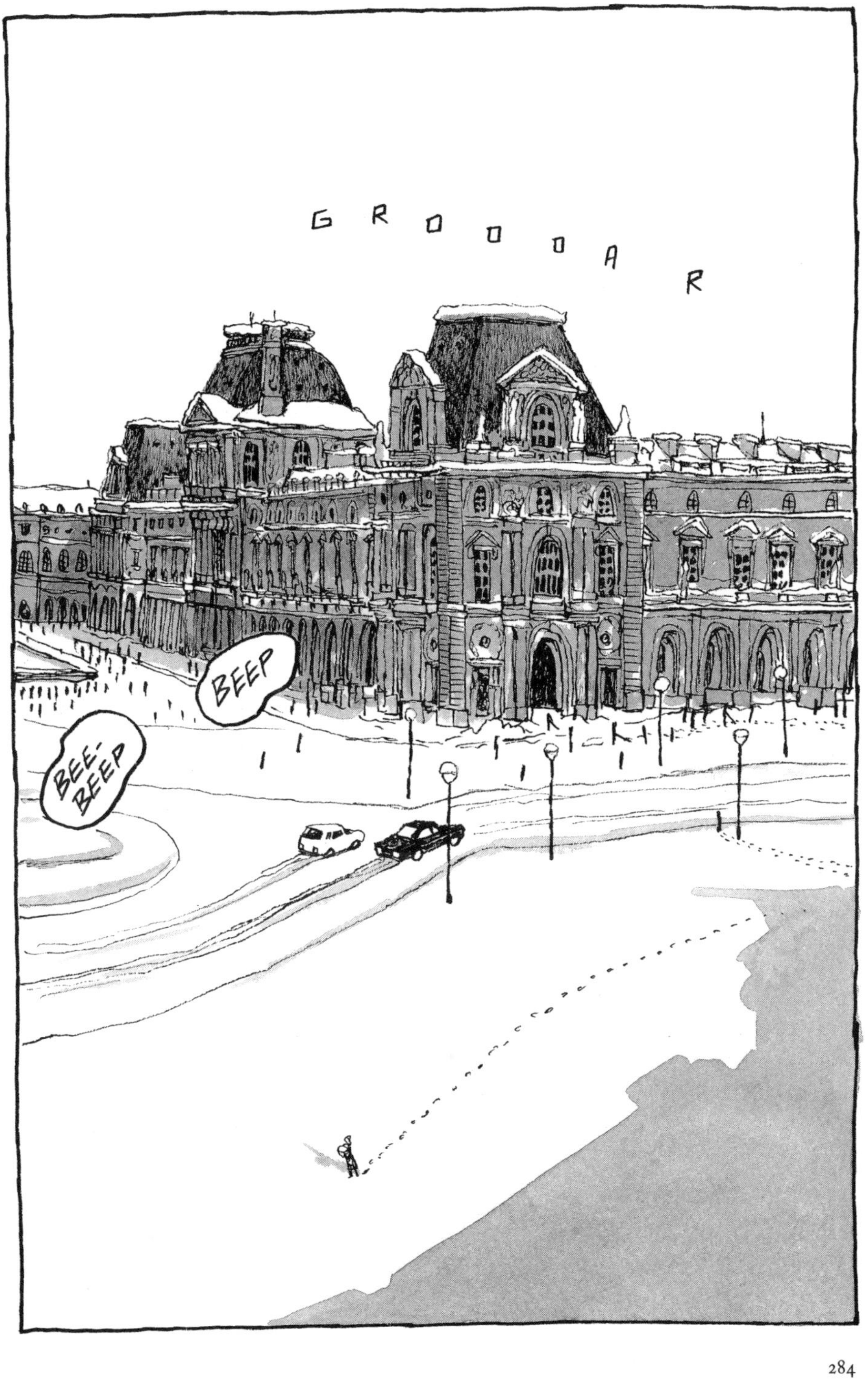
GROOOAR
BEEP
BEE-BEEP

CHAPTER 13

The Secret of the Restorer

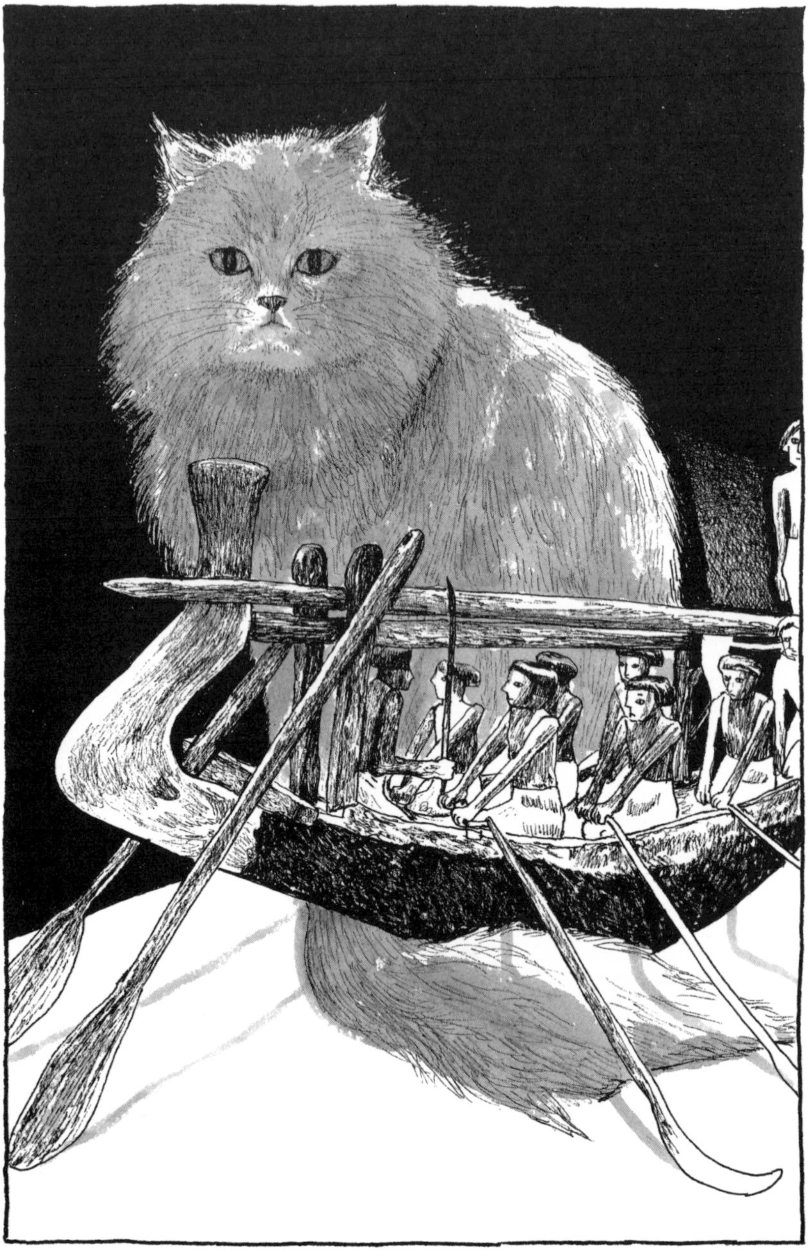

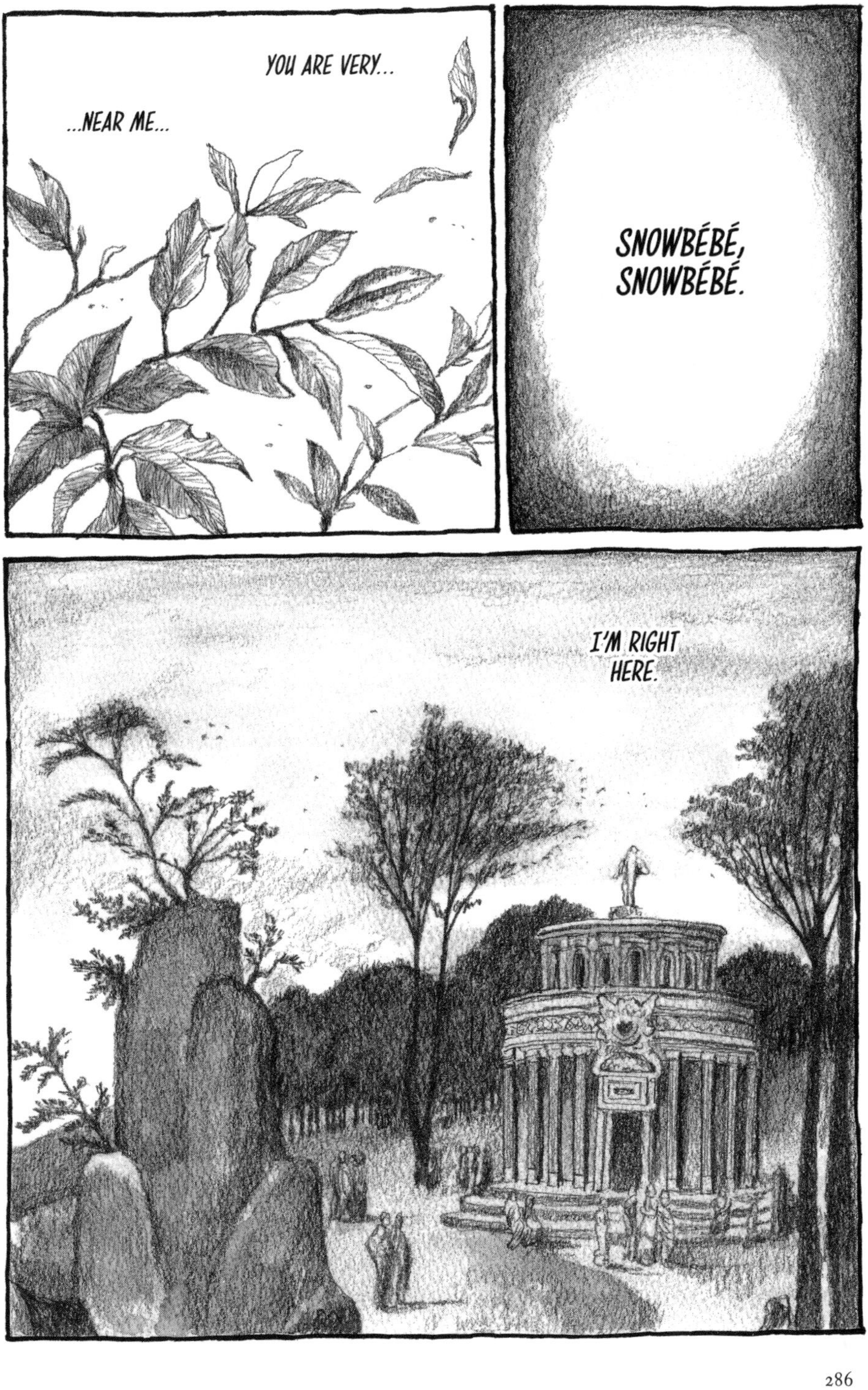
SNOWBÉBÉ, SNOWBÉBÉ.
YOU ARE VERY...
...NEAR ME...
I'M RIGHT HERE.

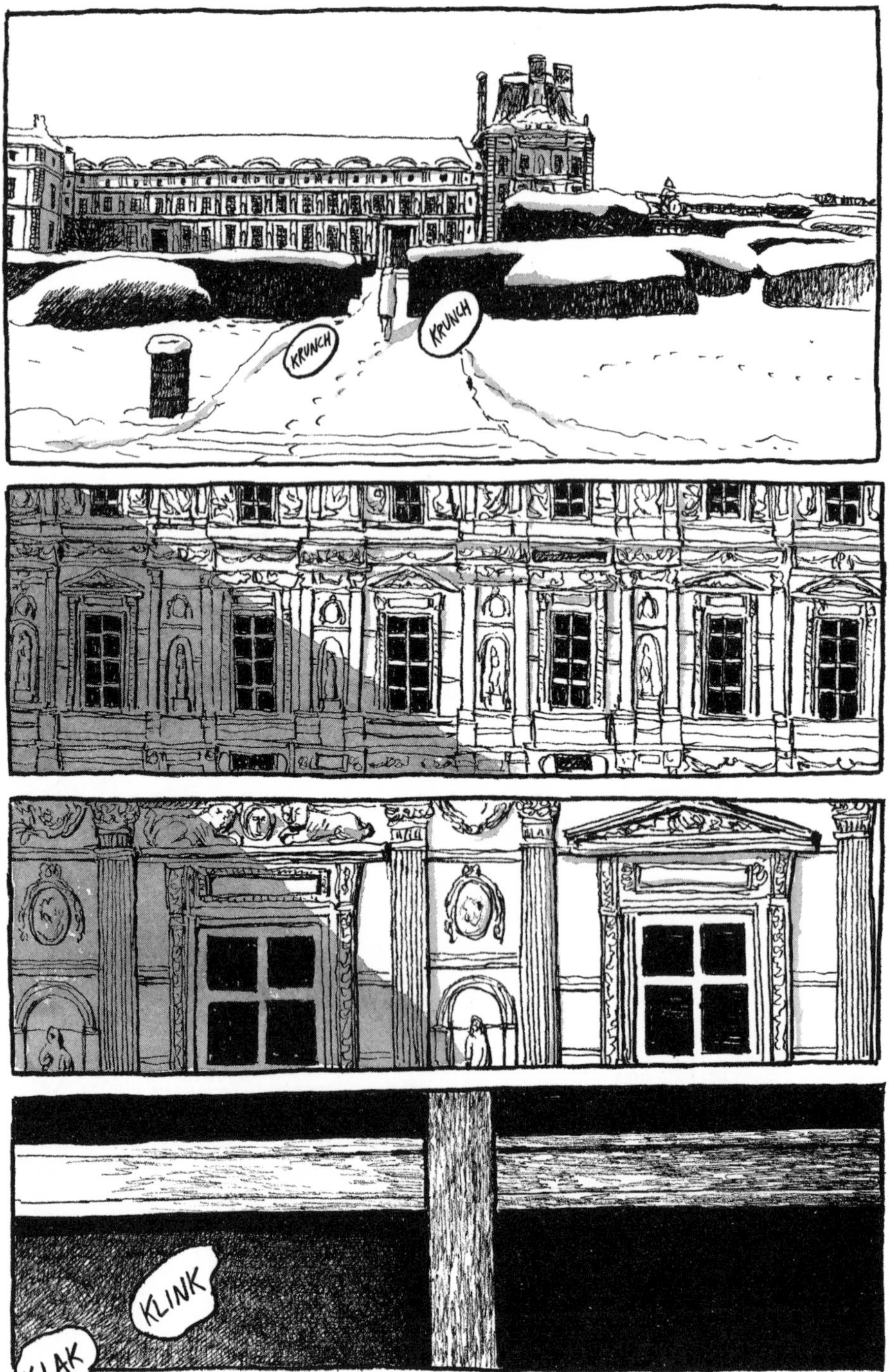

KRUNCH
KRUNCH
KLINK
KLAK

SWP
KLIK
KLAK
SWP
KLUNK
SWP
WP SWP
KLINK KLINK

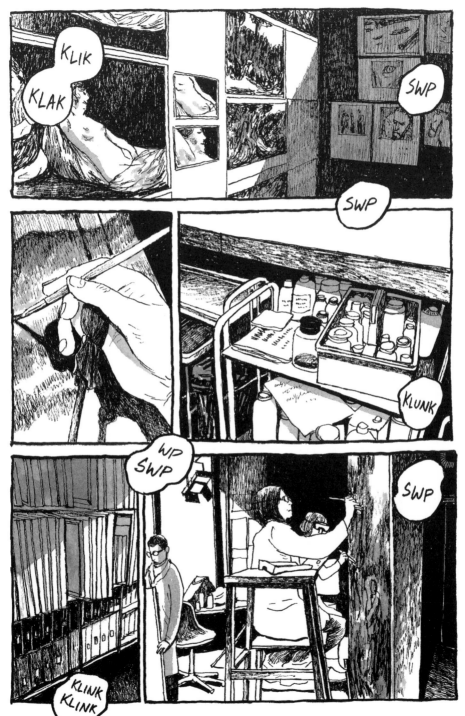

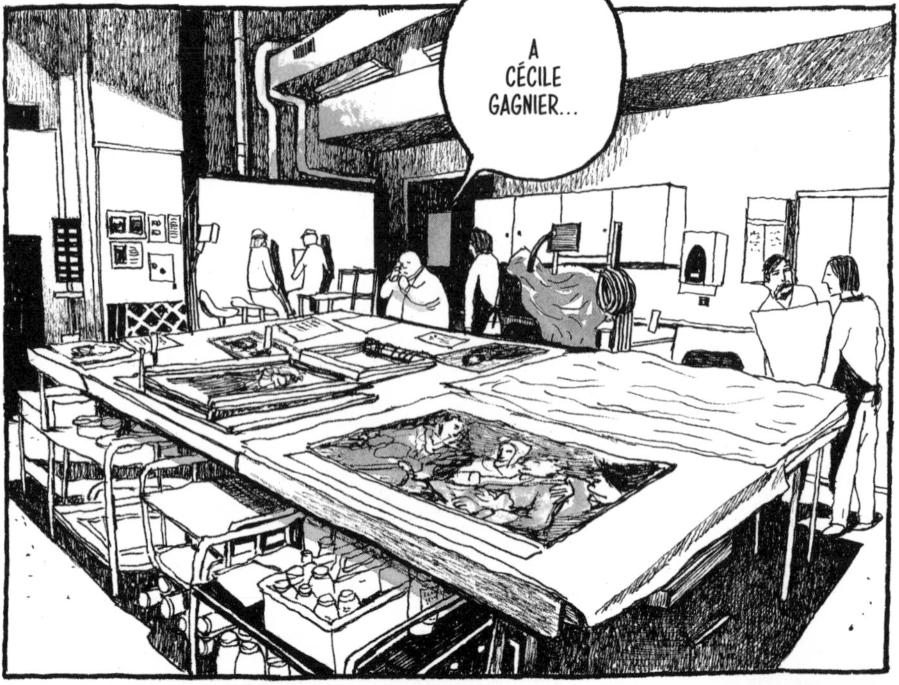
A CÉCILE GAGNIER...
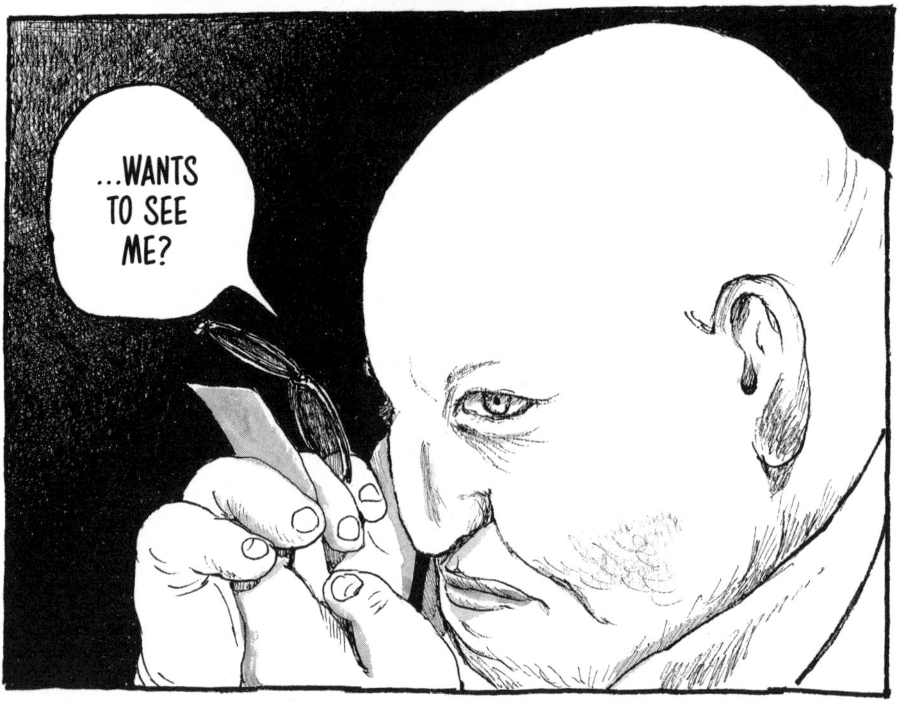
...WANTS TO SEE ME?

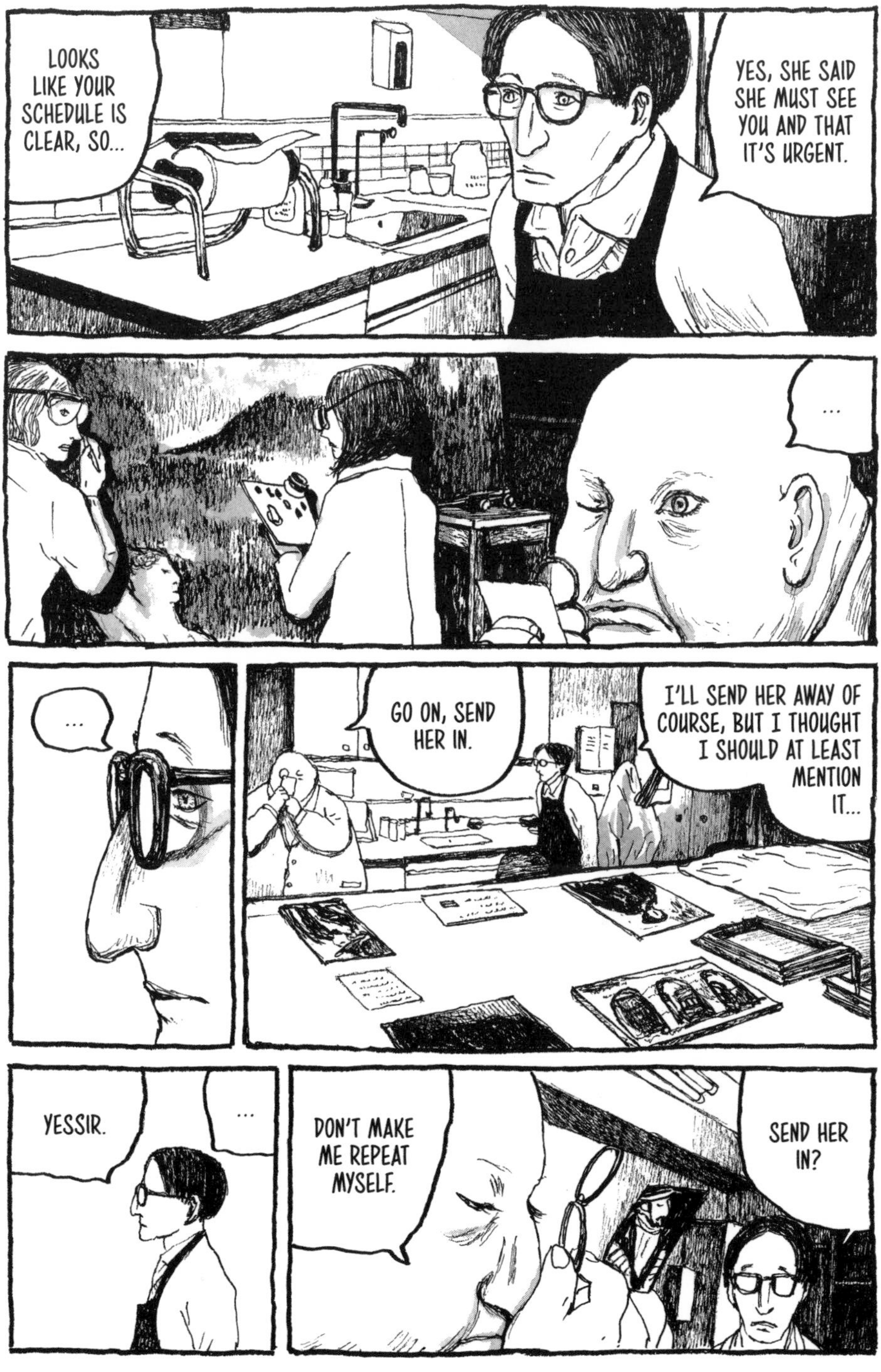
YES, SHE SAID SHE MUST SEE YOU AND THAT IT'S URGENT.
LOOKS LIKE YOUR SCHEDULE IS CLEAR, SO...
...
I'LL SEND HER AWAY OF COURSE, BUT I THOUGHT I SHOULD AT LEAST MENTION IT...
GO ON, SEND HER IN.
...
SEND HER IN?
DON'T MAKE ME REPEAT MYSELF.
...
YESSIR.

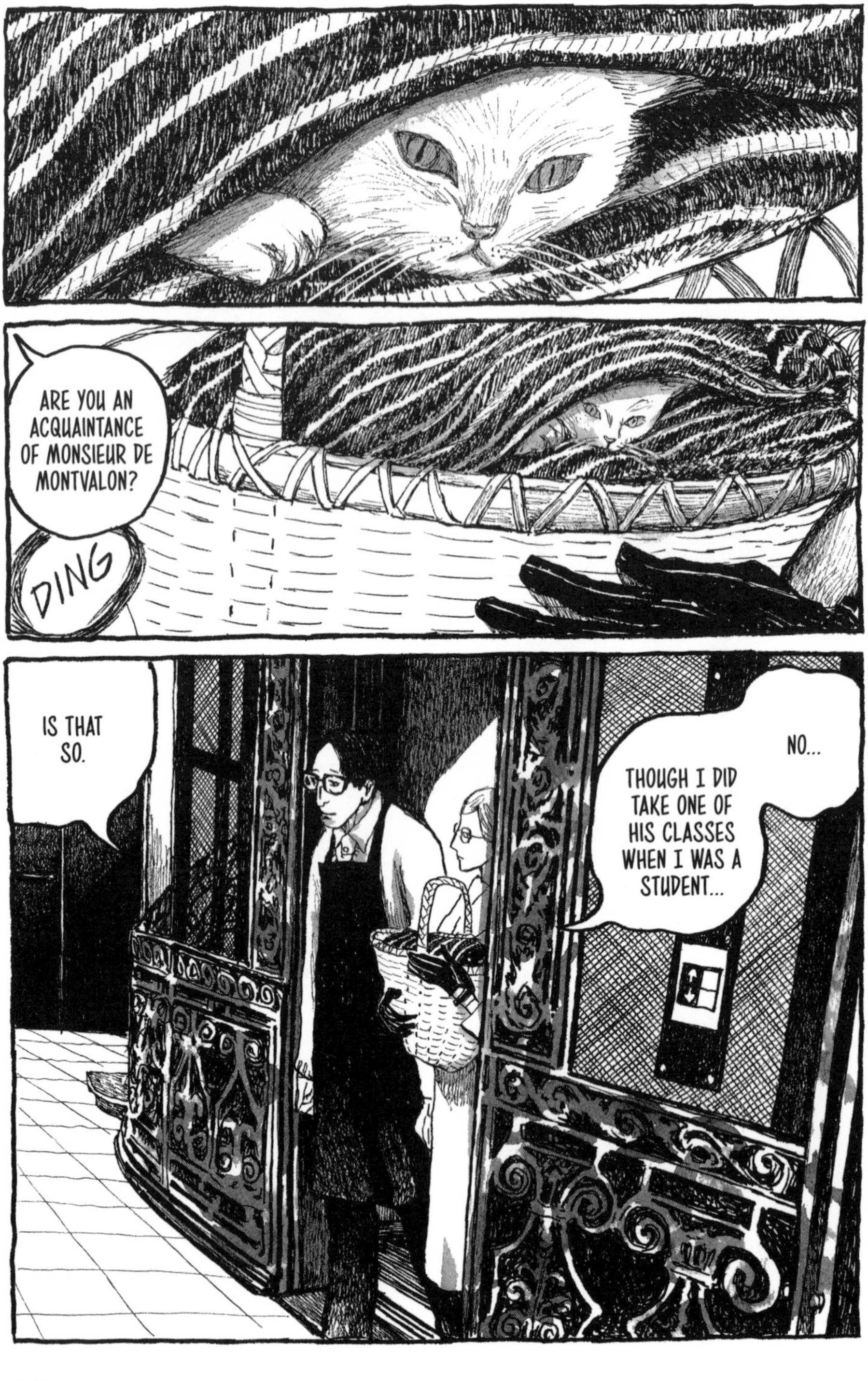
ARE YOU AN ACQUAINTANCE OF MONSIEUR DE MONTVALON?
DING
NO...
THOUGH I DID TAKE ONE OF HIS CLASSES WHEN I WAS A STUDENT...
IS THAT SO.

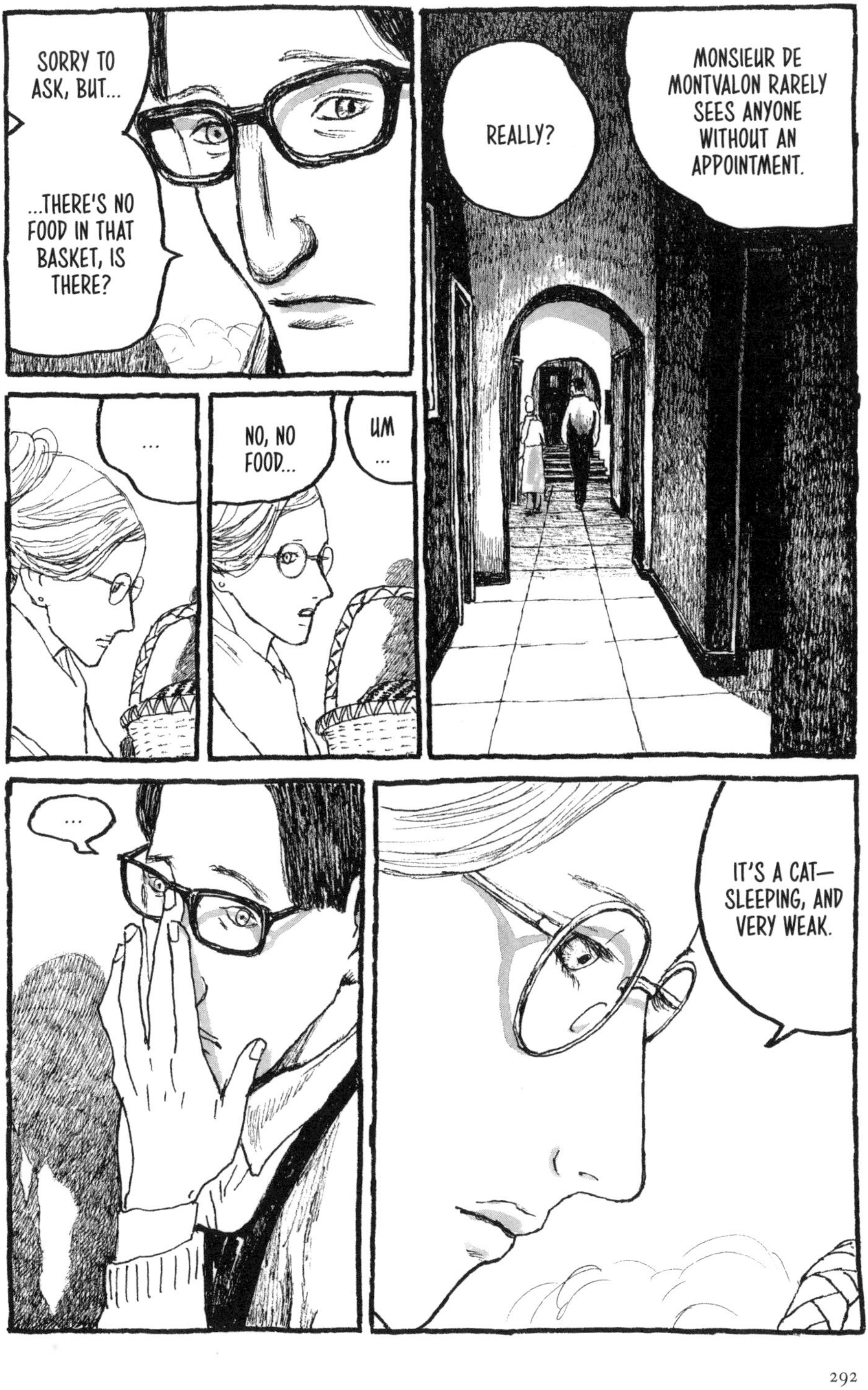
MONSIEUR DE MONTVALON RARELY SEES ANYONE WITHOUT AN APPOINTMENT.
REALLY?
SORRY TO ASK, BUT...
...THERE'S NO FOOD IN THAT BASKET, IS THERE?
UM ...
NO, NO FOOD...
...
IT'S A CAT—SLEEPING, AND VERY WEAK.
...

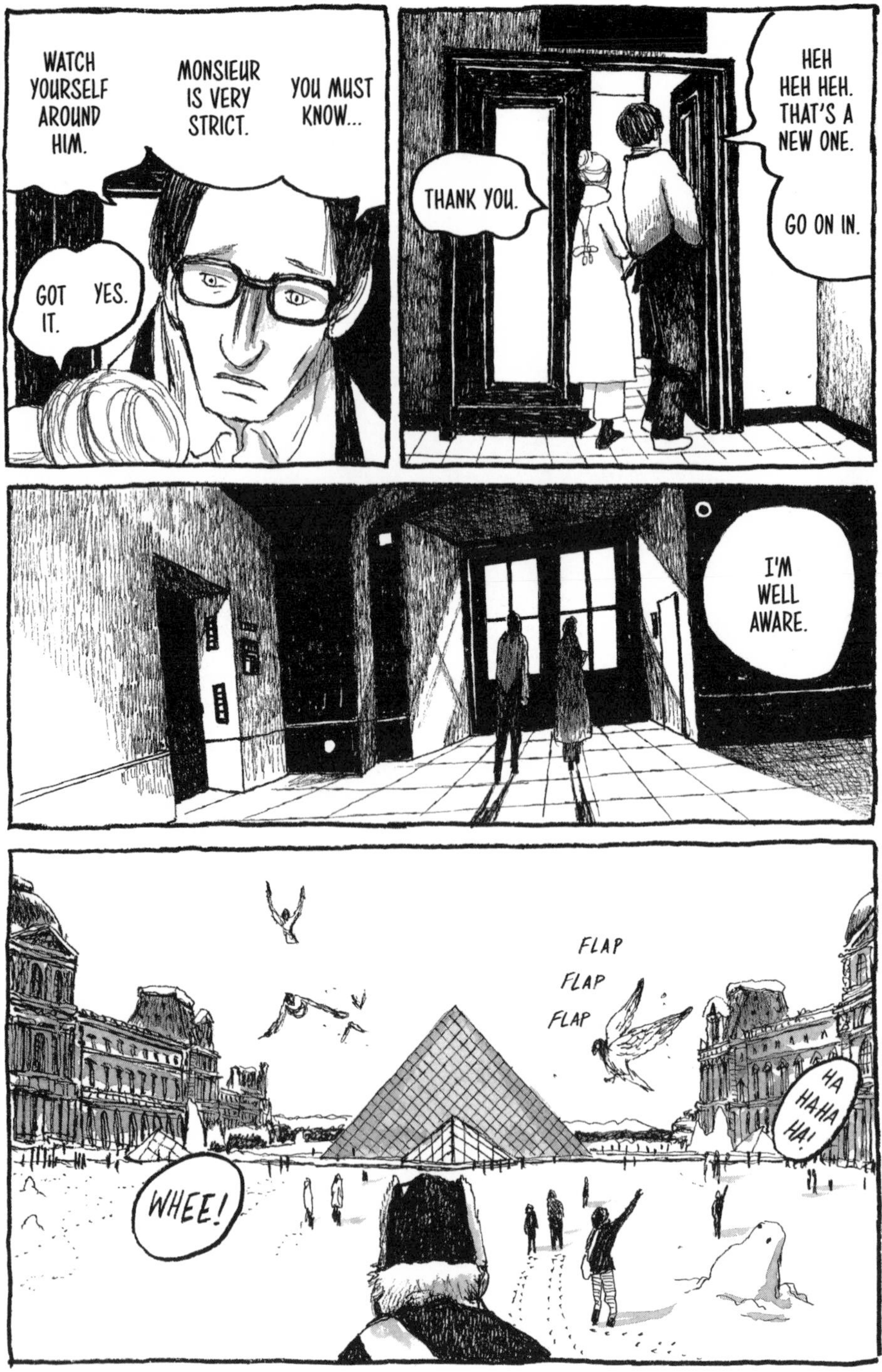
HEH HEH HEH. THAT'S A NEW ONE.
GO ON IN.
THANK YOU.
YOU MUST KNOW...
MONSIEUR IS VERY STRICT.
WATCH YOURSELF AROUND HIM.
YES.
GOT IT.
I'M WELL AWARE.
FLAP FLAP FLAP
HA HAHAHA HA!
WHEE!

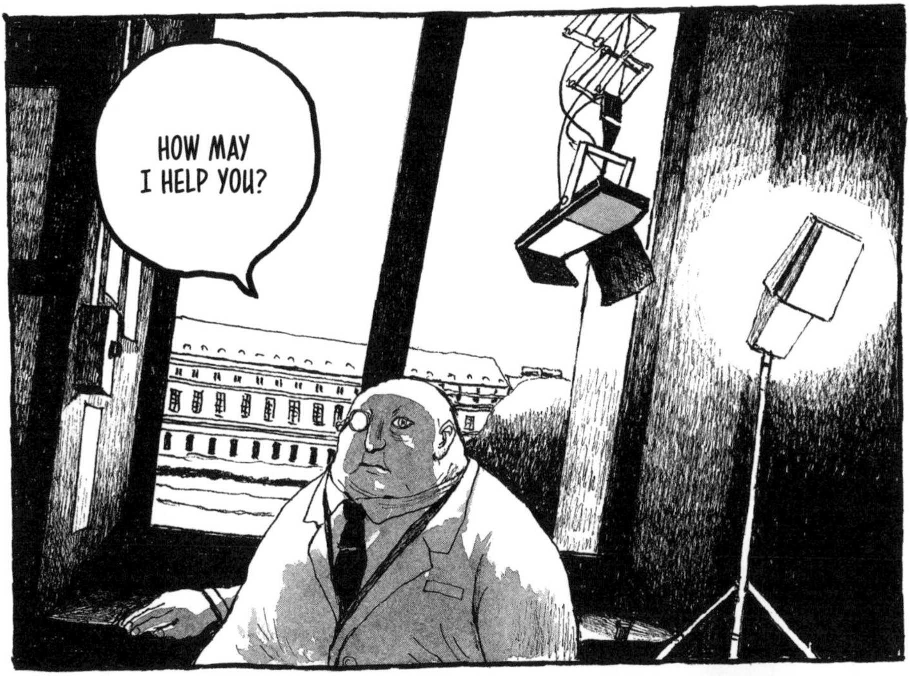
HOW MAY I HELP YOU?

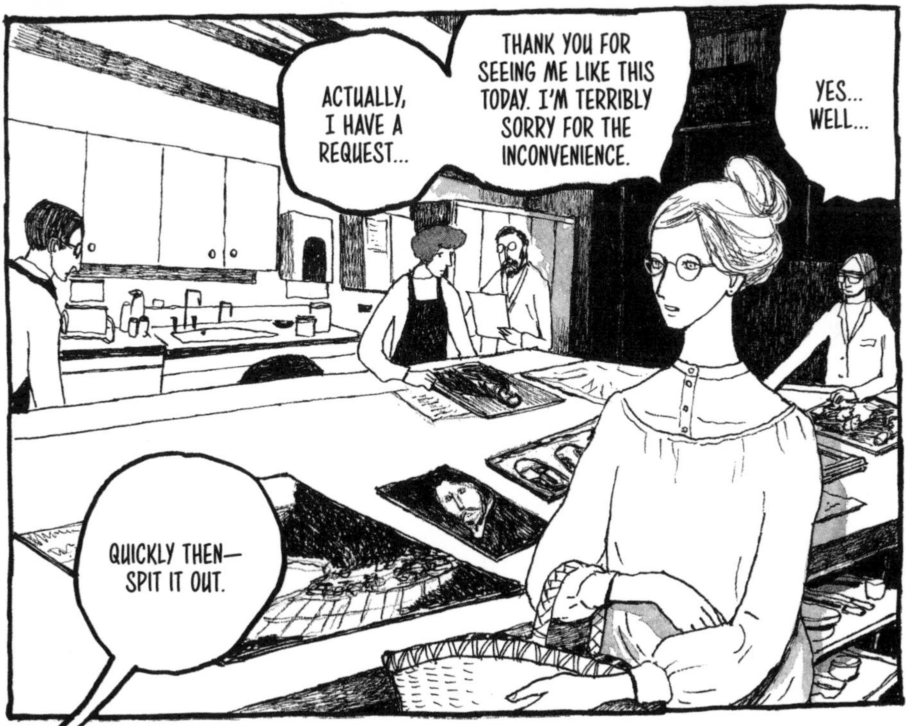
YES... WELL...
THANK YOU FOR SEEING ME LIKE THIS TODAY. I'M TERRIBLY SORRY FOR THE INCONVENIENCE.
ACTUALLY, I HAVE A REQUEST...
QUICKLY THEN— SPIT IT OUT.

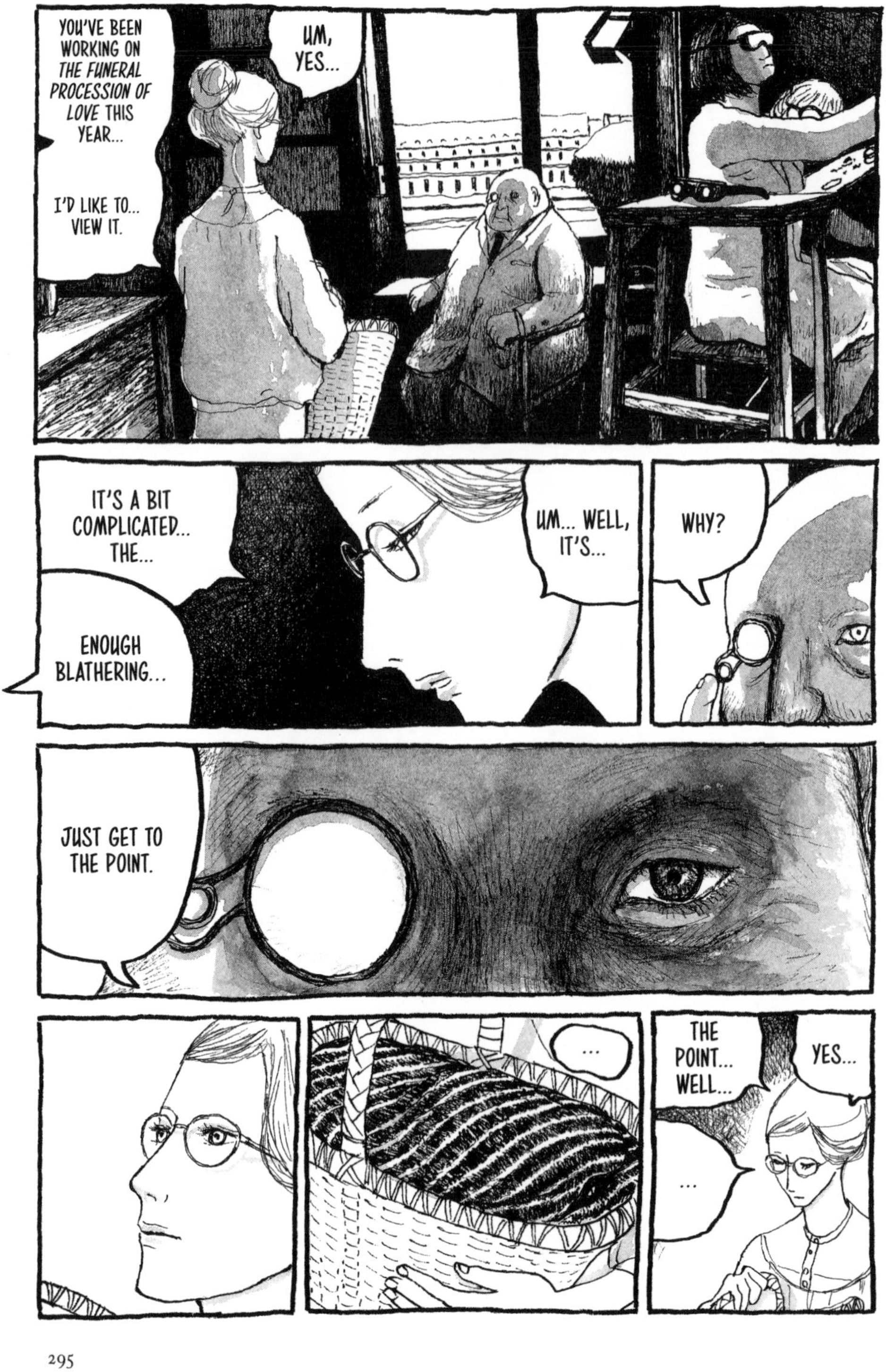
UM, YES...
YOU'VE BEEN WORKING ON *THE FUNERAL PROCESSION OF LOVE* THIS YEAR...
I'D LIKE TO... VIEW IT.
WHY?
UM... WELL, IT'S...
IT'S A BIT COMPLICATED... THE...
ENOUGH BLATHERING...
JUST GET TO THE POINT.
YES...
THE POINT... WELL...
...
...

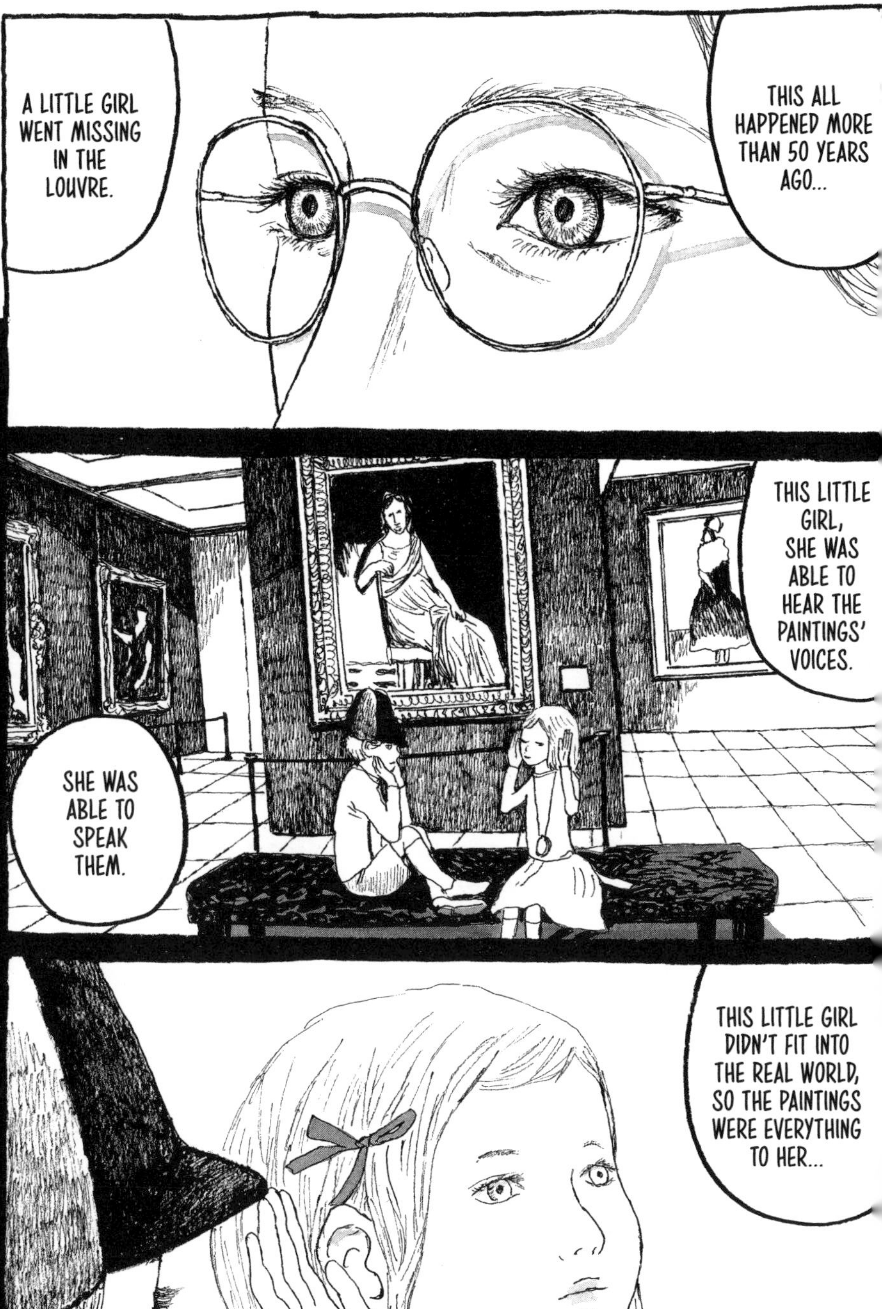
THIS ALL HAPPENED MORE THAN 50 YEARS AGO...
A LITTLE GIRL WENT MISSING IN THE LOUVRE.
THIS LITTLE GIRL, SHE WAS ABLE TO HEAR THE PAINTINGS' VOICES.
SHE WAS ABLE TO SPEAK THEM.
THIS LITTLE GIRL DIDN'T FIT INTO THE REAL WORLD, SO THE PAINTINGS WERE EVERYTHING TO HER...

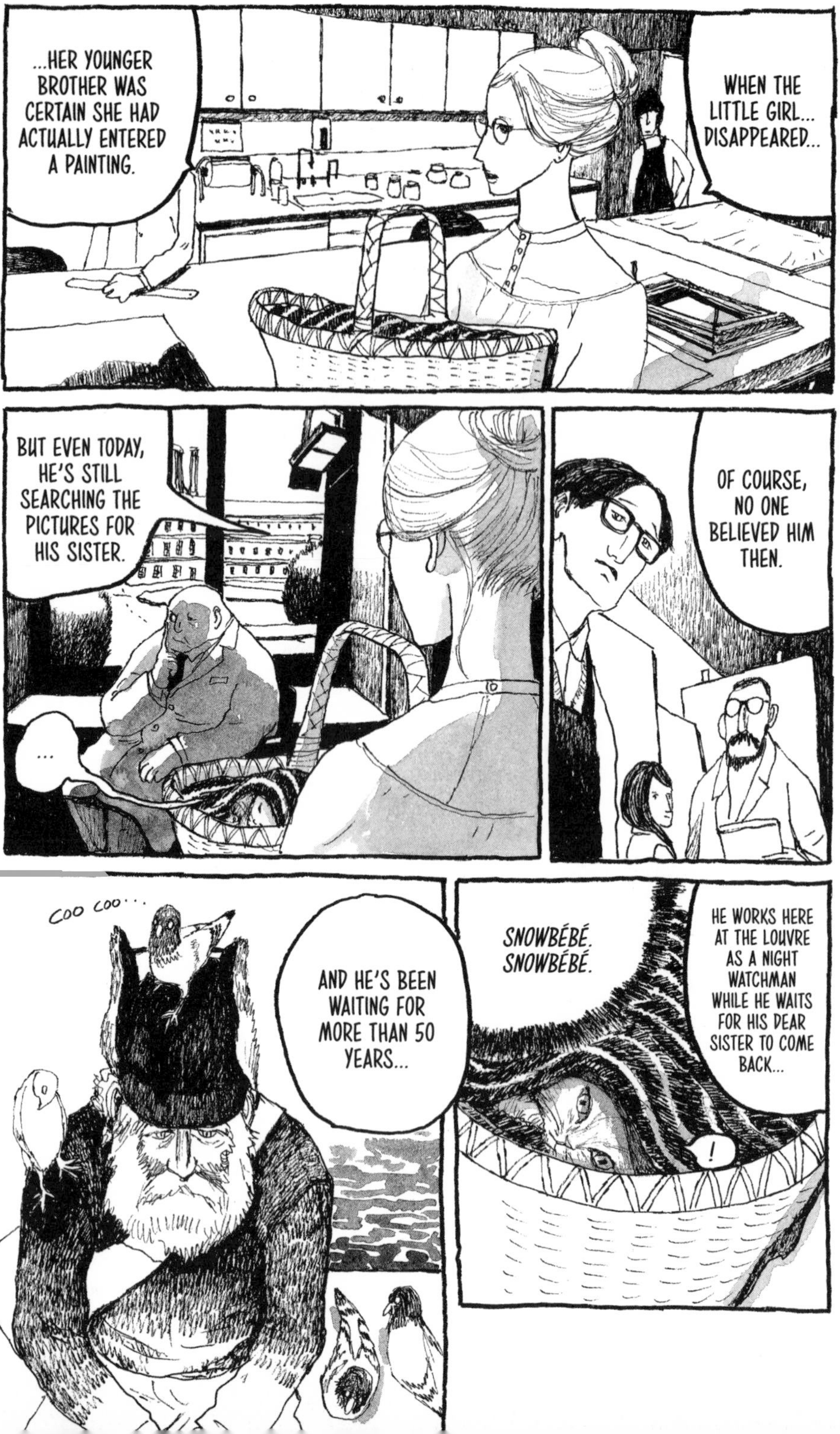
WHEN THE LITTLE GIRL... DISAPPEARED...
...HER YOUNGER BROTHER WAS CERTAIN SHE HAD ACTUALLY ENTERED A PAINTING.
OF COURSE, NO ONE BELIEVED HIM THEN.
BUT EVEN TODAY, HE'S STILL SEARCHING THE PICTURES FOR HIS SISTER.
...
HE WORKS HERE AT THE LOUVRE AS A NIGHT WATCHMAN WHILE HE WAITS FOR HIS DEAR SISTER TO COME BACK...
SNOWBÉBÉ. SNOWBÉBÉ.
!
AND HE'S BEEN WAITING FOR MORE THAN 50 YEARS...
COO COO...

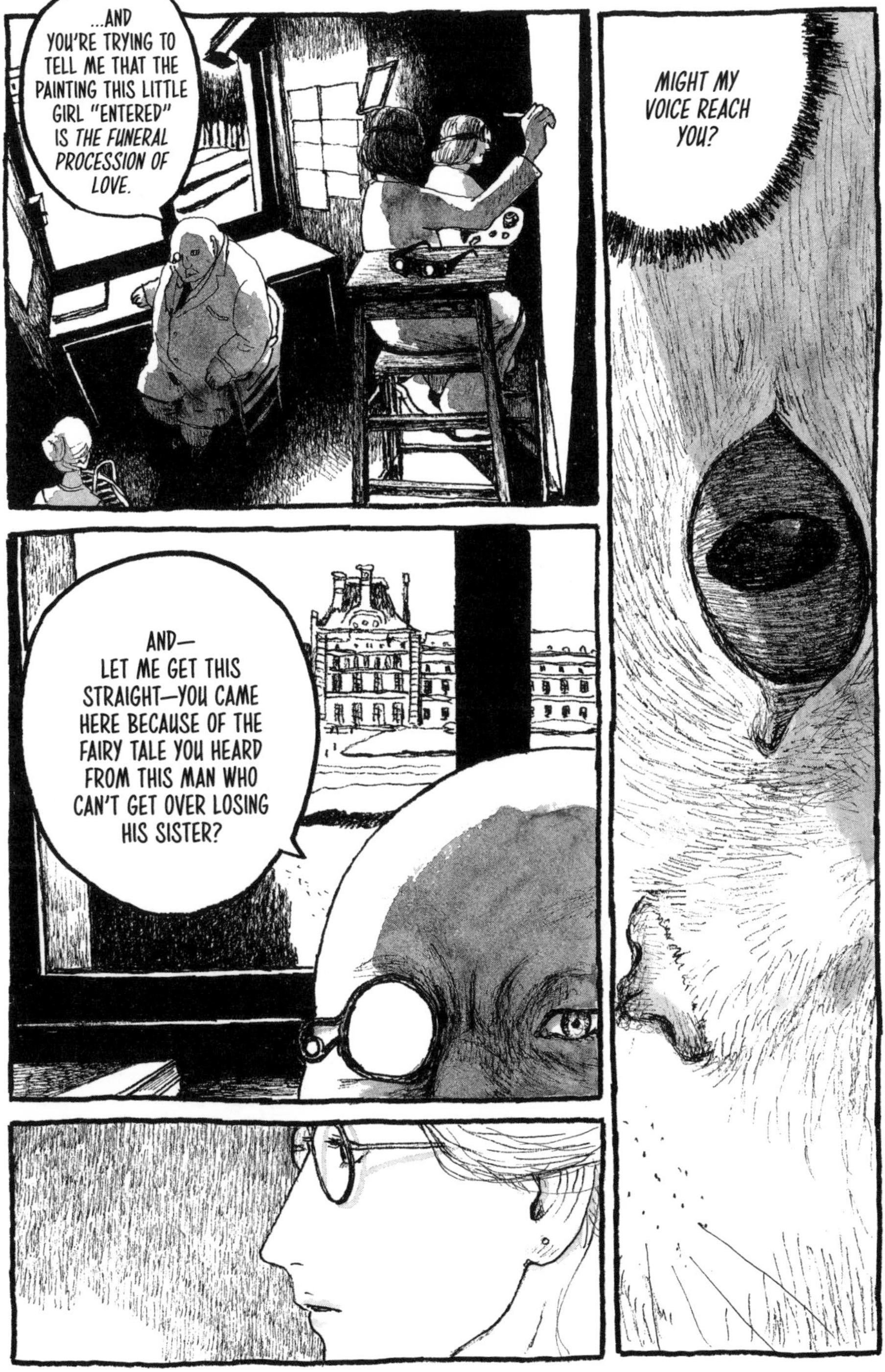
MIGHT MY VOICE REACH YOU?
...AND YOU'RE TRYING TO TELL ME THAT THE PAINTING THIS LITTLE GIRL "ENTERED" IS *THE FUNERAL PROCESSION OF LOVE.*
AND— LET ME GET THIS STRAIGHT—YOU CAME HERE BECAUSE OF THE FAIRY TALE YOU HEARD FROM THIS MAN WHO CAN'T GET OVER LOSING HIS SISTER?

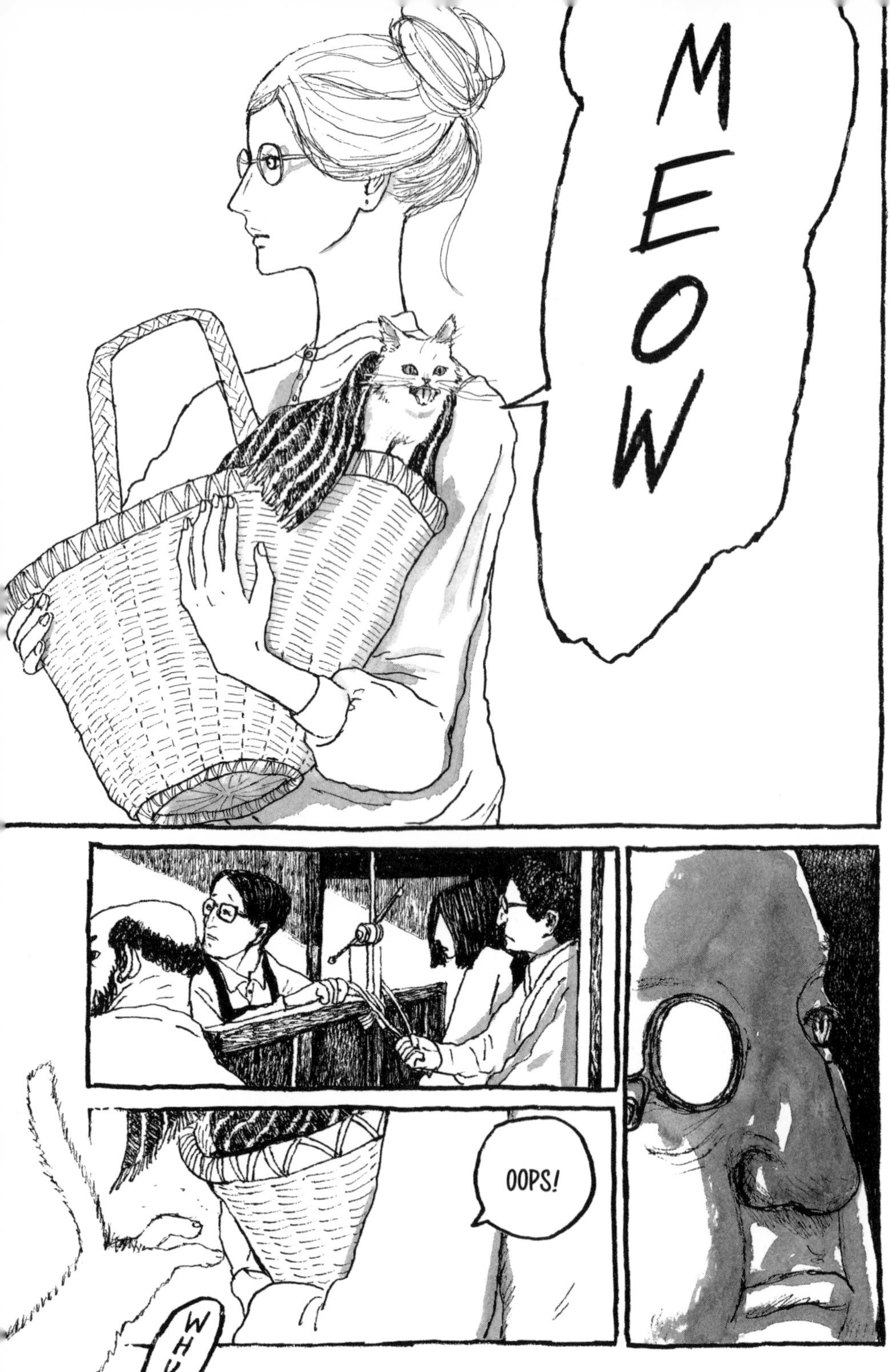
MEOW
OOPS!
WHUP

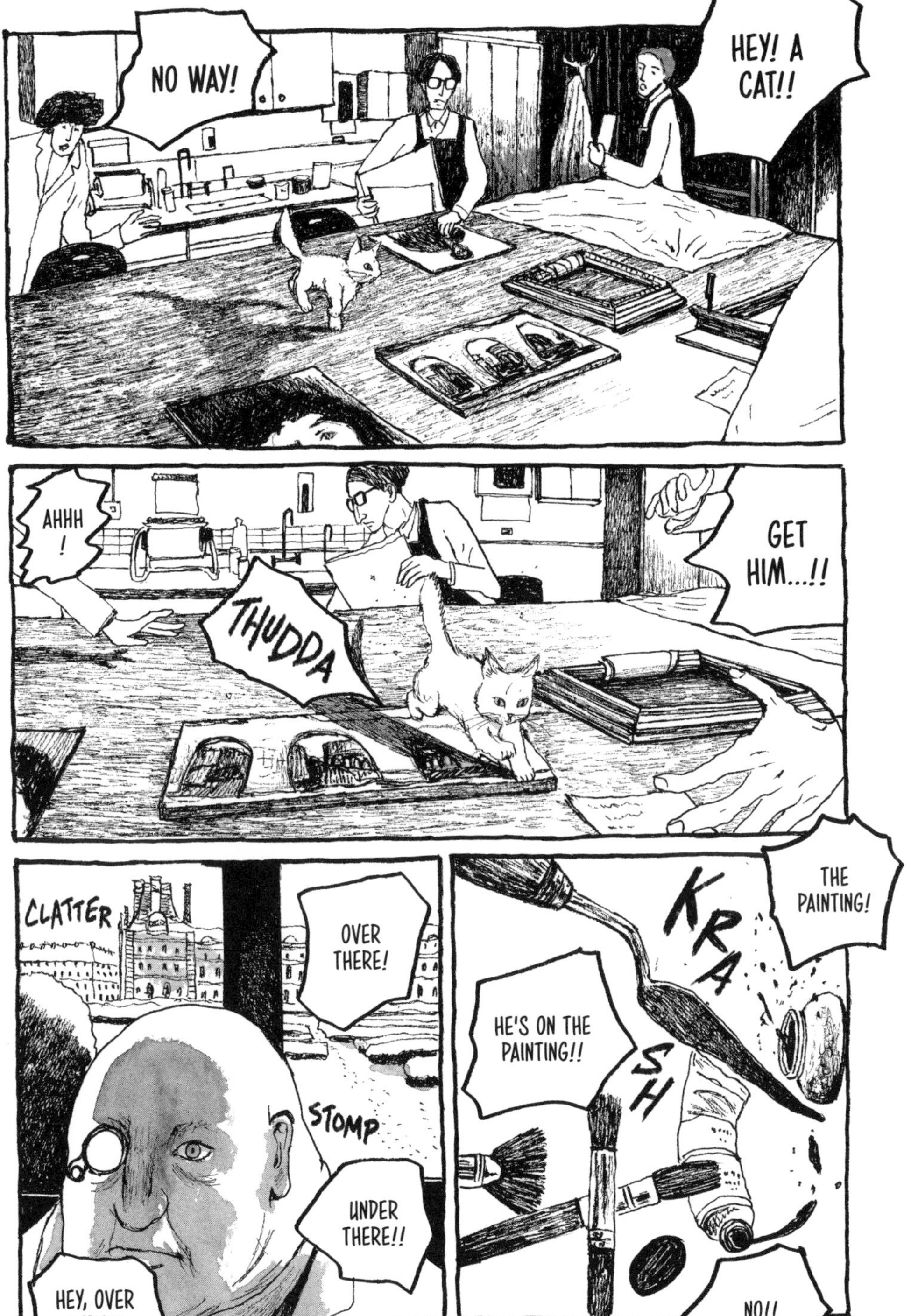
HEY! A CAT!!
NO WAY!
GET HIM...!!
THUDDA
AHHH!
THE PAINTING!
KRASH
HE'S ON THE PAINTING!!
NO!!
OVER THERE!
CLATTER
STOMP
UNDER THERE!!
HEY, OVER HERE!!

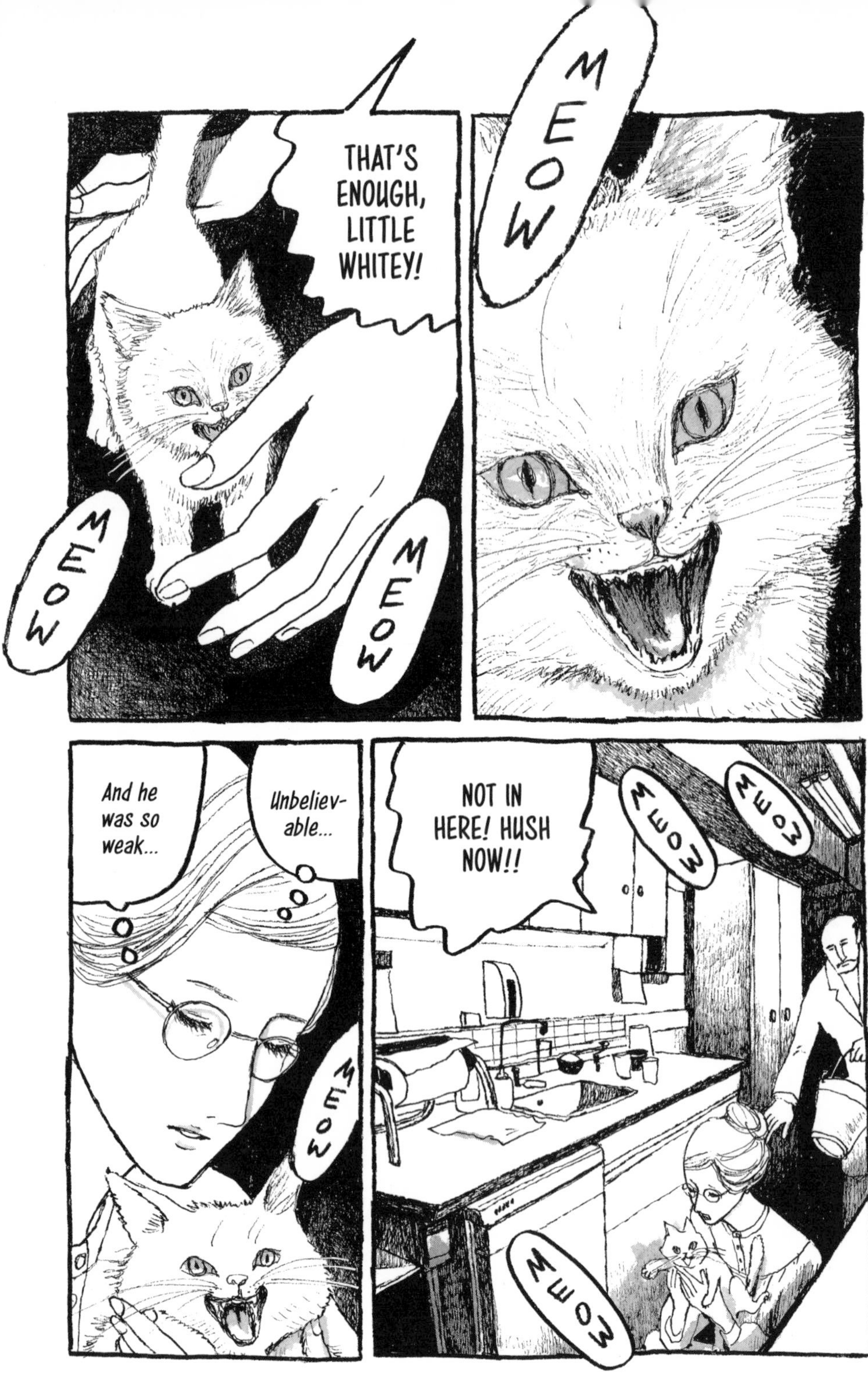
MEOW
THAT'S ENOUGH, LITTLE WHITEY!
MEOW
MEOW
MEOW
MEOW
NOT IN HERE! HUSH NOW!!
MEOW
Unbeliev-able...
And he was so weak...
MEOW

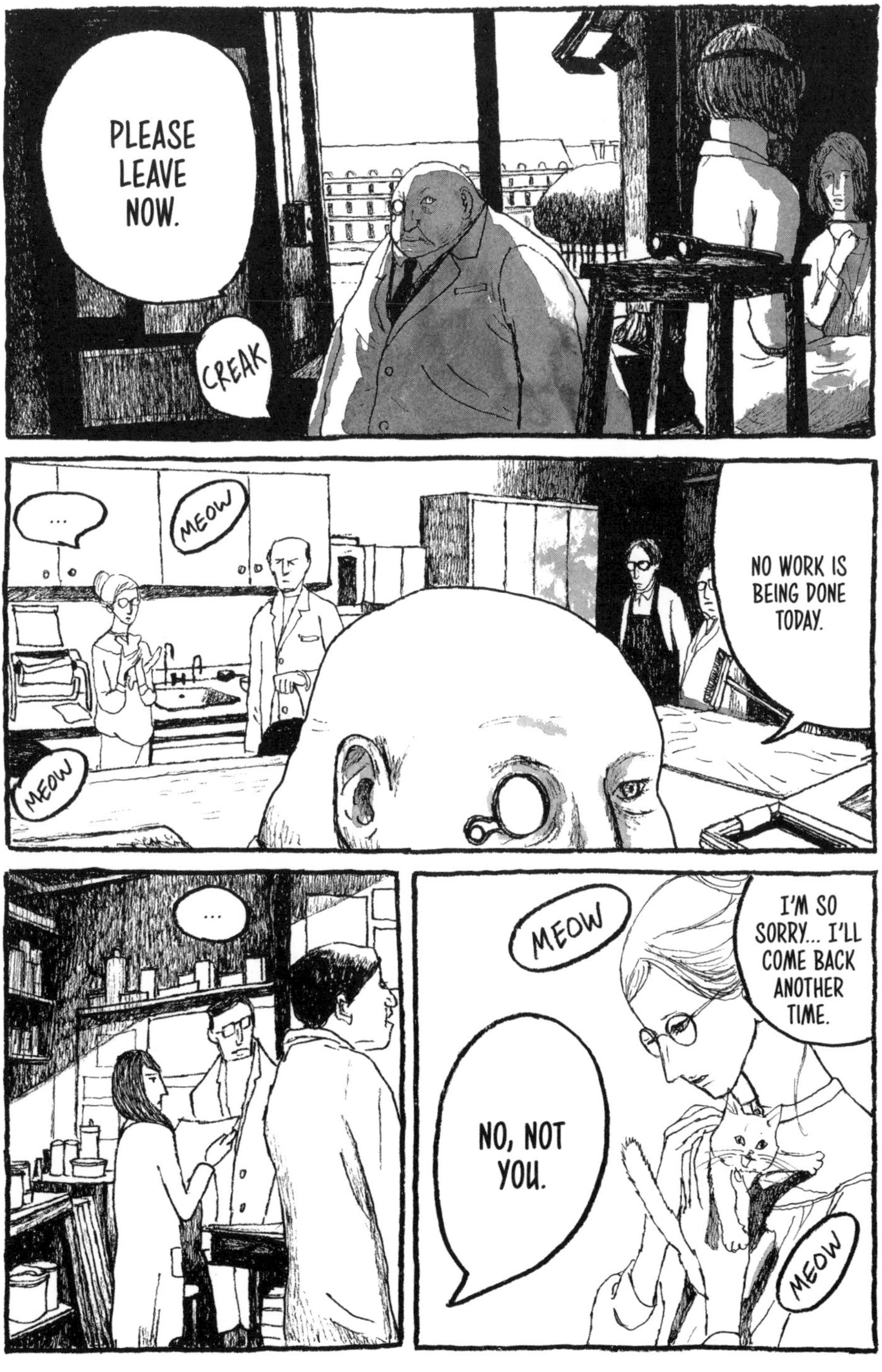
PLEASE LEAVE NOW.
CREAK
NO WORK IS BEING DONE TODAY.
MEOW
...
MEOW
I'M SO SORRY... I'LL COME BACK ANOTHER TIME.
MEOW
NO, NOT YOU.
MEOW
...

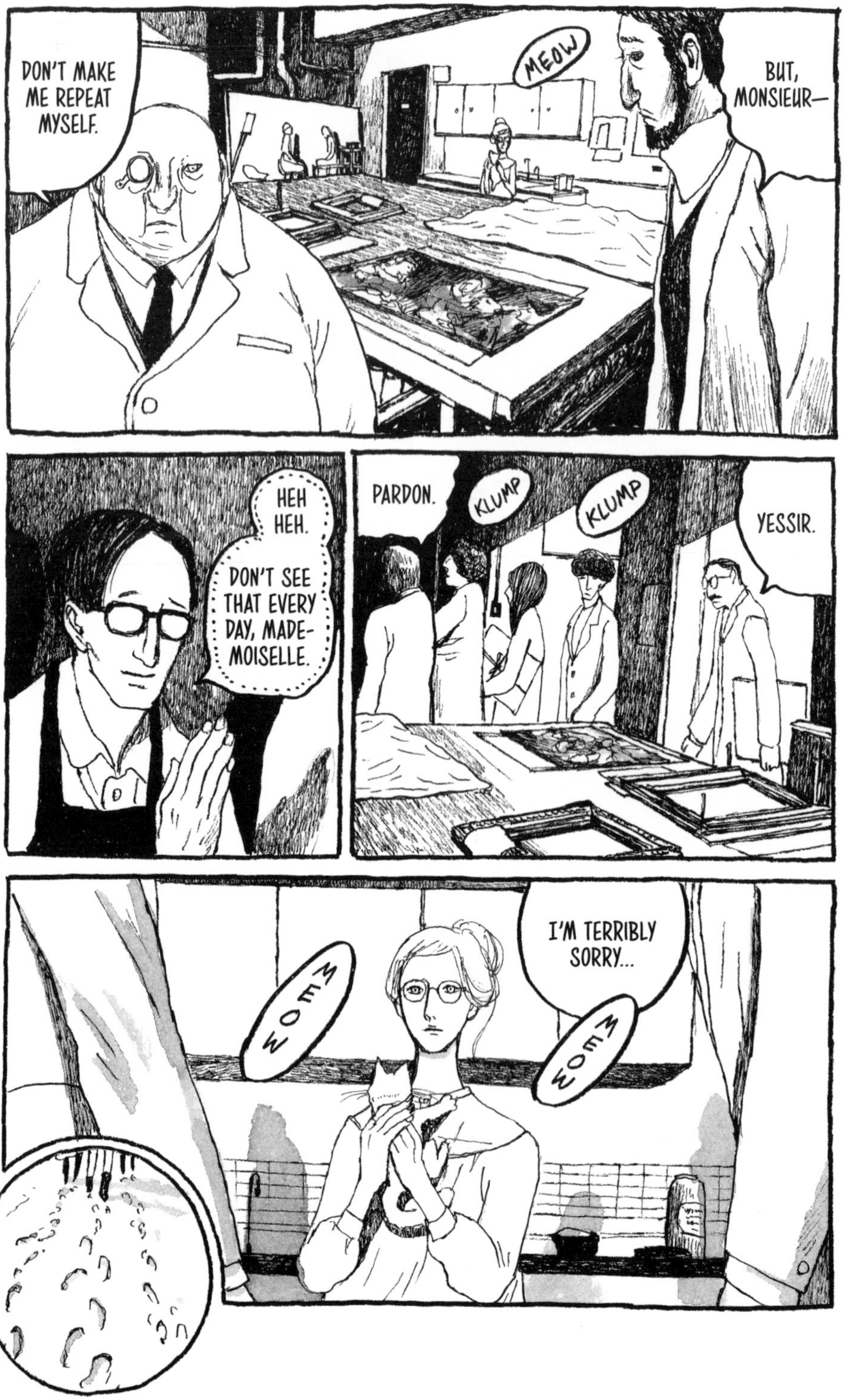
BUT, MONSIEUR—
MEOW
DON'T MAKE ME REPEAT MYSELF.
YESSIR.
KLUMP
KLUMP
PARDON.
HEH HEH.
DON'T SEE THAT EVERY DAY, MADE-MOISELLE.
I'M TERRIBLY SORRY...
MEOW
MEOW

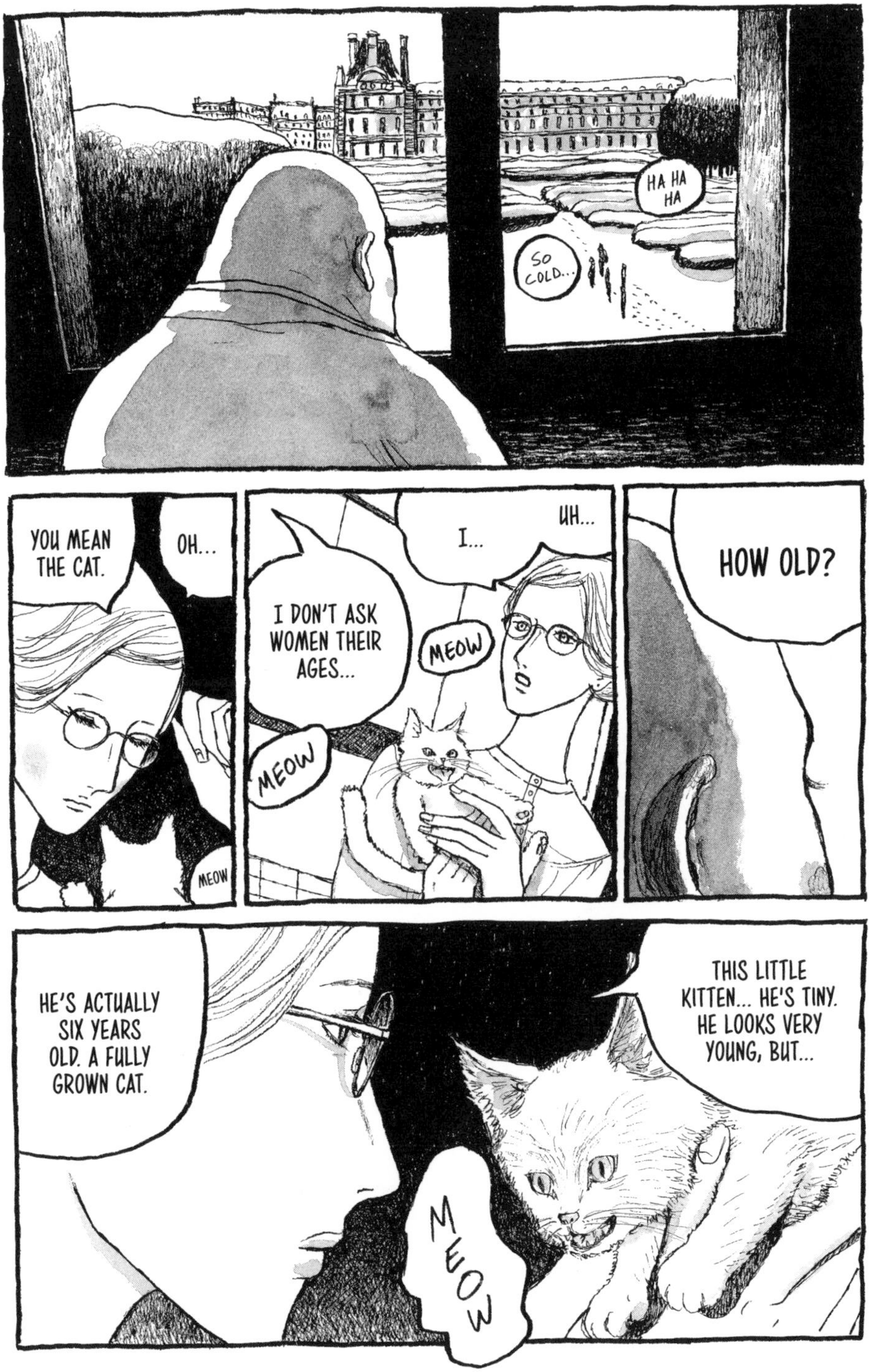
HA HA HA
SO COLD...
HOW OLD?
UH...
I...
I DON'T ASK WOMEN THEIR AGES...
MEOW
MEOW
OH...
YOU MEAN THE CAT.
MEOW
THIS LITTLE KITTEN... HE'S TINY. HE LOOKS VERY YOUNG, BUT...
MEOW
HE'S ACTUALLY SIX YEARS OLD. A FULLY GROWN CAT.

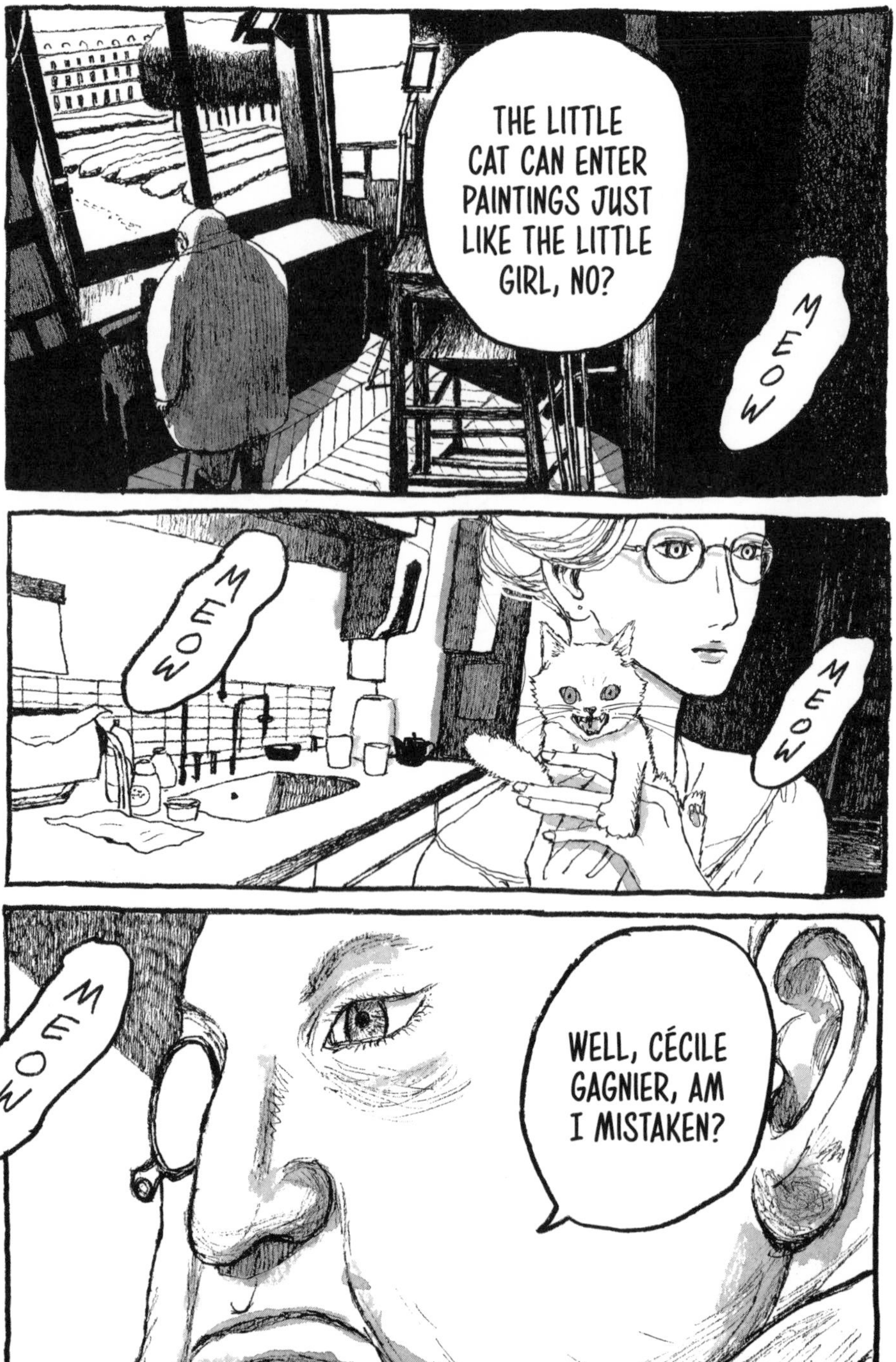
THE LITTLE CAT CAN ENTER PAINTINGS JUST LIKE THE LITTLE GIRL, NO?
MEOW
MEOW
MEOW
WELL, CÉCILE GAGNIER, AM I MISTAKEN?
MEOW

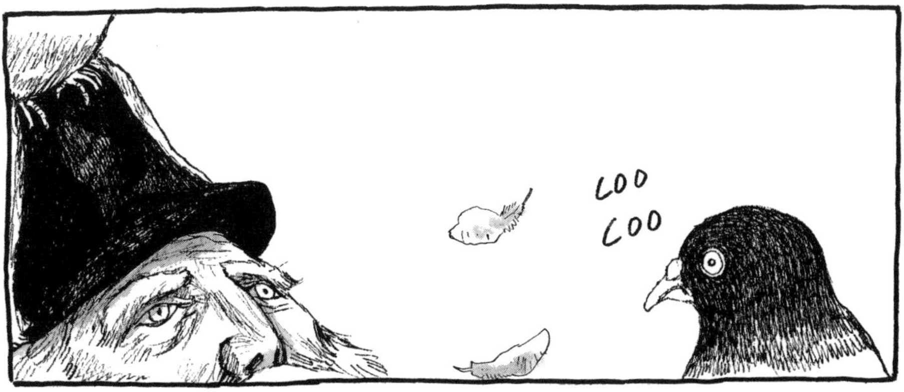
COO
COO
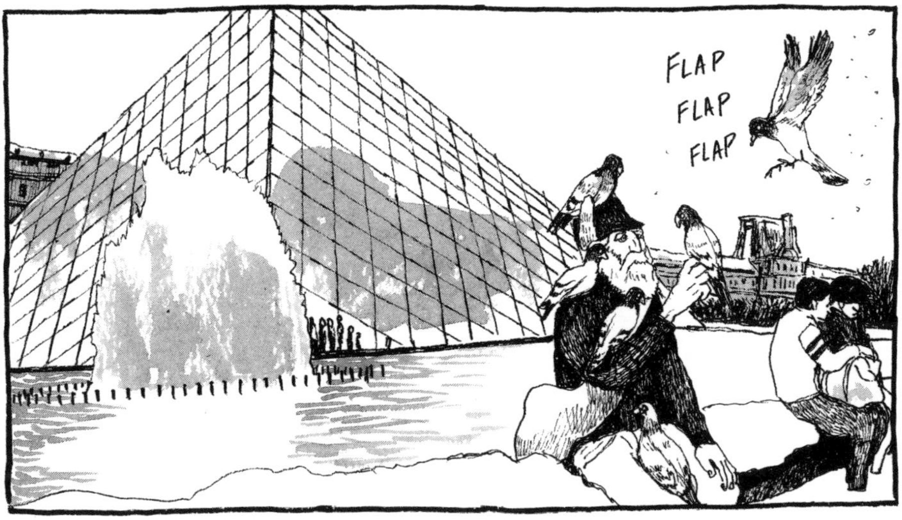
FLAP
FLAP
FLAP
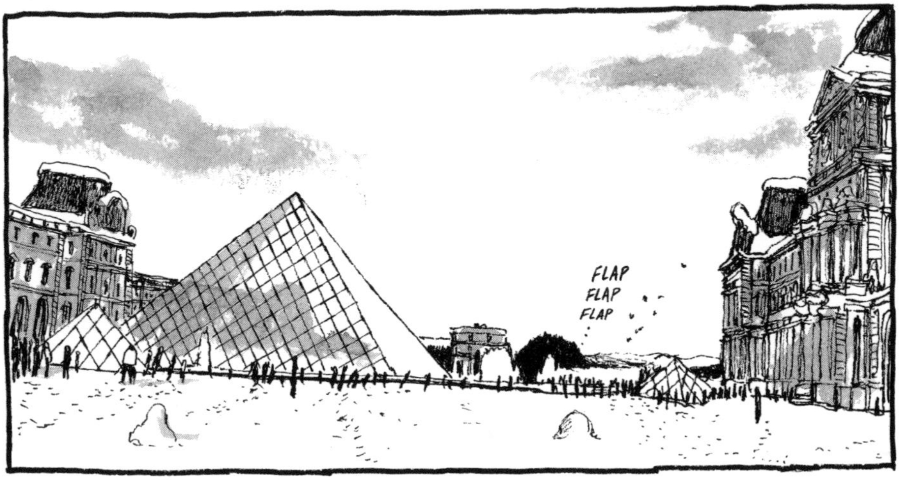
FLAP
FLAP
FLAP

CHAPTER 14

The Secret of Cécile

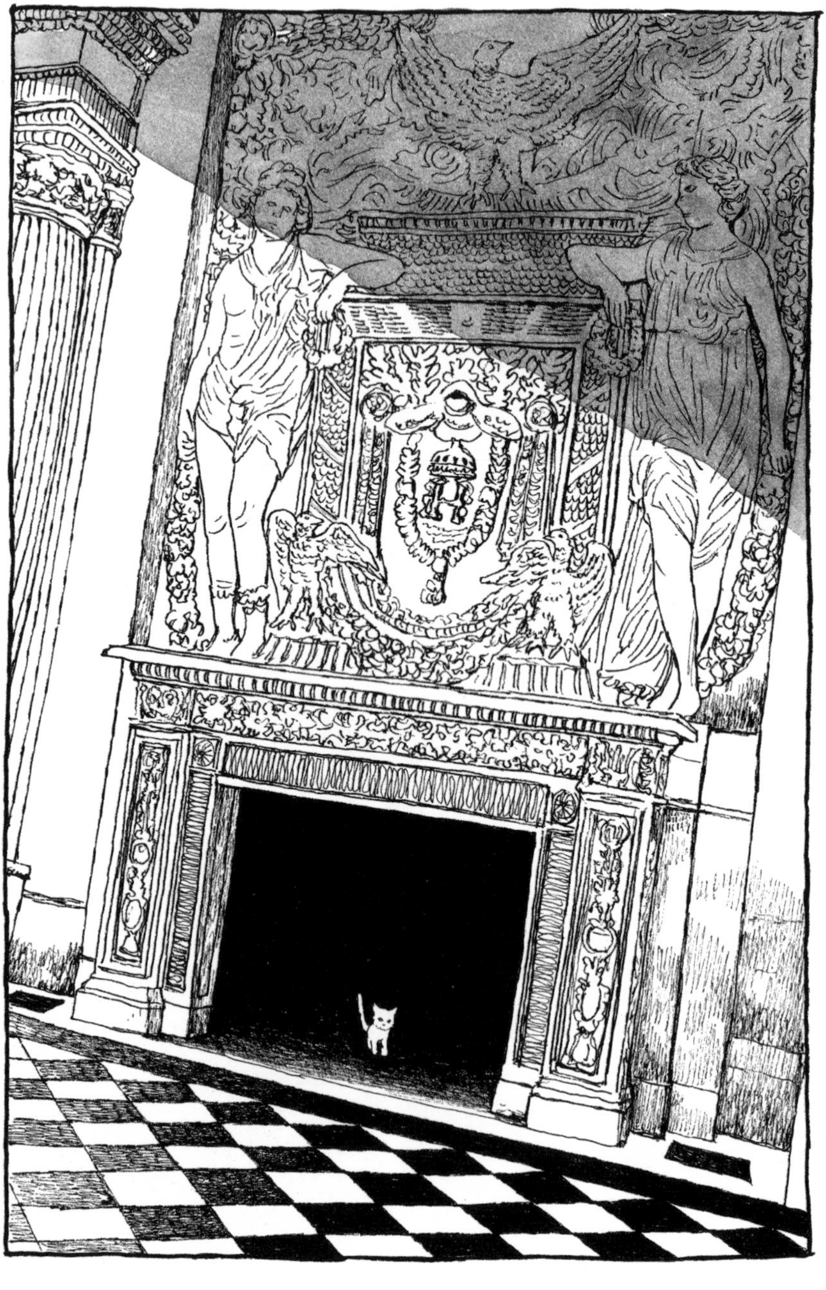

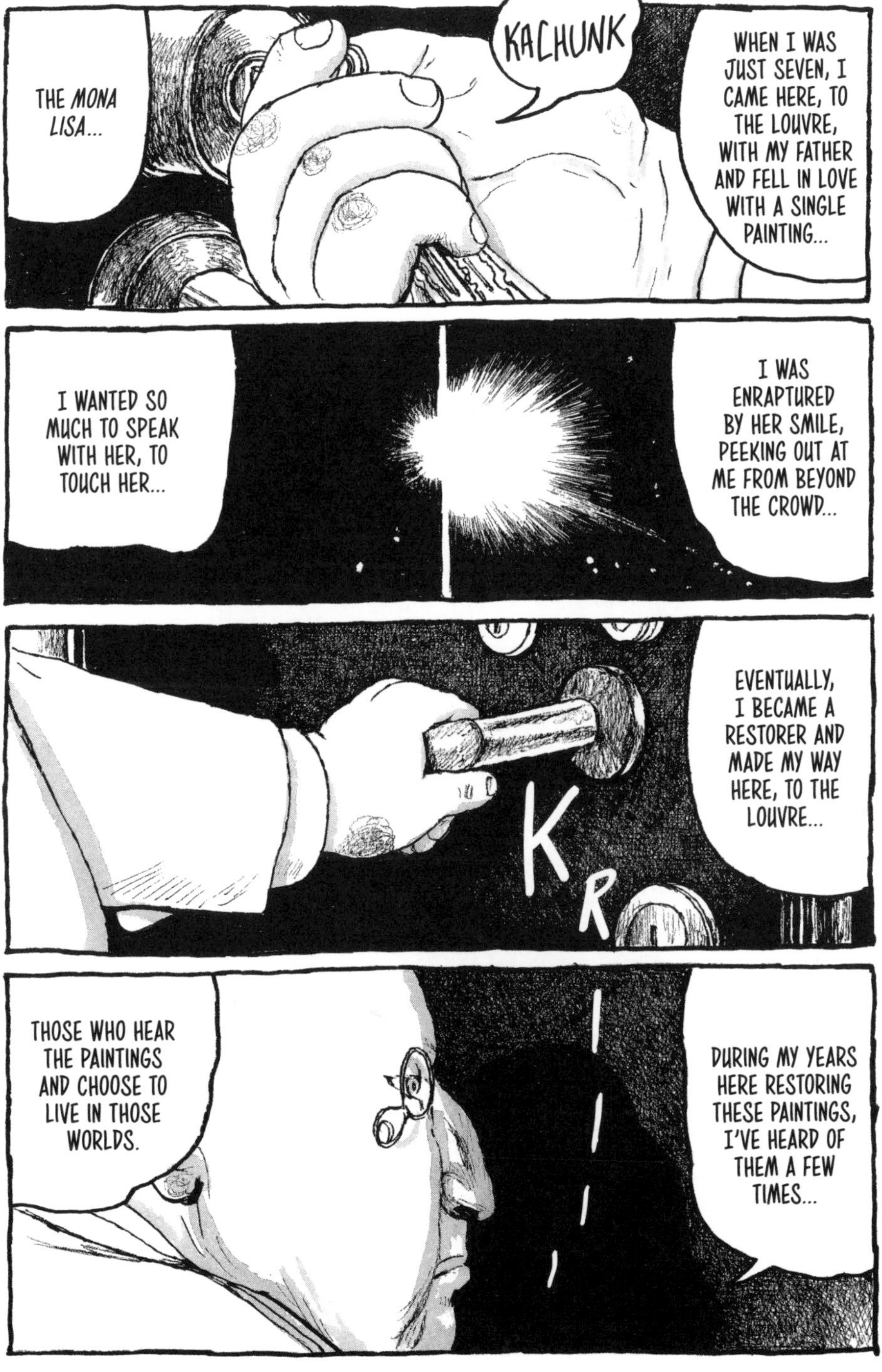
WHEN I WAS JUST SEVEN, I CAME HERE, TO THE LOUVRE, WITH MY FATHER AND FELL IN LOVE WITH A SINGLE PAINTING...
KACHUNK
THE *MONA LISA*...
I WAS ENRAPTURED BY HER SMILE, PEEKING OUT AT ME FROM BEYOND THE CROWD...
I WANTED SO MUCH TO SPEAK WITH HER, TO TOUCH HER...
EVENTUALLY, I BECAME A RESTORER AND MADE MY WAY HERE, TO THE LOUVRE...
KR
DURING MY YEARS HERE RESTORING THESE PAINTINGS, I'VE HEARD OF THEM A FEW TIMES...
THOSE WHO HEAR THE PAINTINGS AND CHOOSE TO LIVE IN THOSE WORLDS.

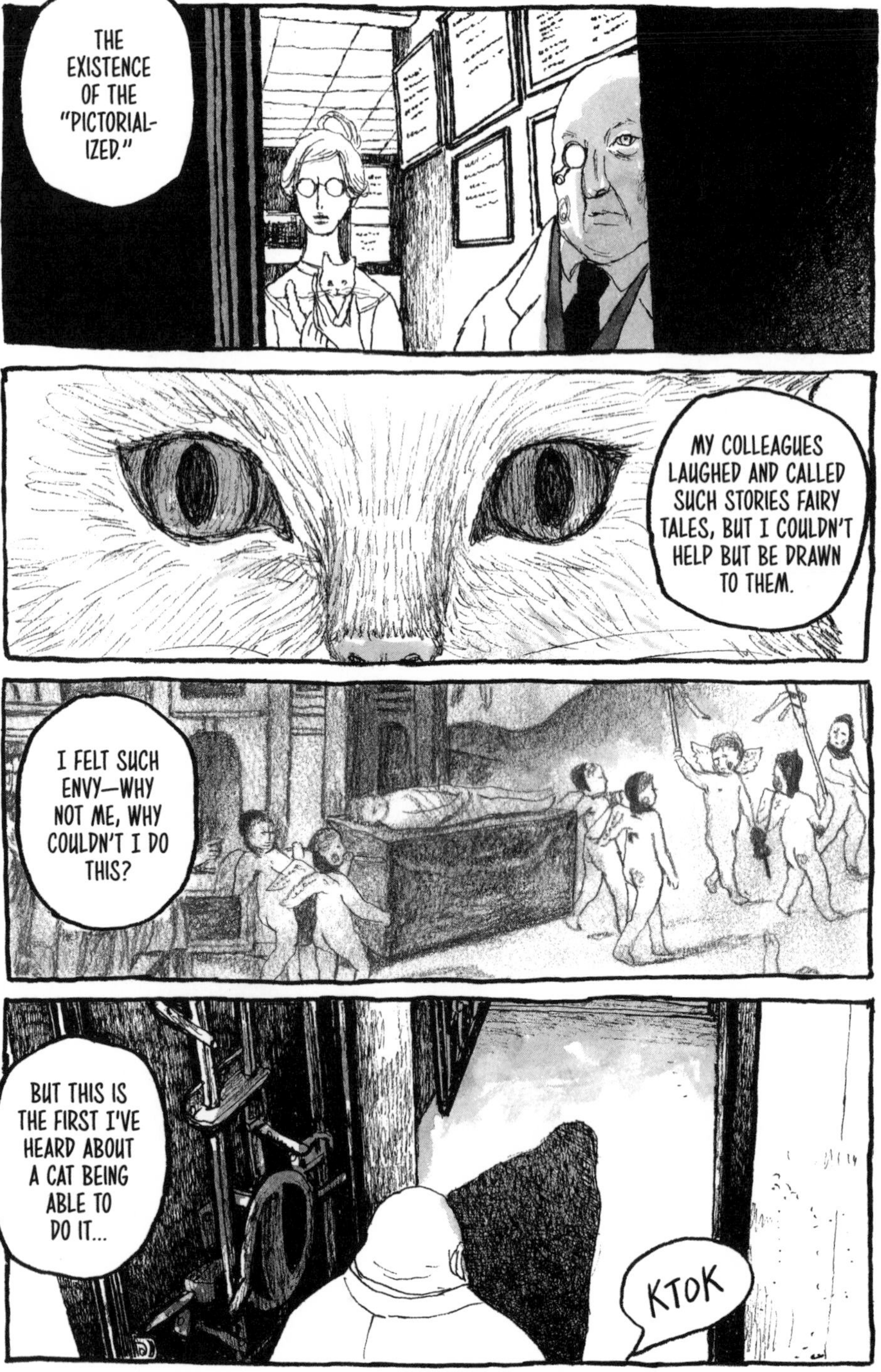
THE EXISTENCE OF THE "PICTORIALIZED."
MY COLLEAGUES LAUGHED AND CALLED SUCH STORIES FAIRY TALES, BUT I COULDN'T HELP BUT BE DRAWN TO THEM.
I FELT SUCH ENVY—WHY NOT ME, WHY COULDN'T I DO THIS?
BUT THIS IS THE FIRST I'VE HEARD ABOUT A CAT BEING ABLE TO DO IT...
KTOK

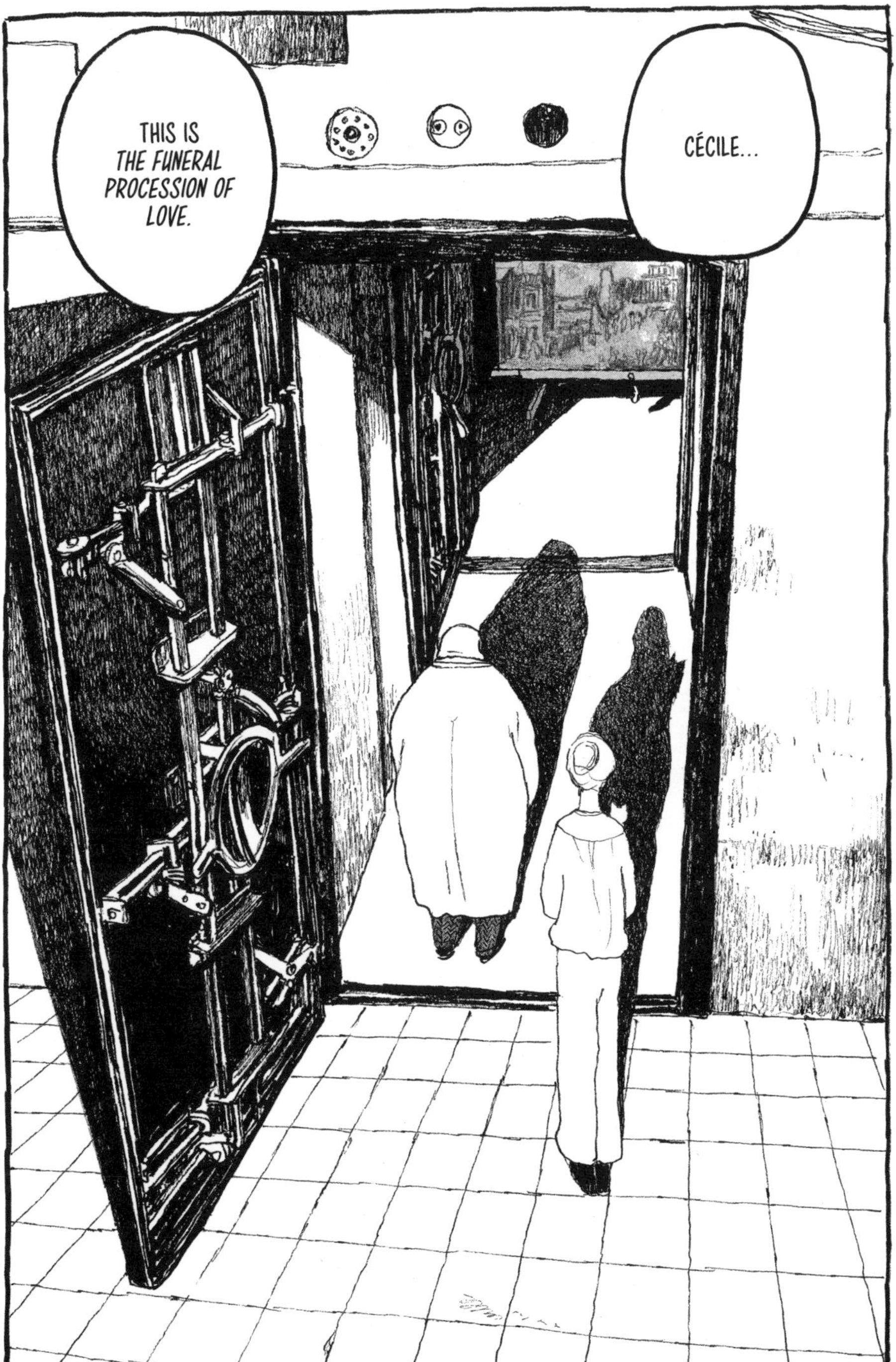
CÉCILE...
THIS IS THE FUNERAL PROCESSION OF LOVE.

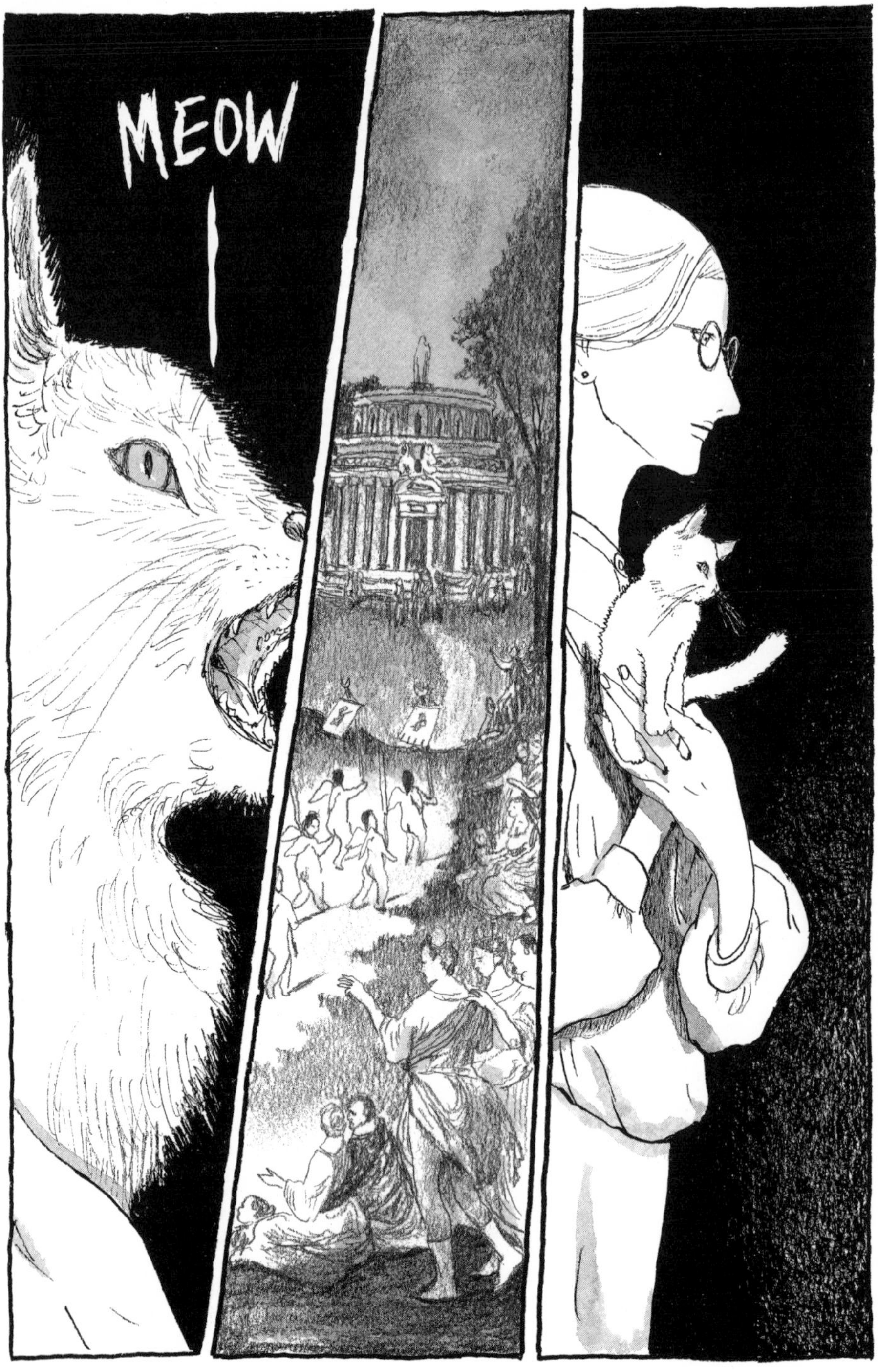
MEOW

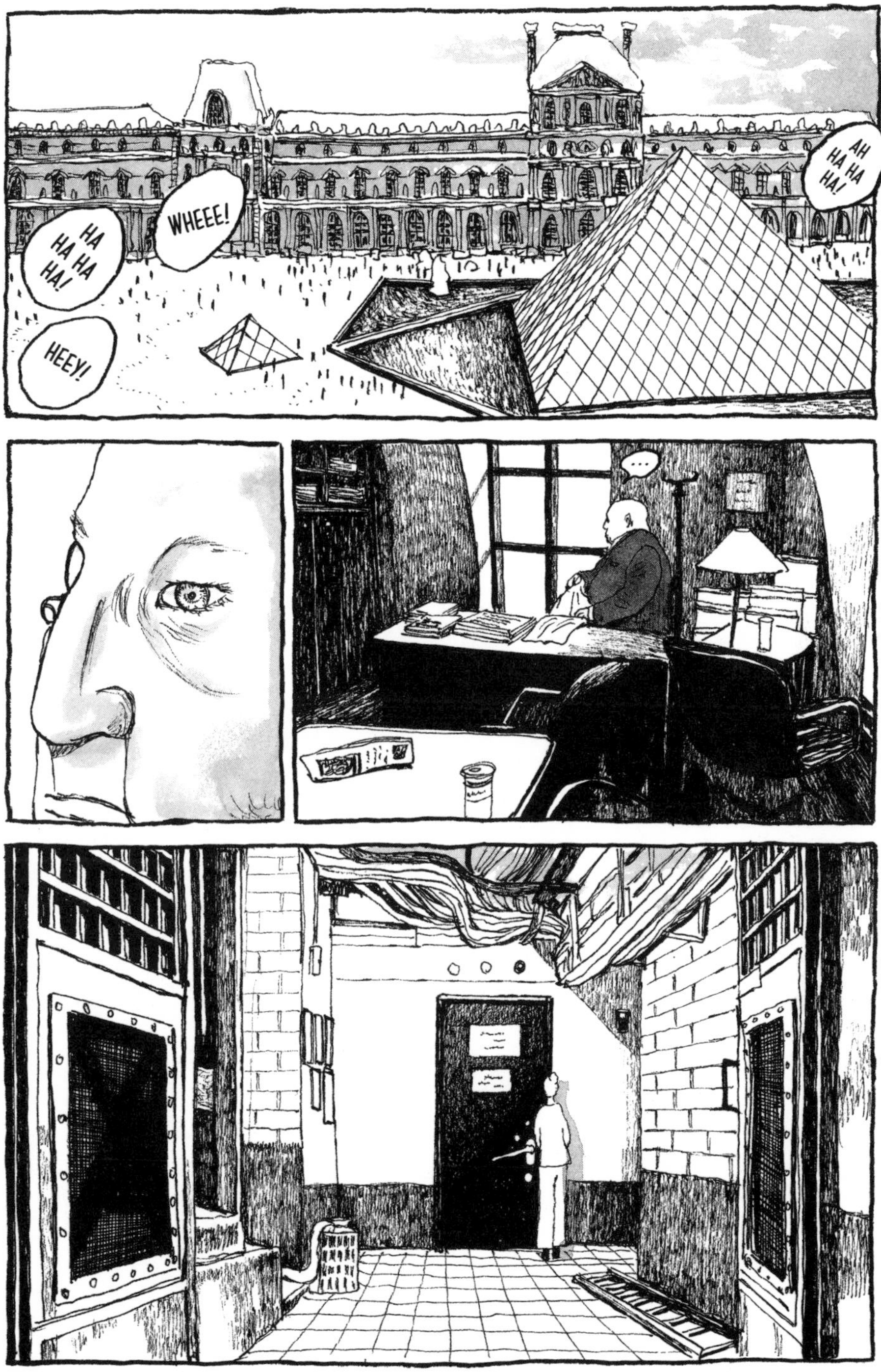
AH HA HA HA!
WHEEE!
HA HA HA HA!
HEEY!
...

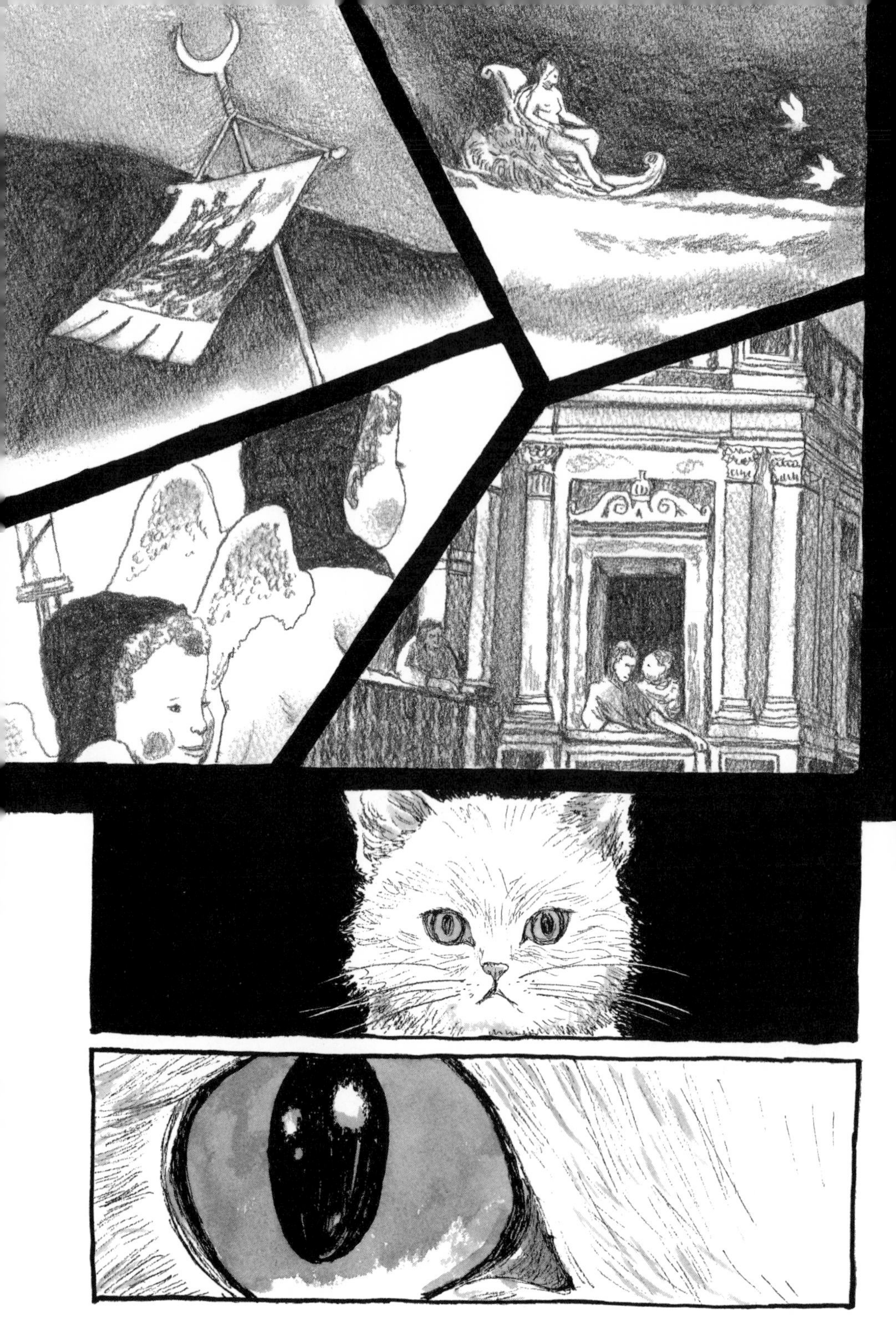

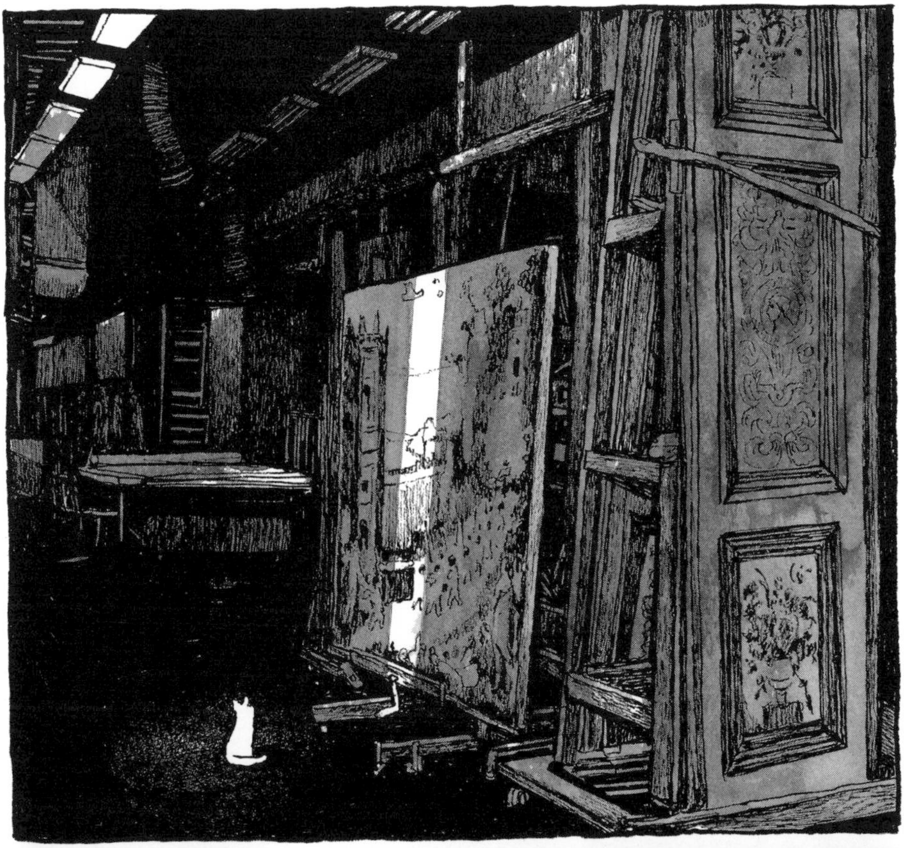

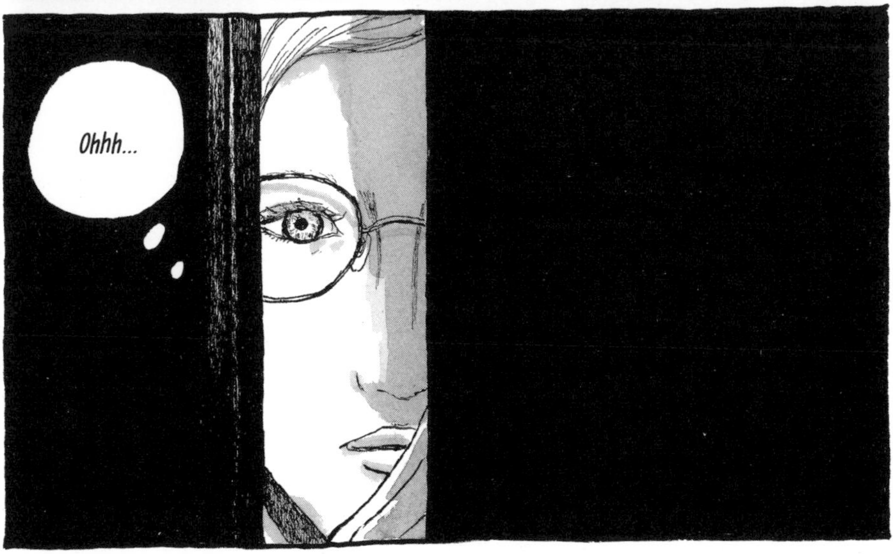
Ohhh...

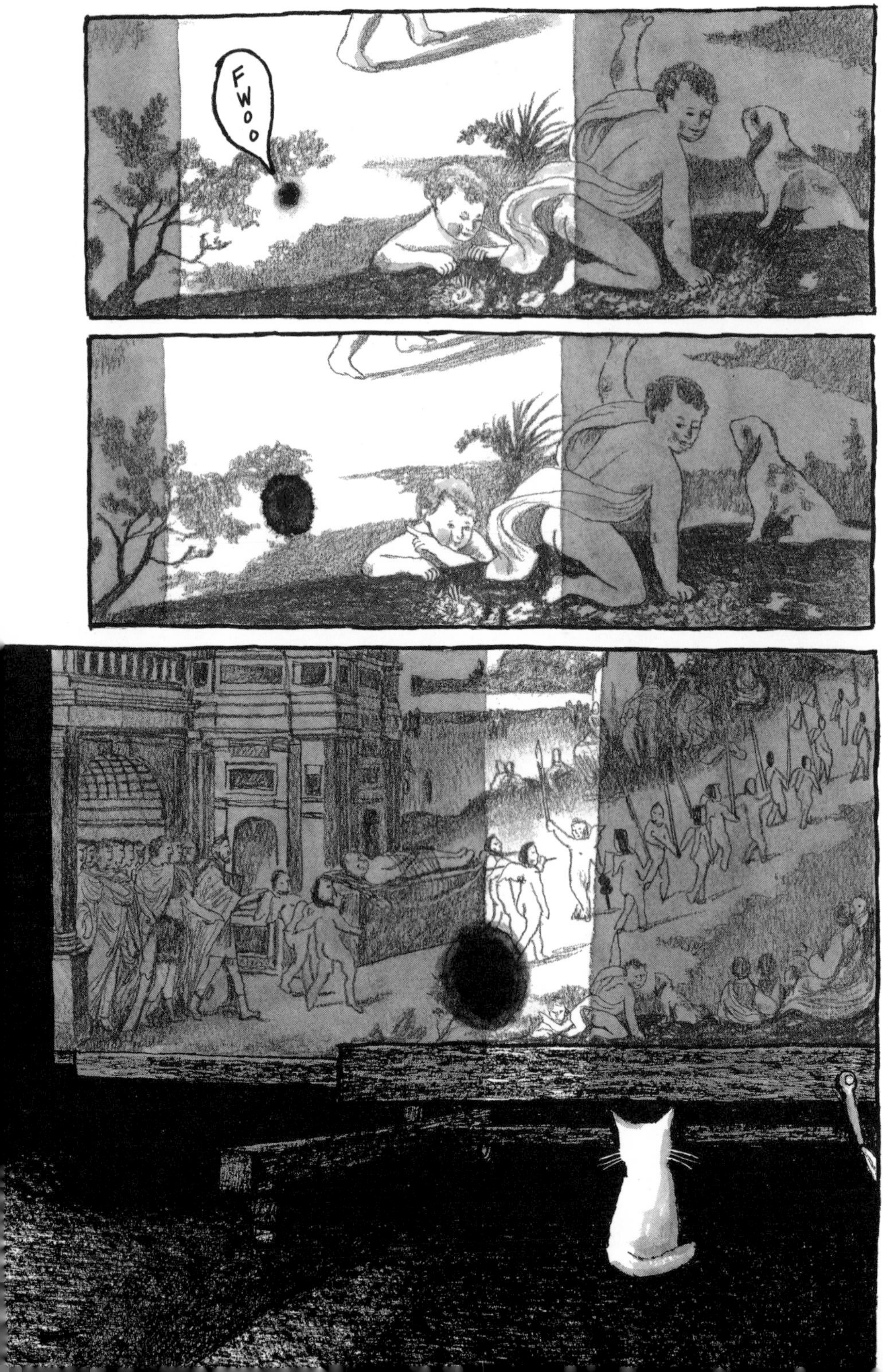
FWOO

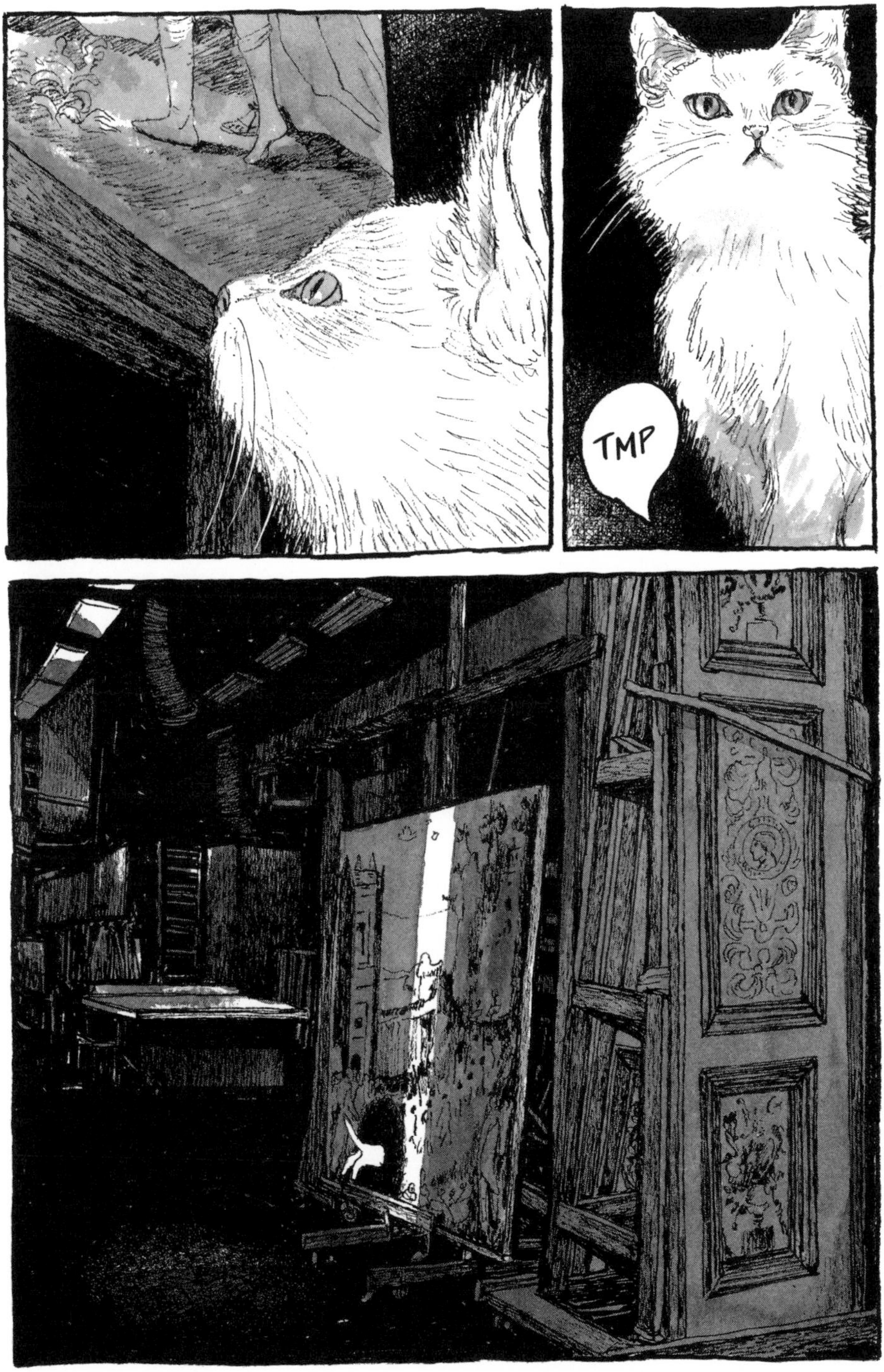
TMP

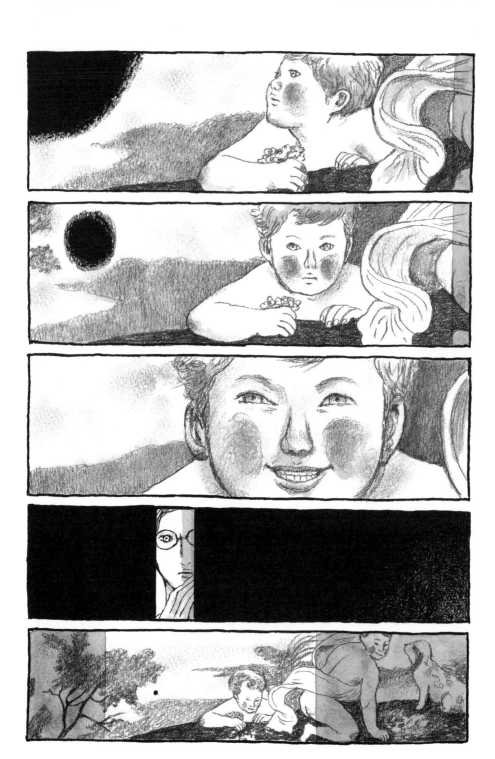

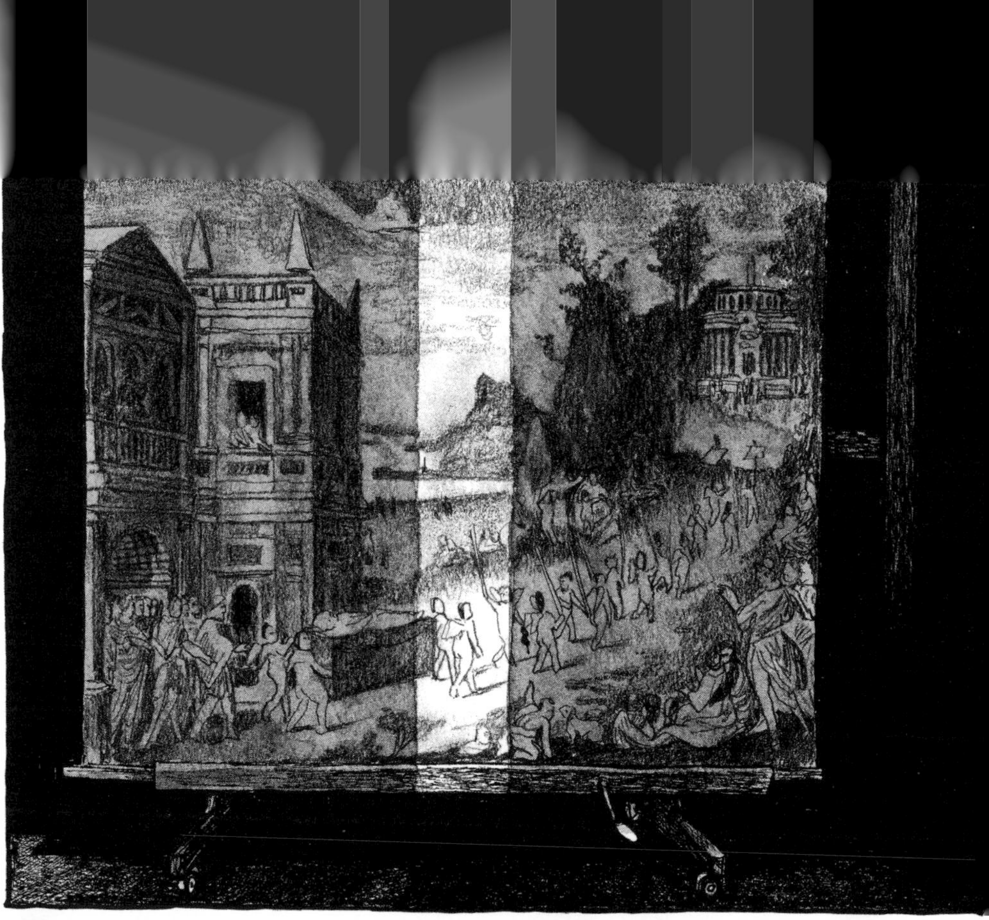

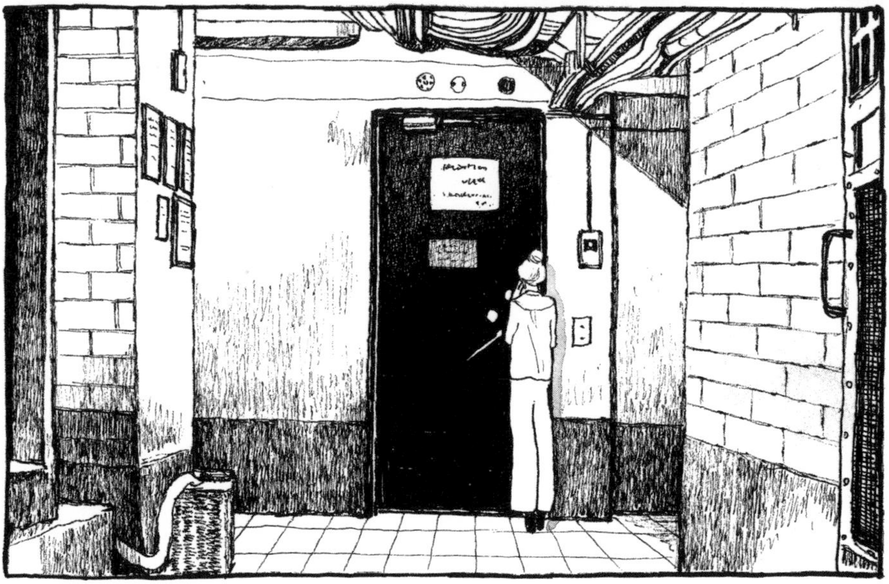

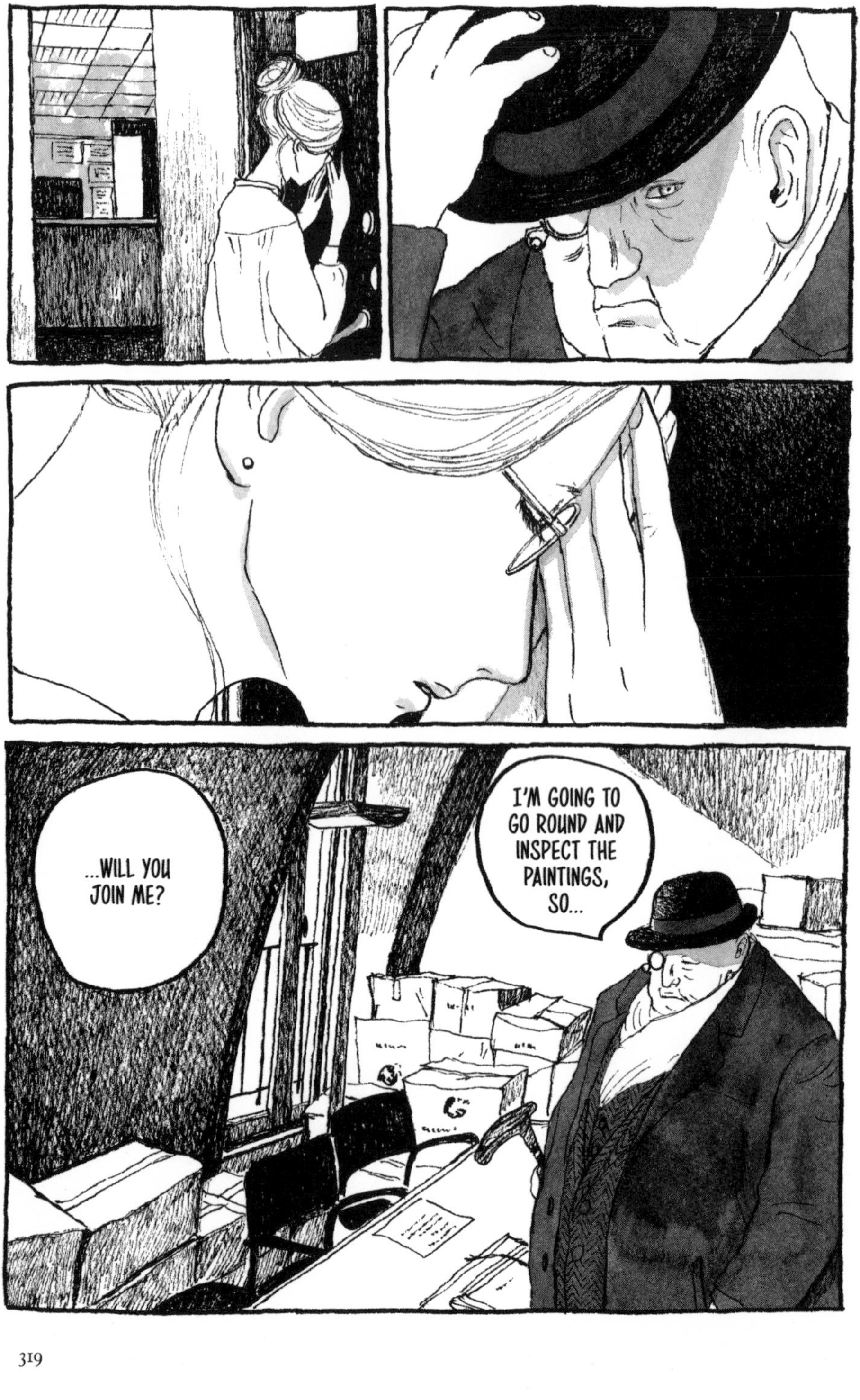
I'M GOING TO GO ROUND AND INSPECT THE PAINTINGS, SO...
...WILL YOU JOIN ME?

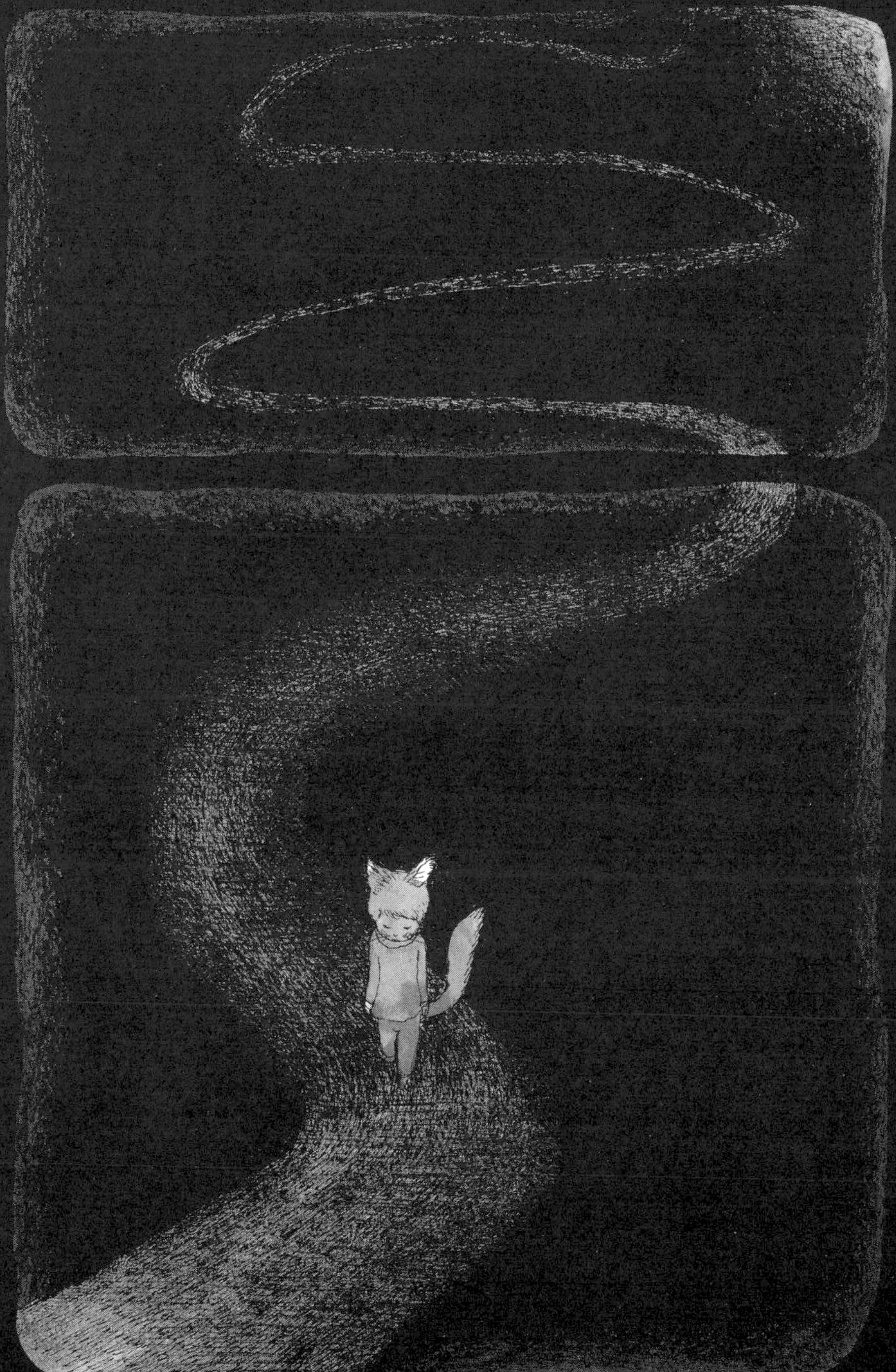

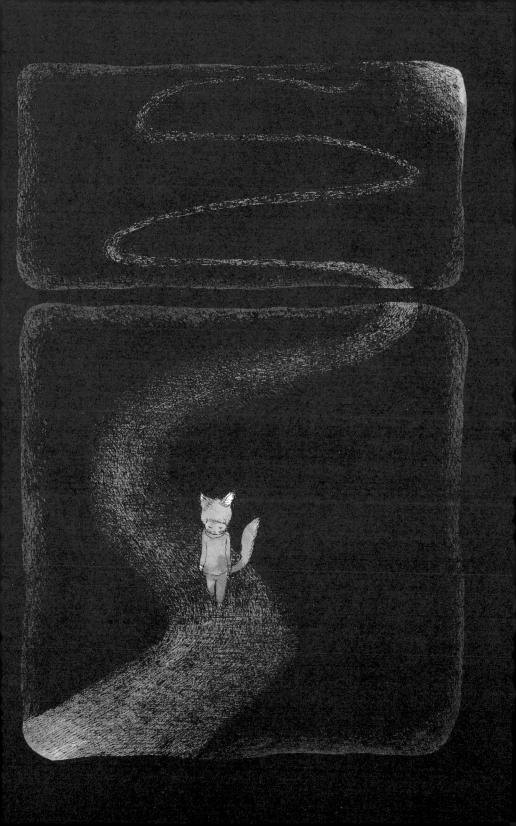

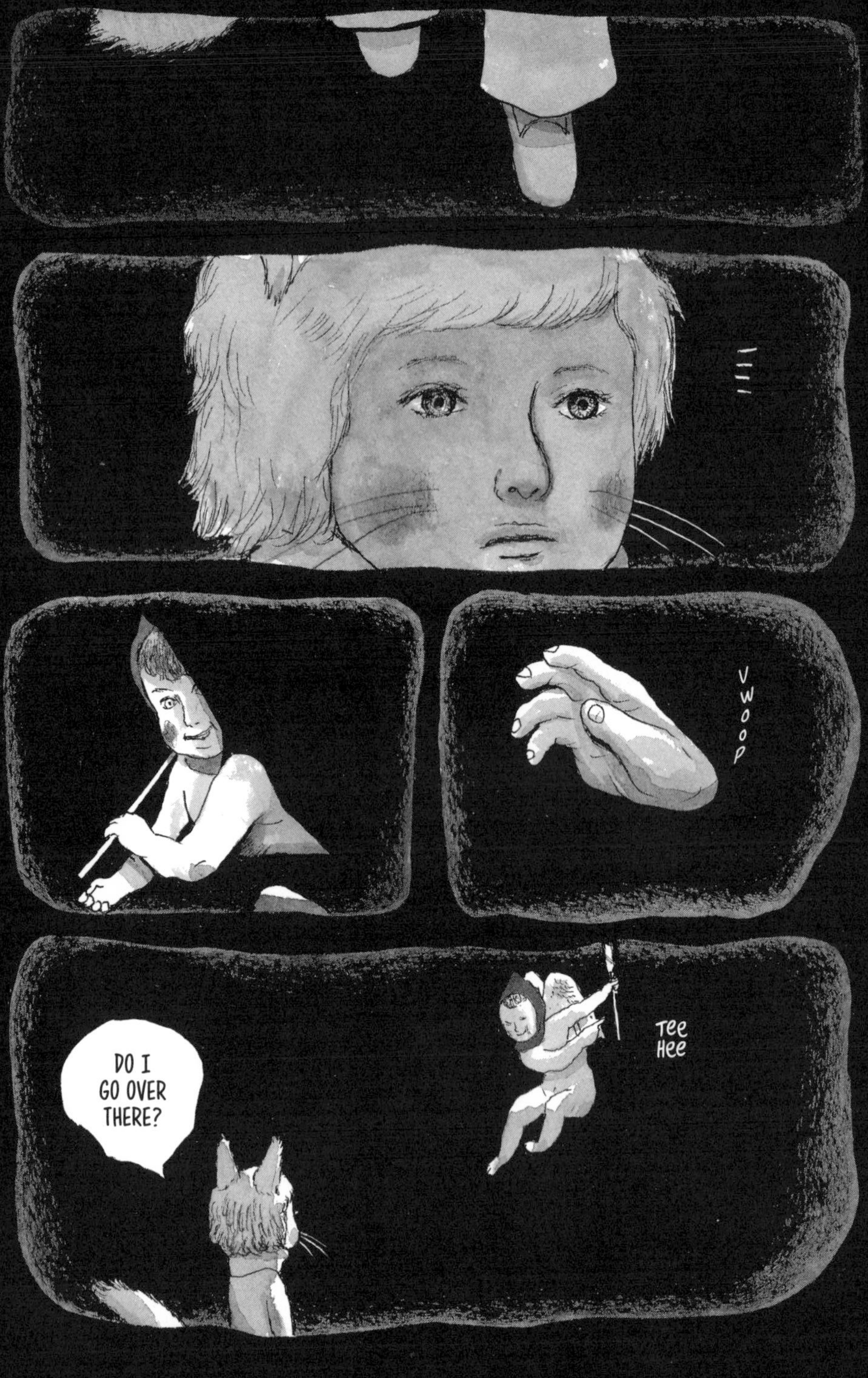
VWOOP
TEE HEE
DO I GO OVER THERE?

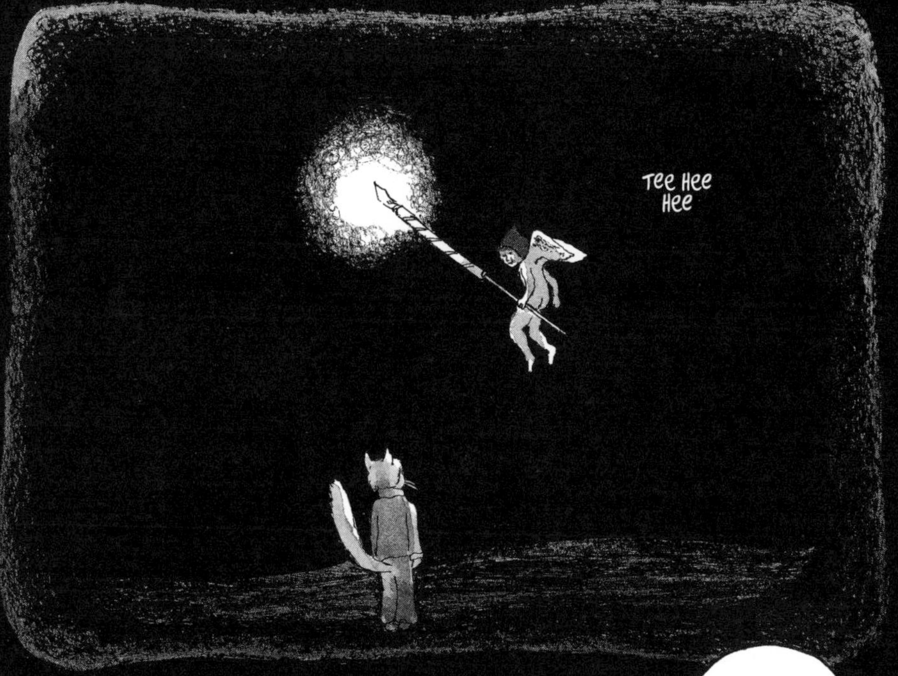
TEE HEE
HEE

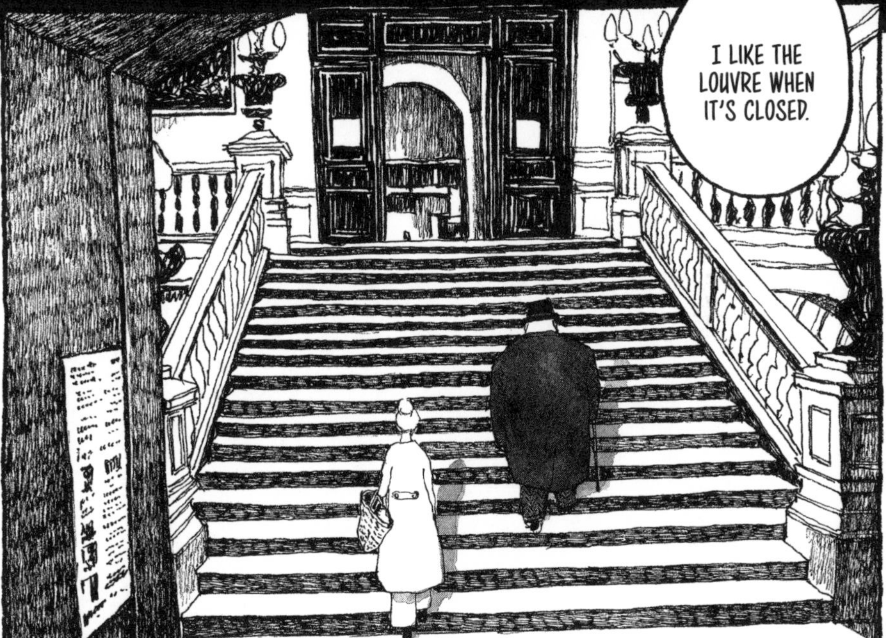
I LIKE THE LOUVRE WHEN IT'S CLOSED.

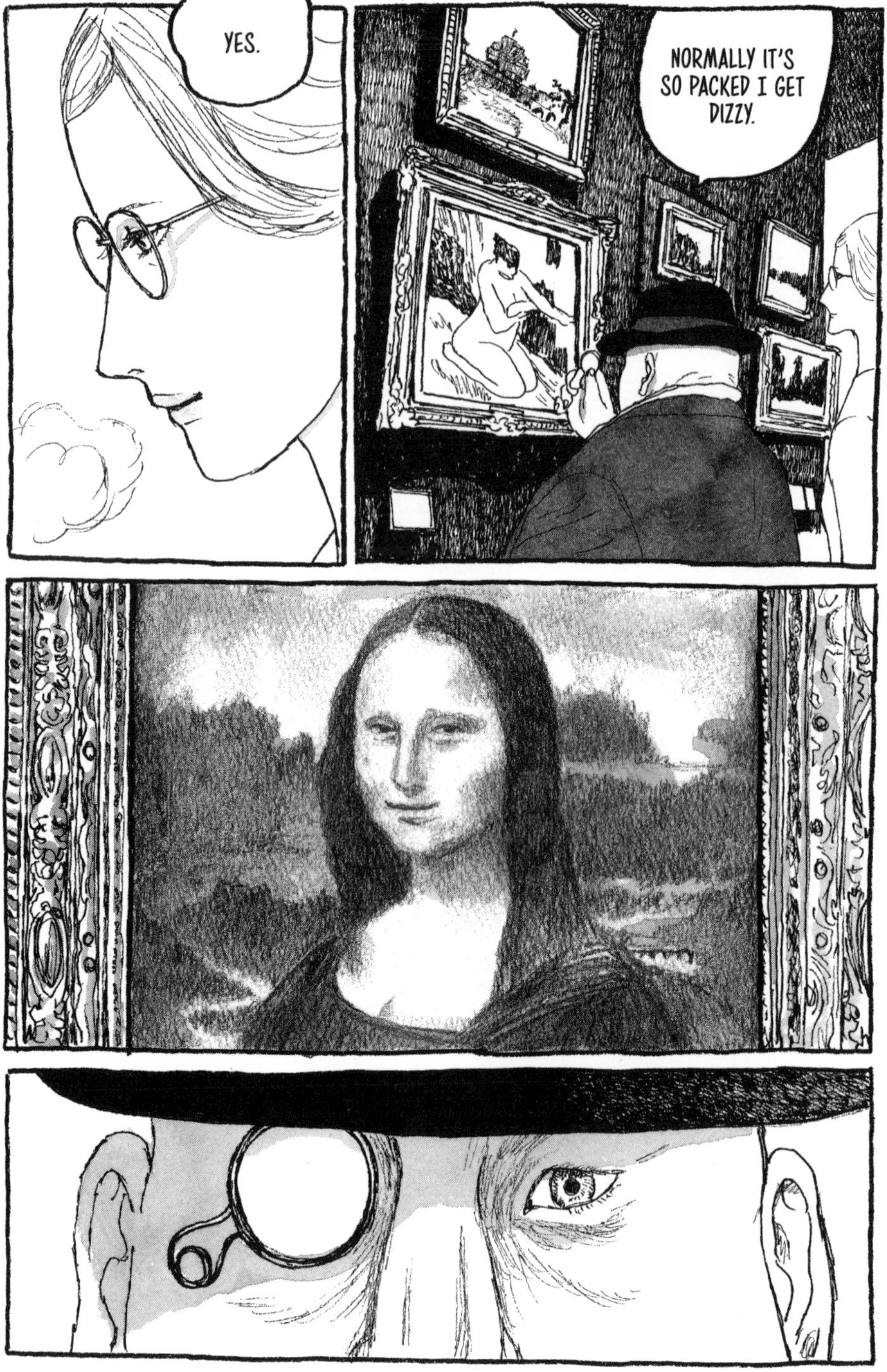
NORMALLY IT'S SO PACKED I GET DIZZY.
YES.

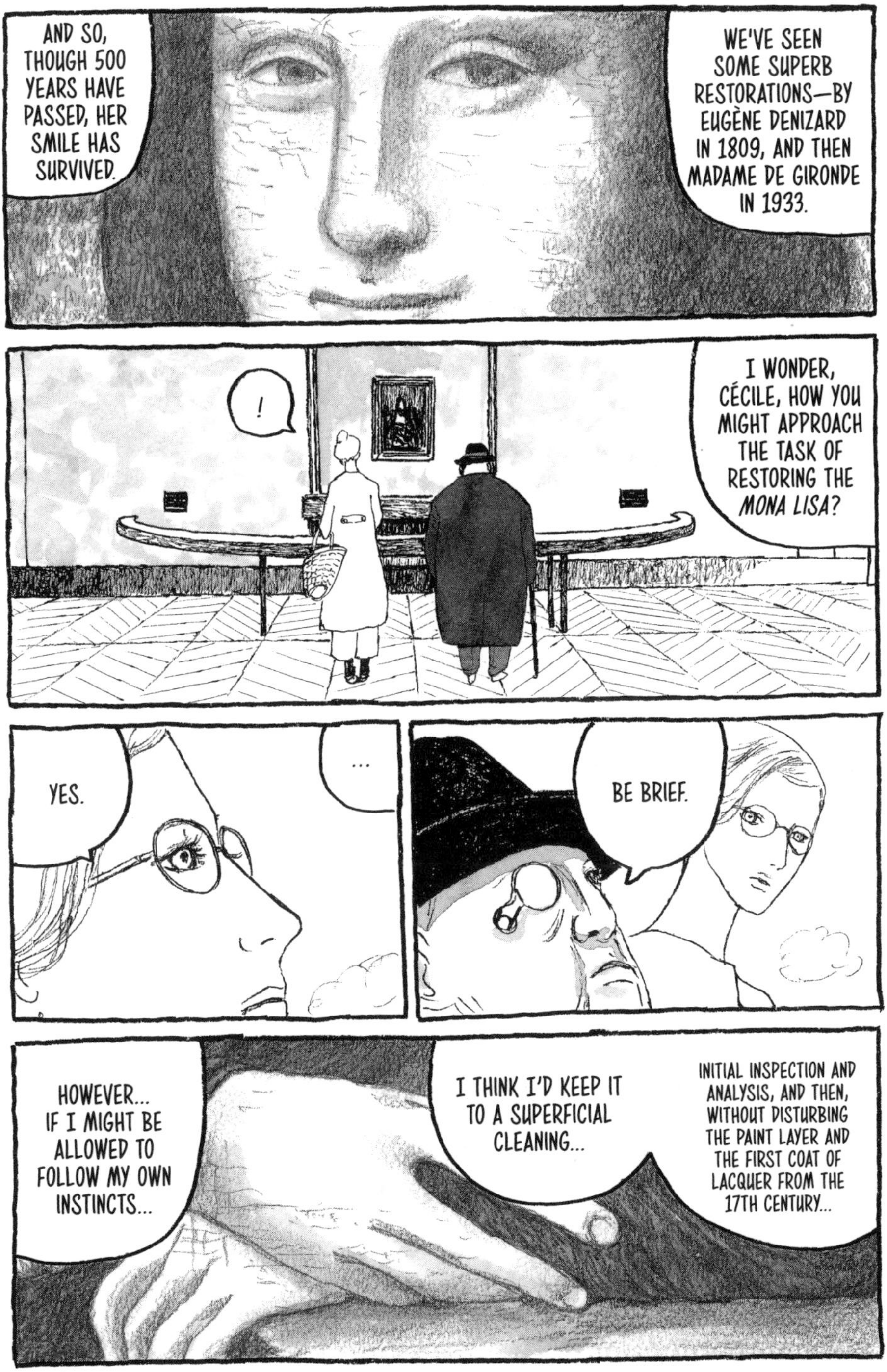
WE'VE SEEN SOME SUPERB RESTORATIONS—BY EUGÈNE DENIZARD IN 1809, AND THEN MADAME DE GIRONDE IN 1933.
AND SO, THOUGH 500 YEARS HAVE PASSED, HER SMILE HAS SURVIVED.
I WONDER, CÉCILE, HOW YOU MIGHT APPROACH THE TASK OF RESTORING THE *MONA LISA?*
!
BE BRIEF.
...
YES.
INITIAL INSPECTION AND ANALYSIS, AND THEN, WITHOUT DISTURBING THE PAINT LAYER AND THE FIRST COAT OF LACQUER FROM THE 17TH CENTURY...
I THINK I'D KEEP IT TO A SUPERFICIAL CLEANING...
HOWEVER... IF I MIGHT BE ALLOWED TO FOLLOW MY OWN INSTINCTS...

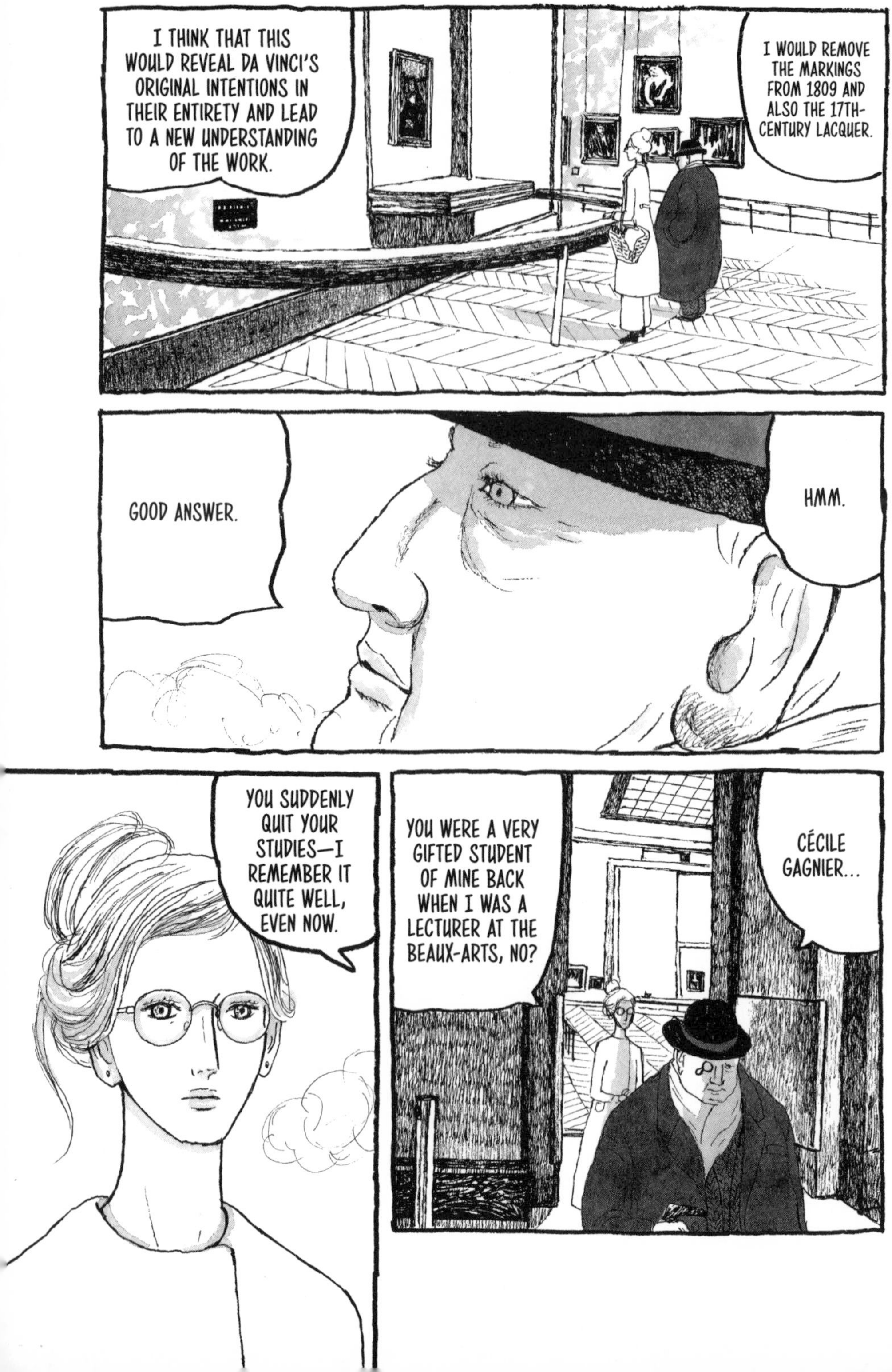
I WOULD REMOVE THE MARKINGS FROM 1809 AND ALSO THE 17TH-CENTURY LACQUER.
I THINK THAT THIS WOULD REVEAL DA VINCI'S ORIGINAL INTENTIONS IN THEIR ENTIRETY AND LEAD TO A NEW UNDERSTANDING OF THE WORK.
HMM.
GOOD ANSWER.
CÉCILE GAGNIER...
YOU WERE A VERY GIFTED STUDENT OF MINE BACK WHEN I WAS A LECTURER AT THE BEAUX-ARTS, NO?
YOU SUDDENLY QUIT YOUR STUDIES—I REMEMBER IT QUITE WELL, EVEN NOW.

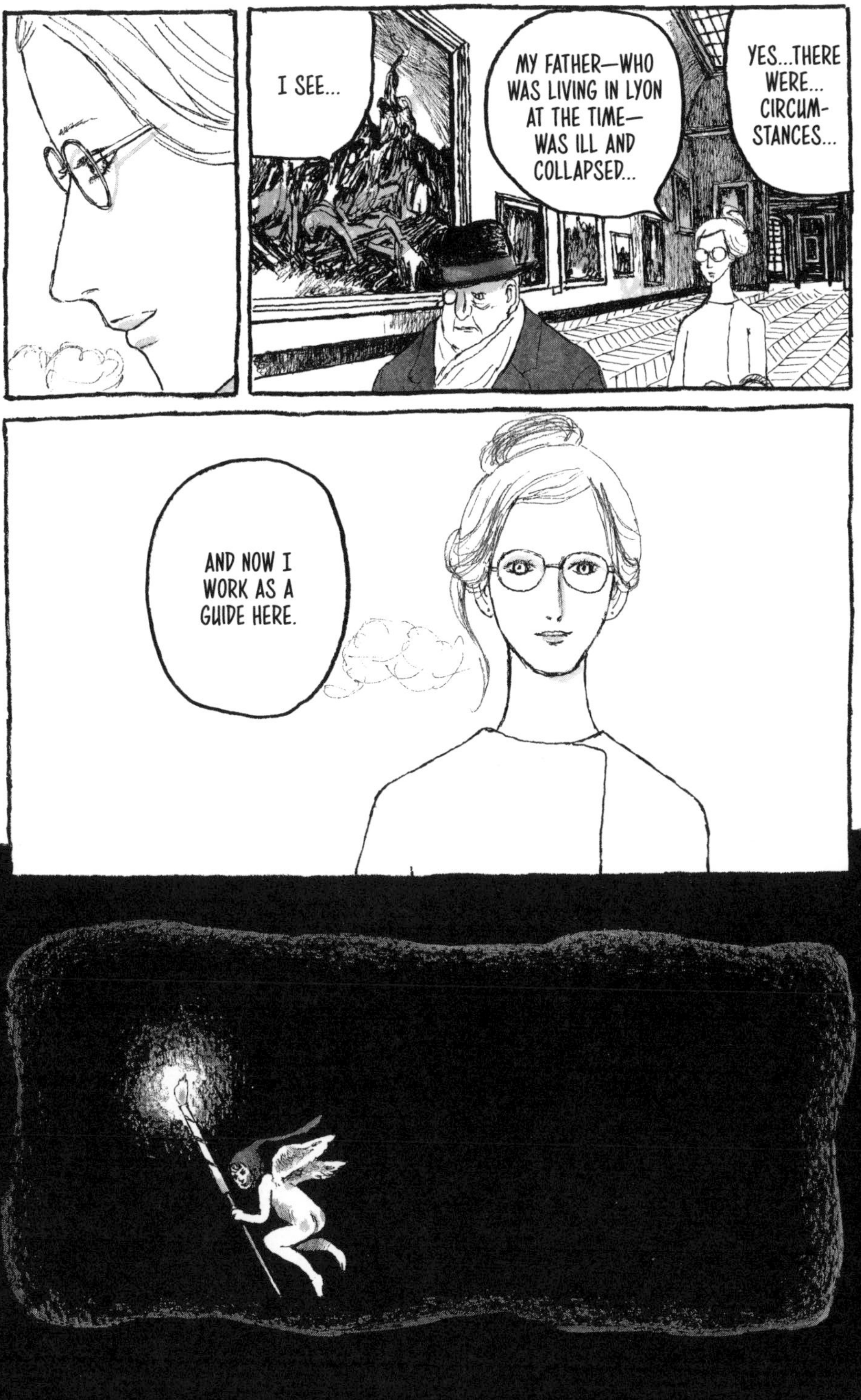
YES...THERE WERE... CIRCUM- STANCES...
MY FATHER—WHO WAS LIVING IN LYON AT THE TIME—WAS ILL AND COLLAPSED...
I SEE...
AND NOW I WORK AS A GUIDE HERE.

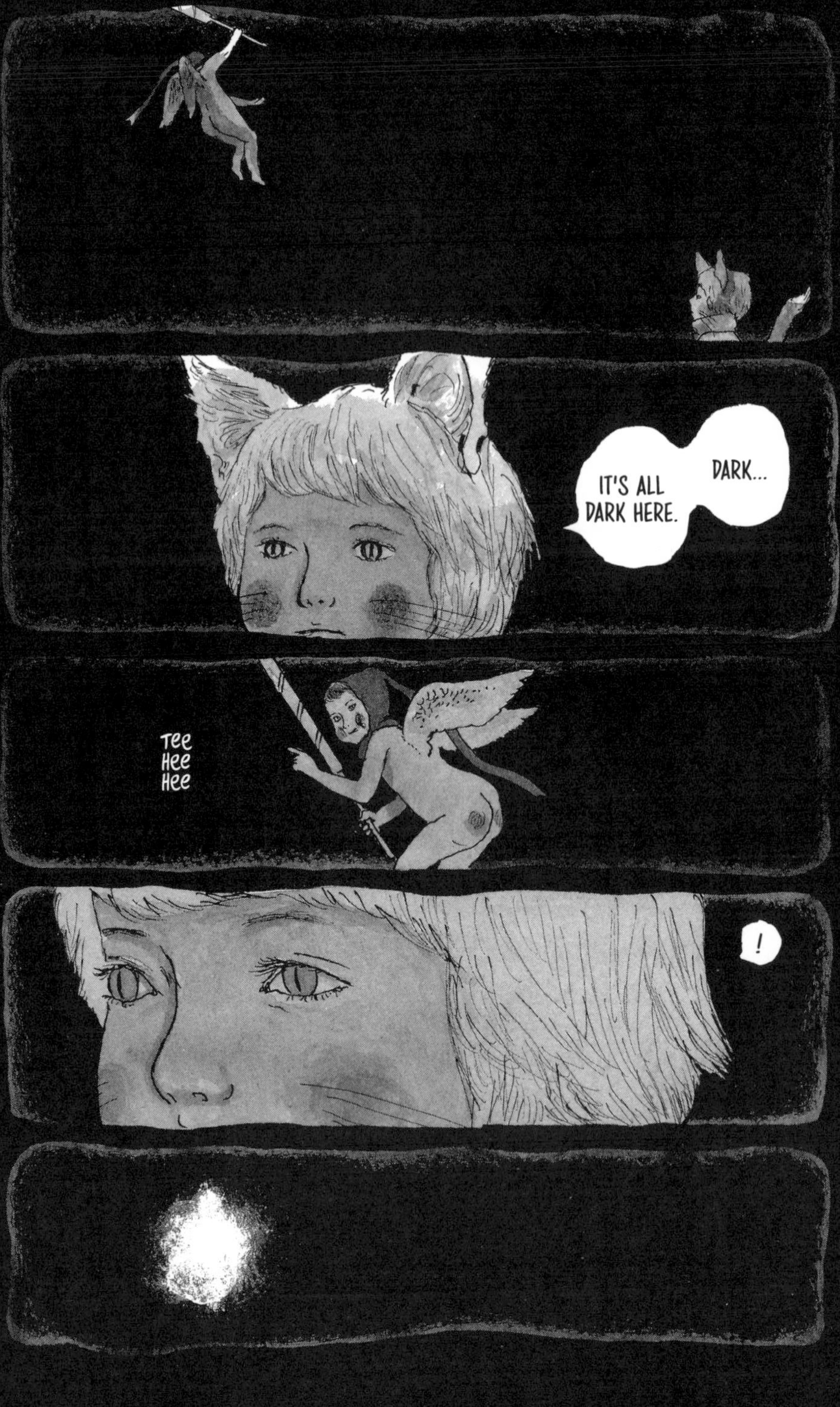
DARK...
IT'S ALL DARK HERE.
TEE HEE HEE
!

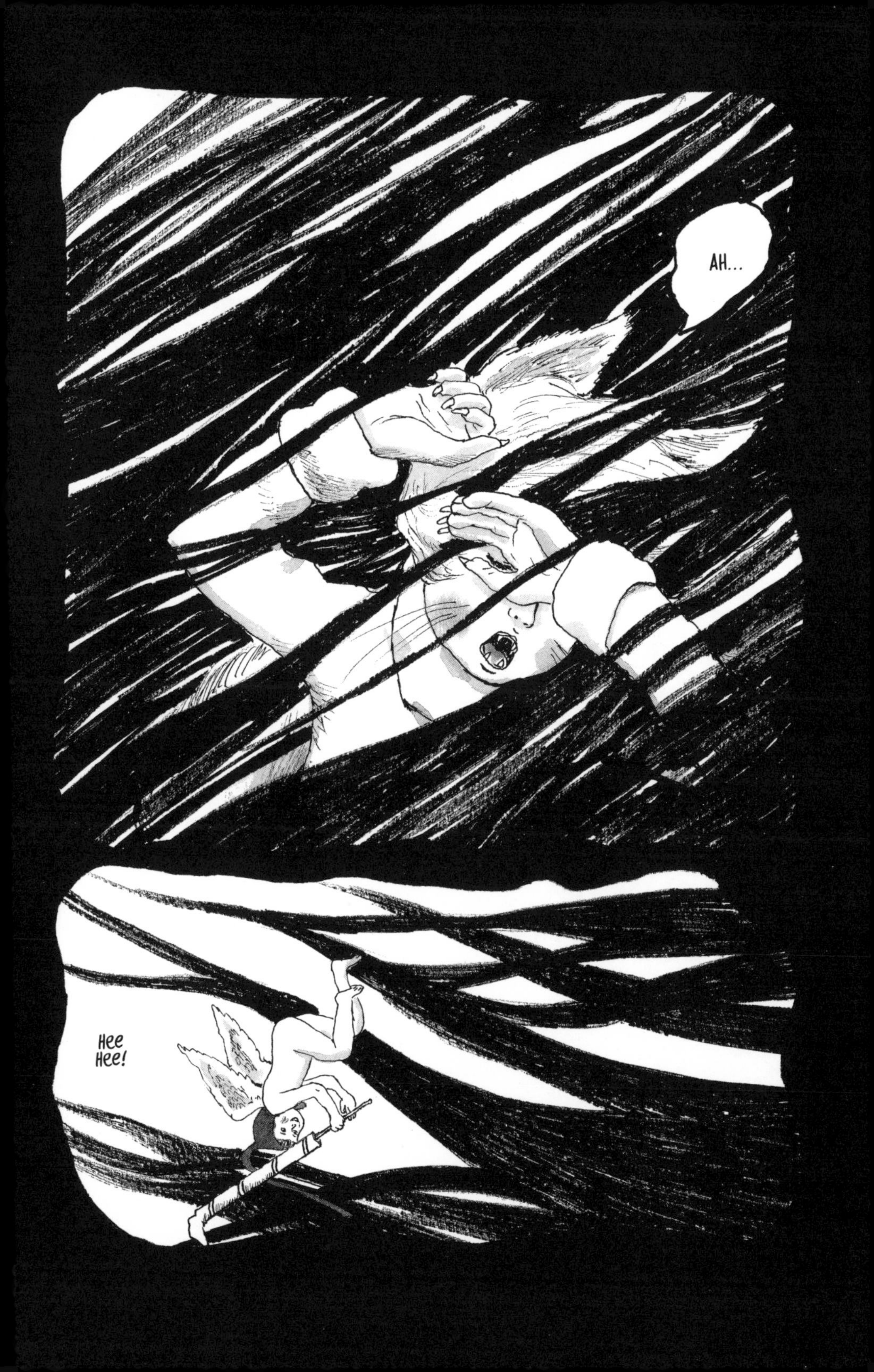
AH...
Hee Hee!

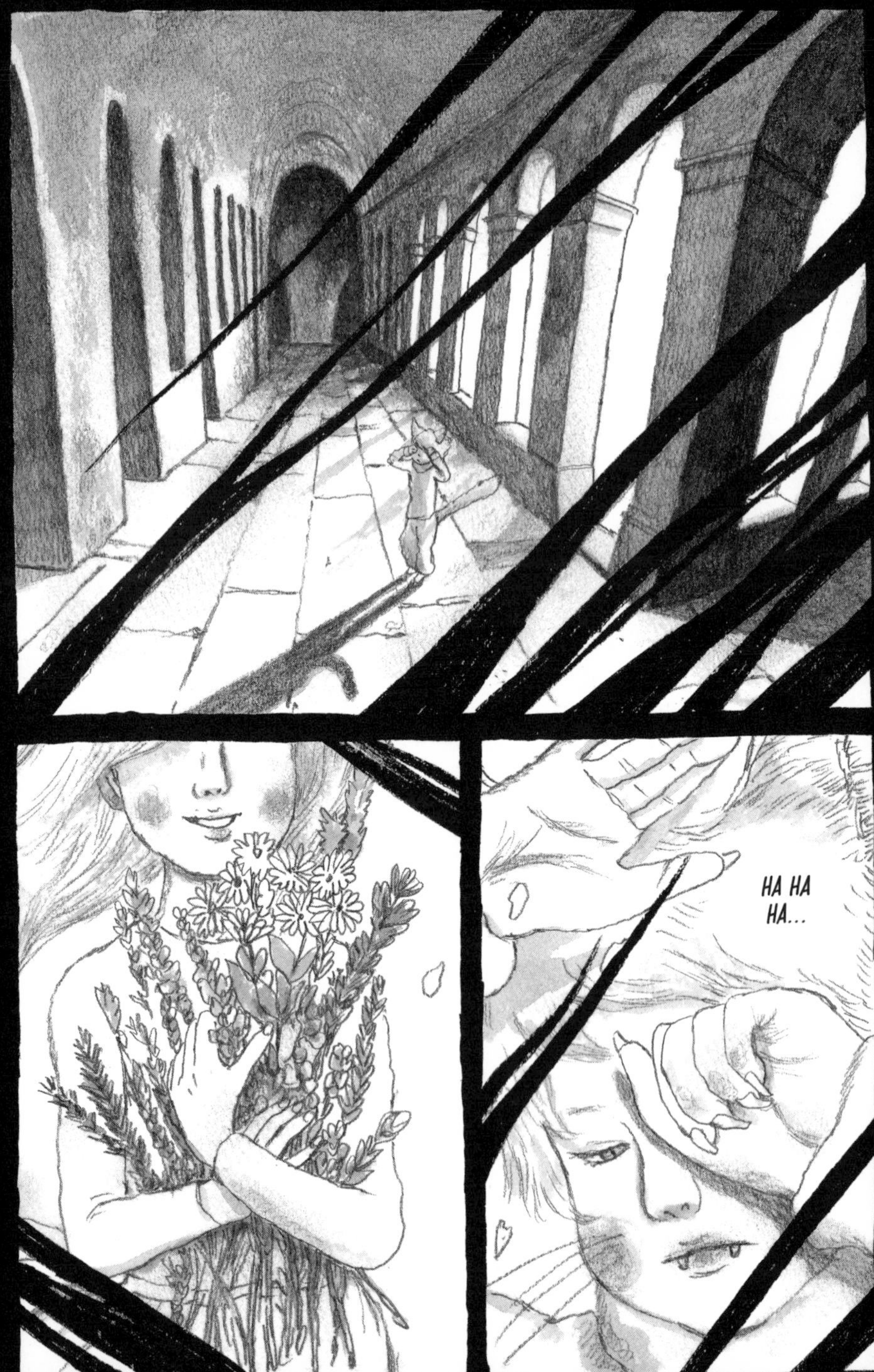
HA HA HA...

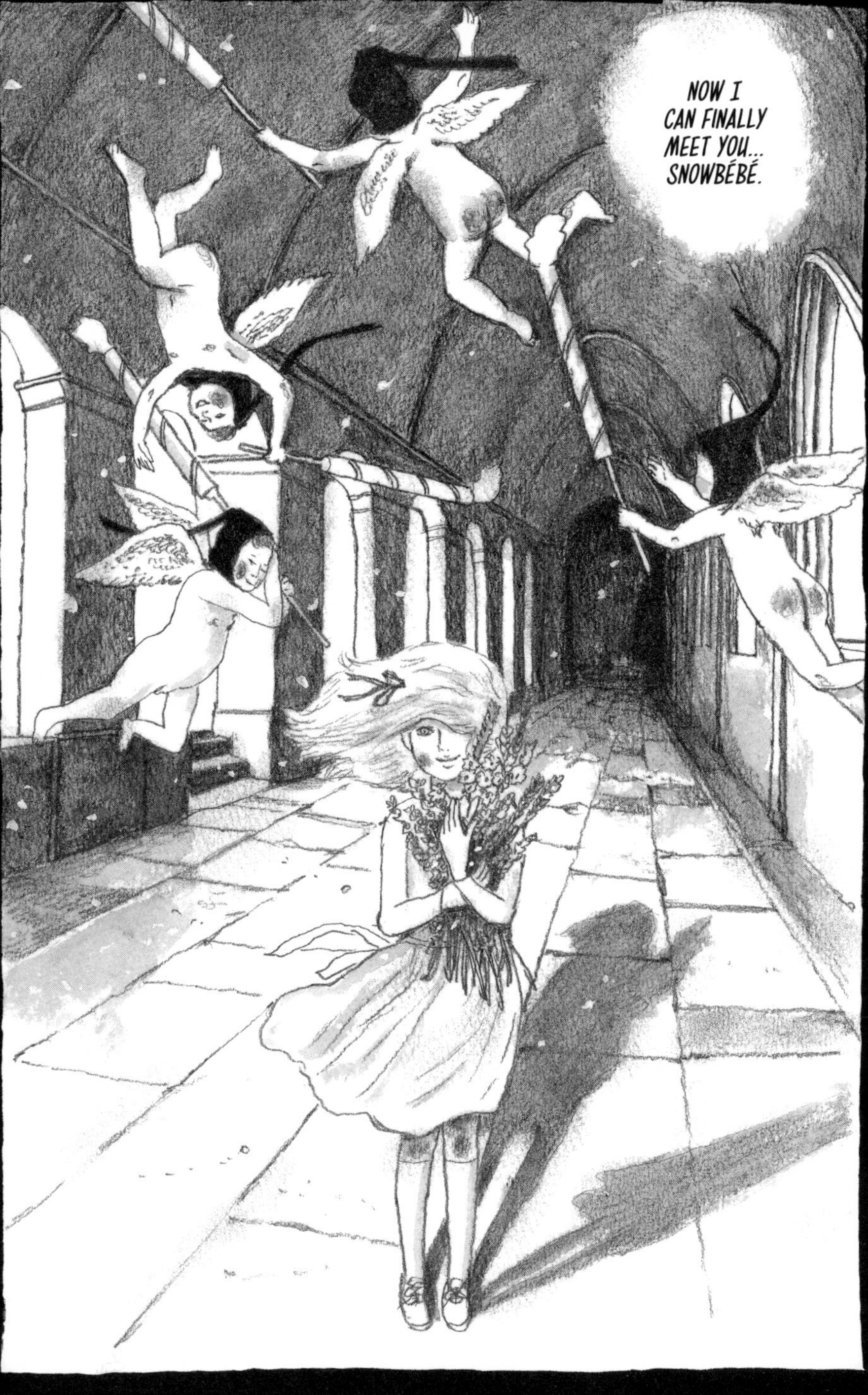
NOW I CAN FINALLY MEET YOU... SNOWBÉBÉ.

CHAPTER 15

The Secret of *The Funeral Procession of Love*

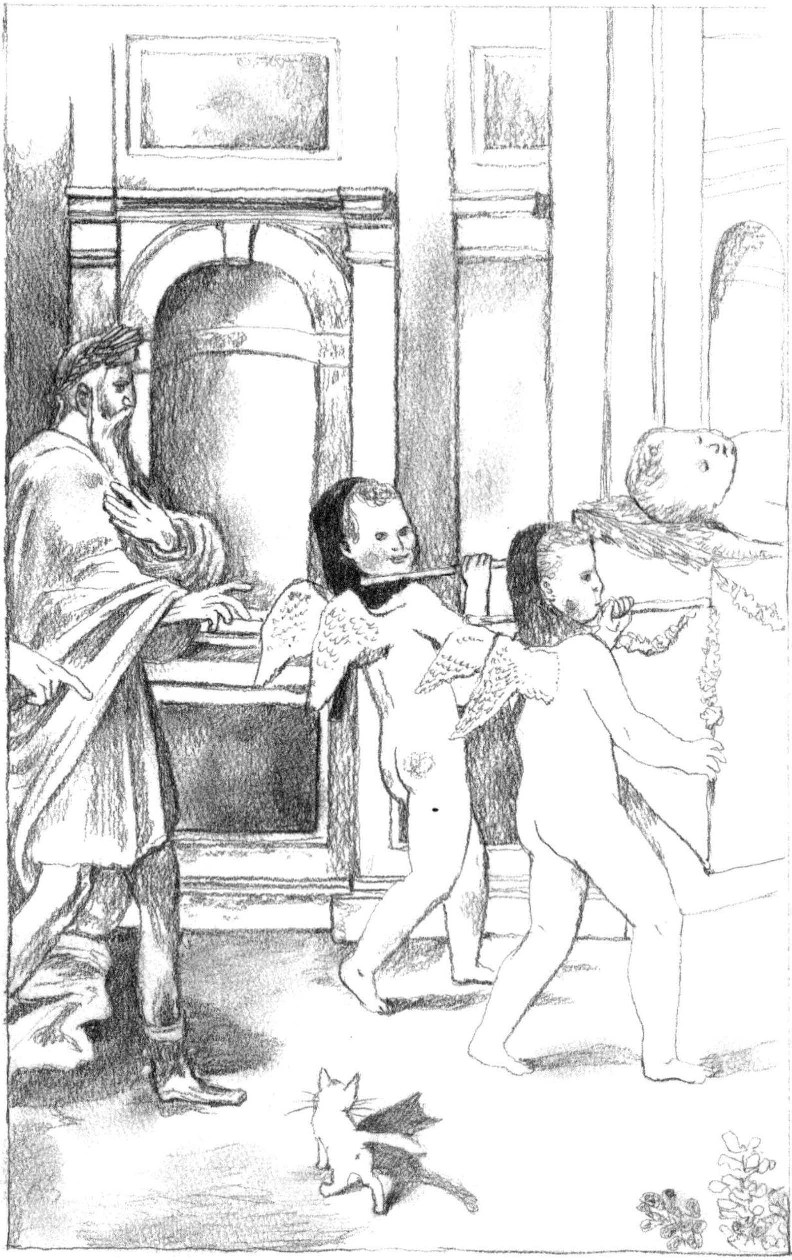

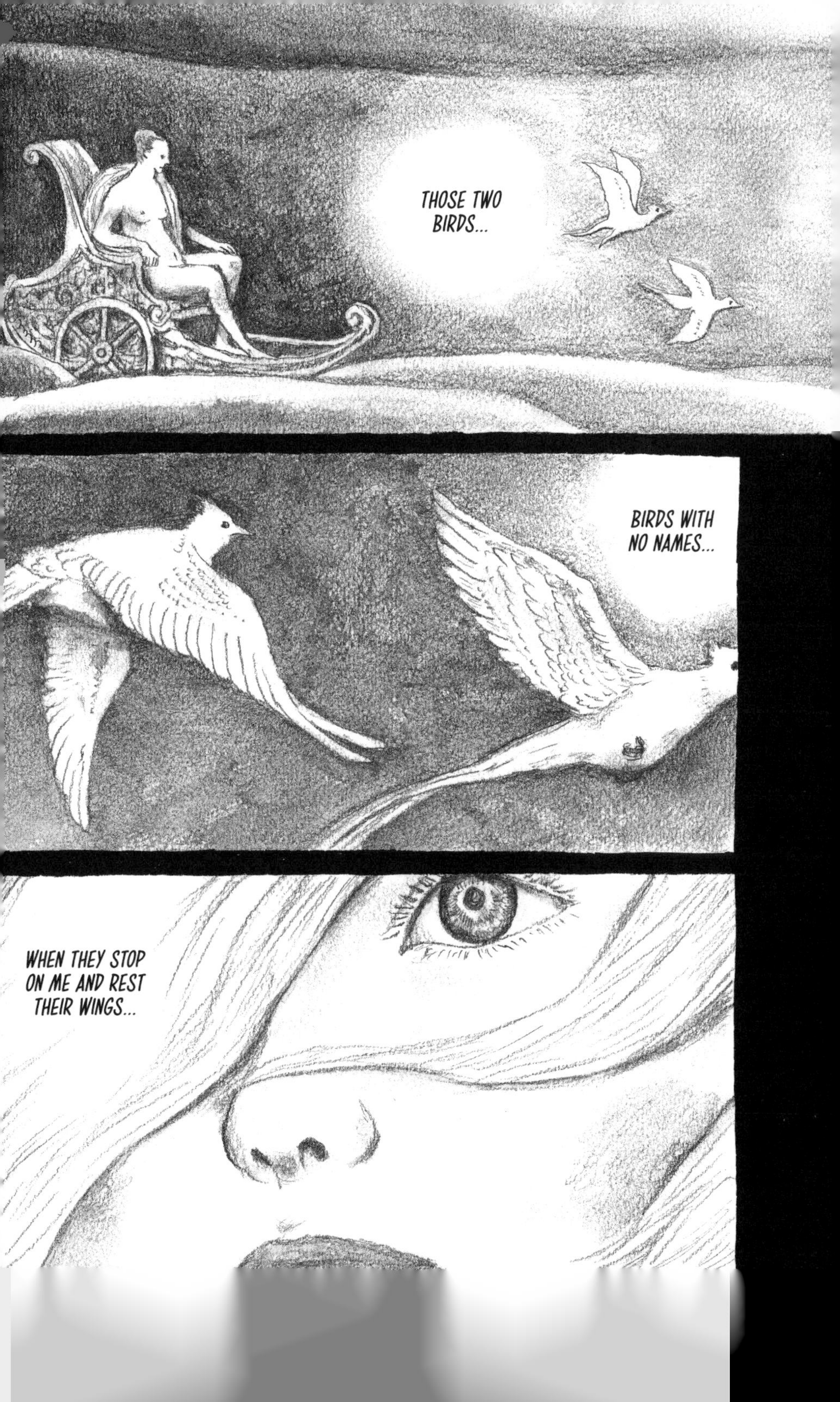
THOSE TWO BIRDS...
BIRDS WITH NO NAMES...
WHEN THEY STOP ON ME AND REST THEIR WINGS...

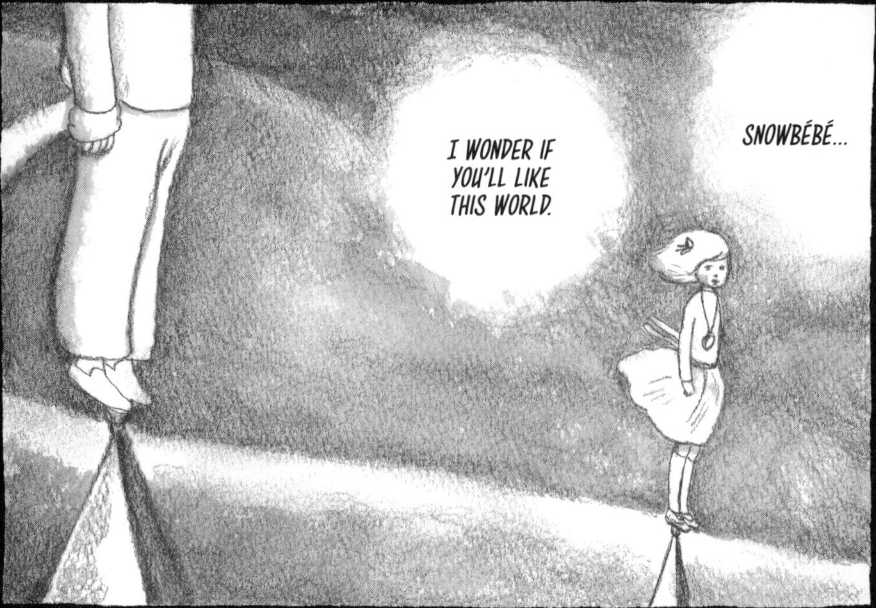
SNOWBÉBÉ...
I WONDER IF YOU'LL LIKE THIS WORLD.
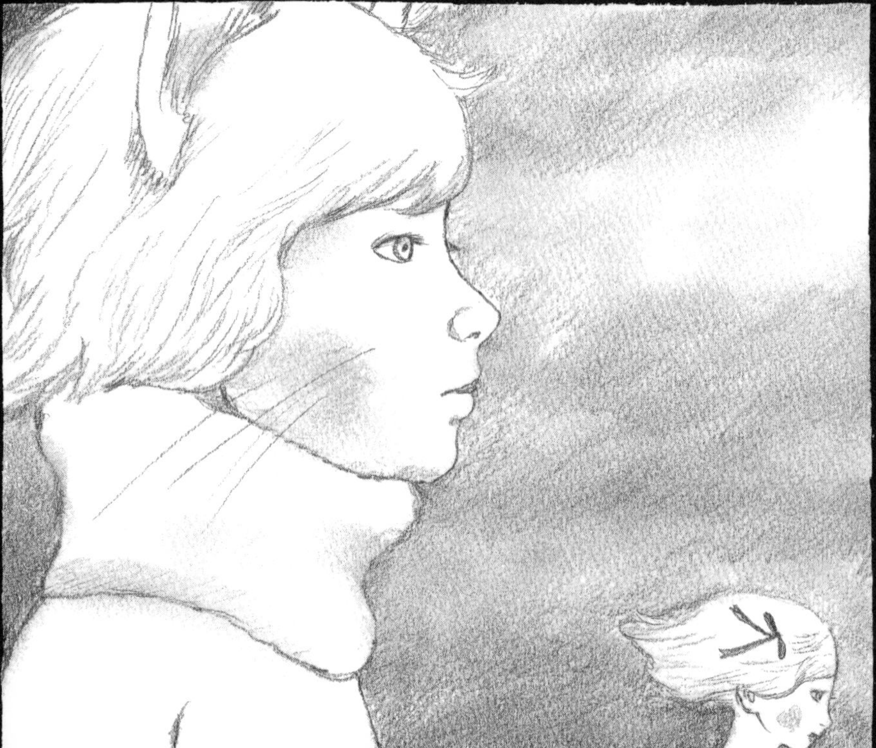

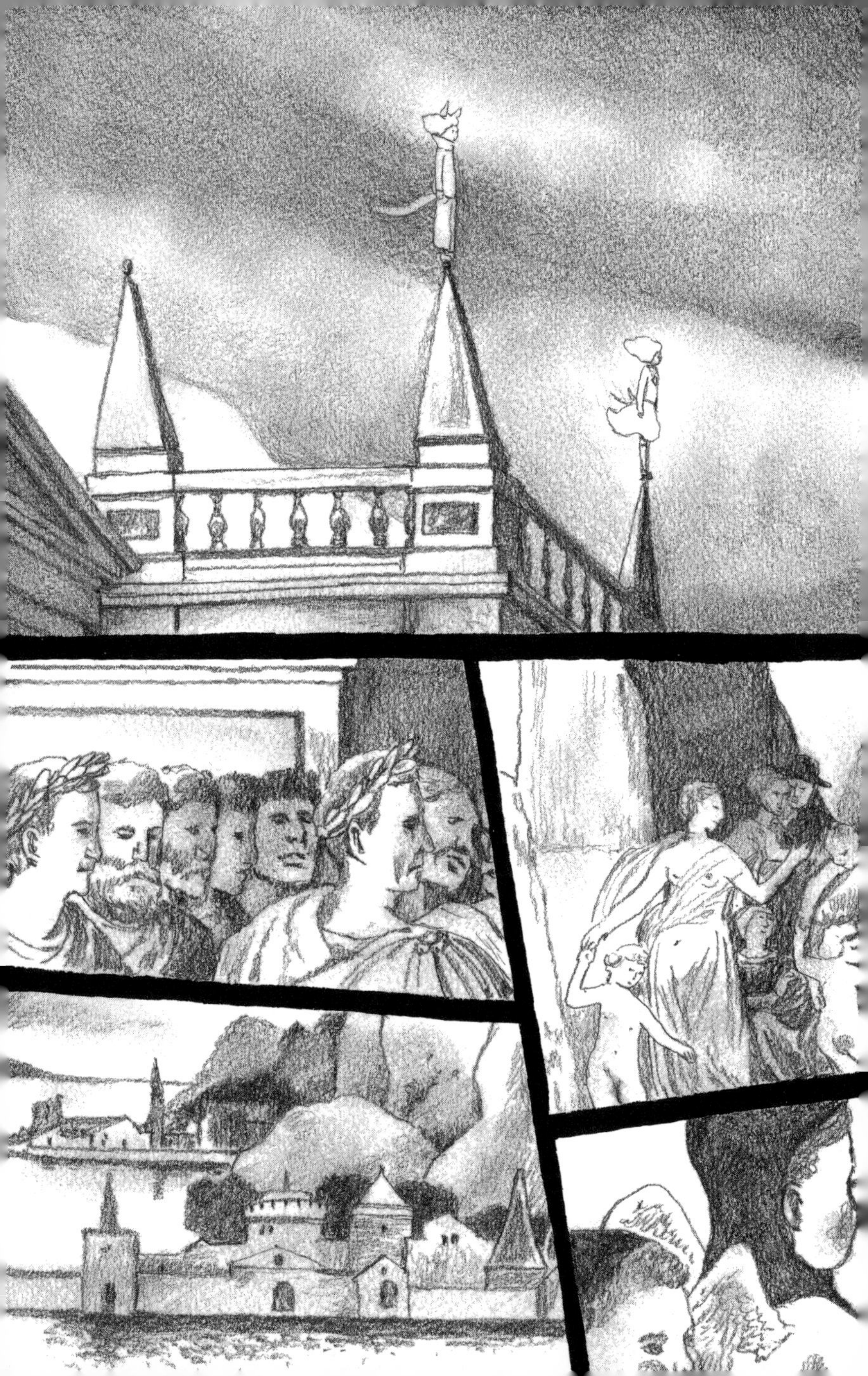

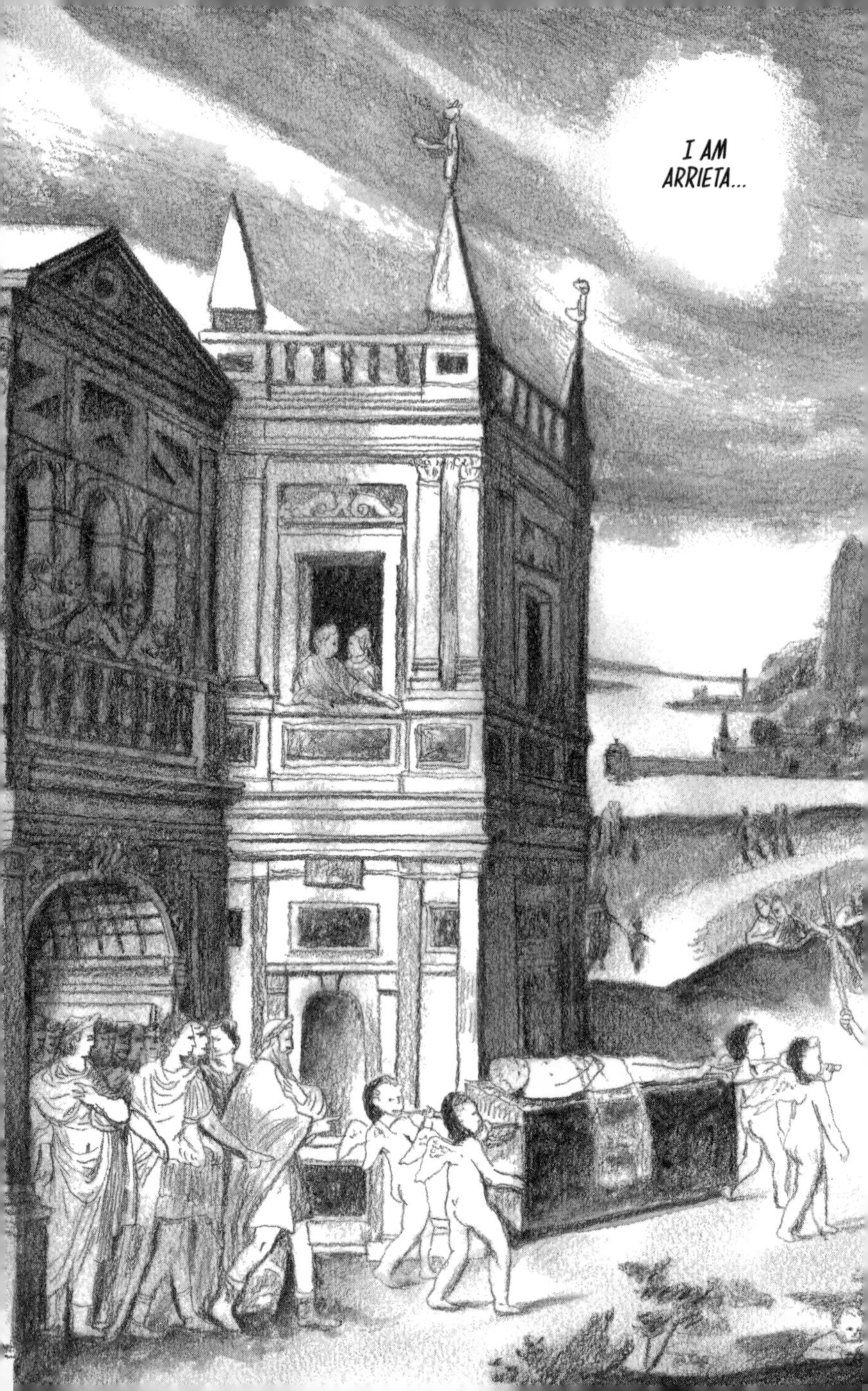
I AM ARRIETA...

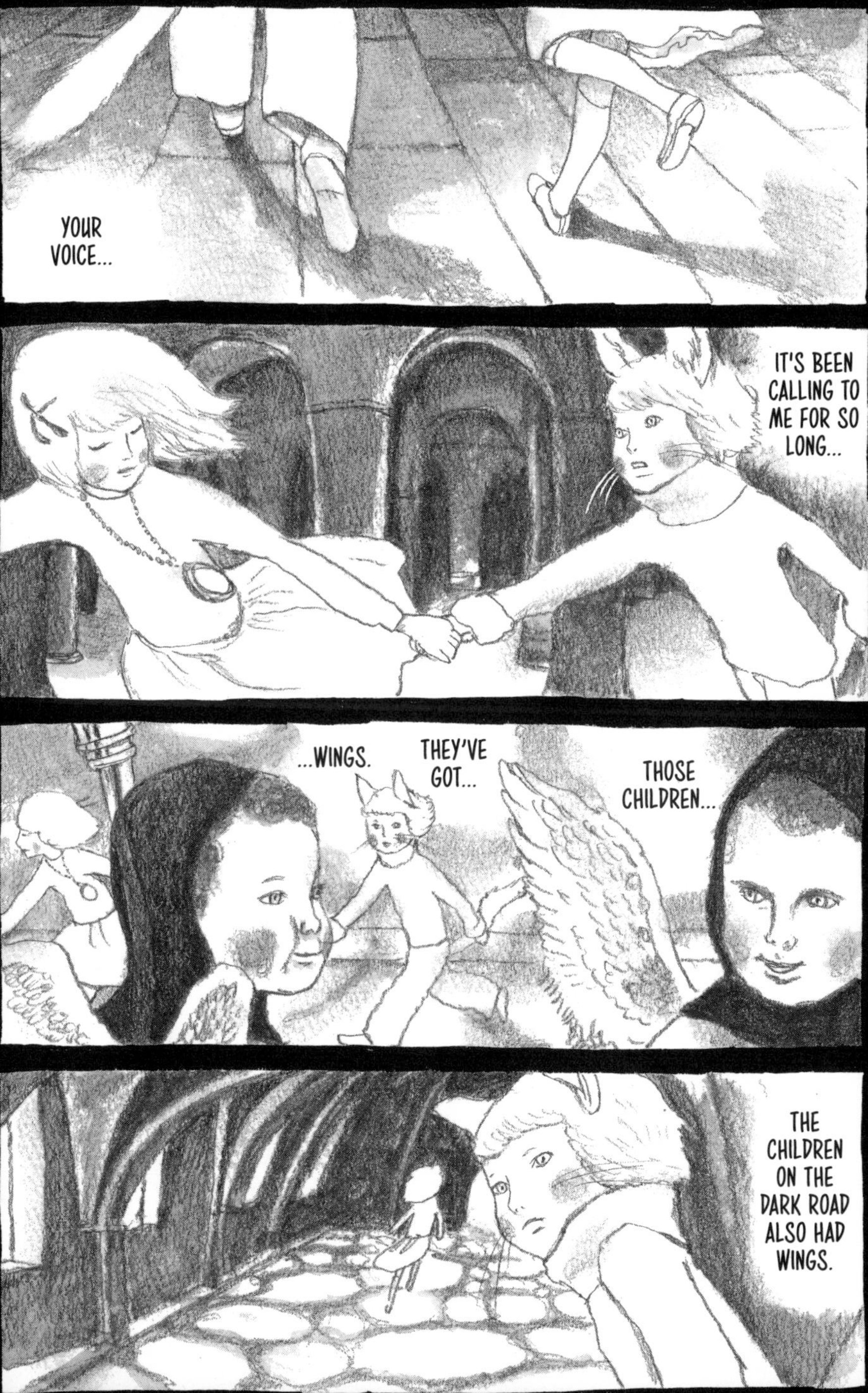
YOUR VOICE...
IT'S BEEN CALLING TO ME FOR SO LONG...
THOSE CHILDREN...
THEY'VE GOT...
...WINGS.
THE CHILDREN ON THE DARK ROAD ALSO HAD WINGS.

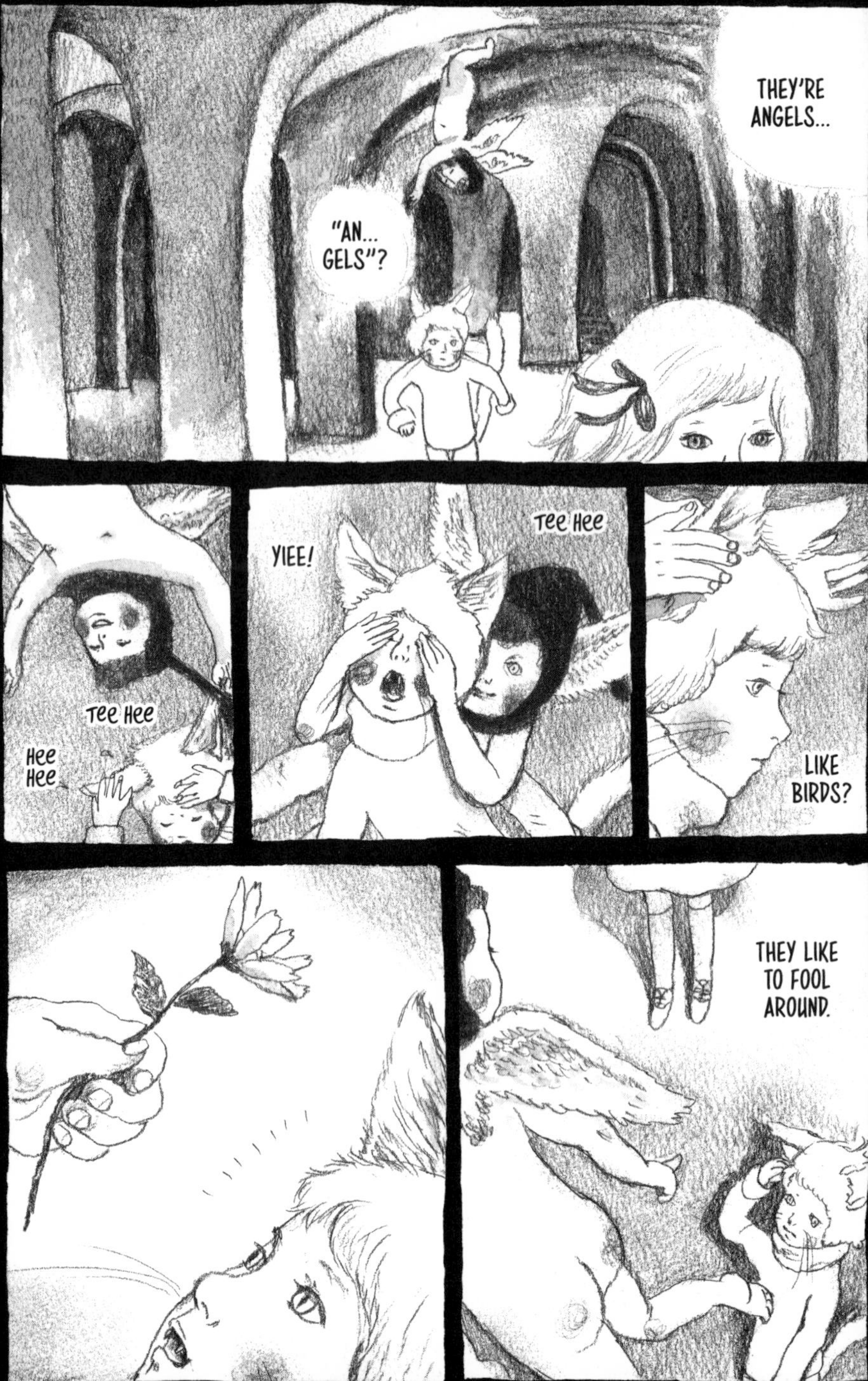
THEY'RE ANGELS...
"AN... GELS"?
LIKE BIRDS?
TEE HEE
YIEE!
TEE HEE
HEE HEE
THEY LIKE TO FOOL AROUND.

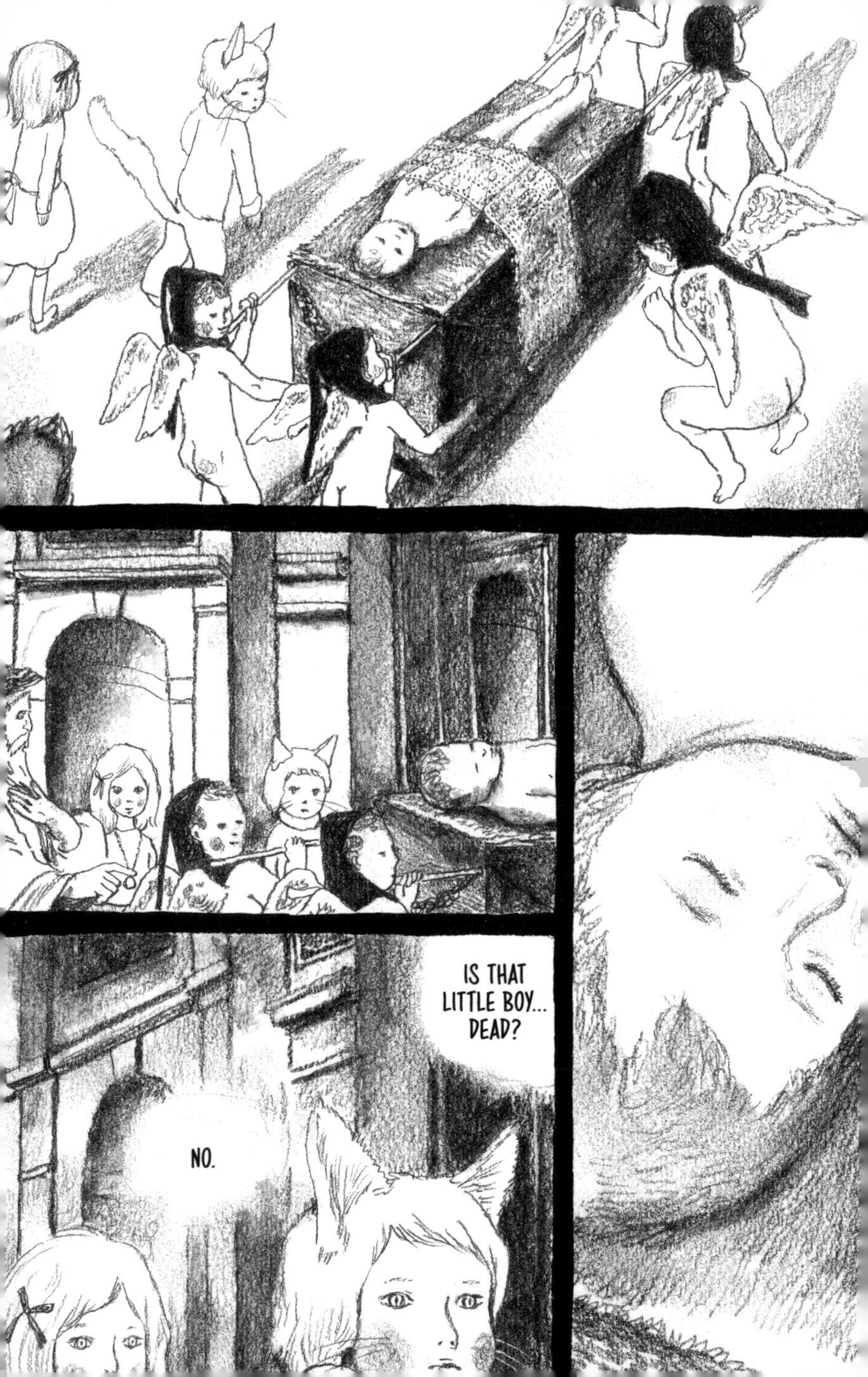
IS THAT LITTLE BOY... DEAD?
NO.

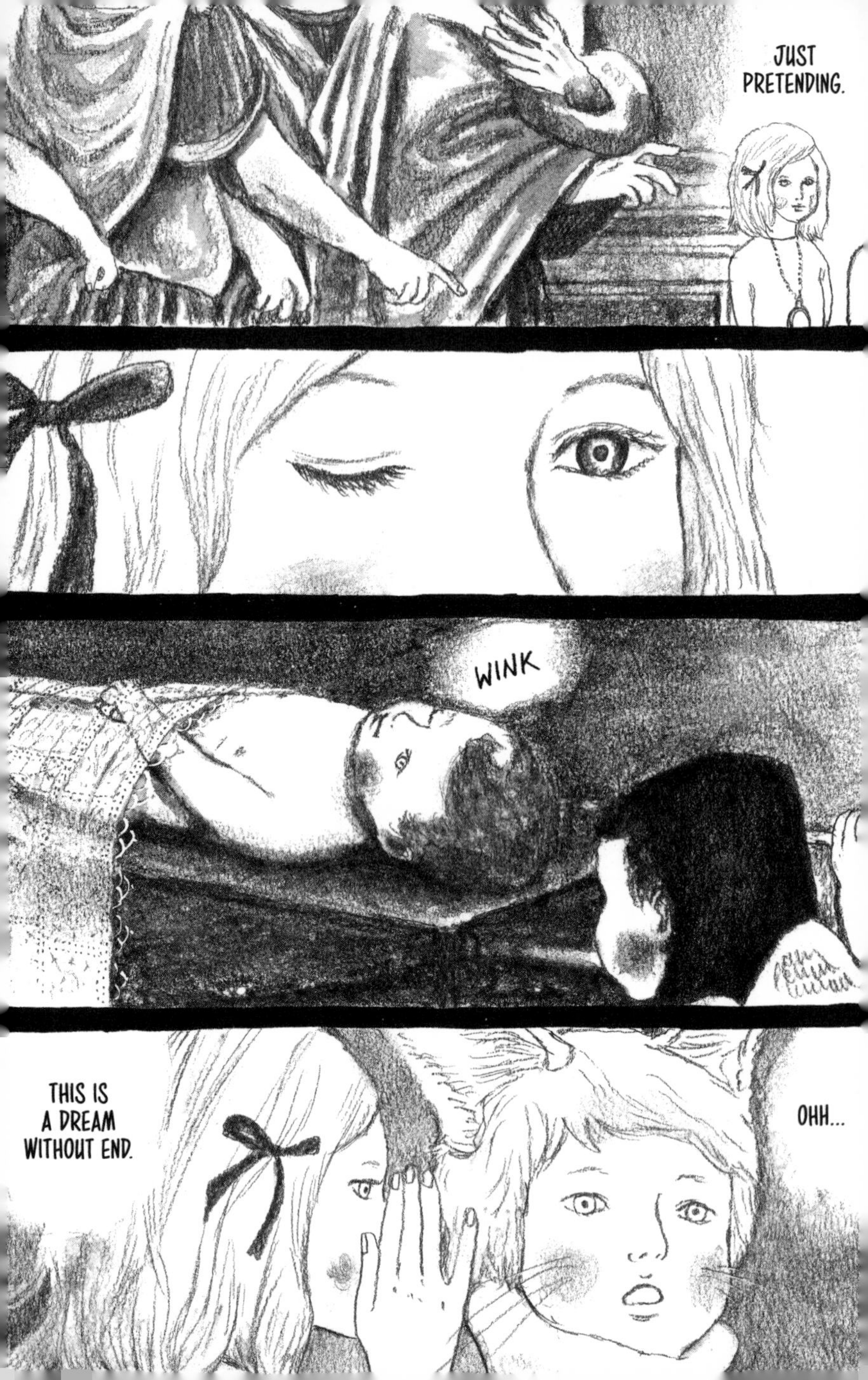
JUST PRETENDING.
WINK
OHH...
THIS IS A DREAM WITHOUT END.

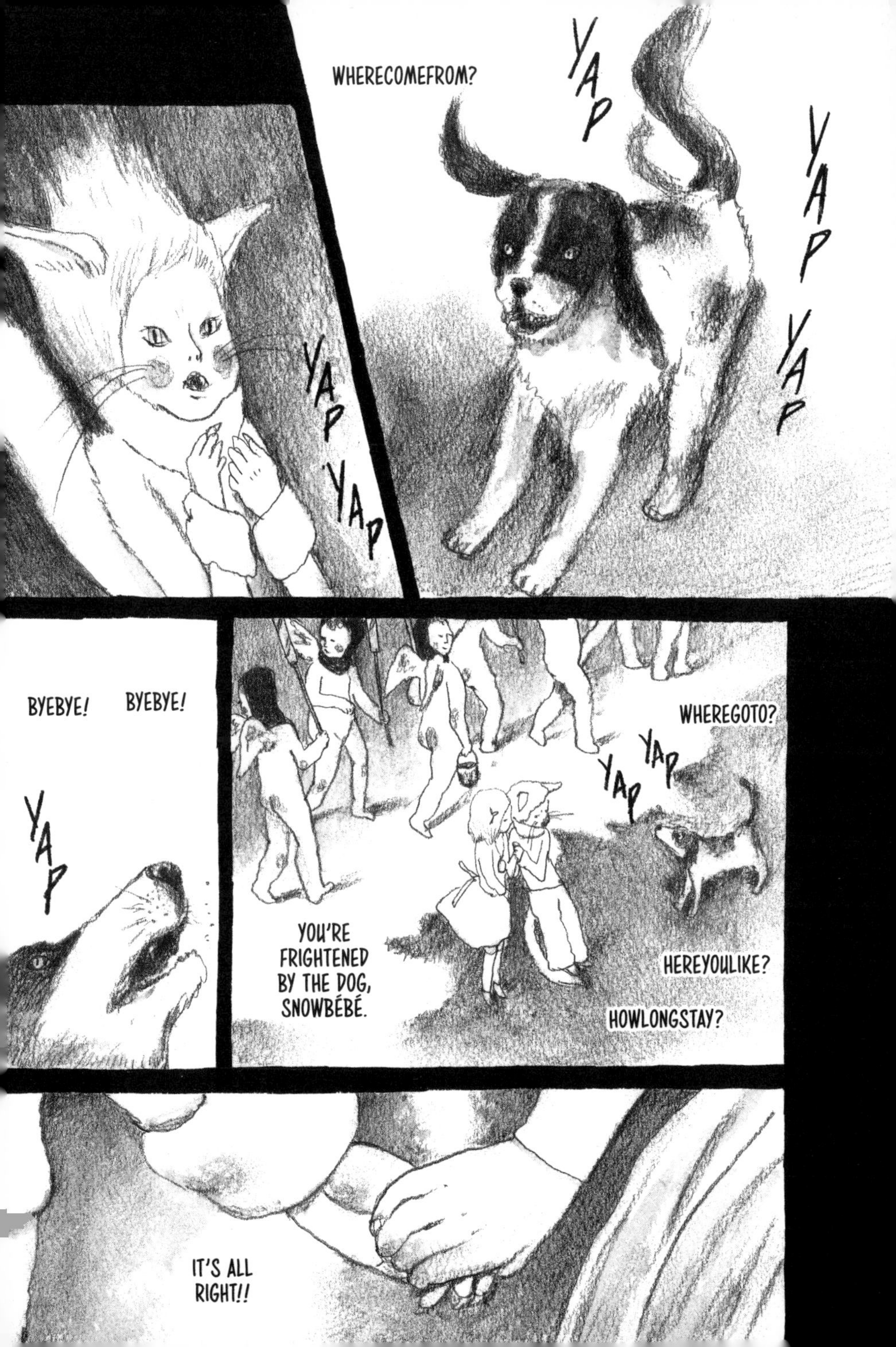

WHERECOMEFROM?
YAP
YAP
YAP
YAP
YAP
YAP
YAP
YAP
YAP
YAP
WHEREGOTO?
YAP
YAP
HEREYOULIKE?
HOWLONGSTAY?
YOU'RE FRIGHTENED BY THE DOG, SNOWBÉBÉ.
BYEBYE!
BYEBYE!
YAP
IT'S ALL RIGHT!!

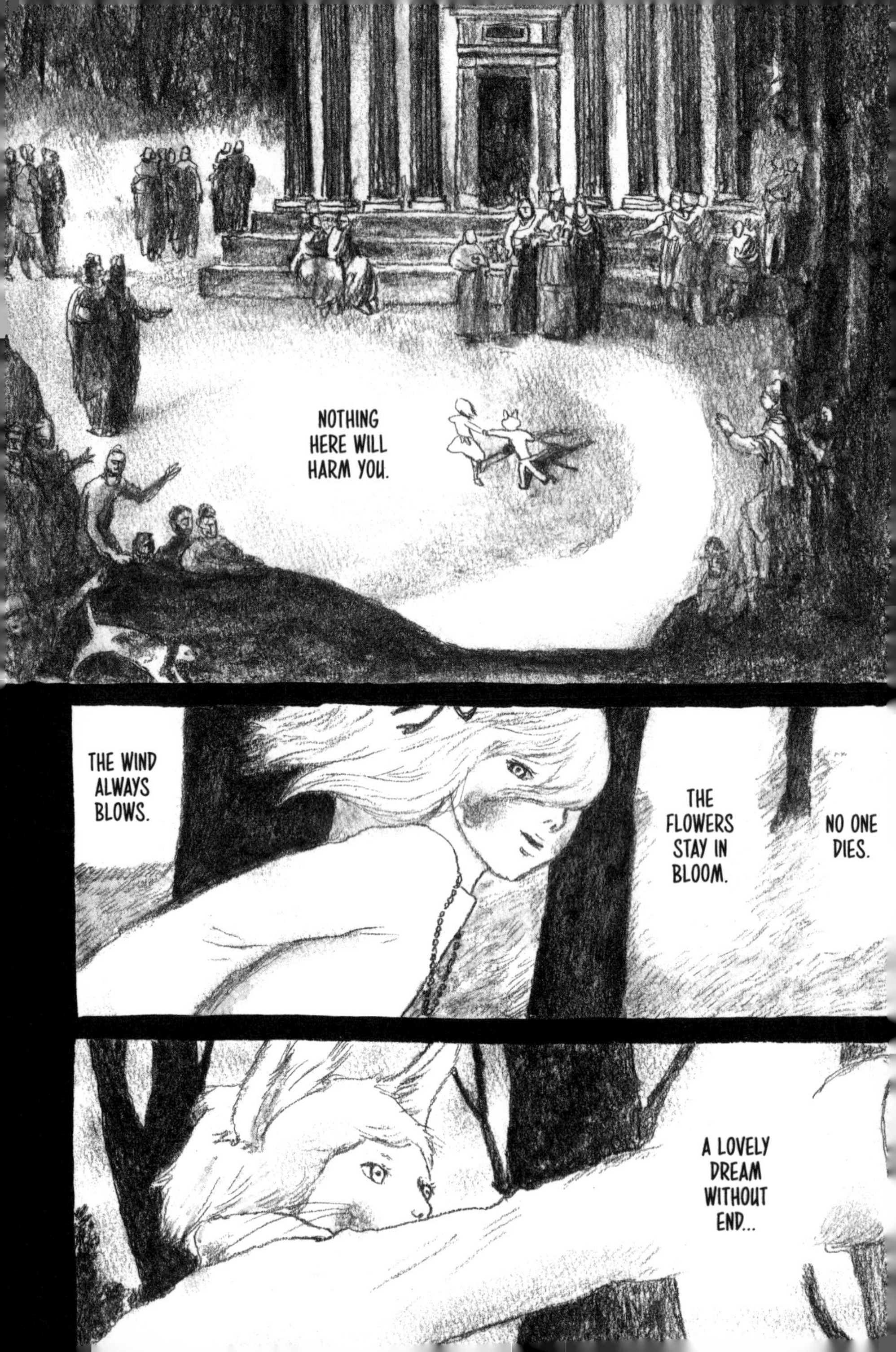
NOTHING HERE WILL HARM YOU.
NO ONE DIES.
THE FLOWERS STAY IN BLOOM.
THE WIND ALWAYS BLOWS.
A LOVELY DREAM WITHOUT END...

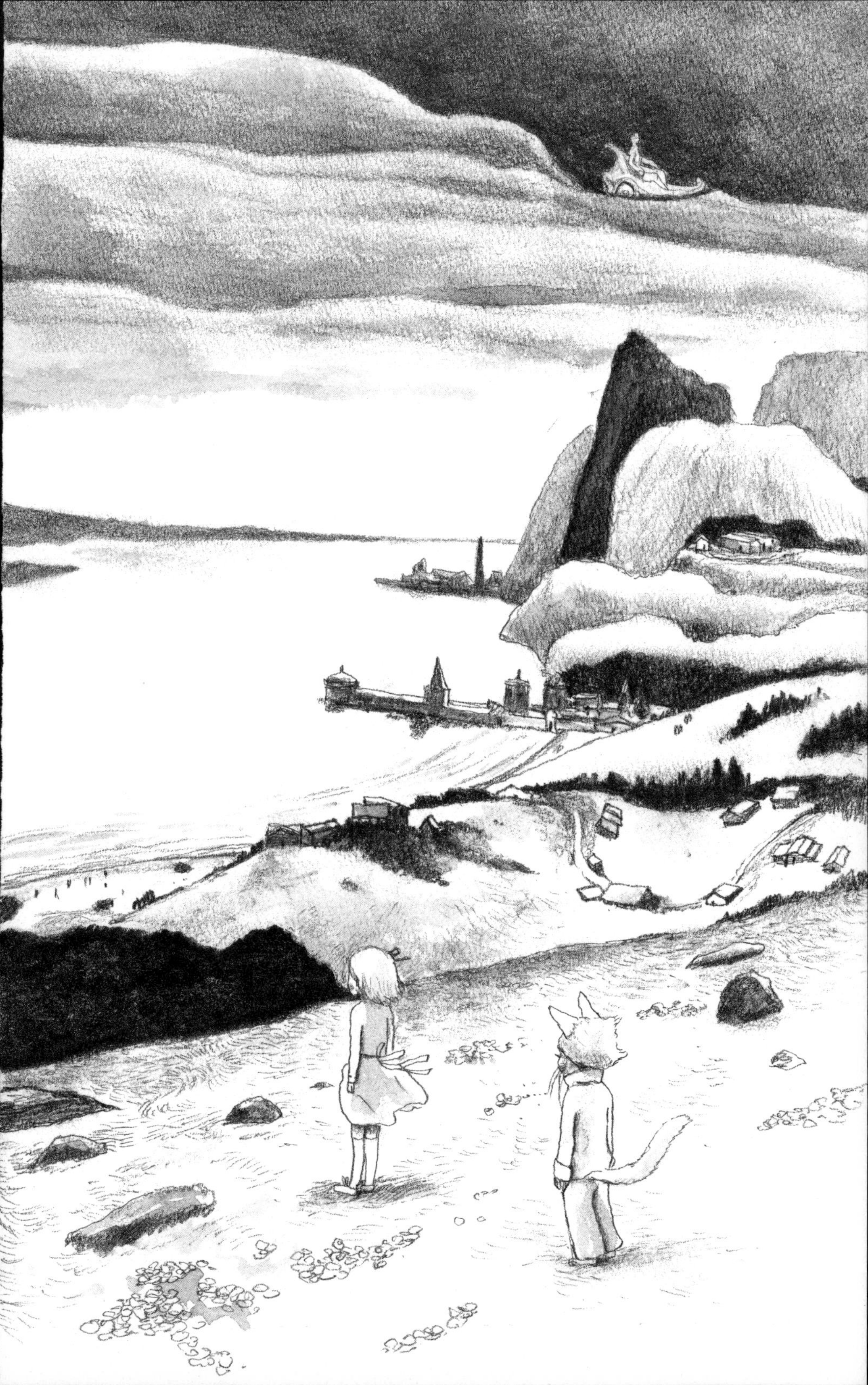

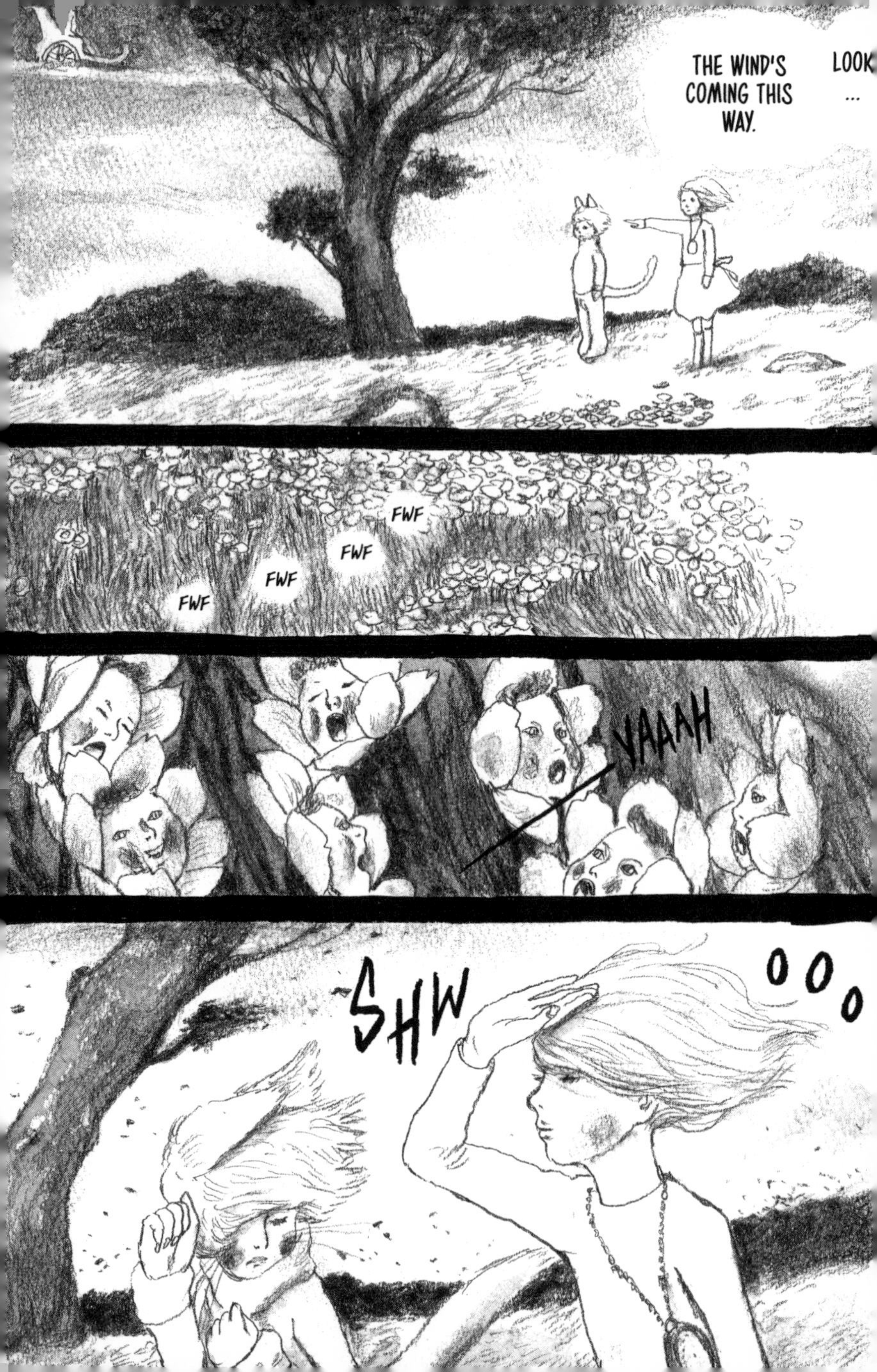
LOOK ...
THE WIND'S COMING THIS WAY.
FWF
FWF
FWF
FWF
VAAAH
SHW OOO

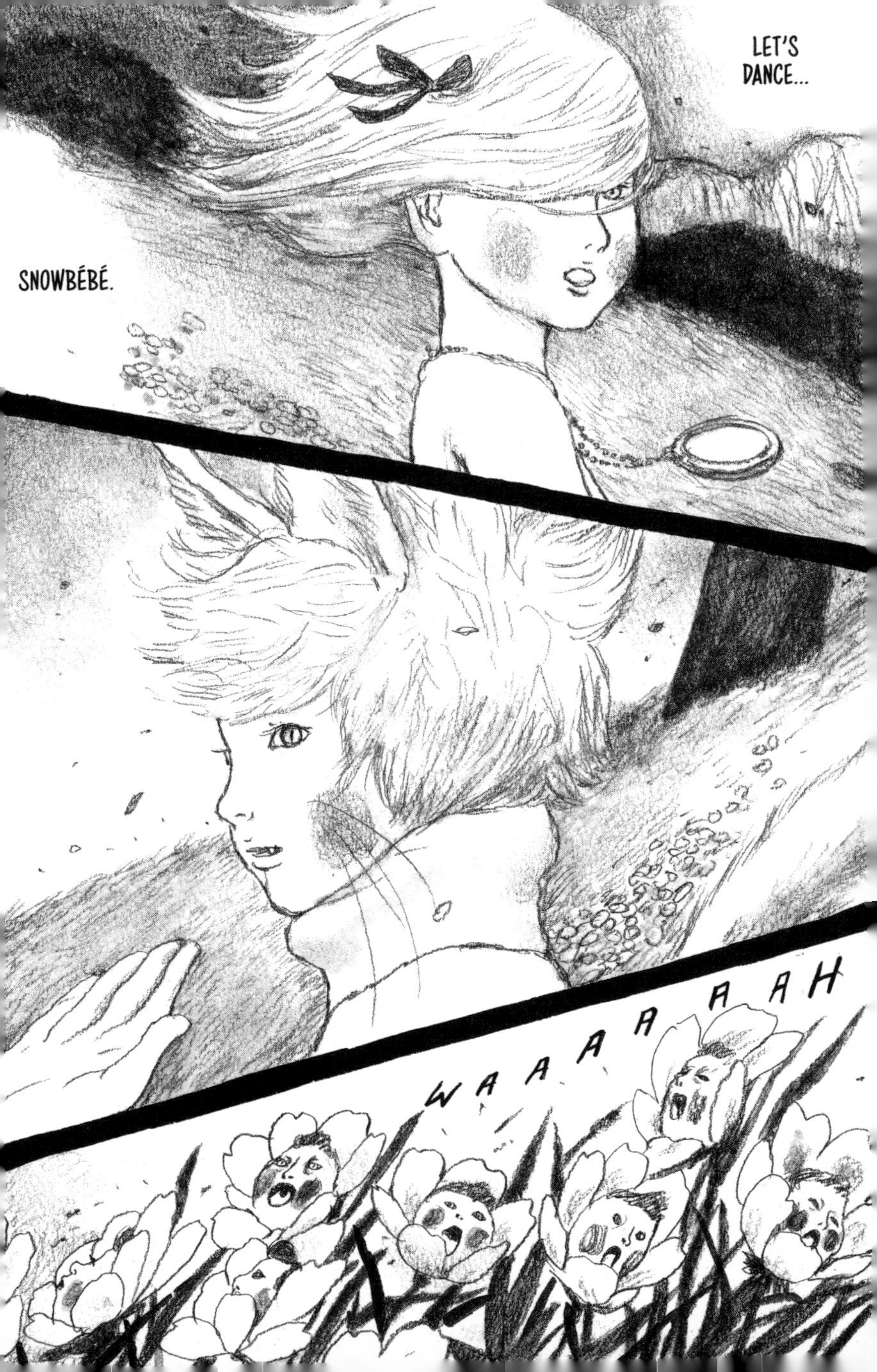
LET'S DANCE...
SNOWBÉBÉ.
WAAAAAAH

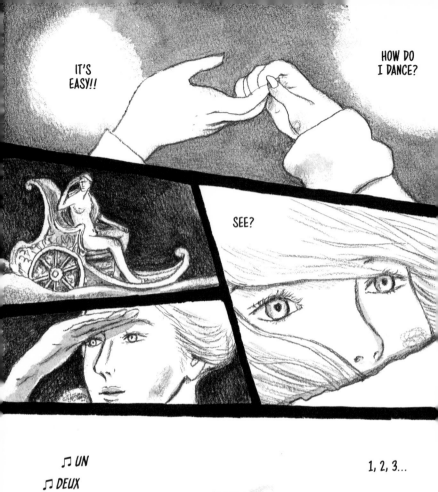

IT'S
EASY!!

HOW DO
I DANCE?

SEE?

♫ *UN*
♪ *DEUX*
♩ *TROIS*

1, 2, 3...

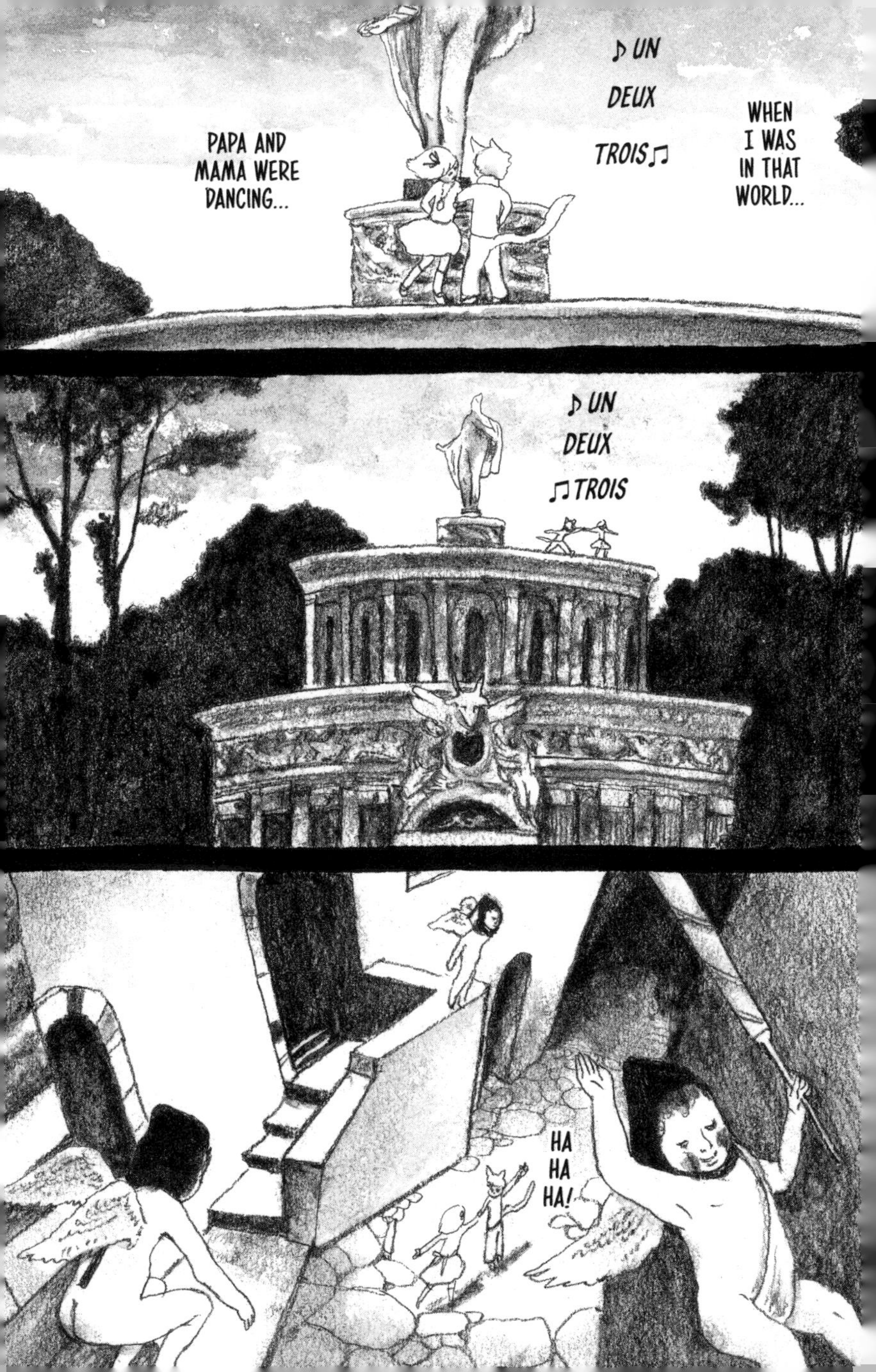
WHEN I WAS IN THAT WORLD...
♪ UN DEUX TROIS ♫
PAPA AND MAMA WERE DANCING...
♪ UN DEUX ♫ TROIS
HA HA HA!

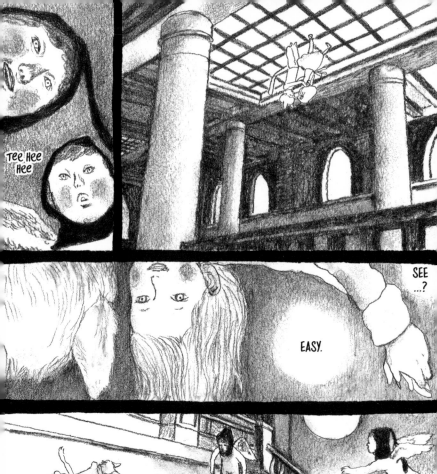

TEE HEE
HEE

SEE
...?

EASY.

TAH ♩
TAH ♩
TADADAH ♫

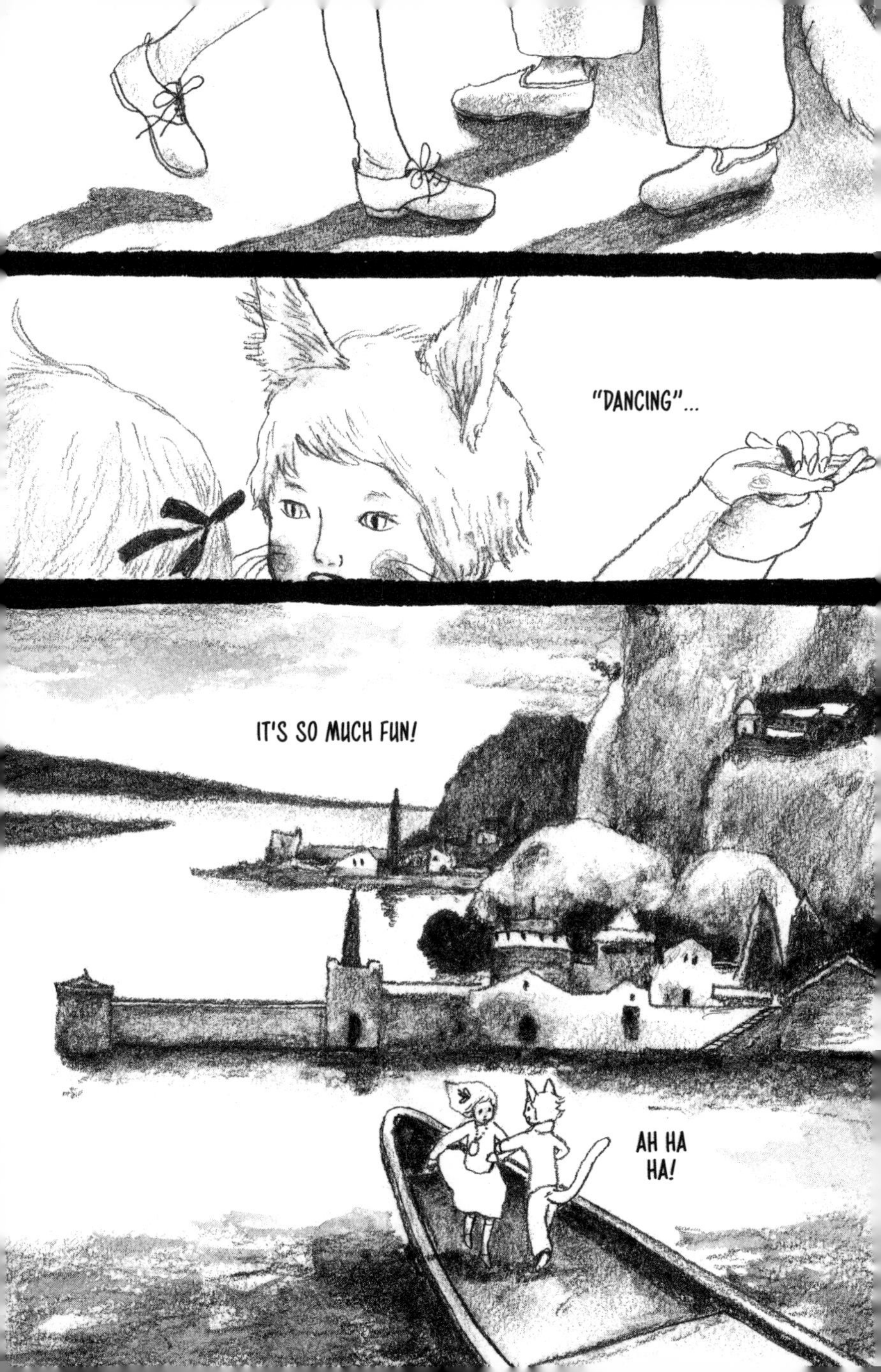
"DANCING"...
IT'S SO MUCH FUN!
AH HA HA!

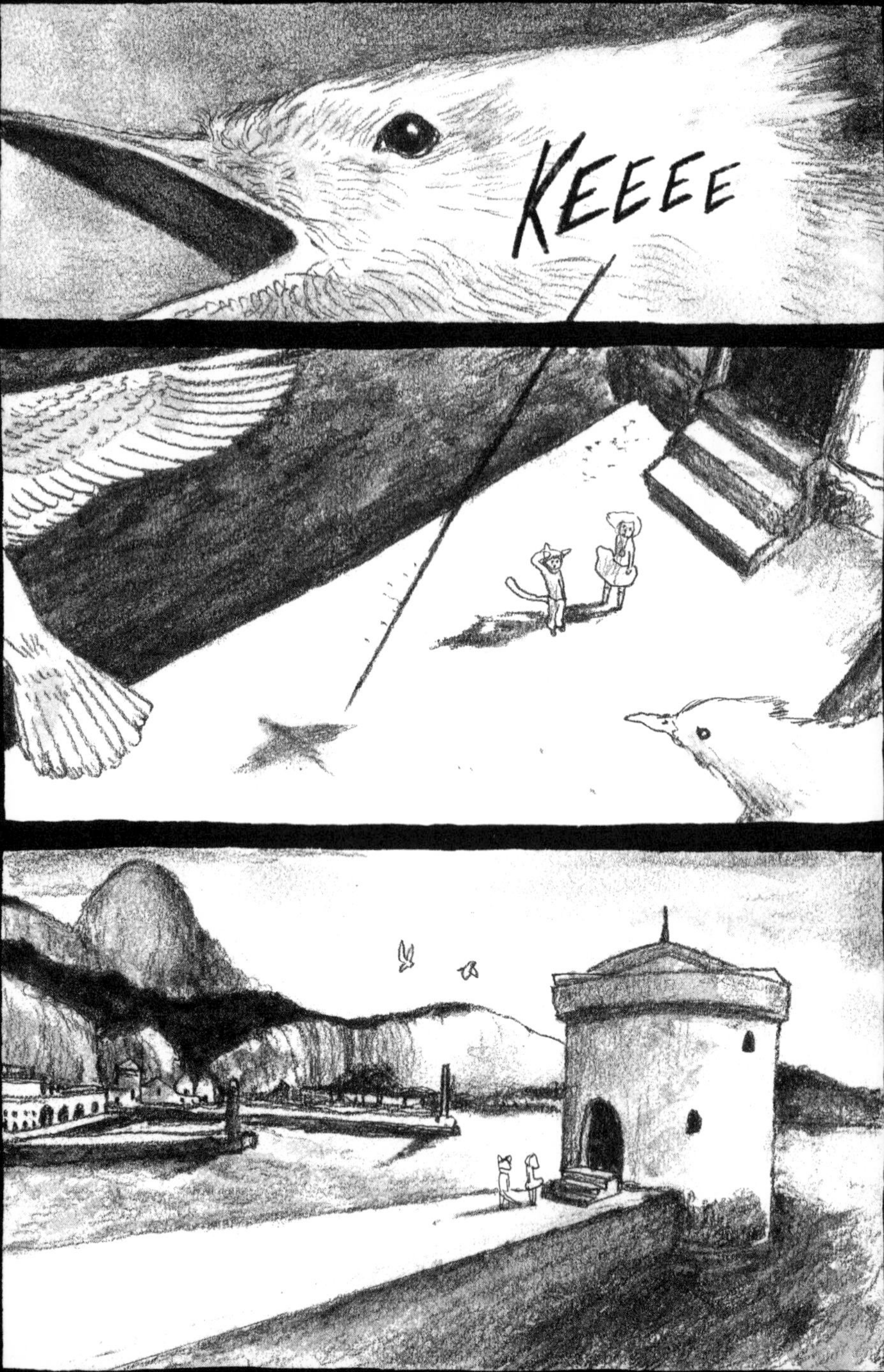
KEEEE

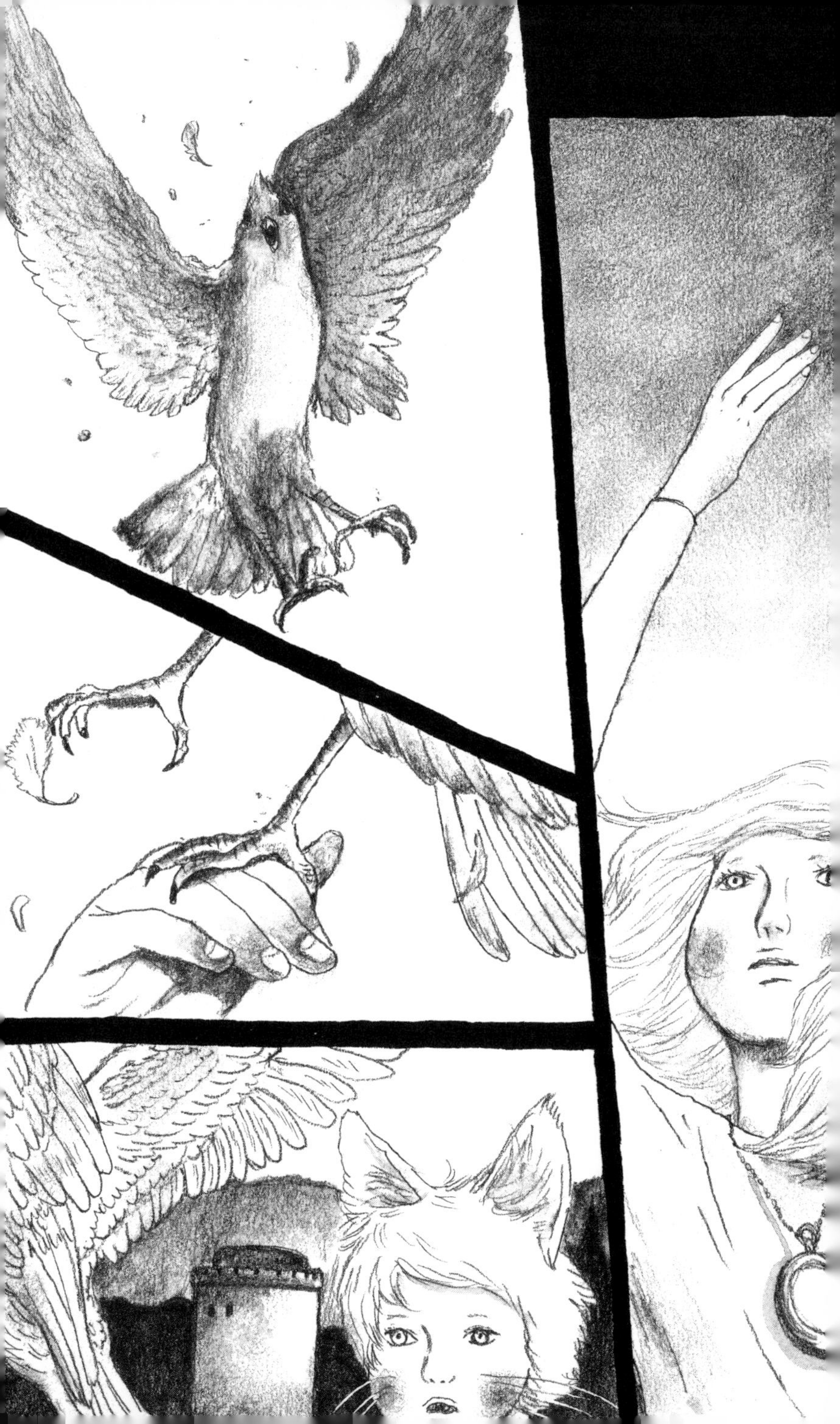

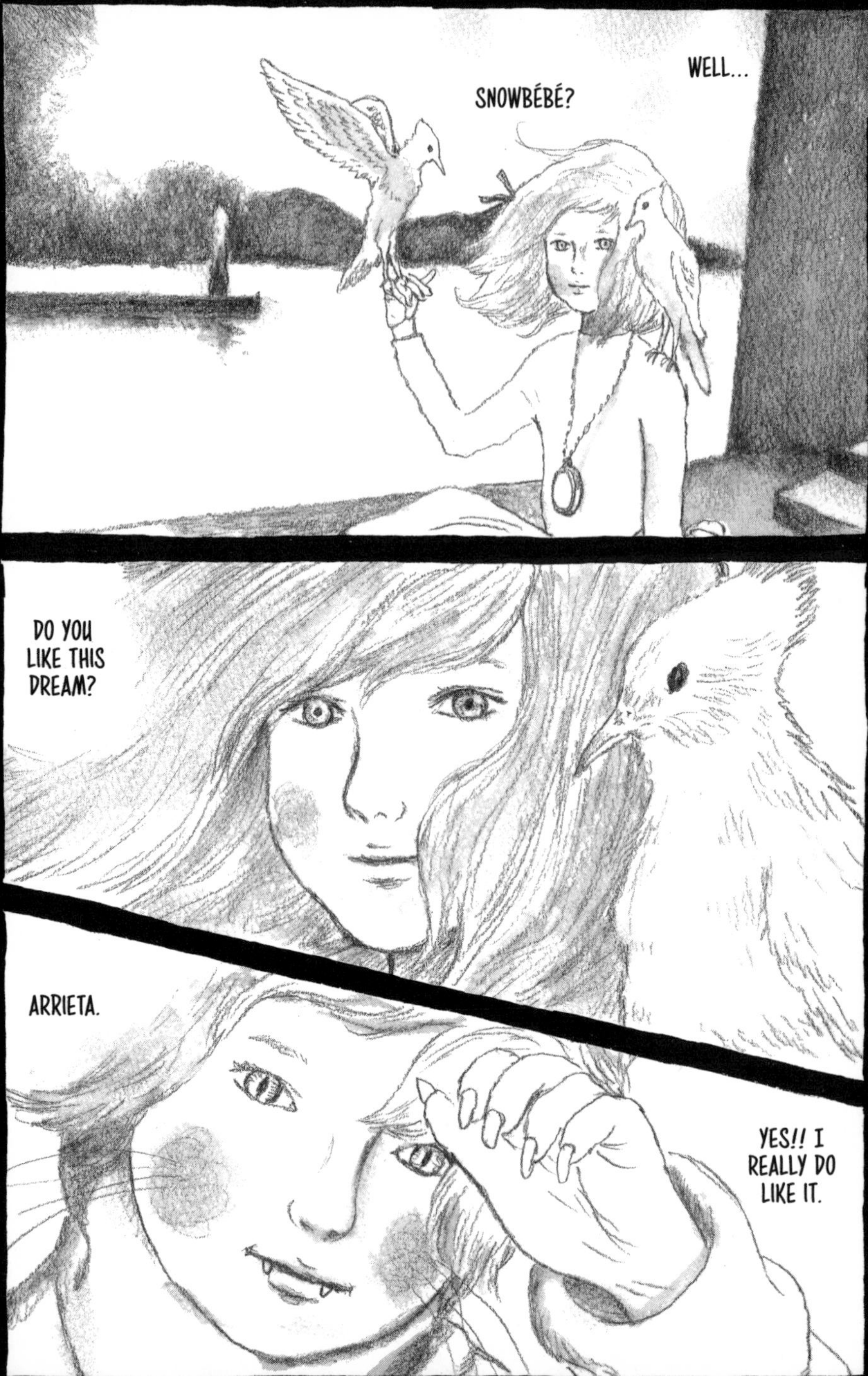
WELL...
SNOWBÉBÉ?
DO YOU LIKE THIS DREAM?
ARRIETA.
YES!! I REALLY DO LIKE IT.

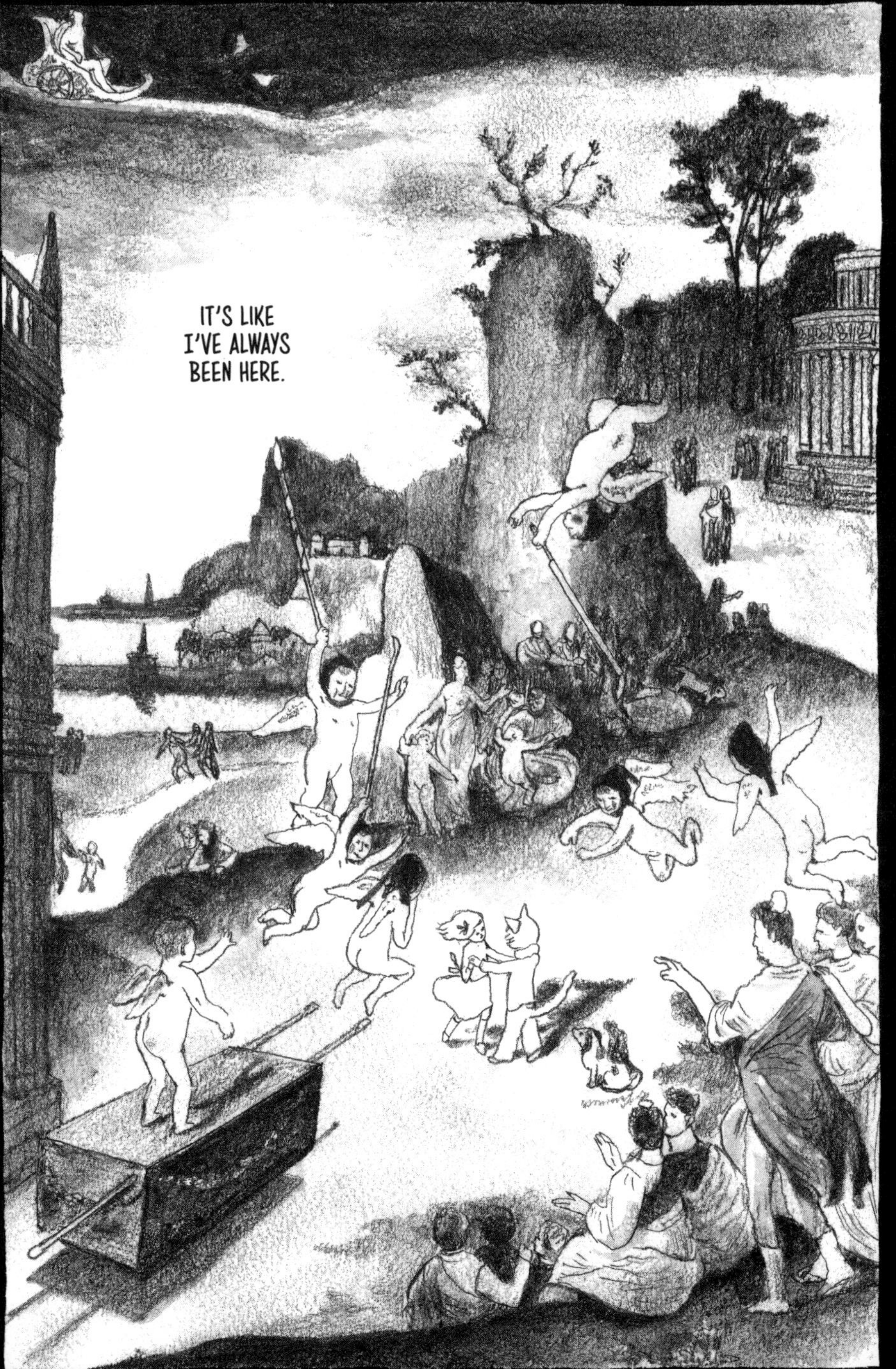
IT'S LIKE
I'VE ALWAYS
BEEN HERE.

CHAPTER 16

The Secret of the Old Pocket Watch

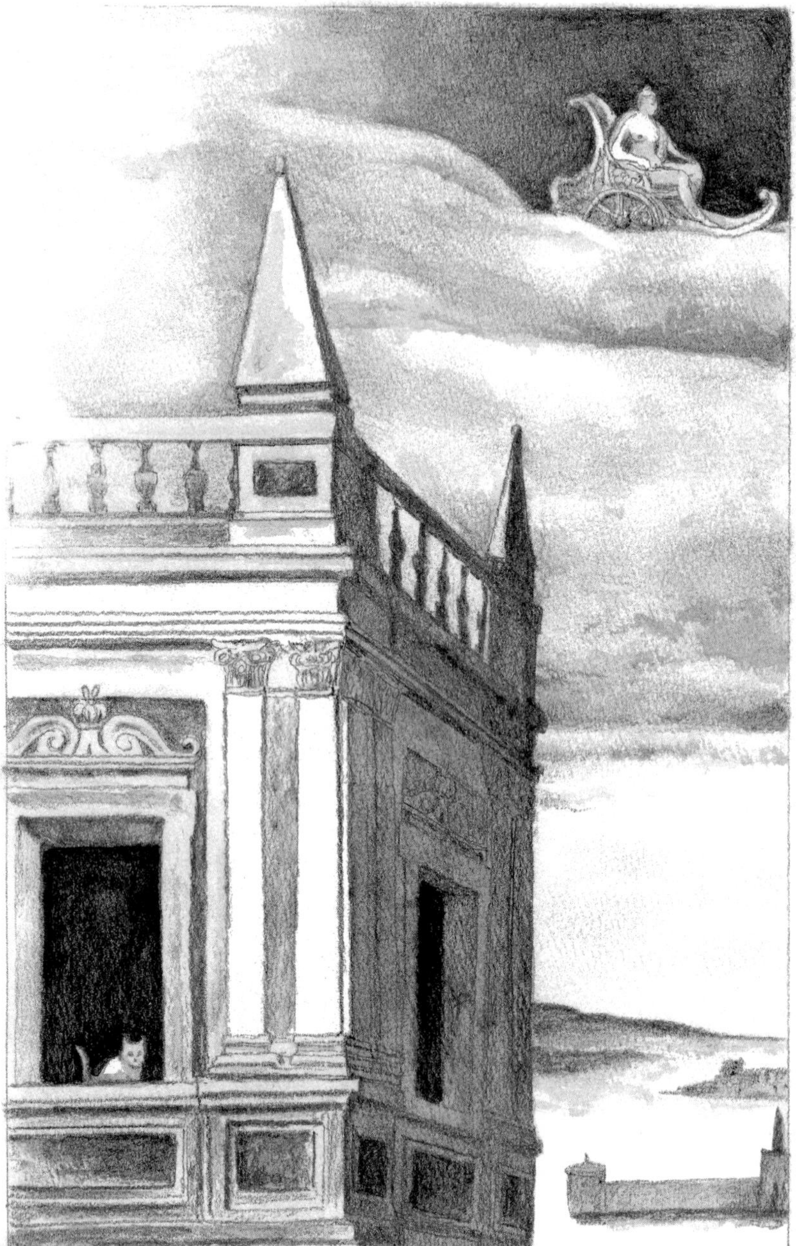

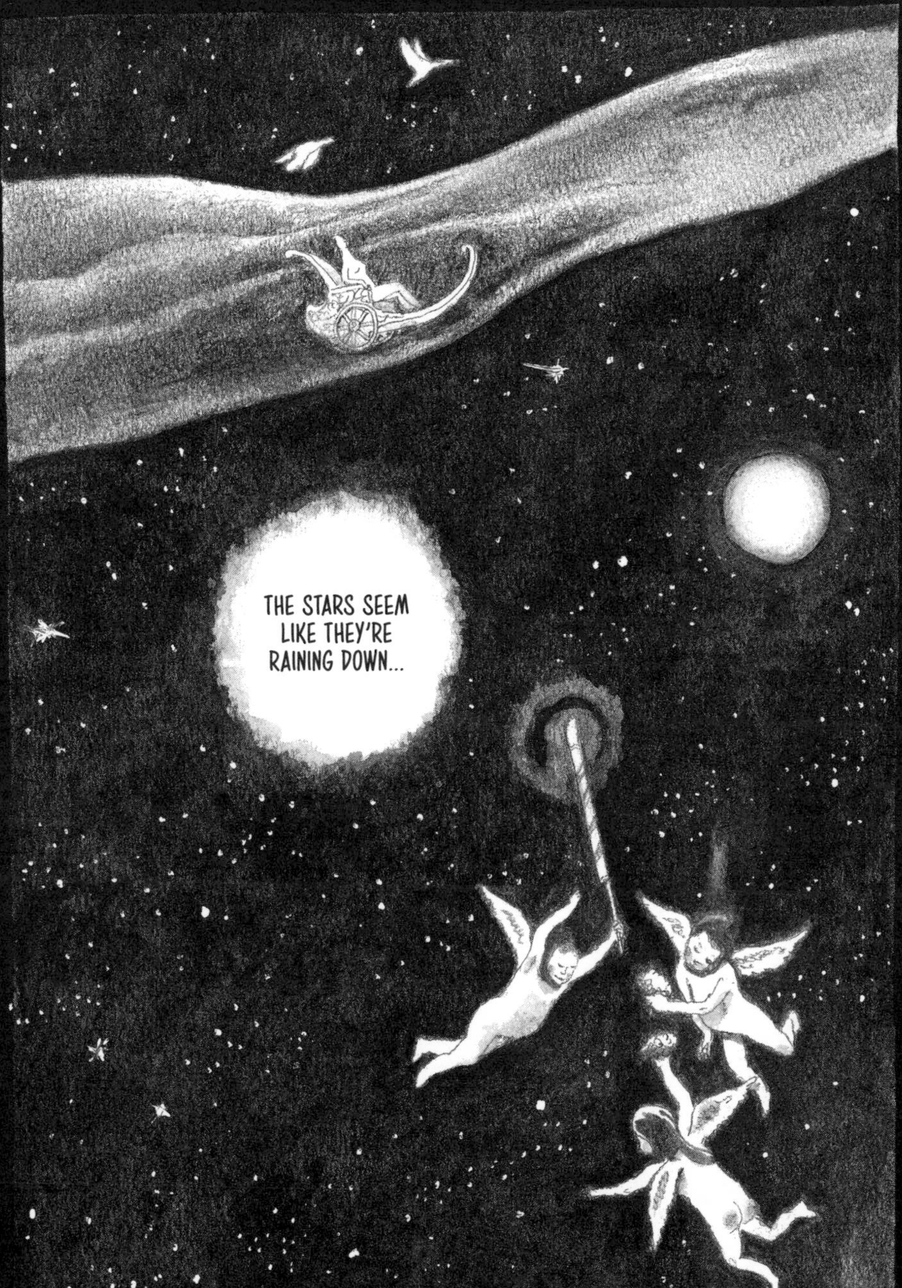
THE STARS SEEM LIKE THEY'RE RAINING DOWN...

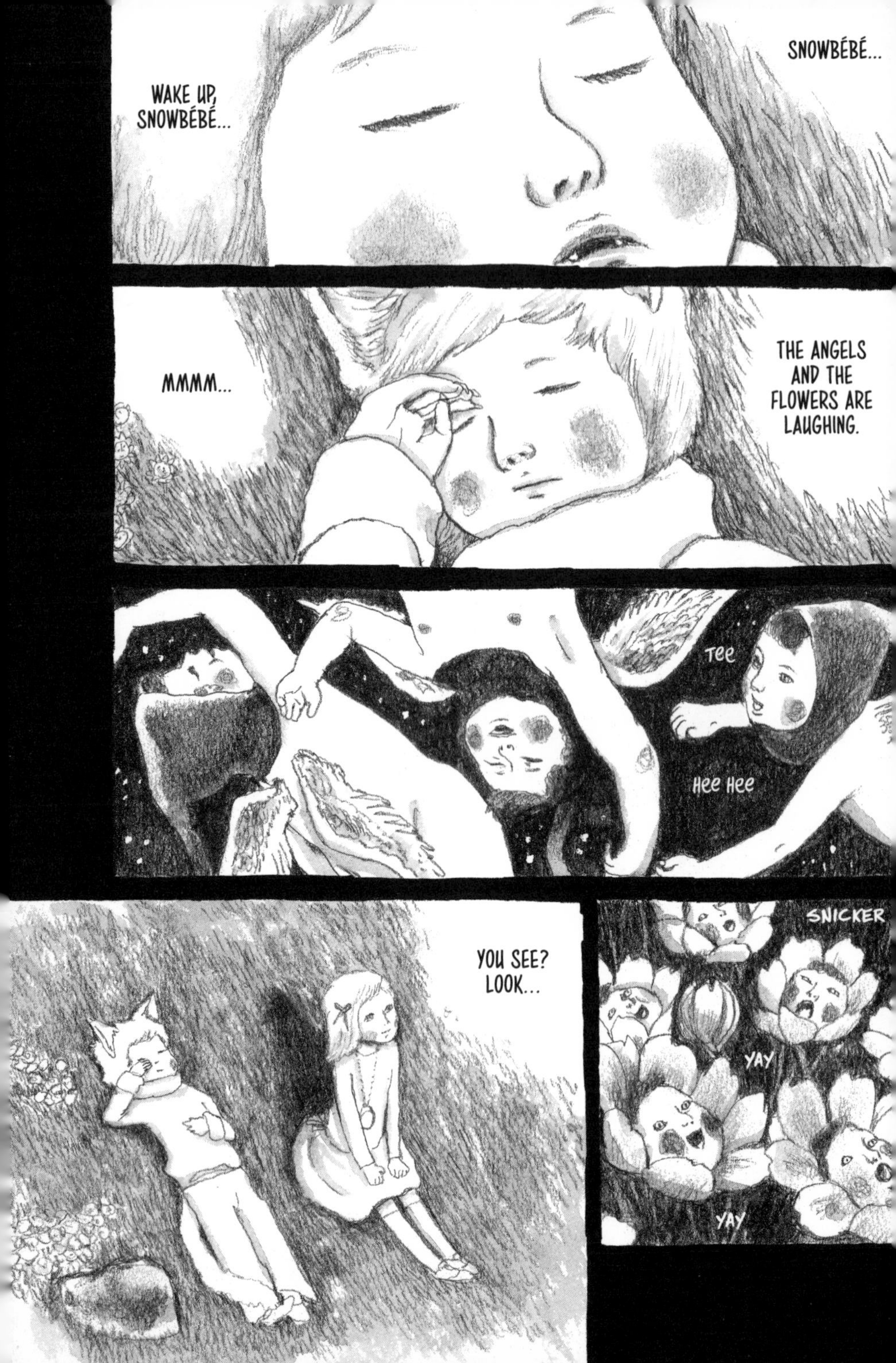
SNOWBÉBÉ...
WAKE UP, SNOWBÉBÉ...
THE ANGELS AND THE FLOWERS ARE LAUGHING.
MMMM...
Tee
Hee Hee
SNICKER
YAY
YAY
YOU SEE? LOOK...

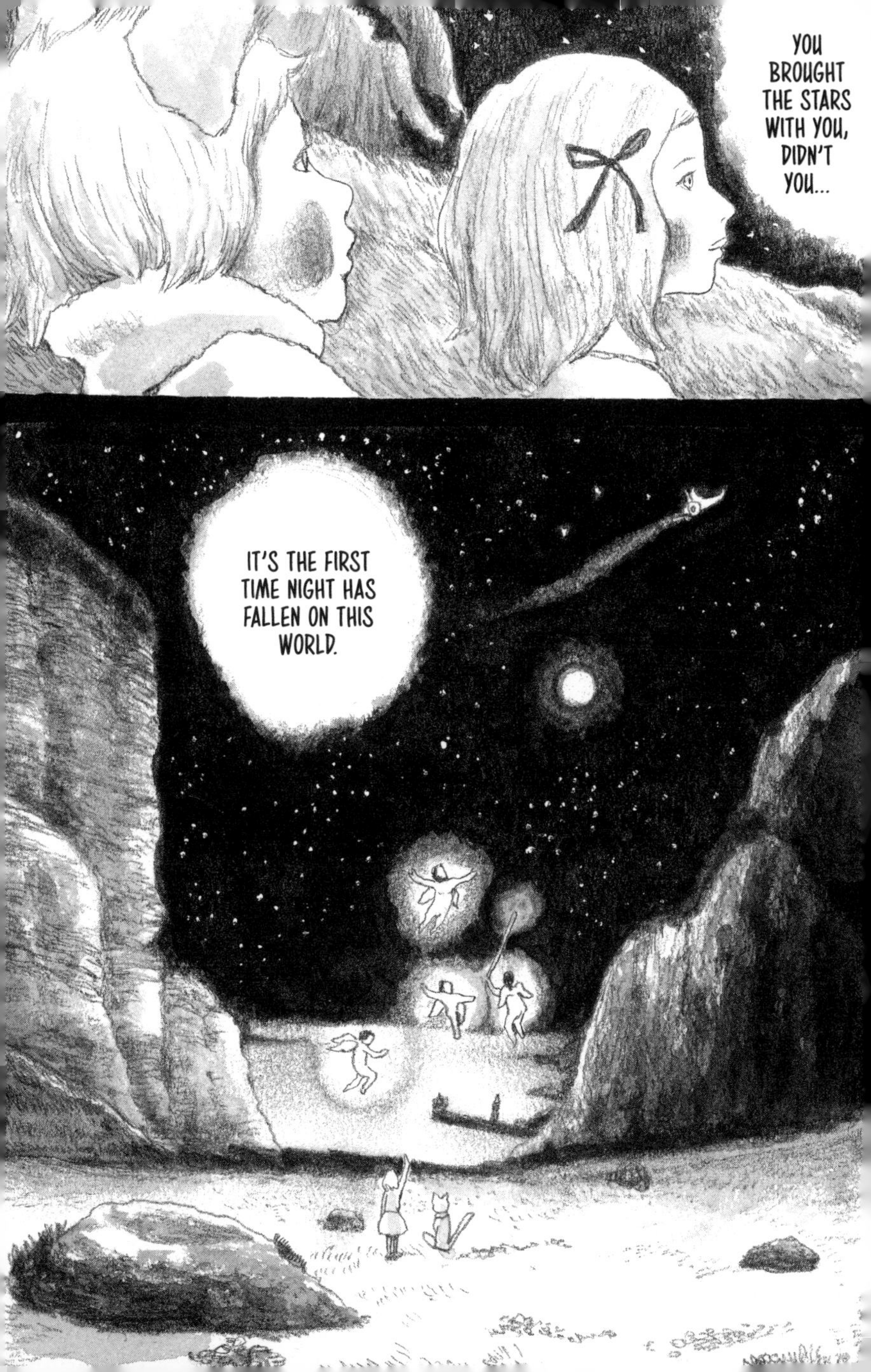
YOU BROUGHT THE STARS WITH YOU, DIDN'T YOU...
IT'S THE FIRST TIME NIGHT HAS FALLEN ON THIS WORLD.

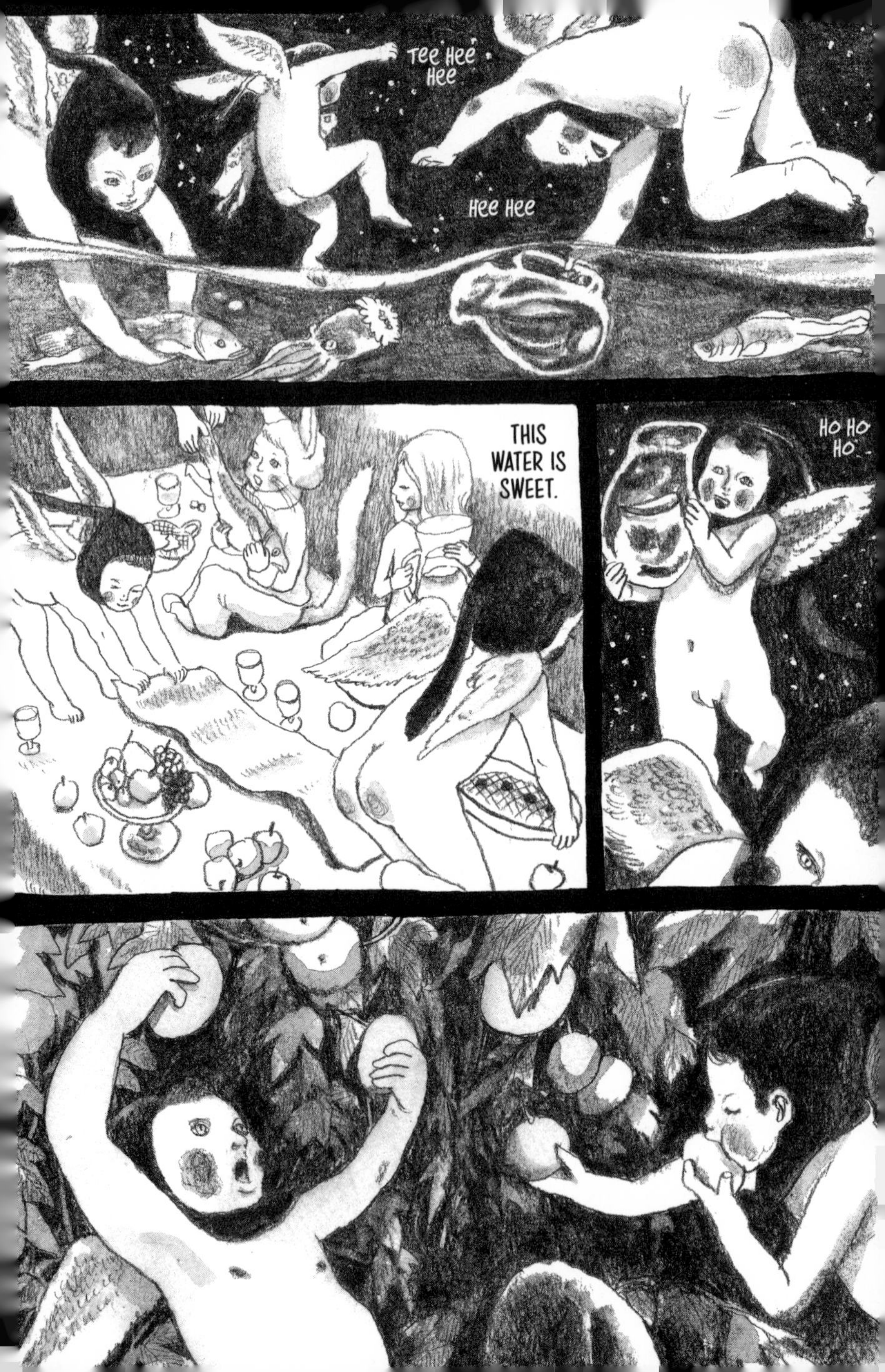
TEE HEE HEE
HEE HEE
HO HO HO
THIS WATER IS SWEET.

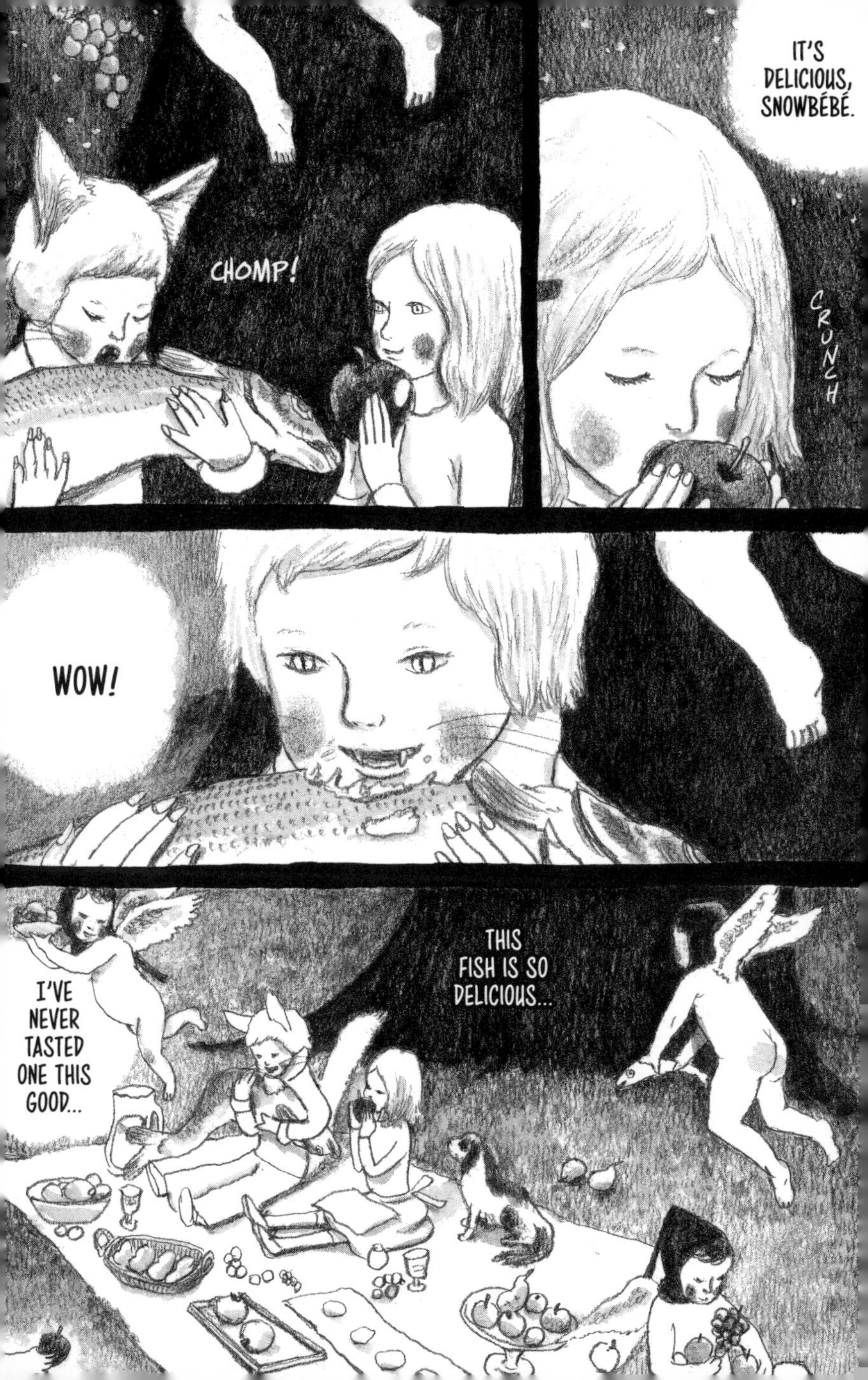
IT'S DELICIOUS, SNOWBÉBÉ.
CRUNCH
CHOMP!
WOW!
THIS FISH IS SO DELICIOUS...
I'VE NEVER TASTED ONE THIS GOOD...

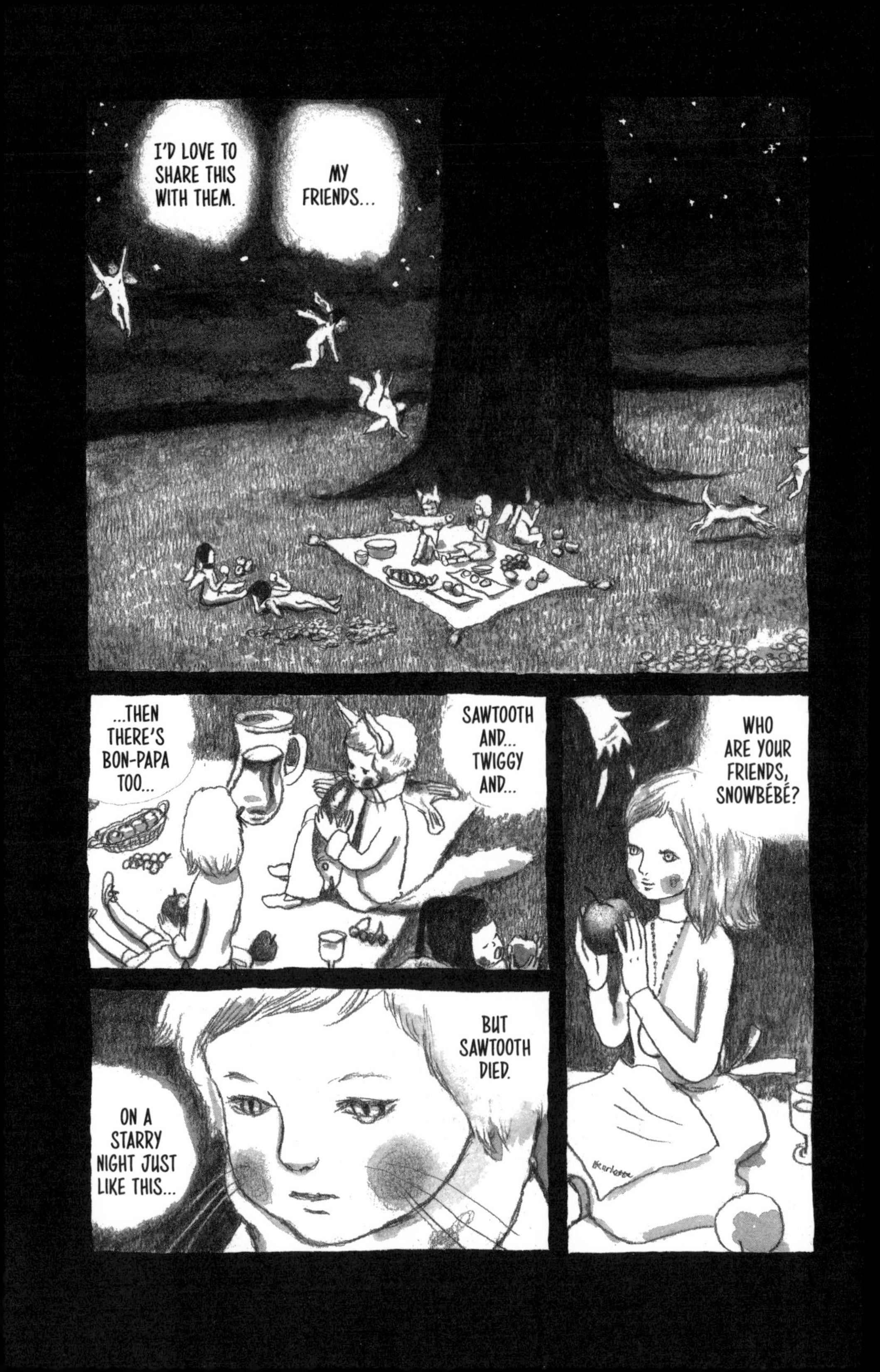
MY FRIENDS…
I'D LOVE TO SHARE THIS WITH THEM.
WHO ARE YOUR FRIENDS, SNOWBÉBÉ?
SAWTOOTH AND… TWIGGY AND…
…THEN THERE'S BON-PAPA TOO…
BUT SAWTOOTH DIED.
ON A STARRY NIGHT JUST LIKE THIS…

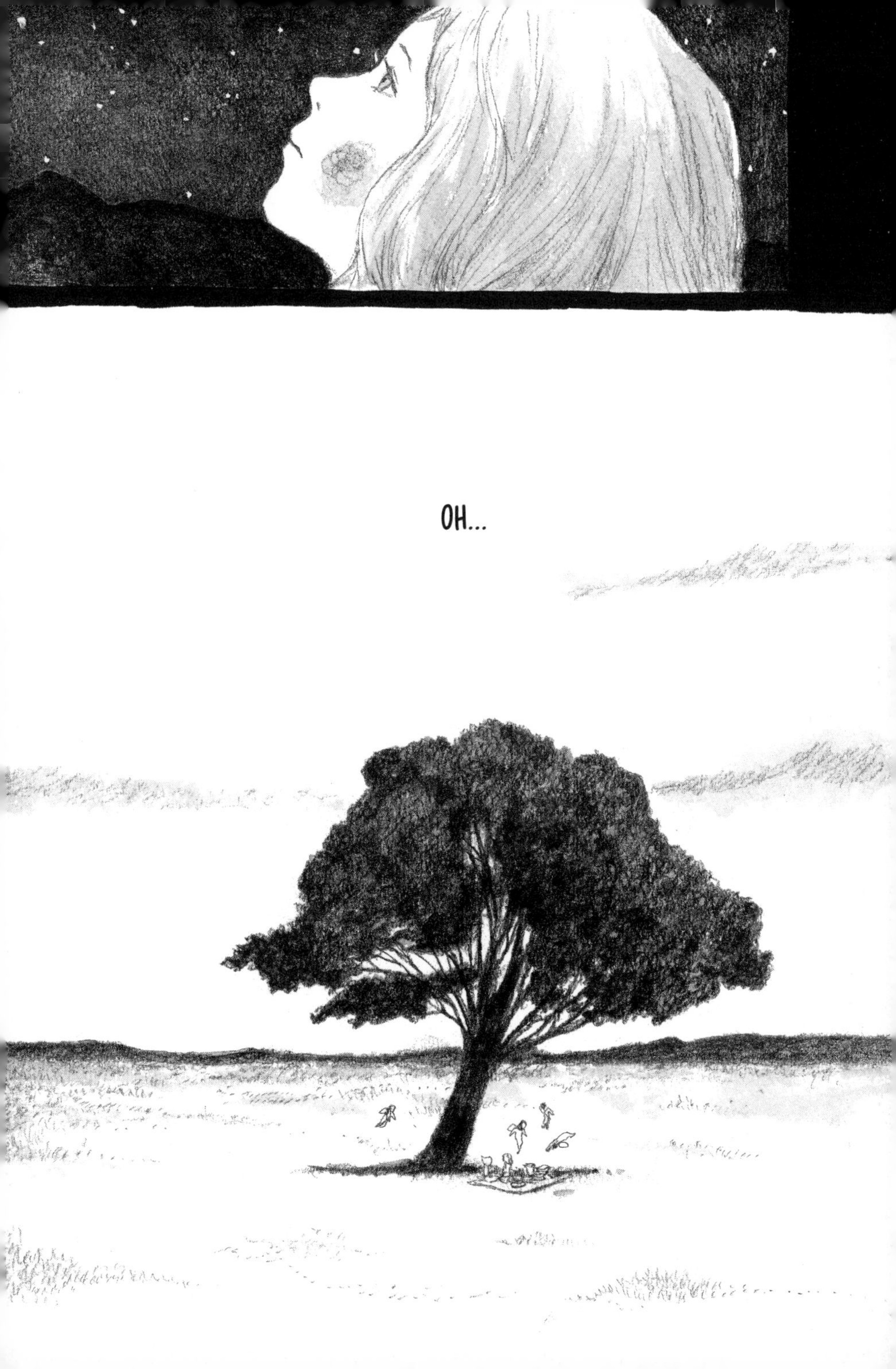
OH...

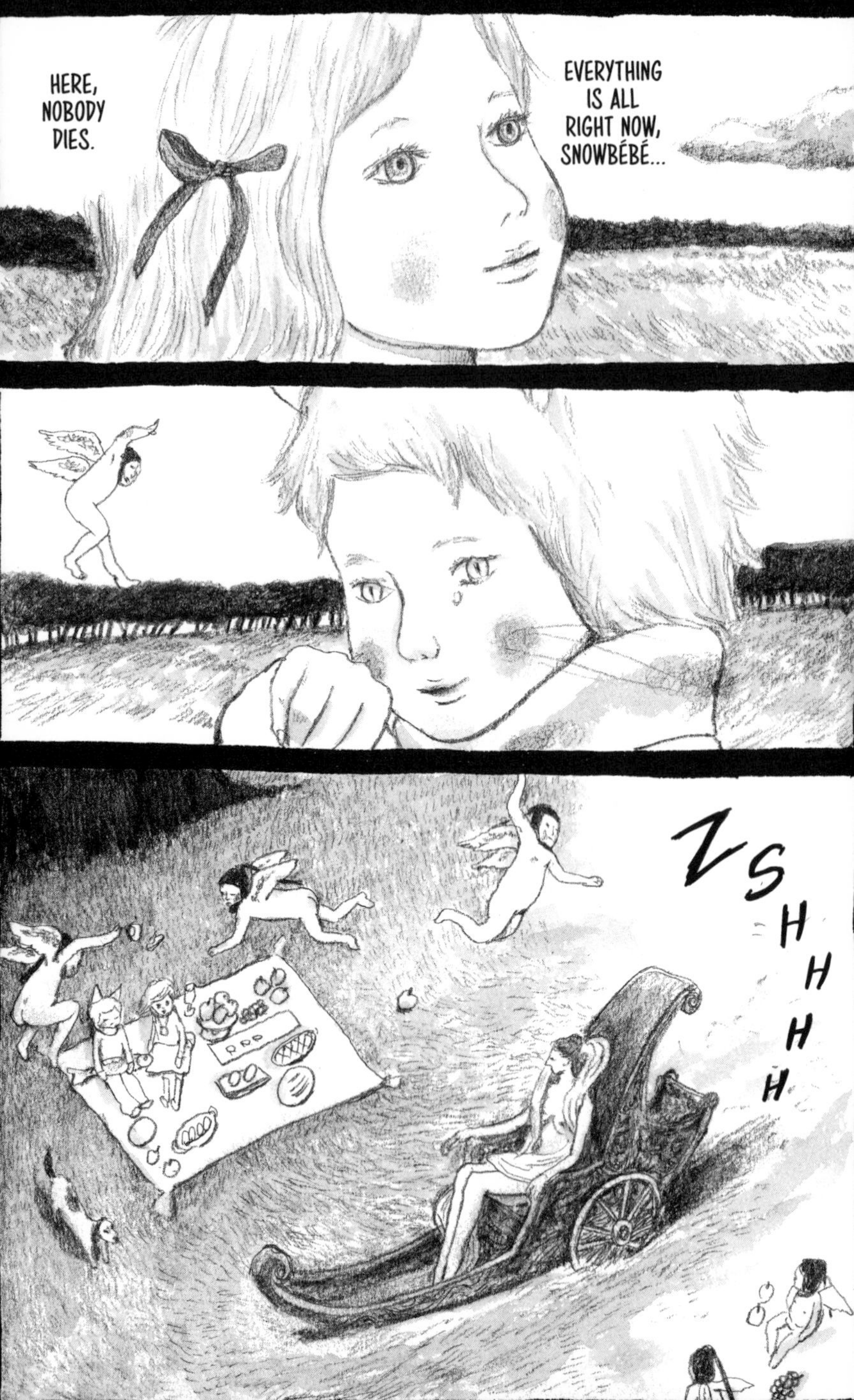
EVERYTHING IS ALL RIGHT NOW, SNOWBÉBÉ...
HERE, NOBODY DIES.
ZSHHHHH

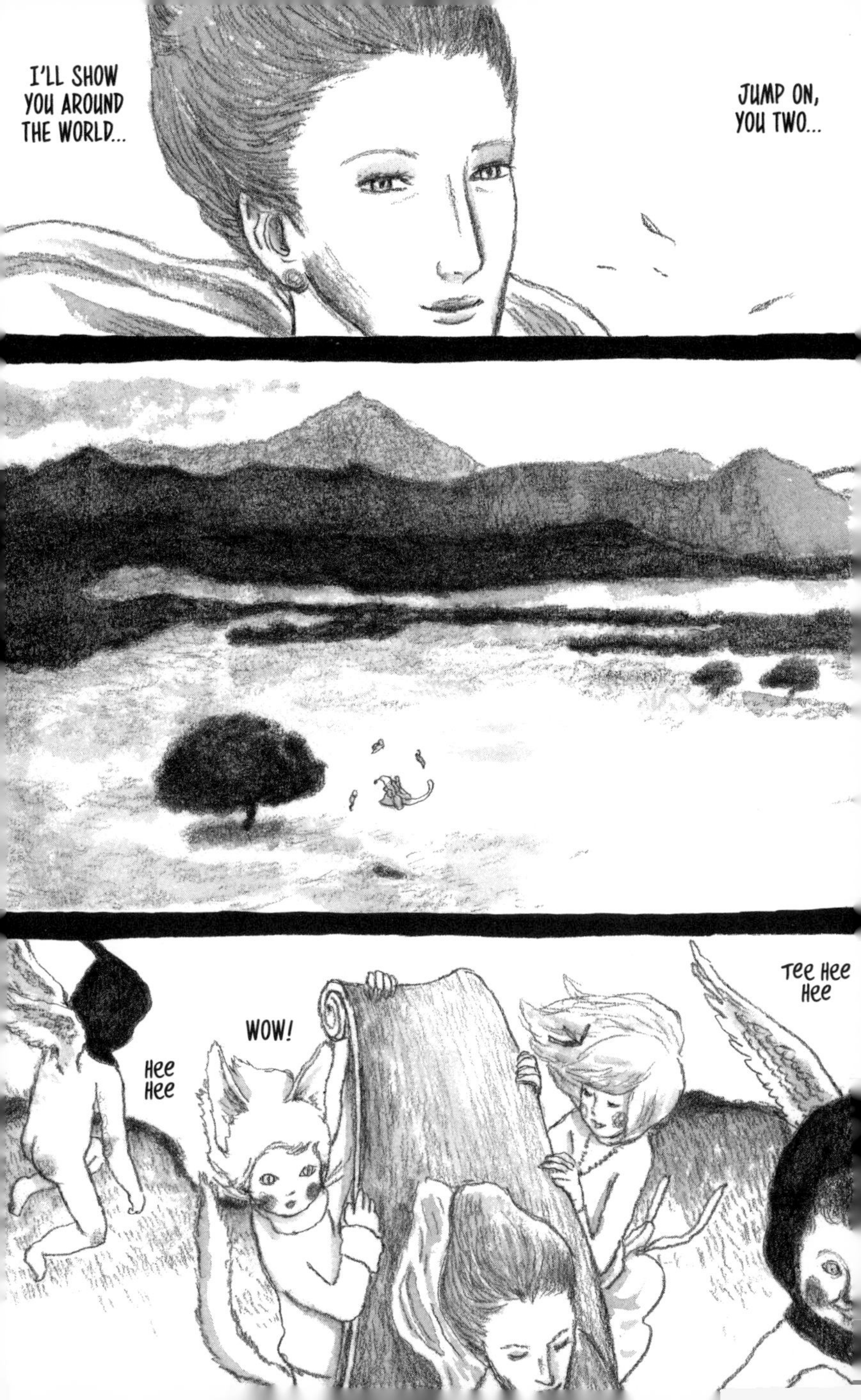
JUMP ON, YOU TWO...
I'LL SHOW YOU AROUND THE WORLD...
Tee Hee Hee
WOW!
Hee Hee

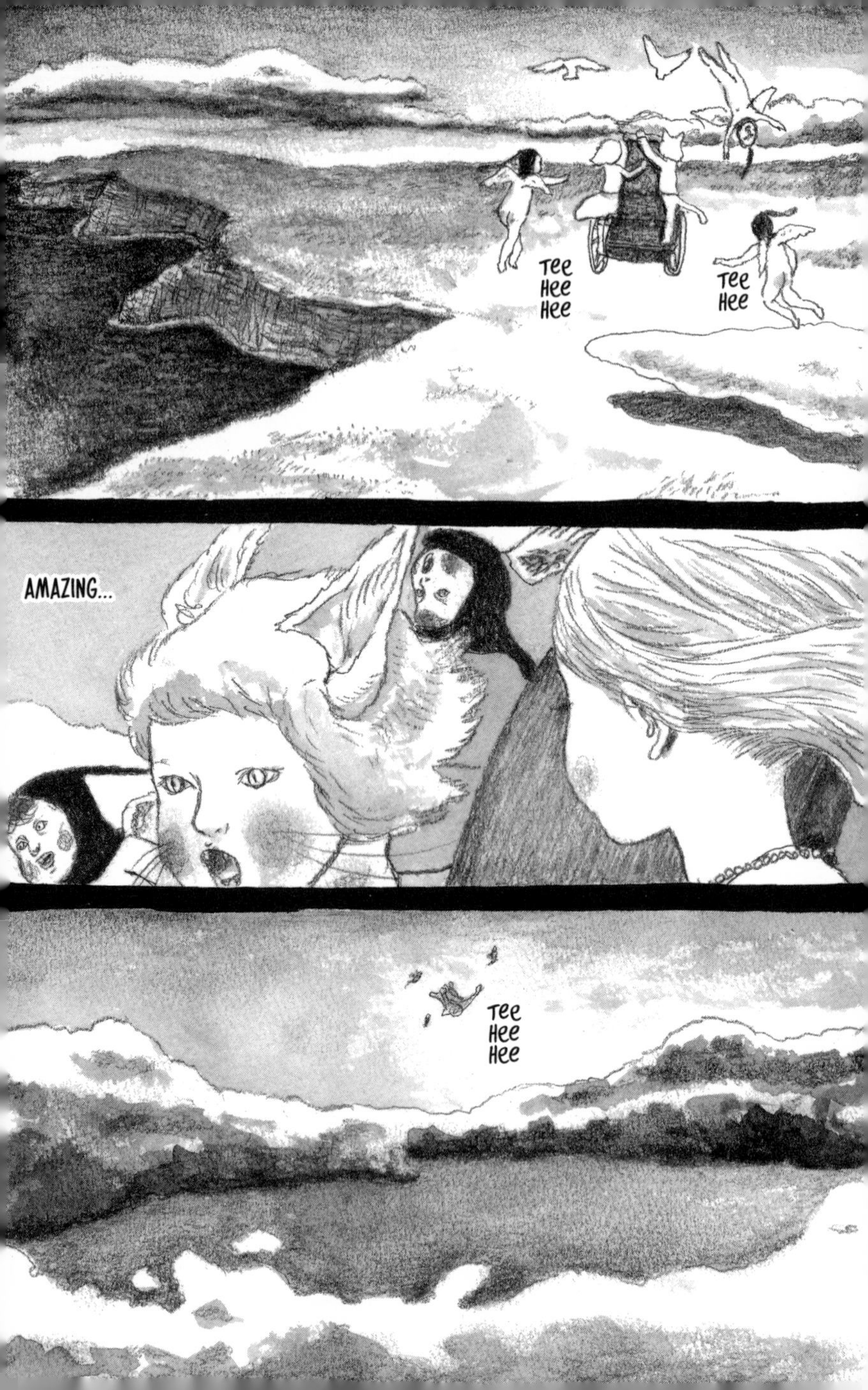
TEE HEE
TEE HEE HEE
AMAZING...
TEE HEE HEE

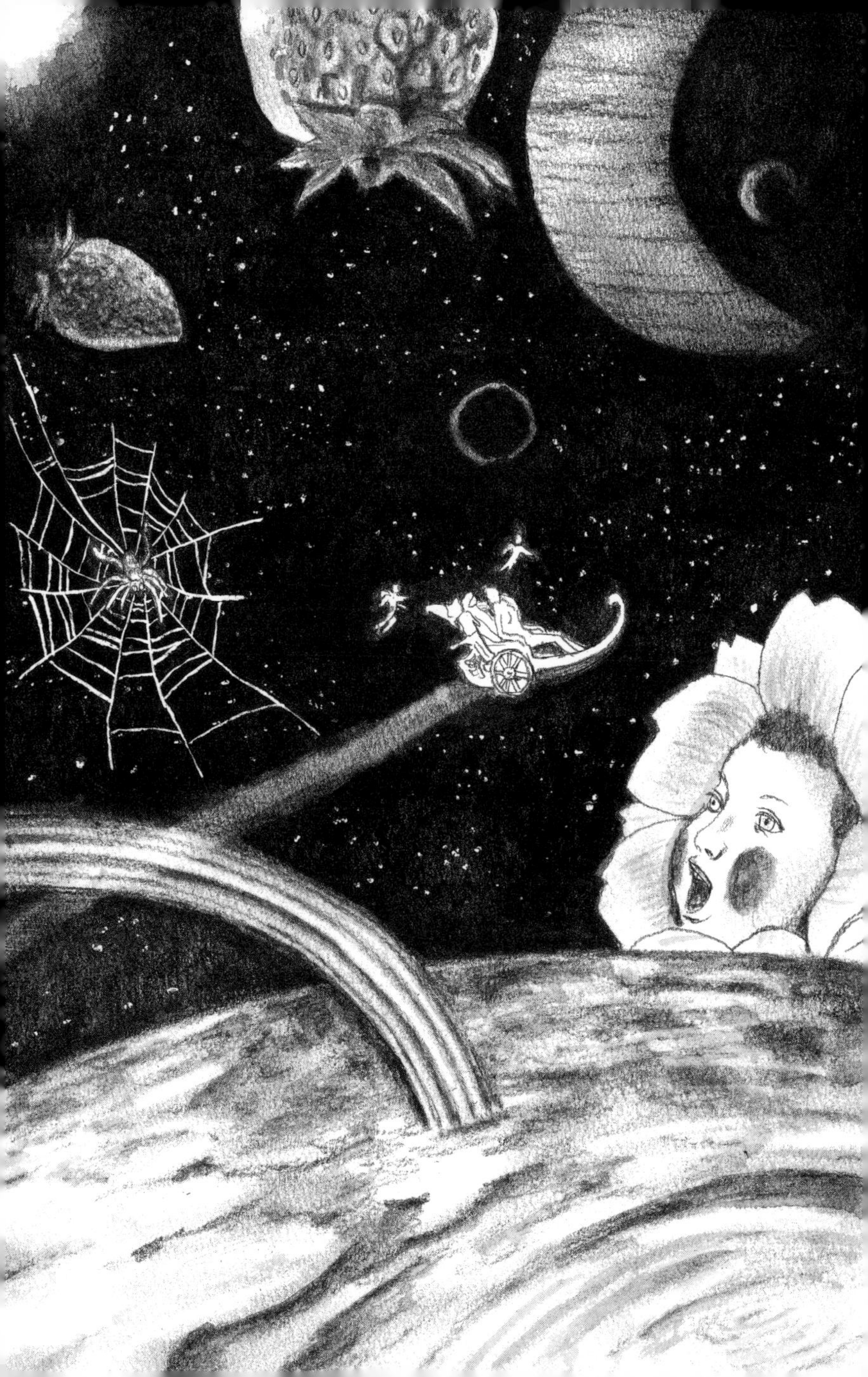

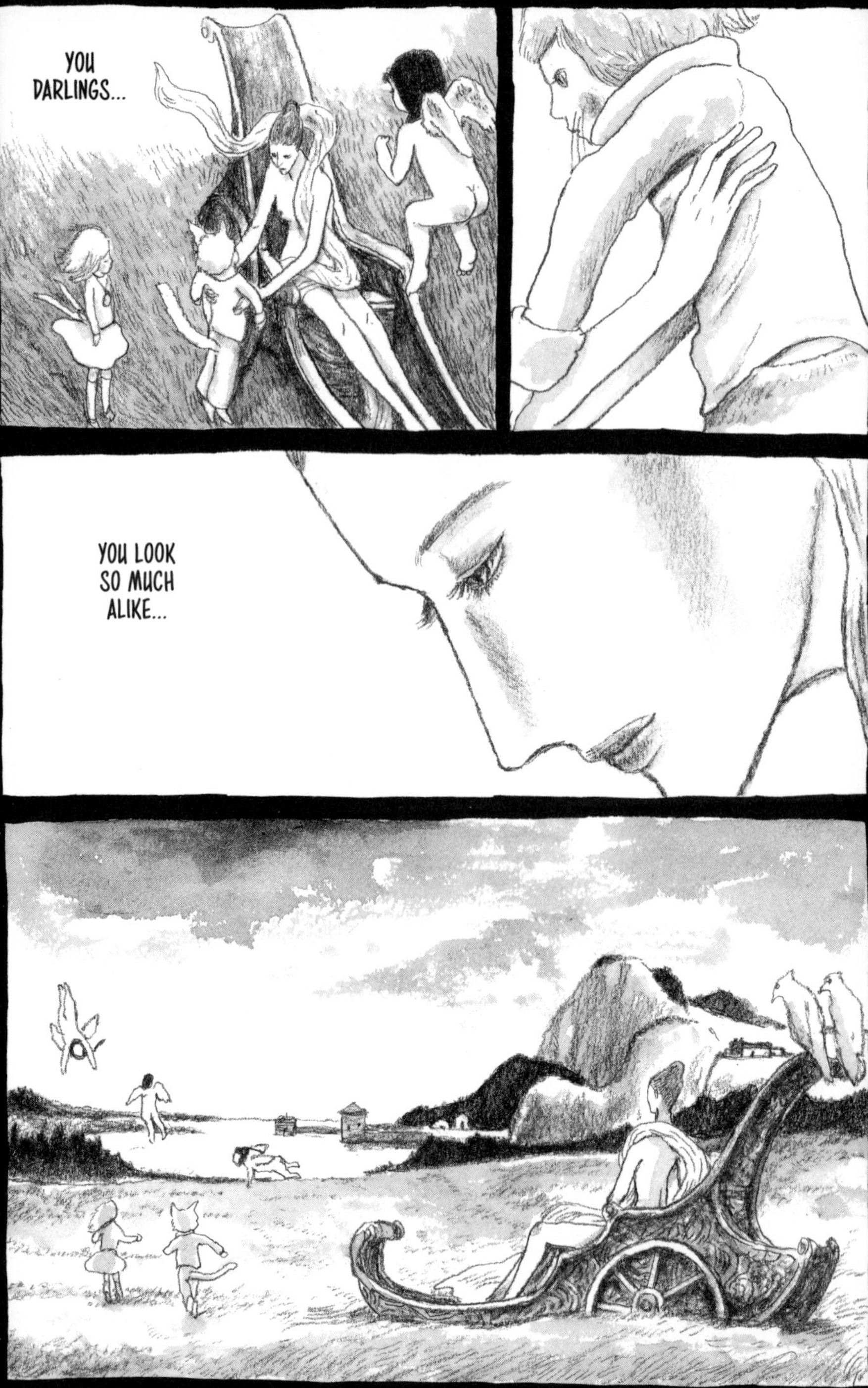
YOU DARLINGS...
YOU LOOK SO MUCH ALIKE...

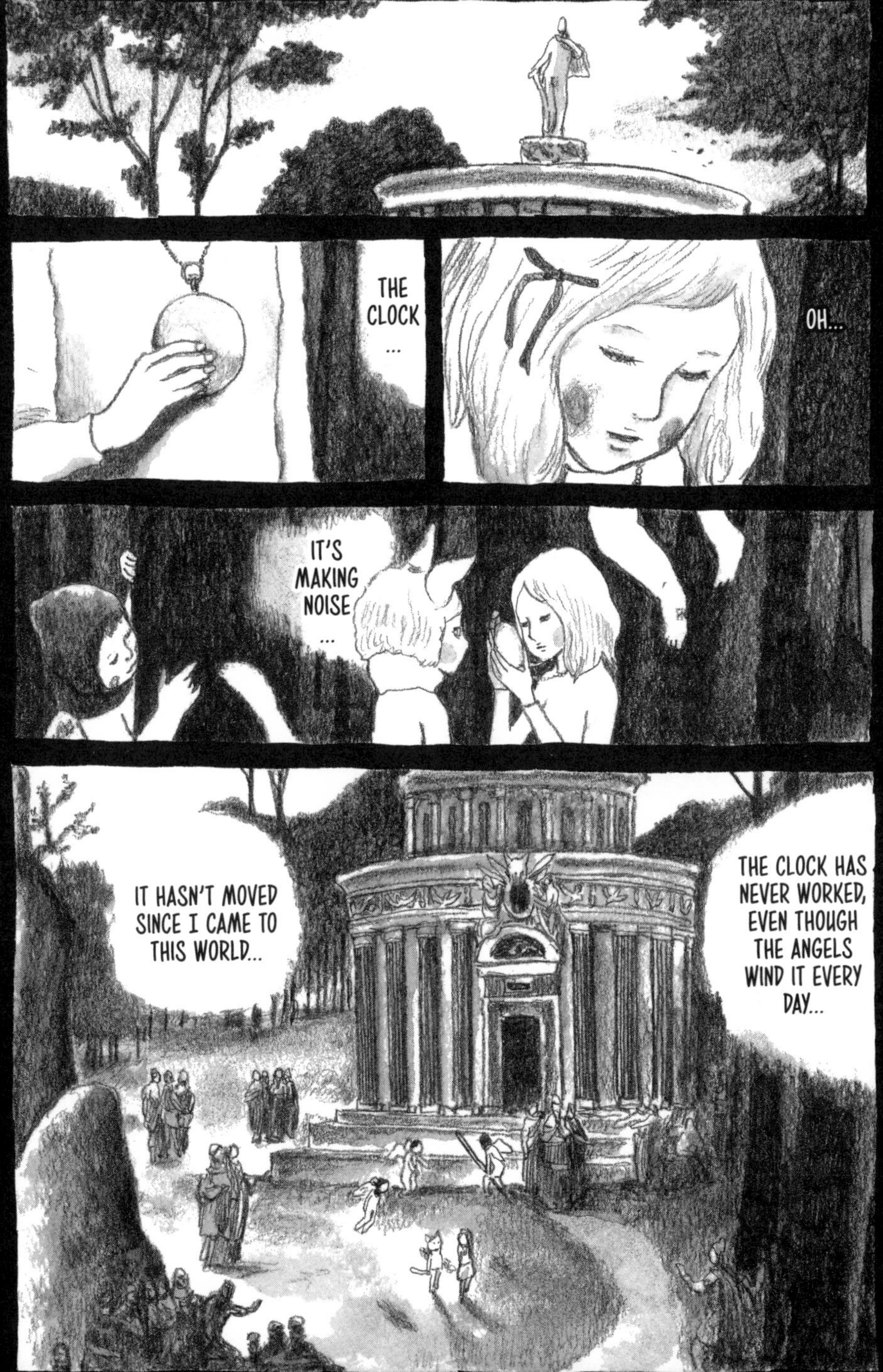
OH...
THE CLOCK ...
IT'S MAKING NOISE ...
THE CLOCK HAS NEVER WORKED, EVEN THOUGH THE ANGELS WIND IT EVERY DAY...
IT HASN'T MOVED SINCE I CAME TO THIS WORLD...

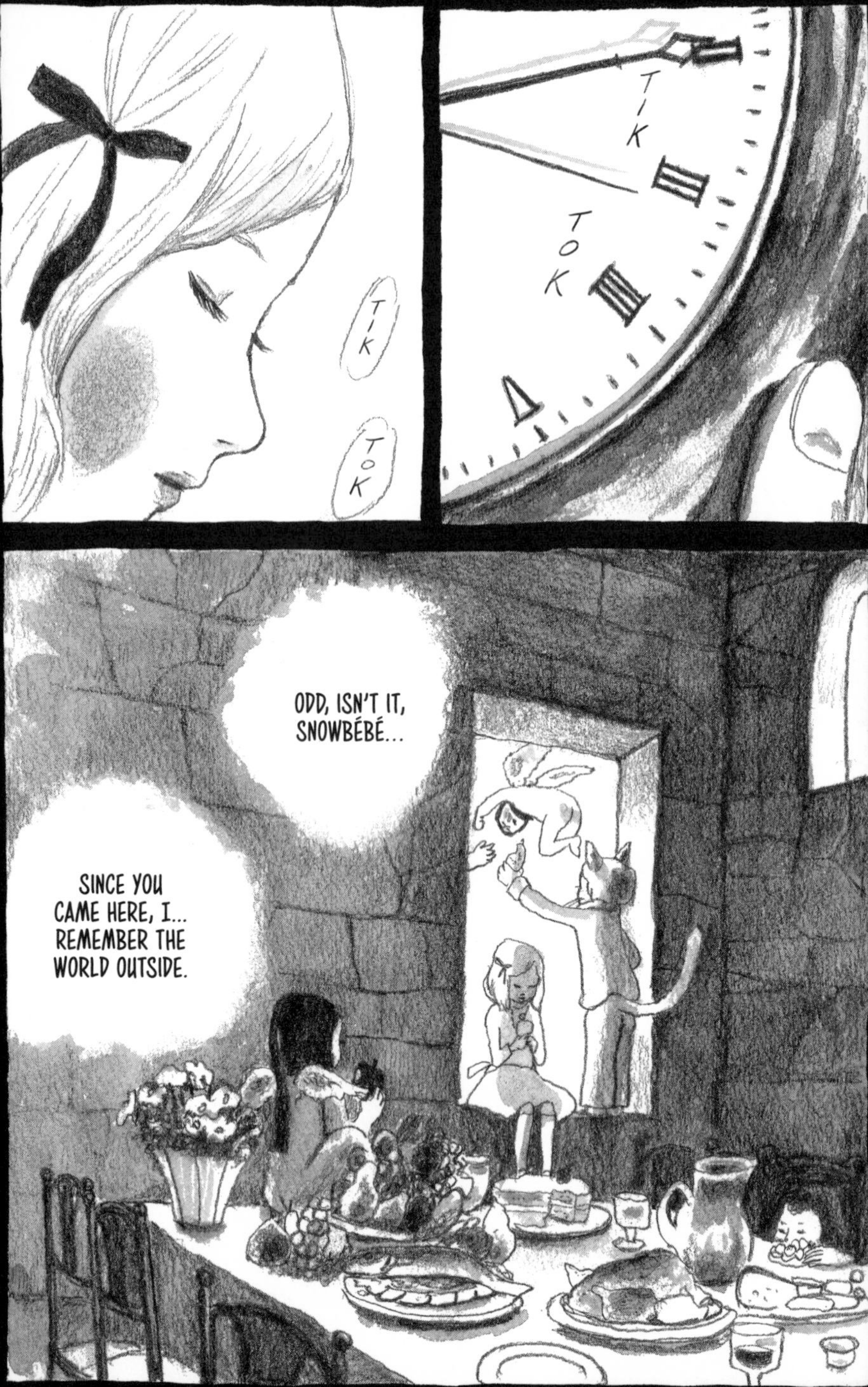
TIK
TOK
TIK
TOK
ODD, ISN'T IT, SNOWBÉBÉ...
SINCE YOU CAME HERE, I... REMEMBER THE WORLD OUTSIDE.

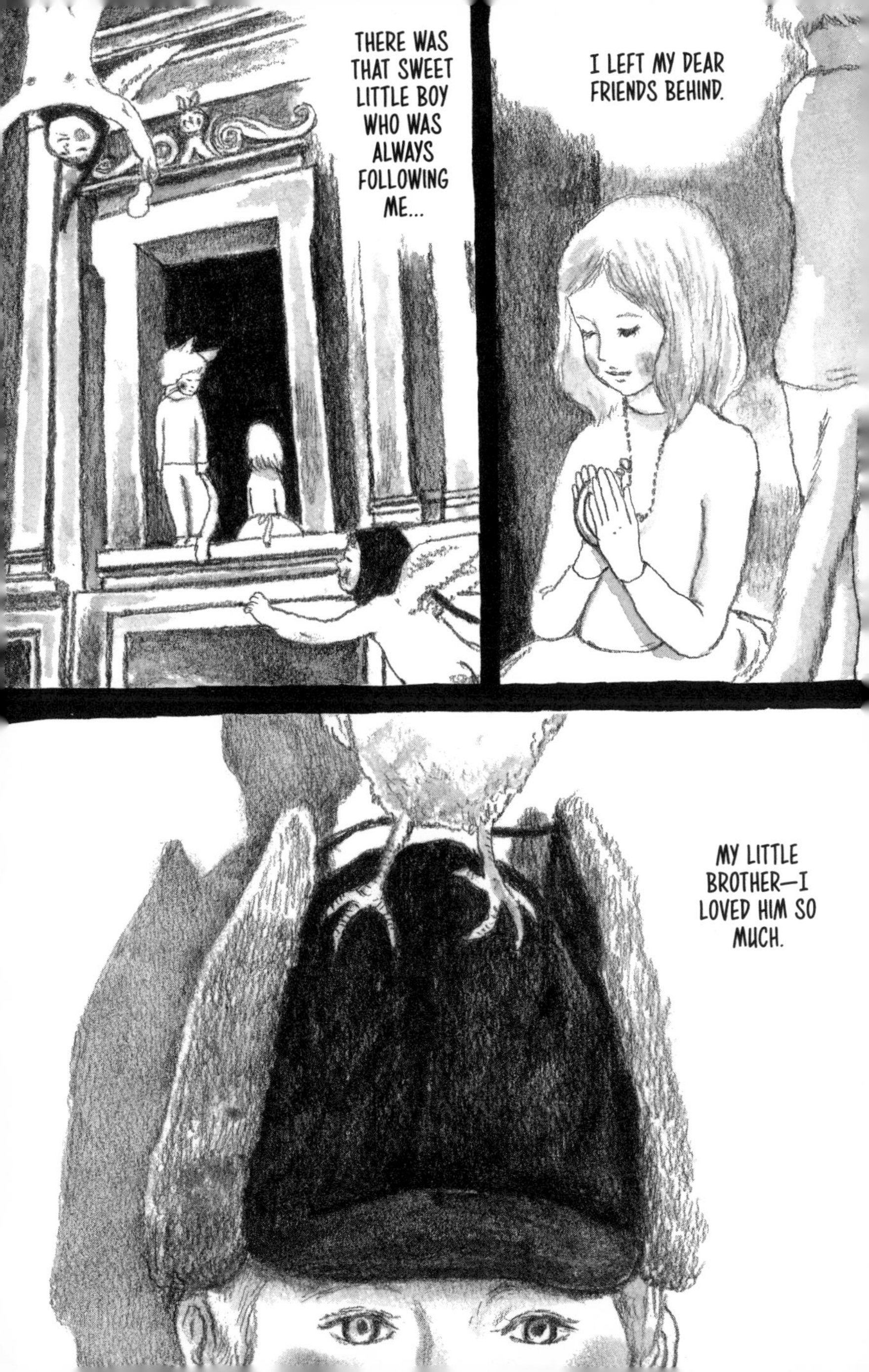
I LEFT MY DEAR FRIENDS BEHIND.
THERE WAS THAT SWEET LITTLE BOY WHO WAS ALWAYS FOLLOWING ME...
MY LITTLE BROTHER—I LOVED HIM SO MUCH.

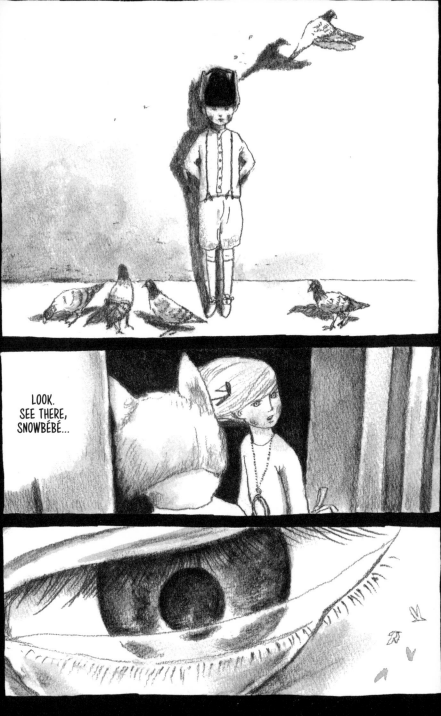

LOOK.
SEE THERE,
SNOWBÉBÉ...

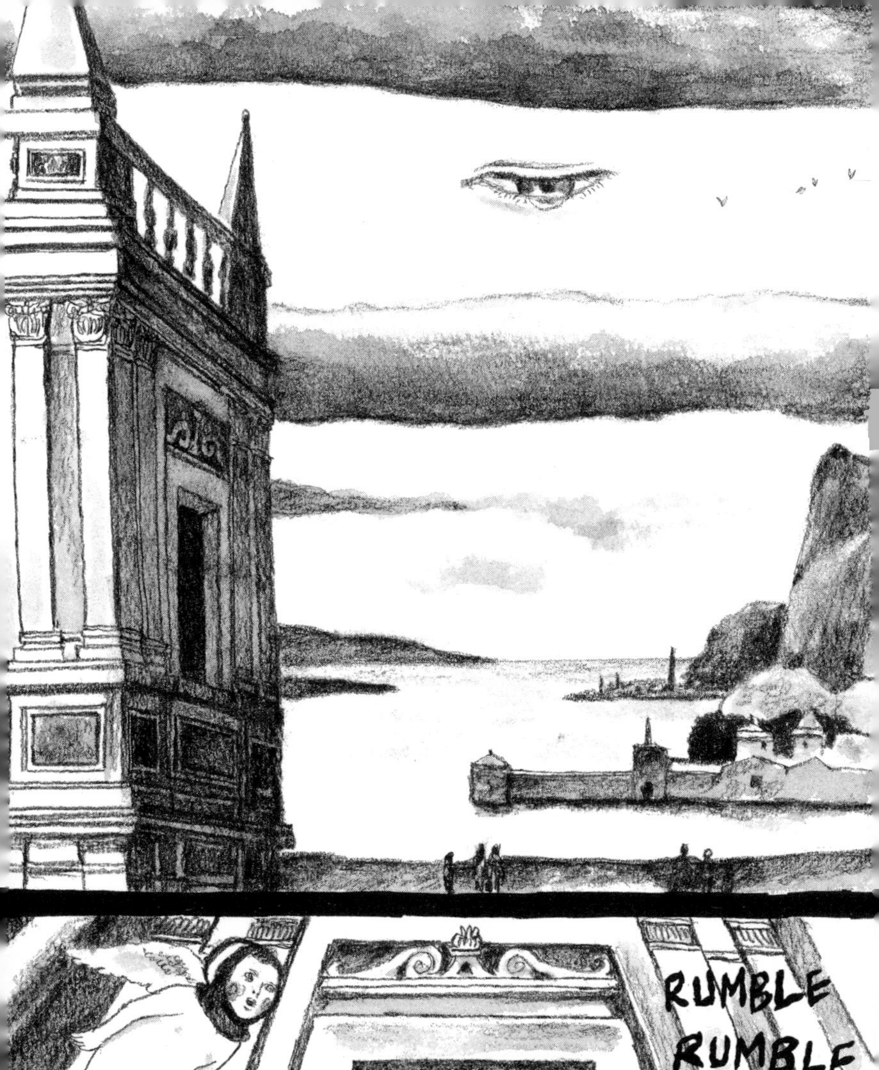

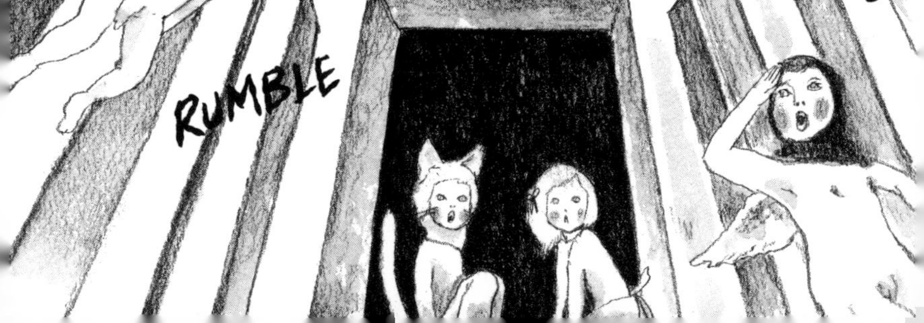
RUMBLE
RUMBLE
RUMBLE

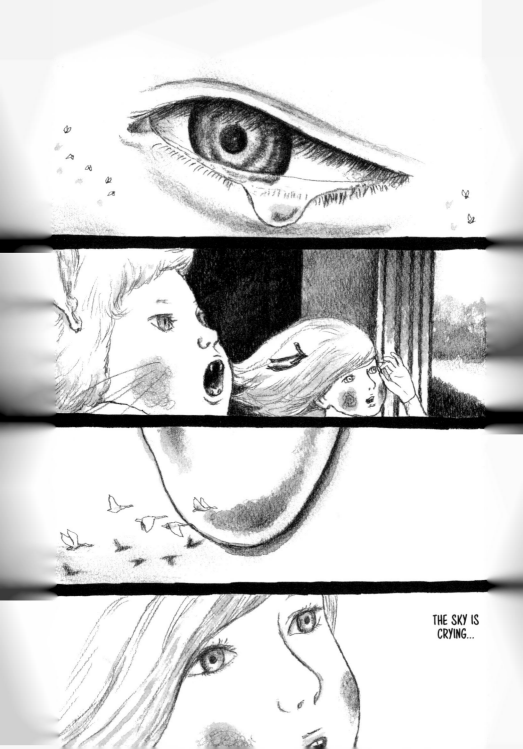

THE SKY IS
CRYING...

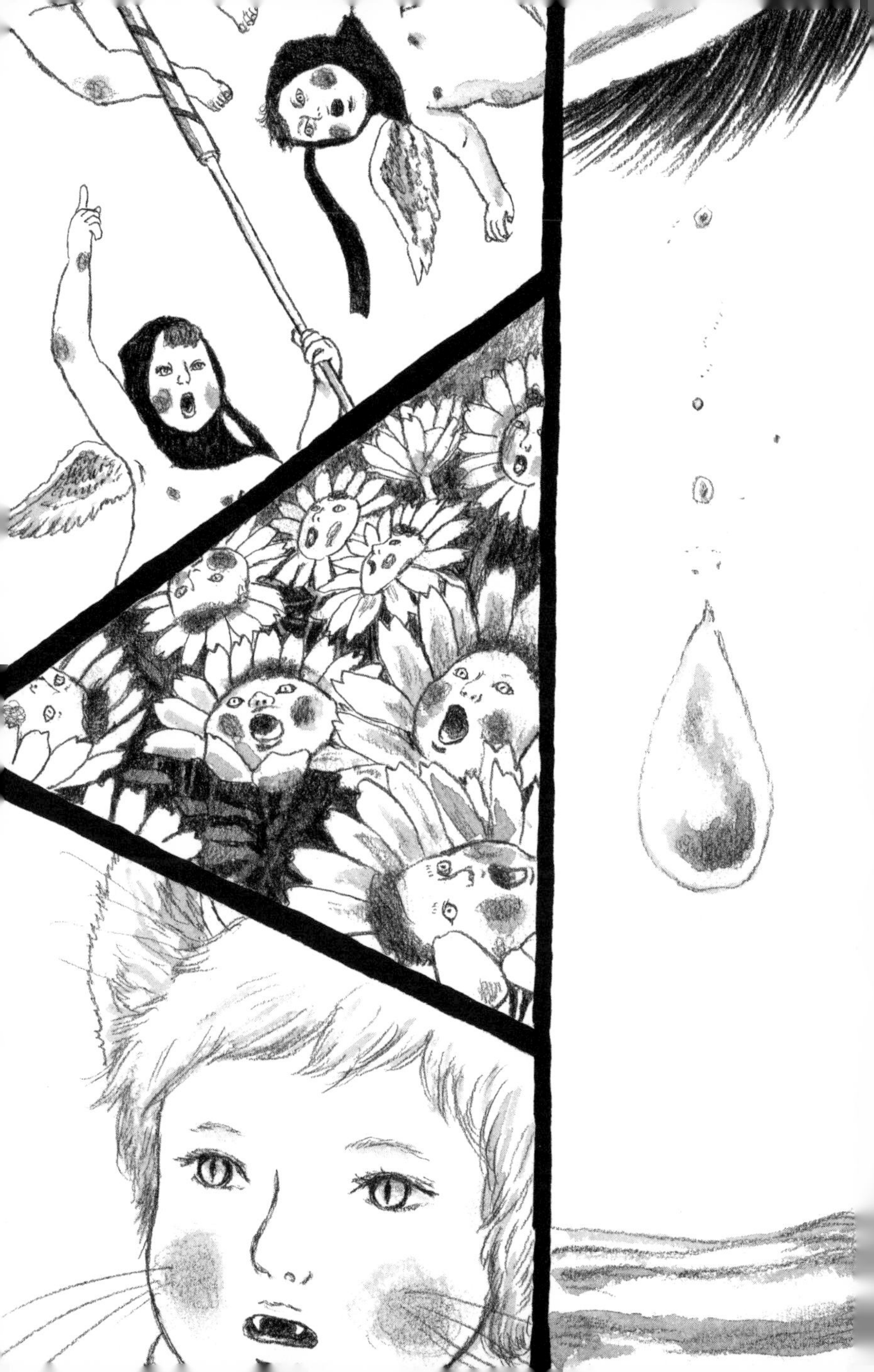

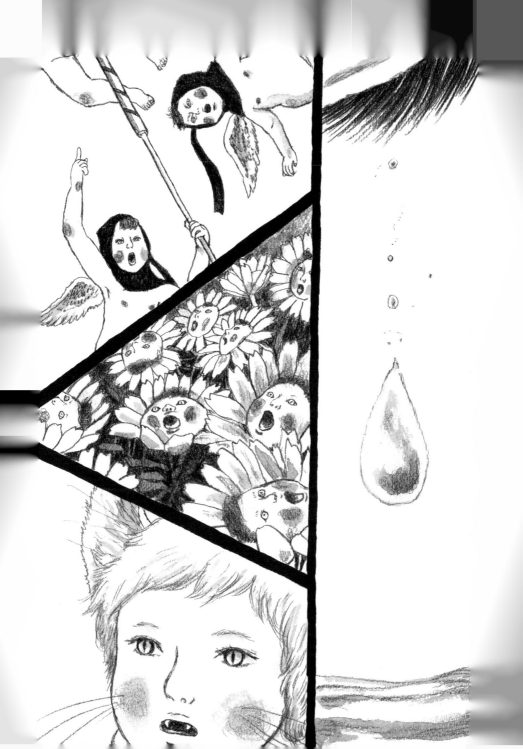

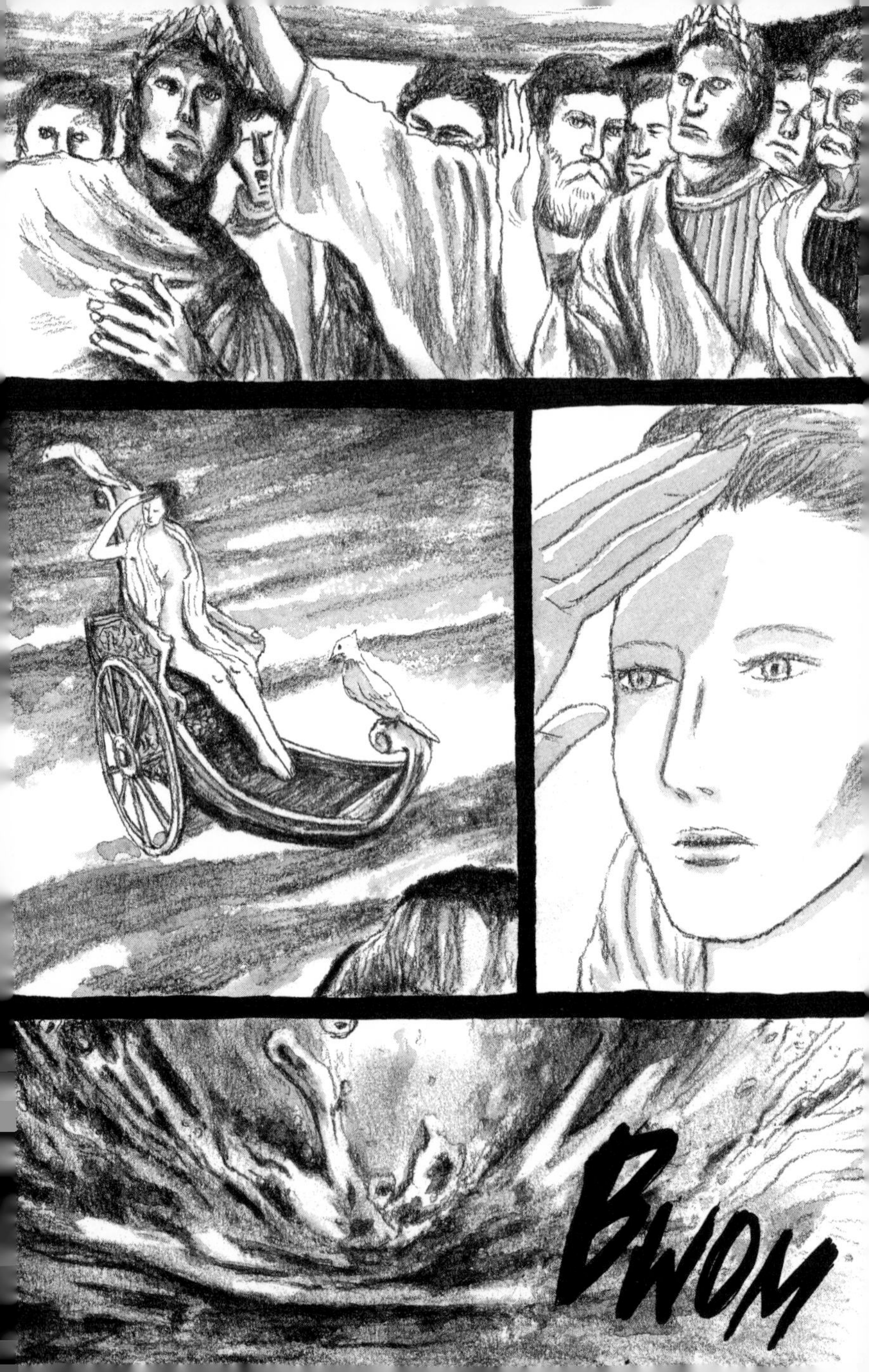
BWOM

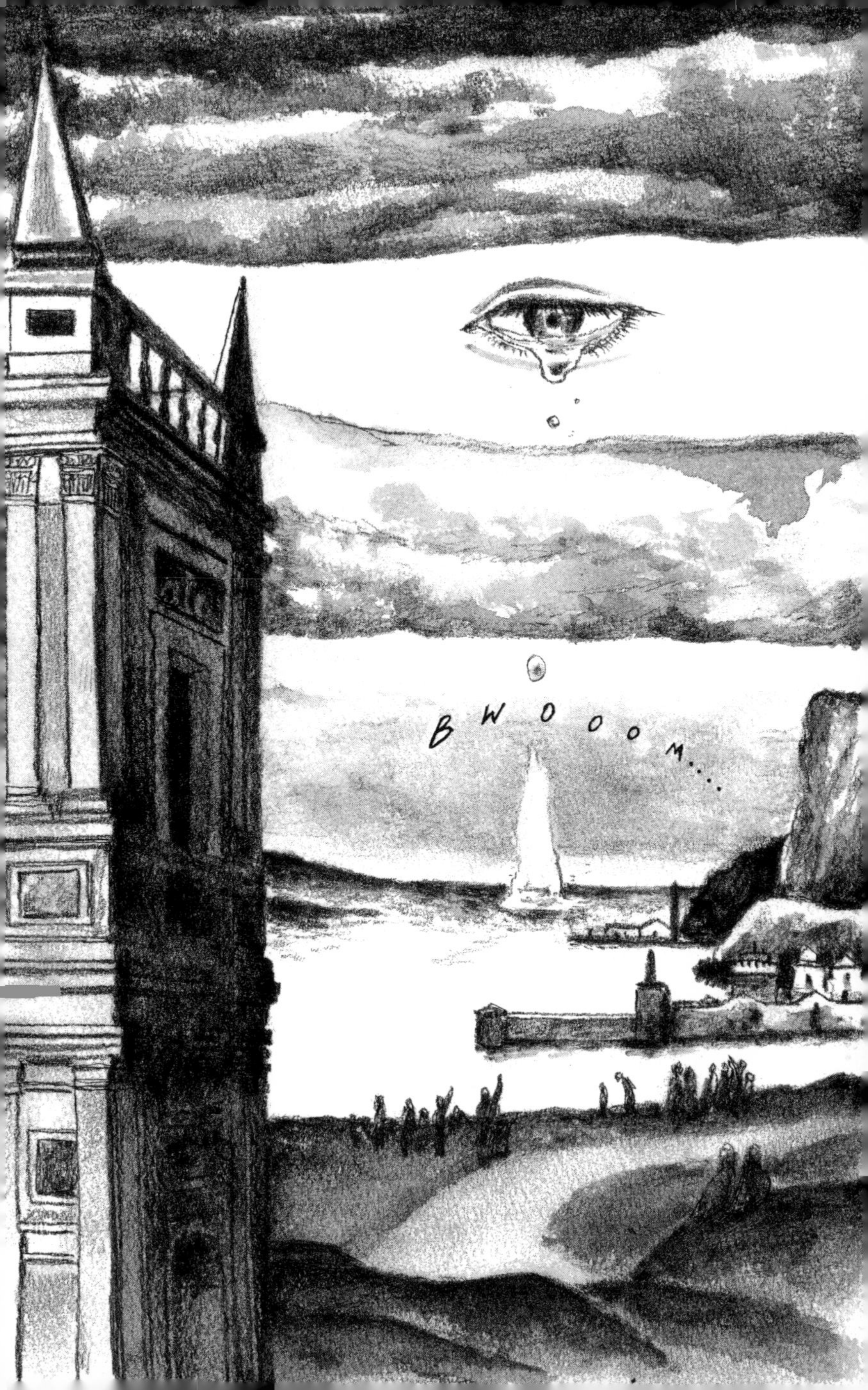
BWOOOM...

CHAPTER 17

The Secret of the White Cat and the Little Girl

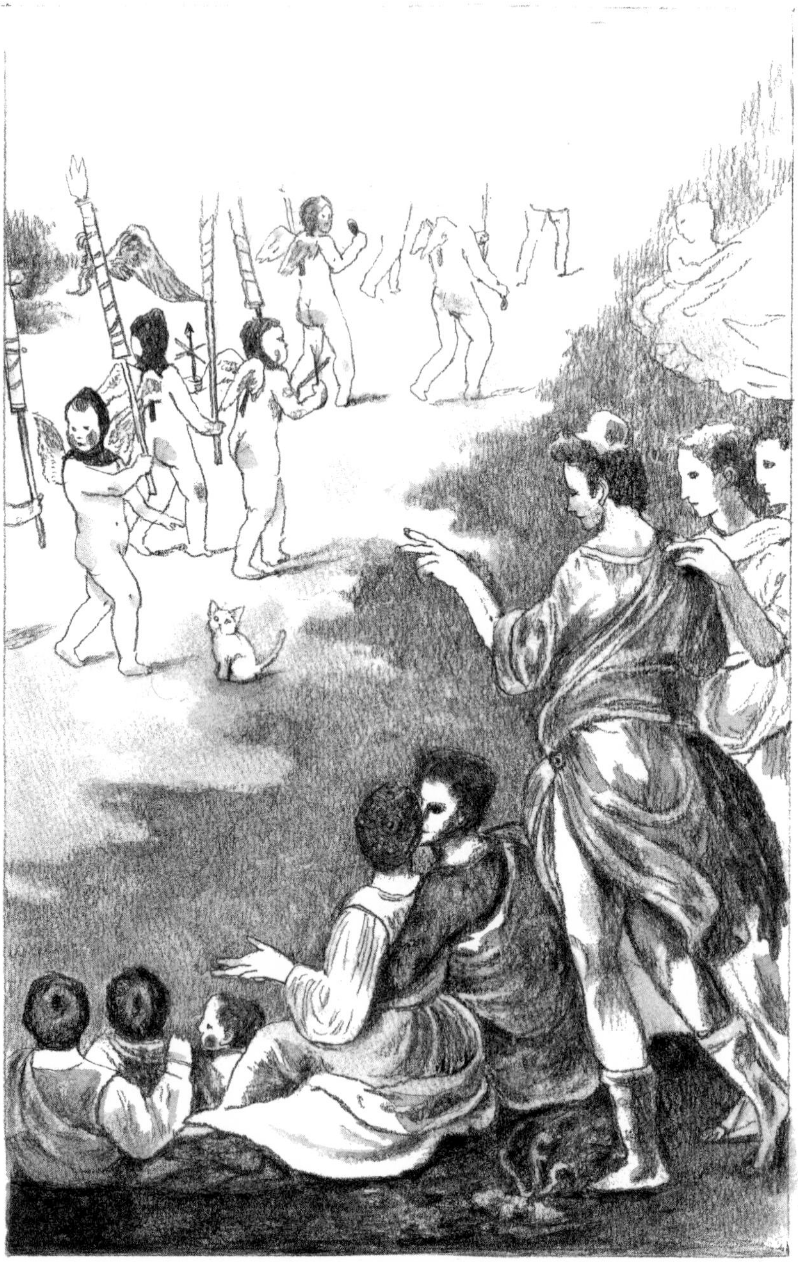

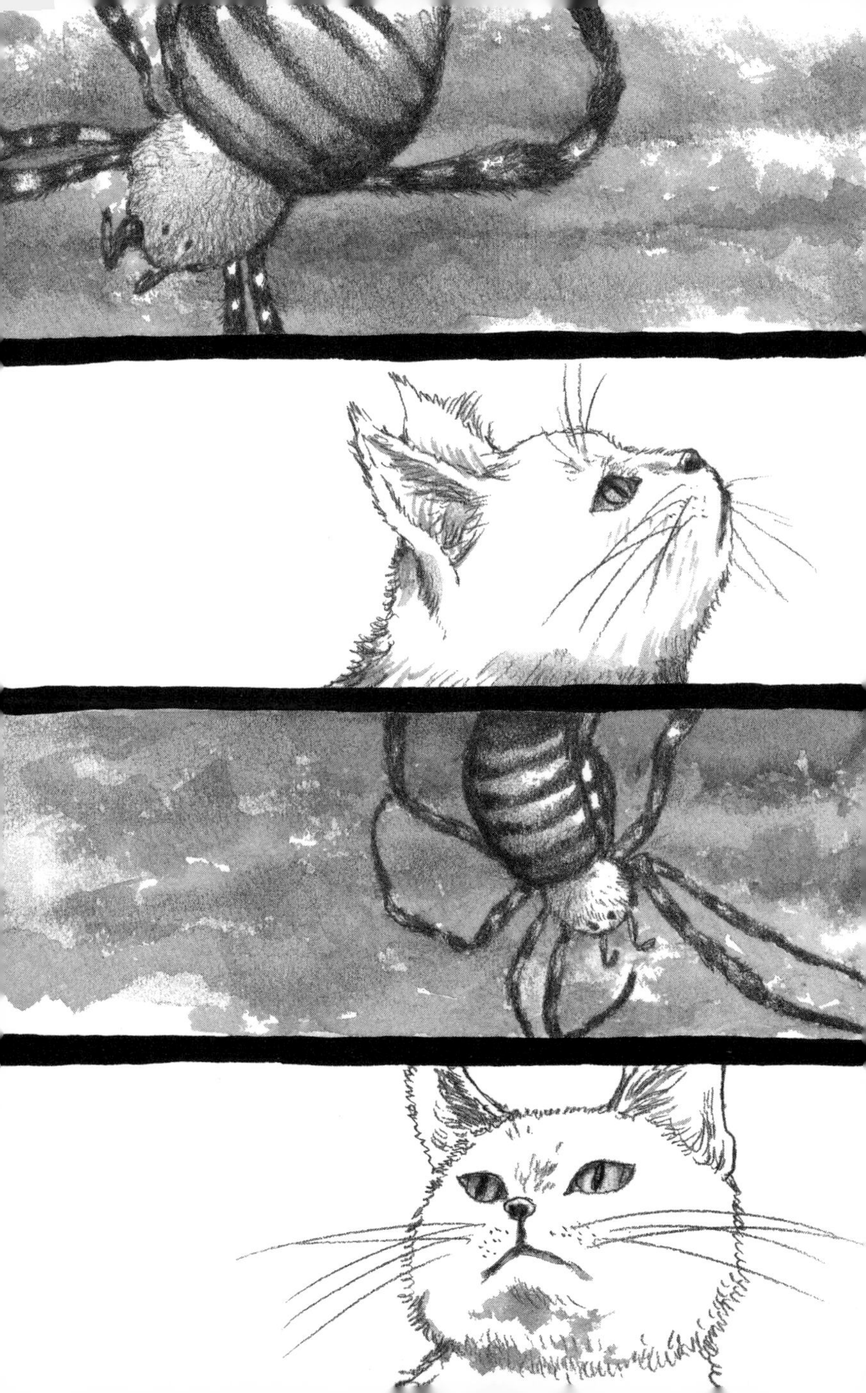

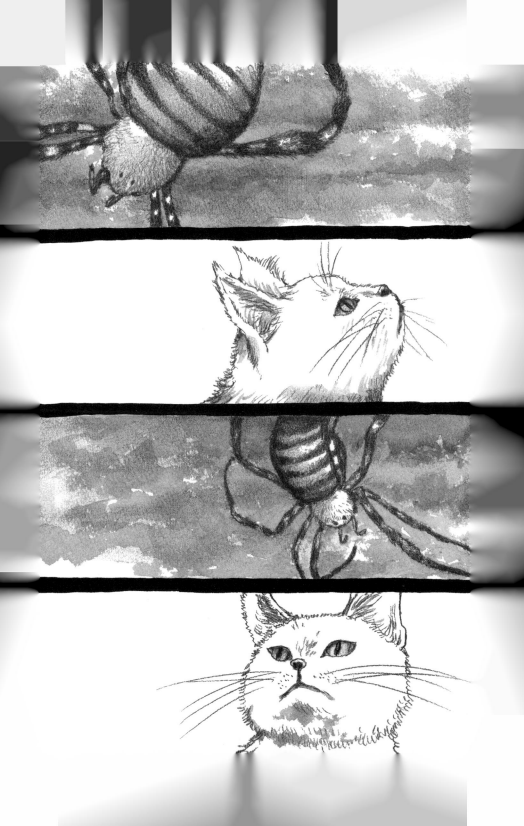

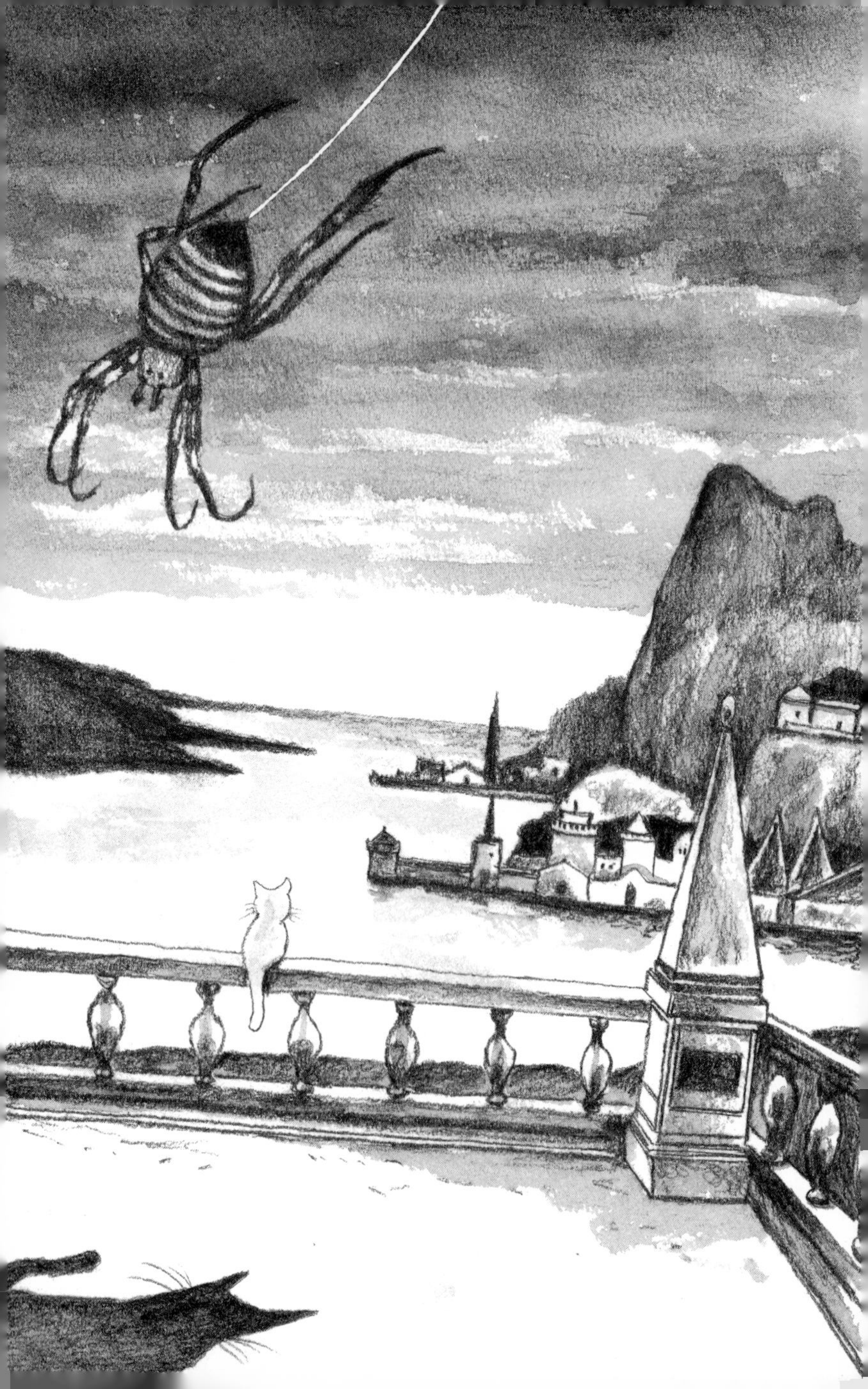

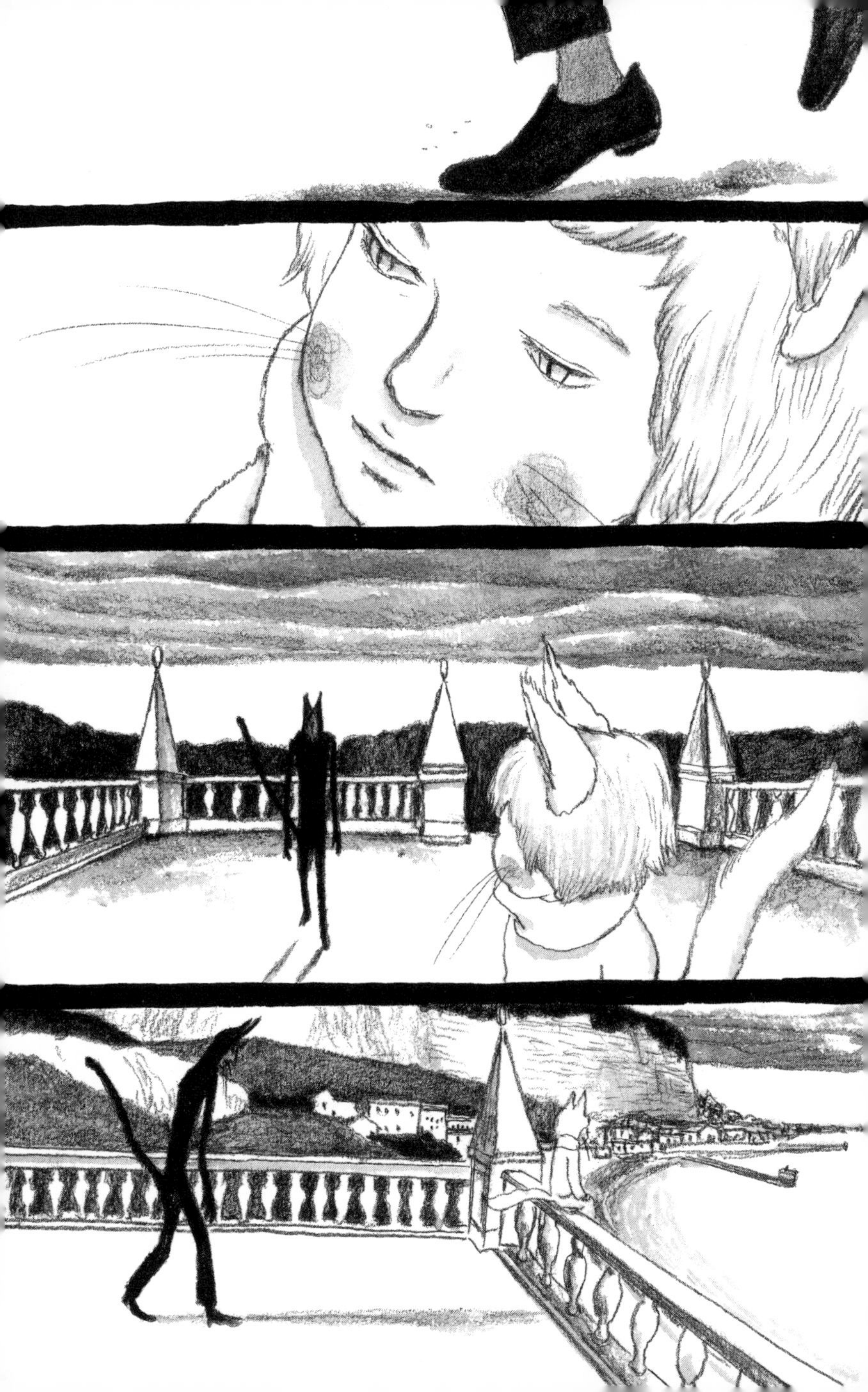

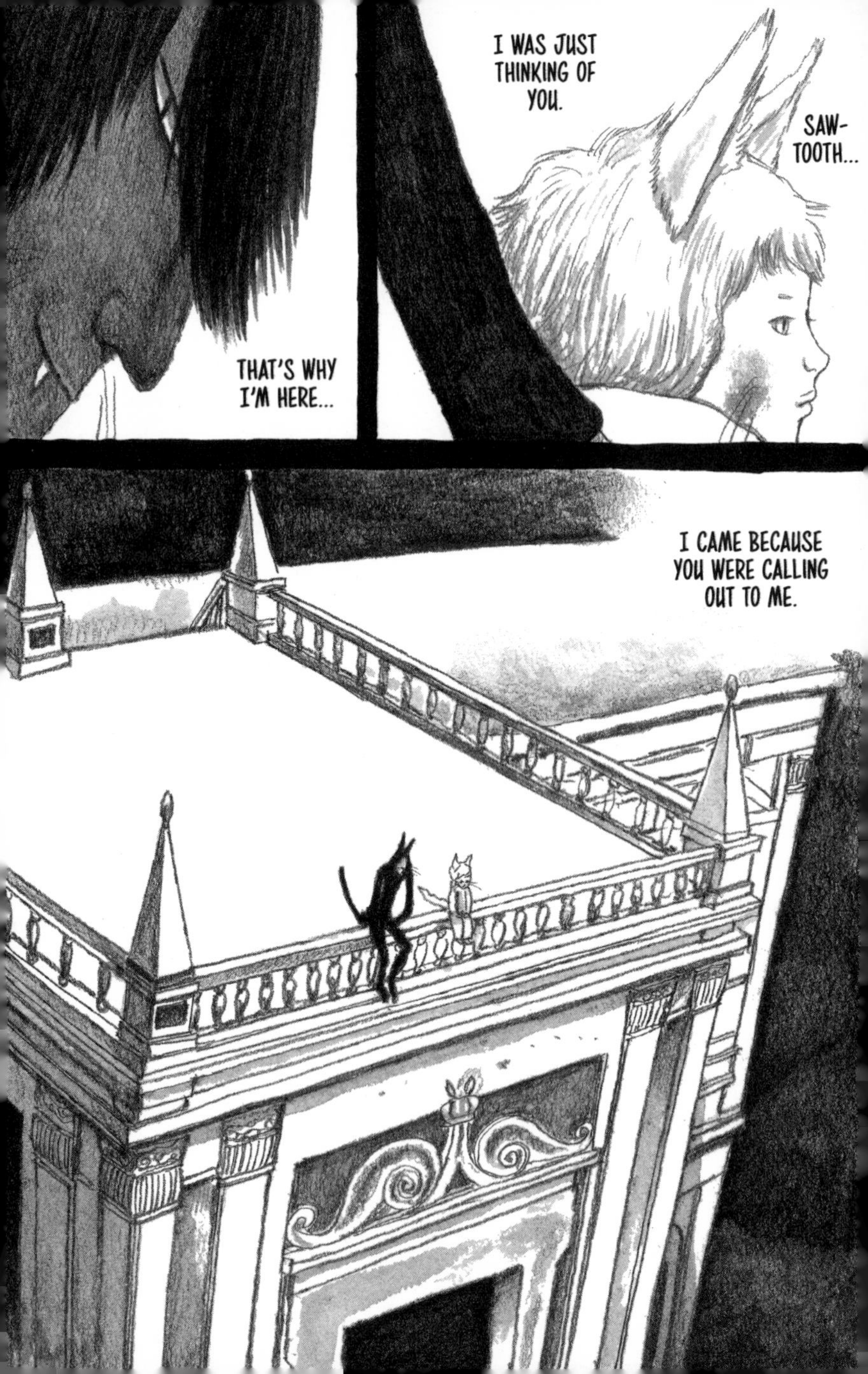
SAW-TOOTH...
I WAS JUST THINKING OF YOU.
THAT'S WHY I'M HERE...
I CAME BECAUSE YOU WERE CALLING OUT TO ME.

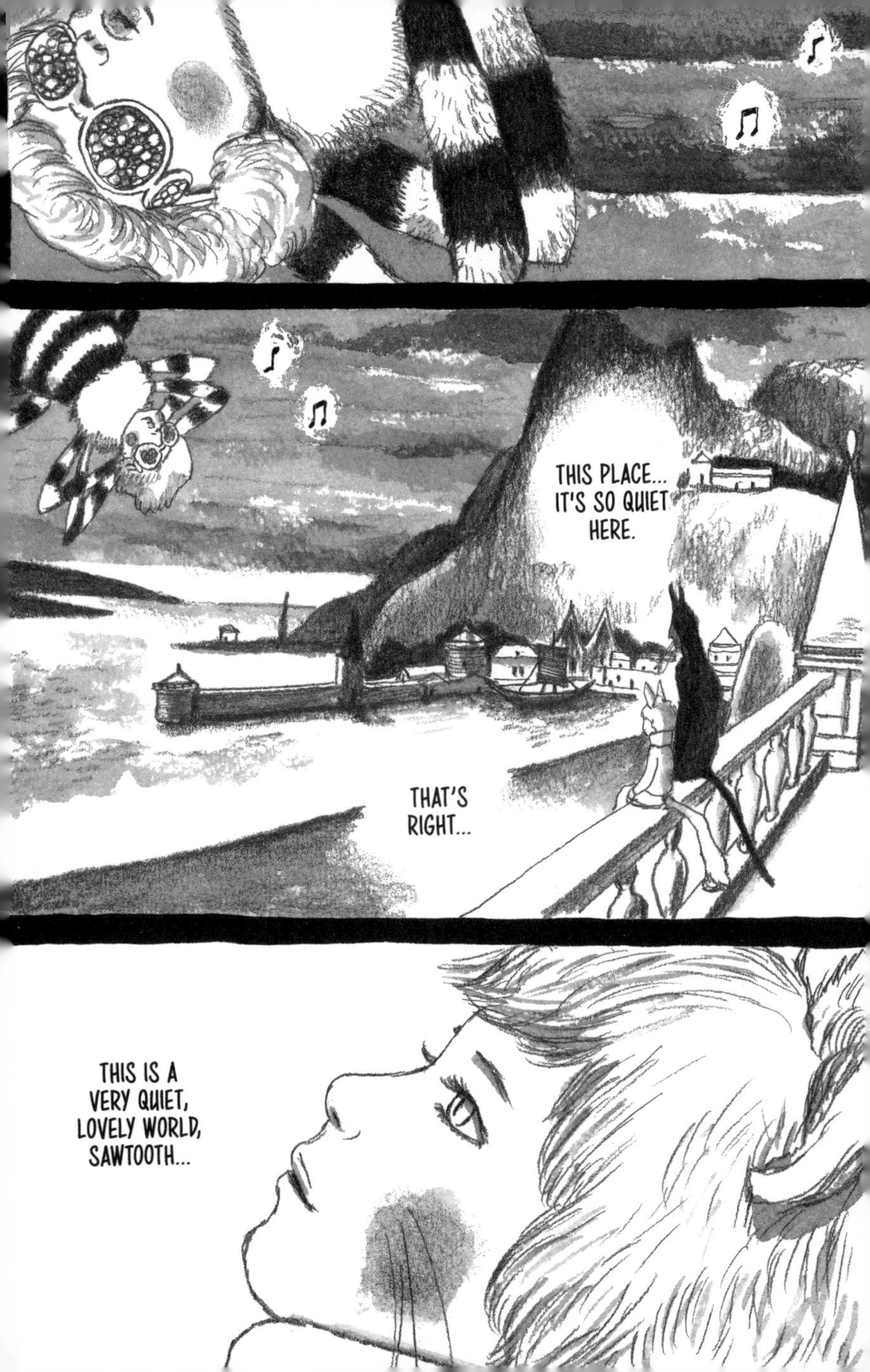
THIS PLACE... IT'S SO QUIET HERE.
THAT'S RIGHT...
THIS IS A VERY QUIET, LOVELY WORLD, SAWTOOTH...

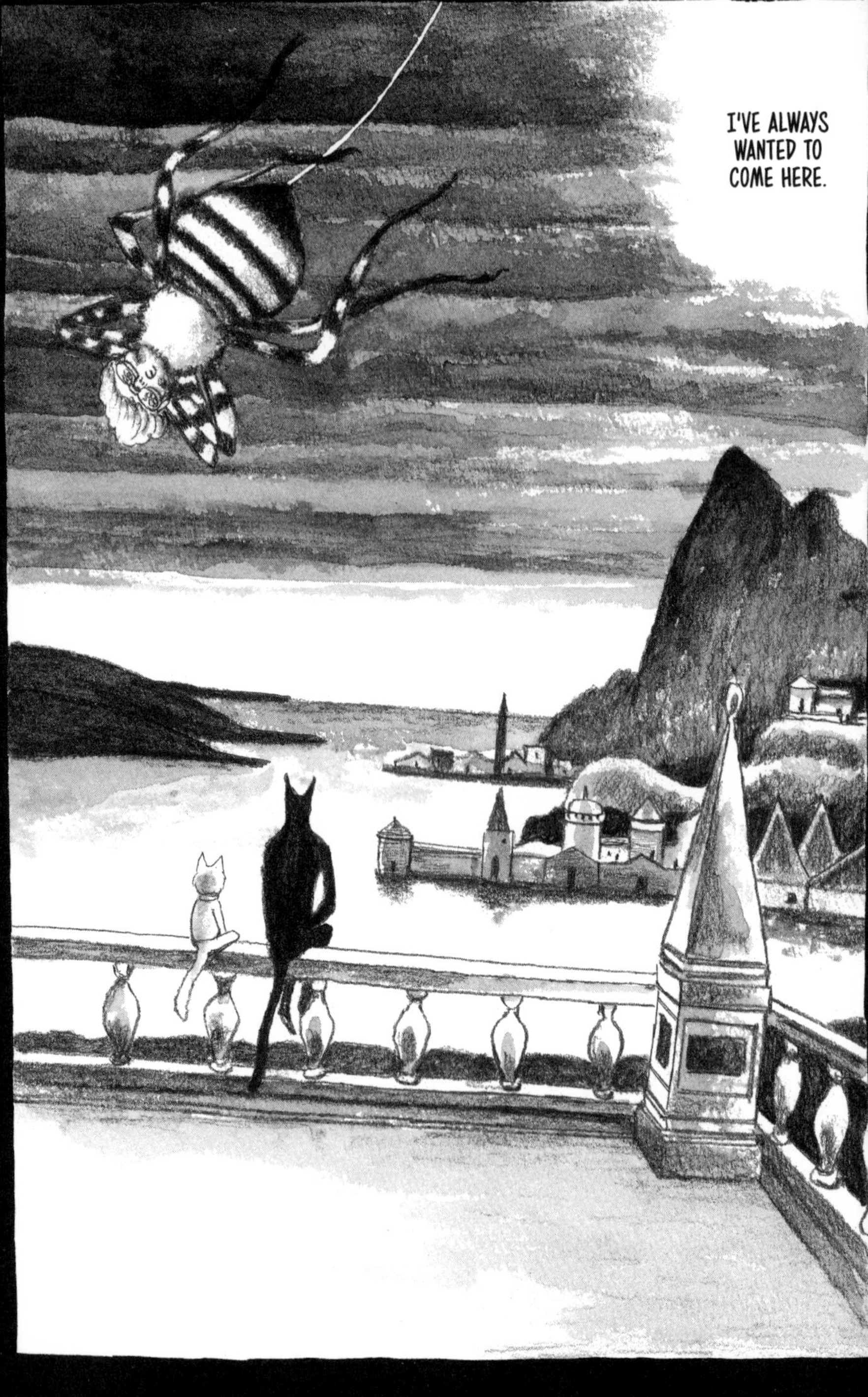
I'VE ALWAYS WANTED TO COME HERE.

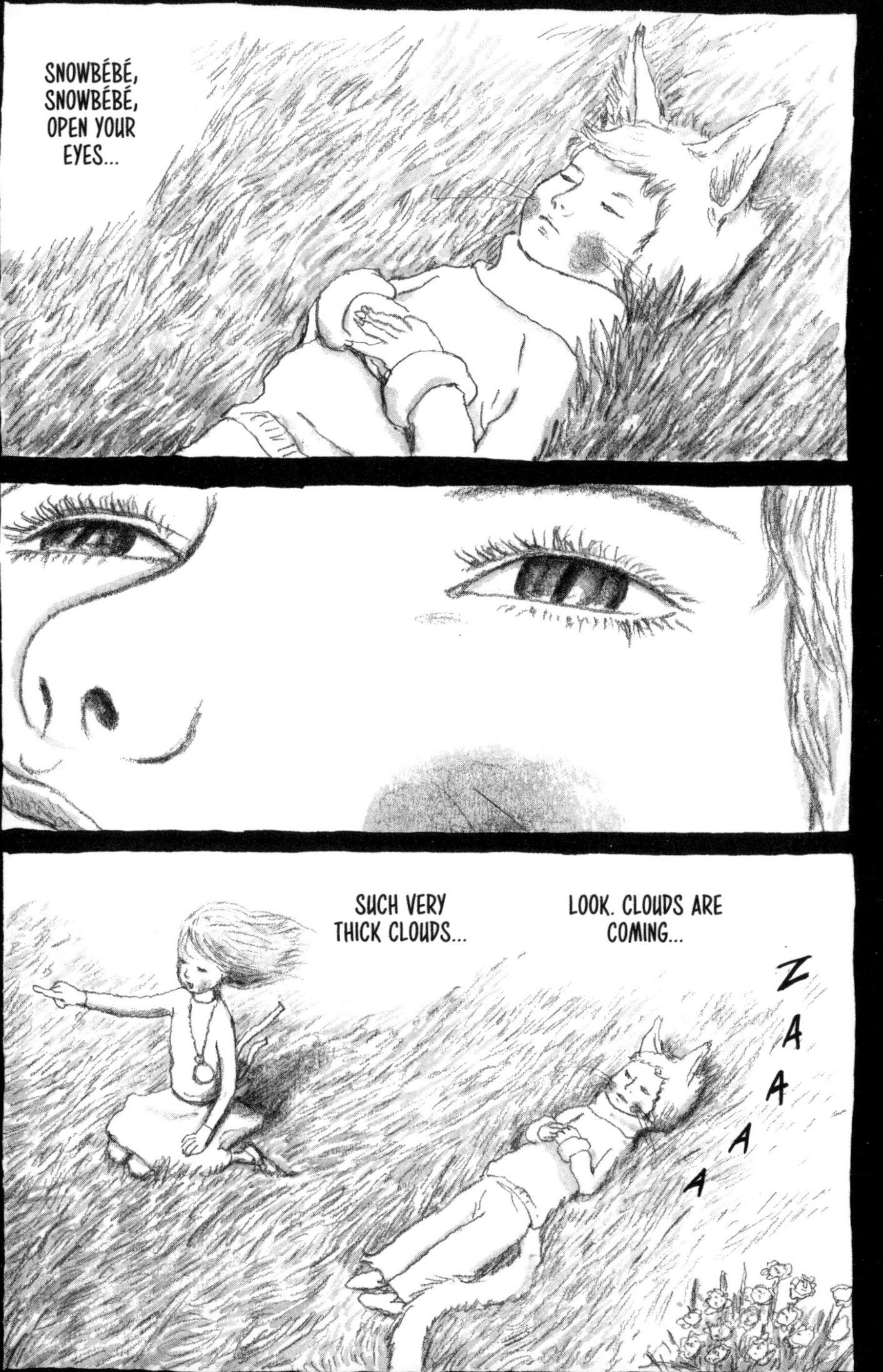
SNOWBÉBÉ, SNOWBÉBÉ, OPEN YOUR EYES...
LOOK. CLOUDS ARE COMING...
SUCH VERY THICK CLOUDS...
ZAAAA

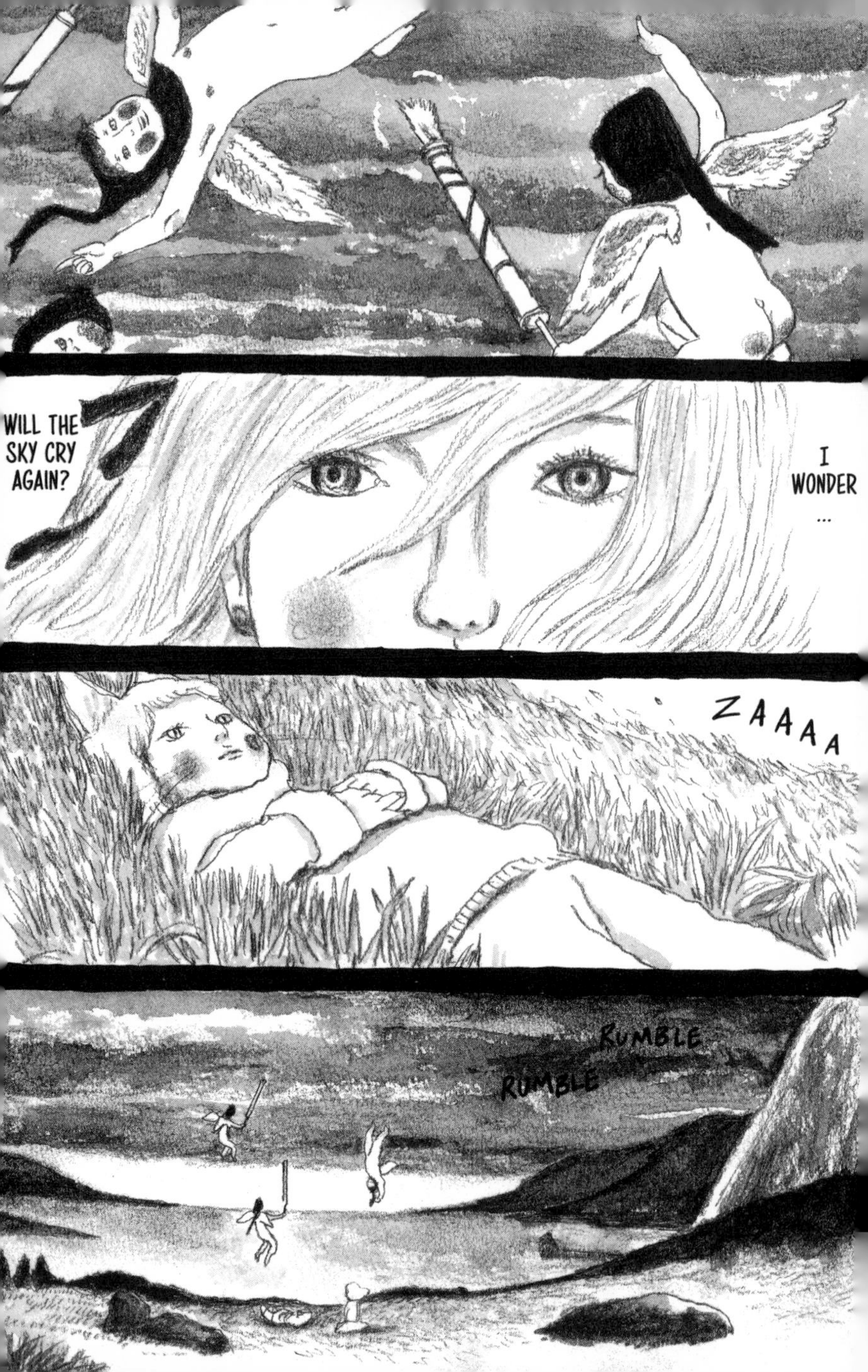
I WONDER ...
WILL THE SKY CRY AGAIN?
ZAAAA
RUMBLE
RUMBLE

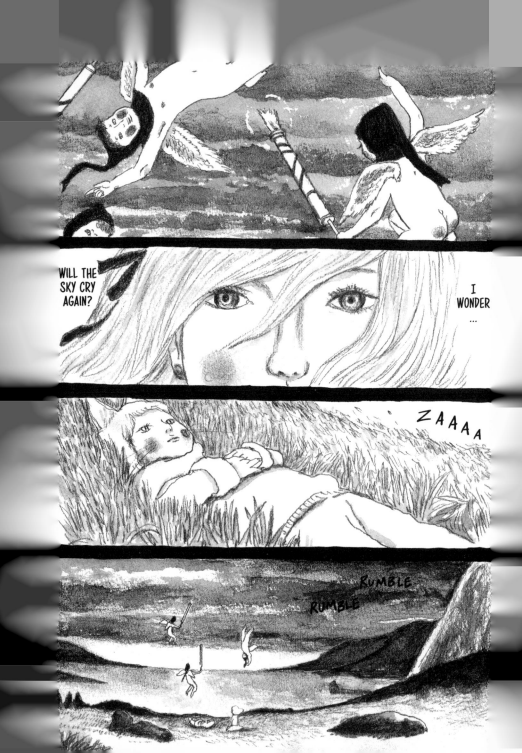

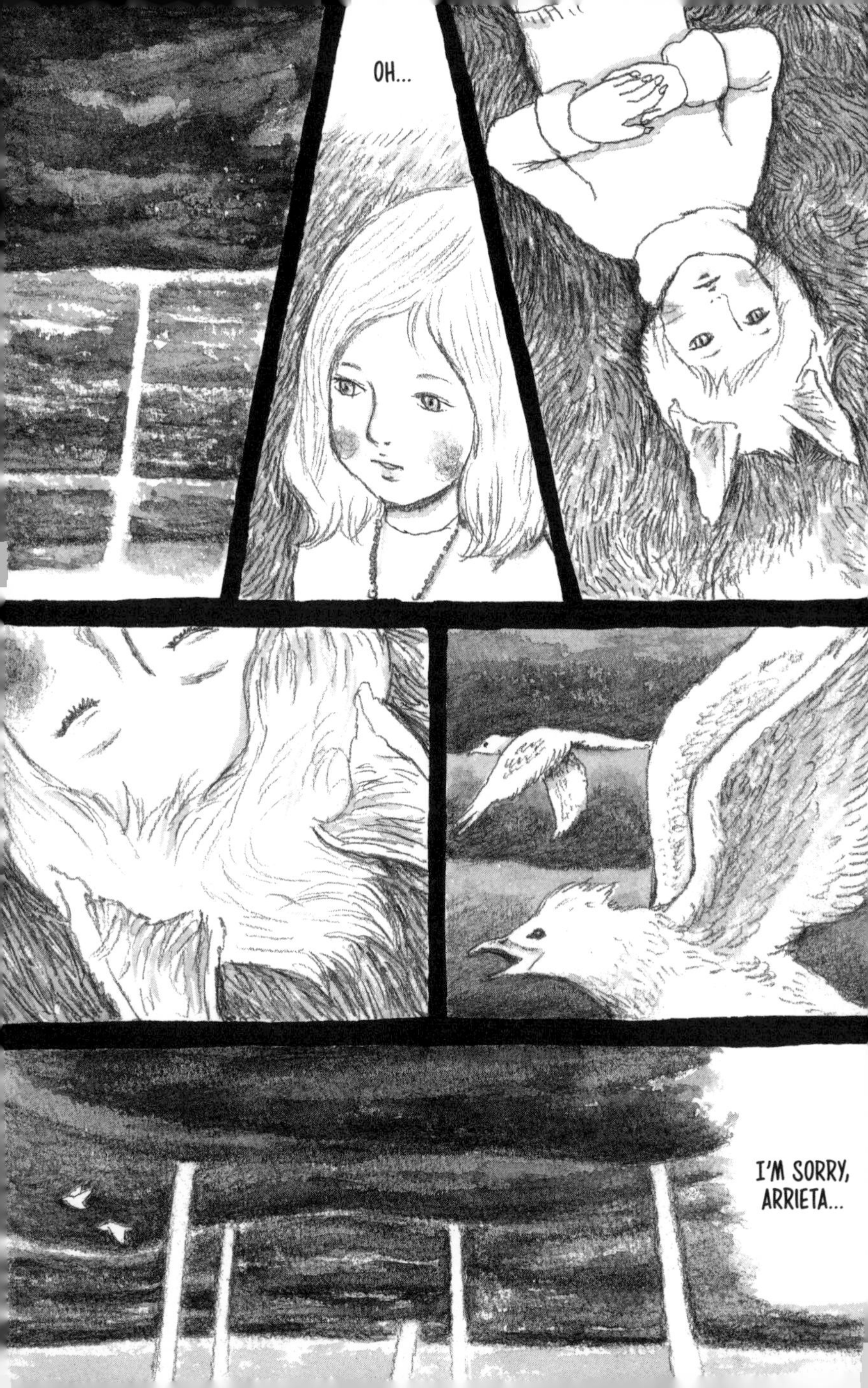
OH...
I'M SORRY, ARRIETA...

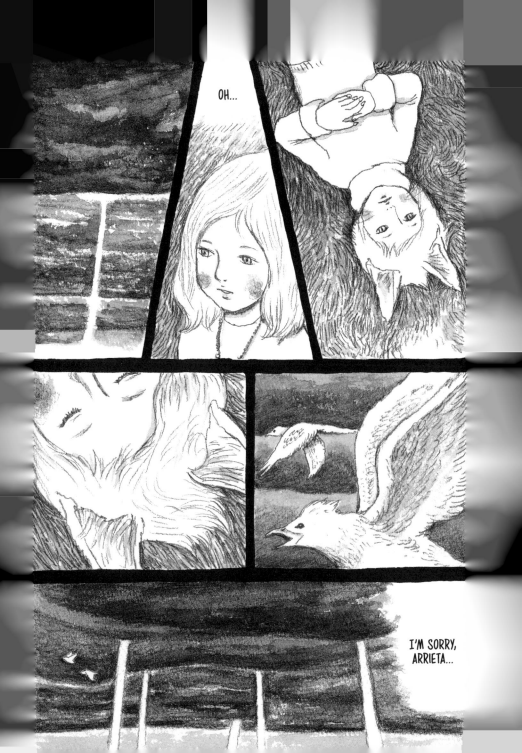

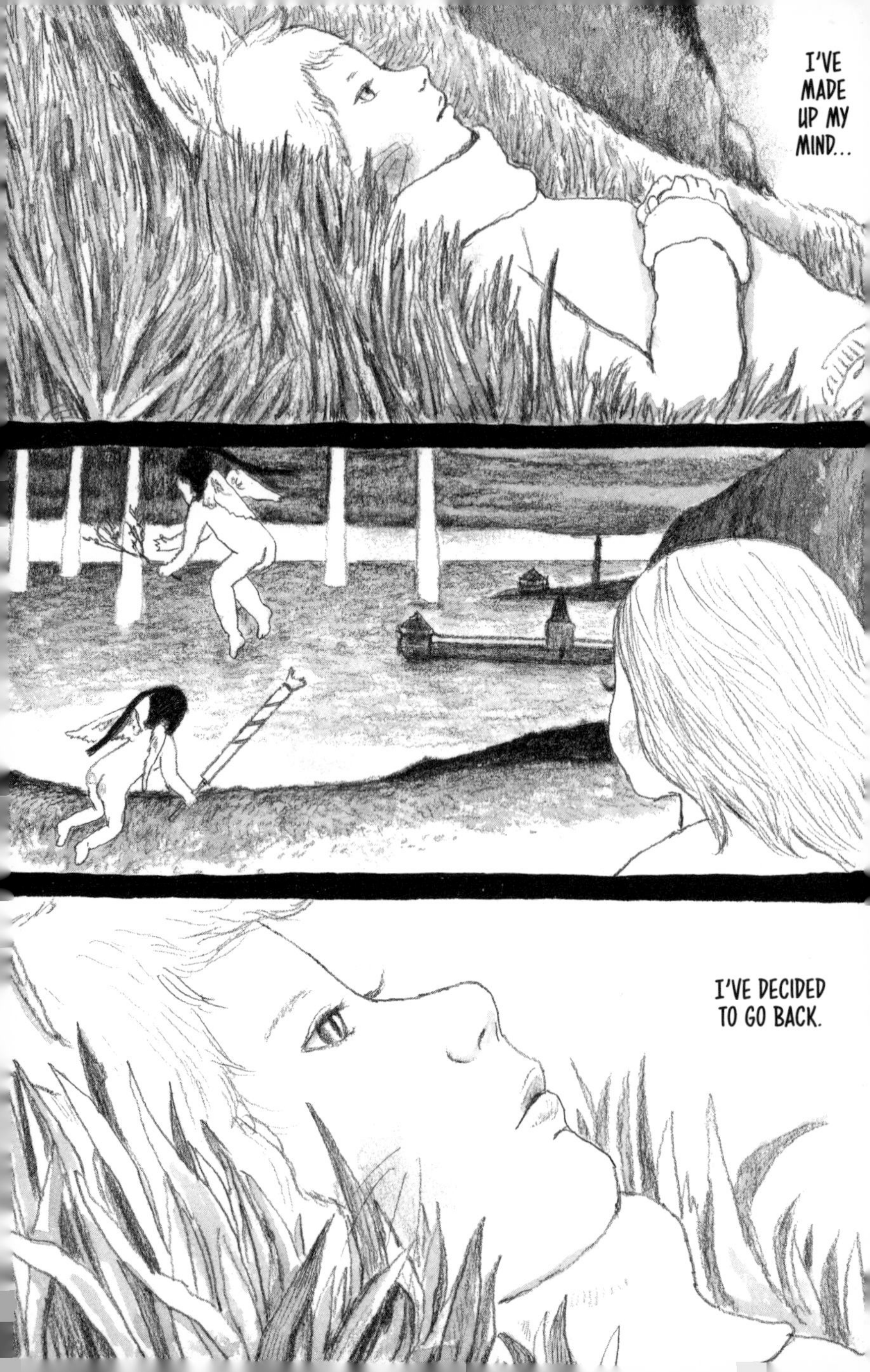
I'VE MADE UP MY MIND...
I'VE DECIDED TO GO BACK.

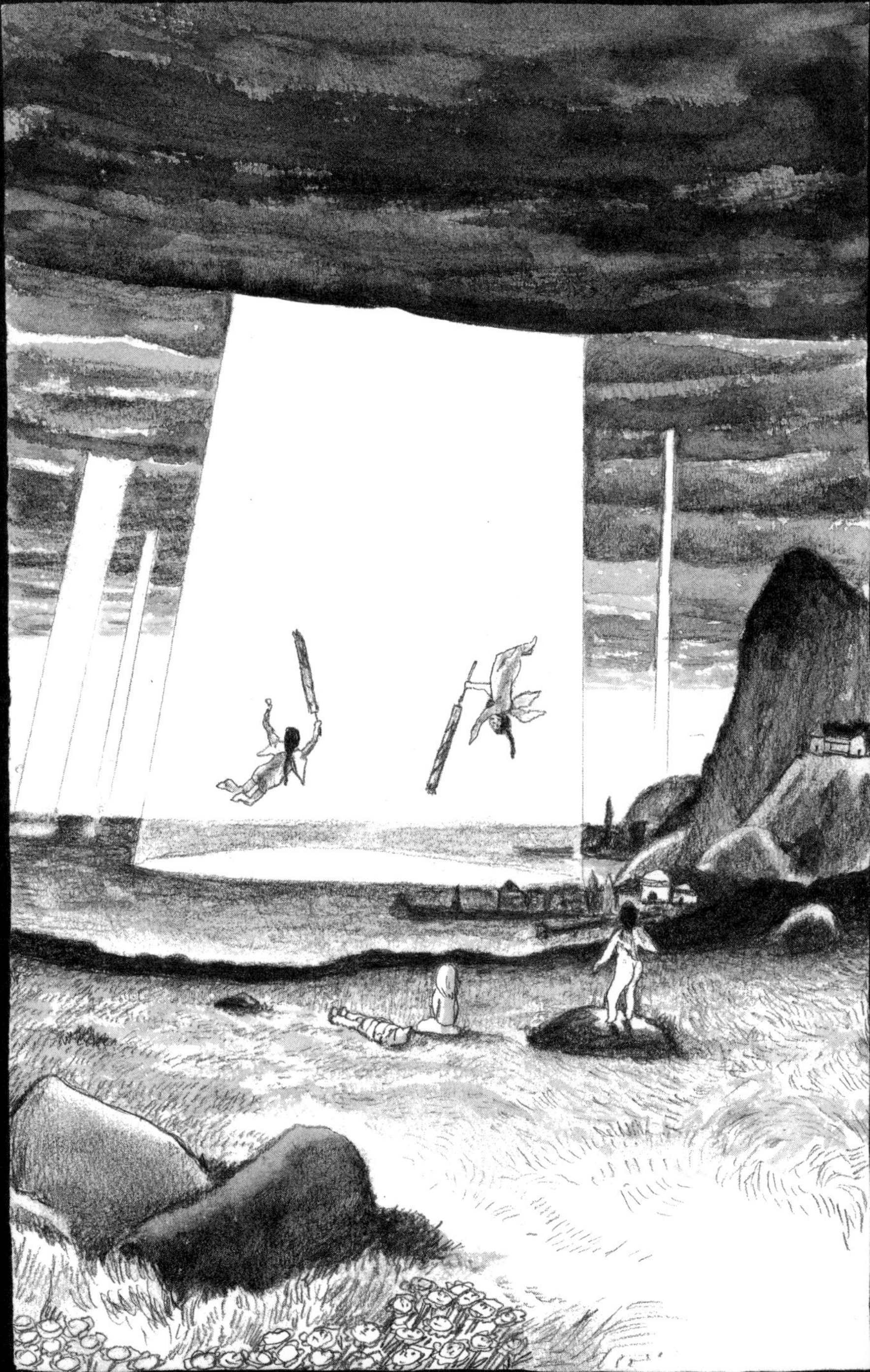

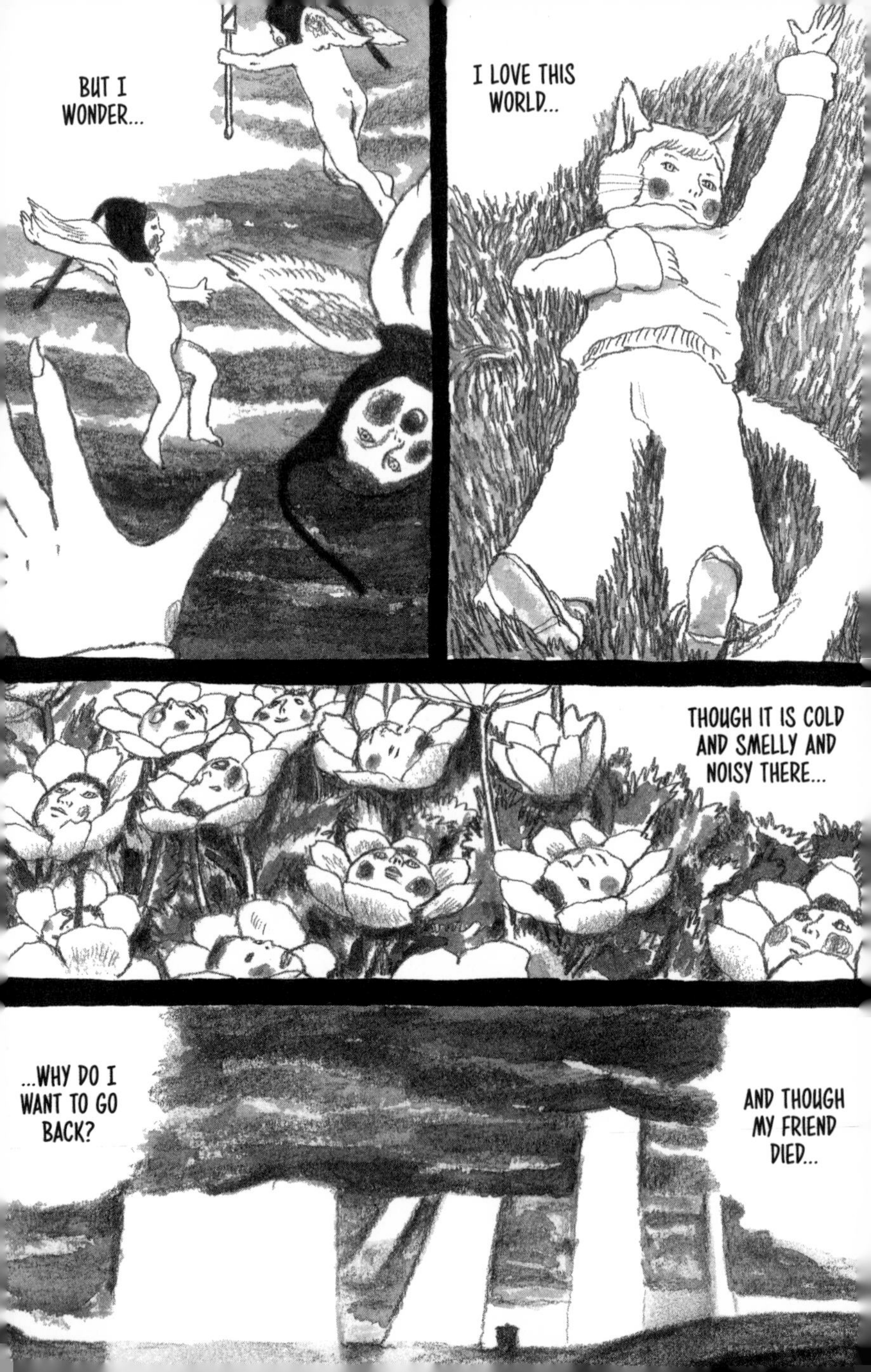
I LOVE THIS WORLD...
BUT I WONDER...
THOUGH IT IS COLD AND SMELLY AND NOISY THERE...
AND THOUGH MY FRIEND DIED...
...WHY DO I WANT TO GO BACK?

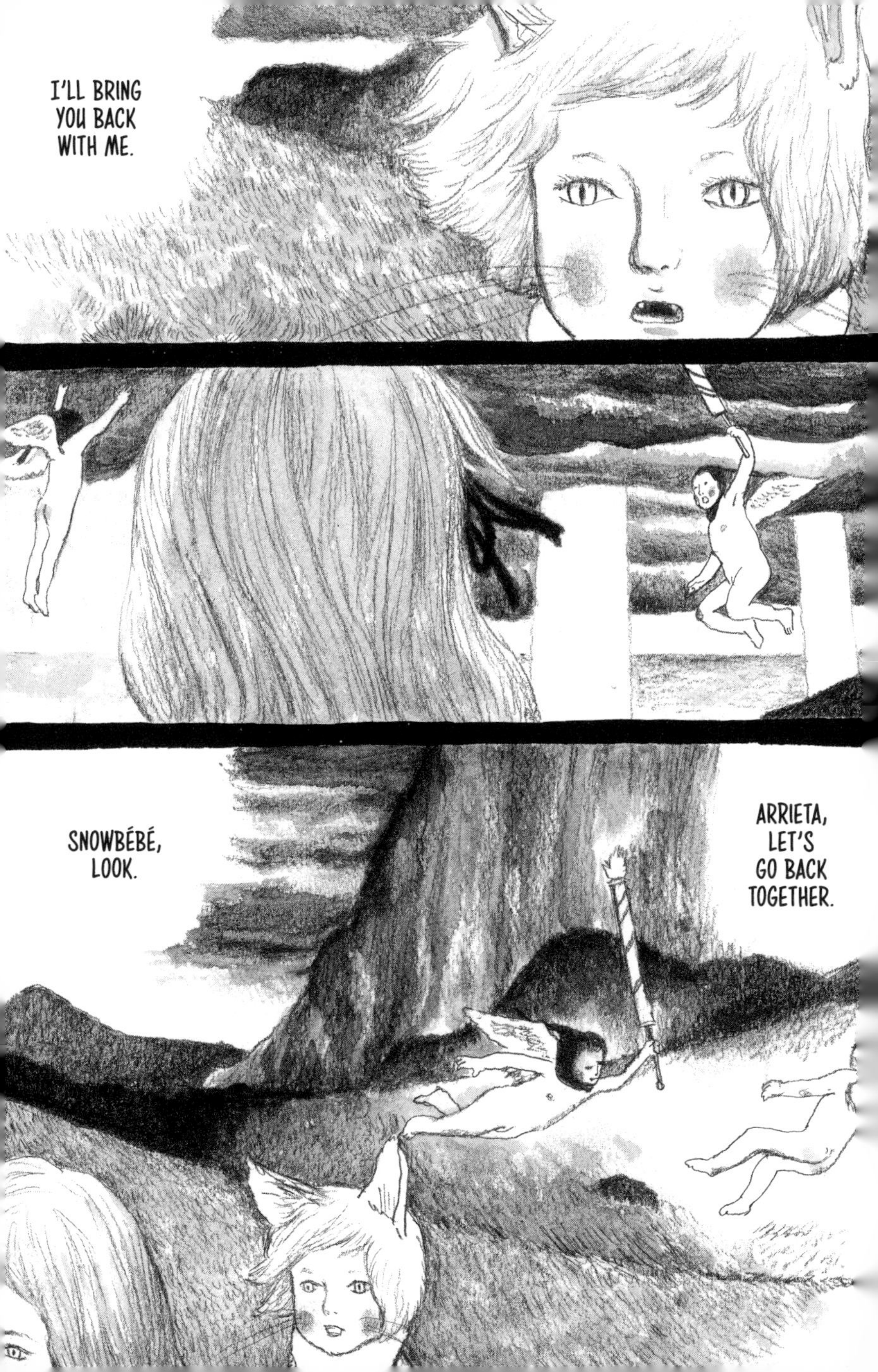
I'LL BRING YOU BACK WITH ME.
ARRIETA, LET'S GO BACK TOGETHER.
SNOWBÉBÉ, LOOK.

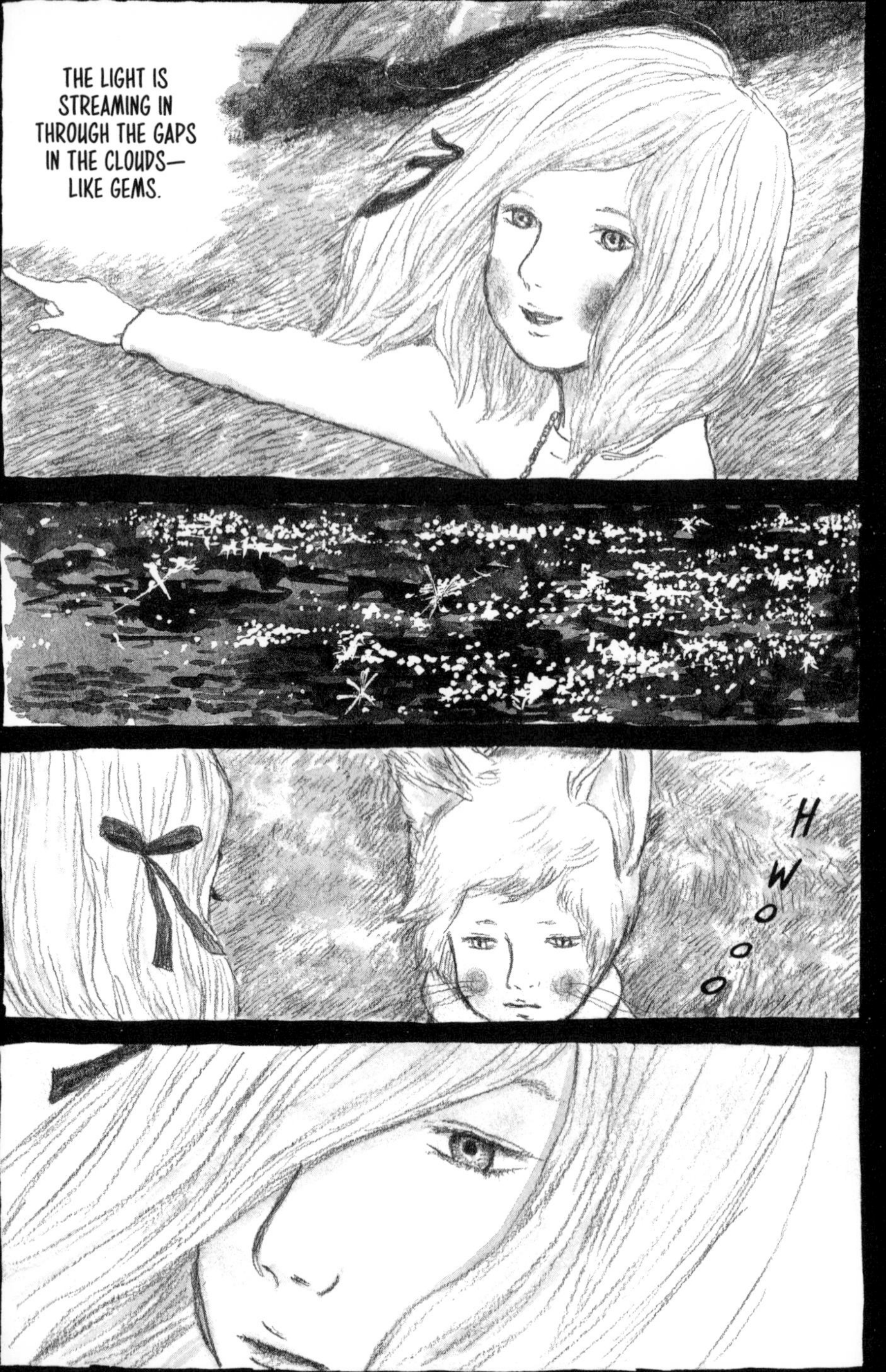
THE LIGHT IS STREAMING IN THROUGH THE GAPS IN THE CLOUDS— LIKE GEMS.
HWOOOO

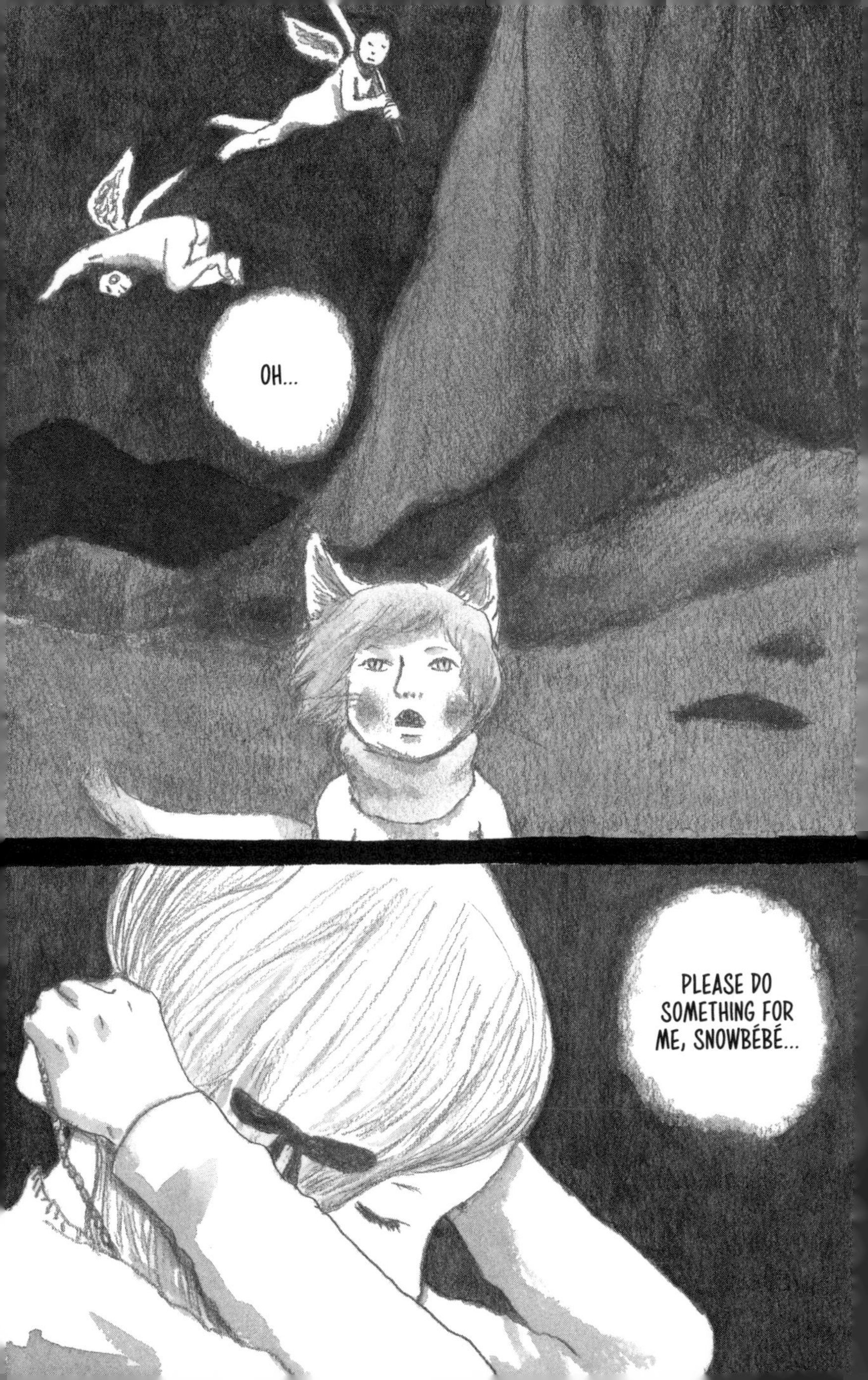
OH...
PLEASE DO SOMETHING FOR ME, SNOWBÉBÉ...

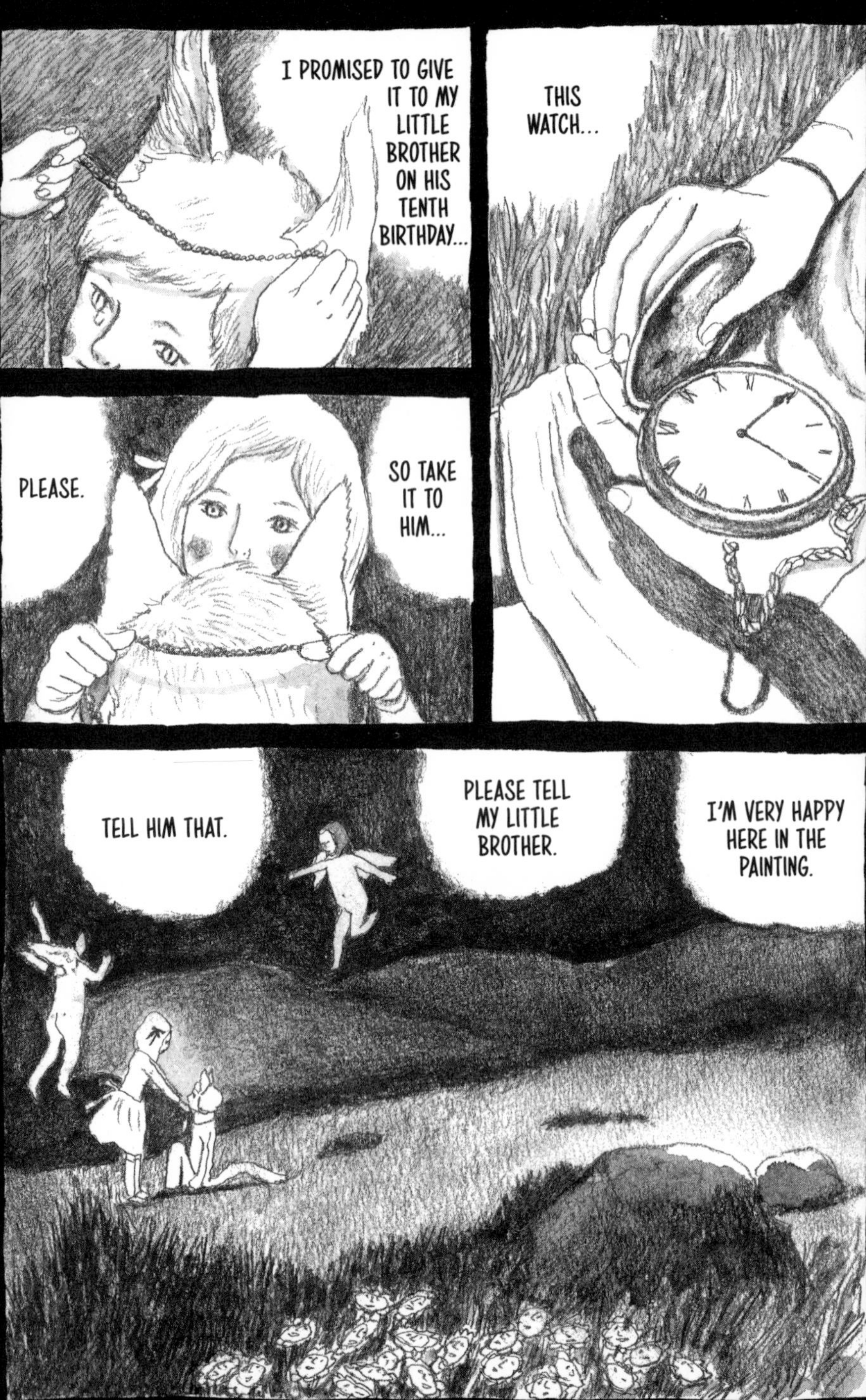
THIS WATCH...
I PROMISED TO GIVE IT TO MY LITTLE BROTHER ON HIS TENTH BIRTHDAY...
SO TAKE IT TO HIM...
PLEASE.
I'M VERY HAPPY HERE IN THE PAINTING.
PLEASE TELL MY LITTLE BROTHER.
TELL HIM THAT.

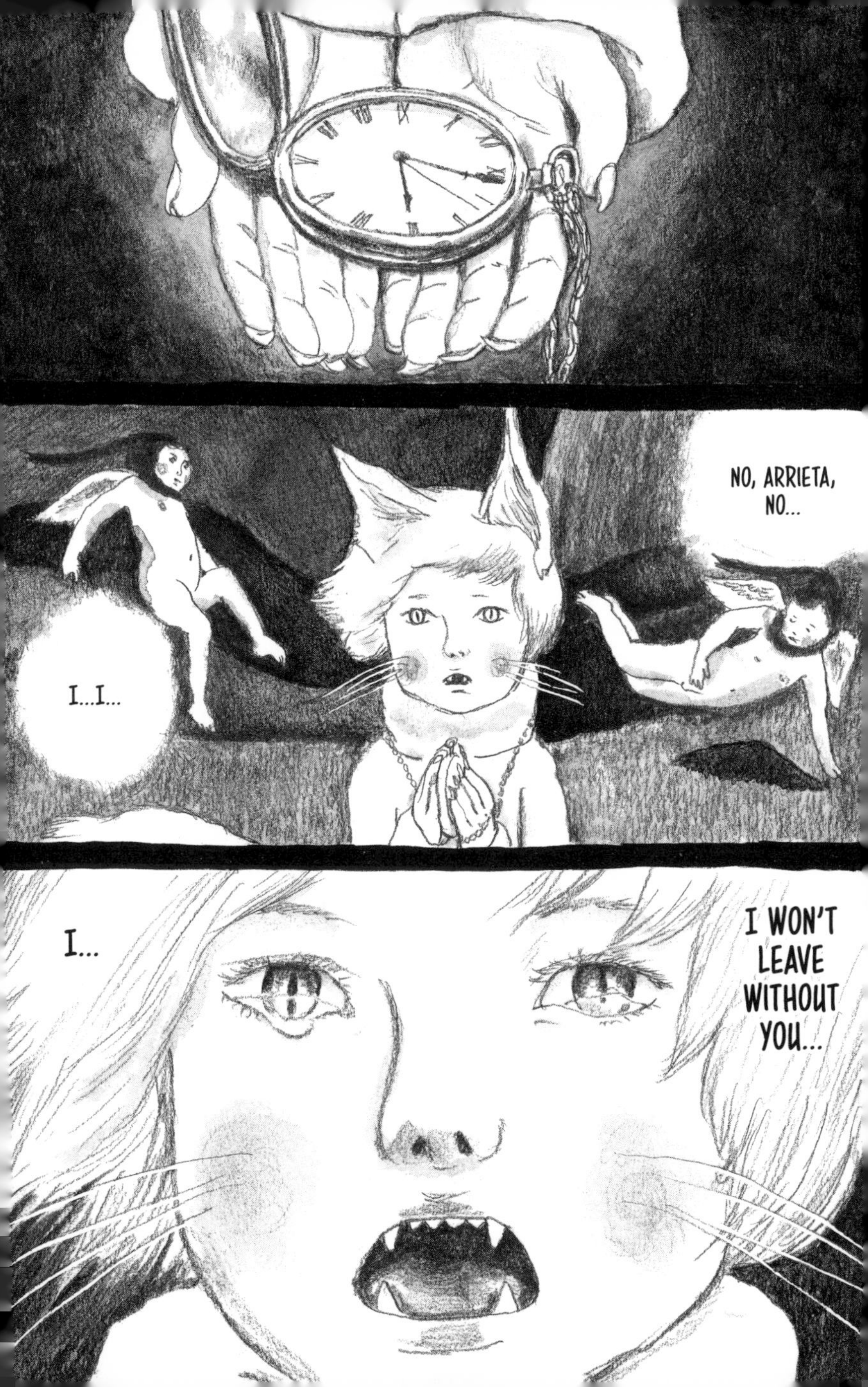
NO, ARRIETA, NO...
I...I...
I WON'T LEAVE WITHOUT YOU...
I...

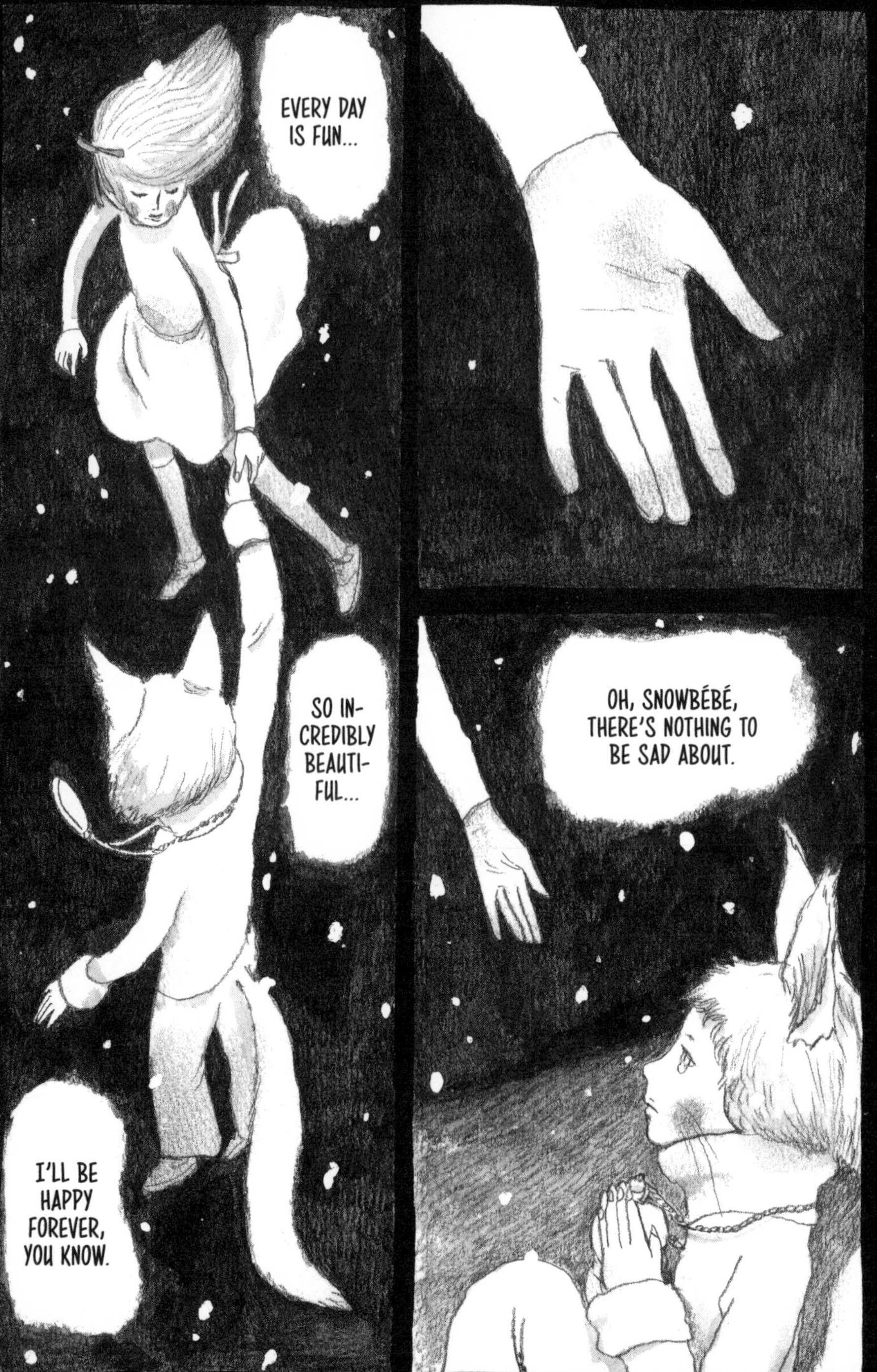
OH, SNOWBÉBÉ, THERE'S NOTHING TO BE SAD ABOUT.
EVERY DAY IS FUN...
SO IN-CREDIBLY BEAUTI-FUL...
I'LL BE HAPPY FOREVER, YOU KNOW.

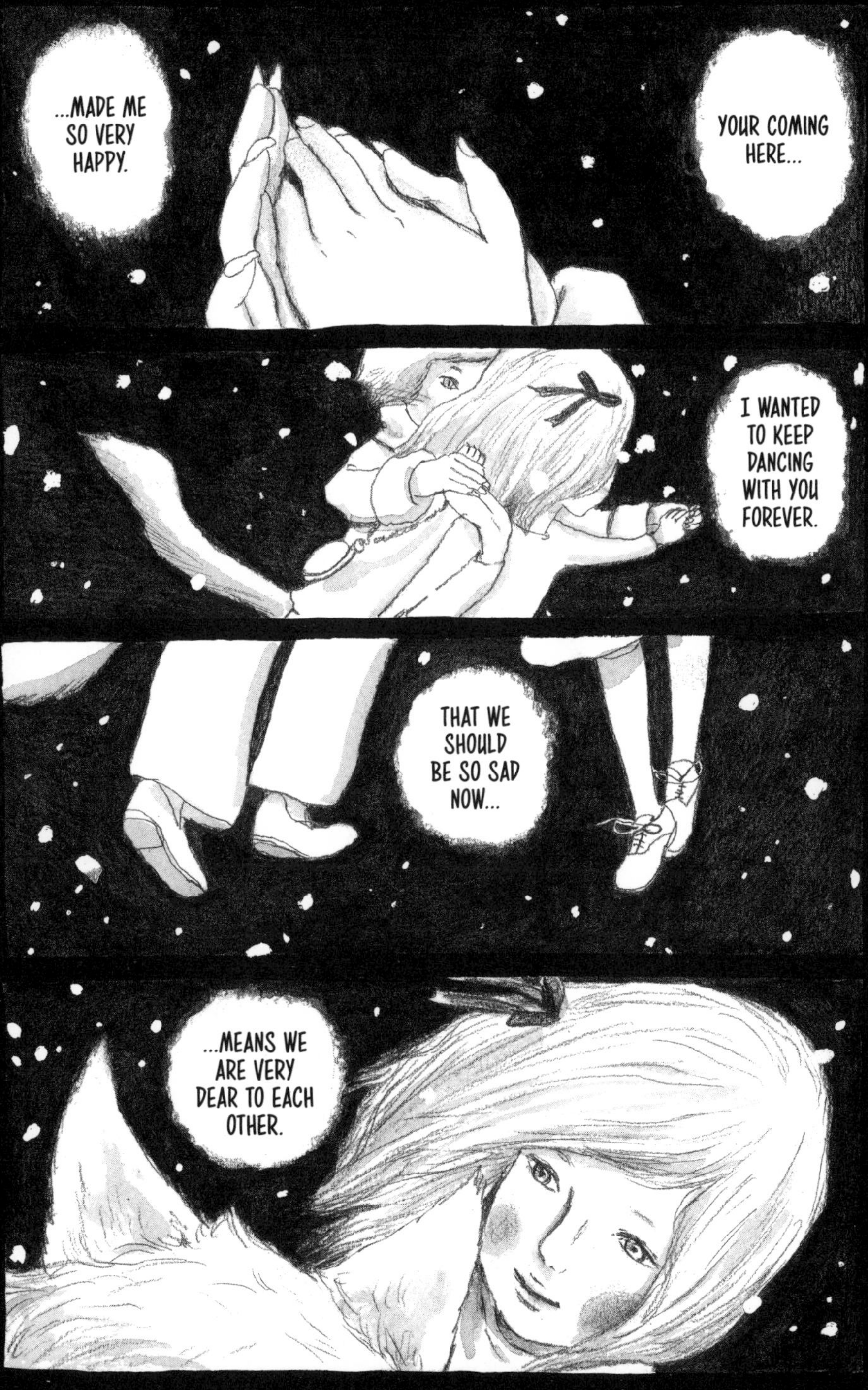
YOUR COMING HERE...
...MADE ME SO VERY HAPPY.
I WANTED TO KEEP DANCING WITH YOU FOREVER.
THAT WE SHOULD BE SO SAD NOW...
...MEANS WE ARE VERY DEAR TO EACH OTHER.

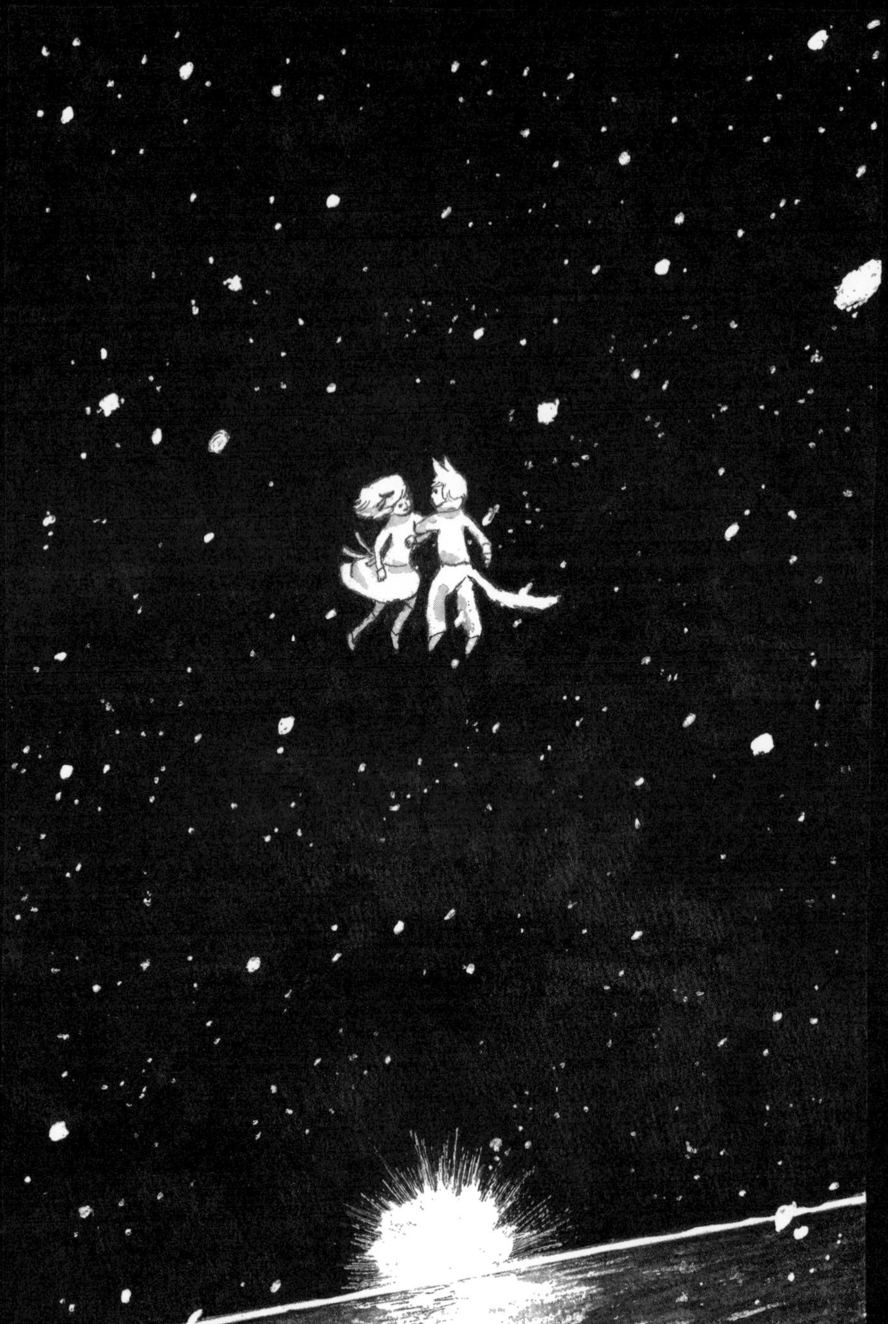

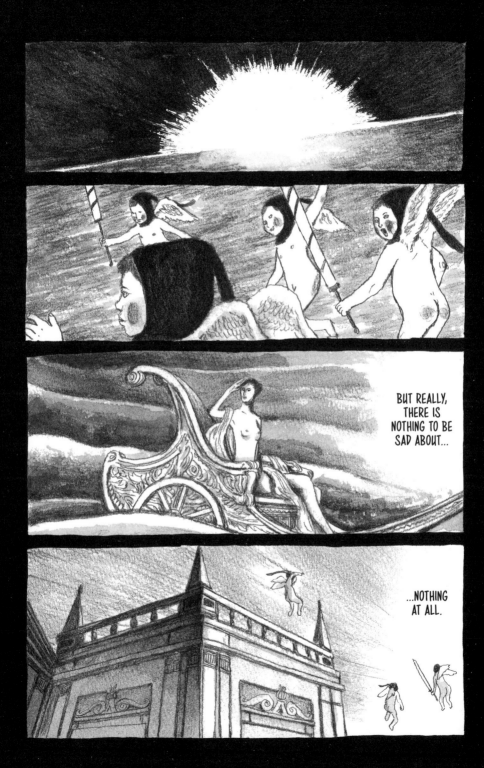

BUT REALLY, THERE IS NOTHING TO BE SAD ABOUT...

...NOTHING AT ALL.

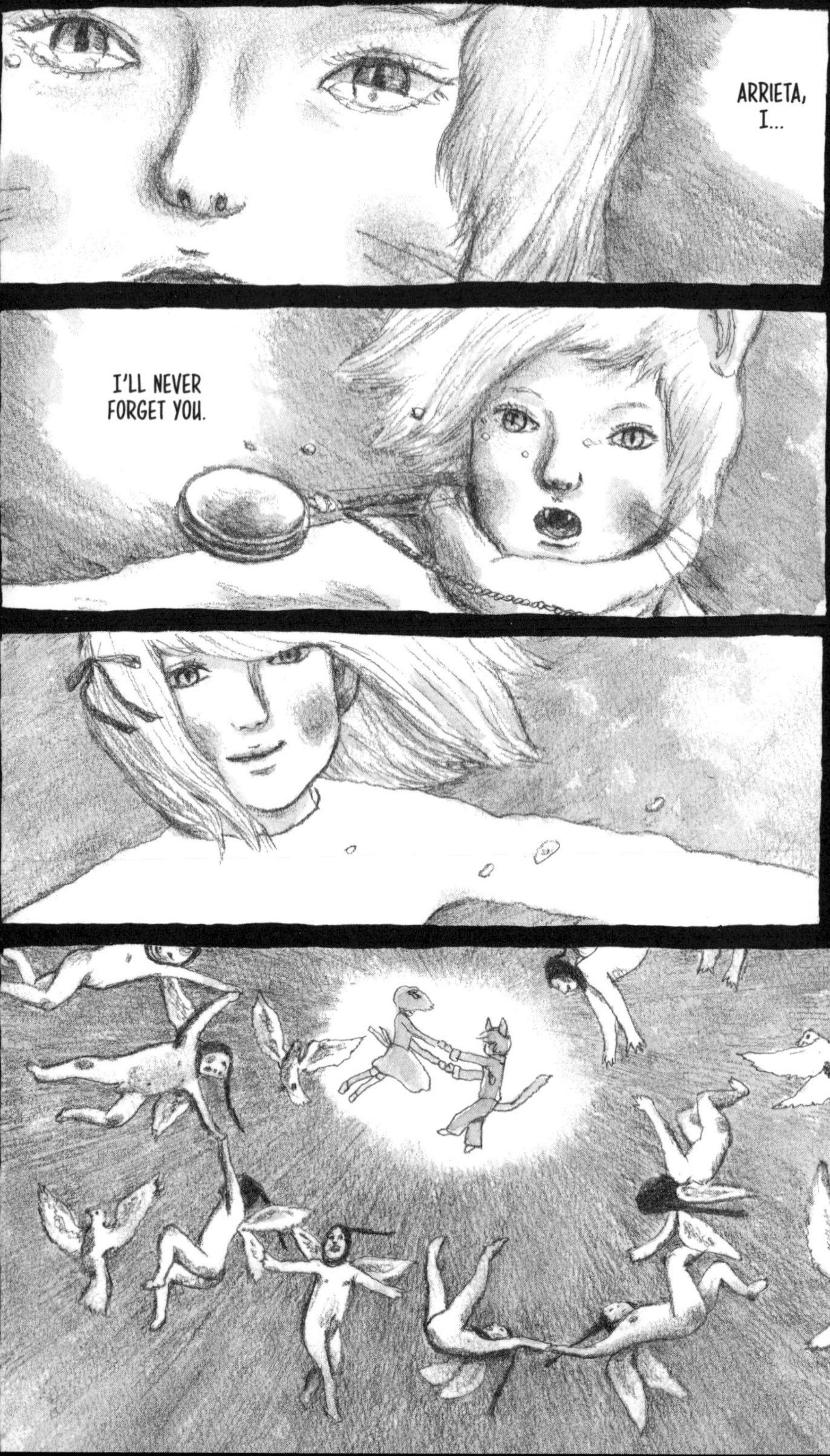
ARRIETA, I...
I'LL NEVER FORGET YOU.

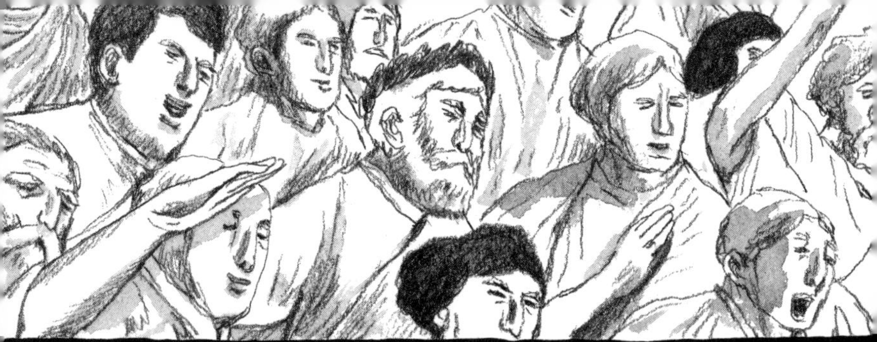

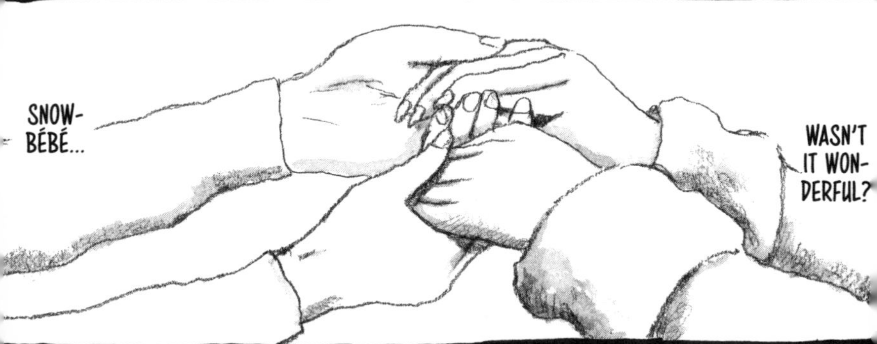
WASN'T IT WON-DERFUL?
SNOW-BÉBÉ...

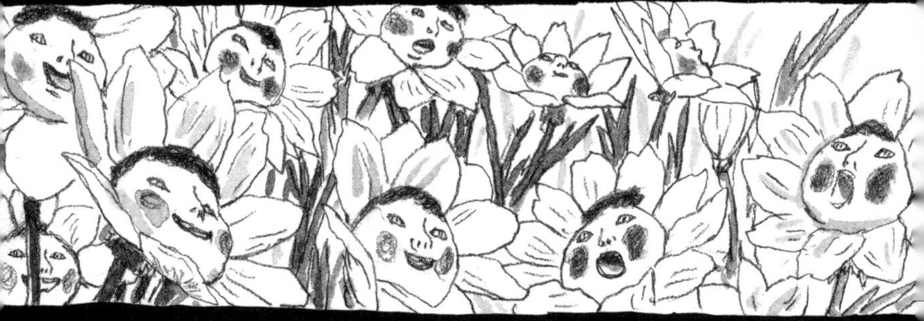

FAREWELL...

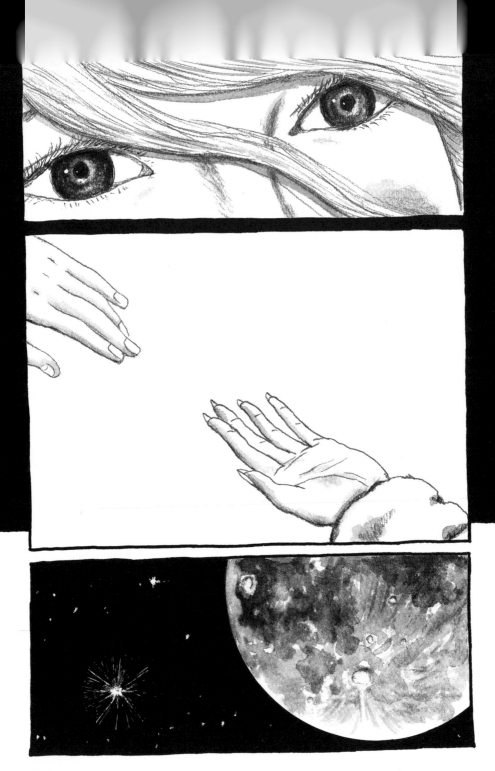

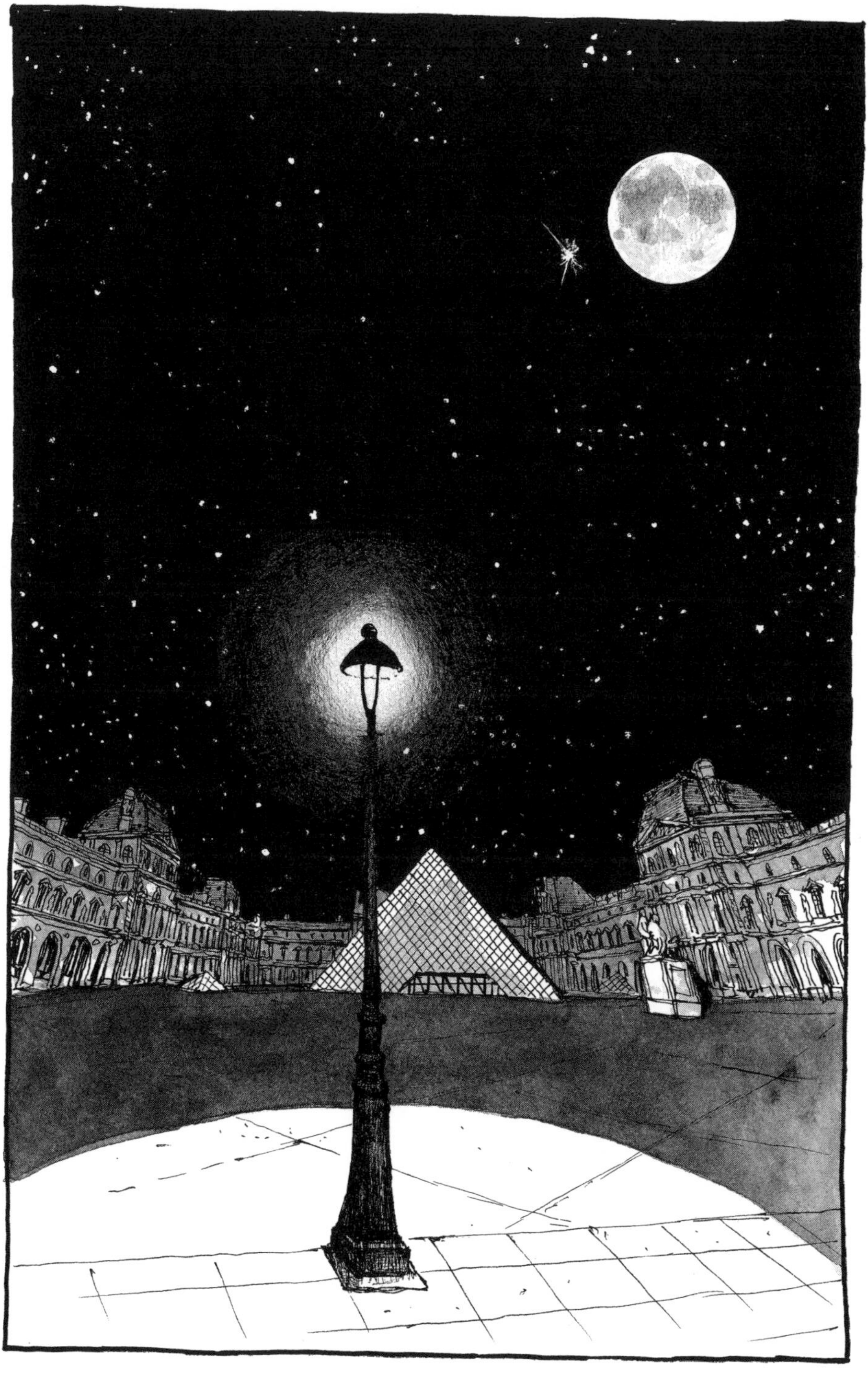

FINAL CHAPTER

The Secret of the Louvre

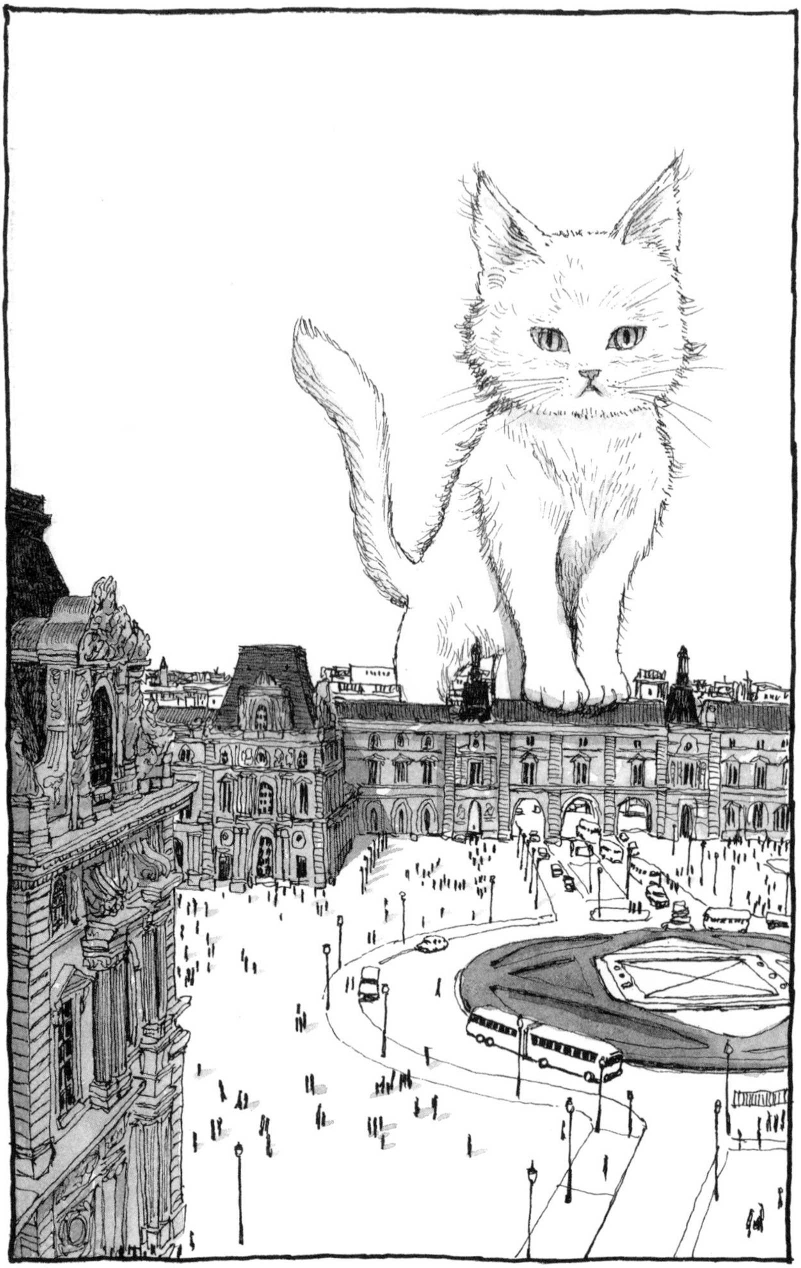

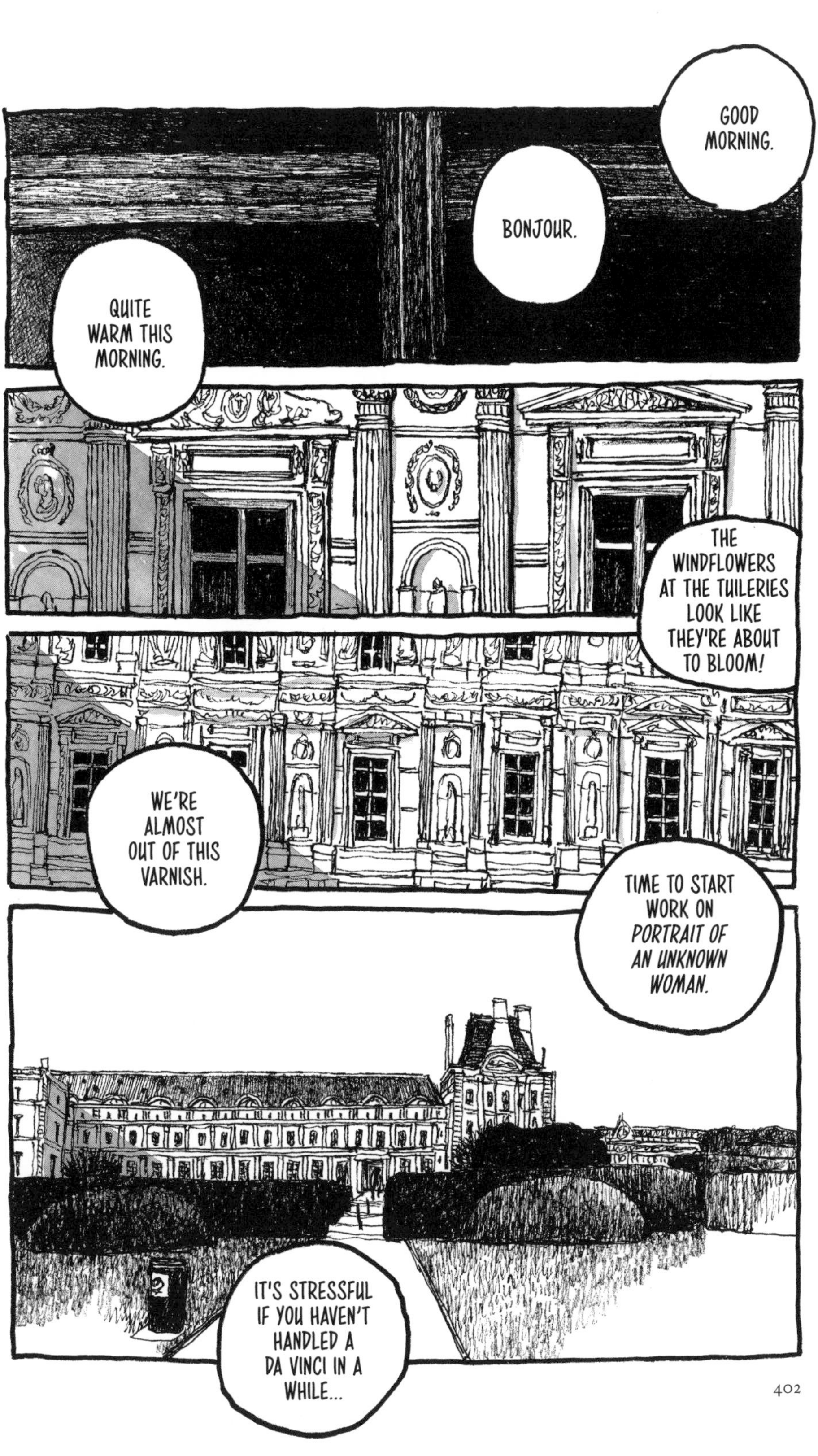
GOOD MORNING.
BONJOUR.
QUITE WARM THIS MORNING.
THE WINDFLOWERS AT THE TUILERIES LOOK LIKE THEY'RE ABOUT TO BLOOM!
WE'RE ALMOST OUT OF THIS VARNISH.
TIME TO START WORK ON *PORTRAIT OF AN UNKNOWN WOMAN.*
IT'S STRESSFUL IF YOU HAVEN'T HANDLED A DA VINCI IN A WHILE...

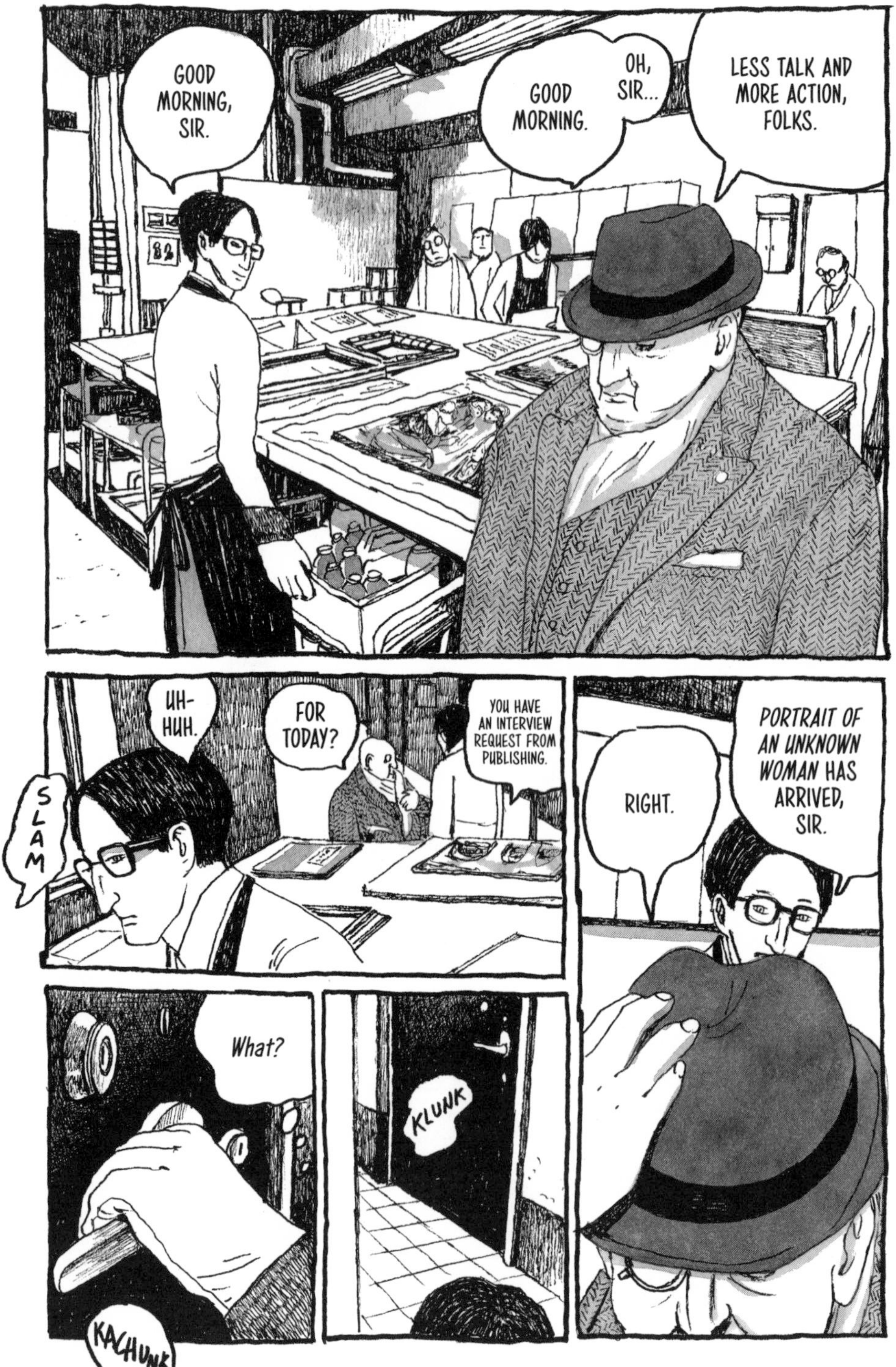
LESS TALK AND MORE ACTION, FOLKS.
OH, SIR...
GOOD MORNING.
GOOD MORNING, SIR.
PORTRAIT OF AN UNKNOWN WOMAN HAS ARRIVED, SIR.
RIGHT.
YOU HAVE AN INTERVIEW REQUEST FROM PUBLISHING.
FOR TODAY?
UH-HUH.
SLAM
KLUNK
What?
KACHUNK

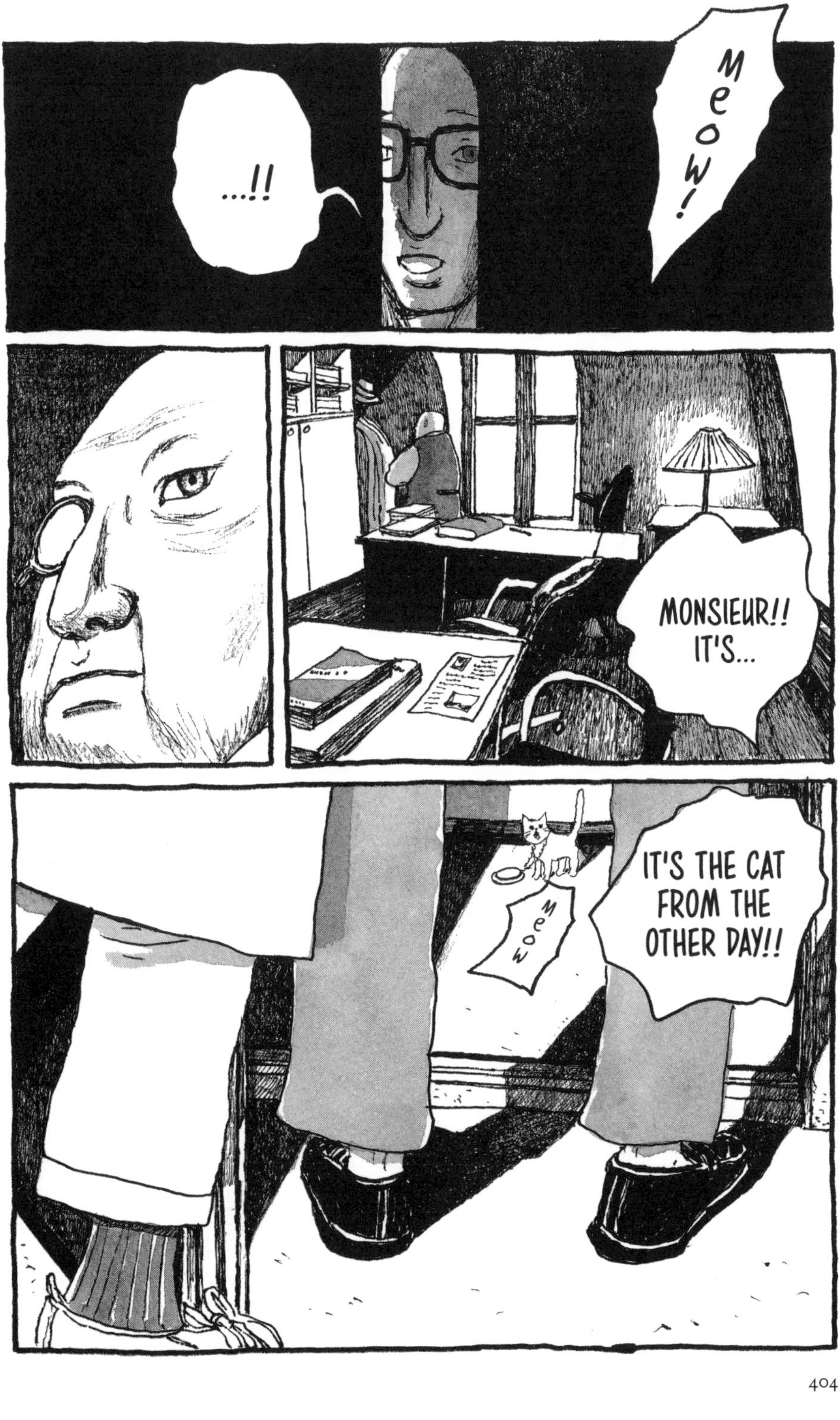
MEOW!
...!!
MONSIEUR!! IT'S...
IT'S THE CAT FROM THE OTHER DAY!!
Meow

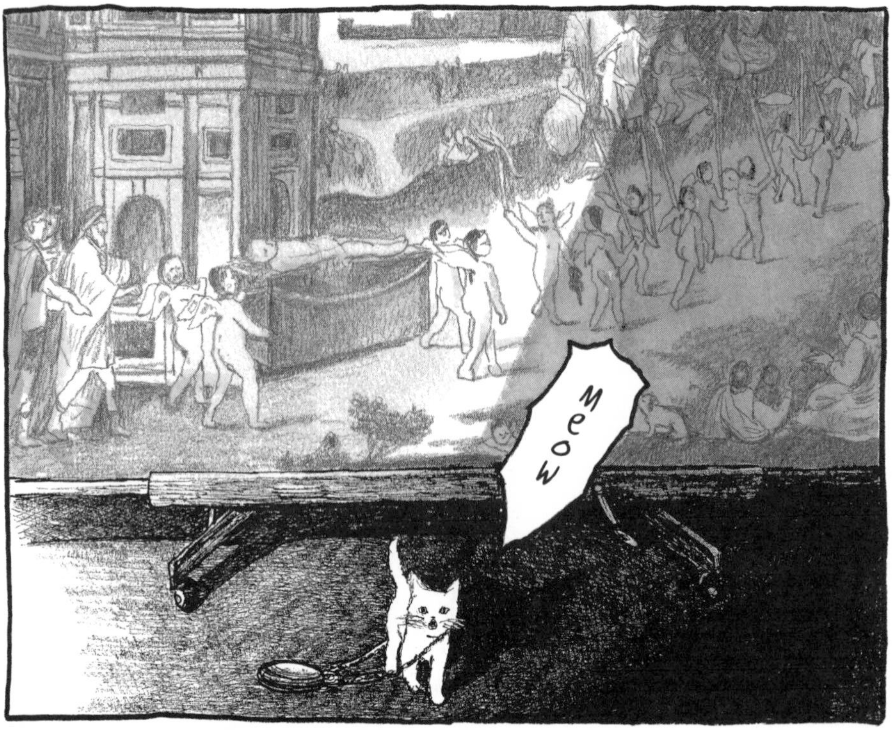
Meow

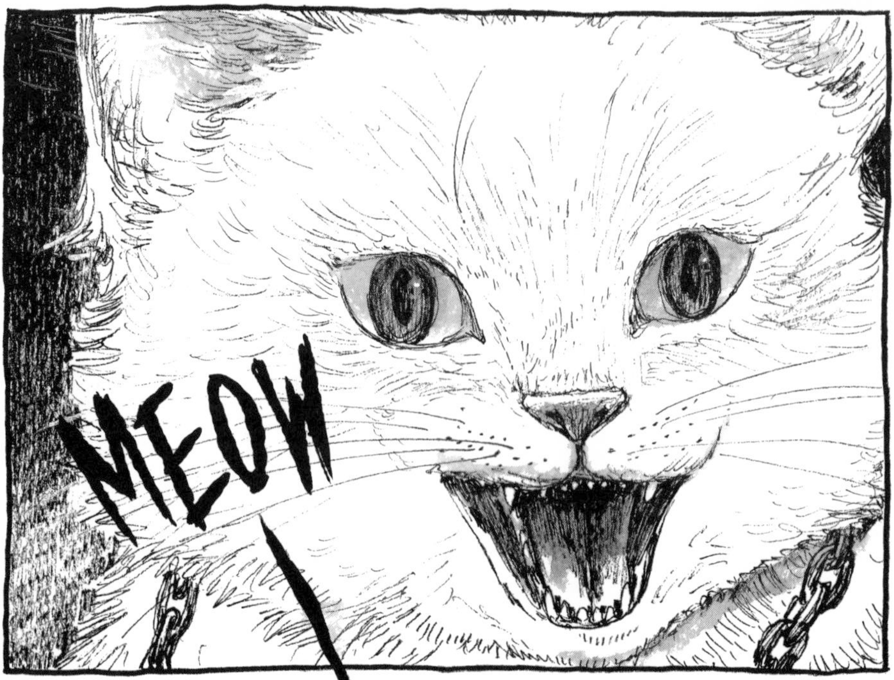
MEOW

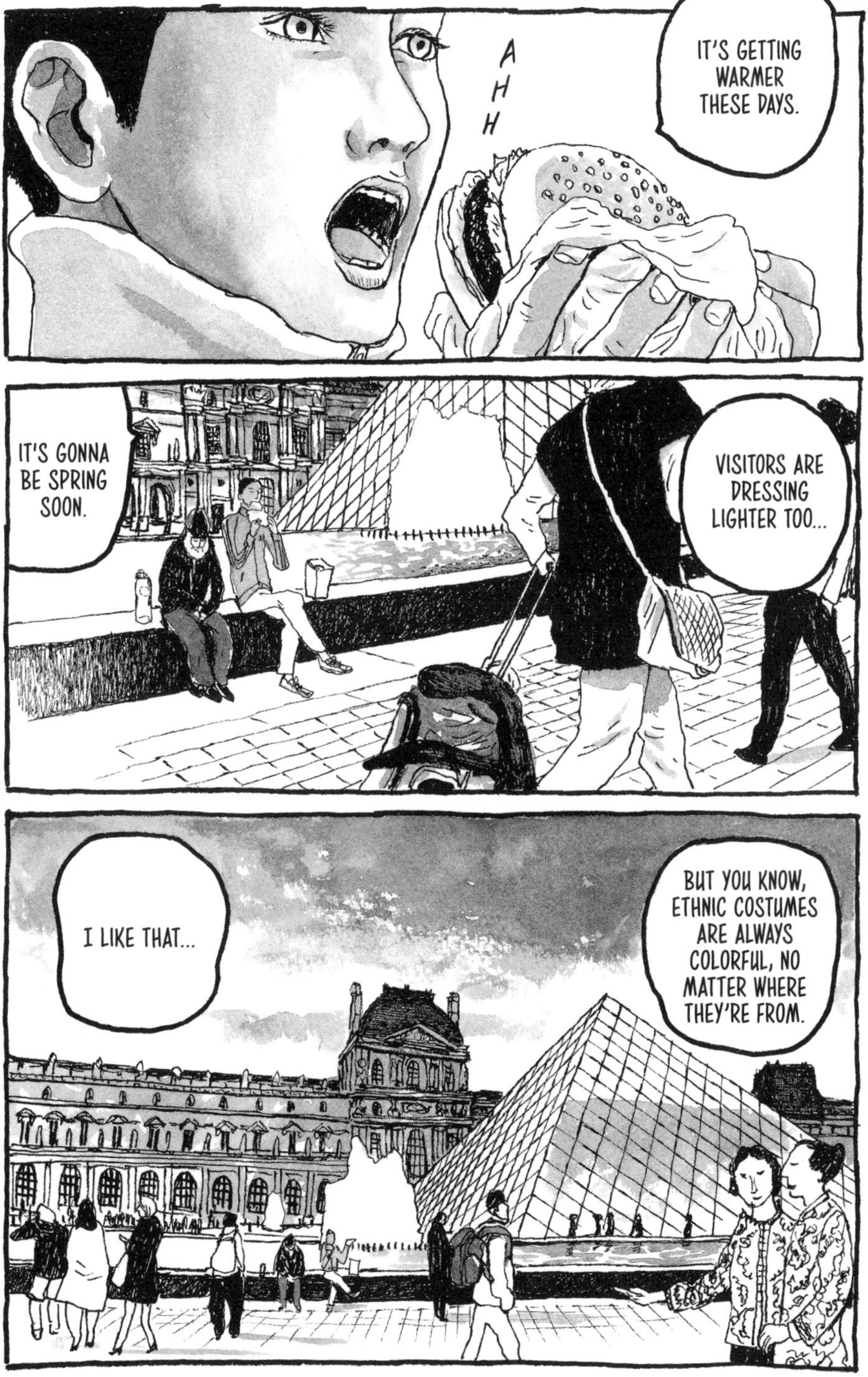
IT'S GETTING WARMER THESE DAYS.
AHH
VISITORS ARE DRESSING LIGHTER TOO...
IT'S GONNA BE SPRING SOON.
BUT YOU KNOW, ETHNIC COSTUMES ARE ALWAYS COLORFUL, NO MATTER WHERE THEY'RE FROM.
I LIKE THAT...

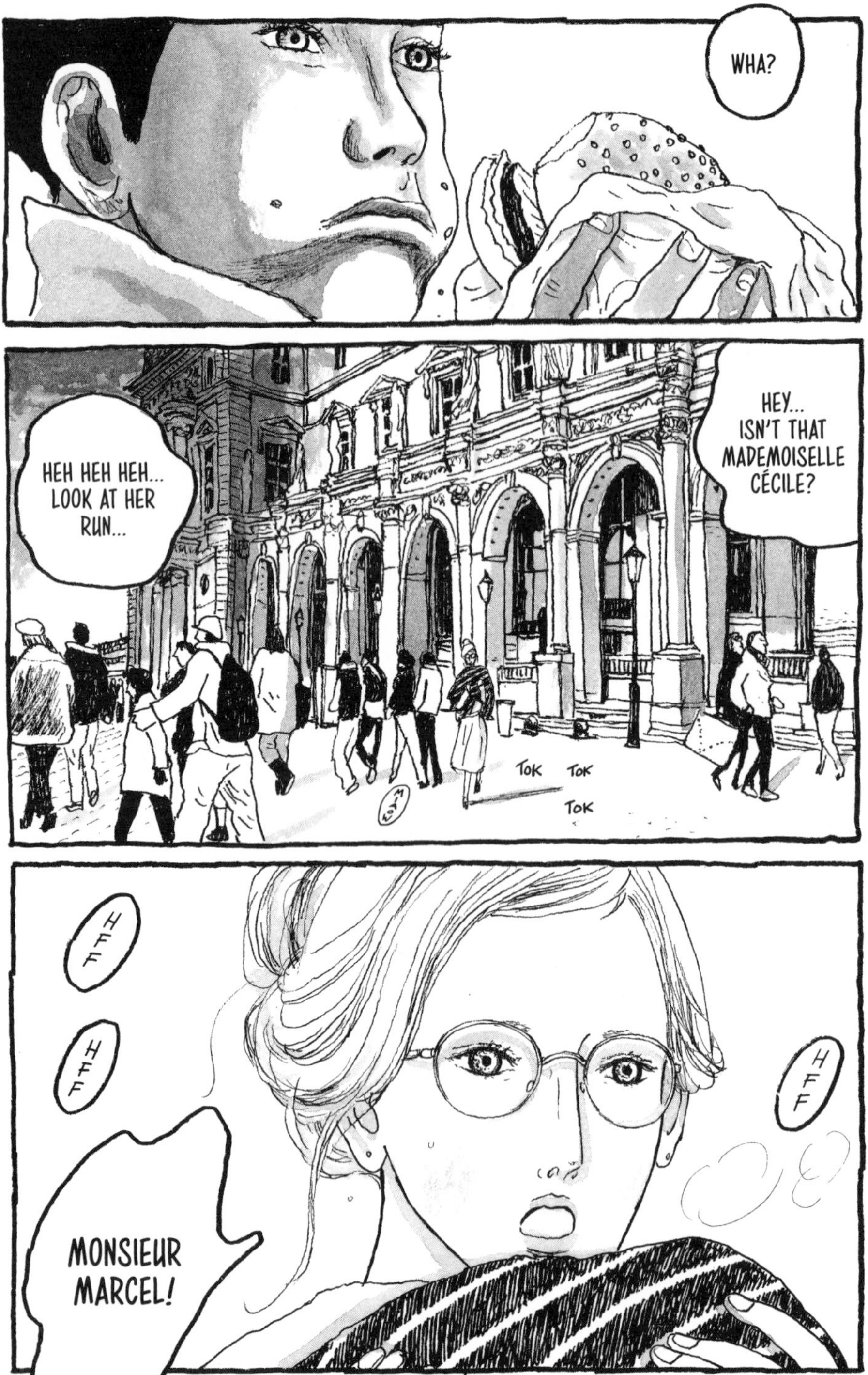
WHA?
HEY... ISN'T THAT MADEMOISELLE CÉCILE?
HEH HEH HEH... LOOK AT HER RUN...
TOK TOK TOK
HFF
HFF
HFF
MONSIEUR MARCEL!

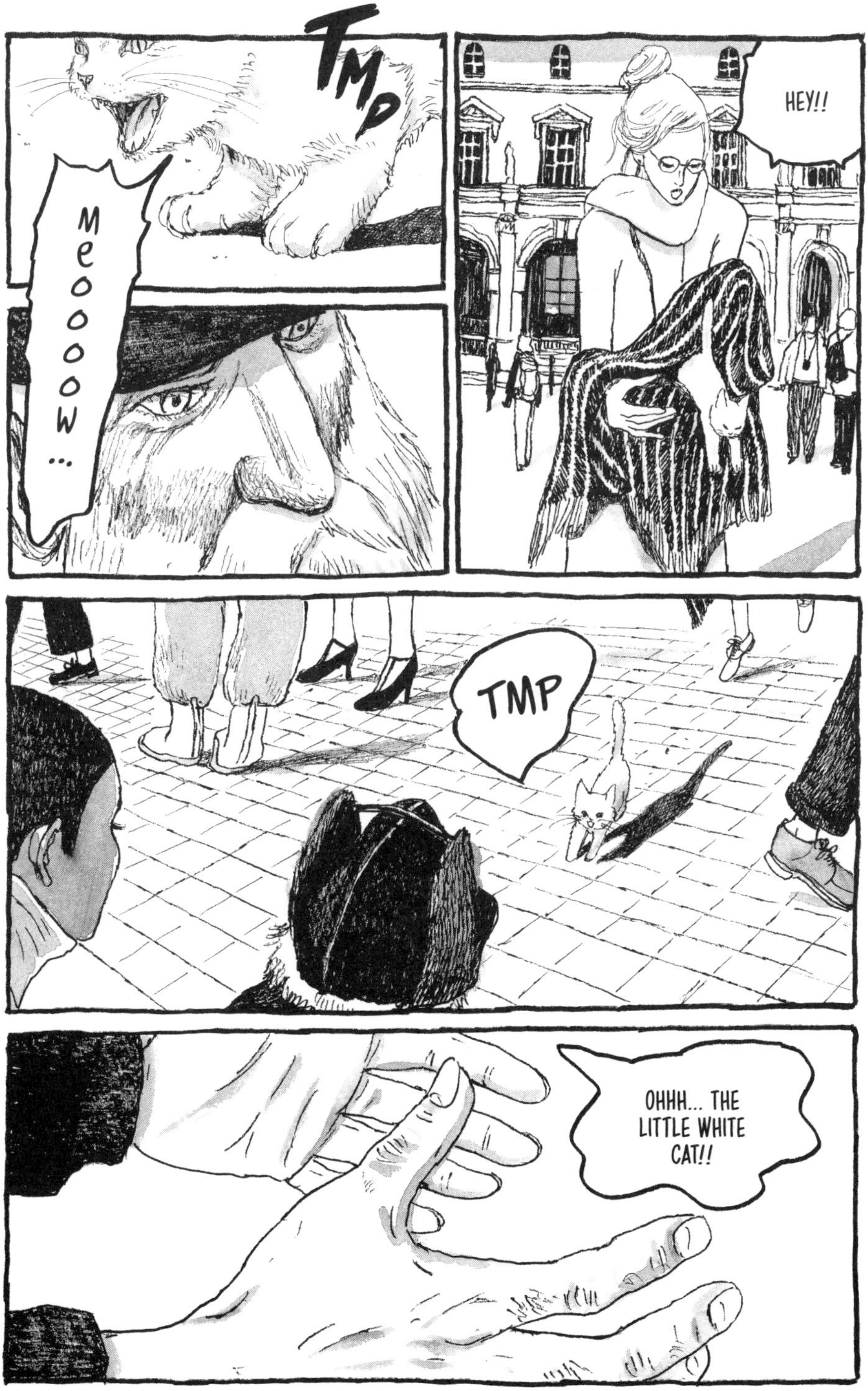
HEY!!
TMP
Meoooooow...
TMP
OHHH... THE LITTLE WHITE CAT!!

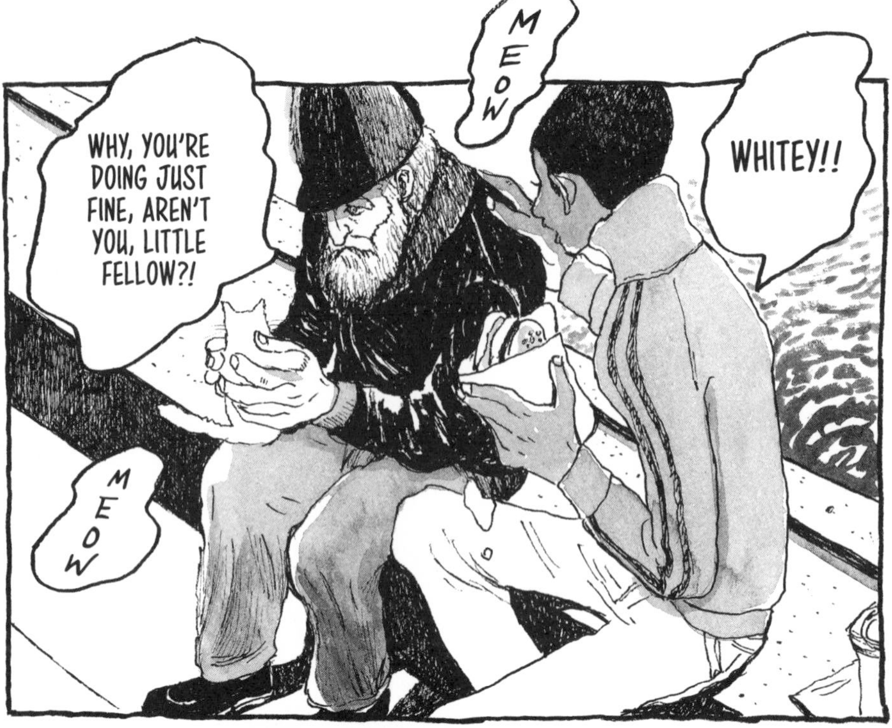
WHITEY!!
MEOW
WHY, YOU'RE DOING JUST FINE, AREN'T YOU, LITTLE FELLOW?!
MEOW

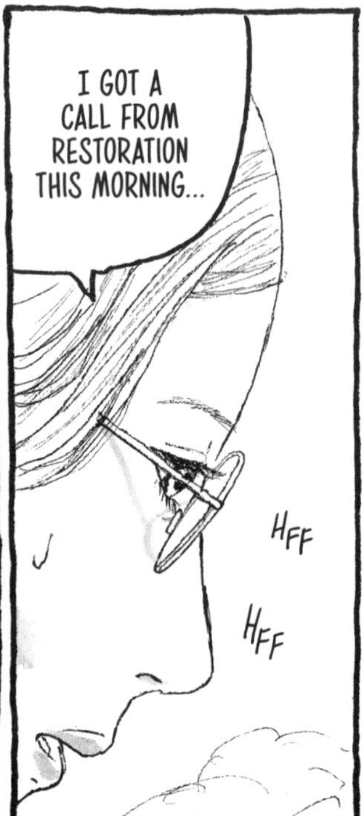
I GOT A CALL FROM RESTORATION THIS MORNING...
HFF
HFF

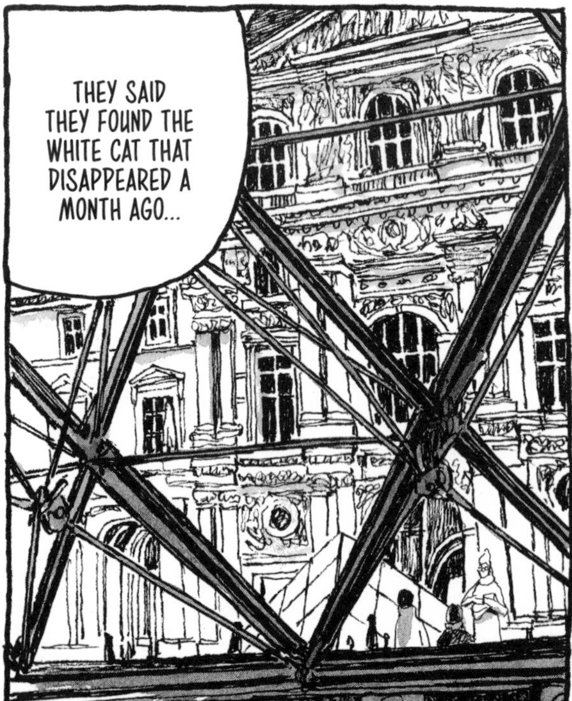
THEY SAID THEY FOUND THE WHITE CAT THAT DISAPPEARED A MONTH AGO...

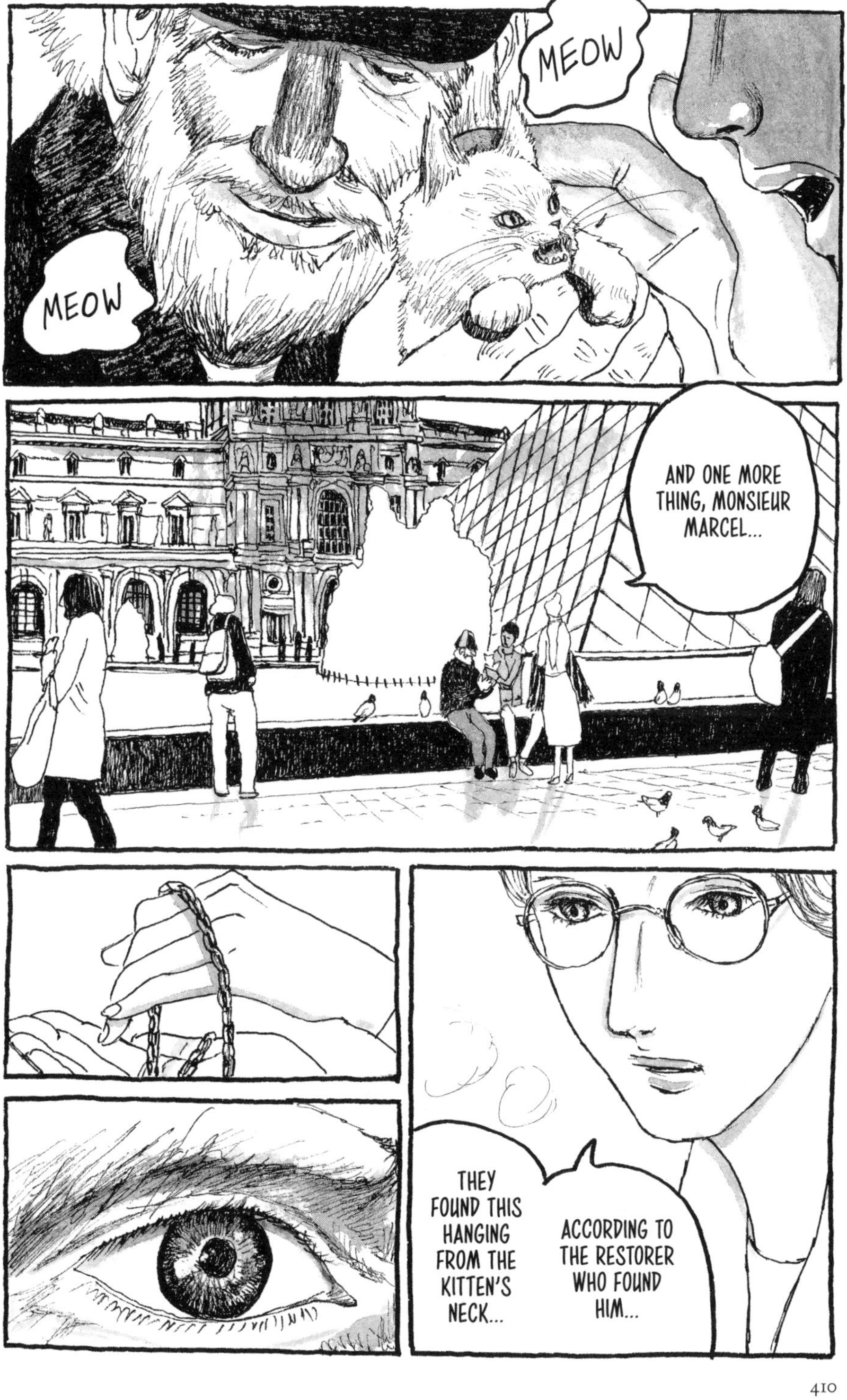
MEOW
MEOW
AND ONE MORE THING, MONSIEUR MARCEL...
ACCORDING TO THE RESTORER WHO FOUND HIM...
THEY FOUND THIS HANGING FROM THE KITTEN'S NECK...

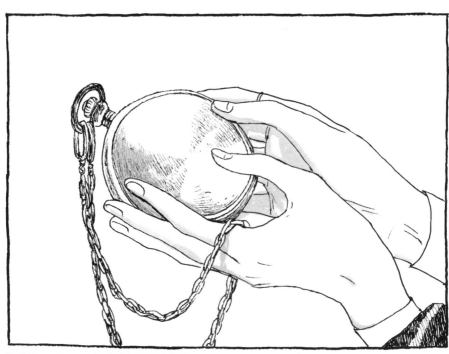

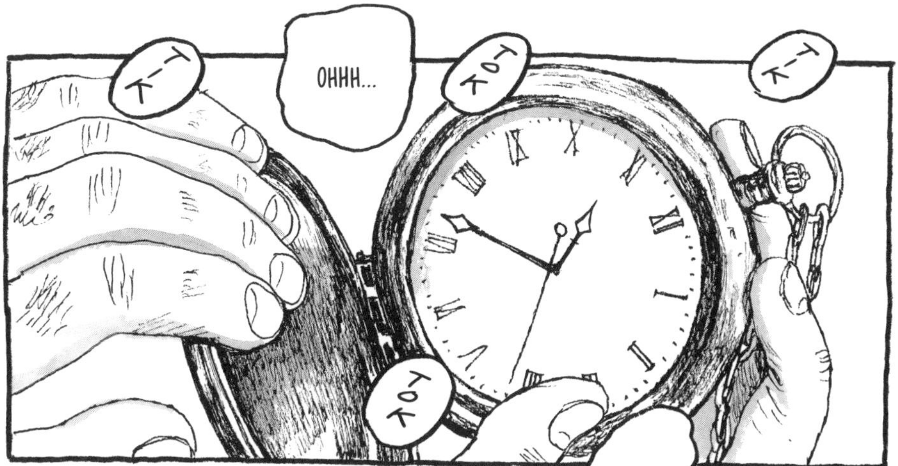
T-K
TOK
OHHH...
T-K
TOK

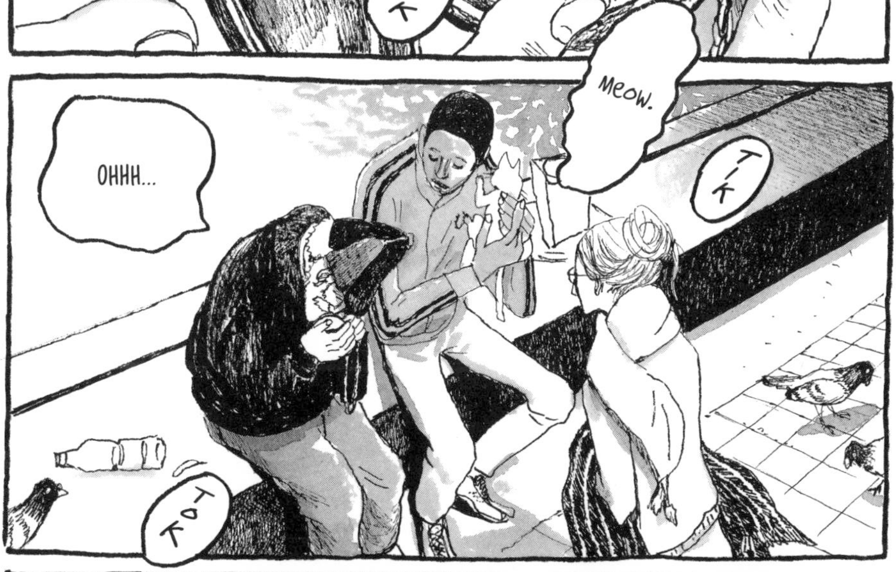
MEOW.
T-K
OHHH...
TOK

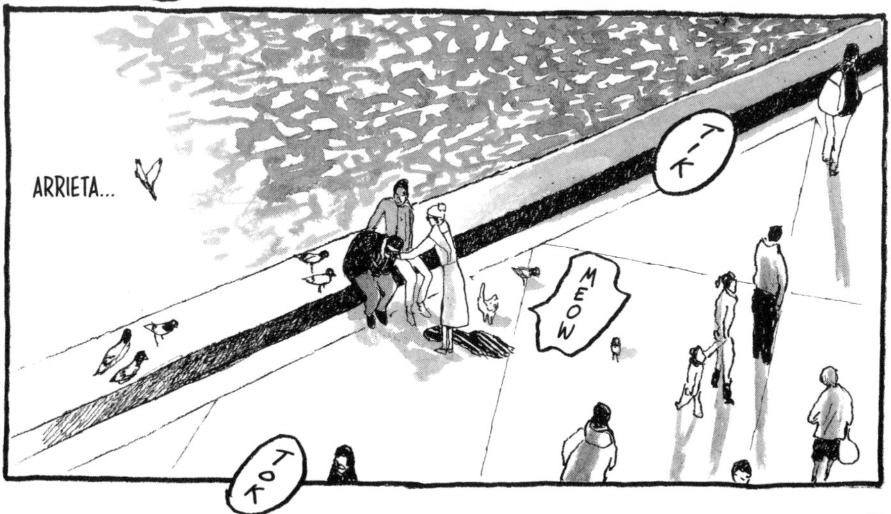
T-K
ARRIETA...
MEOW
TOK

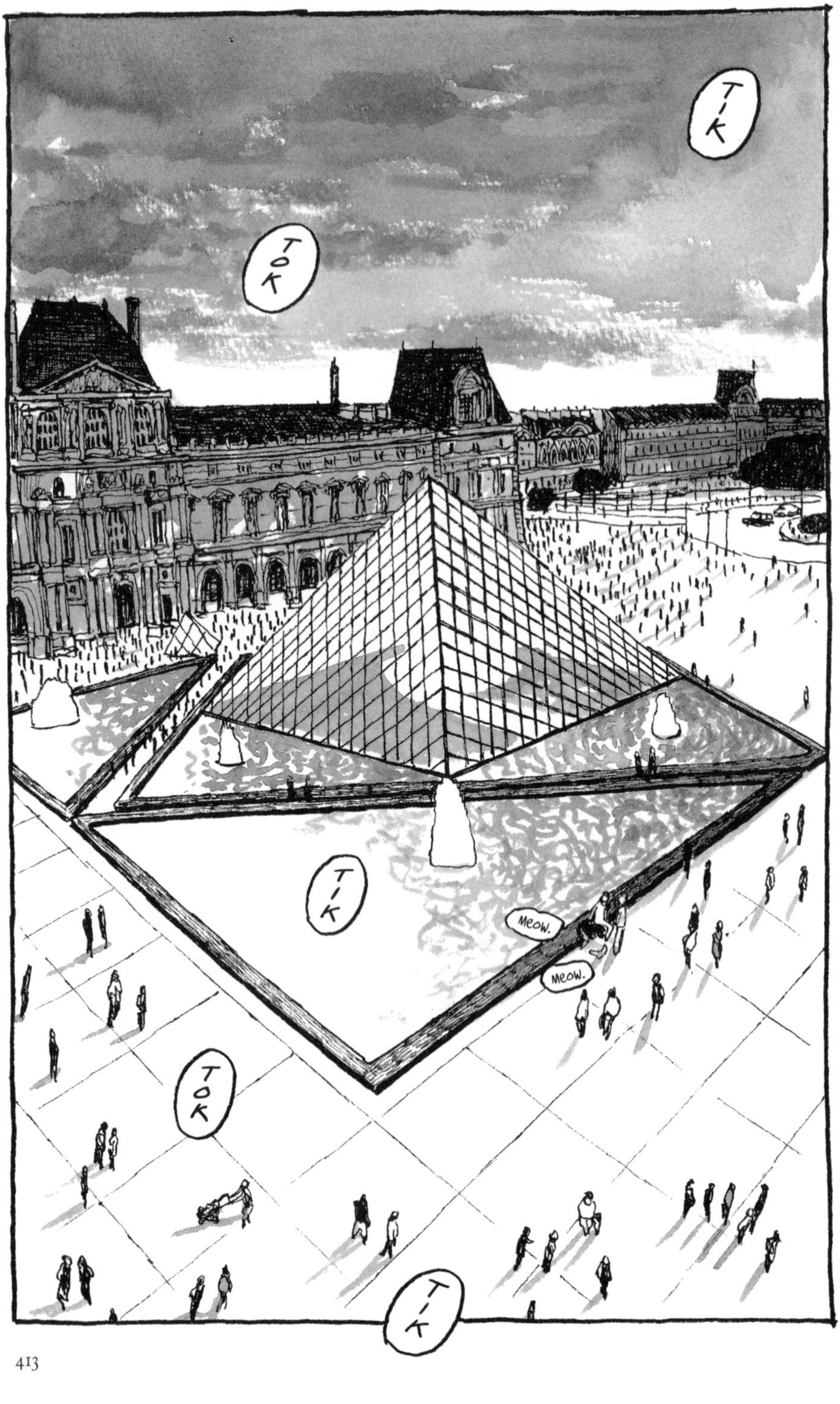
TIK
TOK
TIK
MEOW.
MEOW.
TOK
TIK

SPRING

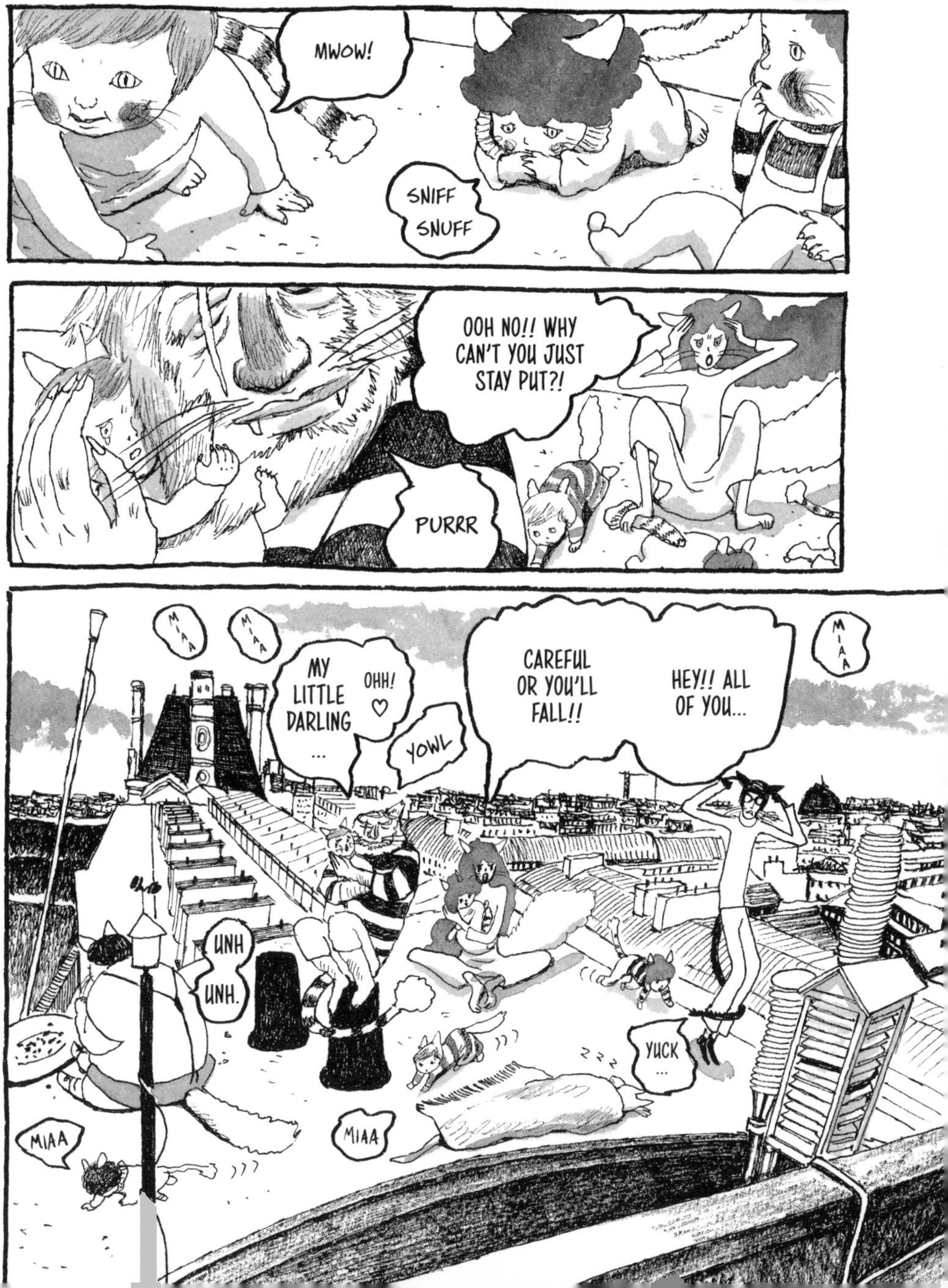
MWOW!
SNIFF SNUFF
OOH NO!! WHY CAN'T YOU JUST STAY PUT?!
PURRR
MIAA
HEY!! ALL OF YOU...
CAREFUL OR YOU'LL FALL!!
OHH! ♡
MY LITTLE DARLING ...
MIAA
MIAA
YOWL
YUCK ...
UNH
UNH.
MIAA
MIAA

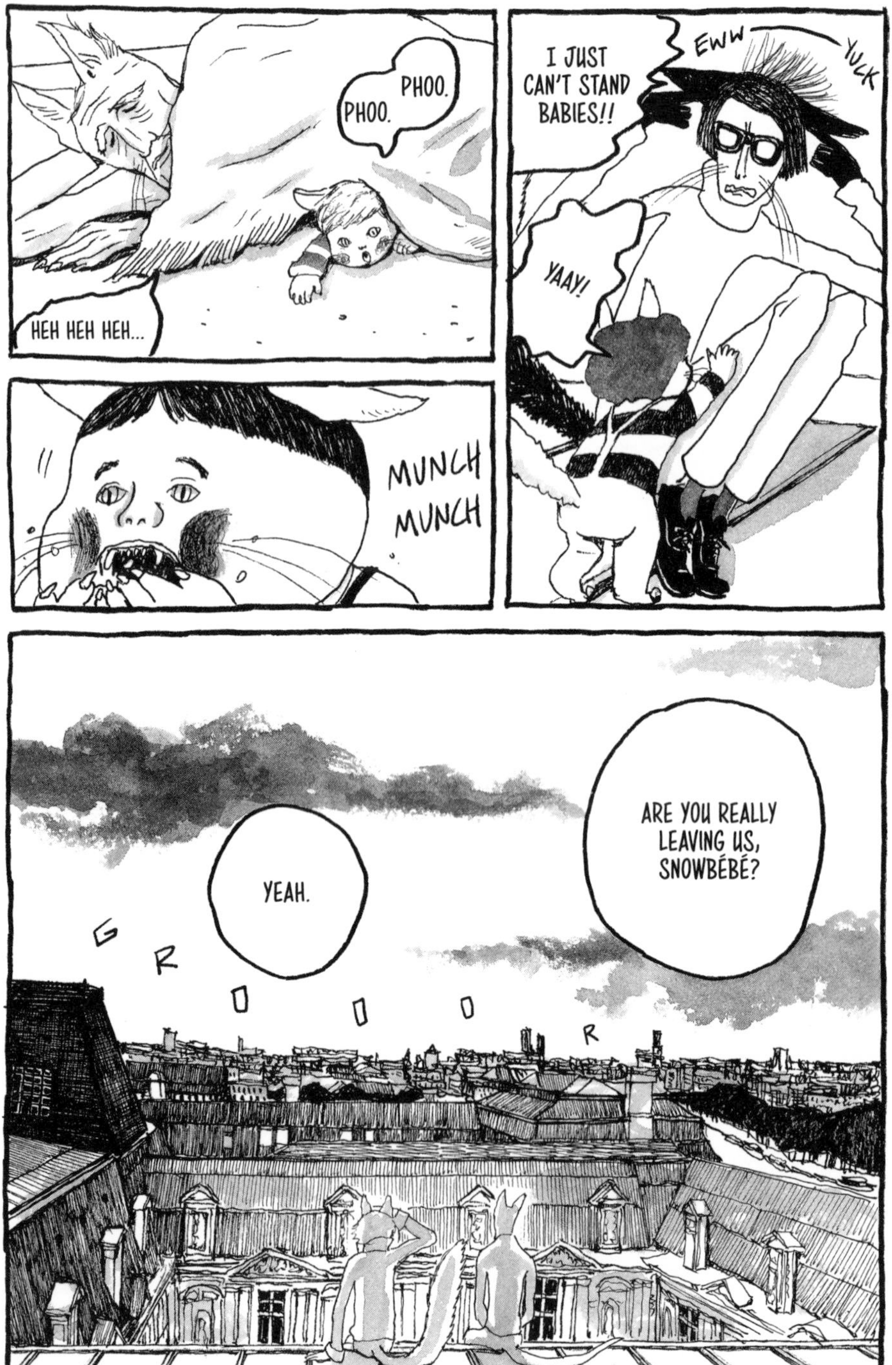
EWW
YUCK
I JUST CAN'T STAND BABIES!!
YAAY!
PHOO. PHOO.
HEH HEH HEH...
MUNCH MUNCH
ARE YOU REALLY LEAVING US, SNOWBÉBÉ?
YEAH.
GROOOR

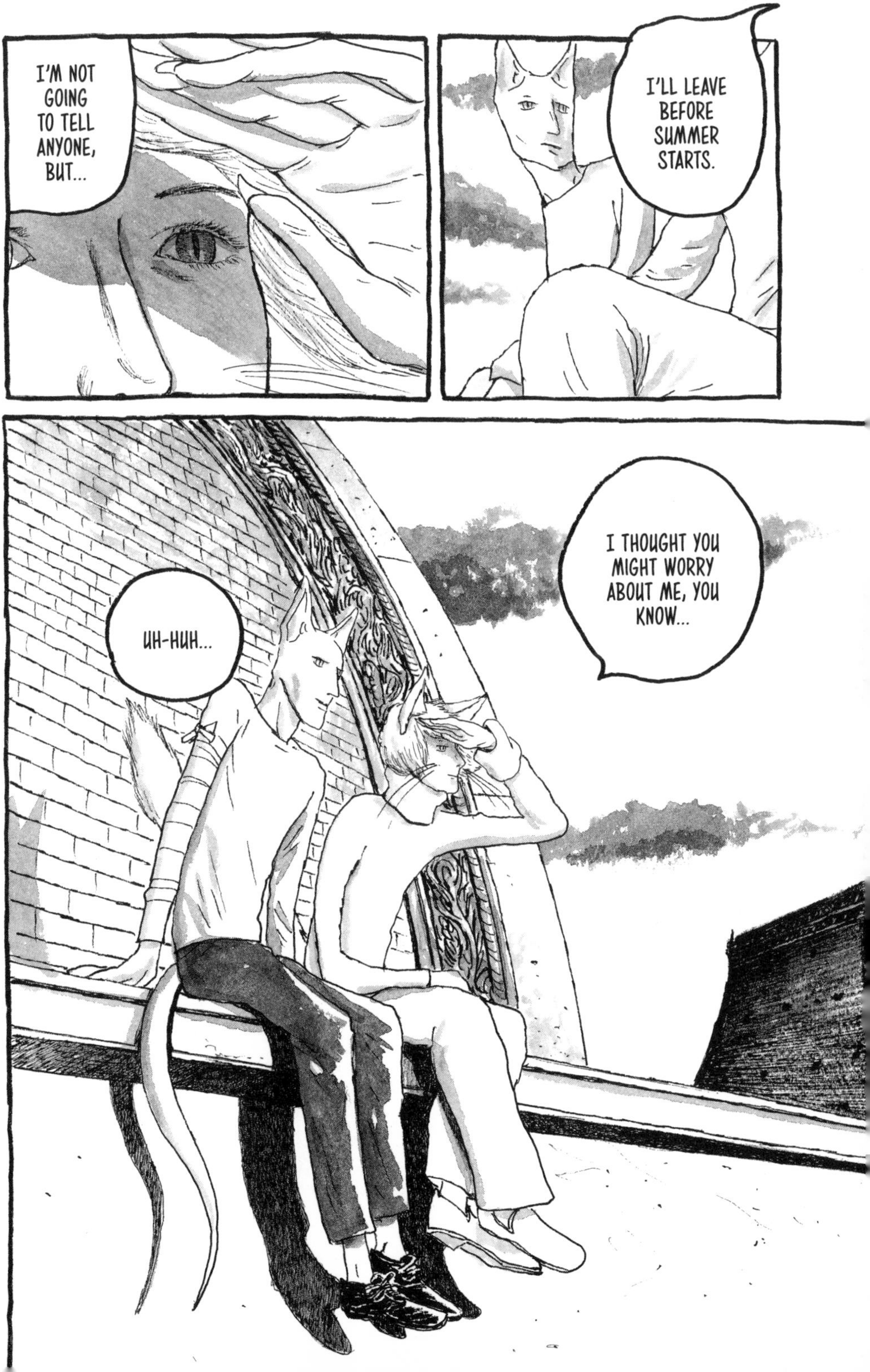
I'LL LEAVE BEFORE SUMMER STARTS.
I'M NOT GOING TO TELL ANYONE, BUT...
I THOUGHT YOU MIGHT WORRY ABOUT ME, YOU KNOW...
UH-HUH...

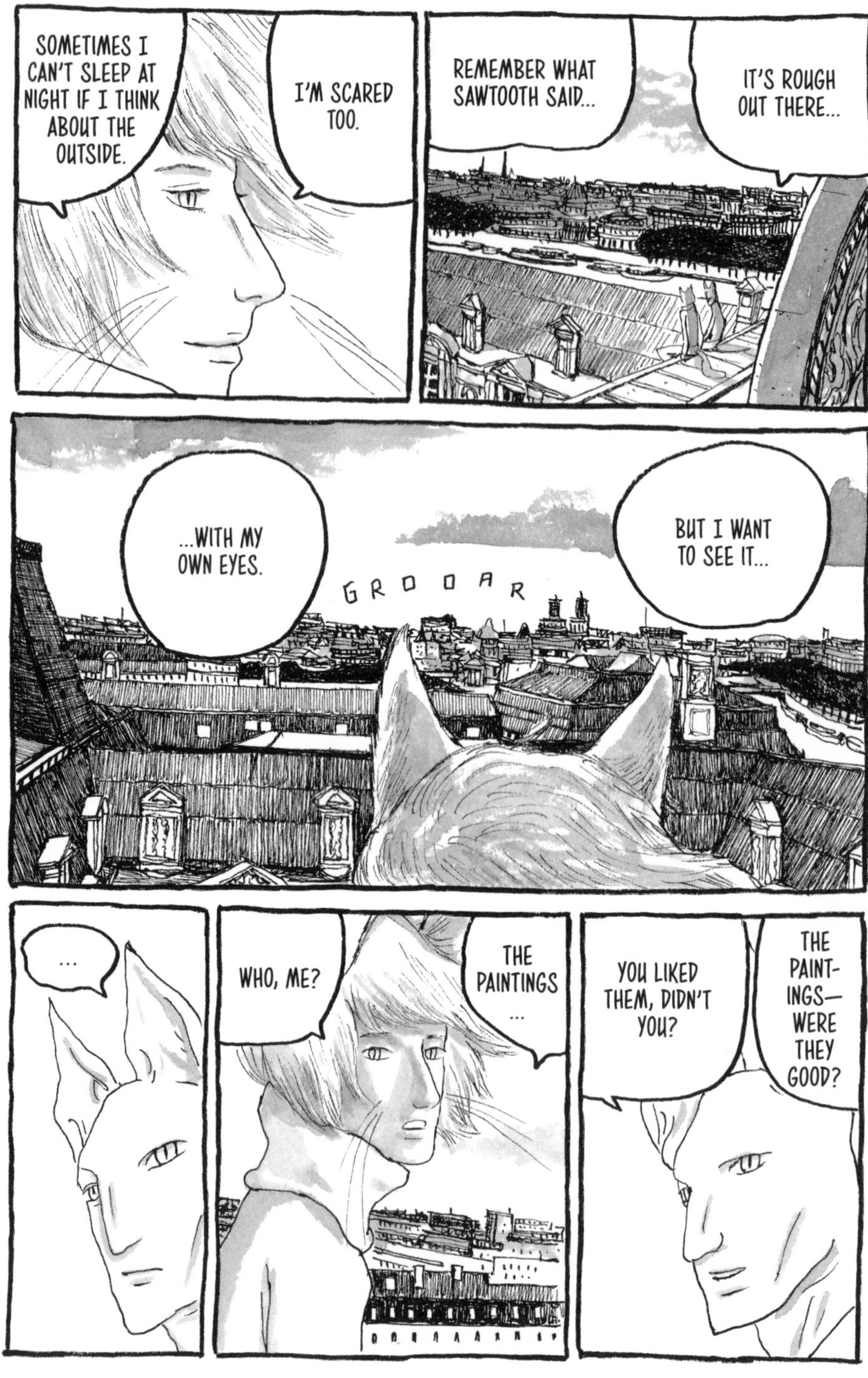
IT'S ROUGH OUT THERE...
REMEMBER WHAT SAWTOOTH SAID...
I'M SCARED TOO.
SOMETIMES I CAN'T SLEEP AT NIGHT IF I THINK ABOUT THE OUTSIDE.
BUT I WANT TO SEE IT...
GROOAR
...WITH MY OWN EYES.
THE PAINT-INGS— WERE THEY GOOD?
YOU LIKED THEM, DIDN'T YOU?
THE PAINTINGS ...
WHO, ME?
...

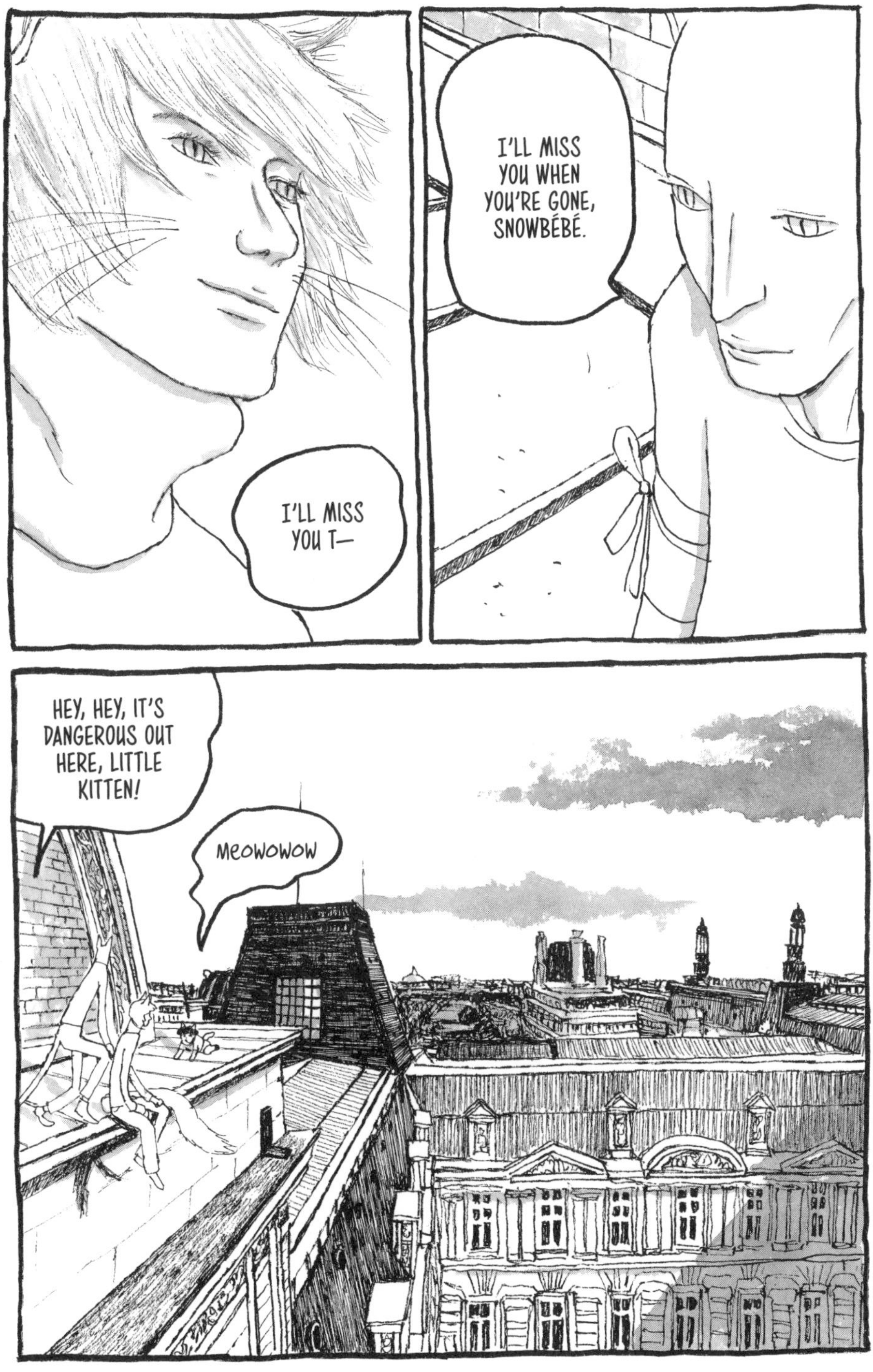
I'LL MISS YOU WHEN YOU'RE GONE, SNOWBÉBÉ.
I'LL MISS YOU T—
HEY, HEY, IT'S DANGEROUS OUT HERE, LITTLE KITTEN!
MEOWOWOW

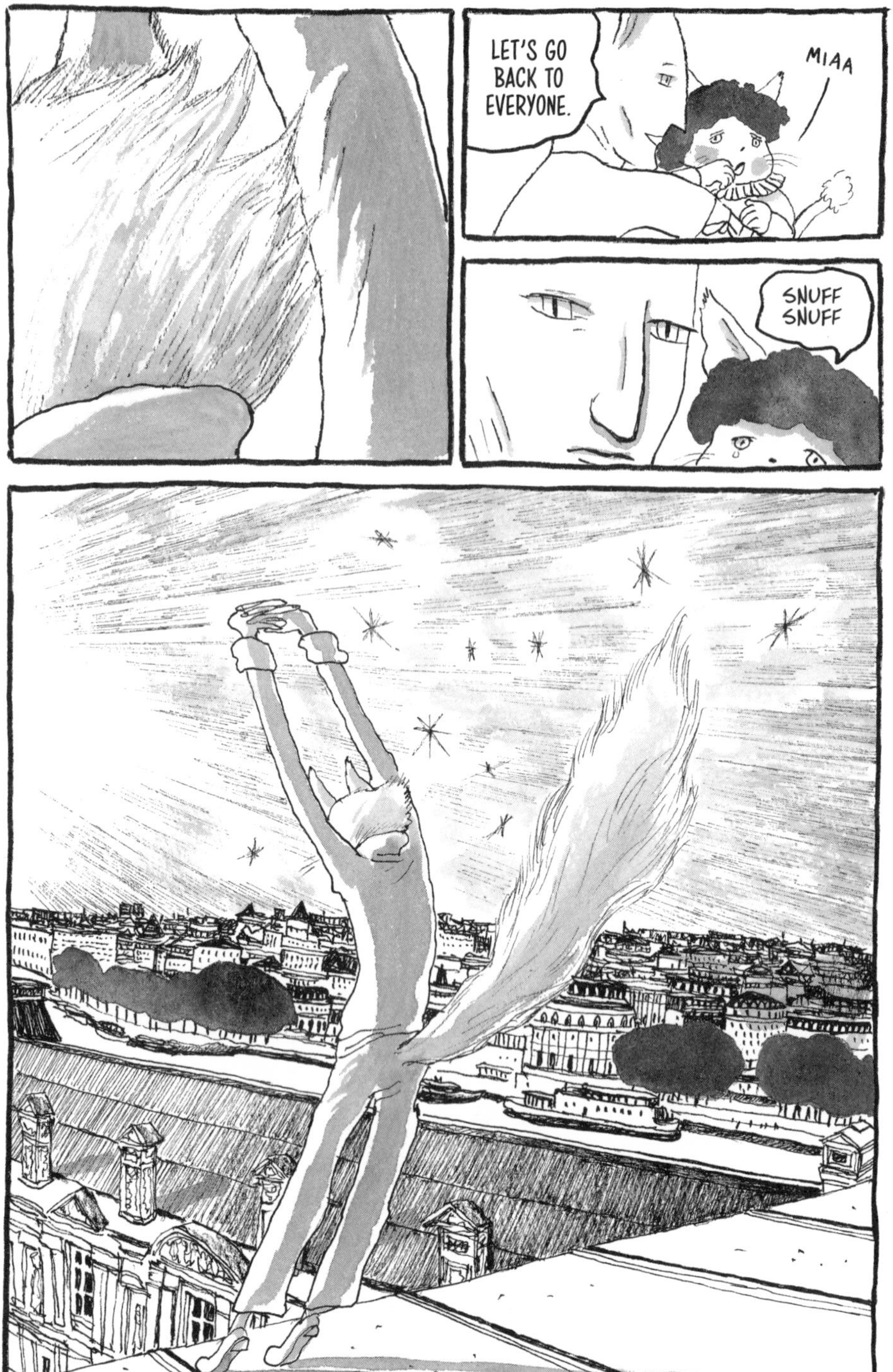
MIAA
LET'S GO BACK TO EVERYONE.
SNUFF SNUFF

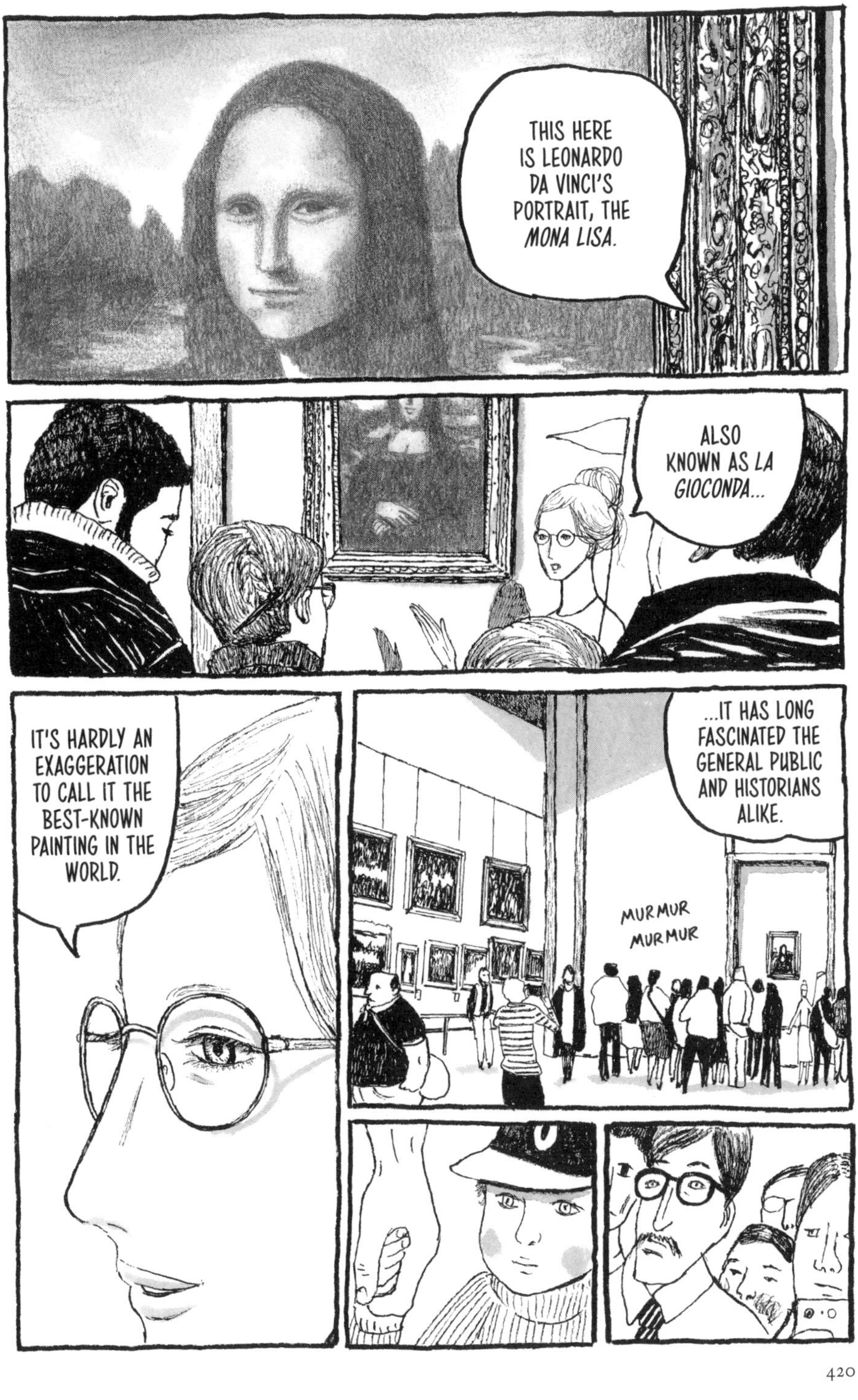
THIS HERE IS LEONARDO DA VINCI'S PORTRAIT, THE *MONA LISA*.
ALSO KNOWN AS *LA GIOCONDA*...
...IT HAS LONG FASCINATED THE GENERAL PUBLIC AND HISTORIANS ALIKE.
MURMUR MURMUR
IT'S HARDLY AN EXAGGERATION TO CALL IT THE BEST-KNOWN PAINTING IN THE WORLD.

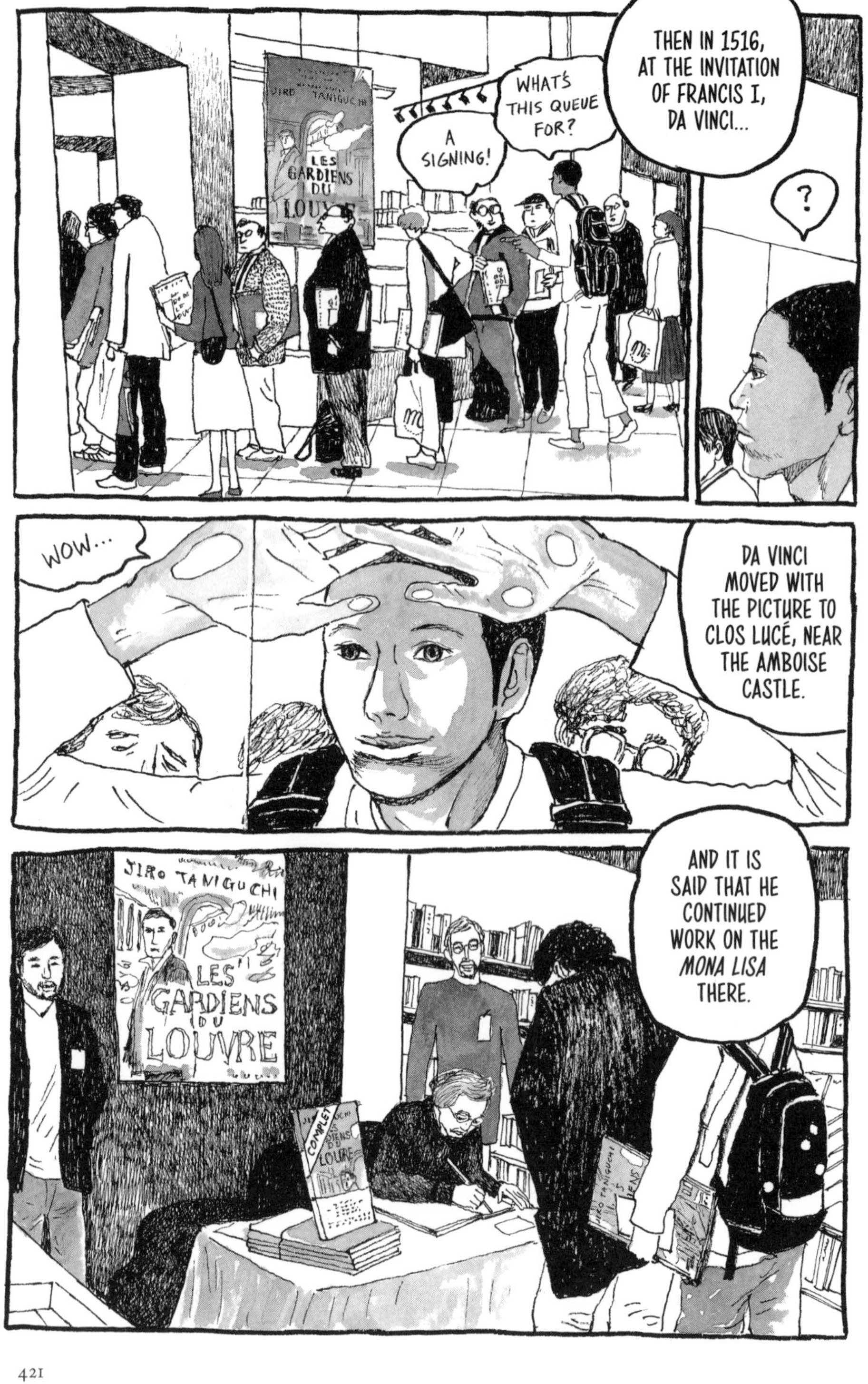
THEN IN 1516, AT THE INVITATION OF FRANCIS I, DA VINCI...
?
WHAT'S THIS QUEUE FOR?
A SIGNING!
JIRO TANIGUCHI
LES GARDIENS DU LOUVRE
DA VINCI MOVED WITH THE PICTURE TO CLOS LUCÉ, NEAR THE AMBOISE CASTLE.
WOW...
AND IT IS SAID THAT HE CONTINUED WORK ON THE *MONA LISA* THERE.
JIRO TANIGUCHI
LES GARDIENS DU LOUVRE
COMPLET

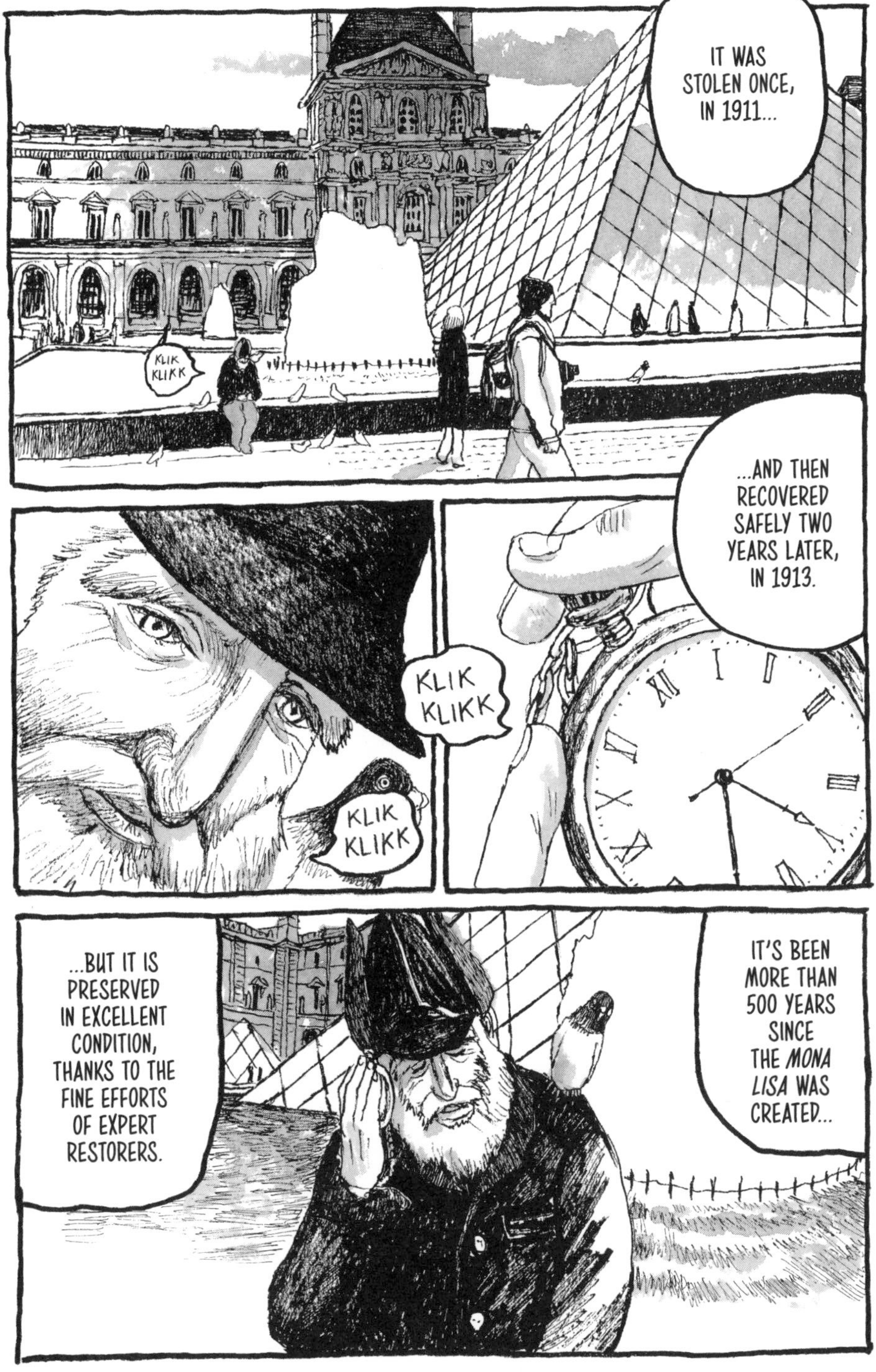
IT WAS STOLEN ONCE, IN 1911...
KLIK KLIKK
...AND THEN RECOVERED SAFELY TWO YEARS LATER, IN 1913.
KLIK KLIKK
KLIK KLIKK
IT'S BEEN MORE THAN 500 YEARS SINCE THE *MONA LISA* WAS CREATED...
...BUT IT IS PRESERVED IN EXCELLENT CONDITION, THANKS TO THE FINE EFFORTS OF EXPERT RESTORERS.

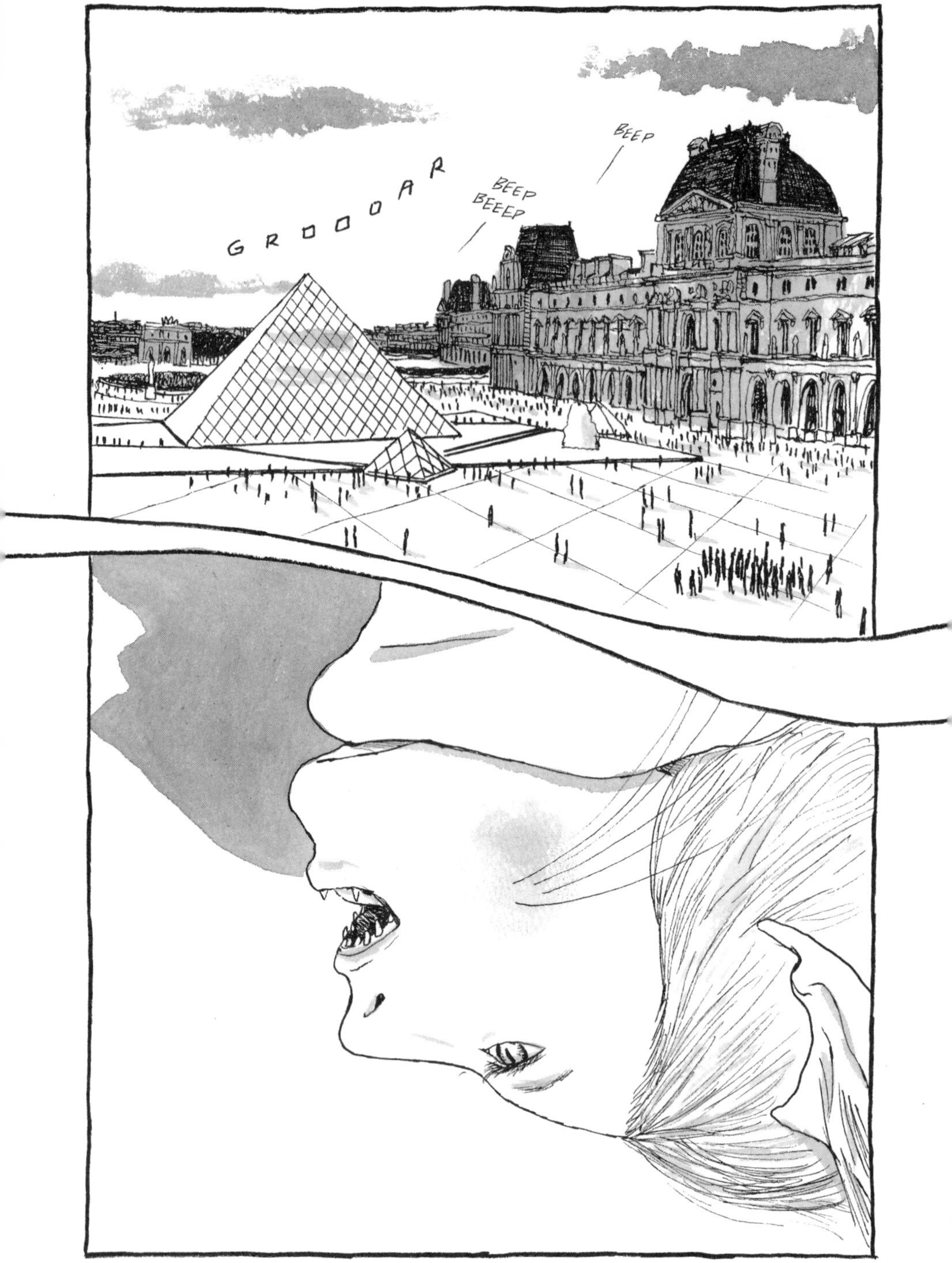
BEEP
BEEP BEEEP
GROOOAR

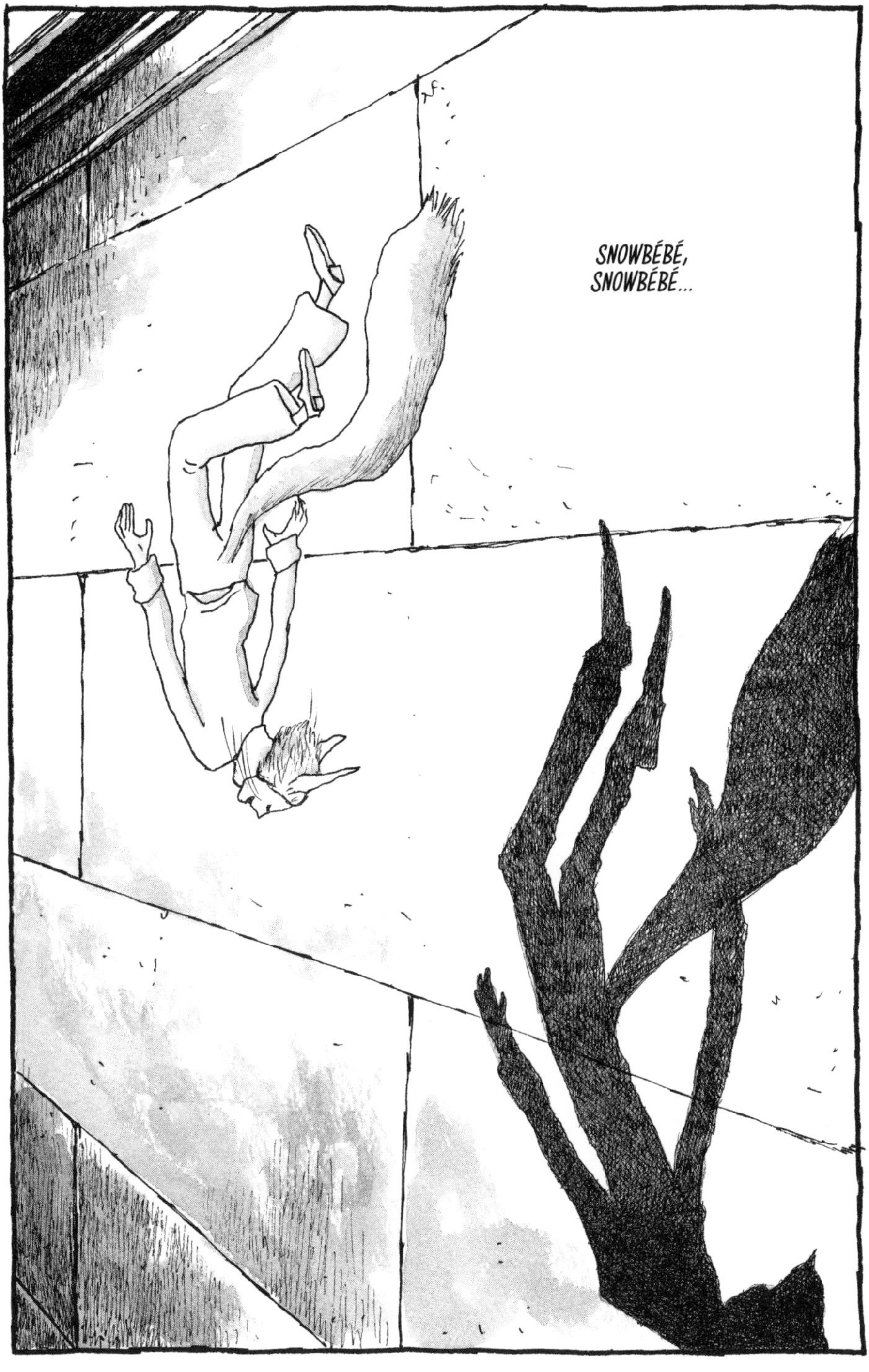
SNOWBÉBÉ,
SNOWBÉBÉ...

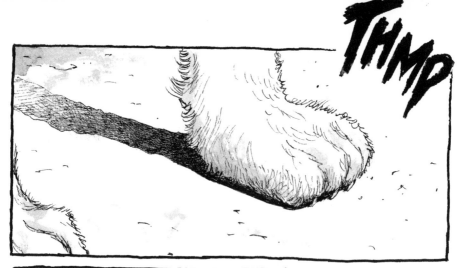

THMP

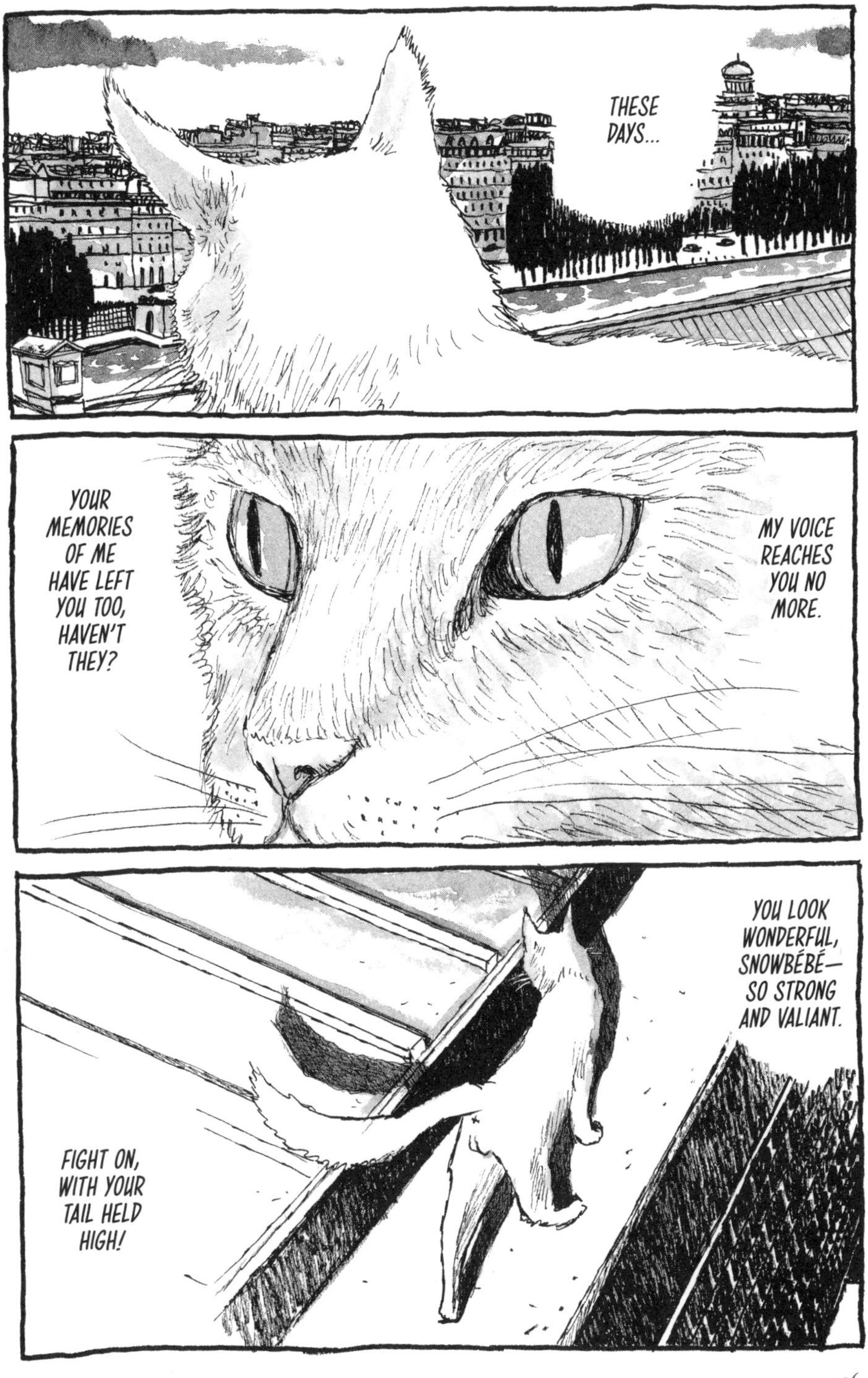
THESE DAYS...
MY VOICE REACHES YOU NO MORE.
YOUR MEMORIES OF ME HAVE LEFT YOU TOO, HAVEN'T THEY?
YOU LOOK WONDERFUL, SNOWBÉBÉ— SO STRONG AND VALIANT.
FIGHT ON, WITH YOUR TAIL HELD HIGH!

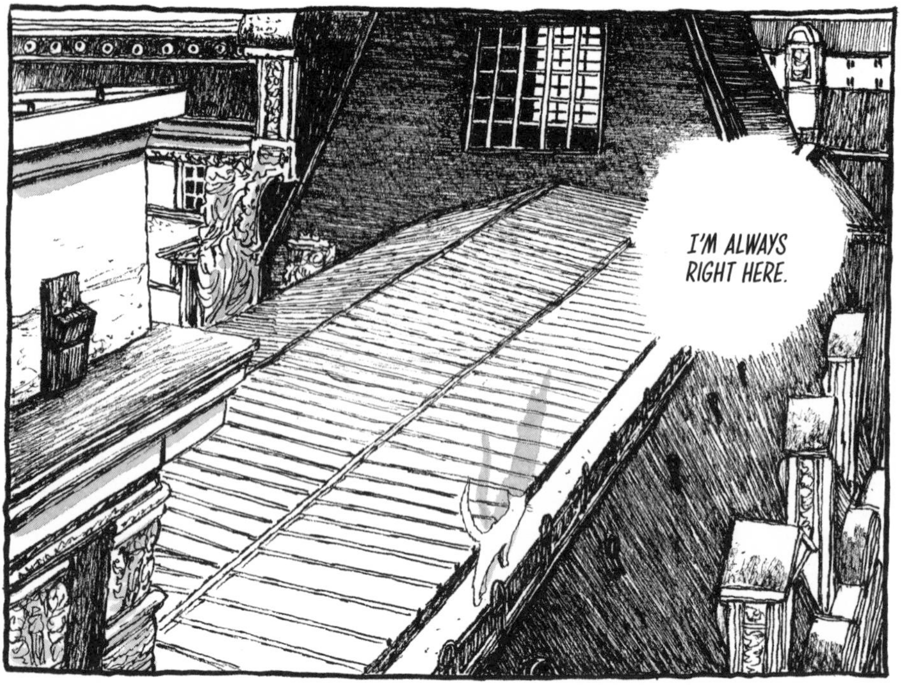
I'M ALWAYS
RIGHT HERE.
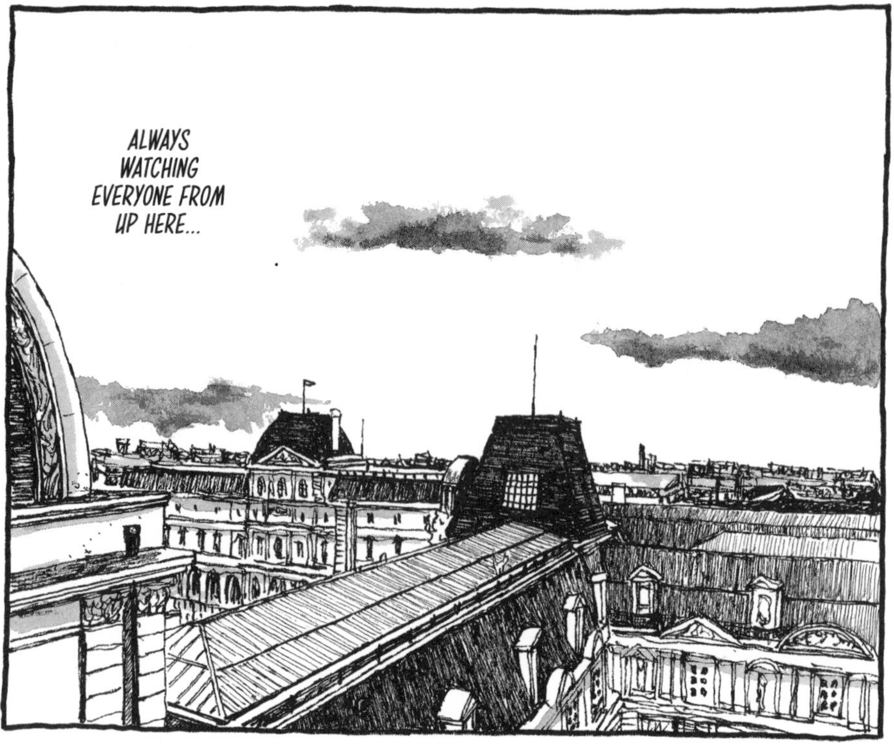
ALWAYS
WATCHING
EVERYONE FROM
UP HERE...

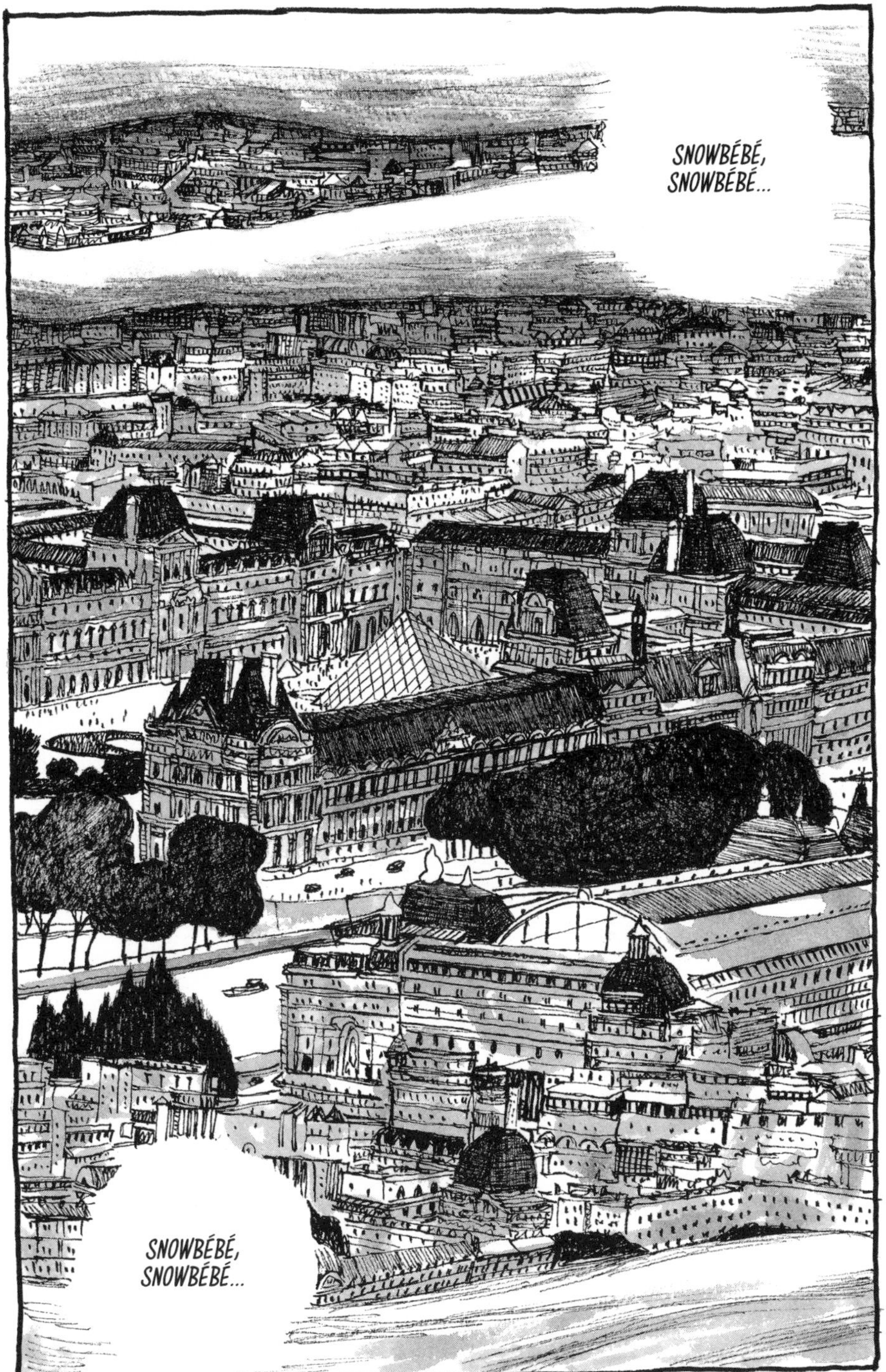
SNOWBÉBÉ,
SNOWBÉBÉ...
SNOWBÉBÉ,
SNOWBÉBÉ...

—FIN—

editor
(japanese edition):

motoyuki oda

story and illustration:

taiyo matsumoto
and saho tono